Standard Normal Distribution Function

$$F(z) = \frac{1}{\sqrt{2\pi}} \int_{-\infty}^{z} e^{-t^2/2}\,dt$$

z	0.00	0.01	0.02	0.03	0.04	0.05	0.06	0.07	0.08	0.09
0.0	0.5000	0.5040	0.5080	0.5120	0.5160	0.5199	0.5239	0.5279	0.5319	0.5359
0.1	0.5398	0.5438	0.5478	0.5517	0.5557	0.5596	0.5636	0.5675	0.5714	0.5753
0.2	0.5793	0.5832	0.5871	0.5910	0.5948	0.5987	0.6026	0.6064	0.6103	0.6141
0.3	0.6179	0.6217	0.6255	0.6293	0.6331	0.6368	0.6406	0.6443	0.6480	0.6517
0.4	0.6554	0.6591	0.6628	0.6664	0.6700	0.6736	0.6772	0.6808	0.6844	0.6879
0.5	0.6915	0.6950	0.6985	0.7019	0.7054	0.7088	0.7123	0.7157	0.7190	0.7224
0.6	0.7257	0.7291	0.7324	0.7357	0.7389	0.7422	0.7454	0.7486	0.7517	0.7549
0.7	0.7580	0.7611	0.7642	0.7673	0.7704	0.7734	0.7764	0.7794	0.7823	0.7852
0.8	0.7881	0.7910	0.7939	0.7967	0.7995	0.8023	0.8051	0.8078	0.8106	0.8133
0.9	0.8159	0.8186	0.8212	0.8238	0.8264	0.8289	0.8315	0.8340	0.8365	0.8389
1.0	0.8413	0.8438	0.8461	0.8485	0.8508	0.8531	0.8554	0.8577	0.8599	0.8621
1.1	0.8643	0.8665	0.8686	0.8708	0.8729	0.8749	0.8770	0.8790	0.8810	0.8830
1.2	0.8849	0.8869	0.8888	0.8907	0.8925	0.8944	0.8962	0.8980	0.8997	0.9015
1.3	0.9032	0.9049	0.9066	0.9082	0.9099	0.9115	0.9131	0.9147	0.9162	0.9177
1.4	0.9192	0.9207	0.9222	0.9236	0.9251	0.9265	0.9279	0.9292	0.9306	0.9319
1.5	0.9332	0.9345	0.9357	0.9370	0.9382	0.9394	0.9406	0.9418	0.9429	0.9441
1.6	0.9452	0.9463	0.9474	0.9484	0.9495	0.9505	0.9515	0.9525	0.9535	0.9545
1.7	0.9554	0.9564	0.9573	0.9582	0.9591	0.9599	0.9608	0.9616	0.9625	0.9633
1.8	0.9641	0.9649	0.9656	0.9664	0.9671	0.9678	0.9686	0.9693	0.9699	0.9706
1.9	0.9713	0.9719	0.9726	0.9732	0.9738	0.9744	0.9750	0.9756	0.9761	0.9767
2.0	0.9772	0.9778	0.9783	0.9788	0.9793	0.9798	0.9803	0.9808	0.9812	0.9817
2.1	0.9821	0.9826	0.9830	0.9834	0.9838	0.9842	0.9846	0.9850	0.9854	0.9857
2.2	0.9861	0.9864	0.9868	0.9871	0.9875	0.9878	0.9881	0.9884	0.9887	0.9890
2.3	0.9893	0.9896	0.9898	0.9901	0.9904	0.9906	0.9909	0.9911	0.9913	0.9916
2.4	0.9918	0.9920	0.9922	0.9925	0.9927	0.9929	0.9931	0.9932	0.9934	0.9936
2.5	0.9938	0.9940	0.9941	0.9943	0.9945	0.9946	0.9948	0.9949	0.9951	0.9952
2.6	0.9953	0.9955	0.9956	0.9957	0.9959	0.9960	0.9961	0.9962	0.9963	0.9964
2.7	0.9965	0.9966	0.9967	0.9968	0.9969	0.9970	0.9971	0.9972	0.9973	0.9974
2.8	0.9974	0.9975	0.9976	0.9977	0.9977	0.9978	0.9979	0.9979	0.9980	0.9981
2.9	0.9981	0.9982	0.9982	0.9983	0.9984	0.9984	0.9985	0.9985	0.9986	0.9986
3.0	0.9987	0.9987	0.9987	0.9988	0.9988	0.9989	0.9989	0.9989	0.9990	0.9990
3.1	0.9990	0.9991	0.9991	0.9991	0.9992	0.9992	0.9992	0.9992	0.9993	0.9993
3.2	0.9993	0.9993	0.9994	0.9994	0.9994	0.9994	0.9994	0.9995	0.9995	0.9995
3.3	0.9995	0.9995	0.9995	0.9996	0.9996	0.9996	0.9996	0.9996	0.9996	0.9997
3.4	0.9997	0.9997	0.9997	0.9997	0.9997	0.9997	0.9997	0.9997	0.9997	0.9998
3.5	0.9998									
4.0	0.99997									
5.0	0.9999997									

D0138507

Miller & Freund's

Probability and Statistics for Engineers

Miller & Freund's

Probability and Statistics for Engineers

Sixth Edition

Richard A. Johnson

University of Wisconsin-Madison

PRENTICE HALL, Upper Saddle River, NJ 07458

Library of Congress Cataloging-in-Publication Data

Miller, Irwin, 1928-
  [Probability and statistics for engineers]
  Miller and Freund's Probability and statistics for engineers /
  Richard A Johnson.- 6th ed.
    p. cm.
  Includes bibliographical references and index.
  ISBN 0-13-014158-5
  1. Engineering-Statistics methods 2. Probabilities.
    I. Freund, John E. II. Johnson, Richard Arnold. III. Title.
TA340 .M5 2000
519.2'02462-dc21   99-053236

Acquisitions Editor: *Kathleen Boothby Sestak*
Assistant Vice President of Production and Manufacturing: *David W. Riccardi*
Executive Managing Editor: *Kathleen Schiaparelli*
Senior Managing Editor: *Linda Mihatov Behrens*
Production Management: *WestWords, Inc.*
Manufacturing Buyer: *Alan Fischer*
Manufacturing Manager: *Trudy Pisciotti*
Marketing Manager: *Melody Marcus*
Marketing Assistant: *Vince Jansen*
Director of Marketing: *John Tweeddale*
Editorial Assistant/Supplements Editor: *Joanne Wendelken*
Art Director: *Heather Scott*
Assistant to Art Director: *John Christiana*
Associate Creative Director/Interior Designer: *Amy Rosen*
Cover Designer/Image: *Elizabeth Nemeth*
Art Editor: *Michele Giusti*
Art Manager: *Gus Vibal*
Director of Creative Services: *Paul Belfanti*
Art Studio: *Scottie Graphics*

© 2000, 1994, 1990, 1985, 1977, 1965 by Prentice-Hall, Inc.
Upper Saddle River, NJ 07458

All rights reserved. No part of this book may be reproduced, in any form or by any means,
without permission in writing from the publisher.

Printed in the United States of America

10 9 8 7 6 5 4 3

ISBN 0-13-014158-5

Prentice-Hall International (UK) Limited, London
Prentice-Hall of Australia Pty. Limited, Sydney
Prentice-Hall Canada Inc. Toronto
Prentice-Hall Hispanoamericana, S.A., Mexico
Prentice-Hall of India Private Limited, New Delhi
Prentice-Hall of Japan, Inc., Tokyo
Pearson Education Asia Pte. Ltd.
Editora Prentice-Hall Do Brasil, Ltd., Rio de Janeiro

CONTENTS

This book has been written for an introductory course in probability and statistics for students of engineering and the physical sciences. Each chapter is keynoted by an introductory statement and has a checklist of key terms (with page numbers) at the end. Important formulas, theorems, and rules are set out from the text in boxes. The steps for hypothesis testing are clearly and consistently delineated in each application. Emphasis is also given to confidence interval procedures.

The text has been tested extensively in courses for university students as well as by in-plant training of engineers. The whole book can be covered in a two-semester or three-quarter course consisting of three lectures a week. The book also makes an excellent basis for a one-semester course where the lecturer can choose topics to emphasize theory or application. The author covers most of the first seven chapters, straight-line regression, and the graphic presentation of factorial designs in one semester.

In this sixth edition we have continued to build on the strengths of the previous editions while bringing in more actual data sets and examples of the application of statistics in scientific investigations.

Important improvements have been made in this revision. Several new data sets have been added. Like many of those already in the text, they arose in the author's consulting activities or in discussions with scientists and engineers about their statistical problems. Data from some companies have been disguised, but they still retain all of the features necessary to illustrate the statistical methods and the reasoning required to make generalizations from data collected in an experiment.

New case studies are given in each of the first two chapters. They illustrate the power of even simple statistical methods to suggest changes that make major improvements in production processes.

Chapter 1 has been expanded to include material on the distinction between sample and population, good and bad samples, and the use of a random number table to choose samples.

The standard normal distribution table now includes both negative and positive z values. Further, graphs of the normal density are used to guide the reader in evaluating normal probabilities.

Graphs of the sampling distribution, showing the critical region and P value, now accompany the examples of testing hypotheses. These graphs help reinforce the understanding of the critical region, significance level, and P value. Additional summary tables of testing procedures have been included.

The introduction to fitting a straight line by least squares in Chapter 11 has been improved, and the role of the correlation coefficient as well as its properties highlighted.

The section on the graphic presentation of 2^2 and 2^3 designs has been further expanded to include blocking. This section works as a stand-alone introduction to the design of experiments when the instructor can only devote two or three lectures to the subject.

To give students an early preview of statistics, descriptive statistics are covered in Chapter 2. Chapters 3 through 6 provide a brief, though rigorous, introduction to the theory of statistics and, together with some of the material in Chapter 15, they are suitable for an introductory semester (or quarter) course on probability and statistics. Chapters 7, 8, and 9 contain conventional material on the key concepts and elementary methods of statistical inference. Chapters 11, 12, and 13 comprise an introduction to some of the standard, though more advanced, topics of experimental design and regression. Chapter 14 stresses the key underlying statistical ideas for quality improvement, and Chapter 15 treats the associated ideas of reliability and the fitting of life length models.

The mathematical background expected of the reader is a year course in calculus; actually, calculus is required mainly for Chapter 5 dealing with basic distribution theory in the continuous case.

We wish to thank MINITAB (State College, Pennsylvania) for permission to include commands and output from their *MINITAB* software package, and the SAS institute (Cary, North Carolina) for permission to include output from their *SAS* package.

Thanks also to Paul M. Berthouex, Michael Brajac, Smiley Cheng, Don Ermer, Jim Evans, Cherilyn Hatfield, David Steinberg, and Steve Verrill for contributing data sets. Kuo-Tsung Wu, Wao Kwong Cheang, and Melissa Schultz provided valuable help in improving the manuscript. Thanks also to Song Yong Sim, Lifei Huang, Erik Johnson, and Wenqing Lu for their help with checking the manuscript.

All revisions in this edition were the responsibility of R. A. Johnson.

Richard A. Johnson

Miller & Freund's

Probability and Statistics for Engineers

Introduction

Everything dealing with the collection, processing, analysis, and interpretation of numerical data belongs to the domain of statistics. In engineering, this includes such diversified tasks as calculating the average length of the downtimes of a computer, collecting and presenting data on the numbers of persons attending seminars on solar energy, evaluating the effectiveness of commercial products, predicting the reliability of a rocket, or studying the vibrations of airplane wings.

In Sections 1.2, 1.3, 1.4, and 1.5 we discuss the recent growth of statistics and, in particular, its applications to problems of engineering. Statistics plays a major role in the improvement of quality of any product or service. An engineer using the techniques described in this book can become much more effective in all phases of work relating to research, development, or production. Section 1.6 emphasizes the distinction between a population and a sample. ▪

1.1 Why Study Statistics?

Answers provided by statistical approaches can provide the basis for making decisions or choosing actions. For example, city officials might examine whether the level of lead in the water supply is within safety standards. Because not all of the water can be checked, answers must be based on the partial information from samples of water that are collected for this purpose. As another example, a civil engineer must determine the strength of supports for

generators at a power plant. A number of those available must be loaded to failure and their strengths will provide the basis for accessing strength. The proportion of all supports available with strengths that lie below a design limit needs to
be determined.

When information is sought, statistical ideas suggest a typical collection process
with four crucial steps.

(a) **Set clearly defined goals for the investigation.**
(b) **Make a plan of what data to collect and how to collect it.**
(c) **Apply appropriate statistical methods to extract information from the data.**
(d) **Interpret the information and draw conclusions.**

These indispensable steps will provide a frame of reference throughout as we develop the key ideas of statistics. Statistical reasoning and methods can help you
become efficient at obtaining information and making accurate conclusions.

1.2   Modern Statistics

The origin of statistics can be traced to two areas of interest that, on the surface,
have little in common: games of chance and what is now called political science.
Mid-eighteenth century studies in probability, motivated largely by interest in
games of chance, led to the mathematical treatment of errors of measurement
and the theory that now forms the foundation of statistics. In the same century,
interest in the numerical description of political units (cities, provinces, counties,
etc.) led to what is now called **descriptive statistics.** At first, descriptive statistics
consisted merely of the presentation of data in tables and charts; nowadays, it includes also the summarization of data by means of numerical descriptions.

In recent decades, the growth of statistics has made itself felt in almost every
major phase of activity, and the most important feature of its growth has been the
shift in emphasis from descriptive statistics to **statistical inference.** Statistical inference concerns generalization based on sample data; it applies to such problems
as estimating an engine's average emission of pollutants from trial runs, testing a
manufacturer's claim on the basis of measurements performed on samples of his
product, and predicting the fidelity of an audio system on the basis of sample data
pertaining to the performance of its components.

When one makes a statistical inference, namely, an inference that goes beyond
the information contained in a set of data, one must always proceed with caution.
One must decide carefully how far one can go in generalizing from a given set of
data, whether such generalizations are at all reasonable or justifiable, whether it
might be wise to wait until there are more data, and so forth. Indeed, some of the
most important problems of statistical inference concern the appraisal of the risks
and the consequences to which one might be exposed by making generalizations
from sample data. This includes an appraisal of the probabilities of making wrong
decisions, the chances of making incorrect predictions, and the possibility of obtaining estimates that do not lie within permissible limits.

We shall approach the subject of statistics as a science, developing each statistical idea insofar as possible from its probabilistic foundation, and applying each idea to problems of physical or engineering science as soon as it has been developed. The great majority of the methods we shall use in stating and solving these problems belong to the **classical approach,** because they do not formally take into account the various subjective factors mentioned above. However we shall endeavor continually to make the reader aware that the subjective factors do exist, and to indicate whenever possible what role they might play in making the final decision. This "bread-and-butter" approach to statistics presents the subject in the form in which it has so successfully contributed to engineering science, as well as to the natural and social sciences, in the last half of the twentieth century.

1.3 Statistics and Engineering

There are few areas where the impact of the recent growth of statistics has been felt more strongly than in engineering and industrial management. Indeed, it would be difficult to overestimate the contributions statistics has made to problems of production, to the effective use of materials and labor, to basic research, and to the development of new products. As in other sciences, statistics has become a vital tool to engineers. It enables them to understand phenomena subject to variation and to effectively predict or control them.

In this text, our attention will be directed largely toward engineering applications, but we shall not hesitate to refer also to other areas to impress upon the reader the great generality of most statistical techniques. Thus, the reader will find that the statistical method which is used to estimate the coefficient of thermal expansion of a metal serves also to estimate the average time it takes a secretary to perform a given task, the average thickness of a pelican eggshell, or the average IQ of an immigrant arriving in the United States. Similarly, the statistical method that is used to compare the strength of two alloys serves also to compare the effectiveness of two teaching methods, the merits of two insect sprays, or the performance of men and women in a current-events test.

1.4 The Role of the Scientist and Engineer in Quality Improvement

Since the 1960's, the United States has found itself in an increasingly competitive world market. At present, we are in the midst of an international revolution in quality improvement. The teaching and ideas of W. Edwards Deming (1900–1993) were instrumental in the rejuvenation of Japan's industry. He stressed that American industry, in order to survive, must mobilize with a continuing commitment to quality improvement. From design to production, processes need to be continually improved. The engineer and scientist, with their technical knowledge and armed with basic statistical skills in data collection and graphical display, can be main participants in attaining this goal.

The **quality improvement** movement is based on the philosophy of "make it right the first time." Furthermore, one should not be content with any process or product but should continue to look for ways of improving it. We emphasize the key statistical components of any modern quality improvement program. In Chapter 14, we outline the basic issues of quality improvement and present some of the specialized statistical techniques for studying production processes. The experimental designs discussed in Chapter 13 are also basic to the process of quality improvement.

Closely related to quality improvement techniques are the statistical techniques that have been developed to meet the **reliability** needs of the highly complex products of space-age technology. Chapter 15 provides an introduction to this area.

1.5 A Case Study: Visually Inspecting Data to Improve Product Quality

This study[1] dramatically illustrates the important advantages gained by appropriately plotting and then monitoring manufacturing data. It concerns a ceramic part used in popular coffee makers. This ceramic part is made by filling the cavity between two dies of a pressing machine with a mixture of clay, water, and oil. After pressing, but before the part is dried to a hardened state, critical dimensions are measured. The depth of the slot is of interest here.

Because of natural uncontrolled variation in the clay-water-oil mixture, the condition of the press, differences in operators and so on, we cannot expect all of the slot measurements to be exactly the same. Some variation in the depth of slots is inevitable but the depth needs to be controlled within certain limits for the part to fit when assembled.

Slot depth was measured on three ceramic parts selected from production every half hour during the first shift from 6 A.M. to 3 P.M. The data in Table 1.1 were obtained on a Friday. The sample mean, or average, for the first sample of 214, 211 and 218 (thousandths of an inch) is

$$\frac{214 + 211 + 218}{3} = \frac{643}{3} = 214.3$$

The graphical procedure, called an **X-bar** chart, consists of plotting the sample averages versus time order. This plot will indicate when changes have occurred and actions need to be taken to correct the process.

From a prior statistical study, it was known that the process was stable about a value of 217.5 thousandths of an inch. This value will be taken as the central line of the chart.

$$\text{central line: } \bar{\bar{x}} = 217.5$$

It was further established that the process was capable of making mostly good ceramic parts if the average slot dimension for a sample remained between the

Lower control limit: LCL = 215.0
Upper control limit: UCL = 220.0

[1]Courtesy of Don Ermer

TABLE 1.1 Slot depth (thousandths of an inch).

Time	6:30	7:00	7:30	8:00	8:30	9:00	9:30	10:00
1	214	218	218	216	217	218	218	219
2	211	217	218	218	220	219	217	219
3	218	219	217	219	221	216	217	218
SUM	643	654	653	653	658	653	652	656
$\bar{x}$	214.3	218.0	217.7	217.7	219.3	217.7	217.3	218.7

Time	10:30	11:00	11:30	12:30	1:00	1:30	2:00	2:30
1	216	216	218	219	217	219	217	215
2	219	218	219	220	220	219	220	215
3	218	217	220	221	216	220	218	214
SUM	653	651	657	660	653	658	655	644
$\bar{x}$	217.7	217.0	219.0	220.0	217.7	219.3	218.3	214.7

(more details on the setting of control limits are given in Chapter 14).
    The X-bar chart is shown in Figure 1.1.

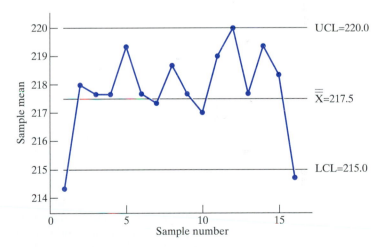

FIGURE 1.1. X-bar Chart for Depth

What does the chart tell us? The mean of 214.3 for the first sample, taken at approximately 6:30 A.M., is outside the lower control limit. Further, the variation in this sample

$$\text{range} = \text{largest} - \text{smallest} = 218 - 211 = 7$$

is large. This evidence suggests that the pressing machine had not yet reached a steady state. The control chart shows that it is necessary to warm up the pressing machine before the first shift begins at 6 A.M. Management and engineering implemented an early start-up and thereby improved the process. The operator and foreman did not have the authority to make this change. Deming claimed that 85% or more of our quality problems are in the system and that the operator and others responsible for the day-to-day operation are responsible for 15% or less of our quality problems.

The X-bar chart further shows that, throughout the day, the process was stable but a little on the high side although no points were out of control until the last sample of the day. Here an unfortunate oversight occurred. The operator did not report the out-of-control value to either the set-up person or the foreman because it was near the end of her shift and the start of her weekend. She also knew the set-up person was already cleaning up for the end of the shift and that the foreman was likely thinking about going across the street to the Legion Bar for some refreshments as soon as the shift ended. She did not want to ruin anyone's plans so she kept quiet.

On Monday morning when the operator started up the pressing machine, one of the dies broke. The cost of the die was over a thousand dollars. But this was not the biggest cost. When a customer was called and told there would be a delay in delivering the ceramic parts, he canceled the order. Certainly the loss of a customer is an expensive item. Deming referred to this type of cost as the unknown and unknowable, but at the same time it is probably the most important cost of poor quality.

On Friday the chart had predicted a problem. Afterwards it was determined that the most likely difficulty was that the clay had dried and stuck to the die, leading to the break. The chart indicated the problem but someone had to act; for a statistical charting procedure to be truly effective action must be taken.

1.6 Two Basic Concepts—Population and Sample

The examples above, where the evaluation of factual information is essential for acquiring new knowledge, motivate the development of statistical reasoning and tools taught in this text. Most experiments and investigations conducted by engineers in the course of investigating, be it a physical phenomenon, production process, or manufactured unit, share some common characteristics.

First, relevant data must be collected. But it is often physically impossible or infeasible from a practical standpoint to obtain a complete set of data. When data are obtained from laboratory experiments, no matter how much experimentation has been performed, more could always be done. To collect an exhaustive set of data related to the damage sustained by all cars of a particular model under collision at a specified speed, every car of that model coming off the production lines would have to be subjected to a collision! In most situations, we must work with only partial information. The distinction between the data actually acquired and the vast collection of all potential observations is a key to understanding statistics. The source of each measurement is called a **unit.** It is usually an object or a person. To emphasize population as the entire collection of units, we term it the **population of units.**

> **unit**   A single entity, usually an object or person, whose characteristics are of interest.
> **population of units**   The complete collection of units about which information is sought.

There is another aspect to any population and that is the value, for each unit, of a characteristic or variable of interest.

There can be several characteristics of interest for a given population of units. Some examples are given in Table 1.2.

TABLE 1.2 Examples of populations, units, and variables.

Population	Unit	Variables/Characteristics
All students currently enrolled in school	student	GPA number of credits hours of work per week major right/left-handed
All printed circuit boards manufactured during a month	board	type of defects number of defects location of defects
All campus fast food restaurants	restaurant	number of employees seating capacity hiring/not hiring
All books in library	book	replacement cost frequency of check-out repairs needed

For a given variable or characteristic of interest, we call the collection of values, evaluated for every unit in the population, the **statistical population** or just the **population.** This collection of values is the population we will address in all later chapters. Here we refer to the collection of units as the **population of units** when there is a need to differentiate it from the collection of values.

> A statistical **population** is the set of all measurements (or record of some quality trait) corresponding to each unit in the entire population of units about which information is sought.

Generally, the strategy for most investigations is to learn about this population by taking a sample.

> A **sample** from a statistical population is the subset of measurements that are actually collected in the course of an investigation.

The sample needs both to be representative of the population and to be large enough to contain information to answer the questions about the population that are crucial to the investigation.

EXAMPLE

Self-selected samples—A bad practice
A magazine which features the latest computer hardware and software for home office use enclosed a short questionnaire on a postcard. Readers were asked to indicate whether or not they owned specific new software packages or hardware products. In past issues, this magazine used similar information from cards that were returned to make such statements as "40% of readers have purchased software package P." Is this sample representative of the population of magazine readers?

Solution
It is clearly impossible to contact all magazine readers since not all are subscribers. One must necessarily settle for taking a sample. Unfortunately the method used by the magazine editors is not representative but is badly biased. Readers who always update and try most of the new software will gladly respond indicating their purchases. In contrast, those who did not purchase any of the software or hardware mentioned in the survey will be very likely not to return the postcard. That is, the proportion of purchasers of software package P in the sample of returned postcards will likely be much higher than it is for the whole population consisting of the *purchase/not purchase* record for each reader. ✔

When we can select the specific units to include in the sample of units, the selection process can be based on random numbers.

Using a Random Number Table to Select Samples

The selection of a sample from a finite population must be done impartially and objectively. But not only is writing the unit names on slips of paper, putting the slips in a box, and drawing them out cumbersome, but proper mixing may not be possible. However, the selection is easy to carry out using a chance mechanism called a **random number table.** Suppose ten balls numbered $0, 1, \ldots, 9$ are placed in an urn and shuffled. Then one is drawn and the digit recorded. It is then replaced, the balls shuffled, another one drawn and the digit recorded. The digits in Table 7 at the end of the book were actually generated by a computer that closely simulates this procedure. A portion of this table is shown as Table 1.3.

The chance mechanism that generated the random number table ensures that each of the single digits has the same chance of occurrence, that all pairs $00, 01, \ldots, 99$ have the same chance of occurrence, and so on. Further, any collection of digits is

TABLE 1.3 Random digits—a portion of Table 7 random digits.

1306	1189	5731	3968	5606	5084	8947	3897	1636	7810
0422	2431	0649	8085	5053	4722	6598	5044	9040	5121
6597	2022	6168	5060	8656	6733	6364	7649	1871	4328
7965	6541	5645	6243	7658	6903	9911	5740	7824	8520
7695	6937	0406	8894	0441	8135	9797	7285	5905	9539
5160	7851	8464	6789	3938	4197	6511	0407	9239	2232
2961	0551	0539	8288	7478	7565	5581	5771	5442	8761
1428	4183	4312	5445	4854	9157	9158	5218	1464	3634
3666	5642	4539	1561	7849	7520	2547	0756	1206	2033
6543	6799	7454	9052	6689	1946	2574	9386	0304	7945
9975	6080	7423	3175	9377	6951	6519	8287	8994	5532
4866	0956	7545	7723	8085	4948	2228	9583	4415	7065
8239	7068	6694	5168	3117	1568	0237	6160	9585	1133
8722	9191	3386	3443	0434	4586	4150	1224	6204	0937
1330	9120	8785	8382	2929	7089	3109	6742	2468	7025

unrelated to any other digit in the table. Because of these properties, the digits are called random.

EXAMPLE

Using the table of random digits

Eighty specialty pumps were manufactured last week. Use Table 1.3 to select a sample of size $n = 5$ to carefully test and recheck for possible defects before they are sent to the purchaser. Select the sample without replacement so that the same pump does not appear twice in the sample.

Solution

The first step is to number the pumps from 1 to 80, or to arrange them in some order so they can be identified. The digits must be selected two at a time because the population size $N = 80$ is a two-digit number. We begin by arbitrarily selecting a row and column. We select row 6 and column 21. Reading the digits in columns 21 and 22, and proceeding downward, we obtain

41   75   91   75   19   69   49

We ignore the number 91 because it is greater than the population size 80. We also ignore any number when it appears a second time, as 75 does here. That is, we continue reading until five different numbers in the appropriate range are selected. Here the five pumps numbered

41   75   19   69   49

will be carefully tested and rechecked for defects.   ✔

For large sample size situations or frequent applications, it is more convenient to use computer software to choose the random numbers.

EXAMPLE   **Selecting a sample by random digit dialing**

Suppose there is a single three-digit exchange for the area in which you wish to conduct a survey. Use the random digit Table 7 to select five phone numbers.

Solution   We arbitrarily decide to start at row 11 and column 21. Reading the digits in columns 21 through 24, and proceeding downward, we obtain

7132   8986   4732   2351   1603

These five numbers, together with the designated exchange, become the phone numbers to be called in the survey. Every phone number, listed or unlisted, has the same chance of being selected. The same holds for every pair, every triplet and so on. Commercial phones may have to be discarded and another number drawn from the table. If there are two exchanges in the area, separate selections could be done for each exchange.   ✔

REVIEW EXERCISES

1.1 A consumer magazine article asks "How Safe Is the Air in Airplanes?"and goes on to say that the air quality was measured on 158 different flights for U.S.-based airlines. Let the variable of interest be a numerical measure of staleness. Identify the population and the sample.

1.2 A radio show host announced that she wanted to know which singer was the favorite among college students in your school. Listeners were asked to call and name their favorite singer. Identify the population, in terms of preferences, and the sample. Is the sample likely to be representative? Comment. Also describe how to obtain a sample that is likely to be more representative.

1.3 A campus engineering club has 40 active members listed on its membership roll. Use Table 7 of random digits to select 5 persons to be interviewed regarding the time they devote to club activities each week.

1.4 A city runs 50 buses daily. Use Table 7 of random digits to select 4 buses to inspect for cleanliness. (We started on the first page of Table 7 at row 31 columns 25 and 26 and read down.)

1.5 Refer to the slot depth data in Table 1.1. After the machine was repaired, a sample of three new ceramic parts had slot depths 215, 216, and 213 (thousandths of an inch).

(a) Redraw the X-bar chart and include the additional mean $\bar{x}$.

(b) Does the new $\bar{x}$ fall within the control limits?

1.6 A Canadian manufacturer identified a critical diameter on a crank bore that needed to be maintained within a close tolerance for the product to be successful. Samples of size 4 were taken every hour. The values of the differences (measurement − specification), in ten-thousandths of an inch, are given in Table 1.4.

(a) Calculate the central line for an X-bar chart for the 24 hourly sample means. The centerline is $\bar{\bar{x}} = (4.25 - 3.00 - \cdots - 1.50 + 3.25)/24$.

(b) Is the average of all the numbers in the table, 4 for each hour, the same as the average of the 24 hourly averages? Should it be?

(c) A computer calculation gives the control limits

$$\text{LCL} = -4.48$$

$$\text{UCL} = 7.88$$

Construct the X-bar chart. Identify hours where the process was out of control.

TABLE 1.4 The differences (measurement − specification), in ten-thousandths of an inch.

Hour	1	2	3	4	5	6	7	8	9	10	11	12
	10	−6	−1	−8	−14	−6	−1	8	−1	5	2	5
	3	1	−3	−3	−5	−2	−6	−3	7	6	1	3
	6	−4	0	−7	−6	−1	−1	9	1	3	1	10
	−2	−3	−7	−2	2	−6	7	11	7	2	4	4
$\bar{x}$	4.25	−3.00	−2.75	−5.00	−5.75	−3.75	−0.25	6.25	3.50	4.00	2.00	5.50

Hour	13	14	15	16	17	18	19	20	21	22	23	24
	5	6	−5	−8	2	7	8	5	8	−5	−2	−1
	9	6	4	−5	8	7	13	4	1	7	−4	5
	9	8	−5	1	−4	5	6	7	0	1	−7	9
	7	10	−2	0	1	3	6	10	−6	2	7	0
$\bar{x}$	7.50	7.50	−2.00	−3.00	1.75	5.50	8.25	6.50	0.75	1.25	−1.50	3.25

KEY TERMS

(with page references)

Classical approach to statistics   3
Descriptive statistics   2
Population   7
Quality improvement   4
Random number table   8

Reliability   4
Sample   8
Statistical inference   2
X-bar chart   4
unit   7

Treatment of Data

Statistical data, obtained from surveys, experiments, or any series of measurements, are often so numerous that they are virtually useless unless they are condensed, or reduced, into a more suitable form. We begin with the use of simple graphics. Next, Sections 2.2 and 2.3 deal with problems relating to the grouping of data and the presentation of such groupings in graphical form; in Section 2.4 we discuss a relatively new way of presenting data.

Sometimes it may be satisfactory to present data just as they are and let them speak for themselves; on other occasions it may be necessary only to group the data and present the result in tabular or graphical form. However, most of the time data have to be summarized further, and in Sections 2.5 through 2.7 we introduce some of the most widely used kinds of statistical descriptions. ▪

2.1 Pareto Diagrams and Dot Diagrams

Data need to be collected to provide the vital information necessary to solve engineering problems. Once gathered, these data must be described and analyzed to produce summary information. Graphical presentations can often be the most effective way to communicate this information. To illustrate the power of graphical techniques, we first describe a **Pareto diagram.** This display, which orders each type of failure or defect according to its frequency, can help engineers identify important defects and their causes.

When a company identifies a process as a candidate for improvement, the first step is to collect data on the frequency of each type of failure. For example, for a computer-controlled lathe whose performance was below par, workers recorded the following causes and their frequencies:

power fluctuations	6
controller not stable	22
operator error	13
worn tool not replaced	2
other	5

These data are presented as a special case of a **bar chart** called a **Pareto diagram** in Figure 2.1. This diagram graphically depicts Pareto's empirical law that any assortment of events consists of a few major and many minor elements. Typically, two or three elements will account for more than half of the total frequency.

Concerning the lathe, 22 or $100(22/48) = 46\%$ of the cases are due to an unstable controller and $22 + 13 = 35$ or $100(35/48) = 73\%$ are due to either unstable controller or operator error. These cumulative percentages are shown in Figure 2.1 as a line graph whose scale is on the right-hand side of the Pareto diagram as in Figure 14.2.

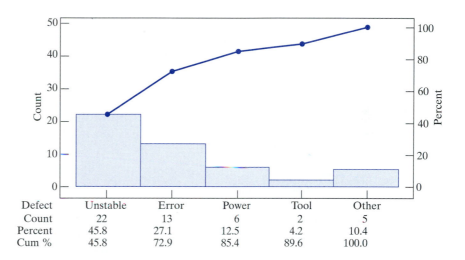

Defect	Unstable	Error	Power	Tool	Other
Count	22	13	6	2	5
Percent	45.8	27.1	12.5	4.2	10.4
Cum %	45.8	72.9	85.4	89.6	100.0

Figure 2.1 A Pareto diagram of failures.

In the context of quality improvement, we want to select the few vital major opportunities for improvement from the many trivial minor opportunities for improvement. This graph visually emphasizes the importance of reducing the frequency of controller misbehavior. An initial goal may be to cut it in half.

As a second step toward improvement of the process, data were collected on the deviations of cutting speed from the target value set by the controller. The seven observed values of (cutting speed) − (target),

$$3 \quad 6 \quad -2 \quad 4 \quad 7 \quad 4 \quad 3$$

are plotted as a **dot diagram** is Figure 2.2. The dot diagram visually summarizes the information that the lathe is, generally, running fast. In Chapters 13 and 14 we

Figure 2.2 Dot diagram of cutting speed deviations.

develop efficient experimental designs and methods for identifying primary causal factors that contribute to the variability in a response such as cutting speed.

When the number of observations is small, it is difficult to identify any pattern of variation. Still, it is a good idea to plot the data and look for unusual features.

EXAMPLE

Dot diagrams expose outliers

In 1987, for the first time, physicists observed neutrinos from a supernova that occurred outside of our solar system. At a site in Kamiokande, the following times (second) between neutrinos were recorded:

0.107   0.196   0.021   0.283   0.179   0.854   0.58   0.19   7.3   1.18   2.0

Draw a dot diagram.

Solution   We plot to the nearest 0.1 second to avoid crowding. (See Figure 2.3.) Note the extremely long gap between 2.0 and 7.3 seconds. Statisticians call such an unusual observation an **outlier.** Usually, outliers merit further attention. Was there a recording error, were neutrinos missed in that long time interval, or were there two separate explosions in the supernova? Important questions in physics hinge on the correct interpretation of this outlier.

Figure 2.3 Dot diagram of times between neutrinos.

EXAMPLE

A dot diagram for multiple samples reveals differences

The vessels that contain the reactions at some nuclear power plants consist of two hemispherical components that are welded together. Copper in the welds could cause them to become brittle after years of service. Samples of welding material from one production run or "heat" that were used in one plant had the copper contents 0.27, 0.35, 0.37. Samples from the next heat had values 0.23, 0.15, 0.25, 0.24, 0.30, 0.33, 0.26. Draw a dot diagram that highlights possible differences in the two production runs (heats) of welding material. If the copper contents for the two runs are different, they should not be combined to form a single estimate.

Solution   We plot the first group as solid circles and the second as open circles. (See Figure 2.4.) It seems unlikely that the two production runs are alike because the top two values are from the first run. (In Chapter 10 we confirm this fact.) The two runs should be treated separately.

The copper content of the welding material used at the power plant is directly related to the determination of safe operating life. Combining the samples would

Figure 2.4 Dot diagram of copper content.

lead to an unrealistically low estimate of copper content and too long an estimate of safe life.   ✔

When a set of data consists of a large number of observations, we take the approach in the next section. The observations are first summarized in the form of a table.

2.2   Frequency Distributions

A **frequency distribution** is a table that divides a set of data into a suitable number of classes (categories), showing also the number of items belonging to each class. Such a table sacrifices some of the information contained in the data; instead of knowing the exact value of each item, we only know that it belongs to a certain class. On the other hand, this kind of grouping often brings out important features of the data, and the gain in "legibility" usually more than compensates for the loss of information. In what follows, we shall consider mainly **numerical distributions,** that is, frequency distributions where the data are grouped according to size; if the data are grouped according to some quality, or attribute, we refer to such a distribution as a **categorical distribution.**

The first step in constructing a frequency distribution consists of deciding how many classes to use and choosing the **limits** for each class, that is, from where to where each class is to go. Generally speaking, the number of classes we use depends on the number of observations, but it is seldom profitable to use fewer than 5 or more than 15. It also depends on the range of the data, namely, the difference between the largest observation and the smallest. Then, we tally the observations and thus determine the **class frequencies,** namely, the number of observations in each class.

To illustrate the construction of a frequency distribution, let us consider the following 80 determinations of the daily emission (in tons) of sulfur oxides from an industrial plant:

15.8	26.4	17.3	11.2	23.9	24.8	18.7	13.9	9.0	13.2
22.7	9.8	6.2	14.7	17.5	26.1	12.8	28.6	17.6	23.7
26.8	22.7	18.0	20.5	11.0	20.9	15.5	19.4	16.7	10.7
19.1	15.2	22.9	26.6	20.4	21.4	19.2	21.6	16.9	19.0
18.5	23.0	24.6	20.1	16.2	18.0	7.7	13.5	23.5	14.5
14.4	29.6	19.4	17.0	20.8	24.3	22.5	24.6	18.4	18.1
8.3	21.9	12.3	22.3	13.3	11.8	19.3	20.0	25.7	31.8
25.9	10.5	15.9	27.5	18.1	17.9	9.4	24.1	20.1	28.5

Since the largest observation is 31.8, the smallest is 6.2, and the range is 25.6, we might choose the six classes having the limits 5.0–9.9, 10.0–14.9, . . . , 30.0–34.9, we might choose the seven classes 5.0–8.9, 9.0–12.9, . . . , 29.0–32.9, or we might choose the nine classes 5.0–7.9, 8.0–10.9, . . . , 29.0–31.9. Note that in each case **the classes do not overlap, they accommodate all the data, and they are all of the same size.**

Deciding on the second of these classifications, we now tally the 80 observations and obtain the results shown in the following table:

Class limits	Tally	Frequency
5.0–8.9	///	3
9.0–12.9	7HL 7HL	10
13.0–16.9	7HL 7HL ////	14
17.0–20.9	7HL 7HL 7HL 7HL 7HL	25
21.0–24.9	7HL 7HL 7HL //	17
25.0–28.9	7HL ////	9
29.0–32.9	//	2
	Total	80

Note that the class limits are given to as many decimal places as the original data. Had the original data been given to two decimal places, we would have used the class limits 5.00–8.99, 9.00–12.99, . . . , 29.00–32.99, and if they had been rounded to the nearest ton, we would have used the class limits 5–8, 9–12, . . . , 29–32.

In the preceding example, the data may be thought of as values of a continuous variable, but if we use classes such as 5.0–9.0, 9.0–13.0, . . . , 29.0–33.0, there exists the possibility of ambiguities: 9.0 could go into the first class or into the second, 13.0 could go into the second class or into the third, and so on. To avoid this difficulty, we can let the first class go from 4.95 to 8.95, the second from 8.95 to 12.95, . . . , and the last from 28.95 to 32.95. We refer to these new limits as the **class boundaries,** and it should be noted that there will be no ambiguities even though the boundaries overlap. These class boundaries are, so to speak, "impossible" values, since the data were given to only one decimal. In practice, we use the class boundaries rather than the original class limits chiefly when we want to stress the fact that we are dealing with continuous kinds of measurements.

An alternative approach, which is popular when graphing frequency distributions, is to make an **endpoint convention.** For the emission data we could take [5, 9) as the first class, [9, 11) as the second, and so on through [29, 33). That is, for this data set, we adopt the convention that the left-hand endpoint is included but the right-hand endpoint is not. For other data sets, we may prefer to reverse the endpoint convention so the right-hand endpoint is included but the left-hand endpoint is not. Whichever endpoint convention is adopted, it should appear in the description of the frequency distribution.

As we pointed out earlier, once data have been grouped, each observation has lost its identity in the sense that its exact value is no longer known. This may lead to difficulties when we want to give further descriptions of the data, but we can avoid them by representing each observation in a class by its midpoint, called the **class mark.** In general, the class marks of a frequency distribution are obtained by averaging successive class limits or successive class boundaries. If the classes of a distribution are all of equal length, as in our example, we refer to the common interval between any successive class marks as the **class interval** of the distribution. Note that the class interval may also be obtained from the difference between any successive class boundaries.

EXAMPLE

Class marks and class interval for grouped data.
With reference to the distribution of the sulfur oxides data, find (a) the class marks, and (b) the class interval.

Solution (a) The class marks are $\dfrac{5.0 + 8.9}{2} = 6.95, \dfrac{9.0 + 12.9}{2} = 10.95, 14.95, 18.95, 22.95,$ 26.95, and 30.95.

(b) The class interval is $10.95 - 6.95 = 4$.

If we use the classes $(5,9], (9,13], \ldots (29,33]$ the class marks are 7, 11, 15, 19, 23, 27, and 31. The class interval is $11 - 7 = 4$. ✔

There are several alternative forms of distributions into which data are sometimes grouped. Foremost among these are the "less than," "or less," "more than," and "or more" **cumulative distributions**. A cumulative "less than" distribution shows the total number of observations that are less than given values. These values must be class boundaries or appropriate class limits, but they may not be class marks.

EXAMPLE

Cumulative distribution for sulfur emission data
Convert the distribution of the sulfur oxides emission data into a distribution showing how many of the observations are less then 4.95, less than 8.95, less than 12.95, . . . , and less then 32.95.

Solution Since none of the values is less than 4.95, 3 are less then 8.95, $3 + 10 = 13$ are less than 12.95, $3 + 10 + 14 = 27$ are less than 16.95, . . . , and all 80 are less than 32.95, we have:

Tons of sulfur oxides	Cumulative frequency
less than 4.95	0
less than 8.95	3
less than 12.95	13
less than 16.95	27
less than 20.95	52
less than 24.95	69
less than 28.95	78
less than 32.95	80

Note that instead of "less than 4.95" we could also have written "less than 5.0" and so on. ✔

Cumulative "more than" and "or more" distributions are constructed similarly by adding the frequencies, one by one, starting at the other end of the frequency distribution. In practice, "less than" cumulative distributions are used most widely, and it is not uncommon to refer to "less than" cumulative distributions simply as cumulative distributions.

If it is desirable to compare frequency distributions, it may be necessary (or at least advantageous) to convert them into **percentage distributions.** We simply divide each class frequency by the total frequency (the total number of observations in the distribution) and multiply by 100; in this way we indicate what percentage of the data falls into each class of the distribution. The same can also be done with cumulative distributions, thus converting them to **cumulative percentage distributions.**

2.3 Graphs of Frequency Distributions

Properties of frequency distributions relating to their shape are best exhibited by means of graphs, and in this section we shall introduce some of the most widely used forms of graphical presentations of frequency distributions and cumulative distributions.

The most common form of graphical presentation of a frequency distribution is the **histogram.** The histogram of a frequency distribution is constructed of adjacent rectangles; the heights of the rectangles represent the class frequencies and the bases of the rectangles extend between successive class boundaries. A histogram of the sulfur oxides emission data is shown in Figure 2.5.

Using our endpoint convention, the interval (5, 9] that defines the first class has frequency 3 so the rectangle has height 3. The second rectangle, over the interval (9, 13], has height 10 and so on. The tallest rectangle is over the interval (17, 21] and it has height 25. The histogram has a single peak and it is reasonably symmetric. About half of the area, representing half of the observations, is over the interval from 15 to 23 tons of sulfur oxides.

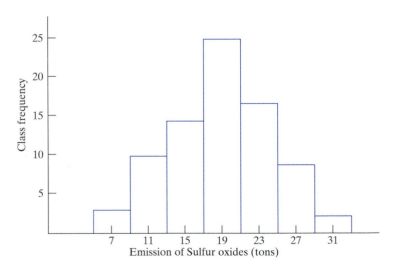

Figure 2.5 Histogram

Inspection of the graph of a frequency distribution as a histogram often brings out features that are not immediately apparent from the data themselves. Aside from the fact that such a graph presents a good overall picture of the data, it can also emphasize irregularities and unusual features. For instance, outlying observations which somehow do not fit the overall picture, that is, the overall pattern of variation in the data, may be due to errors of measurement, equipment failure, and similar causes. Also, the fact that a histogram exhibits two or more *modes* (maxima) can provide pertinent information. The appearance of two modes may imply, for example, a shift in the process that is being measured, or it may imply that the data come from two or more sources. With some experience one learns to spot such irregularities or anomalies, and an experienced engineer would find it just as surprising if the histogram of a distribution of integrated-circuit failure times were symmetrical as if a distribution of American men's hat sizes were bimodal.

Sometimes it can be enough to draw a histogram in order to solve an engineering problem.

EXAMPLE

A histogram reveals the solution to a grinding operation problem
A metallurgical engineer was experiencing trouble with a grinding operation. The grinding action was produced by pellets. After some thought he collected a sample of pellets used for grinding, took them home, spread them out on his kitchen table, and measured their diameters. His histogram is displayed in Figure 2.6. What does the histogram reveal?

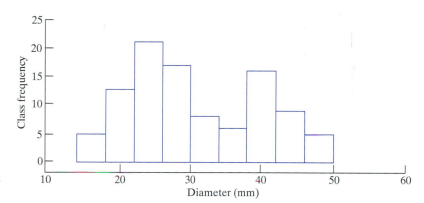

Figure 2.6 Histogram of pellet diameter.

Solution   The histogram exhibits two distinct peaks, one for a group of pellets whose diameters are centered near 25 and the other centered near 40.

By getting his supplier to do a better sort, so all the pellets would be essentially from the first group, the engineer completely solved his problem. ✔

As illustrated by the next example concerning a system of supercomputers, not all histograms are symmetric.

EXAMPLE

A histogram reveals the pattern of a supercomputer systems data
A computer scientist, trying to optimize system performance, collected data on the time, in microseconds, between requests for a particular process service.

2,808	4,201	3,848	9,112	2,082	5,913	1,620	6,719	21,657
3,072	2,949	11,768	4,731	14,211	1,583	9,853	78,811	6,655
1,803	7,012	1,892	4,227	6,583	15,147	4,740	8,528	10,563
43,003	16,723	2,613	26,463	34,867	4,191	4,030	2,472	28,840
24,487	14,001	15,241	1,643	5,732	5,419	28,608	2,487	995
3,116	29,508	11,440	28,336	3,440				

Draw a histogram using the equal length classes $[0, 10{,}000), [10{,}000, 20{,}000), \ldots,$ $[70{,}000, 80{,}000)$ where the left-hand endpoint is included but not the right.

Solution The histogram of this interrequest time data, shown in Figure 2.7, has a long right-hand tail. Notice that two classes are empty with this choice of equal length intervals. To emphasize that it is still possible to observe interrequest times in these intervals, it is preferable to regroup the data in the right-hand tail into classes of unequal lengths (see Exercise 2.58).

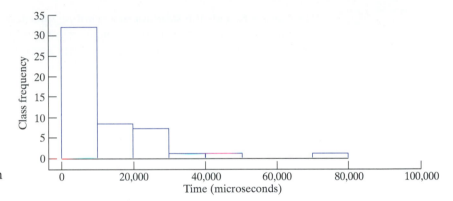

Figure 2.7 Histogram of interrequest time.

When a histogram is constructed from a frequency table having classes of unequal lengths, the height of each rectangle must be changed to $\text{height} = \dfrac{\text{relative frequency}}{\text{width}}$. The area of the rectangle then represents the relative frequency for the class and the total area of the histogram is 1. We call this a **density histogram.**

EXAMPLE

A density histogram has total area 1

Compressive strength was measured on 58 specimens of a new aluminum alloy undergoing development as a material for the next generation of aircraft.

66.4	67.7	68.0	68.0	68.3	68.4	68.6	68.8	68.9	69.0	69.1
69.2	69.3	69.3	69.5	69.5	69.6	69.7	69.8	69.8	69.9	70.0
70.0	70.1	70.2	70.3	70.3	70.4	70.5	70.6	70.6	70.8	70.9
71.0	71.1	71.2	71.3	71.3	71.5	71.6	71.6	71.7	71.8	71.8
71.9	72.1	72.2	72.3	72.4	72.6	72.7	72.9	73.1	73.3	73.5
74.2	74.5	75.3								

Draw a density histogram, that is, a histogram scaled to have a total area of 1 unit. For reasons to become apparent in Chapter 6, we call the vertical scale density.

Solution   We make the height of each rectangle equal to *relative frequency/width*, so that its area equals the relative frequency. The resulting histogram, constructed by computer, has a nearly symmetric shape. (See Figure 2.8.) We have also graphed a continuous curve that approximates the overall shape. In Chapter 6, we will be introduced to this bell-shaped family of curves.

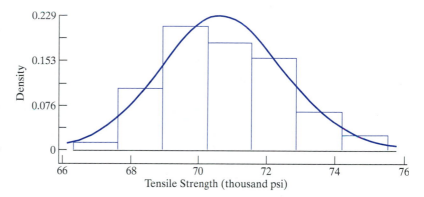

Figure 2.8 Histogram of aluminum alloy compressive strength.

This example suggests that histograms, for observations that come from a continuous scale, can be approximated by smooth curves.

Cumulative distributions are usually presented graphically in the form of **ogives,** where we plot the cumulative frequencies at the class boundaries. The resulting points are connected by means of straight lines, as shown in Figure 2.9, which represents the cumulative "less than" distribution of the sulfur oxides emission data on page 15. The slope is steepest across the class with highest frequency.

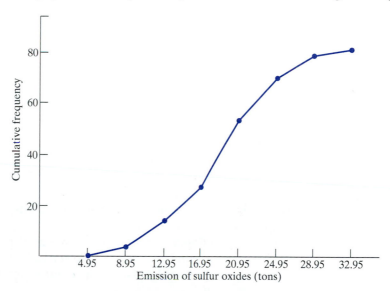

Figure 2.9 Ogive.

2.4   Stem-and-leaf Displays

In the two preceding sections we directed our attention to the grouping of relatively large sets of data, with the objective of putting such data into a manageable form. As we saw, this entailed some loss of information. In recent years, similar techniques have been proposed for the preliminary explorations of small sets of data, which yield a good overall picture of the data without any loss of information.

To illustrate, consider the following humidity readings rounded to the nearest percent:

$$29 \quad 44 \quad 12 \quad 53 \quad 21 \quad 34 \quad 39 \quad 25 \quad 48 \quad 23$$
$$17 \quad 24 \quad 27 \quad 32 \quad 34 \quad 15 \quad 42 \quad 21 \quad 28 \quad 37$$

Proceeding as in Section 2.2, we might group these data into the following distribution:

Humidity readings	Tally	Frequency
10–19	///	3
20–29	ℍℍ ///	8
30–39	ℍℍ	5
40–49	///	3
50–59	/	1

where the tally pictures the overall pattern of the data like a histogram (or bar chart) lying on its side.

If we wanted to avoid the loss of information inherent in the preceding table, we could replace the tally marks with the last digits of the corresponding readings, getting

10–19	2 7 5
20–29	9 1 5 3 4 7 1 8
30–39	4 9 2 4 7
40–49	4 8 2
50–59	3

This can also be written as

1	2 7 5
2	9 1 5 3 4 7 1 8
3	4 9 2 4 7
4	4 8 2
5	3

where the left-hand column gives the tens digits 10, 20, 30, 40, and 50. In this example, the three numbers in the first row are 12, 17, and 15. This table is called a **stem-and-leaf display** (or simply a **stem-leaf display**)—each row has a **stem** and each digit on a stem to the right of the vertical line is a **leaf.** To the left of the vertical line are the **stem labels,** which, in our example, are 1, 2, . . . , 5.

Essentially, a stem-and-leaf display presents the same picture as the corresponding tally, yet it retains all the original information. For instance, if a stem-and-leaf display has the two-digit stem

$$1.2 \quad | \quad 3 \quad 5 \quad 2 \quad 0 \quad 8$$

the corresponding data are 1.23, 1.25, 1.22, 1.20, and 1.28, and if a stem-and-leaf display has the stem

$$0.3 \quad | \quad 17 \quad 03 \quad 55 \quad 89$$

with two-digit leaves, the corresponding data are 0.317, 0.303, 0.355, and 0.389.

There are various ways in which stem-and-leaf displays can be modified to meet particular needs (see Exercises 2.25 and 2.26), but we shall not go into this here in any detail as it has been our objective to present only one of the relatively new techniques, which come under the general heading of **exploratory data analysis.**

EXERCISES

2.1   Accidents at a potato chip plant are categorized according to the area injured.

fingers	17
eyes	5
arm	2
leg	1

Draw a Pareto chart.

2.2   Damage at a paper mill (thousands of dollars) due to breakage can be divided according to the product:

toilet paper	132
hand towels	85
napkins	43
12 other products	50

(a) Draw a Pareto chart.

What percent of the loss occurs in making

(b) toilet paper?

(c) toilet paper or hand towels?

2.3   The following are 15 measurements of the boiling point of a silicon compound (in degrees Celsius): 166, 141, 136, 153, 170, 162, 155, 146, 183, 157, 148, 132, 160, 175, and 150. Construct a dot diagram.

2.4   The following are 14 measurements on the strength (pounds) of paper to be used in cardboard tubes: 121, 128, 129, 132, 135, 133, 127, 115, 131, 125, 118, 114, 120, 116. Construct a dot diagram.

2.5   Civil engineers help municipal wastewater treatment plants operate more efficiently by collecting data on quality of the effluent. On seven occasions, the amounts of suspended solids (parts per million) at one plant were

$$14 \quad 12 \quad 21 \quad 28 \quad 30 \quad 65 \quad 26$$

Display the data in a dot diagram. Comment on your findings.

2.6 Jump River Electric serves part of Northern Wisconsin and because much of the area is forested, it is prone to outages. One August there were 11 power outages (duration in hours).

2.5	2.0	1.5	3.0	1.0	1.5	2.0	1.5	1.0	10.0	1.0

Display the data in a dot diagram.

2.7 The weights of certain mineral specimens, given to the nearest tenth of an ounce, are grouped into a table having the classes 10.5–11.4, 11.5–12.4, 12.5–13.4, and 13.5–14.4 ounces. Find

(a) the class marks;

(b) the class boundaries;

(c) the class interval.

2.8 With reference to the preceding exercise, is it possible to determine from the grouped data how many of the mineral specimens weigh

(a) less than 11.5 ounces;

(b) more than 11.5 ounces;

(c) at least 12.4 ounces;

(d) at most 12.4 ounces;

(e) from 11.5 to 13.5 ounces?

2.9 The following are measurements of the breaking strength (in ounces) of a sample of 60 linen threads:

32.5	15.2	35.4	21.3	28.4	26.9	34.6	29.3	24.5	31.0
21.2	28.3	27.1	25.0	32.7	29.5	30.2	23.9	23.0	26.4
27.3	33.7	29.4	21.9	29.3	17.3	29.0	36.8	29.2	23.5
20.6	29.5	21.8	37.5	33.5	29.6	26.8	28.7	34.8	18.6
25.4	34.1	27.5	29.6	22.2	22.7	31.3	33.2	37.0	28.3
36.9	24.6	28.9	24.8	28.1	25.4	34.5	23.6	38.4	24.0

Group these measurements into a distribution having the classes 15.0–19.9, 20.0–24.9, . . . , 35.0–39.9 and construct a histogram using $[15, 20), [20, 25), . . . , [35, 40)$.

2.10 Convert the distribution obtained in the preceding exercise into a cumulative "less than" distribution and graph its ogive.

2.11 The class marks of a distribution of temperature readings (given to the nearest degree Celsius) are 16, 25, 34, 43, 52, and 61. Find

(a) the class boundaries;

(b) the class limits.

2.12 The following are the ignition times of certain upholstery materials exposed to a flame, given to the nearest hundredth of a second:

2.58	2.51	4.04	6.43	1.58	4.32	2.20	4.19
4.79	6.20	1.52	1.38	3.87	4.54	5.12	5.15
5.50	5.92	4.56	2.46	6.90	1.47	2.11	2.32
6.75	5.84	8.80	7.40	4.72	3.62	2.46	8.75
2.65	7.86	4.71	6.25	9.45	12.80	1.42	1.92
7.60	8.79	5.92	9.65	5.09	4.11	6.37	5.40

11.25	3.90	5.33	8.64	7.41	7.95	10.60	3.81
3.78	3.75	3.10	6.43	1.70	6.40	3.24	1.79
4.90	3.49	6.77	5.62	9.70	5.11	4.50	2.50
5.21	1.76	9.20	1.20	6.85	2.80	7.35	11.75

Group these figures into a table with a suitable number of equal classes and construct a histogram.

2.13 Convert the distribution obtained in Exercise 2.12 into a cumulative "less than" distribution and plot its ogive.

2.14 In a 2-week study of the productivity of workers, the following data were obtained on the total number of acceptable pieces which 100 workers produced:

65	36	49	84	79	56	28	43	67	36
43	78	37	40	68	72	55	62	22	82
88	50	60	56	57	46	39	57	73	65
59	48	76	74	70	51	40	75	56	45
35	62	52	63	32	80	64	53	74	34
76	60	48	55	51	54	45	44	35	51
21	35	61	45	33	61	77	60	85	68
45	53	34	67	42	69	52	68	52	47
62	65	55	61	73	50	53	59	41	54
41	74	82	58	26	35	47	50	38	70

Group these figures into a distribution having the classes 20–29, 30–39, 40–49, . . . , and 80–89, and plot a histogram using $[20, 30), . . . , [80, 90)$.

2.15 Convert the distribution obtained in Exercise 2.14 into a cumulative "less than" distribution and plots its ogive.

2.16 The following are the number of automobile accidents that occurred at 60 major intersections in a certain city during the Fourth of July weekend:

0	2	5	0	1	4	1	0	2	1
5	0	1	3	0	0	2	1	3	1
1	4	0	2	4	1	2	4	0	4
3	5	0	1	3	6	4	2	0	2
0	2	3	0	4	2	5	1	1	2
2	1	6	5	0	3	3	0	0	4

Group these data into a frequency distribution showing how often each of the values occurs and draw a bar chart.

2.17 Convert the distribution obtained in Exercise 2.16 into a cumulative "or more" distribution and draw its ogive.

2.18 Categorical distributions are often presented graphically by means of **pie charts,** in which a circle is divided into sectors proportional in size to the frequencies (or percentages) with which the data are distributed among the categories. Draw a pie chart to represent the following data, obtained in a study in which 40 drivers were asked to judge the maneuverability of a certain make of car:

Very good, good, good, fair, excellent, good, good, good, very good, poor, good, good, good, good, very good, good, fair, good, good, very poor, very good, fair, good, good, excellent, very good, good, good, good, fair, fair, very good, good, very good, excellent, very good, fair, good, good, and very good.

Figure 2.10 Pictogram for Exercise 2.19.　　　Per capita income

2.19 The pictogram of Figure 2.10 is intended to illustrate the fact that per capita income in the United States doubled from $12,000 in 1982 to $24,000 in 1996. Does this pictogram convey a "fair" impression of the actual change? If not, state how it might be modified.

2.20 Convert the distribution of the sulfur oxides emission data on page16 into a distribution having the classes 5.0–8.9, 9.0–20.9, 21.0–28.9, and 29.0–32.9. Draw two histograms of this distribution, one in which the class frequencies are given by the heights of the rectangles and one in which the class frequencies are given by the areas of the rectangles. Explain why the first of these histograms gives a very misleading picture.

2.21 Given a set of observations $x_1, x_2, \ldots,$ and x_n, we define their **empirical cumulative distribution** as the function whose values $F(x)$ equal the proportion of the observations less than or equal to x. Graph the empirical cumulative distribution for the 15 measurements of Exercise 2.3.

2.22 The following are figures on a well's daily production of oil in barrels: 214, 203, 226, 198, 243, 225, 207, 203, 208, 200, 217, 202, 208, 212, 205, and 220. Construct a stem-and-leaf display with the stem labels 19, 20, . . . , and 24.

2.23 The following are determinations of a river's annual maximum flow in cubic meters per second: 405, 355, 419, 267, 370, 391, 612, 383, 434, 462, 288, 317, 540, 295, and 508. Construct a stem-and-leaf display with two-digit leaves.

2.24 List the data that correspond to the following stems of stem-and-leaf displays:

    (a)   1 | 3   2   5   7   1   4   8

    (b)   23 | 4   0   0   1   6

    (c)   2 | 35   18   57   03

    (d)   3.2 | 1   7   4   4   3

2.25 If we want to construct a stem-and-leaf display with more stems than there would be otherwise, we might repeat each stem. The leaves 0, 1, 2, 3, and 4 would be attached to the first stem and leaves 5, 6, 7, 8, and 9 to the second. For the humidity readings on page 22, we would thus get the **double-stem display**

```
1 | 2
1 | 7  5
2 | 1  3  4  1
2 | 9  5  7  8
3 | 4  2  4
3 | 9  7
4 | 4  2
4 | 8
5 | 3
```

where we doubled the number of stems by cutting the interval covered by each stem in half. Construct a double-stem display with one-digit leaves for the data in Exercise 2.14.

2.26 If the double stem display has too few stems, we might wish to have 5 stems where the first holds leaves 0 and 1, the second holds 2 and 3, and so on. The resulting stem-and-leaf display is called a **five-stem display.**

   (a) The following are the IQs of 20 applicants to an undergraduate engineering program: 109, 111, 106, 106, 125, 108, 115, 109, 107, 109, 108, 110, 112, 104, 110, 112, 128, 106, 111, and 108. Construct a five-stem display with one-digit leaves.

   (b) The following is part of a five-stem display:

```
53 | 5  4  4  4  5  4
53 | 6  7  6  6
53 | 9  8
54 | 1
```

List the corresponding measurements.

2.5 Descriptive Measures

Histograms, dot diagrams, and stem-and-leaf diagrams summarize a data set pictorially so we can visually discern the overall pattern of variation. We now develop numerical measures to describe a data set. To proceed, we introduce the notation

$$x_1, x_2, \ldots, x_i, \ldots, x_n$$

for a general sample consisting of n measurements. Here x_i is the i-th observation in the list so x_1 represents the value of the first measurement, x_2 represents the value of the second measurement, and so on.

Given a set of n measurements or observations, $x_1, x_2, \ldots, x_n$, there are many ways in which we can describe their center (middle, or central location). Most popular among these are the **arithmetic mean** and the **median,** although other kinds of "averages" are sometimes used for special purposes. The arithmetic mean—or, more succinctly, the **mean**—is defined by the formula

Sample mean

$$\bar{x} = \frac{\sum_{i=1}^{n} x_i}{n}$$

To emphasize that it is based on a set of observations, we often refer to $\bar{x}$ as the **sample mean.**

Sometimes it is preferable to use the **median** as a descriptive measure of the center, or location, of a set of data. This is true, particularly, if it is desired to minimize the calculations or if it is desired to eliminate the effect of extreme (very large or very small) values. The median of n observations $x_1, x_2, \ldots, x_n$ can be defined loosely as the "middlemost" value once the data are arranged according to size. More precisely, if the observations are arranged according to size and n is an odd number, the median is the value of the observation numbered $\frac{n+1}{2}$; if n is an even number, the median is defined as the mean (average) of the observations numbered $\frac{n}{2}$ and $\frac{n+2}{2}$.

EXAMPLE   **Calculation of the sample mean and median**
Find the mean and the median of 15, 14, 2, 27, and 13.

Solution   The mean is

$$\bar{x} = \frac{15 + 14 + 2 + 27 + 13}{5} = 14.2$$

and, ordering the data from smallest to largest

$$2 \quad 13 \quad \underline{14} \quad 15 \quad 27$$

the median is the third largest value, namely, 14.   ✔

EXAMPLE   **Calculation of the sample median with even sample size**
The engineering group receives email requests for technical information from sales and service persons. The daily numbers for six days were 11, 9, 17, 19, 4, and 15. Find the mean and the median.

Solution   The mean is

$$\bar{x} = \frac{11 + 9 + 17 + 19 + 4 + 15}{6} = 12.5 \text{ requests}$$

and, ordering the data from the smallest to largest

$$4 \quad 9 \quad \underline{11} \quad \underline{15} \quad 17 \quad 19$$

the median, the mean of the third and fourth largest values, is 13 requests.   ✔

Figure 2.11 The interpretation of the sample mean as a balance point.

The sample mean has an interpretation as the balance point, or center, of a data set. Figure 2.11 is the dot diagram for the data on the number of email requests given in the previous example. In the dot diagram, each observation is represented by a ball placed at the appropriate distance along the horizontal axis. If the balls are considered as masses having equal weights and the horizontal axis is weightless, then the mean corresponds to the center of inertia or balance point of the data. This interpretation of the sample mean, as the balance point of the observations, holds for any data set.

Although the mean and the median each provide a single number to represent an entire set of data, the mean is usually preferred in problems of estimation and other problems of statistical inference. An intuitive reason for preferring the mean is that the median does not utilize all the information contained in the observations.

The following is an example where the median actually gives a more useful description of a set of data than the mean.

EXAMPLE

The median is unaffected by a few outliers
A small company employs four young engineers, who each earn $30,000, and the owner (also an engineer), who gets $120,000. Comment on the claim that on the average the company pays $48,000 to its engineers and, hence, is a good place to work.

Solution

The mean of the five salaries is $48,000, but it hardly describes the situation. The median, on the other hand, is $30,000 and it is most representative of what a young engineer earns with the firm. Moneywise, the company is not such a good place for young engineers.

This example illustrates that there is always an inherent danger is summarizing a set of data by means of a single number.

One of the most important characteristics of almost any set of data is that the values are not all alike; indeed, the extent to which they are unalike, or vary among themselves, is of basic importance in statistics. Measures such as the mean and median describe one important aspect of a set of data—their "middle" or their "average"—but they tell us nothing about this other basic characteristic. We observe that the dispersion of a set of data is small if the values are closely bunched about their mean, and that it is large if the values are scattered widely about their mean. It would seem reasonable, therefore, to measure the variation of a set of data in terms of the amounts by which the values deviate from their mean.

If a set of numbers $x_1, x_2, \ldots, x_n$ has mean $\bar{x}$, the differences $x_1 - \bar{x}, x_2 - \bar{x}, \ldots, x_n - \bar{x}$ are called the **deviations from the mean.** It suggests itself that we might use their average as a measure of variation in the data set. Unfortunately, this will not do. For instance, refer to the observations 11 9 17 19 4 15 displayed above in Figure 2.11 where $\bar{x} = 12.5$ is the balance point. The six deviations are -1.5 -3.5 4.5 6.5 -8.5 2.5 and the sum of the positive deviations $4.5 + 6.5 + 2.5 = 13.5$ exactly cancels the sum of the negative deviations $-1.5 - 3.5 - 8.5 = -13.5$ so the sum of all the deviations is 0.

As the reader will be asked to show in Exercise 2.46 on page 40, the sum of the deviations is always zero. That is $\sum_{i=1}^{n}(x_i - \bar{x}) = 0$, so the mean of the deviations is always zero.

Because the deviations sum to zero, an alternative approach is to square each deviation. The **sample variance,** s^2, is essentially the average of the squared deviations from the mean $\bar{x}$, and is defined by the formula

Sample variance

$$s^2 = \frac{\sum_{i=1}^{n}(x_i - \bar{x})^2}{n - 1}$$

Our reason for dividing by $n - 1$ instead of n is that there are only $n - 1$ independent deviations $x_i - \bar{x}$. Because their sum is always zero, the value of any particular one is always equal to the negative of the sum of the other $n - 1$ deviations.

If many of the deviations are large in magnitude, either positive or negative, their squares will be large and s^2 will be large. When all the deviations are small, s^2 will be small.

EXAMPLE   **Calculation of sample variance**
The delay times (handling, setting, and positioning the tools) for cutting 6 parts on an engine lathe are 0.6, 1.2, 0.9, 1.0, 0.6, and 0.8 minutes. Calculate s^2.

Solution   First we calculate the mean:
$$\bar{x} = \frac{0.6 + 1.2 + 0.9 + 1.0 + 0.6 + 0.8}{6} = 0.85$$

Then we set up the work required to find $\sum (x_i - \bar{x})^2$ in the following table:

x_i	$x_i - \bar{x}$	$(x_i - \bar{x})^2$
0.6	-0.25	0.0625
1.2	0.35	0.1225
0.9	0.05	0.0025
1.0	0.15	0.0225
0.6	-0.25	0.0625
0.8	-0.05	0.0025
		0.2750

We divide 0.2750 by $6 - 1 = 5$ to obtain

$$s^2 = \frac{0.2750}{5} = 0.055 \quad (\text{minute})^2 \quad \checkmark$$

Notice that s^2 is in the wrong units. The data are delay times in minutes, so s^2 has the unit $(\text{minute})^2$. Consequently, we define the **standard deviation** of n observations $x_1, x_2, \ldots, x_n$ as the square root of their variance, namely

Sample standard deviation

$$s = \sqrt{\frac{\sum_{i=1}^{n} (x_i - \overline{x})^2}{n - 1}}$$

The standard deviation is by far the most generally useful measure of variation. Its advantage over the variance is that it is given the same units as the observations.

EXAMPLE

Calculation of sample standard deviation
With reference to the previous example, calculate s.

Solution   From the previous example, $s^2 = 0.055$. Take the square root and get

$$s = \sqrt{0.055} = 0.23 \text{ minutes} \quad \checkmark$$

The standard deviation and the variance are measures of **absolute variation,** that is, they measure the actual amount of variation in a set of data, and they depend on the scale of measurement. To compare the variation in several sets of data, it is generally desirable to use a measure of **relative variation,** for instance, the **coefficient of variation,** which gives the standard deviation as a percentage of the mean.

Coefficient of variation

$$V = \frac{s}{\overline{x}} \cdot 100$$

EXAMPLE

The coefficient of variation for comparing relative preciseness
Measurements made with one micrometer of the diameter of a ball bearing have a mean of 3.92 mm and a standard deviation of 0.015 mm, whereas measurements made with another micrometer of the unstretched length of a spring have a mean of 1.54 inches and a standard deviation of 0.008 inch. Which of these two measuring instruments is relatively more precise?

Solution   For the first micrometer the coefficient of variation is

$$V = \frac{0.015}{3.92} \cdot 100 = 0.38\%$$

and for the second micrometer the coefficient of variation is

$$V = \frac{0.008}{1.54} \cdot 100 = 0.52\%$$

Thus, the measurements made with the first micrometer are relatively more precise. ✔

In this section, we have limited the discussion to the mean, the median, the variance, and the standard deviation, but there are many other ways of describing sets of data.

2.6   Quartiles and Other Percentiles

In addition to the median, which divides a set of data into halves, we can consider other division points. When an ordered data set is divided into quarters, the resulting division points are called sample **quartiles.** The **first quartile,** Q_1, is a value that has one-fourth, or 25%, of the observations below its value. The first quartile is also the sample 25th **percentile** $P_{0.25}$. More generally, we define the sample 100 pth percentile as follows.

Sample percentiles

> The sample 100 pth percentile is a value such that at least 100 p% of the observations are at or below this value and at least $100\,(1 - p)\%$ are at or above this value.

As in the case of the median, which is the 50th percentile, this may not uniquely define a percentile. Our convention is to take an observed value for the sample percentile unless two adjacent values both satisfy the definition. In this latter case, take their mean. This coincides with the procedure for obtaining the median when the sample size is even. (Most computer packages linearly interpolate between the two adjacent values. For moderate or large sample sizes, the particular conventions used to locate a sample percentile between the two observations are inconsequential.)

The following rule simplifies the calculation of sample percentiles.

> Calculating the sample 100pth Percentile
> 1. Order the n observations from smallest to largest.
> 2. Determine the product np.
>
>   If np is not an integer, round it up to the next integer and find the corresponding ordered value.
>
>   If np is an integer, say k, calculate the mean of the kth and $(k + 1)$-st ordered observations.

The quartiles are the 25th, 50th, and 75th percentiles.

sample quartiles

> **first quartile** Q_1 = 25th percentile
> **second quartile** Q_2 = 50th percentile
> **third quartile** Q_3 = 75th percentile

EXAMPLE

Calculation of percentiles from the sulfur emission data
Obtain the quartiles and the 95th percentile for the sulfur emission data on page 15.

Solution   The ordered data are:

6.2	7.7	8.3	9.0	9.4	9.8	10.5	10.7	11.0	11.2	11.8
12.3	12.8	13.2	13.3	13.5	13.9	14.4	14.5	14.7	15.2	15.5
15.8	15.9	16.2	16.7	16.9	17.0	17.3	17.5	17.6	17.9	18.0
18.0	18.1	18.1	18.4	18.5	18.7	19.0	19.1	19.2	19.3	19.4
19.4	20.0	20.1	20.1	20.4	20.5	20.8	20.9	21.4	21.6	21.9
22.3	22.5	22.7	22.7	22.9	23.0	23.5	23.7	23.9	24.1	24.3
24.6	24.6	24.8	25.7	25.9	26.1	26.4	26.6	26.8	27.5	28.5
28.6	29.6	31.8								

According to our calculation rule, $np = 80(\frac{1}{4}) = 20$ is an integer, so we take the mean of the 20th and 21st ordered observations.

$$Q_1 = \frac{14.7 + 15.2}{2} = 14.95$$

Since $np = 80(\frac{1}{2}) = 40$, the second quartile, or median, is the mean of the 40th and 41st ordered observations

$$Q_2 = \frac{19.0 + 19.1}{2} = 19.05$$

while the third quartile is the mean of the 60th and 61st:

$$Q_3 = \frac{22.9 + 23.0}{2} = 22.95$$

To obtain the 95th percentile $P_{0.95}$, we determine that $0.95 \times 80 = 76$. Again, a mean is appropriate.

$$P_{0.95} = \frac{27.5 + 28.5}{2} = 28.0$$

The 95th percentile provides a useful description regarding days of high emission. On only 5% of the days are more than 28.0 tons of sulfur put into the air.
In the context of monitoring high values, we also record that the maximum emission was 31.8.

The **minimum** and **maximum** observations also convey information concerning the amount of variability present in a set of data. Together, they describe the interval containing all of the observed values and whose length is the

$$\text{\textbf{range}} = maximum - minimum$$

Care must be taken when interpreting the range since a single large or small observation can greatly inflate its value.

The amount of variation in the middle half of the data is described by the

$$\text{\textbf{interquartile range}} = third\ quartile - first\ quartile = Q_3 - Q_1$$

EXAMPLE   **Calculation of the range and interquartile range**
Obtain the range and interquartile range for the sulfur emission data on page 33.

Solution   The minimum = 6.2. From the previous example, the maximum = 31.8, $Q_1 = 14.95$ and $Q_3 = 22.95$.

$$range = maximum - minimum = 31.8 - 6.2 = 25.6 \text{ tons}$$
$$interquartile\ range = Q_3 - Q_1 = 22.95 - 14.95 = 8.00 \text{ tons} \qquad ✔$$

Boxplots

The summary information contained in the quartiles is highlighted in a graphic display called a **boxplot.** The center half of the data, extending from the first to the third quartile, is represented by a rectangle. The median is identified by a bar within this box. A line extends from the third quartile to the maximum and another line extends from the first quartile to the minimum. (For large data sets the lines may only extend to the 95th and 5th percentiles.)

Figure 2.12 gives the boxplot for the sulfur emission data on page 33. The symmetry seen in the histogram is also evident in this boxplot.

Figure 2.12 Boxplot of the sulfur emission data.

A **modified boxplot** can both identify outliers and reduce their effect on the shape of the boxplot. The outer line extends to the largest observation only if it is not too far from the third quartile. That is, for the line to extend to the largest observation, it must be within 1.5 × (interquartile range) units. The same is true for the smallest observation. Otherwise the line extends to the next most extreme observations that fall within this interval.

EXAMPLE   **A modified boxplot—possible outliers are detached**
Construct a modified boxplot for the neutrino interarrival time data (see page 14)

.021   .107   .179   .190   .196   .283   .580   .854   1.18   2.00   7.30

Construct a modified boxplot.

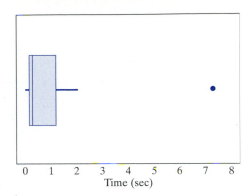

Figure 2.13 Modified boxplot for nutrino data.

Solution   Since $n/4 = 11/4 = 2.75$, the first quartile is the third ordered time .179 and $Q_3 = 1.18$ so the interquartile range is $1.18 - .179 = 1.001$. Further $1.5 \times 1.001 = 1.502$ and the smallest observation is closer than this to $Q_1 = .179$ but

$$\text{maximum} - Q_3 = 7.30 - 1.18 = 6.12 \text{ exceeds } 1.502 = 1.5 \times \text{(interquartile range)}$$

As shown in Figure 2.13, the line extends to 2.00, the most extreme observation within 1.502 units, but not to the largest observation which is shown as detached from the line.   ✔

Boxplots are particularly effective for graphically portraying comparisons among sets of observations. They are easy to understand and have a high visual impact.

EXAMPLE   **Multiple boxplots can reveal differences and similarities**
Sometimes, with rather complicated components like hard disk drives or RAM chips for computers, quality is quantified as an index with target value 100. Typically, a quality index will be based upon the deviations of several physical characteristics from their engineering specifications. Figure 2.14 shows the quality index at 4 manufacturing plants.
Comment on the relationships between quality at different plants.

Solution   It is clear from the graphic that plant 2 needs to reduce its variability and that plants 2 and 4 need to improve their quality level.   ✔

We conclude this section with a warning. Sometimes it is the trend over time that it is the most important feature of the data. This feature would be lost entirely if the set of data were summarized in a dot diagram, stem-and-leaf display, or boxplot. Figure 2.15 illustrates this point by a time plot of the ozone in October, in Dobson units, over a region of the South Pole. The apparent downward trend, if real, is of major scientific interest and, maybe, vital to life on our planet.

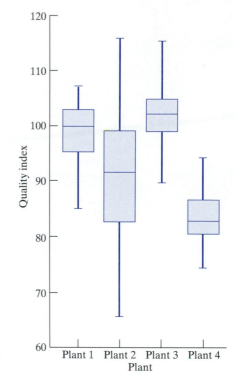

Figure 2.14 Boxplot of the quality index.

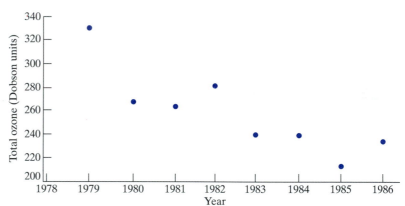

Figure 2.15 The monthly average total atmospheric ozone, for October, over the South Polar latitudes.

2.7 The Calculation of $\bar{x}$ and s

In this section we discuss methods for calculating $\bar{x}$ and s for **raw** (ungrouped) as well as grouped data. These methods are particularly well suited for small hand-held calculators and they are rapid. They are also accurate, except in extreme cases where, say, the data differ only in the seventh or higher digits.

The calculation of $\bar{x}$ for ungrouped data does not pose any problems; we have only to add the values of the observations and divide by n. On the other hand, the calculation of s^2 is usually cumbersome if we directly use the formula defining s^2 on page 30. Instead, we shall use the algebraically equivalent form

Variance (hand-held calculator formula)

$$s^2 = \frac{n \cdot \sum\limits_{i=1}^{n} x_i^2 - \left(\sum\limits_{i=1}^{n} x_i\right)^2}{n(n-1)}$$

which requires less labor to evaluate with a calculator. (In Exercise 2.47 on page 40 the reader will be asked to show that this formula is, in fact, equivalent to the one on page 30.)

EXAMPLE

Calculating variance using the hand-held calculator formula
Find the mean and the standard deviation of the following miles per gallon (mpg) obtained in 20 test runs performed on urban roads with an intermediate-size car:

19.7	21.5	22.5	22.2	22.6
21.9	20.5	19.3	19.9	21.7
22.8	23.2	21.4	20.8	19.4
22.0	23.0	21.1	20.9	21.3

Solution   Using a calculator, we find that the sum of these figures is 427.7 and that the sum of their squares is 9,173.19. Consequently,

$$\overline{x} = \frac{427.7}{20} = 21.38 \text{ mpg}$$

and

$$s^2 = \frac{20(9{,}173.19) - (427.7)^2}{20 \cdot 19} = 1.412$$

and it follows that $s = 1.19$ mpg. In computing the necessary sums we usually retain all decimal places, but as in this example, at the end we usually round to one more decimal than we had in the original data. ✔

See Exercise 2.54 for a computer calculation. This is the recommended procedure because it is easy to check the data entered for accuracy and the calculation is free of human error. Most importantly, the calculation of variance can be done using the square of the deviations $x_i - \overline{x}$ rather than the squares of the observations x_i and this is numerically more stable.

Not too many years ago, one of the main reasons for grouping data was to simplify the calculation of descriptions such as the mean and the standard deviation. With easy access to statistical calculators and computers, this is no longer the case, but we shall nevertheless discuss here the calculation of $\overline{x}$ and s from grouped data, since some data (for instance, from government publications) may be available only in grouped form.

To calculate $\overline{x}$ and s from grouped data, we shall have to make some assumption about the distribution of the values within each class. If we represent all values within a class by the corresponding class mark, the sum of the x's and the sum of their squares can now be written

$$\sum_{i=1}^{k} x_i f_i \quad \text{and} \quad \sum_{i=1}^{k} x_i^2 f_i$$

where x_i is the class mark of the ith class, f_i is the corresponding class frequency, and k is the number of classes in the distribution. Substituting these sums into the formula for $\bar{x}$ and the computing formula for s^2, we get

Mean and variance (grouped data)

$$\bar{x} = \frac{\sum_{i=1}^{k} x_i f_i}{n}$$

$$s^2 = \frac{n \cdot \sum_{i=1}^{k} x_i^2 f_i - \left(\sum_{i=1}^{k} x_i f_i\right)^2}{n(n-1)}$$

EXAMPLE

Calculating a mean and variance from grouped data
Use the distribution obtained on page 16 to calculate the mean and the variance of the sulfur oxides emission data.

Solution   Recording the class marks and the class frequencies in the first two columns, and the products $x_i f_i$ and $x_i^2 f_i$ in the third and fourth columns, we obtain

x_i	f_i	$x_i f_i$	$x_i^2 f_i$
6.95	3	20.85	144.9075
10.95	10	109.50	1,199.0250
14.95	14	209.30	3,129.0350
18.95	25	473.75	8,977.5625
22.95	17	390.15	8,953.9425
26.95	9	242.55	6,536.7225
30.95	2	61.90	1,915.8050
	80	1,508.00	30,857.0000

Then, substitution into the formulas yields

$$\bar{x} = \frac{1,508}{80} = 18.85$$

and

$$s^2 = \frac{80(30,857) - (1,508)^2}{80 \cdot 79} = 30.77$$

EXERCISES

2.27 Referring to Exercise 1.6, we see that the sample of 4 deviations (observation − specification) for a critical crank bore diameter is

$$-6 \quad 1 \quad -4 \quad -3$$

ten-thousandths of an inch during the second hour. For these 4 deviations,

(a) calculate the sample mean $\bar{x}$;

(b) calculate the sample standard deviation s;

(c) on average, is the hole too large or too small?

2.28 A company was experiencing a chronic weld defect problem with a water outlet tube assembly. Each assembly manufactured is leak tested in a water tank. Data were collected on a gap between the flange and the pipe for 6 assemblies that leaked and 6 good assemblies that passed the leak test.

    Leakers   .290   .104   .207   .145   .104   .124

(a) Calculate the sample mean $\bar{x}$.

(b) Calculate the sample standard deviation s.

2.29 Refer to Exercise 2.28. The measurements for 6 assemblies that did not leak were

    Good   .207   .124   .062   .301   .186   .124

(a) Calculate the sample mean $\bar{x}$.

(b) Calculate the sample standard deviation s.

(c) Does there appear to be a major difference in gap between assemblies that leaked and those which did not? The quality improvement group turned their focus to welding process variables.

2.30 A contract for the maintenance of a national railway's high horsepower locomotives was given to a large private company. After one year of experience with the maintenance program, those in charge of the program felt that major improvements could be made in the reliability of the locomotives. To document the current status, they collected data on the cost of materials for rebuilding traction motors. Use the data below to

(a) calculate the sample mean $\bar{x}$.

(b) calculate the sample standard deviation s.

Material costs for rebuilding traction motors (1000s of dollars)

1.41	1.70	1.03	0.99	1.68	1.09	1.68	1.94
1.53	2.25	1.60	3.07	1.78	0.67	1.76	1.17
1.54	0.99	0.99	1.17	1.54	1.68	1.62	0.67
0.67	1.78	2.12	1.52	1.01			

2.31 If the mean annual salary paid to the chief executives of three engineering firms is $125,000, can one of them receive $400,000?

2.32 Records show that in Phoenix, Arizona, the normal daily maximum temperature for each month is 65, 69, 74, 84, 93, 102, 105, 102, 98, 88, 74, and 66 degrees Fahrenheit. Verify that the mean of these figures is 85 and comment on the claim that, in Phoenix, the average daily maximum temperature is a very comfortable 85 degrees.

2.33 The following are the numbers of twists that were required to break 12 forged alloy bars: 33, 24, 39, 48, 26, 35, 38, 54, 23, 34, 29, and 37. Find

   (a) the mean;

   (b) the median.

2.34 With reference to the preceding exercise, find s using

   (a) the formula that defines s;

   (b) the hand-held calculator formula for s.

2.35 The following are the numbers of minutes that a person had to wait for the bus to work on 15 working days: 10, 1, 13, 9, 5, 9, 2, 10, 3, 8, 6, 17, 2, 10, and 15. Find

   (a) the mean;

   (b) the median.

   (c) Draw a boxplot.

2.36 With reference to the preceding exercise, find s^2 using

   (a) the formula that defines s^2;

   (b) the hand-held calculator formula for s^2.

2.37 Material manufactured continuously before being cut and wound into large rolls must be monitored for thickness (caliper). A sample of 10 measurements on paper, in mm, yielded

$$32.2 \quad 32.0 \quad 30.4 \quad 31.0 \quad 31.2 \quad 31.2 \quad 30.3 \quad 29.6 \quad 30.5 \quad 30.7$$

Find the mean and quartiles for this sample.

2.38 For the four observations 9, 7, 15, 5;

   (a) calculate the deviations $(x_i - \bar{x})$ and check that they add to 0;

   (b) calculate the variance and the standard deviation.

2.39 With reference to Exercise 2.14 on page 25, draw a boxplot.

2.40 With reference to Exercise 2.3 on page 23, calculate $\bar{x}$ and s.

2.41 Find the mean and the standard deviation of the 20 humidity readings on page 22 by using

   (a) the raw (ungrouped) data;

   (b) the distribution obtained on page 22.

2.42 Use the distribution in Exercise 2.9 on page 24 to find the mean and the variance of the breaking strengths.

2.43 Use the distribution obtained in Exercise 2.12 on page 24 to find the mean and the standard deviation of the ignition times. Also determine the coefficient of variation.

2.44 Use the distribution obtained in Exercise 2.14 on page 25 to find the coefficient of variation of the productivity data.

2.45 In three recent years, the price of copper was 69.6, 66.8, and 66.3 cents per pound, and the price of bituminous coal was 19.43, 19.82, and 22.40 dollars per short ton. Which of the two sets of prices is relatively more variable?

2.46 Show that $\sum_{i=1}^{n} (x_i - \bar{x}) = 0$ for any set of observations $x_1, x_2, \ldots,$ and x_n.

2.47 Show that the computing formula for s^2 on page 37 is equivalent to the one used to define s^2 on page 30.

2.48 If data are coded so that $x_i = c \cdot u_i + a$, show that $\bar{x} = c \cdot \bar{u} + a$ and $s_x = |c| \cdot s_u$.

2.49 To find the **median** of a distribution obtained for n observations, we first determine the class into which the median must fall. Then, if there are j values in this class and

k values below it, the median is located $\dfrac{(n/2) - k}{j}$ of the way into this class, and to obtain the median we multiply this fraction by the class interval and add the result to the lower class boundary of the class into which the median must fall. This method is based on the assumption that the observations in each class are "spread uniformly" throughout the class interval, and this is why we count $\dfrac{n}{2}$ of the observations instead of $\dfrac{n+1}{2}$ as on page 28. To illustrate, let us refer to the distribution of the sulfur oxides emission data on page 33. Since $n = 80$, it can be seen that the median must fall into the class 17.0–20.9, and since $j = 25$ and $k = 27$, it follows that the median is $16.95 + \dfrac{40 - 27}{25} \cdot 4 = 19.03$.

(a) Use the distribution obtained in Exercise 2.9 on page 24 to find the median of the grouped breaking strengths.

(b) Use the distribution obtained in Exercise 2.12 on page 24 to find the median of the grouped ignition times.

2.50 For each of the following distributions, decide whether it is possible to find the mean and/or the median. Explain your answers.

(a)

Grade	Frequency
40–49	5
50–59	18
60–69	27
70–79	15
80–89	6

(b)

IQ	Frequency
less than 90	3
90–99	14
100–109	22
110–119	19
more than 119	7

(c)

Weight	Frequency
100 or less	41
101–110	13
111–120	8
121–130	3
131–140	1

2.51 To find the quartiles Q_1 and Q_3 for grouped data, we proceed as in Exercise 2.49, but count $\dfrac{n}{4}$ and $\dfrac{3n}{4}$ of the observations instead of $\dfrac{n}{2}$.

   (a) With reference to the distribution of the sulfur oxides emission data on page 33, find Q_1, Q_3, and the interquartile range.

   (b) Find Q_1 and Q_3 for the distribution of the ignition time data given on page 24.

2.52 If k sets of data consist, respectively, of $n_1, n_2, \ldots, n_k$ observations and have the means $\bar{x}_1, \bar{x}_2, \ldots, \bar{x}_k$, then the overall mean of all the data is given by the formula

$$\bar{x} = \frac{\displaystyle\sum_{i=1}^{k} n_i \bar{x}_i}{\displaystyle\sum_{i=1}^{k} n_i}$$

   (a) The average annual salaries paid to top-level management in three companies are \$94,000, \$102,000, and \$99,000. If the respective numbers of top-level executives in these companies are 4, 15, and 11, find the average salary paid to these 30 executives.

   (b) In a nuclear engineering class there are 22 juniors, 18 seniors, and 10 graduate students. If the juniors averaged 71 in the midterm examination, the seniors averaged 78, and the graduate students averaged 89, what is the mean for the entire class?

2.53 The formula of the preceding exercise is a special case of the following formula for the **weighted mean**

$$\bar{x}_w = \frac{\displaystyle\sum_{i=1}^{k} w_i x_i}{\displaystyle\sum_{i=1}^{k} w_i}$$

where w_i is a weight indicating the relative importance of the ith observation.

   (a) If an instructor counts the final examination in a course four times as much as each 1-hour examination, what is the weighted average grade of a student who received grades of 69, 75, 56, and 72 in four 1-hour examinations and a final examination grade of 78?

   (b) From 1995 to 2000 the cost of food increased by 53% in a certain city, the cost of housing increased by 40%, and the cost of transportation increased by 34%. If the average salaried worker spent 28% of his or her income on food, 35% on housing, and 14% on transportation, what is the combined percentage increase in the cost of these items?

2.54 Modern computer software packages have come a long way towards removing the tedium of calculating statistics. *MINITAB* is one common and easy-to-use package. We illustrate the use of the computer using *MINITAB* commands. Other easy-to-use packages have a quite similar command structure.

   The lumber used in the construction of buildings must be monitored for strength. Data for strength, in pounds per square inch, for 2 × 4 pieces of lumber are in the file 2.54.dat. We give the basic commands that calculate $n, \bar{x}$ and s as well as the quartiles.

   The session commands require the data to be set in the first column, C1, of the *MINITAB* work sheet. The command for creating a box plot is also included.

Data in (2.54.dat)

strength

Dialog box:	**Session command**
Stat > Basic Statistics > Descriptive Statistics	MTB > DESCRIBE C1
Type *strength* in **Variables.** Click **Graphs** Click **Graphical Summary**.	MTB > BOXPLOT C1
Click **OK**. Click **OK**.	

Output: (partial)

Variable	N	Mean	Median	StDev
Strength	30	1908.8	1863.0	327.1

Variable	Minimum	Maximum	Q1	Q3
Strength	1325.0	2983.0	1711.5	2071.8

Use *MINITAB*, or some other statistical package, to find $\bar{x}$ and s for

   (a)   the decay times on page 167;

   (b)   the interrequest times on page 20.

2.55 (Further *MINITAB* calculation and graphs) With the observations on the strength (in pounds per square inch) of 2×4 pieces of lumber already set in C1, the sequence of choices and clicks

Stat > Basic Statistics > Descriptive Statistics

Type *strength* in **Variables.** Click **OK**

produces an even more complete summary.

Descriptive Statistics

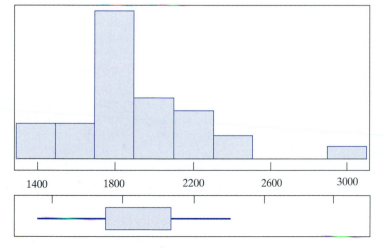

Variable: Strength

Mean	1908.77
StDev	327.12
Variance	107004
N	30
Minimum	1325.00
1st Quartile	1711.50
Median	1863.00
3rd Quartile	2071.75
Maximum	2983.00

The ordered strength data are

1325	1419	1490	1633	1645	1655	1710	1712	1725	1727	1745
1828	1840	1856	1859	1867	1889	1899	1943	1954	1976	2046
2061	2104	2168	2199	2276	2326	2403	2983			

From the ordered data

(a) obtain the quartiles;

(b) construct a histogram and locate the mean, median, Q_1, and Q_3 on the horizontal axes;

(c) repeat parts (a) and (b) with the aluminum alloy data on page 20.

2.8 A Case Study: Problems with Aggregating Data[1]

As circuit boards and other components move through a company's surface mount technology assembly line, a significant amount of data is collected for each assembly. The data are recorded at several stages of manufacture in a serial tracking database by means of computer terminals located throughout the factory. The data include the board serial number, the type of defect, number of defects and their location. The challenge here is to transform a large amount of data into manageable and useful information. When there is a variety of products and lots of data are collected on each, record management and the extraction of appropriate data for product improvement must be done well.

Originally, an attempt was made to understand this large database by *aggregating,* or grouping together, data from all products and performing an analysis of the data as if it were one product! This was a poor practice that decreased the resolution of the information obtained from the database. The products on the assembly line ranged in complexity, maturity, method of processing, and lot size.

To see the difficulties caused by aggregation, consider a typical week's production where 100 printed circuits of Product A were produced; 40 boards of Product B; and 60 boards of Product C. Following a wave soldering process, a total of 400 solder defects was reported. This translates to an overall average of $400/200 = 2$ defects per board. It was this company's practice to circulate the weekly aggregate average throughout the factory floor for review and comment. It was then the operator's responsibility to take action according to the *misleading* report. Over time, it became apparent that this process was ineffective for improving quality.

However, further analysis of this data on a product by product basis revealed that products A, B, and C actually contributed 151, 231, and 18 defects. Thus, the number of defects per board was 1.51, 5.78, and 0.30 for products A, B and C, respectively. Figure 2.16 correctly shows the average defects. Product C has a significantly lower and Product B has a significantly higher defect rate relative to the incorrect aggregated average. These latter are also the more complex boards.

These data concern the number of defects that occurred when boards were wave soldered after an assembly stage. The next step was to implement control

[1]Courtesy of Don Ermer

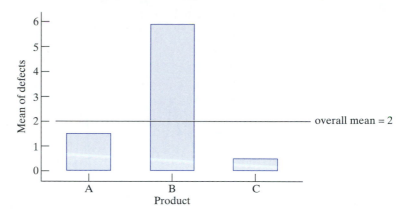

Figure 2.16 Average number of defects per product type.

charts for the number of defects for each of the three products. The numbers of defects for Product B were

10	8	8	4	6	8	8	10	6	7	4	2	4	5	5
5	2	11	6	6	5	7	3	4	3	2	6	5	1	7
3	1	1	5	4	5	12	13	11	8					

The appropriate control chart is a time plot where the serial numbers of the product or sample are on the horizontal axis and the corresponding number of defects on the vertical axis. In this C-chart, the central line labeled $\bar{C}$ is the average number of defects over all cases in the plot. The dashed lines are the control limits set at three standard deviations above the central line. (For reasons explained in Section 14.6, we use $\sqrt{\bar{C}}$ rather than s when the data are numbers of defects.)

$$\text{LCL} = \bar{C} - 3\sqrt{\bar{C}}$$
$$\text{UCL} = \bar{C} + 3\sqrt{\bar{C}}$$

Figure 2.17(a) gives a C-chart constructed for Product B, but where the centerline is incorrectly calculated from the aggregated data as $\bar{C} = 2.0$. This is far too low and so is the upper control limit 6.24. The lower control limit is negative so we use 0. It looks like a great many of the observations are out of control because they exceed the upper control limit.

When the C-chart is correctly constructed on the basis of data from Product B alone, the centerline is $\bar{C} = 231/40 = 5.775$ and the upper control limit is 12.98. The lower control limit is again negative so we use 0. From Figure 2.17(b), the correct C-chart, the wave soldering process for Product B appears to be in control except for time 38 when 13 defects were observed.

With the data segregated into products, separate charts were constructed for each of the three products. With this new outlook on data interpretation, a number of improvement opportunities surfaced that were previously disguised by aggregation. For example, by reducing the dimensions of an electrical pad a significant

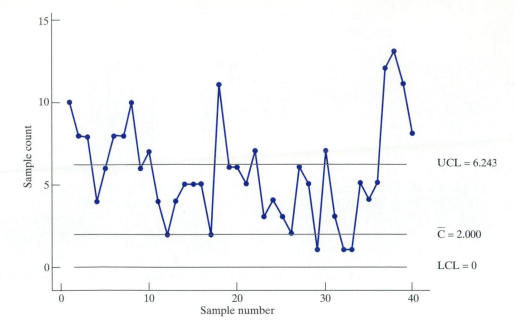

Figure 2.17a
Incorrect C-Chart
for Defects

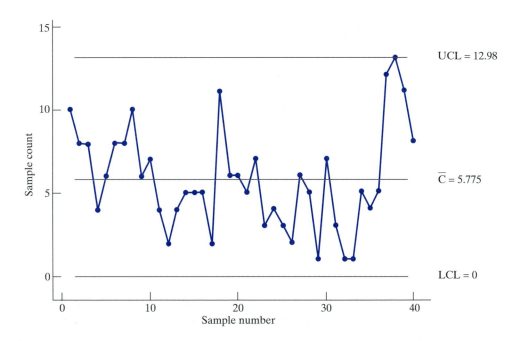

Figure 2.17b
Correct C-Chart
for Defects

reduction was achieved in the number of solder bridges between pins. This same design change was added to all of the board specifications and improvements were obtained on all products.

In summary, the aggregation of data from different products, or more generally from different sources, can lead to incorrect conclusions and mask opportunities for quality improvement. Segregating data by product, although more time-consuming initially, can lead to significant reduction in waste and manufacturing costs.

REVIEW EXERCISES

2.56 From 2000 computer chips inspected by the manufacturer, the following numbers of defects were recorded.

holes not open	182
holes too large	55
poor connections	31
incorrect size chip	5
other	7

Draw a Pareto chart.

2.57 Draw

(a) a frequency table of the aluminum alloy strength data on page 20 using the classes [66.0,67.5), [67.5, 69.0), [69.0, 70.5), [70.5–72.0), [72.0, 73.5), [73.5, 75.0), [75.0–76.5), where the right-hand endpoint is excluded.

(b) a histogram using the frequency table in part (a).

2.58 Draw

(a) a frequency table of the interrequest time data on page 20 using the intervals 0–2,499, 2,500–4,999, 5,000–9,999, 10,000–19,999, 20,000–39,999, 40,000–59,999, 60,000–79,999;

(b) a histogram using the frequency table in part (a) (note that the intervals are unequal, so make the height of the rectangle equal relative frequency/width).

2.59 Direct evidence of Newton's universal law of gravitation was provided from a renowned experiment by Henry Cavendish (1731–1810). In the experiment, masses of objects were determined by weighing and the measured force of attraction was used to calculate the density of the earth. The values of the earth's density, in time order by row, are

5.36	5.29	5.58	5.65	5.57	5.53	5.62	5.29
5.44	5.34	5.79	5.10	5.27	5.39	5.42	5.47
5.63	5.34	5.46	5.30	5.75	5.68	5.85	

(Source: *Philosophical Transactions* 17 (1798): 469.)

(a) Find the mean and standard deviation.

(b) Find the median, Q_1, and Q_3.

(c) Plot the observations versus time order. Is there any obvious trend?

2.60 J. J. Thomson (1856–1940) discovered the electron by isolating negatively charged particles for which he could measure the mass-charge ratio. This ratio appeared to be constant over a wide range of experimental conditions and, consequently, could be a characteristic of a new particle. His observations, from two different cathode-ray tubes that used air as the gas, are

Tube 1	0.57	0.34	0.43	0.32	0.48	0.40	0.40
Tube 2	0.53	0.47	0.47	0.51	0.63	0.61	0.48

(Source: *Philosophical Magazine* 44; 5 (1897): 293.)

(a) Draw a dot diagram with solid dots for Tube 1 observations and circles for Tube 2 observations.

(b) Calculate the mean and standard deviation for the Tube 1 observations.

(c) Calculate the mean and standard deviation for the Tube 2 observations.

2.61 With reference to Exercise 2.60,

(a) calculate the median, maximum, minimum, and range for Tube 1 observations;

(b) calculate the median, maximum, minimum, and range for the Tube 2 observations.

2.62 A. A. Michelson (1852–1931) made many series of measurements of the speed of light. Using a revolving mirror technique, he obtained

$$12 \quad 30 \quad 30 \quad 27 \quad 30 \quad 39 \quad 18 \quad 27 \quad 48 \quad 24 \quad 18$$

for the differences (velocity of light in air) – (229,700) km/s. (Source: *The Astrophysical Journal* 65 (1927): 11.)

(a) Draw a dot diagram.

(b) Find the median and the mean. Locate both on the dot diagram.

(c) Find the variance and standard deviation.

2.63 With reference to Exercise 2.62

(a) find the quartiles;

(b) find the minimum, maximum, range, and interquartile range;

(c) draw a boxplot.

2.64 A civil engineer monitors water quality by measuring the amount of suspended solids in a sample of river water. Over 11 weekdays, she observed

$$14 \quad 12 \quad 21 \quad 28 \quad 30 \quad 63 \quad 29 \quad 63 \quad 55 \quad 19 \quad 20$$

suspended solids (parts per million).

(a) Draw a dot diagram.

(b) Find the median and the mean. Locate both on the dot diagram.

(c) Find the variance and standard variation.

2.65 With reference to Exercise 2.64

(a) find the quartiles;

(b) find the minimum, maximum, range, and interquartile range;

(c) construct a boxplot.

2.66 With reference to the aluminum alloy strength data in the example on page 20

(a) find the quartiles;

(b) find the minimum, maximum, range, and interquartile range;

(c) find the 10th percentile and the 20th percentile.

2.67 With reference to Exercise 2.66, draw a boxplot.

2.68 With reference to the aluminum alloy strength data in the example on page 20, make a stem-and-leaf display.

2.69 In five tests, one student averaged 63.2 with a standard deviation of 3.3, whereas another student averaged 78.8 with a standard deviation of 5.3. Which student is relatively more consistent?

2.70 With reference to the lumber strength data in Exercise 2.55, the statistical software package *SAS* produced the output in Figure 2.17. Using this output

(a) identify the mean and standard deviation and compare these answers with the values given in Exercise 2.55;

(b) draw a boxplot.

UNIVARIATE PROCEDURE

VARIABLE = STRENGTH

Moments

N	30	Sum Wgts	30
Mean	1908.767	Sum	57263
Std Dev	327.115	Variance	107004.3
Skewness	1.118406	Kurtosis	2.883349
USS	1.124E8	CSS	3103123
CV	17.13751	Std Mean	59.72276

Quantiles (Def = 5)

100%	Max	2983	99%	2983
75%	Q3	2061	95%	2403
50%	Med	1863	90%	2301
25%	Q1	1712	10%	1561.5
0%	Min	1325	5%	1419
			1%	1325

Range	1658
Q3 − Q1	349

Figure 2.17 Selected SAS output to describe the lumber strength data from Exercise 2.55.

2.71. Civil engineers must monitor flow on rivers where power is generated. The following are the daily mean flow rates (MGD) on the Namekagon River during the month of May for 47 years.

602.0	517.5	572.5	392.4	505.8	547.5	389.1	497.2
794.8	657.6	904.7	595.5	611.9	482.9	698.6	606.7
986.4	567.7	400.1	634.9	448.4	479.1	1156.0	718.5
575.6	743.3	1146.0	461.6	644.0	480.8	429.1	626.9
833.9	889.0	752.6	516.5	817.2	895.8	572.2	563.7
679.3	738.0	618.9	390.8	550.9	425.9	760.6	

(a) obtain the quartiles;

(b) obtain the 90th percentile;

(c) construct a histogram.

2.72 The National Highway Traffic Safety Administration reported the relative speed (rounded to the nearest 5 mph) of automobiles involved in accidents one year. The percentages at different speeds were

20 mph or less	2.0%
25 or 30 mph	29.7%
35 or 40 mph	30.4%
45 or 50 mph	16.5%
55 mph	19.2%
60 or 65 mph	2.2%

(a) From these data can we conclude that it is quite safe to drive at high speeds? Why or why not?

(b) Why do most accidents occur in the 35 or 40 mph and in the 25 or 30 mph ranges?

(c) Construct a density histogram using the endpoints 0, 22.5, 32.5, 42.5, 52.5, 57.5, 67.5 for the intervals.

KEY TERMS

(with page references)

Absolute variation   31

Arithmetic mean   27

Bar chart   13

Boxplot   34

Categorical distribution   15

Class boundary   16

Class frequency   15

Class interval   17

Class limit   15

Class mark   16

Coefficient of variation   31

Cumulative distribution   17

Cumulative percentage distribution   18

Density histogram   20

Dot diagram   13

Double-stem display   26

Empirical cumulative distribution   26

Endpoint convention   16

Exploratory data analysis   23

Five-stem display   27

Frequency distribution   15

Histogram   18

Interquartile range   34

Leaf   22

Mean   28

Median   28

Modified boxplot   34

Numerical distribution   15

Ogive   21

Outlier   14

Pareto diagram   13

Percentage distribution   18

Percentile   32

Pie chart   25

Quartile   33

Range   34

Raw data   36

Relative variation   31

Sample mean   28

Sample variance   30

Standard deviation   31

Stem   22

Stem-and-leaf display   22

Stem label   22

Variance   30

Weighted mean   42

Probability

In the study of probability there are basically three kinds of questions: (1) What do we mean when we say that the probability of an event is, say, 0.50, 0.02, or 0.81? (2) How are the numbers we call probabilities determined, or measured in actual practice? (3) What are the mathematical rules which probabilities must obey?

After some mathematical preliminaries in Sections 3.1 and 3.2, we study the first two kinds of questions in Section 3.3 and the third kind of question in Sections 3.4 through 3.7. The related concept of a mathematical expectation is introduced in Section 3.8. ■

3.1   Sample Spaces and Events

Probability allows us to quantify the variability in the outcome of any experiment whose exact outcome cannot be predicted with certainty. However, before we can introduce probability, it is necessary to specify the space of outcomes and the events on which it will be defined.

In statistics, a set of all possible outcomes of an experiment is called a **sample space,** owing to the fact that it usually consists of all the things that can happen when one takes a sample. Sample spaces are usually denoted by the letter S. To avoid misunderstandings about the words "experiment" and "outcome" as we have used them here, it should be understood that statisticians use these terms in a very wide sense. An **experiment** may consist of the simple process of noting whether a switch is turned on or off; it may consist of determining the time it takes a car to accelerate to 30 miles per hour; or it may consist of the complicated process of finding the mass of an electron. Thus, the **outcome** of an experiment may be a simple choice between two alternatives; it may be the result of a direct measurement or count; or it may be an answer obtained after extensive measurements and calculations.

When we study the outcomes of an experiment, we usually identify the various possibilities with numbers, points, or some other kinds of symbols. For instance, if four contractors bid on a highway construction job and we let $a, b, c,$ and d denote that it is awarded to Mr. Adam, Mrs. Brown, Mr. Clark, or Ms. Dean, then the sample space for this experiment is the set $S = \{a, b, c, d\}$.

Also, if a government agency must decide where to locate two new computer research facilities and that (for a certain purpose) it is of interest to indicate how many of them will be located in Texas and how many in California, we can write the sample space as

$$S = \{(0, 0), (1, 0), (0, 1), (2, 0), (1, 1), (0, 2)\}$$

where the first coordinate is the number of research facilities that will be located in Texas and the second coordinate is the number that will be located in California. Geometrically, this sample space may be pictured as in Figure 3.1, from which it is apparent, for example, that in two of the six possibilities Texas and California will get an equal number of the new research facilities. The use of points rather than letters or numbers has the advantage that it makes it easier to visualize the various possibilities, and perhaps discover some special features which several of the outcomes may have in common.

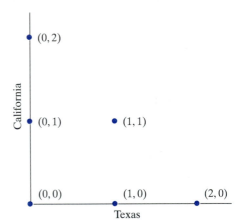

FIGURE 3.1 Sample space for the number of new computer research facilities to be located in Texas and in California

Generally, sample spaces are classified according to the number of elements (points) that they contain. In the two preceding examples, the sample spaces had four and six elements, and they are both referred to as **finite.** Other examples of finite sample spaces are the one for the various ways in which a president and a vice-president can be selected from among the 25 members of a union local and the one for the various ways in which a student can answer the 12 questions on a true-false test. As we see on page 57, the first of these sample spaces has 600 elements and the other has 4,096.

The following are examples of sample spaces that are not finite. If persons checking the nitrogen oxide emission of cars are interested in the number of cars they have to inspect before they observe the first one that does not meet government regulations, it could be the first, the second, . . . , the fiftieth, . . . , and for all we know they may have to check thousands of cars before they find one that does not meet government regulations. Not knowing how far they may have to go, it is appropriate in an example like this to take as the sample space the whole set of natural numbers, of which there is a countable infinity. To go one step further, if they were interested in the nitrogen oxide emission of a given car in grams per mile, the sample space would have to consist of all the points on a continuous scale (a certain interval on the line of real numbers), of which there is a continuum.

In general, a sample space is said to be **discrete** if it has finitely many or a countable infinity of elements. If the elements (points) of a sample space constitute a continuum, for example, all the points on a line, all the points on a line segment, or all the points in a plane, the sample space is said to be **continuous.** In the remainder of this chapter we shall consider only discrete and mainly finite sample spaces.

In statistics, any subset of a sample space is called an **event.** By subset we mean any part of a set, including the whole set and, trivially, a set called the **empty set** and denoted by ϕ, which has no elements at all. For instance, with reference to Figure 3.1,

$$C = \{(1, 0), (0, 1)\}$$

is the event that, between them, Texas and California will get one of the two research facilities,

$$D = \{(0, 0), (0, 1), (0, 2)\}$$

is the event that Texas will not get either of the two research facilities, and

$$E = \{(0, 0), (1, 1)\}$$

is the event that Texas and California will get an equal number of the facilities. Note that events C and E have no elements in common—they are **mutually exclusive events.**

In many probability problems we are interested in events which can be expressed in terms of two or more events by forming **unions, intersections,** and **complements.** Although the reader must surely be familiar with these terms, let us review briefly that if A and B are any two sets in a sample space S, their union $A \cup B$ is the subset of S that contains all elements that are either in A, in B, or in both; their intersection $A \cap B$ is the subset of S that contains all elements that are in both A and B; and the complement $\overline{A}$ of A is the subset of S that contains all the elements of S that are not in A.

<table>
<tr><td>EXAMPLE</td><td>

Combining events by union, intersection, and complement
With reference to the sample space of Figure 3.1 and the events C, D, and E just defined, list the outcomes comprising each of the following events and also express the events in words:
</td></tr>
</table>

(a) $C \cup E$;

(b) $C \cap D$;

(c) $\overline{D}$.

Solution   (a) Since $C \cup E$ contains all the elements that are in C, in E, or in both,

$$C \cup E = \{(1, 0), (0, 1), (0, 0), (1, 1)\}$$

is the event that neither Texas nor California will get both of the new research facilities.

(b) Since $C \cap D$ contains all the elements that are in both C and D,

$$C \cap D = \{(0, 1)\}$$

is the event that Texas will not get either of the two new facilities and California will get one.

(c) Since $\overline{D}$ contains all the elements of the sample space that are not in D,

$$\overline{D} = \{(1, 0), (1, 1), (2, 0)\}$$

is the event that Texas will get at least one of the new computer research facilities. ✔

Sample spaces and events, particularly relationships among events, are often depicted by means of **Venn diagrams** like those of Figures 3.2 and 3.4. In each case the sample space is represented by a rectangle, whereas events are represented by regions within the rectangle, usually by circles or parts of circles. The shaded regions of the four Venn diagrams of Figure 3.2 represent event A, the complement of event A, the union of events A and B, and the intersection of events A and B.

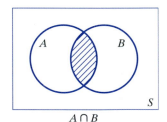

FIGURE 3.2 Venn diagrams showing complement, union, and intersection

EXAMPLE

Relating regions in Venn diagrams to events

If A is the event that a certain student is taking a course in calculus and B is the event that the student is taking a course in applied mechanics, what events are represented by the shaded regions of the four Venn diagrams of Figure 3.2?

Solution   The shaded region of the first diagram represents the event that the student is taking a course in calculus; that of the second diagram represents the event that the student is not taking a course in calculus; that of the third diagram represents the event that the student is taking a course in calculus and/or a course in applied mechanics; and that of the fourth diagram represents the event that the student is taking a course in calculus as well as a course in applied mechanics. ✔

Venn diagrams are often used to verify relationships among sets, thus making it unnecessary to give formal proofs based on the algebra of sets. To illustrate, let us show that $\overline{(A \cup B)} = \overline{A} \cap \overline{B}$, which expresses the fact that the complement of the union of two sets equals the intersection of their complements. To begin, note that the shaded region of the first Venn diagram of Figure 3.3 represents the set $\overline{(A \cup B)}$ (compare this diagram with the third diagram of Figure 3.2). The crosshatched region of the second Venn diagram of Figure 3.3 was obtained by shading the region representing $\overline{A}$ with lines going in one direction and that representing $\overline{B}$ with lines going in another direction. Thus, the crosshatched region represents the intersection of $\overline{A}$ and $\overline{B}$, and it can be seen that it is identical with the shaded region of the first Venn diagram of Figure 3.3.

FIGURE 3.3 Use of Venn diagrams to show that $\overline{(A \cup B)} = \overline{A} \cap \overline{B}$

$\overline{(A \cup B)}$

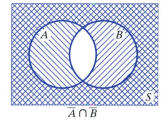
$\overline{A} \cap \overline{B}$

When we deal with three events, we draw the circles as in Figure 3.4. In this diagram, the circles divide the sample space into eight regions, numbered 1 through 8, and it is easy to determine whether the corresponding events are parts of A or $\overline{A}$, B or $\overline{B}$, and C or $\overline{C}$.

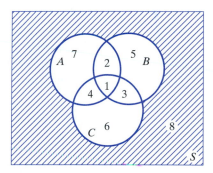

FIGURE 3.4 Venn diagram

EXAMPLE

Relating events to regions of the Venn diagram

A manufacturer of small motors is concerned with three major types of defects. If A is the event that the shaft size is too large, B is the event that the windings are improper, and C is the event that the electrical connections are unsatisfactory, express in words what events are represented by the following regions of the Venn diagram of Figure 3.4:

(a) region 2;
(b) regions 1 and 3 together;
(c) regions 3, 5, 6, and 8 together.

Solution

(a) Since this region is contained in A and B but not in C, it represents the event that the shaft is too large and the windings improper, but the electrical connections are satisfactory.
(b) Since this region is common to B and C, it represents the event that the windings are improper and the electrical connections are unsatisfactory.
(c) Since this is the entire region outside A, it represents the event that the shaft size is not too large.

3.2 Counting

At times it can be quite difficult, or at least tedious, to determine the number of elements in a finite sample space by direct enumeration. To illustrate, suppose that a consumer testing service rates lawn mowers as being easy, average, or difficult to operate; as being expensive or inexpensive; and as being costly, average, or cheap to repair. In how many different ways can a lawn mower be rated by this testing service?

Clearly, there are many possibilities; a lawn mower may be rated easy to operate, inexpensive, but costly to repair; it may be rated difficult to operate, expensive, and cheap to repair; it may be rated as neither easy nor difficult to operate, inexpensive, with average cost of repairs; and so on. Continuing this way, we may be able to list all 18 possibilities, but the chances are that we will omit at least one or two.

To handle this kind of problem systematically, it helps to draw a **tree diagram** like that of Figure 3.5, where the three alternatives for ease of operation are denoted by E_1, E_2, and E_3; the price is either P_1, or P_2; and the three alternatives for the cost of repairs are denoted by C_1, C_2, and C_3. Following a given path from left to right along the branches of the tree, we obtain a particular rating, namely, a particular element of the sample space, and it can be seen that altogether there are 18 possibilities.

This result could also have been obtained by observing that there are three E-branches, that each E-branch forks into two P-branches, and that each P-branch forks into three C-branches. Thus, there are $3 \cdot 2 \cdot 3 = 18$ combinations of branches, or paths. This result is a special case of the following theorem:

Multiplication of
choices

Theorem 3.1 If sets $A_1, A_2, \ldots, A_k$ contain, respectively, $n_1, n_2, \ldots, n_k$ elements, there are $n_1 \cdot n_2 \cdots n_k$ ways of choosing first an element of A_1, then an element of $A_2, \ldots,$ and finally an element of A_k.

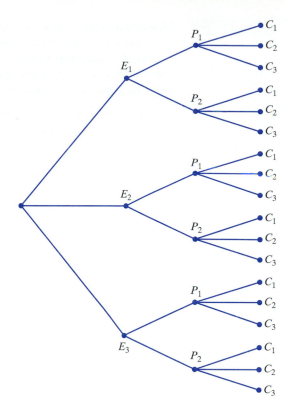

FIGURE 3.5 Tree
diagram for rating of
lawn mowers

In our example we had $n_1 = 3$, $n_2 = 2$, and $n_3 = 3$, and hence, $3 \cdot 2 \cdot 3 = 18$ possibilities.

EXAMPLE   **The multiplication rule for $k = 2$ stages of choices**
In how many different ways can a union local with a membership of 25 choose a vice president and a president?

Solution   Since the vice president can be chosen in 25 ways and, subsequently, the president in 24 ways, there are altogether $25 \cdot 24 = 600$ ways in which the whole choice can be made.   ✔

EXAMPLE   **The multiplication rule with $k = 12$ stages of choices**
If a test consists of 12 true-false questions, in how many different ways can a student mark the test paper with one answer to each question?

Solution   Since each question can be answered in two ways, there are altogether

$$2 \cdot 2 \cdot 2 \cdot 2 \cdot 2 \cdot 2 \cdot 2 \cdot 2 \cdot 2 \cdot 2 \cdot 2 \cdot 2 = 2^{12} = 4,096 \text{ possibilities}$$ ✔

EXAMPLE

Determining the size of an experiment

A manufacturer is experiencing difficulty getting consistent readings of tensile strength between three machines located on the production floor, research lab, and quality control lab, respectively. There are also four possible technicians—Tom, Joe, Ken, and Carol—who operate at least one of the test machines regularly.

(a) How many operator-machine pairs must be included in a designed experiment where every operator tries every machine?

(b) If each operator-machine pair is required to test eight specimens, how many test specimens are required for the entire procedure? Note: A specimen is destroyed when its tensile strength is measured.

Solution

(a) There are $n_1 = 4$ operators and $n_2 = 3$ machines, so $4 \cdot 3 = 12$ pairs are required.

(b) There are $n_3 = 8$ test specimens required for each operator-machine pair, so $8 \cdot 12 = 96$ test specimens are required for the designed experiment. ✔

As in the first of these three examples, the rule for the multiplication of choices is often used when several choices are made from one set and we are concerned with the order in which they are made. In general, if r objects are chosen from a set of n distinct objects, any particular arrangement, or order, of these objects is called a **permutation.** For instance, 4 1 2 3 is a permutation of the first four positive integers, and Maine, Vermont, and Connecticut is a permutation, a particular ordered arrangement, of three of the six New England states.

To find a formula for the total number of permutations of r objects selected from a set of n distinct objects, we observe that the first selection is made from the whole set of n objects, the second selection is made from the $n - 1$ objects which remain after the first selection has been made, . . . , and the rth selection is made from the $n - (r - 1) = n - r + 1$ objects which remain after the first $r - 1$ selections have been made. Therefore, by the rule for the multiplication of choices, the total number of permutations of r objects selected from a set of n distinct objects is

$$_nP_r = n(n - 1)(n - 2) \cdots (n - r + 1)$$

for $r = 1, 2, \ldots, n$.

Since products of consecutive integers arise in many problems relating to permutations or other kinds of special selections, it will be convenient to introduce here the **factorial notation,** where $1! = 1, 2! = 2 \cdot 1 = 2, 3! = 3 \cdot 2 \cdot 1 = 6$, $4! = 4 \cdot 3 \cdot 2 \cdot 1 = 24, \ldots$, and in general $n! = n(n - 1)(n - 2) \cdots 3 \cdot 2 \cdot 1$. Also, to make various formulas more generally applicable, we let $0! = 1$ by definition.

To express the formula for $_nP_r$ in terms of factorials, we multiply and divide by $(n - r)!$ getting

$$_nP_r = \frac{n(n - 1)(n - 2) \cdots (n - r + 1)(n - r)!}{(n - r)!} = \frac{n!}{(n - r)!}$$

To summarize

Number of permuta-
tions of *n* objects
taken *r* at a time

> **Theorem 3.2**   The number of permutations of *r* objects selected from a set of *n* distinct objects is
>
> $$_nP_r = n(n - 1)(n - 2) \cdots (n - r + 1)$$
>
> or, in factorial notation,
>
> $$_nP_r = \frac{n!}{(n - r)!}$$

Note that the second formula also holds for $r = 0$.

EXAMPLE

Evaluating a permutation
In how many different ways can one make a first, second, third, and fourth choice among 12 firms leasing construction equipment?

Solution   For $n = 12$ and $r = 4$, the first formula yields

$$_{12}P_4 = 12 \cdot 11 \cdot 10 \cdot 9 = 11{,}880$$

and the second formula yields

$$_{12}P_4 = \frac{12!}{(12 - 4)!} = \frac{12!}{8!} = \frac{12 \cdot 11 \cdot 10 \cdot 9 \cdot 8!}{8!} = 11{,}880 \qquad ✔$$

EXAMPLE

The number of ways to assemble chips in a controller
An electronic controlling mechanism requires 5 identical memory chips. In how many ways can this mechanism be assembled by placing the 5 chips in the 5 positions within the controller?

Solution   For $n = 5$ and $r = 5$, the first formula yields

$$_5P_5 = 5 \cdot 4 \cdot 3 \cdot 2 \cdot 1 = 120$$

and the second formula yields

$$_5P_5 = \frac{5!}{(5 - 5)!} = \frac{5!}{0!} = 5! = 120 \qquad ✔$$

The first formula for $_nP_r$ is generally easier to use unless we can use a calculator which directly yields factorials and/or ratios of factorials.

There are many problems in which we must find the number of ways in which *r* objects can be selected from a set of *n* objects, but we do not care about the order in which the selection is made. For instance, we may want to know in how many ways 3 of 20 laboratory assistants can be chosen to assist with an experiment. In general, there are *r*! permutations of any *r* objects we select from a set of *n* distinct objects. So, the $_nP_r$ permutations of *r* objects, selected from a set of *n* objects, contains each set of *r* objects *r*! times. Therefore, to find the number of ways in which *r* objects can be selected from a set of *n* distinct objects, also called the number of

combinations of n objects taken r at a time and denoted by $_nC_r$ or $\binom{n}{r}$, we divide $_nP_r$ by $r!$ and get

---

Number of combinations of n objects taken r at a time

Theorem 3.3 The number of ways in which r objects can be selected from a set of n distinct objects is

$$\binom{n}{r} = \frac{n(n-1)(n-2)\cdots(n-r+1)}{r!}$$

or, in factorial notation,

$$\binom{n}{r} = \frac{n!}{r!(n-r)!}$$

EXAMPLE

Evaluating a combination
In how many different ways can 3 of 20 laboratory assistants be chosen to assist with an experiment?

Solution   For $n = 20$ and $r = 3$, the first formula for $\binom{n}{r}$ yields

$$\binom{20}{3} = \frac{20 \cdot 19 \cdot 18}{3!} = 1,140 \qquad \checkmark$$

EXAMPLE

Selection of machines for an experiment
A calibration study needs to be conducted to see if the readings on 15 test machines are giving similar results. In how many ways can 3 of the 15 be selected for the initial investigation?

Solution
$$\binom{15}{3} = \frac{15 \cdot 14 \cdot 13}{3 \cdot 2 \cdot 1} = 455 \text{ ways}$$

Note that selecting which 3 machines to use is the same as selecting which 12 not to include. That is, according to the second formula

$$\binom{15}{12} = \frac{15!}{12!3!} = \frac{15!}{3!12!} = \binom{15}{3} \qquad \checkmark$$

EXAMPLE

The number of choices of new researchers
In how many different ways can the director of a research laboratory choose 2 chemists from among 7 applicants and 3 physicists from among 9 applicants?

Solution   The 2 chemists can be chosen in $\binom{7}{2} = 21$ ways and the 3 physicists can be chosen in $\binom{9}{3} = 84$ ways. By the multiplication rule, the whole selection can be made in $21 \cdot 84 = 1,764$ ways. $\qquad \checkmark$

EXERCISES

3.1 A technician has to check the suitability of 3 solid crystal lasers and 2 carbon dioxide lasers for a given task.

   (a) Using two coordinates so that $(2, 1)$, for example, represents the event that the technician will find two of the solid crystal lasers and one of the carbon dioxide lasers suitable for the task, draw a diagram similar to that of Figure 3.1 showing the 12 points of the sample space.

   (b) If R is the event that equally many solid crystal lasers and carbon dioxide lasers are suitable for the task, T is the event that none of the carbon dioxide lasers is suitable for the task, and U is the event that fewer solid crystal lasers than carbon dioxide lasers are suitable for the task, express each of these events symbolically by listing its elements.

3.2 With reference to Exercise 3.1, which of the three pairs of events, R and T, R and U, and T and U, are mutually exclusive?

3.3 With reference to Exercise 3.1, list the outcomes comprising each of the following events, and also express the events in words.

   (a) $R \cup U$

   (b) $R \cap T$

   (c) $\overline{T}$

3.4 With reference to the sample space of Figure 3.1, express each of the following events in words.

   (a) $F = \{(1, 0), (1, 1)\}$

   (b) $G = \{(0, 2), (1, 1), (2, 0)\}$

   (c) $F \cap G$

3.5 To construct sample spaces for experiments in which we deal with nonnumeric data, we often code the various alternatives by assigning them numbers. For instance, if a mechanic is asked whether work on a certain model car is very easy, easy, average, difficult, or very difficult, we might assign these alternatives the codes, $1, 2, 3, 4$, and 5. If $A = \{3, 4\}$, $B = \{2, 3\}$, and $C = \{4, 5\}$, express each of the following symbolically by listing its elements and also in words.

   (a) $A \cup B$

   (b) $A \cap B$

   (c) $A \cup \overline{B}$

   (d) $\overline{C}$

3.6 With reference to Exercise 3.5, which of the three pairs of events, A and B, A and C, and A and C, are mutually exclusive?

3.7 Two professors and 3 graduate assistants are responsible for the supervision of a physics lab, and at least one professor and one graduate assistant has to be present at all times.

   (a) Using two coordinates so that $(1, 3)$, for example, represents the event that one professor and 3 graduate assistants are present, draw a diagram similar to that of Figure 3.1 showing the points of the corresponding sample space.

(b) Describe in words the events which are represented by $B = \{(1, 3), (2, 3)\}$, $C = \{(1, 1), (2, 2)\}$, and $D = \{(1, 2), (2, 1)\}$.

(c) With reference to part (b), express $C \cup D$ symbolically by listing its elements, and also express this event in words.

(d) With reference to part (b), are B and D mutually exclusive?

3.8 For each of the following experiments decide whether it would be appropriate to use a sample space which is finite, countably infinite, or continuous.

(a) The amount of cosmic radiation to which passengers are exposed during a transcontinental jet flight is measured by means of a suitable counter.

(b) Five of the members of a professional society with 12,600 members are chosen to serve on a nominating committee.

(c) An experiment is conducted to measure the heat of vaporization of water.

(d) A study is made to determine in how many of 450 airplane accidents the main cause is pilot error.

(e) Measurements are made to determine the uranium content of a certain ore.

(f) In a torture test, a watch is dropped a number of times from a tall building until it stops running.

3.9 In Figure 3.6, C is the event that an ore contains copper and U is the event that it contains uranium. Explain in words what events are represented by regions 1, 2, 3, and 4.

3.10 With reference to Exercise 3.9, what events are represented by

(a) regions 1 and 3 together;

(b) regions 3 and 4 together;

(c) regions 1, 2, and 3 together?

3.11 With reference to Figure 3.4, what events are represented by

(a) region 5;

(b) regions 4 and 6 together;

(c) regions 7 and 8 together;

(d) regions 1, 2, 3, and 5 together?

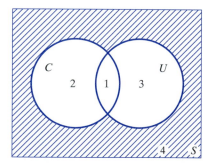

FIGURE 3.6 Venn diagram for exercises 3.9 and 3.10

3.12 With reference to Figure 3.4, what regions or combinations of regions represent the events that a motor will have

  (a) none of the major defects;

  (b) shaft that is large and windings improper;

  (c) shaft that is large and/or windings improper but the electrical connections are satisfactory;

  (d) the shaft is large and the windings improper and/or the electrical connections are unsatisfactory.

3.13 Use Venn diagrams to verify that

  (a) $(\overline{A \cap B}) = \overline{A} \cup \overline{B}$;

  (b) $A \cup (A \cap B) = A$;

  (c) $(A \cap B) \cup (A \cap \overline{B}) = A$;

  (d) $A \cup B = (A \cap B) \cup (A \cap \overline{B}) \cup (\overline{A} \cap B)$;

  (e) $A \cup (B \cap C) = (A \cup B) \cap (A \cup C)$.

3.14 A building inspector has to check the wiring in a new apartment building either on Monday, Tuesday, Wednesday, or Thursday, and at 8 A.M., 1 P.M., or 2 P.M. Draw a tree diagram which shows the various ways in which the inspector can schedule the inspection of the wiring of the new apartment building.

3.15 If the five finalists in an international volleyball tournament are Spain, United States, Uruguay, Portugal, and Japan, draw a tree diagram which shows the various possible first and second place finishers.

3.16 A biomechanical device for medical emergencies can operate for 0, 1, or 2 times a night. Construct a tree diagram to show that there are 10 different ways that it can be operated for a total of 6 times over 4 nights.

3.17 In an optics kit there are 6 concave lenses, 4 convex lenses, and 3 prisms. In how many ways can one choose one of the concave lenses, one of the convex lenses, and one of the prisms?

3.18 A special-purpose computer contains 3 switches, each of which can be set in 3 different ways. In how many ways can the computer's bank of switches be set?

3.19 In a small geology class, each of the 4 students must write a report on one of 8 field trips. In how many different ways can they each choose one of the field trips if

  (a) no 2 students may choose the same field trip;

  (b) there is no restriction on their choice?

3.20 If there are 9 cars in a race, in how many different ways can they place first, second, and third?

3.21 In how many ordered ways can a television director schedule 6 different commercials during the 6 time slots allocated to commercials during the telecast of the first period of a hockey game?

3.22 If among n objects k are alike and the others are all distinct, the number of permutations of these n objects taken all together is $\dfrac{n!}{k!}$.

  (a) How many permutations are there of the letters of the word *class*?

  (b) In how many ways can the television director of Exercise 3.21 fill the 6 time slots allocated to commercials, if there are 4 different commercials, of which a given one is to be shown 3 times while each of the others is to be shown once?

3.23 Determine the number of ways in which a manufacturer can choose 2 of 15 locations for a new warehouse.

3.24 If the order does not matter, in how many different ways can 4 of 18 robotic arms be chosen for a special welding job?

3.25 A carton of 12 rechargeable batteries contains one that is defective. In how many ways can an inspector choose 3 of the batteries and

  (a) get the one that is defective;

  (b) not get the one that is defective;

3.26 With reference to Exercise 3.25, suppose that two of the batteries are defective. In how many ways can the inspector choose 3 of the batteries and get

  (a) none of the defective batteries;

  (b) one of the defective batteries;

  (c) both of the defective batteries?

3.27 The supply department has 8 different electric motors and 5 different starting switches. In how many ways can 2 motors and 2 switches be selected for an experiment concerning a tracking antenna?

3.3   Probability

So far we have studied only what is possible in a given situation; now we shall go one step further and judge also what is probable and what is improbable. Historically, the oldest way of measuring uncertainties is the **classical probability concept,** which was developed originally in connection with games of chance. It applies when all possible outcomes are equally likely, in which case we say that

The classical probability concept

> If there are n equally likely possibilities, of which one must occur and s are regarded as favorable, or as a "success," then the probability of a "success" is given by $\dfrac{s}{n}$.

In the application of this rule, the terms favorable and success are used rather loosely—favorable may mean that a television set does not work and success may mean that someone catches the flu.

EXAMPLE

Well-shuffled cards are equally likely to be selected

What is the probability of drawing an ace from a well-shuffled deck of 52 playing cards?

Solution   There are $s = 4$ aces among the $n = 52$ cards, so we get

$$\frac{s}{n} = \frac{4}{52} = \frac{1}{13}$$

Although equally likely possibilities are found mostly in games of chance, the classical probability concept applies also to a great variety of situations where gambling devices are used to make random selections; say, when offices are assigned to research assistants by lot, when laboratory animals are chosen for an experiment so that each one has the same chance of being selected, or when washing machine parts are chosen for inspection so that each part produced has the same chance of being selected.

EXAMPLE

Random selection results in the equally likely case
If 3 of 20 tires in storage are defective and 4 of them are randomly chosen for inspection (that is, each tire has the same chance of being selected), what is the probability that only one of the defective tires will be included?

Solution

There are $\binom{20}{4} = 4{,}845$ equally likely ways of choosing 4 of 20 tires, so $n = 4{,}845$. The number of favorable outcomes is the number of ways in which one of the defective tires and three of the nondefective tires can be selected, or $s = \binom{3}{1}\binom{17}{3} = 3 \cdot 680 = 2{,}040$. It follows that the probability is

$$\frac{s}{n} = \frac{2{,}040}{4{,}845} = \frac{8}{19}$$

or approximately 0.42. ✔

A major shortcoming of the classical probability concept is its limited applicability, for there are many situations in which the various possibilities cannot all be regarded as equally likely. This would be the case, for example, if we are concerned with the question of whether it will rain the next day, whether a missile launching will be a success, whether a newly designed engine will function for at least 1,000 hours, or whether a certain candidate will win an election.

Among the various probability concepts, most widely held is the **frequency interpretation,** according to which

The frequency interpretation of probability

> The probability of an event (or outcome) is the proportion of times the event would occur in a long run of repeated experiments.

If we say that the probability is 0.78 that a jet from New York to Boston will arrive on time, we mean that such flights arrive on time 78% of the time. Also, if the Weather Service predicts that there is a 40% chance for rain (that the probability is 0.40), this means that under the same weather conditions it will rain 40% of the time. More generally, we say that an event has a probability of, say, 0.90, in the same sense in which we might say that in cold weather our car will start 90% of the time. We cannot guarantee what will happen on any particular occasion—the car may start and then it may not—but if we kept records over a long period of time, we should find that the proportion of "successes" is very close to 0.90.

In accordance with the frequency interpretation of probability, we estimate the probability of an event by observing what fraction of the time similar events have occurred in the past.

Long-run relative frequency approximation to probability
If records show that 294 of 300 ceramic insulators tested were able to withstand a certain thermal shock, what is the probability that any one untested insulator will be able to withstand the thermal shock?

Solution   Among the insulators tested, $\frac{294}{300} = 0.98$ were able to withstand the thermal shock, and we use this figure as an estimate of the probability.   ✔

An alternative point of view which is currently gaining in favor is to interpret probabilities as **personal** or **subjective evaluations.** Such probabilities express the strength of one's belief with regard to the uncertainties that are involved, and they apply especially when there is little or no direct evidence, so that there is no choice but to consider collateral (indirect) evidence, educated guesses, and perhaps intuition and other subjective factors. Subjective probabilities are best determined by referring to risk taking, or betting situations, as will be explained in Exercise 3.53.

3.4   The Axioms of Probability

In this section we define probabilities mathematically as the values of **additive set functions.** Since the reader is probably most familiar with functions for which the elements of the domain and the range are all numbers, let us first give a very simple example where the elements of the domain are sets while the elements of the range are nonnegative integers, namely, a **set function** that assigns to each subset A of a finite sample space S the number of elements in A, written $N(A)$. Suppose that 500 machine parts are inspected before they are shipped, that I denotes that a machine part is improperly assembled, D denotes that it contains one or more defective components, and the distribution of the 500 machine parts among the various categories is as shown in the Venn diagram of Figure 3.7. The numbers in Figure 3.7 are $N(I \cap \overline{D}) = 20$, $N(I \cap D) = 10$, $N(\overline{I} \cap D) = 5$, and $N(\overline{I} \cap \overline{D}) = 465$. Using these values and the fact that the set function is **additive** (meaning that the number which it assigns to the union of two subsets which have no elements in common

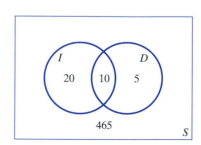

FIGURE 3.7 Classification of 500 machine parts

is the sum of the numbers assigned to the individual subsets), we can determine the value of $N(A)$ for any other subset A of S. For instance,

$$N(\bar{I}) = N(\bar{I} \cap D) + N(\bar{I} \cap \bar{D}) = 5 + 465 = 470$$
$$N(I \cup D) = N(I \cap \bar{D}) + N(I \cap D) + N(\bar{I} \cap D)$$
$$= 20 + 10 + 5 = 35$$
$$N(\bar{I} \cup D) = N(I \cap D) + N(\bar{I} \cap D) + N(\bar{I} \cap \bar{D})$$
$$= 10 + 5 + 465 = 480$$

and

$$N(D) = N(I \cap D) + (\bar{I} \cap D) = 10 + 5 = 15$$

Using the concept of an additive set function, let us now explain what we mean by the probability of an event. Given a finite sample space S and an event A in S, we define $P(A)$, the probability of A, to be a value of an additive set function that satisfies the following three conditions:

The axioms of probability for a finite sample space

Axiom 1 $0 \le P(A) \le 1$ for each event A in S.
Axiom 2 $P(S) = 1$.
Axiom 3   If A and B are mutually exclusive events in S, then
$P(A \cup B) = P(A) + P(B)$.

The first axiom states that probabilities are real numbers on the interval from 0 to 1. The second axiom states that the sample space as a whole is assigned a probability of 1 and this expresses the idea that the probability of a certain event, an event which must happen, is equal to 1. The third axiom states that probability functions must be additive.

Axioms for a mathematical theory require no proof, but if such a theory is to be applied to the physical world, we must show somehow that the axioms are "realistic." Thus, let us show that the three postulates are consistent with the classical probability concept and the frequency interpretation.

So far as the first axiom is concerned, fractions of the form $\frac{s}{n}$, where $0 \le s \le n$ and n is a positive integer, cannot be negative or exceed 1, and the same is true also for the proportion of the time that an event will occur. To show that the second axiom is consistent with the classical probability concept and the frequency interpretation for a long series of repeated experiments, we have only to observe that for the whole sample space $P(S) = \frac{n}{n} = 1$ and that an event which is certain to occur must happen 100% of the time. So far as the third axiom is concerned, if $P(A) = \frac{s_1}{n}$, $P(B) = \frac{s_2}{n}$, and A and B are mutually exclusive, then $P(A \cup B) = \frac{s_1 + s_2}{n} = P(A) + P(B)$; also, if one event occurs in proportion .36 or 36% of the time, another event occurs 41% of the time, and the two events are mutually exclusive, then one or the other will occur in proportion $.36 + .41 = .77$ or 77% of the time.

Before we go any further, it is important to stress the point that the axioms of probability do not tell us how to assign probabilities to the various outcomes of an experiment; they merely restrict the ways in which it can be done. In actual practice, probabilities are assigned on the basis of past experience, on the basis of a careful analysis of conditions underlying the experiment, on the basis of subjective evaluations, or on the basis of assumptions—say, the common assumption that all the outcomes are equiprobable.

EXAMPLE

Checking possible assignments of probability

If an experiment has the three possible and mutually exclusive outcomes A, B, and C, check in each case whether the assignment of probabilities is permissible:

(a) $P(A) = \frac{1}{3}$, $P(B) = \frac{1}{3}$, and $P(C) = \frac{1}{3}$
(b) $P(A) = 0.64$, $P(B) = 0.38$, and $P(C) = -0.02$
(c) $P(A) = 0.35$, $P(B) = 0.52$, and $P(C) = 0.26$
(d) $P(A) = 0.57$, $P(B) = 0.24$, and $P(C) = 0.19$

Solution

(a) The assignment of probabilities is permissible because the values are all on the interval from 0 to 1 and their sum is $\frac{1}{3} + \frac{1}{3} + \frac{1}{3} = 1$.
(b) The assignment is not permissible because $P(C)$ is negative.
(c) The assignment is not permissible because $0.35 + 0.52 + 0.26 = 1.13$, which exceeds 1.
(d) The assignment is permissible because the values are all on the interval from 0 to 1 and their sum is $0.57 + 0.24 + 0.19 = 1$. ✔

3.5 Some Elementary Theorems

With the use of mathematical induction, the third axiom of probability can be extended to include any number of mutually exclusive events; in other words, the following can be shown.

Generalization of third axiom of probability

> **Theorem 3.4** If $A_1, A_2, \ldots, A_n$ are mutually exclusive events in a sample space S, then
>
> $$P(A_1 \cup A_2 \cup \cdots \cup A_n) = P(A_1) + P(A_2) + \cdots + P(A_n)$$

In the next chapter we shall see how the third axiom of probability must be modified so that the axioms apply also to sample spaces which are not finite.

EXAMPLE

Probabilities add for mutually exclusive events

The probability that a consumer testing service will rate a new antipollution device for cars very poor, poor, fair, good, very good, or excellent are 0.07, 0.12, 0.17, 0.32, 0.21, and 0.11. What are the probabilities that it will rate the device

(a) very poor, poor, fair, or good;

(b) good, very good, or excellent?

Solution   Since the possibilities are all mutually exclusive, direct substitution into the formula of Theorem 3.4 yields

$$0.07 + 0.12 + 0.17 + 0.32 = 0.68$$

for part (a) and

$$0.32 + 0.21 + 0.11 = 0.64$$

for part (b).   ✔

As it can be shown that a sample space of n points (outcomes) has 2^n subsets, it would seem that the problem of specifying a probability function (namely, a probability for each subset or event) can easily become very tedious. Indeed, for $n = 20$ there are already more than 1 million possible events. Fortunately, this task can be simplified considerably by the use of the following theorem:

Rule for calculating probability of an event

> **Theorem 3.5**   If A is an event in the finite sample space S, then $P(A)$ equals the sum of the probabilities of the individual outcomes comprising A.

To prove this theorem, let $E_1, E_2, \ldots, E_n$ be the n outcomes comprising event A, so that we can write $A = E_1 \cup E_2 \cup \cdots \cup E_n$. Since the E's are individual outcomes they are mutually exclusive, and by Theorem 3.4 we have

$$
\begin{aligned}
P(A) &= P(E_1 \cup E_2 \cup \cdots \cup E_n) \\
&= P(E_1) + P(E_2) + \cdots + P(E_n)
\end{aligned}
$$

which completes the proof.

EXAMPLE

Using a Venn diagram to determine probabilities

With reference to the lawn-mower-rating example on page 56, suppose that the probabilities of the 18 outcomes are as shown in Figure 3.8 (which, except for the probabilities, is identical with Figure 3.5). Find $P(E_1)$, $P(P_1)$, $P(C_1)$, $P(E_1 \cap P_1)$, and $P(E_1 \cap C_1)$.

Solution   Adding the probabilities of the outcomes comprising the respective events, we get

$$P(E_1) = 0.07 + 0.13 + 0.06 + 0.05 + 0.07 + 0.02 = 0.40$$
$$P(P_1) = 0.07 + 0.13 + 0.06 + 0.07 + 0.14 + 0.07 + 0.02$$
$$+0.03 + 0.01 = 0.60$$
$$P(C_1) = 0.07 + 0.05 + 0.07 + 0.08 + 0.02 + 0.01 = 0.30$$
$$P(E_1 \cap P_1) = 0.07 + 0.13 + 0.06 = 0.26$$

and

$$P(E_1 \cap C_1) = 0.07 + 0.05 = 0.12$$ ✔

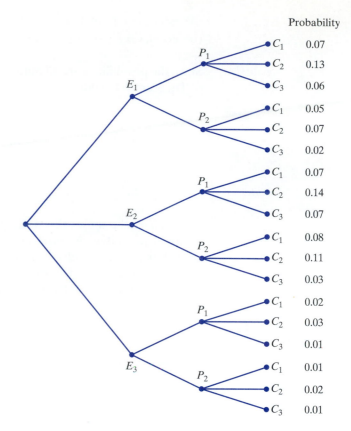

Probability

			C_1	0.07
	P_1		C_2	0.13
			C_3	0.06
E_1			C_1	0.05
	P_2		C_2	0.07
			C_3	0.02
			C_1	0.07
	P_1		C_2	0.14
			C_3	0.07
E_2			C_1	0.08
	P_2		C_2	0.11
			C_3	0.03
			C_1	0.02
	P_1		C_2	0.03
			C_3	0.01
E_3			C_1	0.01
	P_2		C_2	0.02
			C_3	0.01

FIGURE 3.8 Ratings of lawn mowers and their probabilities

In Theorem 3.4 we saw that the third axiom of probability can be extended to include more than two mutually exclusive events. Another useful and important extension of this axiom allows us to find the probability of the union of any two events in S regardless of whether they are mutually exclusive. To motivate the theorem which follows, let us consider the Venn diagram of Figure 3.9, which concerns the job offers received by recent engineering school graduates. The letter I and G stand for a job offer from industry and a job offer from the government, respectively. It follows from the Venn diagram that

$$P(I) = 0.18 + 0.12 = 0.30$$
$$P(G) = 0.12 + 0.24 = 0.36$$

and

$$P(I \cup G) = 0.18 + 0.12 + 0.24 = 0.54$$

We were able to add the various probabilities because they represent mutually exclusive events.

Had we erroneously used the third axiom of probability to calculate $P(I \cup G)$, we would have obtained $P(I) + P(G) = 0.30 + 0.36$, which exceeds the correct value by 0.12. This error results from adding in $P(I \cap G)$ twice, once in $P(I) = 0.30$

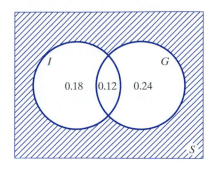

FIGURE 3.9 Venn diagram for job offers

and once in $P(G) = 0.36$, and we could correct for it by subtracting 0.12 from 0.66. Thus, we would get

$$P(I \cup G) = P(I) + P(G) - P(I \cap G)$$
$$= 0.30 + 0.36 - 0.12$$
$$= 0.54$$

and this agrees, as it should, with the result obtained before.

In line with this motivation, let us now state and prove the following theorem:

General addition rule for probability

> Theorem 3.6 If A and B are any events in S, then
>
> $$P(A \cup B) = P(A) + P(B) - P(A \cap B)$$

To prove this theorem, we make use of the identities of parts (c) and (d) of Exercise 3.13, getting

$$P(A \cup B) = P(A \cap B) + P(A \cap \overline{B}) + P(\overline{A} \cap B)$$
$$= [P(A \cap B) + P(A \cap \overline{B})] + [P(A \cap B) + P(\overline{A} \cap B)] - P(A \cap B)$$
$$= P(A) + P(B) - P(A \cap B)$$

Note that when A and B are mutually exclusive so that $P(A \cap B) = 0$, Theorem 3.6 reduces to the third axiom of probability. For this reason, we sometimes refer to the third axiom of probability as the **special addition rule.**

EXAMPLE **Using the general addition rule for probability**
With reference to the lawn-mower-rating example, find the probability that a lawn mower will be rated easy to operate or having a high average cost of repairs, namely, $P(E_1 \cup C_1)$.

Solution Making use of the results obtained on page 69, $P(E_1) = 0.40$, $P(C_1) = 0.30$, and $P(E_1 \cap C_1) = 0.12$, we substitute into the formula of Theorem 3.6 and get

$$P(E_1 \cup C_1) = 0.40 + 0.30 - 0.12$$
$$= 0.58$$

EXAMPLE   **The probability of requiring repair under warranty**
If the probabilities are $0.87, 0.36$, and 0.29 that, while under warranty, a new car will require repairs on the engine, drive train, or both, what is the probability that a car will require one or the other or both kinds of repairs under the warranty?

Solution   Substituting these given values into the formula of Theorem 3.6, we get

$$0.87 + 0.36 - 0.29 = 0.94$$ ✔

Note that the general addition rule, Theorem 3.6, can be generalized further so that it applies to more than two events (see Exercise 3.49).

Using axioms of probability, we can derive many other theorems which play important roles in applications. For instance, let us show the following:

Probability rule of the complement

> **Theorem 3.7**   If A is any event in S, then $P(\overline{A}) = 1 - P(A)$.

To prove this theorem, we make use of the fact that A and $\overline{A}$ are mutually exclusive by definition, and that $A \cup \overline{A} = S$ (namely, that among them A and $\overline{A}$ contain all the elements in S). Hence, we can write

$$\begin{aligned} P(A) + P(\overline{A}) &= P(A \cup \overline{A}) \\ &= P(S) \\ &= 1 \end{aligned}$$

so that $P(\overline{A}) = 1 - P(A)$. As a special case we find that $P(\phi) = 1 - P(S) = 0$, since the empty set ϕ is the complement of S.

EXAMPLE   **Using the probability rule of the complement**
Referring again to the lawn-mower-rating example and the results on page 69, find

(a) the probability that a lawn mower will not be rated easy to operate;
(b) the probability that a lawn mower will be rated as either not being easy to operate or not having a high average repair cost.

Solution   (a) $P(\overline{E_1}) = 1 - P(E_1) = 1 - 0.40 = 0.60$.
(b) Since $\overline{E_1} \cup \overline{C_1} = \overline{(E_1 \cap C_1)}$ according to the identity of part (a) of Exercise 3.13, we get

$$P(\overline{E_1} \cup \overline{C_1}) = P[\overline{(E_1 \cap C_1)}] = 1 - P(E_1 \cap C_1) = 1 - 0.12 = 0.88$$ ✔

EXERCISES

3.28 If a card is drawn from a well-shuffled deck of 52 playing cards, what is the probability of drawing

(a) a red king;
(b) a 3, 4, 5, or 6;

(c) a black card;

(d) a red ace or a black queen?

3.29 When we roll a pair of balanced dice, what are the probabilities of getting

(a) 7;

(b) 11;

(c) 7 or 11;

(d) 3;

(e) 2 or 12;

(f) 2, 3, or 12?

3.30 A lottery sells tickets numbered from 00001 through 50000. What is the probability of drawing a number that is divisible by 200?

3.31 A car rental agency has 18 compact cars and 12 intermediate-size cars. If four of the cars are randomly selected for a safety check, what is the probability of getting two of each kind?

3.32 Among the first 842 convection ovens sold to consumers, 143 required some adjustment during the warranty period. Estimate the probability that a newly purchased convection oven will require some adjustment during the warranty period.

3.33 In a group of 160 graduate engineering students, 92 are enrolled in an advanced course in statistics, 63 are enrolled in a course in operations research, and 40 are enrolled in both. How many of these students are not enrolled in either course?

3.34 Among 150 persons interviewed as part of an urban mass transportation study, some live more than 3 miles from the center of the city (A), some now regularly drive their own car to work (B), and some would gladly switch to public mass transportation if it were available (C). Use the information given in Figure 3.10 to find

(a) $N(A)$;

(b) $N(B)$;

(c) $N(C)$;

(d) $N(A \cap B)$;

(e) $N(A \cap C)$;

(f) $N(A \cap B \cap C)$;

(g) $N(A \cup B)$;

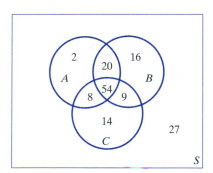

FIGURE 3.10 Diagram for Exercise 3.34

(h) $N(B \cup C)$;

(i) $N(\overline{A} \cup \overline{B} \cup C)$;

(j) $N[B \cap (A \cup C)]$.

3.35 An experiment has the four possible mutually exclusive outcomes A, B, C, and D. Check whether the following assignments of probability are permissible:

(a) $P(A) = 0.38$, $P(B) = 0.16$, $P(C) = 0.11$, $P(D) = 0.35$;

(b) $P(A) = 0.31$, $P(B) = 0.27$, $P(C) = 0.28$, $P(D) = 0.16$;

(c) $P(A) = 0.32$, $P(B) = 0.27$, $P(C) = -0.06$, $P(D) = 0.47$;

(d) $P(A) = \frac{1}{2}$, $P(B) = \frac{1}{4}$, $P(C) = \frac{1}{8}$, $P(D) = \frac{1}{16}$;

(e) $P(A) = \frac{5}{18}$, $P(B) = \frac{1}{6}$, $P(C) = \frac{1}{3}$, $P(D) = \frac{2}{9}$.

3.36 With reference to Exercise 3.1, suppose that the points $(0, 0)$, $(0, 1)$, $(0, 2)$, $(1, 0)$, $(1, 1)$, $(1, 2)$, $(2, 0)$, $(2, 1)$, $(2, 2)$, $(3, 0)$, $(3, 1)$, and $(3, 2)$ have the probabilities 0.001, 0.002, 0.006, 0.001, 0.017, 0.078, 0.004, 0.069, 0.311, 0.004, 0.092, and 0.415.

(a) Verify that this assignment of probabilities is permissible.

(b) Find the probabilities of events R, T, and U given in part (b) of that exercise.

(c) Calculate the probabilities that zero, one, or two carbon dioxide lasers will be suitable for the given task.

3.37 With reference to Exercise 3.7, suppose that each point (i, j) of the sample space is assigned the probability $\dfrac{15/28}{i + j}$.

(a) Verify that this assignment of probabilities is permissible.

(b) Find the probabilities of events B, C, and D described in part (b) of that exercise.

(c) Find the probabilities that one, two, or three of the graduate students will be supervising the physics lab.

3.38 Explain why there must be a mistake in each of the following statements;

(a) The probability that a mineral sample will contain silver is 0.38 and the probability that it will not contain silver is 0.52.

(b) The probability that a drilling operation will be a success is 0.34 and the probability that it will not be a success is -0.66.

(c) An air-conditioning repairperson claims that the probability is 0.82 that the compressor is all right, 0.64 that the fan motor is all right, and 0.41 that they are both all right.

3.39 Refer to parts (c) and (d) of Exercise 3.13 to show that

(a) $P(A \cap B) \leq P(A)$;

(b) $P(A \cup B) \geq P(A)$.

3.40 Explain why there must be a mistake in each of the following statements:

(a) The probability that a student will get an A in a geology course is 0.32, and the probability that he or she will get either an A or a B is 0.27.

(b) A company is working on the construction of two shopping centers; the probability that the larger one will be completed on time is 0.35 and the probability that both will be completed on time is 0.42.

3.41 If A and B are mutually exclusive events, $P(A) = 0.29$, and $P(B) = 0.43$, find

    (a) $P(\overline{A})$;

    (b) $P(A \cup B)$;

    (c) $P(A \cap \overline{B})$;

    (d) $P(\overline{A} \cap \overline{B})$.

3.42 With reference to Exercise 3.34, suppose that the questionnaire filled in by one of the 150 persons is to be double-checked. If it is chosen in such a way that each questionnaire has a probability of $\frac{1}{150}$ of being selected, find the probabilities that the person

    (a) lives more than 3 miles from the center of the city;

    (b) regularly drives his or her car to work;

    (c) does not live more than 3 miles from the center of the city and would not want to switch to public mass transportation if it were available;

    (d) regularly drives his or her car to work but would gladly switch to public mass transportation if it were available.

3.43 A police department needs new tires for its patrol cars and the probabilities are 0.17, 0.22, 0.03, 0.29, 0.21, and 0.08 that it will buy Uniroyal tires, Goodyear tires, Michelin tires, General tires, Goodrich tires, or Armstrong tires. Find the probabilities that it will buy

    (a) Goodyear or Goodrich tires;

    (b) Uniroyal, General, or Goodrich tires;

    (c) Michelin or Armstrong tires;

    (d) Goodyear, General, or Armstrong tires.

3.44 The probabilities that a TV station will receive $0, 1, 2, 3, \ldots, 8$, or at least 9 complaints after showing a controversial program are, respectively, 0.01, 0.03, 0.07, 0.15, 0.19, 0.18, 0.14, 0.12, 0.09, and 0.02. What are the probabilities that after showing such a program the station will receive

    (a) at most 4 complaints;

    (b) at least 6 complaints;

    (c) from 5 to 8 complaints?

3.45 If each point of the sample space of Figure 3.11 represents an outcome having the probability $\frac{1}{32}$, find

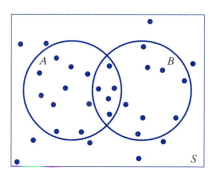

FIGURE 3.11 Diagram for Exercise 3.45

(a) $P(A)$;

(b) $P(B)$;

(c) $P(A \cap B)$;

(d) $P(A \cup B)$;

(e) $P(\overline{A} \cap B)$;

(f) $P(\overline{A} \cap \overline{B})$.

3.46 The probability that an integrated circuit chip will have defective etching is 0.12, the probability that it will have a crack defect is 0.29, and the probability that it has both defects is 0.07.

(a) What is the probability that a newly manufactured chip will have either an etching or a crack defect?

(b) What is the probability that a newly manufactured chip will have neither defect?

3.47 The probability that a new airport will get an award for its design is 0.16, the probability that it will get an award for the efficient use of materials is 0.24, and the probability that it will get both awards is 0.11.

(a) What is the probability that it will get at least one of the two awards?

(b) What is the probability that it will get only one of two awards?

3.48 Given $P(A) = 0.35$, $P(B) = 0.73$, and $P(A \cap B) = 0.14$, find

(a) $P(A \cup B)$;

(b) $P(\overline{A} \cap B)$;

(c) $P(A \cap \overline{B})$;

(d) $P(\overline{A} \cup \overline{B})$.

3.49 It can be shown that for any three events A, B, and C, the probability that at least one of them will occur is given by

$$P(A \cup B \cup C) = P(A) + P(B) + P(C) - P(A \cap B) - P(A \cap C)$$
$$- P(B \cap C) + P(A \cap B \cap C)$$

Verify that this formula holds for the probabilities of Figure 3.12.

3.50 Suppose that in the maintenance of a large medical-records file for insurance purposes the probability of an error in processing is 0.0010, the probability of an error

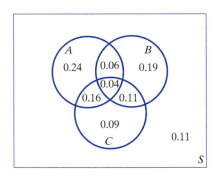

Figure 3.12 Diagram for Exercise 3.49

in filing is 0.0009, the probability of an error in retrieving is 0.0012, the probability of an error in processing as well as filing is 0.0002, the probability of an error in processing as well as retrieving is 0.0003, the probability of an error in filing as well as retrieving is 0.0003, and the probability of an error in processing and filing as well as retrieving is 0.0001. What is the probability of making at least one of these errors?

3.51 If the probability of event A is p, then the **odds** that it will occur are given by the ratio of p to $1 - p$. Odds are usually given as a ratio of two positive integers having no common factor, and if an event is more likely not to occur than to occur, it is customary to give the odds that it will not occur rather than the odds that it will occur. What are the odds for or against the occurrence of an event if its probability is

(a) $\frac{4}{7}$;

(b) 0.05;

(c) 0.80?

3.52 Use the definition of Exercise 3.51 to show that if the odds for the occurrence of event A are a to b, where a and b are positive integers, then $p = \dfrac{a}{a + b}$.

3.53 The formula of Exercise 3.52 is often used to determine subjective probabilities. For instance, if an applicant for a job "feels" that the odds are 7 to 4 of getting the job, the subjective probability the applicant assigns to getting the job is $p = \dfrac{7}{7 + 4} = \dfrac{7}{11}$.

(a) If a businessperson feels that the odds are 3 to 2 that a new venture will succeed (say, by betting \$300 against \$200 that it will succeed), what subjective probability is he or she assigning to its success?

(b) If a student is willing to bet \$30 against \$10, but not \$40 against \$10, that he or she will get a passing grade in a certain course, what does this tell us about the subjective probability the student assigns to getting a passing grade in the course?

3.54 Subjective probabilities may or may not satisfy the third axiom of probability. When they do, we say that they are **consistent;** when they do not, they ought not to be taken too seriously.

(a) The supplier of delicate optical equipment feels that the odds are 7 to 5 against a shipment arriving late and 11 to 1 against it not arriving at all. Furthermore, he feels that there is a fifty-fifty chance (the odds are 1 to 1) that such a shipment will either arrive late or not at all. Are the corresponding probabilities consistent?

(b) There are two Ferraris in a race, and an expert feels that the odds against their winning are, respectively, 2 to 1 and 3 to 1. Furthermore, she claims that there is a less-than-even chance that either of the two Ferraris will win. Discuss the consistency of these claims.

3.6 Conditional Probability

As we have defined probability, it is meaningful to ask for the probability of an event only if we refer to a given sample space S. To ask for the probability that an engineer earns at least \$40,000 a year is meaningless unless we specify whether we are referring to all engineers in the western hemisphere, all engineers in the United States, all those in a particular industry, all those affiliated with a university, and so forth. Thus, when we use the symbol $P(A)$ for the probability of A, we really mean the probability of A given some sample space S. Since the choice of S is by no means always evident, and since there are problems in which we are interested in the probabilities of A with respect to more sample spaces than one, the notation $P(A|S)$ is used to make it clear that we are referring to a particular sample space S. We read $P(A|S)$ as the conditional probability of A relative to S, and every probability is thus a conditional probability. Of course, we use the simplified notation $P(A)$ whenever the choice of S is clearly understood.

To illustrate some of the ideas connected with conditional probabilities, let us consider again the 500 machine parts of which some are improperly assembled and some contain one or more defective components as shown in Figure 3.7. Assuming equal probabilities in the selection of one of the machine parts for inspection, it can be seen that the probability of getting one with one or more defective components is $P(D) = \dfrac{10 + 5}{500} = \dfrac{3}{100}$. To check whether the probability is the same if the choice is restricted to the machine parts that are improperly assembled, we have only to look at the reduced sample space of Figure 3.13 and assume that each of the 30 improperly assembled parts has the same chance of being selected. We thus get

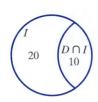

FIGURE 3.13
Reduced sample space

$$P(D|I) = \frac{N(D \cap I)}{N(I)} = \frac{10}{30} = \frac{1}{3}$$

and it can be seen that the probability of getting a machine part with one or more defective components has increased from $\frac{3}{100}$ to $\frac{1}{3}$. Note that if we divide the numerator and denominator of the preceding formula for $P(D|I)$ by $N(S)$, we get

$$P(D|I) = \frac{\dfrac{N(D \cap I)}{N(S)}}{\dfrac{N(I)}{N(S)}} = \frac{P(D \cap I)}{P(I)}$$

where $P(D|I)$ is given by the ratio of $P(D \cap I)$ to $P(I)$.

Looking at this example in another way, note that with respect to the whole sample space S we have

$$P(D \cap I) = \frac{10}{500} = \frac{1}{50} \quad \text{and} \quad P(\overline{D} \cap I) = \frac{20}{500} = \frac{2}{50}$$

assuming, as before, that each of the 500 machine parts has the same chance of being selected. Thus, the probabilities that the machine part selected will or will not contain one or more defective components, given that it is improperly assembled, should be in the ratio 1 to 2. Since the probabilities of D and $\overline{D}$ in the reduced sample space must add up to 1, it follows that

$$P(D|I) = \frac{1}{3} \quad \text{and} \quad P(\overline{D}|I) = \frac{2}{3}$$

and this agrees with the result obtained before. This explains why we had to divide by $P(I)$ when we wrote

$$P(D|I) = \frac{P(D \cap I)}{P(I)}$$

above—division by $P(I)$, or multiplication by $1/P(I)$, takes care of the proportionality factor which makes the sum of the probabilities over the reduced sample space equal to 1.

Following these observations, let us now make the following general definition:

Conditional probability

> If A and B are any events in S and $P(B) \neq 0$, the conditional probability of A given B is
>
> $$P(A|B) = \frac{P(A \cap B)}{P(B)}$$

EXAMPLE

Calculating a conditional probability
If the probability that a communication system will have high fidelity is 0.81 and the probability that it will have high fidelity and high selectivity is 0.18, what is the probability that a system with high fidelity will also have high selectivity?

Solution   If A is the event that a communication system has high selectivity and B is the event that it has high fidelity, we have $P(B) = 0.81$ and $P(A \cap B) = 0.18$, and substitution into the formula yields

$$P(A|B) = \frac{0.18}{0.81} = \frac{2}{9}$$

EXAMPLE

The conditional probability that a lawn mower is easy to operate given that repairs are costly
Referring to the lawn-mower-rating example, for which the probabilities of the individual outcomes are given in Figure 3.8, use the results obtained on page 69 to find $P(E_1|C_1)$.

Solution   Since we had $P(E_1 \cap C_1) = 0.12$ and $P(C_1) = 0.30$, substitution into the formula for a conditional probability yields

$$P(E_1|C_1) = \frac{0.12}{0.30} = 0.40$$

It is of interest to note that the value obtained here for $P(E_1|C_1)$ equals that obtained on page 69 for $P(E_1)$. This means that the probability of a lawn mower being rated easy to repair is the same regardless of whether or not it is given that it has a high average cost of repairs, and we say that E_1 is **independent** of C_1. As the reader will be asked to verify in Exercise 3.59 on page 87, it also follows from the results on page 69 that E_1 is not independent of P_1, namely, that a lawn mower's ease of operation is related to its retail price.

In general, if A and B are any two events in a sample space S, we say that **A is independent of B if and only if $P(A|B) = P(A)$,** but as it can be shown that B is independent of A whenever A is independent of B, it is customary to say simply that **A and B are independent events.**

The following theorem is an immediate consequence of the definition of conditional probability:

General multiplication rule of probability

> **Theorem 3.8**   If A and B are any events in S, then
>
> $$P(A \cap B) = P(A) \cdot P(B|A) \qquad \text{if } P(A) \neq 0$$
> $$= P(B) \cdot P(A|B) \qquad \text{if } P(B) \neq 0$$

The second of these rules is obtained directly from the definition of conditional probability by multiplying both sides by $P(B)$; the first is obtained from the second by interchanging the letters A and B.

EXAMPLE

Using the general multiplication rule of probability
The supervisor of a group of 20 construction workers wants to get the opinion of 2 of them (to be selected at random) about certain new safety regulations. If 12 workers favor the new regulations and the other 8 are against them, what is the probability that both of the workers chosen by the supervisor will be against the new safety regulations?

Solution

Assuming equal probabilities for each selection (which is what we mean by the selections being random), the probability that the first worker selected will be against the new safety regulations is $\frac{8}{20}$, and the probability that the second worker selected will be against the new safety regulations given that the first one is against them is $\frac{7}{19}$. Thus, the desired probability is $\frac{8}{20} \cdot \frac{7}{19} = \frac{14}{95}$.   ✔

In the special case where A and B are independent so $P(A|B) = P(A)$, Theorem 3.8 leads to the following result:

Special product rule of probability

> **Theorem 3.9**   Two events A and B are independent events if and only if
> $$P(A \cap B) = P(A) \cdot P(B)$$

Thus, the probability that two independent events will both occur is simply the product of their probabilities. This rule is sometimes used as the definition of independence; in any case, it may be used to determine whether two given events are independent.

EXAMPLE

The outcomes to unrelated parts of an experiment can be treated as independent
What is the probability of getting two heads in two flips of a balanced coin?

Solution

Since the probability of heads is $\frac{1}{2}$ for each flip and the two flips are independent, the probability is $\frac{1}{2} \cdot \frac{1}{2} = \frac{1}{4}$.   ✔

EXAMPLE

Independence and selection with and without replacement
Two cards are drawn at random from an ordinary deck of 52 playing cards. What is the probability of getting two aces if

(a) the first card is replaced before the second card is drawn;
(b) the first card is not replaced before the second card is drawn?

Solution

(a) Since there are four aces among the 52 cards, we get $\frac{4}{52} \cdot \frac{4}{52} = \frac{1}{169}$.
(b) Since there are only three aces among the 51 cards that remain after one ace has been removed from the deck, we get $\frac{4}{52} \cdot \frac{3}{51} = \frac{1}{221}$.

Note that $\frac{1}{221} \neq \frac{4}{52} \cdot \frac{4}{52}$, so independence is violated when the sampling is without replacement. ✔

EXAMPLE

Checking if two events are independent under an assigned probability
If $P(C) = 0.65$, $P(D) = 0.40$, and $P(C \cap D) = 0.24$, are the events C and D independent?

Solution

Since $P(C) \cdot P(D) = (0.65)(0.40) = 0.26$ and not 0.24, the two events are not independent. ✔

In the preceding examples we have used the assigned probabilities to check if two events are independent. The concept of independence can be—and frequently is—employed when probabilities are assigned to events that concern unrelated parts of an experiment.

EXAMPLE

Assigning probability by the special product rule
Let A be the event that raw material is available when needed and B be the event that the machining time is less than 1 hour. If $P(A) = 0.8$ and $P(B) = 0.7$, assign probability to the event $A \cap B$.

Solution

Since the events A and B concern unrelated steps in the manufacturing process, we invoke independence and make the assignment

$$P(A \cap B) = P(A)P(B) = (0.8)(0.7) = 0.56$$ ✔

The special product rule can easily be extended so that it applies to more than two independent events—again, we multiply together all the individual probabilities.

EXAMPLE

The extended special product rule of probability
What is the probability of not rolling any 6's in four rolls of a balanced die?

Solution

The probability is $\frac{5}{6} \cdot \frac{5}{6} \cdot \frac{5}{6} \cdot \frac{5}{6} = \frac{625}{1,296}$. ✔

For three or more dependent events the multiplication rule becomes more complicated, as is illustrated in Exercise 3.70.

EXAMPLE **The probability of falsely signaling a pollution problem**
Many companies must monitor the effluent that is discharged from their plants
into rivers and waterways. In some states, it is the law that some substances have
water-quality limits that are below the limit of detection, *L,* for the current method
of measurement. The effluent is judged to satisfy the quality limit if every test specimen is below the limit of detection *L.* Otherwise it will be declared to fail compliance with the quality limit. Suppose the water does not contain the contaminant
of interest but that the variability in the chemical analysis still gives a 1% chance
that a measurement on a test specimen will exceed *L.*

(a) Find the probability that neither of two test specimens, both free of the contaminant, will fail to be in compliance.

(b) If one test specimen is taken each week for two years, and they are all free
of the contaminant, find the probability that none of the test specimens will
fail to be in compliance.

(c) Comment on the incorrect reasoning of having a fixed limit of detection no
matter how many tests are conducted.

Solution (a) If the two samples are not taken too close in time or space, we treat them as
independent. We use the special product rule to obtain the probability that
both are in compliance

$$(.99) \times (.99) = .9801$$

(b) Treating the results for different weeks as independent

$$(.99)^{104} = .35$$

so, even with excellent water quality, there is almost a two-thirds chance that
at least once the water quality will be declared to fail to be in compliance
with the law.

(c) With this type of law, no company would want to collect test specimens
more than maybe once a year. This is in direct opposition to the scientific
idea that more information is better than less information on water quality.
Some effort should be made to allow for higher limits when the testing is
more frequent. ✔

EXAMPLE **Using probability to compare the accuracy of two schemes for sending messages**
Electrical engineers are considering two alternative systems for sending messages.
A message consists of a word that is either a 0 or a 1. However, because of random
noise in the channel, a 1 that is transmitted could be received as a 0 and vice versa.
That is, there is a small probability, *p,* that

$$P[\text{A transmitted 1 is received as 0}] = p$$
$$P[\text{A transmitted 0 is received as 1}] = p$$

One scheme is to send a single digit. The message is short but may be unreliable.
A second scheme is to repeat the selected digit three times in succession. At the
receiving end, the majority rule will be used to decode. For instance, when any of
101, 110, or 011 are received, it is interpreted to mean a 1 was sent.

(a) Evaluate the probability that a transmitted 1 will be received as a 1 under the three-digit scheme when $p = .01, .02,$ or $.05$. Compare with the scheme where a single digit is transmitted as a word. Treat the results for different digits as independent.

(b) Suppose a message, consisting of the two words, a 1 followed by 0, is to be transmitted using the three-digit scheme. What is the probability that the total message will be correctly decoded under the majority rule with $p = .05$? Compare with the scheme where a single digit is transmitted as a word.

Solution   (a) The three digits 111 are transmitted. By independence, the sequence 111 has probability $(1 - p)(1 - p)(1 - p)$ of being received as 111. Also the probability of receiving 011 is $p(1 - p)(1 - p)$, so the probability of exactly one 0 among the three received is $3p(1 - p)^2$. Using the majority rule,

$$P[\text{Correct}] = P[\text{transmitted 1 received as 1}] = (1 - p)^3 + 3p(1 - p)^2$$

p	.01	.02	.05
$P[\text{Correct}]$	.9997	.9988	.9928

All three probabilities are considerably above the corresponding single-digit scheme probabilities .99, .98, and .95 respectively.

(b) Both of the words 1 and 0 must be received correctly. As in part (a), the probability that a 0 is received correctly is also .9928. Consequently, using independence, the probability that the total message is correctly received is $(.9928)^2 = .986$. This improves over the scheme where single digits are sent for each word since that scheme has only probability $(.95)^2 = .903$ of correctly receiving the total message.

Redundancy helps improve accuracy but more digits need to be transmitted, which results in a significantly lower throughput.   ✔

3.7   Bayes' Theorem

The general multiplication rules are useful in solving many problems in which the ultimate outcome of an experiment depends on the outcomes of various intermediate stages. Suppose, for instance, that an assembly plant receives its voltage regulators from three different suppliers, 60% from supplier B_1, 30% from supplier B_2, and 10% from supplier B_3. In other words, the probabilities that any one voltage regulator received by the plant comes from these three suppliers are 0.60, 0.30, and 0.10. If 95% of the voltage regulators from B_1, 80% of those from B_2, and 65% of those from B_3 perform according to specifications, what we would like to know is the probability that any one voltage regulator received by the plant will perform according to specifications.

on

If A denotes the event that a voltage regulator received by the plant performs according to specifications, and B_1, B_2, and B_3 are the events that it comes from the respective suppliers, we can write

$$A = A \cap [B_1 \cup B_2 \cup B_3]$$
$$= (A \cap B_1) \cup (A \cap B_2) \cup (A \cap B_3)$$

and

$$P(A) = P(A \cap B_1) + P(A \cap B_2) + P(A \cap B_3)$$

since $A \cap B_1$, $A \cap B_2$, and $A \cap B_3$ are mutually exclusive. Then, if we apply the second of the general multiplication rules to $P(A \cap B_1)$, $P(A \cap B_2)$, and $P(A \cap B_3)$, we get

$$P(A) = P(B_1) \cdot P(A|B_1) + P(B_2) \cdot P(A|B_2) + P(B_3) \cdot P(A|B_3)$$

and substitution of the given numerical values yields

$$P(A) = (0.60)(0.95) + (0.30)(0.80) + (0.10)(0.65)$$
$$= 0.875$$

for the probability that any one voltage regulator received by the given plant will perform according to specifications.

To visualize this result, we have only to construct a tree diagram like that of Figure 3.14, where the probability of the final outcome is given by the sum of the products of the probabilities corresponding to each branch of the tree.

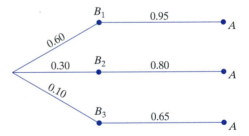

FIGURE 3.14 Tree diagram for example dealing with three suppliers of voltage regulators

In the preceding example there were only three alternatives at the intermediate stage, but if there are n mutually exclusive alternatives $B_1, B_2, \ldots, B_n$ at the intermediate stage, a similar argument will lead to the following result, sometimes called the **rule of elimination** or the **rule of total probability**:

Rule of elimination

Theorem 3.10 If $B_1, B_2, \ldots, B_n$ are mutually exclusive events of which one must occur, then

$$P(A) = \sum_{i=1}^{n} P(B_i) \cdot P(A|B_i)$$

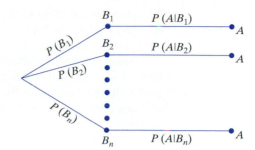

FIGURE 3.15 Tree diagram for rule of elimination

To visualize this result, we have only to construct a tree diagram like that of Figure 3.15, where the probability of the final outcome is again given by the sum of the products of the probabilities corresponding to each branch of the tree.

To consider a problem that is closely related to the one we have just discussed, suppose we want to know the probability that a particular voltage regulator, which is known to perform according to specifications, came from supplier B_3. Symbolically, we want to know the value of $P(B_3|A)$, and to find a formula for this probability we first write

$$P(B_3|A) = \frac{P(A \cap B_3)}{P(A)}$$

Then, substituting $P(B_3) \cdot P(A|B_3)$ for $P(A \cap B_3)$ and $\sum_{i=1}^{3} P(B_i) \cdot P(A|B_i)$ for $P(A)$ in accordance with Theorems 3.8 and 3.10, we get the formula

$$P(B_3|A) = \frac{P(B_3) \cdot P(A|B_3)}{\sum\limits_{i=1}^{3} P(B_i) \cdot P(A|B_i)}$$

which expresses $P(B_3|A)$ in terms of given probabilities. Substituting the values from page 83 (or from Figure 3.14), we finally obtain

$$P(B_3|A) = \frac{(0.10)(0.65)}{(0.60)(0.95) + (0.30)(0.80) + (0.10)(0.65)}$$
$$= 0.074$$

Note that the probability that a voltage regulator is supplied by B_3 decreases from 0.10 to 0.074 once it is known that it performs according to specifications.

The method used to solve the preceding example can easily be generalized to yield the following formula, called **Bayes' Theorem:**

Bayes' theorem

Theorem 3.11   If $B_1, B_2, \ldots, B_n$ are mutually exclusive events of which one must occur, then

$$P(B_r|A) = \frac{P(B_r) \cdot P(A|B_r)}{\sum\limits_{i=1}^{n} P(B_i) \cdot P(A|B_i)}$$

for $r = 1, 2, \ldots, n$.

Note that the expression in the numerator is the probability of reaching A via the rth branch of the tree and that the expression in the denominator is the sum of the probabilities of reaching A via the n branches of the tree.

Bayes' theorem provides a formula for finding the probability that the "effect" A was "caused" by the event B_r. For instance, in our example we found the probability that an acceptable voltage regulator was made by supplier B_3. The probabilities $P(B_i)$ are called the "prior," or "a priori," probabilities of the "causes" B_i, and in practice it is often difficult to assign them numerical values. For many years Bayes' theorem was looked upon with suspicion because it was used with the often erroneous assumption that the prior probabilities are all equal. A good deal of the controversy once surrounding Bayes' theorem has been cleared up with the realization that the probabilities $P(B_i)$ must be determined separately in each case from the nature of the problem, preferably on the basis of past experience.

EXAMPLE

Using Bayes' theorem

Four technicians regularly make repairs when breakdowns occur on an automated production line. Janet, who services 20% of the breakdowns, makes an incomplete repair 1 time in 20; Tom, who services 60% of the breakdowns, makes an incomplete repair 1 time in 10; Georgia, who services 15% of the breakdowns, makes an incomplete repair 1 time in 10; and Peter, who services 5% of the breakdowns, makes an incomplete repair 1 time in 20. For the next problem with the production line diagnosed as being due to an initial repair that was incomplete, what is the probability that this initial repair was made by Janet?

Solution   Substituting the various probabilities into the formula of Theorem 3.11, we get

$$P(B_1|A) = \frac{(0.20)(0.05)}{(0.20)(0.05) + (0.60)(0.10) + (0.15)(0.10) + (0.05)(0.05)}$$

$$= 0.114$$

and it is of interest to note that although Janet makes an incomplete repair only 1 out of 20 times, namely, 5% of the breakdowns, more than 11% of the incomplete repairs are her responsibility.   ✔

EXERCISES

3.55 With reference to Figure 3.7, find $P(I|D)$ and $P(I|\overline{D})$, assuming that originally each of the 500 machine parts has the same chance of being chosen for inspection.

3.56 With reference to the example on page 79, the probability is 0.75 that the system will have high fidelity. What is the probability that a system with high fidelity will have high selectivity?

3.57 With reference to Exercise 3.34 and Figure 3.10, assume that each of 150 persons has the same chance of being selected and find the probabilities that he or she

   (a) lives more than 3 miles from the center of the city given that he or she would gladly switch to public mass transportation;

(b) regularly drives his or her car to work given that he or she lives more than 3 miles from the center of the city;

(c) would not want to switch to public mass transportation given that he or she does not regularly drive his or her car to work.

3.58 With reference to Figure 3.12, find

(a) $P(A|B)$;

(b) $P(B|\overline{C})$;

(c) $P(A \cap B|C)$;

(d) $P(B \cup C|\overline{A})$;

(e) $P(A|B \cup C)$;

(f) $P(A|B \cap C)$;

(g) $P(A \cap B \cap C|B \cap C)$;

(h) $P(A \cap B \cap C|B \cup C)$.

3.59 With reference to the lawn-mower-rating example and the probabilities given in Figure 3.8, find

(a) $P(E_1|P_1)$ and compare its value with that of $P(E_1)$;

(b) $P(C_2|P_2)$ and compare its value with that of $P(C_2)$;

(c) $P(E_1|P_1 \cap C_1)$ and compare its value with that of $P(E_1)$.

3.60 With reference to Exercise 3.47, find the probabilities that the airport will get the design award given that

(a) it got the award for the efficient use of materials;

(b) it did not get the award for the efficient use of materials.

3.61 Prove that $P(A|B) = P(A)$ implies that $P(B|A) = P(B)$ provided that $P(A) \neq 0$ and $P(B) \neq 0$.

3.62 If the probabilities are 0.58, 0.25, and 0.19 that a person in a certain income bracket will invest in money market funds, common stocks, or both, find the probabilities that a person in that income bracket

(a) who invests in money market funds will also invest in common stocks;

(b) who invests in common stock will also invest in money market funds.

3.63 Given $P(A) = 0.50$, $P(B) = 0.30$, and $P(A \cap B) = 0.15$, verify that

(a) $P(A|B) = P(A)$;

(b) $P(A|\overline{B}) = P(A)$;

(c) $P(B|A) = P(B)$;

(d) $P(B|\overline{A}) = P(B)$.

3.64 Among the 24 invoices prepared by a billing department, 4 contain errors while the others do not. If we randomly check 2 of these invoices, what are the probabilities that

(a) both will contain errors;

(b) neither will contain an error?

3.65 Among 60 automobile repair parts loaded on a truck in San Francisco, 45 are destined for Seattle and 15 for Vancouver. If two of the parts are unloaded in Portland by mistake and the "selection" is random, what are the probabilities that

(a) both parts should have gone to Seattle;

(b) both parts should have gone to Vancouver;

(c) one should have gone to Seattle and one to Vancouver?

3.66 For two rolls of a balanced die, find the probabilities of getting

(a) two 4's;

(b) first a 4 and then a number less than 4.

3.67 If $P(A) = 0.80$, $P(C) = 0.35$, and $P(A \cap C) = 0.28$, are events A and C independent?

3.68 If the odds are 5 to 3 that an event M will not occur, 2 to 1 that event N will occur, and 4 to 1 that they will not both occur, are the two events M and N independent?

3.69 Find the probabilities of getting

(a) eight heads in a row with a balanced coin;

(b) three 3's and then a 4 or a 5 in four rolls of a balanced die;

(c) five multiple-choice questions answered correctly, if for each question the probability of answering it correctly is $\frac{1}{3}$.

3.70 For three or more events which are not independent, the probability that they will all occur is obtained by multiplying the probability that one of the events will occur times the probability that a second of the events will occur given that the first event has occurred times the probability that a third of the events will occur given that the first two events have occurred, and so on. For instance, for three events we can write

$$P(A \cap B \cap C) = P(A) \cdot P(B|A) \cdot P(C|A \cap B)$$

and we find that the probability of drawing without replacement three aces in a row from an ordinary deck of 52 playing cards is

$$\frac{4}{52} \cdot \frac{3}{51} \cdot \frac{2}{50} = \frac{1}{5,525}$$

(a) If six bullets, of which three are blanks, are randomly inserted into a gun, what is the probability that the first three bullets fired will all be blanks?

(b) In a certain city during the month of May, the probability that a rainy day will be followed by another rainy day is 0.80 and the probability that a sunny day will be followed by a rainy day is 0.60. Assuming that each day is classified as being either rainy or sunny and that the weather on any given day depends only on the weather the day before, find the probability that in the given city a rainy day in May is followed by two more rainy days, then a sunny day, and finally another rainy day.

(c) A department store which bills its charge-account customers once a month has found that if a customer pays promptly one month, the probability is 0.90 that he will also pay promptly the next month; however, if a customer does not pay promptly one month, the probability that he will pay promptly the next month is only 0.50. What is the probability that a customer who has paid promptly one month will not pay promptly the next three months?

(d) If 5 of a company's 12 delivery trucks do not meet emission standards and 4 of the 12 trucks are randomly picked for inspection, what is the probability that none of them meets emission standards?

3.71 At an electronics plant, it is known from past experience that the probability is 0.86 that a new worker who has attended the company's training program will meet the production quota and that the corresponding probability is 0.35 for a new worker who has not attended the company's training program. If 80% of all new workers attend the training program, what is the probability that a new worker will meet the production quota?

3.72 With reference to the preceding exercise, find the probability that a new worker who meets the production quota will have attended the company's training program.

3.73 A consulting firm rents cars from three agencies, 20% from agency D, 20% from agency E, and 60% from agency F. If 10% of the cars from D, 12% of the cars from E, and 4% of the cars from F have bad tires, what is the probability that the firm will get a car with bad tires?

3.74 With reference to Exercise 3.73, what is the probability that a car with bad tires rented by the firm came from agency F?

3.75 Use the information on the tree diagram of Figure 3.16 to determine the value of

  (a) $P(A)$;

  (b) $P(B|A)$;

  (c) $P(B|\overline{A})$.

3.76 With reference to the example on page 83, find the probabilities that a voltage regulator that performs according to specifications came

  (a) from supplier B_1;

  (b) from supplier B_2.

3.77 With reference to the example on page 86, for a problem diagnosed as being due to an incomplete initial repair, find the probability that the initial repair was made by

  (a) Tom;

  (b) Georgia;

  (c) Peter.

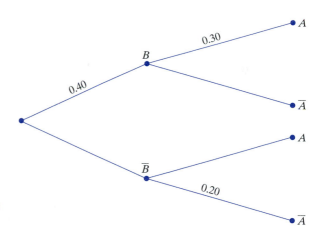

FIGURE 3.16 Diagram for Exercise 3.75

3.78 Two firms V and W consider bidding on a road-building job, which may or may not be awarded depending on the amounts of the bids. Firm V submits a bid and the probability is $\frac{3}{4}$ that it will get the job provided firm W does not bid. The probability is $\frac{3}{4}$ that W will bid, and if it does, the probability that V will get the job is only $\frac{1}{3}$.

   (a) What is the probability that V will get the job?

   (b) If V gets the job, what is the probability that W did not bid?

3.79 Engineers in charge of maintaining our nuclear fleet must continually check for corrosion inside the pipes that are part of the cooling systems. The inside condition of the pipes cannot be observed directly but a nondestructive test can give an indication of possible corrosion. This test is not infallible. The test has probability .7 of detecting corrosion when it is present but it also has probability .2 of falsely indicating internal corrosion. Suppose the probability that any section of pipe has internal corrosion is .1.

   (a) Determine the probability that a section of pipe has internal corrosion given that the test indicates its presence.

   (b) Determine the probability that a section of pipe has corrosion given that the test is negative.

3.80 An East Coast manufacturer of printed circuit boards exposes all finished boards to an online automated verification test. During one period, 900 boards were completed and 890 passed the test. The test is not infallible. Of 30 boards intentionally made to have noticeable defects, 25 were detected by the test. Use the relative frequencies to approximate the conditional probabilities needed below.

   (a) Give an approximate value for $P[\text{Pass test} \mid \text{board has defects}]$.

   (b) Explain why your answer in (a) may be too small.

   (c) Give an approximate value for the probability that a manufactured board will have defects. In order to answer the question, you need information about the conditional probability that a good board will fail the test. This is important to know but was not available at the time an answer was required. To proceed, you can assume that this probability is zero.

   (d) Approximate the probability that a board has defects given that it passed the automated test.

3.8   Mathematical Expectation and Decision Making

If an insurance agent tells us that in the United States a 40-year-old woman can expect to live 38 more years, this does not mean that anyone really expects a 40-year-old woman to live until her seventy-eighth birthday and then die the next day. Similarly, if we read that a radial tire can be expected to last 40,000 miles, that in the coal mining industry we can expect 41.5 nonfatal injuries per million work-hours, or that the U.S. Patent Office can expect to issue 27,000 certificates of trademarks each year, it must be understood that the word "expect" is not used in its colloquial sense. So far as the first statement is concerned, some 40-year-old women will live another 15 years, some will live another 30 years, some will live another 50 years, . . . , and the life expectancy of "38 more years" will have to be interpreted as an average, namely, as a **mathematical expectation.**

Originally, the concept of a mathematical expectation arose in connection with games of chance, and in its simplest form it is the product of the amount a player stands to win and the probability that he or she will win.

EXAMPLE

Calculating mathematical expectation

What is our mathematical expectation if we stand to win $8 if and only if a balanced coin comes up heads?

Solution The probability of heads is $\frac{1}{2}$ and our mathematical expectation is $8 \cdot \frac{1}{2} = \$4$. ✔

EXAMPLE

The mathematical expectation for a raffle

What is our mathematical expectation if we are given one of 1,000 raffle tickets for a grand prize of $500?

Solution The probability of winning the grand prize is $\frac{1}{1,000}$ and the mathematical expectation is $500 \cdot \frac{1}{1,000} = \$0.50$. ✔

In both of these examples there was a single prize, but in each case there were two possible payoffs—$8 or $0 in the first example and $500 or $0 in the other. Indeed, in the second example we can argue that 999 of the tickets will pay $0 and one of the tickets will pay $500; altogether, the 1,000 tickets will thus pay $500, or on the average $0.50 per ticket, and this is the mathematical expectation.

To generalize the concept of a mathematical expectation, let us consider the following example:

EXAMPLE

Mathematical expectation of net profit

A distributor makes a profit of $20 on an item if it is shipped from the factory in perfect condition and arrives on time, but it is reduced by $2 if it does not arrive on time, and by $12 regardless of whether it arrives on time if it is not shipped from the factory in perfect condition. If 70% of such items are shipped in perfect condition and arrive on time, 10% are shipped in perfect condition but do not arrive on time, and 20% are not shipped in perfect condition, what is the distributor's expected profit per item?

Solution We can argue that the distributor will make the $20 profit 70% of the time, the $18 profit 10% of the time, and the $8 profit 20% of the time, so that the average profit per item (the expected profit) is

$$20(0.70) + 18(0.10) + 8(0.20) = \$17.40$$

The result is the sum of the products obtained by multiplying each amount by the corresponding proportion or probability. ✔

Generalizing from this example, let us now make the following definition:

Mathematical expectation

> If the probabilities of obtaining the amounts $a_1, a_2, \ldots$, or a_k are $p_1, p_2, \ldots$, and p_k, then the mathematical expectation is
> $$E = a_1 p_1 + a_2 p_2 + \cdots + a_k p_k$$

As far as the a's are concerned, it is important to keep in mind that they are positive when they represent profits, winnings, or gains and that they are negative when they represent losses, deficits, or penalties.

EXAMPLE

Evaluating expected net profit

An engineering firm is faced with the task of preparing a proposal for a research contract. The cost of preparing the proposal is $5,000 and the probabilities for potential gross profits of $50,000, $30,000, $10,000, or $0 are 0.20, 0.50, 0.20, and 0.10, provided that the proposal is accepted. If the probability is 0.30 that the firm's proposal will be accepted, what is its expected net profit?

Solution   The probability that the firm will make a net profit of $45,000 ($50,000 minus the cost of the proposal) is $(.30)(0.20) = 0.06$. Similarly, the probabilities that the firm will make net profits of $25,000 or $5,000 are $(0.30)(0.50) = 0.15$ and $(0.30)(0.20) = 0.06$, whereas the probability of a $5,000 loss is $(0.30)(0.10) + 0.70 = 0.73$, allowing for the possibility that the proposal will not be accepted. Thus, the expected net profit is

$$45,000(0.06) + 25,000(0.15) + 5,000(0.06) - 5,000(0.73) = \$3,100$$

Whether or not it is wise to risk $5,000 to make an expected profit of $3,100 is not a question of statistics. If a company has little capital and can make only few such proposals, the 0.73 chance of losing $5,000 may well make the venture unattractive. On the other hand, if a company is well capitalized and prepares many such proposals, the risk may be worth taking, for it promises an expected return of 62% on the original investment.   ✔

The following is a typical inventory problem in which expected values are used to determine optimum conditions:

EXAMPLE

Using expected profit to determine inventory

It is known from past experience that the daily demand for a perishable product is as shown in the following table:

Number of orders	3	4	5	6	7	8	9
Probability	0.05	0.12	0.20	0.24	0.17	0.14	0.08

If each item costs $35 (including the cost of carrying it in stock), it sells for $50 provided that it is in stock, and it represents a total loss if it remains in stock at the end of a day, how many items should be stocked each day so as to maximize the expected profit?

Solution   If 3 items are stocked, the profit is $150 - $105 = $45, since there is a probability of 1 that there will be a demand for 3 or more. If 4 items are stocked, there is a probability of 0.05 that 3 items will be sold, a probability of 0.95 that there will be a demand for 4 or more, and the expected profit is

$$150(0.05) + 200(0.95) - 140 = \$57.50$$

Similarly, if 5 items are stocked, there is a probability of 0.05 that 3 items will be sold, a probability of 0.12 that 4 items will be sold, a probability of 0.83 that there will be a demand for 5 or more, and the expected profit is

$$150(0.05) + 200(0.12) + 250(0.83) - 175 = \$64.00$$

Continuing in this way (see Exercise 3.87), it can be shown that if 6 items are stocked the expected profit is $60.50, if 7 items are stocked the expected profit is $45.00, and that the expected profit is a maximum when the number of items stocked is 5.

In recent years, mathematical expectations have been playing an increasingly important role in scientific decision making, as it is generally considered rational to select whichever alternative has the most promising mathematical expectation: the one that maximizes the expected profit, minimizes the expected cost, maximizes tax advantages, minimizes the expected loss, and so forth.

In applying the methods of decision making illustrated in this section, there are essentially two practical limitations: First, we must be able to assign "cash values" to the various outcomes, and second, we must have adequate information concerning all relevant probabilities. The problem of assigning cash values to the various outcomes can be much more difficult than it was in our examples. For instance, if a government agency were faced with the decision of whether to require crash barriers for interstate highway construction, it would be extremely difficult to assign a cash value to the savings in life and reductions in injuries that might result.

The specification of probabilities concerning the various outcomes can be equally difficult. In our examples, the probabilities were presumably based on past experience, and, hence, are really only estimates (or approximations). This may be questioned with respect to the example dealing with the preparation of the research proposal, where it would be extremely difficult even to estimate the probability that a given proposal will be accepted. This would have to depend not only on the quality of the proposal itself, but on such unknown factors as the number and quality of competing proposals as well as the policy of the sponsoring agency. The estimate of 0.30 in our example, on page 92, was purely subjective, being based on some executive's "feeling" about the situation measured against the background of his personal experience. While such estimates of probabilities are not without value, they do leave open the possibility that different individuals (acting in the same situation and having the same information) would arrive at different "optimum" decisions.

EXERCISES

3.81 If a service club sells 4,000 raffle tickets for a cash prize of $800, what is the mathematical expectation of a person who is given one of the tickets?

3.82 A charitable organization raises funds by selling 2,000 raffle tickets for a first prize worth $500 and a second prize worth $100. What is the mathematical expectation of a person who is given one of the tickets?

3.83 What is our mathematical expectation if we win $10 if a balanced coin comes up heads and lose $10 if it comes up tails?

3.84 A game between two players is fair if each player has the same mathematical expectation. If someone gives us $5 each time we roll a 1 or a 2 with a balanced die, how much must we pay that person each time we roll a 3, 4, 5, or 6 to make the game fair?

3.85 When the American League and National League champions are evenly matched, the probabilities that a World Series will end in 4, 5, 6, or 7 games are, respectively, $\frac{1}{8}, \frac{1}{4}, \frac{5}{16}$, and $\frac{5}{16}$. What is the expected length of a World Series when the two teams are evenly matched?

3.86 The two finalists in a golf tournament play 18 holes, with the winner getting $50,000 and the runner-up getting $30,000. What are the two players' mathematical expectations if

   (a) they are evenly matched;

   (b) one of the two players should be favored by odds of 3 to 1?

3.87 With reference to the example on page 92, show that for six and seven items stocked, the expected profits are $60.50 and $45.00.

3.88 An importer is offered a shipment of machine tools for $140,000, and the probabilities that he will be able to sell them for $180,000, $170,000, or $150,000 are 0.32, 0.55, and 0.13. What is the importer's expected gross profit?

3.89 The manufacturer of a new battery additive has to decide whether to sell her product for $0.80 a can or for $1.20 with a "double-your-money-back-if-not-satisfied" guarantee. How does she feel about the chances that a person will ask for double his or her money back if

   (a) she decides to sell the product for $0.80;

   (b) she decides to sell the product for $1.20 with the guarantee;

   (c) she cannot make up her mind?

3.90 A merchant can buy an item for $2.10 and sell it for $4.50. The probabilities for a demand of 0, 1, 2, 3, 4, or "5 or more" items are, respectively, 0.05, 0.15, 0.30, 0.25, 0.15, and 0.10. Calculate the expected profit resulting from stocking 0, 1, 2, 3, 4, or 5 items and determine how many the merchant should stock so as to maximize expected profit.

3.91 Mr. Brown and Mr. Jones are betting on repeated flips of a balanced coin. At the beginning Mr. Brown has m dollars, Mr. Jones has n dollars; at each flip the loser pays the winner one dollar, and they continue playing until one of them has lost all the money with which he began. To find p, the probability that Mr. Brown will win Mr. Jones' n dollars before he loses his m dollars, set up an equation in m, n and p which makes use of the fact that in a fair game each player's mathematical expectation is the same. What is the probability that Mr. Brown will win if he begins with $12 and Mr. Jones begins with $4?

3.92 The management of a mining company must decide whether to continue an operation at a certain location. If they continue and are successful, this will be worth $1,000,000; if they continue and are not successful, this will entail a loss of $600,000; if they do not continue but would have been successful, this will entail a loss of $400,000 (for competitive reasons); and if they do not continue and would not have been successful anyhow, this will be worth $100,000 to the company (because funds allocated to the operation remain unspent). What decision would maximize the company's expected profit if the probabilities for and against success are 0.40 and 0.60?

3.93 With reference to Exercise 3.92, what decision would maximize the company's expected profit if the probabilities for and against success are 0.20 and 0.80?

3.94 With reference to Exercise 3.92, suppose that it is possible to continue the operation for two months at a cost of $300,000, after which it will be possible to know for certain whether the operation will be a success. At that point, the only relevant costs are the $1,000,000 and $100,000 gains. Would it be worthwhile to spend these additional funds?

3.95 A power company is faced with the choice of whether to construct a light-water reactor (LWR) or a fossil-fuel power plant (FF). The LWR plant will cost $300 per kilowatt to construct, and the FF plant will cost $150 per kilowatt. Due to uncertainties concerning fuel availability and the impact of future air- and water-quality regulations, the useful operating life of each plant is unknown, but the following probabilities have been estimated:

Useful life (years)		10	20	30	40
Probabilities {	*LWR plant*	0.05	0.25	0.50	0.20
	FF plant	0.10	0.50	0.30	0.10

    (a) Obtain the expected useful operation life for each plant.

    (b) Compare the two plants by calculating the ratio of construction cost per kilowatt to expected useful operating life.

REVIEW EXERCISES

3.96 A salesperson of industrial chemicals has four customers in Sacramento, whom he may or may not be able to visit on a 2-day trip to this city. He will not visit any of these customers more than once.

    (a) Using two coordinates so that (2, 1), for example, represents the event that he will visit two of his customers on the first day and one on the second day, draw a diagram similar to that of Figure 3.1 showing the points of the corresponding sample space.

    (b) List the points of the sample space that constitute the events A, B, and C that he will visit all four of his customers, that he will visit more of his customers on the first day than on the second day, and that he will visit at least three of his customers on the second day.

    (c) Which of the three pairs of events, A and B, B and C, and A and C, are mutually exclusive?

3.97 With reference to the preceding exercise, express each of the following events symbolically by listing its elements, and also express it in words:

    (a) $\overline{A}$;

    (b) $A \cup B$;

    (c) $A \cap C$;

    (d) $\overline{A} \cap B$.

3.98 Use Venn diagrams to verify that

(a) $\overline{(A \cup B)} = \overline{A} \cap \overline{B}$;

(b) $\overline{(A \cap \overline{B})} = \overline{A} \cup B$.

3.99 If the tone quality of four audio systems is to be rated superior, average, or inferior and we are interested only in how many of the systems get each of these ratings, draw a tree diagram which shows the 15 different possibilities.

3.100 Alarm units are to be connected at four fixed positions along a pipeline. In how many ways can the four available alarm units be connected to the four positions along the line?

3.101 In how many ways can two out of seven chemical engineers be assigned to a new project?

3.102 An experiment has three possible mutually exclusive outcomes, A, B, and C. Check whether the following assignments of probability are possible.

(a) $P(A) = 0.3$, $P(B) = 0.4$, and $P(C) = 0.34$

(b) $P(A) = 0.5$, $P(B) = 0.1$, and $P(C) = 0.4$

(c) $P(A) = 0.4$, $P(B) = 0.64$, and $P(C) = -0.04$

3.103 Given $P(A) = 0.3$, $P(B) = 0.5$, and $P(A \cap B) = 0.24$, find

(a) $P(A \cup B)$;

(b) $P(\overline{A} \cap B)$;

(c) $P(A \cap \overline{B})$;

(d) $P(\overline{A} \cup \overline{B})$.

(e) Are A and B independent?

3.104 In a sample of 446 cars stopped at a roadblock, only 67 of the drivers had their seatbelts fastened. Estimate the probability that a driver stopped on that road will have his or her seatbelt fastened.

3.105 The personnel manager of a manufacturing plant claims that among the 400 employees 312 got a raise in 2000, 248 got increased pension benefits, 173 got both, and 43 got neither. Explain why this claim should be questioned.

3.106 If the probabilities that a satellite launching rocket will explode during lift-off or have its guidance system fail in flight are 0.0002 and 0.0005, find the probabilities that such a rocket will

(a) not explode during lift-off;

(b) explode during lift-off or have its guidance system fail in flight;

(c) neither explode during lift-off nor have its guidance system fail in flight.

3.107 Given $P(A) = 0.4$, $P(B) = 0.5$, and $P(A \cap B) = 0.2$ verify that

(a) $P(A|B) = P(A)$;

(b) $P(A|\overline{B}) = P(A)$;

(c) $P(B|A) = P(B)$;

(d) $P(B|\overline{A}) = P(B)$;

3.108 If events A and B are independent and $P(A) = 0.25$ and $P(B) = 0.40$, find

(a) $P(A \cap B)$;

(b) $P(A|B)$;

(c) $P(A \cup B)$;

(d) $P(\overline{A} \cap \overline{B})$.

3.109 The following frequency table shows the classification of 58 landfills in a state according to their concentration of the three hazardous chemicals arsenic, barium, and mercury.

		Barium			
		High		Low	
		Mercury		Mercury	
		High	Low	High	Low
Arsenic	High	1	3	5	9
	Low	4	8	10	18

If a landfill is selected at random, find the probability that it has a

(a) high concentration of mercury;

(b) high concentration of barium and low concentrations of arsenic and mercury;

(c) high concentrations of any two of the chemicals and low concentration of the third;

(d) high concentration of any one of the chemicals and low concentrations of the other two.

3.110 Refer to Exercise 3.109. Given that a landfill, selected at random, is found to have a high concentration of barium, what is the probability that its concentration is

(a) high in mercury?

(b) low in both arsenic and mercury?

(c) high in either arsenic or mercury?

3.111 An explosion in an LNG storage tank in the process of being repaired could have occurred as the result of static electricity, malfunctioning electrical equipment, an open flame in contact with the liner, or purposeful action (industrial sabotage). Interviews with engineers who were analyzing the risks involved led to estimates that such an explosion would occur with probability 0.25 as a result of static electricity, 0.20 as a result of malfunctioning electric equipment, 0.40 as a result of an open flame, and 0.75 as a result of purposeful action. These interviews also yielded subjective estimates of the prior probabilities of these four causes of 0.30, 0.40, 0.15, and 0.15, respectively. What was the most likely cause of the explosion?

3.112 It costs $60 to test a certain component of a machine. If a defective component is installed, it costs $1,200 to repair the resulting damage to the machine. Is it more profitable to install the component without testing if it is known that

(a) 3% of all components produced are defective;

(b) 5% of all components produced are defective;

(c) 8% of all components produced are defective?

3.113 A contractor has to choose between two jobs. The first job promises a profit of $240,000 with a probability of 0.75 or a loss of $60,000 (due to strikes and other delays) with a probability of 0.25; the second job promises a profit of $360,000 with a probability of 0.50 or a loss of $90,000 with a probability of 0.50.

(a) Which job should the contractor choose if she wants to maximize her expected profit?

(b) Which job would the contractor probably choose if her business is in bad shape and she will go broke unless she can make a profit of at least $300,000 on her next job?

3.114 An engineer wants to move across the country from City A to City B to work. On different days, she mails a cover letter and resume to three different companies in City B. Suppose that a letter sent from City A to City B has a probability of .7 of reaching City B within 3 days.

(a) What is the probability that exactly 2 of the 3 letters will reach City B within 3 days?

(b) If the three letters are mailed together at the same time and location how does your conclusion in part(a) change? Explain.

3.115 Amy commutes to work by two different routes A and B. If she comes home by route A, then she will be home no later than 6 P.M. with probability .8 but if she comes home by route B, then she will be home no later than 6 P.M. with probability .7. In the past, the proportion of times that Amy chose route A is .4.

(a) What proportion of times is Amy home no later than 6 P.M.?

(b) If Amy is home after 6 P.M. today, what is the probability that she took route B?

KEY TERMS

(with page references)

Probability Distributions

In most statistical problems we are concerned with one number or a few numbers that are associated with the outcomes of experiments. In the inspection of a manufactured product we may be interested only in the number of defectives; in the analysis of a road test we may be interested only in the average speed and the average fuel consumption; and in the study of the performance of a rotary switch we may be interested only in its lubrication, the current, and the humidity. All these numbers are associated with situations involving an element of chance—in other words, they are values of random variables.

In the study of random variables we are usually interested in their probability distributions, namely, in the probabilities with which they take on the various values in their range. The introduction to random variables and probability distributions in Section 4.1 is followed by a discussion of various special probability distributions in Sections 4.2, 4.3, 4.7, 4.8, and 4.9, and descriptions of the most important features of probability distributions in Sections 4.4 and 4.5. ∎

CHAPTER OUTLINE

4.1   Random Variables

To be more explicit about the concept of a random variable, let us refer again to the lawn-mower-rating example on page 56, and the corresponding probabilities shown in Figure 3.8. Now let us suppose that we refer to E_1 (easy to operate), P_2 (inexpensive),

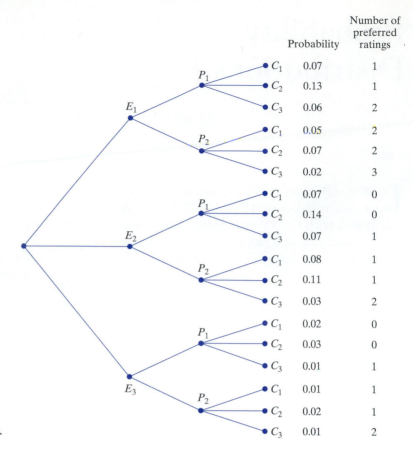

	Probability	Number of preferred ratings
C_1	0.07	1
C_2	0.13	1
C_3	0.06	2
C_1	0.05	2
C_2	0.07	2
C_3	0.02	3
C_1	0.07	0
C_2	0.14	0
C_3	0.07	1
C_1	0.08	1
C_2	0.11	1
C_3	0.03	2
C_1	0.02	0
C_2	0.03	0
C_3	0.01	1
C_1	0.01	1
C_2	0.02	1
C_3	0.01	2

FIGURE 4.1 Ratings of lawn mowers and numbers of preferred ratings.

and C_3 (low average cost of repairs) as preferred ratings, and that we are interested only in the number of preferred ratings a lawn mower will get. To find the probabilities that a lawn mower will get 0, 1, 2, or 3 preferred ratings, let us refer to Figure 4.1, which is like Figure 3.8 except that we indicate for each outcome the number of preferred ratings. Adding the respective probabilities, we find that for zero preferred ratings the probability is $0.07 + 0.14 + 0.02 + 0.03 = 0.26$, for one preferred rating the probability is $0.07 + 0.13 + 0.07 + 0.08 + 0.11 + 0.01 + 0.01 + 0.02 = 0.50$, for two preferred ratings the probability is $0.06 + 0.05 + 0.07 + 0.03 + 0.01 = 0.22$, and for three preferred ratings the probability is 0.02. These results may be summarized as in the following table, where x denotes the number of preferred ratings:

x	0	1	2	3
Probability	0.26	0.50	0.22	0.02

The numbers 0, 1, 2, and 3 in this table are values of a **random variable**—the number of preferred ratings. Corresponding to each elementary outcome in the sample space there is exactly one value x for this random variable. That is, the random variable may be thought of as a function defined over the elements of the sample space. This is how we define random variables in general; they are functions defined over the elements of a sample space.

Random variables are denoted by capital letters X, Y and so on to distinguish them from their possible values given in lower case.

To find the probability that a random variable will take on any one value within its range, we proceed as in the above example. Indeed, the table which we obtained displays another function, called the **probability distribution** of the random variable. To denote the values of a probability distribution we shall use such symbols as $f(x), g(x), \varphi(y), h(z)$, and so on. Strictly speaking, it is the function $f(x) = P(X = x)$ which assigns probability to each possible outcome x that is called the probability distribution. However, we will follow the common practice of also calling $f(x)$ the probability distribution, with the understanding that we are referring to the function and that the range of x values is part of the definition.

Random variables are usually classified according to the number of values which they can assume. In this chapter we shall limit our discussion to **discrete random variables,** which can take on only a finite number, or a countable infinity of values; **continuous random variables** are taken up in Chapter 5.

Whenever possible, we try to express probability distributions by means of equations; otherwise we must give a table that actually exhibits the correspondence between the values of the random variable and the associated probabilities. For instance,

$$f(x) = \frac{1}{6} \quad \text{for } x = 1, 2, 3, 4, 5, 6$$

gives the probability distribution for the number of points we roll with a balanced die.

Of course, not every function defined for the values of a random variable can serve as a probability distribution. Since the values of probability distributions are probabilities and one value of a random variable must always occur, it follows that if $f(x)$ is a probability distribution, then

$$f(x) \geq 0 \quad \text{for all } x$$

and

$$\sum_{\text{all } x} f(x) = 1$$

EXAMPLE

Checking for nonnegativity and total probability equals one
Check whether the following can serve as probability distributions:

(a) $f(x) = \dfrac{x - 2}{2} \quad$ for $x = 1, 2, 3, 4$

(b) $h(x) = \dfrac{x^2}{25} \quad$ for $x = 0, 1, 2, 3, 4$

Solution   (a) This function cannot serve as a probability distribution because $f(1)$ is negative.

FIGURE 4.2 Graphs of the probability distribution of the number of preferred ratings

(b) The function cannot serve as a probability distribution because the sum of the five probabilities is $\frac{6}{5}$ and not 1. ✔

It is often helpful to visualize probability distributions by means of graphs like those of Figure 4.2. The one on the left is called a **probability histogram;** the heights of the rectangles are proportional to the corresponding probabilities and the bases touch so that there are no gaps between the rectangles representing the successive values of the random variable. The one on the right is called a **bar chart;** the heights of the rectangles are also proportional to the corresponding probabilities, but they are narrow and their width is of no significance.

As we see later in this chapter, there are many problems in which we are interested not only in the probability $f(x)$ that the value of a random variable is x, but also in the probability $F(x)$ that the value of a random variable is less than or equal to x. We refer to the function $F(x)$ as the **cumulative distribution function** or just the **distribution function** of the random variable. Referring again to the lawn-mower-rating example and basing our calculations on the table on page 100, we get

x	0	1	2	3
$F(x)$	0.26	0.76	0.98	1.00

for the distribution function of the number of preferred ratings.

4.2 The Binomial Distribution

Many statistical problems deal with the situations referred to as **repeated trials.** For example, we may want to know the probability that one of five rivets will rupture in a tensile test, the probability that 9 of 10 VCRs will run at least 1,000 hours, the probability that 45 of 300 drivers stopped at a road block will be wearing seatbelts, or the probability that 66 of 200 television viewers (interviewed by a rating service) will recall what products were advertised on a given program. To borrow from the language of games of chance, we might say that in each of these examples we are interested in the probability of getting x **successes** in n **trials,** or in other words, x successes and $n - x$ failures in n attempts.

In the problems we study in this section, we shall always make the following assumptions:

1. **There are only two possible outcomes for each trial** (arbitrarily called "success" and "failure," without inferring that a success is necessarily desirable).
2. **The probability of a success is the same for each trial.**
3. **There are n trials, where n is a constant.**
4. **The n trials are independent.**

Trials satisfying these assumptions are referred to as **Bernoulli trials;** if the assumptions cannot be met, the theory we shall develop here does not apply.

Let X be the random variable that equals the number of successes in n trials. To obtain probabilities concerning X, we proceed as follows: If p and $1 - p$ are the probabilities of success and failure on any one trial, then the probability of getting x successes and $n - x$ failures *in some specific order* is $p^x(1 - p)^{n-x}$; clearly, in this product of p's and $(1 - p)$'s there is one factor p for each success, one factor $1 - p$ for each failure. The x factors p and $n - x$ factors $1 - p$ are all multiplied together by virtue of the generalized multiplication rule for more than two independent events. Since this probability applies to any point of the sample space that represents x successes and $n - x$ failures (in any specific order), we have only to count how many points of this kind there are, and then multiply $p^x(1 - p)^{n-x}$ by this number. Clearly, the number of ways in which we can select the x trials on which there is to be a success is $\binom{n}{x}$, the number of combinations of x objects selected from a set of n objects, and we thus arrive at the following result:

Binomial distribution

$$b(x; n, p) = \binom{n}{x} p^x (1 - p)^{n-x} \quad for \; x = 0, 1, 2, \ldots, n$$

This probability distribution is called the **binomial distribution** because for $x = 0, 1, 2, \ldots,$ and n, the values of the probabilities are the successive terms of binomial expansion of $[p + (1 - p)]^n$; for the same reason, the combinatorial quantities $\binom{n}{x}$ are referred to as **binomial coefficients.** Actually, the preceding equation defines a family of probability distributions with each member characterized by a given value of the **parameter** p and the number of trials n.

EXAMPLE

Evaluating binomial probabilities

It has been claimed that in 60% of all solar heat installations the utility bill is reduced by at least one-third. Accordingly, what are the probabilities that the utility bill will be reduced by at least one-third in

(a) four of five installations;

(b) at least four of five installations?

Solution   (a) Substituting $x = 4, n = 5,$ and $p = 0.60$ into the formula for the binomial distribution, we get

$$b(4; 5, 0.60) = \binom{5}{4}(0.60)^4(1 - 0.60)^{5-4}$$

$$= 0.259$$

(b) Substituting $x = 5, n = 5,$ and $p = 0.60$ into the formula for the binomial distribution, we get

$$b(5; 5, 0.60) = \binom{5}{5}(0.60)^5(1 - 0.60)^{5-5}$$

$$= 0.078$$

and the answer is $b(4; 5, 0.60) + b(5; 5, 0.60) = 0.259 + 0.078 = 0.337.$ ✔

If n is large, the calculation of binomial probabilities can become quite tedious. Many statistical software packages have binomial distribution commands (see Exercises 4.28 and 4.29). Otherwise it is convenient to refer to special tables. Values of the binomial distribution and the corresponding cumulative distribution function have been tabulated for $n = 2$ to $n = 49$ by the National Bureau of Standards and for $n = 50$ to $n = 100$ by H. G. Romig (see the bibliography at the end of the book). Table 1 at the end of the book gives the values of

$$B(x; n, p) = \sum_{k=0}^{x} b(k; n, p) \quad \text{for } x = 0, 1, 2, \ldots, n$$

for $n = 2$ to $n = 20$ and $p = 0.05, 0.10, 0.15, \ldots, 0.90, 0.95.$ We tabulated the **cumulative probabilities** rather than the values of $b(x; n, p)$, because the values of $B(x; n, p)$ are the ones needed more often in statistical applications. Note, however, that the values of $b(x; n, p)$ can be obtained by subtracting adjacent entries in Table 1. Because the two cumulative probabilities $B(x; n, p)$ and $B(x - 1; n, p)$ differ by the single term $b(x; n, p)$

$$b(x; n, p) = B(x; n, p) - B(x - 1; n, p)$$

The examples that follow illustrate the direct use of Table 1 and the use of this relationship.

EXAMPLE   **Evaluating cumulative binomial probabilities**

If the probability is 0.05 that a certain wide-flange column will fail under a given axial load, what are the probabilities that among 16 such columns

(a) at most two will fail;

(b) at least four will fail?

Solution   (a) Table 1 shows that $B(2; 16, 0.05) = 0.9571.$

(b) Since

$$\sum_{x=4}^{16} b(x; 16, 0.05) = 1 - B(3; 16, 0.05)$$

Table 1 yields $1 - 0.9930 = 0.0070$.   ✔

EXAMPLE

Finding a binomial probability using cumulative binomial probabilities
If the probability is 0.20 that any one person will dislike the taste of a new tooth-paste, what is the probability that 5 of 18 randomly selected persons will dislike it?

Solution   Using the relationship to cumulative probabilities and then looking up these probabilities in Table 1, we get

$$\begin{aligned} b(5; 18, 0.20 &= B(5; 18, 0.20) - B(4; 18, 0.20) \\ &= 0.8671 - 0.7164 \\ &= 0.1507 \end{aligned}$$ ✔

The following example illustrates the use of the binomial distribution in a problem of decision making.

EXAMPLE

A binomial probability to guide decision making
A manufacturer of fax machines claims that only 10% of his machines require repairs within the warranty period of 12 months. If 5 of 20 of his machines required repairs within the first year, does this tend to support or refute the claim?

Solution   Let us first find the probability that five or more of 20 of the fax machines will require repairs within a year when the probability that any one will require repairs within a year is 0.10. Using Table 1, we get

$$\begin{aligned} \sum_{x=5}^{20} b(x; 20, 0.10) &= 1 - B(4; 20, 0.10) \\ &= 1 - 0.9568 \\ &= 0.0432 \end{aligned}$$

Since this probability is very small, it would seem reasonable to reject the fax machine manufacturer's claim.   ✔

Important information about the shape of binomial distributions is shown in Figures 4.3 and 4.4. First, if $p = 0.50$ the equation for the binomial distribution is

$$b(x; n, 0.50) = \binom{n}{x}(0.5)^n$$

and since $\binom{n}{n-x} = \binom{n}{x}$, it follows that $b(x; n, 0.50) = b(n - x; n, 0.50)$. This means that the probability histograms of such binomial distributions are **symmetrical,** as is illustrated in Figure 4.3. Note, however, that if p is less than 0.50, it is more likely that X will be small rather than large compared to $n/2$ and that the opposite is true if p is greater than 0.50. This is illustrated in Figure 4.4, showing the histograms

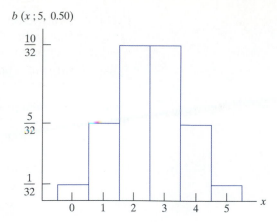

$b(x; 5, 0.50)$

FIGURE 4.3 Symmetrical binomial distribution with $n = 5$ and $p = 0.50$

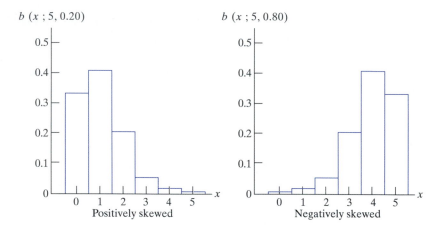

$b(x; 5, 0.20)$

$b(x; 5, 0.80)$

FIGURE 4.4 Skewed binomial distributions with $n = 5$ and $p = 0.20$ and $p = 0.80$

Positively skewed

Negatively skewed

of binomial distributions with $n = 5$ and $p = 0.20$ and $p = 0.80$. These two are mirror images of each other as can be verified more generally in Exercise 4.7.

Finally, a probability distribution that has a probability histogram like either of those in Figure 4.4 is said to be **skewed** (or long-tailed). It is said to be **positively skewed** if the tail is on the right, and it is said to be **negatively skewed** if the tail is on the left.

4.3 The Hypergeometric Distribution

Suppose that we are interested in the number of defectives in a sample of n units drawn from a lot containing N units, of which a are defective. Let the sample be drawn in such a way that at each successive drawing whatever units are left in the lot have the same chance of being selected. The probability that the first drawing will yield a defective unit is $\dfrac{a}{N}$, but for the second drawing it is $\dfrac{a-1}{N-1}$ or $\dfrac{a}{N-1}$, depending on whether or not the first unit drawn was defective. Thus, the trials are not independent, the fourth assumption underlying the binomial distribution is not met, and the binomial distribution does not apply. Note that the binomial distribution would apply if we do **sampling with replacement,** namely, if each unit selected for the sample is replaced before the next one is drawn.

To solve the problem of **sampling without replacement** (that is, as we originally formulated the problem), let us proceed as follows: The x successes (defectives) can be chosen in $\binom{a}{x}$ ways, the $n - x$ failures (nondefectives) can be chosen in $\binom{N - a}{n - x}$ ways, and hence, x successes and $n - x$ failures can be chosen in $\binom{a}{x}\binom{N - a}{n - x}$ ways. Also, n objects can be chosen from a set of N objects in $\binom{N}{n}$ ways, and if we consider all these possibilities as equally likely, it follows that for sampling without replacement the probability of getting "x successes in n trials" is

Hypergeometric
distribution

$$h(x; n, a, N) = \frac{\binom{a}{x}\binom{N - a}{n - x}}{\binom{N}{n}} \qquad for\ x = 0, 1, \ldots, n$$

where x cannot exceed a and $n - x$ cannot exceed $N - a$. This equation defines the **hypergeometric distribution,** whose parameters are the sample size n, the lot size (or population size) N, and the number of "successes" in the lot a.

EXAMPLE **Calculating a probability using the hypergeometric distribution**
A shipment of 20 tape recorders contains 5 that are defective. If 10 of them are randomly chosen for inspection, what is the probability that 2 of the 10 will be defective?

Solution Substituting $x = 2, n = 10, a = 5$, and $N = 20$ into the formula for the hypergeometric distribution, we get

$$h(2; 10, 5, 20) = \frac{\binom{5}{2}\binom{15}{8}}{\binom{20}{10}} = \frac{10 \cdot 6{,}435}{184{,}756} = 0.348$$

In the preceding example, n was large compared to N, and if we had made the mistake of using the binomial distribution with $n = 10$ and $p = \frac{5}{20} = 0.25$ to calculate the probability of two defectives, the result would have been 0.282, which is much too small. However, when n is small compared to N, the composition of the lot is not seriously affected by drawing the sample, and the binomial distribution with the parameters n and $p = \dfrac{a}{N}$ will yield a good approximation.

EXAMPLE

A numerical comparison of the hypergeometric and binomial distributions
Repeat the preceding example for a lot of 100 tape recorders, of which 25 are defective, by using

(a) the formula for the hypergeometric distribution;
(b) the formula for the binomial distribution as an approximation.

Solution (a) Substituting $x = 2, n = 10, a = 25$, and $N = 100$ into the formula for the hypergeometric distribution, we get

$$h(2; 10, 25, 100) = \frac{\binom{25}{2}\binom{75}{8}}{\binom{100}{10}} = 0.292$$

(b) Substituting $x = 2, n = 10$, and $p = \frac{25}{100} = 0.25$ into the formula for the binomial distribution, we get

$$b(2; 10, 0.25) = \binom{10}{2}(0.25)^2(1 - 0.25)^{10-2}$$

$$= 0.282 \qquad\qquad ✔$$

Observe that the difference between the two values is only 0.010. In general, it can be shown that $h(x; n, a, N)$ approaches $b(x; n, p)$ with $p = \dfrac{a}{N}$ when $N \to \infty$, and a good rule of thumb is to use the binomial distribution as an approximation to the hypergeometric distribution if $n \leq \dfrac{N}{10}$.

Although we have introduced the hypergeometric distribution in connection with a problem of sampling inspection, it has many other applications. For instance, it can be used to find the probability that 3 of 12 housewives prefer Brand A detergent to Brand B, if they are selected from among 200 housewives among whom 40 actually prefer Brand A to Brand B. Also, it can be used in connection with a problem of selecting industrial diamonds, some of which have superior qualities and some of which do not, or in connection with a problem of sampling income tax returns, where a among N returns filed contain questionable deductions, and so on.

EXERCISES

4.1 Suppose that a probability of $\frac{1}{12}$ is assigned to each point of the sample space of part (a) of Exercise 3.1 on page 61. Find the probability distribution of the total number of lasers that are suitable for the given task.

4.2 An experiment consists of four tosses of a coin. Denoting the outcomes *HHTH,
THTT, . . .* , and assuming that all 16 outcomes are equally likely, find the probability distribution for the total number of heads.

4.3 Determine whether the following can be probability distributions of a random variable which can take on only the values 1, 2, 3, and 4.

   (a) $f(1) = 0.26, f(2) = 0.26, f(3) = 0.26,$ and $f(4) = 0.26$

   (b) $f(1) = 0.15, f(2) = 0.28, f(3) = 0.29,$ and $f(4) = 0.28$

   (c) $f(1) = 0.33, f(2) = 0.37, f(3) = -0.03,$ and $f(4) = 0.33$

4.4 Check whether the following can define probability distributions, and explain your answers.

   (a) $f(x) = \dfrac{x}{15}$ for $x = 0, 1, 2, 3, 4, 5$

   (b) $f(x) = \dfrac{5 - x^2}{6}$ for $x = 0, 1, 2, 3$

   (c) $f(x) = \dfrac{1}{4}$ for $x = 3, 4, 5, 6$

   (d) $f(x) = \dfrac{x + 1}{25}$ for $x = 1, 2, 3, 4, 5$

4.5 Given that $f(x) = \dfrac{k}{2^x}$ is a probability distribution for a random variable that can take on the values $x = 0, 1, 2, 3,$ and 4, find k.

4.6 With reference to Exercise 4.5, find an expression for the distribution function $F(x)$ of the random variable.

4.7 Prove that $b(x; n, p) = b(n - x; n, 1 - p)$.

4.8 Prove that $B(x; n, p) = 1 - B(n - x - 1; n, 1 - p)$.

4.9 Prove that

$$\frac{b(x + 1; n, p)}{b(x; n, p)} = \frac{p(n - x)}{(1 - p)(x + 1)}$$

for $x = 0, 1, 2, \ldots , n - 1$, and use this recursion formula to calculate the values of the binomial distribution with $n = 6$ and $p = 0.30$. Also, verify the results by means of Table 1.

4.10 Use Table 1 to find

   (a) $B(8; 16, 0.40)$;

   (b) $b(8; 16, 0.40)$:

   (c) $B(9; 12, 0.60)$;

   (d) $b(9; 12, 0.60)$;

   (e) $\displaystyle\sum_{k=6}^{20} b(k; 20, 0.15)$;

   (f) $\displaystyle\sum_{k=6}^{9} b(k; 9, 0.70)$.

4.11 Use Table 1 to find

   (a) $B(7; 19, 0.45)$;

   (b) $b(7; 19, 0.45)$;

(c) $B(8; 10, 0.95)$;

(d) $b(8; 10, 0.95)$;

(e) $\sum_{k=4}^{10} b(k; 10, 0.35)$;

(f) $\sum_{k=2}^{4} b(k; 9, 0.30)$.

4.12 Rework the decision problem on page 105, supposing that only 3 of the 20 fax machines required repairs within the first year.

4.13 Human error is given as the reason for 75% of all accidents in a plant. Use the formula for the binomial distribution to find the probability that human error will be given as the reason for two of the next four accidents.

4.14 If the probability is 0.40 that steam will condense in a thin-walled aluminum tube at 10 atm pressure, use the formula for the binomial distribution to find the probability, that under the stated conditions steam will condense in 4 of 12 such tubes.

4.15 During one stage in the manufacture of integrated circuit chips, a coating must be applied. If 70% of chips receive a thick enough coating, use Table 1 to find the probabilities that among 15 chips

(a) at least 12 will have thick enough coatings.;

(b) at most 6 will have thick enough coatings;

(c) exactly 10 will have thick enough coatings.

4.16 The probability that the noise level of a wide-band amplifier will exceed 2 dB is 0.05. Use Table 1 to find the probabilities that among 12 such amplifiers the noise level of

(a) one will exceed 2 dB;

(b) at most two will exceed 2 dB;

(c) two or more will exceed 2 dB.

4.17 An agricultural cooperative claims that 90% of the watermelons shipped out are ripe and ready to eat. Find the probabilities that among 18 watermelons shipped out

(a) all 18 are ripe and ready to eat;

(b) at least 16 are ripe and ready to eat;

(c) at most 14 are ripe and ready to eat.

4.18 A quality-control engineer wants to check whether (in accordance with specifications) 95% of the electronic components shipped by his company are in good working condition. To this end, he randomly selects 15 from each large lot ready to be shipped and passes the lot if the selected components are all in good working condition; otherwise, each of the components in the lot is checked. Find the probabilities that the quality-control engineer will commit the error of

(a) holding a lot for further inspection even though 95% of the components are in good working condition;

(b) letting a lot pass through without further inspection even though only 90% of the components are in good working condition;

(c) letting a lot pass through without further inspection even though only 80% of the components are in good working condition.

4.19 A food processor claims that at most 10% of her jars of instant coffee contain less coffee than claimed on the label. To test this claim, 16 jars of her instant coffee are randomly selected and the contents are weighed; her claim is accepted if fewer than 3 of the jars contain less coffee than claimed on the label. Find the probabilities that the food processor's claim will be accepted when the actual percentage of her jars containing less coffee than claimed on the label is

    (a) 5%;

    (b) 10%;

    (c) 15%;

    (d) 20%.

4.20 A study shows that a computer firm answers 70% of all inquiries within 6 days. Find the probabilities that the firm will answer 0, 1, 2, . . . , or 10 of 10 inquiries within 6 days, and draw a probability histogram of the probability distribution.

4.21 What is the probability that an IRS auditor will catch only 2 income tax returns with illegitimate deductions, if she randomly selects 6 returns from among 18 returns, of which 8 contain illegitimate deductions?

4.22 Among the 12 solar collectors on display at a trade show, 9 are flat-plate collectors and the others are concentrating collectors. If a person visiting the show randomly selects 4 of the solar collectors to check out, what is the probability that 3 of them will be flat-plate collectors?

4.23 A quality-control engineer inspects a random sample of 3 batteries from each lot of 24 car batteries that is ready to be shipped. If such a lot contains 6 batteries with slight defects, what are the probabilities that the inspector's sample will contain

    (a) none of the batteries with defects;

    (b) only one of the batteries with defects;

    (c) at least two of the batteries with defects?

4.24 If 6 of 18 new buildings in a city violate the building code, what is the probability that a building inspector, who randomly selects 4 of the new buildings for inspection, will catch

    (a) none of the buildings that violate the building code;

    (b) 1 of the new buildings that violate the building code;

    (c) 2 of the new buildings that violate the building code;

    (d) at least 3 of the new buildings that violate the building code?

4.25 Among the 16 cities that a professional society is considering for its next 3 annual conventions, 7 are in the western part of the United States. To avoid arguments, the selection is left to chance. If none of the cities can be chosen more than once, what are the probabilities that

    (a) none of the conventions will be held in the western part of the United States;

    (b) all of the conventions will be held in the western part of the United States?

4.26 A shipment of 120 burglar alarms contains 5 that are defective. If 3 of these alarms are randomly selected and shipped to a customer, find the probability that the customer will get one bad unit by using

    (a) the formula for the hypergeometric distribution;

    (b) the formula for the binomial distribution as an approximation.

4.27 Among the 300 employees of a company, 240 are union members, while the others are not. If 8 of the employees are chosen by lot to serve on the committee which administers the pension fund, find the probability that 5 of them will be union members while the others are not, by using

(a) the formula for hypergeometric distribution;

(b) the formula for binomial distribution as an approximation.

4.28 Binomial probabilities can be calculated using MINITAB.

Dialog box:	**Session command**
Calc > Probability Distribution > Binomial	MTB > PDF 2;
Choose **Probability.**	MTB > BINOMIAL with n = 7, p = .33
Enter 7 in **Number of trials** and	
.33 in **Probability of success.**	
Choose **Input constant** and enter 2.	
Click **OK.**	

Output:
Binomial with n = 7 and p = 0.330000

x	P(X = x)
2.00	0.3088

Find the binomial probabilities with $n = 27$ and $p = 0.47$.

4.29 Cumulative binomial probabilities can be calculated using MINITAB.

Dialog box:	**Session command**
Calc > Probability Distribution > Binomial	MTB > CDF 2;
Choose **Cumulative Distribution.**	MTB > BINOMIAL with n = 7, p = .33
Enter 7 in **Number of trials** and	
.33 in **Probability of success.**	
Choose **Input constant** and enter 2.	
Click **OK.**	

Output:
Binomial with n = 7 and p = 0.330000

x	P(X <= x)
2.00	0.5783

Find the cumulative binomial probabilities with $n = 27$ and $p = 0.47$.

4.4 The Mean and the Variance of a Probability Distribution

Besides the binomial and hypergeometric distributions, there are many other probability distributions that have important engineering applications. However, before we go any further, let us discuss some general characteristics of probability distributions.

One such characteristic, that of the symmetry or skewness of a probability distribution, was illustrated by means of Figure 4.3 and 4.4; two others will be presented here with reference to Figure 4.5, which shows the probability histograms of two binomial distributions. One of these binomial distributions has the parameters $n = 4$ and $p = \frac{1}{2}$, and the other has the parameters $n = 16$ and $p = \frac{1}{2}$. Essentially, these two probability distributions differ in two respects. The first probability distribution is centered about $x = 2$, whereas the other (whose histogram is shaded) is centered about $x = 8$, and we say that the two distributions differ in their **location.** Another distinction is that the histogram of the second distribution is more spread out, and we say that the two distributions differ in **variation.** To make such comparisons more specific, we shall introduce in this section two of the most important statistical measures, describing, respectively, the location and the variation of a probability distribution—the **mean** and the **variance.**

The mean of a probability distribution is simply the mathematical expectation of a corresponding random variable. If a random variable X takes on the values $x_1, x_2, \ldots,$ or x_k, with the probabilities $f(x_1), f(x_2), \ldots,$ and $f(x_k)$, its mathematical expectation or expected value is

$$x_1 \cdot f(x_1) + x_2 \cdot f(x_2) + \cdots + x_k \cdot f(x_k) = \sum (\text{value}) \times (\text{probability})$$

using the $\sum$ notation. We can thus write

Mean of discrete probability distribution

$$\mu = \sum_{\text{all } x} x \cdot f(x)$$

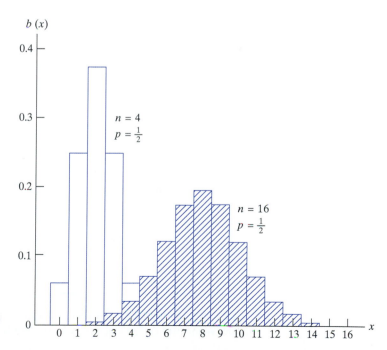

FIGURE 4.5 Probability histograms of two binomial distributions.

where the **mean** is denoted by the Greek letter μ (*mu*). The mean of a probability distribution measures its center in the sense of an average, or better, in the sense of a center of gravity. Note that the above formula for μ is, in fact, that for the **first moment about the origin** of a discrete system of masses $f(x)$ arranged on a straight line at distances x from the origin. We do not have to divide here by $\sum_{\text{all } x} f(x)$, as we do in the usual formula for the x-coordinate of the center of gravity, since the sum equals 1 by definition.

EXAMPLE

The mean number of heads in three tosses
Find the mean of the probability distribution of the number of heads obtained in 3 flips of a balanced coin.

Solution   The probabilities for 0, 1, 2, or 3 heads are $\frac{1}{8}$, $\frac{3}{8}$, $\frac{3}{8}$, and $\frac{1}{8}$, as can easily be verified by counting equally likely possibilities or by using the formula for the binomial distribution with $n = 3$ and $p = \frac{1}{2}$. Thus,

$$\mu = 0 \cdot \frac{1}{8} + 1 \cdot \frac{3}{8} + 2 \cdot \frac{3}{8} + 3 \cdot \frac{1}{8} = \frac{3}{2}$$ ✔

EXAMPLE

The mean number of preferred lawn mower ratings
With reference to the lawn-mower-rating example and the probabilities given on page 100, find the mean of the probability distribution of the number of preferred ratings.

Solution   Substituting $x = 0, 1, 2$, and 3, and the corresponding probabilities, into the formula for μ, we get

$$\mu = 0(0.26) + 1(0.50) + 2(0.22) + 3(0.02)$$

$$= 1.00$$ ✔

Returning to the second probability distribution of Figure 4.5, we could find its mean by calculating all the necessary probabilities (or by looking them up in Table 1) and substituting them into the formula for μ. However, if we reflect for a moment, we might argue that there is a fifty-fifty chance for a success on each trial, there are 16 trials, and it would seem reasonable to expect 8 heads and 8 tails (in the sense of a mathematical expectation). Similarly, we might argue that if a binomial distribution has the parameters $n = 200$ and $p = 0.20$, we can expect a success 20% of the time and, hence, on the average $200(0.20) = 40$ successes in 200 trials. These two values are, indeed, correct, and it can be shown in general that

Mean of binomial distribution

$$\mu = n \cdot p$$

for the mean of a binomial distribution. To prove this formula, we substitute the expression that defines $b(x; n, p)$ into the formula for μ, and we get

$$\mu = \sum_{x=0}^{n} x \cdot \frac{n!}{x!(n-x)!} p^x (1-p)^{n-x}$$

Then, making use of the fact that $\frac{x}{x!} = \frac{1}{(x-1)!}$ and $n! = n(n-1)!$, and factoring out n and p, we obtain

$$\mu = np \sum_{x=1}^{n} \frac{(n-1)!}{(x-1)!(n-x)!} p^{x-1}(1-p)^{n-x}$$

where the summation starts with $x = 1$ since the original summand is zero for $x = 0$. If we now let $y = x - 1$ and $m = n - 1$, we obtain

$$\mu = np \sum_{y=0}^{m} \frac{m!}{y!(m-y)!} p^y (1-p)^{m-y}$$

and this last sum can easily be recognized as that of all the terms of the binomial distribution with the parameters m and p. Hence, this sum equals 1 and it follows that $\mu = np$.

EXAMPLE

Using $\mu = np$ to find the mean number of heads in three tosses
Find the mean of the probability distribution of the number of heads obtained in 3 flips of a balanced coin.

Solution   For a binomial distribution with $n = 3$ and $p = \frac{1}{2}$, we get $\mu = 3 \cdot \frac{1}{2} = \frac{3}{2}$, and this agrees with the result obtained on page 114.

The formula $\mu = np$ applies, of course, only to binomial distributions, but for other special distributions, we can, similarly, express the mean in terms of their parameters. For instance, for the mean of the hypergeometric distribution with the parameters n, a, and N, we can write

Mean of hyper-geometric distribution

$$\mu = n \cdot \frac{a}{N}$$

In Exercise 4.41 on page 123, the reader will be asked to derive this formula by a method similar to the one we used to derive the formula for the mean of a binomial distribution.

EXAMPLE

Using the formula for the mean of a hypergeometric distribution
With reference to the example on page 107, where 5 of 20 tape recorders were defective, find the mean of the probability distribution of the number of defectives in a sample of 10 randomly chosen for inspection.

Solution   Substituting $n = 10$, $a = 5$, and $N = 20$ into the above formula for μ, we get

$$\mu = 10 \cdot \frac{5}{20} = 2.5$$

In other words, if we inspect 10 of the tape recorders, we can expect 2.5 defectives, where "expect" is to be interpreted in the sense of a mathematical expectation. ✔

To study the second of the two properties of probability distributions mentioned on page 113, their variation, let us refer again to the two probability distributions of Figure 4.5. For the one where $n = 4$ there is a high probability of getting values close to the mean, but for the one where $n = 16$ there is a high probability of getting values scattered over considerable distances away from the mean. Using this property, it may seem reasonable to measure the variation of a probability distribution with the quantity

$$\sum_{\text{all } x} (x - \mu) \cdot f(x)$$

namely, the average amount by which the values of the random variable deviate from the mean. Unfortunately,

$$\sum_{\text{all } x} (x - \mu) \cdot f(x) = \sum_{\text{all } x} x \cdot f(x) - \sum_{\text{all } x} \mu \cdot f(x)$$

$$= \mu - \mu \cdot \sum_{\text{all } x} f(x) = \mu - \mu = 0$$

so that this expression is always equal to zero. However, since we are really interested in the magnitude of the deviations $x - \mu$ and not in their signs, it suggests itself that we average the absolute values of these deviations from the mean. This would, indeed, provide a measure of variation, but on purely theoretical grounds we prefer to work instead with the squares of the deviations from the mean. These quantities are also nonnegative, and their average is indicative of the spread or dispersion of a probability distribution. We thus define the **variance** of a probability distribution $f(x)$, or that of X which has that probability distribution, as

Variance of probability distribution

$$\sigma^2 = \sum_{\text{all } x} (x - \mu)^2 \cdot f(x)$$

where σ is the lowercase Greek letter for s. This measure is not in the same units (or dimension) as the values of the random variable, but we can adjust for this by taking the square root. The **standard deviation** is defined as

Standard deviation of probability distribution

$$\sigma = \sqrt{\sum_{\text{all } x} (x - \mu)^2 \cdot f(x)}$$

EXAMPLE   **Calculating the standard deviations of two probability distributions**
Compare the standard deviations of the two probability distributions of Figure 4.5, on page 113.

Solution   Since $\mu = 4 \cdot \frac{1}{2} = 2$ for the binomial distribution with $n = 4$ and $p = \frac{1}{2}$, we find that the variance of this probability distribution is

$$\sigma^2 = (0-2)^2 \cdot \frac{1}{16} + (1-2)^2 \cdot \frac{4}{16} + (2-2)^2 \cdot \frac{6}{16} + (3-2)^2 \cdot \frac{4}{16} + (4-2)^2 \cdot \frac{1}{16}$$

$$= 1$$

and, hence, that its standard deviation is $\sigma = 1$. Similarly, it can be shown that for the other distribution $\sigma = 2$, and we find that the second (shaded) distribution with the greater spread also has the greater standard deviation.   ✔

Given any probability distribution, we can always calculate σ^2 by substituting the corresponding probabilities $f(x)$ into the formula which defines the variance. As in the case of the mean, however, this work can be simplified to a considerable extent when we deal with special kinds of distributions. For instance, it can be shown that the variance of the binomial distribution with the parameters n and p is given by the formula

Variance of binomial
distribution

$$\sigma^2 = n \cdot p \cdot (1 - p)$$

The variance of the hypergeometric distribution with the parameters n, a, and N is given by the formula

Variance of
hypergeometric
distribution

$$\sigma^2 = \frac{n \cdot a \cdot (N - a) \cdot (N - n)}{N^2 \cdot (N - 1)}$$

EXAMPLE   **Using the formula for variance of the binomial distribution**

Verify the result stated in the preceding example, that $\sigma = 2$ for the binomial distribution with $n = 16$ and $p = \frac{1}{2}$.

Solution   Substituting $n = 16$ and $p = \frac{1}{2}$ into the formula for the variance of a binomial distribution, we get

$$\sigma^2 = 16 \cdot \frac{1}{2} \cdot \frac{1}{2} = 4$$

and, hence, $\sigma = \sqrt{4} = 2$.   ✔

EXAMPLE   **Using the formula for variance of the hypergeometric distribution**

With reference to the example of page 107, where 5 of 20 tape recorders were defective, find the standard deviation of the probability distribution of the number of defectives in a sample of 10 randomly chosen for inspection.

Solution   Substituting $n = 10$, $a = 5$, and $N = 20$ into the formula for the variance of a hypergeometric distribution, we get

$$\sigma^2 = \frac{10 \cdot 5 \cdot (20 - 5) \cdot (20 - 10)}{20^2 \cdot 19} = \frac{75}{76}$$

and, hence, $\sigma = \sqrt{75/76} = 0.99$.   ✓

When we first defined the variance of a probability distribution, it may have occurred to the reader that the formula looked exactly like the one which we use in physics to define second moments, or moments of inertia. Indeed, it is customary in statistics to define the **kth moment about the origin** as

$$\mu'_k = \sum_{all\ x} x^k \cdot f(x)$$

and the **kth moment about the mean** as

$$\mu_k = \sum_{all\ x} (x - \mu)^k \cdot f(x)$$

Thus, the mean μ is the first moment about the origin, and the variance σ^2 is the second moment about the mean. Higher moments are often used in statistics to give further descriptions of probability distributions. For instance, the third moment about the mean (divided by σ^3 to make this measure independent of the scale of measurement) is used to describe the symmetry or skewness of a distribution; the fourth moment about the mean (divided by σ^4) is, similarly, used to describe its "peakedness," or **kurtosis.** To determine moments about the mean, it is usually easiest to express moments about the mean in terms of moments about the origin and then to calculate the necessary moments about the origin. For the second moment about the mean we thus have the important formula

Computing formula
for the variance

$$\sigma^2 = \mu'_2 - \mu^2$$

which the reader will be asked to prove in part (a) of Exercise 4.47 on page 124; part (b) of that exercise pertains to a similar formula for expressing μ_3, in terms of moments about the origin.

EXAMPLE   **Calculating variance using the alternative computing formula**
Use the preceding computing formula to determine the variance of the probability distribution of the number of points rolled with a balanced die.

Solution   Since $f(x) = \dfrac{1}{6}$ for $x = 1, 2, 3, 4, 5$, and 6, we get

$$\mu = 1 \cdot \frac{1}{6} + 2 \cdot \frac{1}{6} + 3 \cdot \frac{1}{6} + 4 \cdot \frac{1}{6} + 5 \cdot \frac{1}{6} + 6 \cdot \frac{1}{6}$$

$$= \frac{7}{2}$$

$$\mu_2' = 1^2 \cdot \frac{1}{6} + 2^2 \cdot \frac{1}{6} + 3^2 \cdot \frac{1}{6} + 4^2 \cdot \frac{1}{6} + 5^2 \cdot \frac{1}{6} + 6^2 \cdot \frac{1}{6}$$

$$= \frac{91}{6}$$

and, hence, $\sigma^2 = \dfrac{91}{6} - \left(\dfrac{7}{2}\right)^2 = \dfrac{35}{12}.$ ✔

EXAMPLE   **The mean and variance of the number of incorrect addresses**
As part of a quality-improvement project focused on the delivery of mail at a department office within a large company, data were gathered on the number of different addresses that had to be changed so the mail could be redirected to the
correct mail stop. The distribution, given in the first two columns of the table below,
describes the number of redirects per delivery. Compute the mean and variance.

Solution   We determine the columns $xf(x)$ and $x^2f(x)$

x	$f(x)$	$xf(x)$	$x^2f(x)$
0	.05	.0	0.0
1	.20	.2	0.2
2	.45	.9	1.8
3	.20	.6	1.8
4	.10	.4	1.6
Total		2.1	5.4

so $\mu = 2.1$ and $\sigma^2 = 5.4 - (2.1)^2 = 0.990.$ ✔

4.5 Chebyshev's Theorem

Earlier in this chapter we used examples to show how the standard deviation measures the variation of a probability distribution, that is, how it controls the concentration of probability in the neighborhood of the mean. If σ is small, there is a
high probability of getting values close to the mean; if σ is large there is a correspondingly higher probability of getting values farther away from the mean. Formally, the idea is expressed by the following theorem.

Chebyshev's theorem

> **Theorem 4.1** If a probability distribution has mean μ and standard deviation
> σ, the probability of getting a value which deviates from μ by at least $k\sigma$ is at
> most $\dfrac{1}{k^2}$.

Symbolically,

$$P(|X - \mu| \geq k\sigma) \leq \frac{1}{k^2}$$

where $P(|X - \mu| \geq k\sigma)$ is the probability associated with the set of outcomes for which x, the value of a random variable having the given probability distribution, is such that $|x - \mu| \geq k\sigma$.

Thus, the probability that a random variable will take on a value which deviates (differs) from the mean by at least 2 standard deviations is at most $\frac{1}{4}$, the probability that is will take on a value which deviates from the mean by at least 5 standard deviations is at most $\frac{1}{25}$, and the probability that it will take on a value which deviates from the mean by 10 standard deviations or more is less than or equal to $\frac{1}{100}$.

To prove this theorem, consider any probability distribution $f(x)$, having mean μ, and variance σ^2. Dividing the sum defining the variance into three parts as indicated in Figure 4.6, we have

$$\sigma^2 = \sum_{\text{all } x} (x - \mu)^2 f(x)$$

$$= \sum_{R_1} (x - \mu)^2 f(x) + \sum_{R_2} (x - \mu)^2 f(x) + \sum_{R_3} (x - \mu)^2 f(x)$$

where R_1 is the region for which $x \leq \mu - k\sigma$, R_2 is the region for which $\mu - k\sigma < x < \mu + k\sigma$, and R_3 is the region for which $x \geq \mu + k\sigma$. Since $(x - \mu)^2 f(x)$ cannot be negative, the above sum over R_2 is nonnegative, and without it the sum of the summations over R_1 and R_3 is less than or equal to σ^2, that is

$$\sigma^2 \geq \sum_{R_1} (x - \mu)^2 f(x) + \sum_{R_3} (x - \mu)^2 f(x)$$

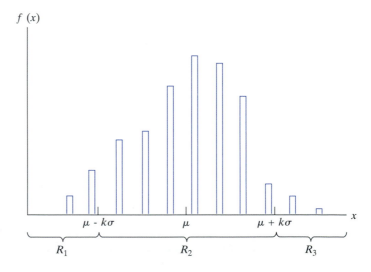

FIGURE 4.6 Diagram for proof of Chebyshev's theorem.

But $x - \mu \leq -k\sigma$ in the region R_1 and $x - \mu \geq k\sigma$ in the region R_3, so that in either case $|x - \mu| \geq k\sigma$; hence, in both regions $(x - \mu)^2 \geq k^2\sigma^2$. If we now re-place $(x - \mu)^2$ in each sum by $k^2\sigma^2$, a number less than or equal to $(x - \mu)^2$, we obtain the inequality

$$\sigma^2 \geq \sum_{R_1} k^2\sigma^2 f(x) + \sum_{R_3} k^2\sigma^2 f(x)$$

or

$$\frac{1}{k^2} \geq \sum_{R_1} f(x) + \sum_{R_3} f(x)$$

Since $\sum_{R_1} f(x) + \sum_{R_3} f(x)$ represents the probability assigned to the region $R_1 \cup R_3$, namely, $P(|X - \mu| \geq k\sigma)$, this completes the proof of Theorem 4.1.

To obtain an alternative form of Chebyshev's theorem, note that the event $|x - \mu| < k\sigma$ is the complement of the event $|x - \mu| \geq k\sigma$; hence, the probability of getting a value which deviates from μ by less than $k\sigma$ is at least $1 - \dfrac{1}{k^2}$.

EXAMPLE

A probability bound using Chebyshev's theorem
The number of customers who visit a car dealer's showroom on a Saturday morning is a random variable with $\mu = 18$ and $\sigma = 2.5$. With what probability can we assert that there will be between 8 and 28 customers?

Solution Since $k = \dfrac{28 - 18}{2.5} = \dfrac{18 - 8}{2.5} = 4$, the probability is at least $1 - \dfrac{1}{4^2} = \dfrac{15}{16}$. ✔

Theoretically speaking, the most important feature of Chebyshev's theorem is that it applies to any probability distribution for which μ and σ exist. However, so far as applications are concerned, this generally is also its greatest weakness—it provides only an upper limit (often a very poor one) to the probability of getting a value that deviates from the mean by k standard deviations or more. For instance, we can assert in general that the probability of getting a value which differs from the mean by at least 2 standard deviations is at most 0.25, whereas the corresponding exact probability for the binomial distribution with $n = 16$ and $p = \frac{1}{2}$ is only 0.0768—"at most 0.25" is correct, but it does not tell us that the actual probability may be as small as 0.0768.

An important result is obtained if we apply Chebyshev's theorem to the binomial distribution when the number of trials is large. To illustrate this result, consider the following example.

EXAMPLE

Chebyshev's theorem with a large number of trials
Show that for 40,000 flips of a balanced coin, the probability is at least 0.99 that the proportion of heads will fall between 0.475 and 0.525.

Solution Since $\mu = 40,000 \cdot \frac{1}{2} = 20,000$, $\sigma = \sqrt{40,000 \cdot \frac{1}{2} \cdot \frac{1}{2}} = 100$, and $1 - \dfrac{1}{k^2} = 0.99$ yields $k = 10$, the alternative form of Chebyshev's theorem tells us that the probability is at least 0.99 that we will get between $20,000 - 10(100) = 19,000$ and

$20,000 + 10(100) = 21,000$ heads. Hence, the probability is at least 0.99 that the proportion of heads will fall between $\dfrac{19,000}{40,000} = 0.475$ and $\dfrac{21,000}{40,000} = 0.525.$ ✔

Correspondingly, the reader will be asked to show in Exercise 4.45 that for 1,000,000 flips of a balanced coin the probability is at least 0.99 that the proportion of heads will fall between 0.495 and 0.505, and these results suggest that when n is large, the chances are that the proportion of heads will be very close to $p = \frac{1}{2}$. When formulated for any binomial distribution with the parameters n and p, this result is referred to as the **law of large numbers.**

EXERCISES

4.30 Suppose that the probabilities are $0.4, 0.3, 0.2,$ and 0.1 that there will be $0, 1, 2,$ or 3 power failures in a certain city during the month of July. Use the formulas which define μ and σ^2 to find

    (a) the mean of this probability distribution;

    (b) the variance of this probability distribution.

4.31 Use the computing formula for σ^2 to rework part (b) of the preceding exercise.

4.32 The following table gives the probabilities that a certain computer will malfunction $0, 1, 2, 3, 4, 5,$ or 6 times on any one day:

Number of malfunctions: x	0	1	2	3	4	5	6
Probability: $f(x)$	0.17	0.29	0.27	0.16	0.07	0.03	0.01

Use the formulas which define μ and σ to find

    (a) the mean of this probability distribution;

    (b) the standard deviation of this probability distribution.

4.33 Use the computing formula for σ^2 to rework part (b) of the preceding exercise.

4.34 Find the mean and the variance of the uniform probability distribution given by

$$f(x) = \frac{1}{n} \quad \text{for } x = 1, 2, 3, \ldots, n$$

[*Hint:* The sum of the first n positive integers is $\frac{1}{2}n(n+1)$, and the sum of their squares is $\frac{1}{6}n(n+1)(2n+1)$.]

4.35 Find the mean and the variance of the binomial distribution with $n = 4$ and $p = 0.70$ by using

    (a) Table 1 and the formulas defining μ and σ^2;

    (b) the special formulas for the mean and the variance of a binomial distribution.

4.36 As can easily be verified by means of the formula for the binomial distribution (or by listing all 32 possibilities), the probabilities of getting $0, 1, 2, 3, 4,$ or 5 heads in five flips of a balanced coin are $\frac{1}{32}, \frac{5}{32}, \frac{10}{32}, \frac{10}{32}, \frac{5}{32},$ and $\frac{1}{32}$. Find the mean of this probability distribution using

    (a) the formula that defines μ ;

    (b) the special formula for the mean of a binomial distribution.

4.37 With reference to Exercise 4.36, find the variance of the probability distribution using

  (a) the formula that defines σ^2;

  (b) the computing formula for σ^2;

  (c) the special formula for the variance of a binomial distribution.

4.38 If 95% of certain high-performance radial tires last at least 30,000 miles, find the mean and the standard deviation of the distribution of the number of these tires, among 20 selected at random, that last at least 30,000 miles, using

  (a) Table 1, the formula which defines μ, and the computing formula for σ^2.

  (b) the special formulas for the mean and the variance of a binomial distribution.

4.39 Find the mean and the standard deviation of the distribution of each of the following random variables (having binomial distributions):

  (a) The number of heads obtained in 676 flips of a balanced coin.

  (b) The number of 4's obtained in 720 rolls of a balanced die.

  (c) The number of defectives in a sample of 600 parts made by a machine, when the probability is 0.04 that any one of the parts is defective.

  (d) The number of students among 800 interviewed who do not like the food served at the university cafeteria, when the probability is 0.65 that any one of them does not like the food.

4.40 Find the mean and the standard deviation of the hypergeometric distribution with the parameters $n = 3$, $a = 4$, and $N = 8$

  (a) by first calculating the necessary probabilities and then using the formulas which define μ and σ;

  (b) by using the special formulas for the mean and the variance of a hypergeometric distribution.

4.41 Prove the formula for the mean of the hypergeometric distribution with the parameters n, a, and N, namely, $\mu = n \cdot \dfrac{a}{N}$. [*Hint:* Make use of the identity

$$\sum_{r=0}^{k} \binom{m}{r}\binom{s}{k-r} = \binom{m+s}{k}$$

which can be obtained by equating the coefficients of x^k in $(1 + x)^m(1 + x)^s$ and in $(1 + x)^{m+s}$.]

4.42 Construct a table showing the upper limits provided by Chebyshev's theorem for the probabilities of obtaining values differing from the mean by at least 1, 2, and 3 standard deviations and also the corresponding probabilities for the binomial distribution with $n = 16$ and $p = \frac{1}{2}$.

4.43 The tensile strength of some synthetic fibers can be determined by tying two strands together and pulling until either the right- or left-hand strand breaks. If 144 pairs of strands will be broken, what does Chebyshev's theorem with $k = 4$ tell us about the number of cases where the left-hand strand broke?

4.44 In one out of 6 cases, material for bulletproof vests fails to meet puncture standards. If 405 specimens are tested, what does Chebyshev's theorem tell us about the probability of getting at most 30 or more than 105 cases that do not meet puncture standards?

4.45 Show that for 1,000,000 flips of a balanced coin the probability is at least 0.99 that the proportion of heads will fall between 0.495 and 0.505.

4.46 How many times do we have to flip a balanced coin to be able to assert with a probability of at most 0.01 that the difference between the proportion of tails and 0.50 will be at least 0.04?

4.47 Prove that

(a) $\sigma^2 = \mu_2' - \mu^2$;

(b) $\mu_3 = \mu_3' - 3\mu_2' \cdot \mu + 2\mu^3$.

4.6 The Poisson Approximation to the Binomial Distribution

The Poisson distribution often serves as a model for counts which do not have a natural upper bound. The Poisson distribution, with mean λ (lambda), has probabilities given by

Poisson distribution

$$f(x; \lambda) = \frac{\lambda^x e^{-\lambda}}{x!} \quad \text{for } x = 0, 1, 2, \ldots$$

When n is large and p is small, binomial probabilities are often approximated by means of the Poisson distribution with λ equal to the product np. Before we justify this approximation, let us point out that $x = 0, 1, 2, \ldots$ means that there is a countable infinity of possibilities, and this requires that we modify the third axiom of probability given on page 67. In its place we substitute the following axiom.

Modification of third axiom of probability

Axiom 3' If $A_1, A_2, A_3, \ldots$ is a finite or infinite sequence of mutually exclusive events in S, then

$$P(A_1 \cup A_2 \cup A_3 \cup \cdots) = P(A_1) + P(A_2) + P(A_3) + \cdots$$

The other postulates remain unchanged. To verify that $P(S) = 1$ for this formula, we make use of Axiom 3' and write

$$\sum_{x=0}^{\infty} f(x; \lambda) = \sum_{x=0}^{\infty} \frac{e^{-\lambda}\lambda^x}{x!} = e^{-\lambda} \sum_{x=0}^{\infty} \frac{\lambda^x}{x!}$$

Since the infinite series in the expression on the right is the Maclaurin's series for e^λ, it follows that

$$\sum_{x=0}^{\infty} f(x; \lambda) = e^{-\lambda} \cdot e^\lambda = 1$$

Let us now show that when $n \to \infty$ and $p \to 0$, while $np = \lambda$ remains constant, the limiting form of the binomial distribution is as given in the beginning of the preceding paragraph. First let us substitute $\dfrac{\lambda}{n}$ for p into the formula for the binomial distribution and simplify the resulting expression; thus, we get

$$b(x; n, p) = \frac{n!}{x!(n-x)!}\left(\frac{\lambda}{n}\right)^x\left(1 - \frac{\lambda}{n}\right)^{n-x}$$

$$= \frac{n(n-1)(n-2)\cdots(n-x+1)}{x!n^x}(\lambda)^x\left(1 - \frac{\lambda}{n}\right)^{n-x}$$

$$= \frac{\left(1 - \frac{1}{n}\right)\left(1 - \frac{2}{n}\right)\cdots\left(1 - \frac{x-1}{n}\right)}{x!}(\lambda)^x\left(1 - \frac{\lambda}{n}\right)^{n-x}$$

If we now let $n \to \infty$, we find that

$$\left(1 - \frac{1}{n}\right)\left(1 - \frac{2}{n}\right)\cdots\left(1 - \frac{x-1}{n}\right) \to 1$$

that

$$\left(1 - \frac{\lambda}{n}\right)^{n-x} = \left[\left(1 - \frac{\lambda}{n}\right)^{n/\lambda}\right]^{\lambda}\left(1 - \frac{\lambda}{n}\right)^{-x} \to e^{-\lambda}$$

and, hence, that the binomial distribution approaches

$$\frac{\lambda^x e^{-\lambda}}{x!} \qquad \text{for } x = 0, 1, 2, \ldots$$

This completes our proof; the distribution at which we arrived is called the **Poisson distribution,** as we already indicated on page 124.

Since the Poisson distribution has many important applications besides approximating binomial probabilities (see Section 4.7), it has been extensively tabulated. Table 2 at the end of the book gives the values of the probabilities $F(x; \lambda) = \sum_{k=0}^{x} f(k; \lambda)$ for values of λ in varying increments from 0.02 to 25, and its use is very similar to that of Table 1. Poisson probabilities are also calculated by many statistical software packages (see Exercise 4.68 and 4.69).

The following are some examples illustrating the Poisson approximation of binomial probabilities. An acceptable rule of thumb is to use this approximation if $n \geq 20$ and $p \leq 0.05$; if $n \geq 100$, the approximation is generally excellent so long as $np \leq 10$.

EXAMPLE

Comparing Poisson and binomial probabilities
It is known that 5% of the books bound at a certain bindery have defective bindings. Find the probability that 2 of 100 books bound by this bindery will have defective bindings using

(a) the formula for the binomial distribution;
(b) the Poisson approximation to the binomial distribution.

Solution (a) Substituting $x = 2$, $n = 100$, and $p = 0.05$ into the formula for the binomial distribution, we get

$$b(2; 100, 0.05) = \binom{100}{2}(0.05)^2(0.95)^{98} = 0.081$$

(b) Substituting $x = 2$ and $\lambda = 100(0.05) = 5$ into the formula for the Poisson distribution, we get

$$f(2; 5) = \frac{5^2 \cdot e^{-5}}{2!} = 0.084$$

It is of interest to note that the difference between the two values we obtained (the error we would make by using the Poisson approximation) is only 0.003. [Had we used Table 2 instead of using a calculator to obtain e^{-5}, we would have obtained $f(2; 5) = F(2; 5) - F(1; 5) = 0.125 - 0.040 = 0.085.$] ✔

EXAMPLE **A Poisson approximation to binomial probabilities**
A heavy machinery manufacturer has 3,840 large generators in the field that are under warranty. If the probability is 1/1,200 that any one will fail during the given year, find the probabilities that $0, 1, 2, 3, 4 \ldots$ of the generators will fail during the given year.

Solution The binomial distribution could be used when appropriate computer software is available. However, the expected number is small and the number of generators is large so the Poisson approximation is valid. We take

$$\lambda = 3840 \cdot \frac{1}{1200} = 3.2$$

Consulting Table 2 with $\lambda = 3.2$, and using the identity $f(x; \lambda) = F(x; \lambda) - F(x - 1; \lambda)$ we obtain the results shown in the probability histogram of Figure 4.7. ✔

Using a method similar to that employed on page 115 to derive the formula for the mean of the binomial distribution, we can show that the mean and the variance of the Poisson distribution with the parameter λ are given by

Mean and variance of
Poisson distribution

$$\mu = \lambda \quad \text{and} \quad \sigma^2 = \lambda$$

The first of these results should really have been expected, for in our justification of the Poisson approximation to the binomial distribution we let $\lambda = np$. For the variance we can write $\sigma^2 = np(1 - p) = \lambda(1 - p)$, which approaches λ as $p \to 0$.

EXAMPLE **A Poisson distribution for counts of particles**
Over a 10-minute period, a counter records an average of 1.3 gamma particles per millisecond coming from a radioactive substance. To a good approximation, the distribution of the count, X, of gamma particles during the next millisecond is Poisson. Determine (a) λ, (b) the probability of one or more gamma particles, and (c) the variance.

Solution (a) The mean of the Poisson distribution is λ, so we approximate that $\lambda = 1.3$ to agree with the long-run average.

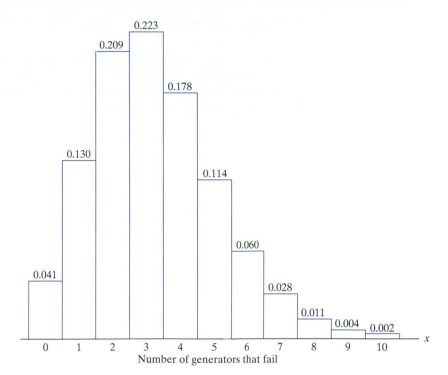

FIGURE 4.7 Probability histogram of Poisson distribution with $\lambda = 3.2$.

(b) $1 - P(X = 0) = 1 - e^{-1.3} = .727$

(c) For the Poisson, the variance is also equal to λ, so $\sigma^2 = 1.3$.   ✔

4.7   Poisson Processes

In general, a **random process** is a physical process that is wholly or in part controlled by some sort of chance mechanism. It may be a sequence of repeated flips of a coin, measurements of the quality of manufactured products coming off an assembly line, the vibrations of airplane wings, the noise in a radio signal, or any one of numerous other phenomena. What characterizes such processes is their time dependence, namely, the fact that certain events do or do not take place (depending on chance) at regular intervals of time or throughout continuous intervals of time.

In this section we shall be concerned with processes taking place over continuous intervals of time, such as the occurrence of imperfections on a continuously produced bolt of cloth, the recording of radiation by means of a Geiger counter, the arrival of telephone calls at a switchboard, or the passing by cars over an electronic counting device. We will now show that the mathematical model which we can use to describe many situations like these is that of the Poisson distribution. To find the probability of x successes during a time interval of length T, we divide the interval into n equal parts of length Δt, so that $T = n \cdot \Delta t$, and we assume that:

1. The probability of a success during a very small interval of time Δt is given by $\alpha \cdot \Delta t$.

2. The probability of more than one success during such a small time interval Δt is negligible.

3. The probability of a success during such a time interval does not depend on what happened prior to that time.

This means that the assumptions underlying the binomial distribution are satisfied, and the probability of x successes in the time interval T is given by the binomial probability $b(x; n, p)$ with $n = \dfrac{T}{\Delta t}$ and $p = \alpha \cdot \Delta t$. Then, following the argument on page 125, we find that when $n \to \infty$ the probability of x successes during the time interval T is given by the corresponding Poisson probability with the parameter $\lambda = n \cdot p = \dfrac{T}{\Delta t} \cdot (\alpha \cdot \Delta t) = \alpha T$. Since λ is the mean of this Poisson distribution, note that α is the average (mean) number of successes per unit time.

EXAMPLE   **Calculating probabilities concerning bad checks**
If a bank receives on the average $\alpha = 6$ bad checks per day, what are the probabilities that it will receive

(a) 4 bad checks on any given day;

(b) 10 bad checks over any 2 consecutive days?

Solution   (a) Substituting $x = 4$ and $\lambda = \alpha T = 6 \cdot 1 = 6$ into the formula for the Poisson distribution, we get

$$f(4; 6) = \frac{6^4 \cdot e^{-6}}{4!} = \frac{1{,}296(0.00248)}{24} = 0.134$$

(b) Here $\lambda = \alpha \cdot 2 = 12$ so we want to find $f(10; 12)$. We write

$$
\begin{aligned}
f(10; 12) &= F(10; 12) - F(9; 12) \\
&= 0.347 - 0.242 \\
&= 0.105
\end{aligned}
$$

where the values of $F(10; 12)$ and $F(9; 12)$ were obtained from Table 2.   ✔

EXAMPLE   **Calculating the probabilities of imperfections**
In the inspection of tin plate produced by a continuous electrolytic process, 0.2 imperfection is spotted on the average per minute. Find the probabilities of spotting

(a) one imperfection in 3 minutes;

(b) at least two imperfections in 5 minutes;

(c) at most one imperfection in 15 minutes.

Solution   Referring in each case to Table 2, with $\lambda = (0.2) \cdot 3 = 0.6$, we get

$$
\begin{aligned}
F(1; 0.6) - F(0; 0.6) &= 0.878 - 0.549 \\
&= 0.329
\end{aligned}
$$

for part (a). With $\lambda = (0.2) \cdot 5 = 1.0$, we get

$$1 - F(1; 1.0) = 1 - 0.736$$
$$= 0.264$$

for part (b), and with $\lambda = (0.2) \cdot 15 = 3.0$, we get

$$F(1; 3.0) = 0.199$$

for part (c).   ✔

The Poisson distribution has many important applications in *queueing* problems, where we may be interested, for example, in the number of customers arriving for service at a cafeteria, the number of ships or trucks arriving to be unloaded at a receiving dock, the number of aircraft arriving at an airport, and so forth. Thus, if on the average 0.3 customer arrives per minute at a cafeteria, then the probability that exactly 3 customers will arrive during a 5-minute span is

$$F(3; 1.5) - F(2; 1.5) = 0.934 - 0.809 = 0.125$$

and if on the average 3 trucks arrive per hour to be unloaded at a warehouse, then the probability that at most 20 will arrive during an 8-hour day is

$$F(20; 24) = 0.243$$

Also, if on the average 14.5 planes arrive per day at a private airport, then the probability that the number of arrivals on any one day will be anywhere from 12 to 15, inclusive, is

$$F(15; 14.5) - F(11; 14.5) = 0.619 - 0.220 = 0.399$$

4.8 The Geometric Distribution

On page 53 we indicated that a countably infinite sample space would be needed if we are interested in the number of cars persons have to inspect until they find one whose nitrogen oxide emission does not meet government standards. To treat this kind of problem in general, suppose that in a sequence of trials we are interested in the number of the trial on which the first success occurs, and that all but the third of the assumptions underlying the binomial distributions are satisfied; in other words, n is not fixed.

Clearly, if the first success is to come on the xth trial, it has to be preceded by $x - 1$ failures, and if the probability of a success is p, the probability of $x - 1$ failures in $x - 1$ trials is $(1 - p)^{x-1}$. Then, if we multiply this expression by the probability p of a success on the xth trial, we find that the probability of getting the first success on the xth trial is given by

Geometric distribution

$$g(x; p) = p(1 - p)^{x-1} \quad \text{for } x = 1, 2, 3, 4, \ldots$$

This probability distribution is called the **geometric distribution,** and, as the reader will be asked to verify in Exercise 4.66 on page 132, its mean is

Mean of geometric
distribution

$$\mu = \frac{1}{p}$$

EXAMPLE

Calculating a probability using the geometric distribution
If the probability is 0.05 that a certain kind of measuring device will show excessive drift, what is the probability that the sixth measuring device tested will be the first to show excessive drift?

Solution   Substituting $x = 6$ and $p = 0.05$ into the formula for the geometric distribution, we get

$$g(6; 0.05) = (0.05)(1 - 0.05)^{6-1}$$
$$= 0.039$$ ✔

EXERCISES

4.48 Prove that for the Poisson distribution

$$\frac{f(x + 1; \lambda)}{f(x; \lambda)} = \frac{\lambda}{x + 1}$$

for $x = 0, 1, 2, \ldots$.

4.49 Use the recursion formula of Exercise 4.48 to calculate the values of the Poisson distribution with $\lambda = 3$ for $x = 0, 1, 2, \ldots$, and 9, and draw the probability histogram of this distribution. Verify your results by referring to Table 2.

4.50 Use Table 2 to find

(a) $F(4; 7)$;

(b) $f(4; 7)$;

(c) $\sum_{k=6}^{19} f(k; 8)$.

4.51 Use Table 2 to find

(a) $F(9; 12)$;

(b) $f(9; 12)$;

(c) $\sum_{k=3}^{12} f(k; 7.5)$.

4.52 Use the Poisson distribution to approximate the binomial probability $b(3; 100, 0.03)$.

4.53 In a given city, 6% of all drivers get at least one parking ticket per year. Use the Poisson approximation to the binomial distribution to determine the probabilities that among 80 drivers (randomly chosen in this city)

(a) 4 will get at least one parking ticket in any given year;

(b) at least 3 will get at least one parking ticket in any given year;

(c) anywhere from 3 to 6, inclusive, will get at least one parking ticket in any given year.

4.54 If 0.8% of the fuses delivered to an arsenal are defective, use the Poisson approximation to determine the probability that 4 fuses will be defective in a random sample of 400.

4.55 The number of gamma rays emitted per second by a certain radioactive substance is a random variable having the Poisson distribution with $\lambda = 5.8$. If a recording instrument becomes inoperative when there are more than 12 rays per second, what is the probability that this instrument becomes inoperative during any given second?

4.56 Given that the switchboard of a consultant's office receives on the average 0.6 calls per minute, find the probabilities that

(a) in a given minute there will be at least 1 call;

(b) in a 4-minute interval there will be at least 3 calls.

4.57 At a checkout counter customers arrive at an average of 1.5 per minute. Find the probabilities that

(a) at most 4 will arrive in any given minute;

(b) at least 3 will arrive during an interval of 2 minutes;

(c) at most 15 will arrive during an interval of 6 minutes.

4.58 A company rents out time on a computer for periods of t hours, for which it receives $600 an hour. The number of times the computer breaks down during t hours is a random variable having the Poisson distribution with $\lambda = (0.8)t$, and if the computer breaks down x times during t hours it costs $50x^2$ dollars to fix it. How should the company select t in order to maximize its expected profit?

4.59 The determination of geometric probabilities is often simplified by making use of the identity

$$g(x; p) = \frac{1}{x} \cdot b(1; x, p)$$

and looking up $b(1; x, p)$ in a table of binomial probabilities. Verify this identity and use it (and Table 1) to evaluate

(a) $g(12; 0.10)$;

(b) $g(10; 0.30)$.

4.60 An expert shot hits a target 95% of the time. What is the probability that the expert will miss the target for the first time on the fifteenth shot?

4.61 In a "torture test" a light switch is turned on and off until it fails. If the probability that the switch will fail any time it is turned on or off is 0.001, what is the probability that the switch will fail *after* it has been turned on or off 1,200 times? Assume that the conditions underlying the geometric distribution are met. [*Hint:* Use the formula for the value of an infinite geometric progression and logarithms.]

4.62 A pool company's records show that the probability is 0.20 that one of its new pools will require repairs within a year. What is the probability that the sixth pool it builds in a given year will be the first one to require repairs within a year?

4.63 In the example on page 129 we considered customers arriving at a cafeteria at an average rate of 0.3 per minute.

(a) Find the probability that exactly 2 customers arrive in a 10-minute span.

(b) Find the probability that 2 or more customers arrive in a 10-minute span.

(c) Find the probability that exactly one customer arrives in a 5-minute span and one customer arrives in the next 5-minute span.

4.64 The arrival of trucks at a receiving dock is a Poisson process with a mean arrival rate of 2 per hour.

(a) Find the probability that exactly 5 trucks arrive in a two hour period.

(b) Find the probability that 8 or more trucks arrive in a two hour period.

(c) Find the probability that exactly two trucks arrive in a one hour period and exactly 3 trucks arrive in the next one hour period.

4.65 The number of flaws in a fiber optic cable follows a Poisson process with an average of 0.6 per 100 feet.

(a) Find the probability of exactly 2 flaws in a 200 foot cable.

(b) Find the probability of exactly 1 flaw in the first 100 feet and exactly 1 flaw in the second 100 feet.

4.66 Differentiating with respect to p on both sides of the equation

$$\sum_{x=1}^{\infty} p(1-p)^{x-1} = 1$$

show that the geometric distribution

$$f(x) = p(1-p)^{x-1} \qquad \text{for } x = 1, 2, 3, \ldots$$

has the mean $1/p$.

4.67 Use the formulas defining μ and σ^2 to show that the mean and the variance of the Poisson distribution are both equal to λ.

4.68 Poisson probabilities can be calculated using MINITAB.

Dialog box:	**Session command**
Calc > Probability Distribution > Poisson	MTB > PDF 2;
Choose **Probability.**	MTB > POISSON mean=1.64.
Type 1.64 in **Mean.**	
Choose **Input constant** and enter 2.	
Click **OK.**	

Output:

Poisson with mu = 1.64000

x	P(X = x)
2.00	0.2609

Find the Poisson probabilities for x = 2 and x = 3 when

(a) $\lambda = 2.73$

(b) $\lambda = 4.33$

4.69 Cumulative Poisson probabilities can be calculated using MINITAB.

Dialog box:	**Session command**
Calc > Probability Distribution > Poisson	MTB > CDF 2;
Choose **Cumulative Distribution.**	MTB > POISSON mean=1.64.
Type 1.64 in **Mean.**	
Choose **Input constant** and enter 2.	
Click **OK.**	

Output:

Poisson with mu = 1.64000

$$\begin{array}{cc} x & P(X <= x) \\ 2.00 & 0.7730 \end{array}$$

Find the cumulative Poisson probabilities for x = 2 and x = 3 when

(a) $\lambda = 2.73$

(b) $\lambda = 4.33$

4.9 The Multinomial Distribution

An immediate generalization of the binomial distribution arises when each trial can have more than two possible outcomes. This happens, for example, when a manufactured product is classified as superior, average, or poor, when a student's performance is graded as an A, B, C, D, or F, or when an experiment is judged successful, unsuccessful, or inconclusive. To treat this kind of problem in general, let us consider the case where there are n independent trials, with each trial permitting k mutually exclusive outcomes whose respective probabilities are $p_1, p_2, \ldots, p_k$ (with $\sum_{i=1}^{k} p_i = 1$). Referring to the outcomes as being of the first kind, the second kind, . . . , and the kth kind, we shall be interested in the probability $f(x_1, x_2, \ldots x_k)$ of getting x_1 outcomes of the first kind, x_2 outcomes of the second kind, . . . , and x_k outcomes of the kth kind, with $\sum_{i=1}^{k} x_i = n$. Using arguments similar to those which we employed in deriving the equation for the binomial distribution in Section 4.2, it can be shown that the desired probability is given by

Multinomial
distribution

$$f(x_1, x_2, \ldots, x_k) = \frac{n!}{x_1! x_2! \cdots x_k!} p_1^{x_1} \cdot p_2^{x_2} \cdots p_k^{x_k}$$

for $x_i = 0, 1, \ldots, n$ for each i, subject to the restriction $\sum_{i=1}^{k} x_i = n$. The **joint probability distribution** whose values are given by these probabilities is called the **multinomial distribution;** it owes its name to the fact that for the various values of the x_i the probabilities are given by the corresponding terms of the multinomial expansion of $(p_1 + p_2 + \cdots + p_k)^n$.

EXAMPLE **Calculating a probability using the multinomial distribution**
The probabilities that the light bulb of a certain kind of slide projector will last fewer than 40 hours of continuous use, anywhere from 40 to 80 hours of continuous use, or more than 80 hours of continuous use, are 0.30, 0.50, and 0.20. Find the probability that among eight such bulbs 2 will last fewer than 40 hours, 5 will last anywhere from 40 to 80 hours, and 1 will last more than 80 hours.

Solution   Substituting $n = 8$, $x_1 = 2$, $x_2 = 5$, $x_3 = 1$, $p_1 = 0.30$, $p_2 = 0.50$, and $p_3 = 0.20$ into the formula, we get

$$f(2, 5, 1) = \frac{8!}{2!5!1!}(0.30)^2(0.50)^5(0.20)^1$$

$$= 0.0945 \qquad \qquad \checkmark$$

EXERCISES

4.70 Suppose that the probabilities are, respectively, 0.40, 0.40, and 0.20 that in city driving a certain kind of imported car will average less than 22 miles per gallon, anywhere from 22 to 25 miles per gallon, or more than 25 miles per gallon. Find the probability that among 12 such cars tested, 4 will average less than 22 miles per gallon, 6 will average anywhere from 22 to 25 miles per gallon, and 2 will average more than 25 miles per gallon.

4.71 As can easily be shown, the probabilities of getting 0, 1, or 2 heads with a pair of balanced coins are $\frac{1}{4}$, $\frac{1}{2}$, and $\frac{1}{4}$. What is the probability of getting 2 tails twice, 1 head and 1 tail 3 times, and 2 heads once in 6 tosses of a pair of balanced coins?

4.72 Suppose that the probabilities are, respectively, 0.60, 0.20, 0.10, and 0.10 that an income tax form will be filled out correctly, that it will contain an error favoring the taxpayer, that it will contain an error favoring the government, or that it will contain both kinds of errors. Find the probability that among 10 of the income tax forms randomly selected for audit 5 will be correct, 3 will contain an error favoring the taxpayer, 1 will contain an error favoring the government, and 1 will contain both kinds of errors.

4.73 Using the same sort of reasoning as in the derivation of the formula for the hypergeometric distribution, we can derive a formula which is analogous to the multinomial distribution but applies to sampling without replacement. If a set of N objects contains a_1 objects of the first kind, a_2 objects of the second kind, ..., and a_k objects of the kth kind, so that $a_1 + a_2 + \cdots + a_k = N$, the number of ways in which we can select x_1 objects of the first kind, x_2 objects of the second kind, ..., and x_k objects of the kth kind is given by the product of the number of ways in which we can select x_1 of the a_1 objects of the first kind, x_2 of the a_2 objects of the second kind, ..., and x_k of the a_k objects of the kth kind. Thus, the probability of getting that many objects of each kind is simply this product divided by the total number of ways in which $x_1 + x_2 + \cdots + x_k = n$ objects can be selected from the whole set of N objects.

(a) Write a formula for the probability of obtaining x_1 objects of the first kind, x_2 objects of the second kind, ... and x_k objects of the kth kind.

(b) If 20 defective glass bricks include 10 that have cracks but no discoloration, 7 that are discolored but have no cracks, and 3 that have cracks and discoloration, what is the probability that among 6 of the bricks chosen at random for further checks 3 will have cracks only, 2 will only be discolored, and 1 will have cracks as well as discoloration?

4.10 Simulation

In recent years, simulation techniques have been applied to many problems in the various sciences, and if the processes which are being simulated involve an element of chance, these techniques are referred to as **Monte Carlo methods.** Very often, the use of Monte Carlo simulation eliminates the cost of building and operating expensive equipment; it is used, for instance, in the study of collisions of photons with electrons, the scattering of neutrons, and similar complicated phenomena. Monte Carlo methods are also useful in situations where direct experimentation is impossible—say, in studies of the spread of cholera epidemics, which, of course, are not induced experimentally on human populations. In addition, Monte Carlo techniques are sometimes applied to the solution of mathematical problems which actually cannot be solved by direct means, or where a direct solution is too costly or requires too much time.

A classical example of the use of Monte Carlo methods in the solution of a problem of pure mathematics is the determination of π (the ratio of the circumference of a circle to its diameter) by probabilistic means. Early in the eighteenth century, George de Buffon, a French naturalist, proved that if a very fine needle of length a is thrown at random on a board ruled with equidistant parallel lines, the probability that the needle will intersect one of the lines is $2a/\pi b$, where b is the distance between the parallel lines. What is remarkable about this fact is that it involves the constant $\pi = 3.1415926\ldots$, which in elementary geometry is approximated by the circumferences of regular polygons enclosed in a circle of radius $\frac{1}{2}$. Buffon's result implies that if such a needle is actually tossed a great many times, the proportion of the time it crosses one of the lines gives an estimate of $2a/\pi b$ and, hence, an estimate of π since a and b are known. Early experiments of this kind yielded an estimate of 3.1596 (based on 5,000 trials) and an estimate of 3.155 (based on 3,204 trials) in the middle of the nineteenth century.

Although Monte Carlo methods are sometimes based on actual gambling devices (for example, the needle tossing in the estimation of π), it is usually expedient to use so-called tables of **random digits** or **random numbers.** Tables of random numbers consist of many pages on which the digits of $0, 1, 2, \ldots$, and 9 are set down in a "random" fashion, much as they would appear if they were generated one at a time by a gambling device giving each digit an equal probability of being selected. Actually, we could construct such tables ourselves—say, by repeatedly drawing numbered slips out of a hat or by using a perfectly constructed spinner—but in practice such tables are usually generated by means of electronic computers.

Although tables of random numbers are constructed so that the digits can be looked upon as values of a random variable having the discrete uniform distribution $f(x) = \frac{1}{10}$ for $x = 0, 1, 2, \ldots$, or 9, they can be used to simulate values of any discrete random variable, and even continuous random variables.

To illustrate the use of a table of random numbers, let us show how we can play "head or tails" without actually flipping a coin. Letting 0, 2, 4, 6, and 8 represent heads and 1, 3, 5, 7, and 9 represent tails, we might arbitrarily choose the fourth column of the first page of Table 7, start at the top and go down the page. Thus, we get 6, 2, 7, 5, 5, 0, 1, 8, 6, 3, . . . , and we interpret this as head, head, tail, tail, tail, head, tail, head, head, tail, ...

Repeated flips of any number of coins, say, three coins, can be simulated in the same way. If we arbitrarily choose the ninth, tenth, and eleventh columns of the second page of Table 7, start at row 11 and go down the page, we get 480, 280, 085, 265, 303, 288, 295, 388, 127, 222, . . . , and, counting the number of even digits in each case, we interpret this as 3, 3, 2, 2, 1, 3, 1, 2, 1, 3 . . . , heads. If we did not want to count even digits, we could make use of the fact that the probabilities of getting 0, 1, 2, or 3 heads are $\frac{1}{8}, \frac{3}{8}, \frac{3}{8}$, and $\frac{1}{8}$, and use the following scheme:

Number of heads	Probability	Random digits
0	$\frac{1}{8}$	0
1	$\frac{3}{8}$	1, 2, 3
2	$\frac{3}{8}$	4, 5, 6
3	$\frac{1}{8}$	7

Ignoring the digits 8 and 9 wherever they may occur, we would thus interpret the random digits 4, 8, 1, 1, 1, 9, 3, 3, 3, 7, 6, 3, 6, 2, 6, 5, 8, 9, 3, 1, 0, and 6 (in the twenty-fifth row of the third page of Table 7) as getting 2, 1, 1, 1, 1, 1, 1, 3, 2, 1, 2, 1, 2, 2, 1, 1, 0, and 2 heads in 18 tosses of three coins.

Of the two methods used in the proceeding example, the first has the disadvantage that we have to count how many even digits there are in each case, and the second has the disadvantage that we have to ignore 8 and 9. To avoid such waste of effort and time, we could have used the following scheme:

Number of heads	Probability	Cumulative probability	Random numbers
0	0.125	0.125	000–124
1	0.375	0.500	125–499
2	0.375	0.875	500–874
3	0.125	1.000	875–999

Here we used three-digit random numbers because the probabilities are given to three decimals, and we allocated 125 (or one-eighth) of the 1,000 random numbers from 000 to 999 to 0 heads, 375 (or three-eighths) to 1 head, 375 (or three-eighths) to 2 heads, and 125 (or one-eighth) to 3 heads. The column of "or less" **cumulative probabilities** was added to facilitate the assignment of the random numbers. Observe that in each case the last random digit is one less than the number formed by the three decimal digits of the corresponding cumulative probability.

With this scheme, if we arbitrarily use the twenty-second, twenty-third, and twenty-fourth columns of the first page of Table 7, starting with the sixth row and going down the page, we get 197, 565, 157, 520, 946, 951, 948, 568, 586, and 089, and we interpret this as 1, 2, 1, 2, 3, 3, 3, 2, 2, and 0 heads.

The method we have illustrated here with reference to a game of chance can be used to simulate observations of any random variable with a given probability distribution.

EXAMPLE

Suppose that the probabilities are 0.082, 0.205, 0.256, 0.214, 0.134, 0.067, 0.028, 0.010, 0.003, and 0.001 that 0, 1, 2, 3, ..., or 9 cars will arrive at a toll booth of a turnpike during any one-minute interval in the early afternoon.

(a) Distribute the three-digit random numbers from 000 to 999 among the 10 values of this random variable, so that they can be used to simulate the arrival of cars at the toll booth.

(b) Use the fifth, sixth, and seventh columns of the fifth page of Table 7, starting from the top and going down the page, to simulate the arrival of cars at the toll booth during 20 one-minute intervals in the early afternoon.

Solution

(a) Calculating the cumulative probabilities and following the suggestion given above, we arrive at the following scheme:

Number of cars	Probability	Cumulative probability	Random numbers
0	0.082	0.082	000–081
1	0.205	0.287	082–286
2	0.256	0.543	287–542
3	0.214	0.757	543–756
4	0.134	0.891	757–890
5	0.067	0.958	891–957
6	0.028	0.986	958–985
7	0.010	0.996	986–995
8	0.003	0.999	996–998
9	0.001	1.000	999

(b) Following the instructions, we get the random numbers 036, 417, 962, 458, 778, 541, 869, 379, 973, 553, 325, 674, 907, 710, 709, 499, 493, 384, 346, and 301, and this means that 0, 2, 6, 2, 4, 2, 4, 2, 6, 3, 2, 3, 5, 3, 3, 2, 2, 2, 2, and 2 cars arrived at the toll booth during the 20 one-minute intervals. ✔

EXERCISES

4.74 Letting any 5 digits represent heads and the other 5 digits represent tails, use random numbers to simulate 100 flips of a balanced coin.

4.75 Using the digits 1, 2, 3, 4, 5, and 6 to represent the corresponding faces of a die (and omitting 0, 7, 8, and 9), simulate 120 rolls of a balanced die.

4.76 The probabilities that a computer software salesperson will make 0, 1, 2, 3, 4, or 5 sales on any one day are 0.14, 0.28, 0.27, 0.18, 0.09, and 0.04.

(a) Distribute the two-digit random numbers from 00 to 99 among the 6 values of this random variable, so that the corresponding random numbers can be used to simulate the salesperson's sales.

(b) Use the result of part (a) to simulate the salesperson's sales on 25 days.

4.77 With reference to the example on page 126 and the probabilities shown in Figure 4.7, distribute the 3-digit random numbers from 000 to 999 among the 11 values of the random variable, and simulate the number of generators that fail within the given year, over a period of 20 years.

4.78 Depending on the availability of parts, a company can manufacture 3, 4, 5, or 6 units of a certain item per week with corresponding probabilities of 0.10, 0.40, 0.30, and 0.20. The probabilities that there will be a weekly demand for 0, 1, 2, 3, . . . , or 8 units are, respectively, 0.05, 0.10, 0.30, 0.30, 0.10, 0.05, 0.05, 0.04, and 0.01. If a unit is sold during the week that it is made, it will yield a profit of $100; this profit is reduced by $20 for each week that a unit has to be stored. Use random numbers to simulate the operations of this company for 50 consecutive weeks and estimate its expected weekly profit.

REVIEW EXERCISES

4.79 A manufacturer of digital phones has the following probability distribution for the number of defects per phone

x	f(x)
0	.89
1	.07
2	.03
3	.01

(a) Determine the probability of 2 or more defects.

(b) Is a randomly selected phone more likely to have 0 defects or 1 or more defects?

4.80 Upon reviewing recent usage of conference rooms at an engineering consulting firm, an industrial engineer determined the following probability distribution for the number of requests for a conference room per half day.

x	f(x)
0	.07
1	.15
2	.45
3	.25
4	.08

(a) Currently, the building has two conference rooms. What is the probability that the number of requests will exceed the number of rooms for a given half-day?

(b) What is the probability that the two conference rooms will not be fully utilized on a given half day?

(c) How many additional conference rooms are required so that the probability of denying a request is no more than .10?

4.81 Refer to Exercise 4.80 and obtain the

(a) mean;

(b) variance;

(c) standard deviation;

for the number of requests for conference rooms.

4.82 Determine whether the following can be probability distributions of a random variable that can take on only the values of 0, 1, and 2.

(a) $f(0) = 0.34, f(1) = 0.34$, and $f(2) = 0.34$

(b) $f(0) = 0.2, f(1) = 0.6$, and $f(2) = 0.2$

(c) $f(0) = 0.7, f(1) = 0.4$, and $f(2) = -0.1$

4.83 Check whether the following can define probability distributions, and explain your answers.

(a) $f(x) = \dfrac{x}{10}$, for $x = 0, 1, 2, 3, 4$

(b) $f(x) = \dfrac{1}{3}$, for $x = -1, 0, 1$

(c) $f(x) = \dfrac{(x-1)^2}{4}$, for $x = 0, 1, 2, 3$

4.84 A basketball player makes 90% of her free throws. What is the probability she will miss for the first time on the seventh shot?

4.85 If the probabiltiy is 0.20 that a downtime of an automated production process will exceed 2 minutes, find the probability that 3 of 8 downtimes of the process will exceed 2 minutes using

(a) the formula for the binomial distribution;

(b) Table 1.

4.86 If the probability that a fluorescent light has a useful life of at least 500 hours is 0.85, find the probabilities that among 20 such lights

(a) 18 will have a useful life of at least 500 hours;

(b) at least 15 will have a useful life of at least 500 hours;

(c) at least two will not have a useful life of at least 500 hours.

4.87 In 15 experiments studying the electrical behavior of single cells, 11 use microelectrodes made of metal and the other 4 use microelectrodes made from glass tubing. If 2 of the experiments are to be terminated for financial reasons, and they are selected at random, what are the probabilities that

(a) neither uses microeletrodes made from glass tubing;

(b) only one uses microelectrodes made from glass tubing;

(c) both use microelectrodes made from glass tubing?

4.88 As can be easily verified by means of the formula for the binomial distribution, the probabilities of getting 0, 1, 2, or 3 heads in 3 flips of a coin whose probability of heads is 0.4 are 0.216, 0.432, 0.288 and 0.064. Find the mean of this probability distribution using

(a) the formula that defines μ;

(b) the special formula for the mean of a binomial distribution.

4.89 With reference to Exercise 4.88, find the variance of the probability distribution using

(a) the formula that defines σ^2;

(b) the special formula for the variance of a binomial distribution.

4.90 Find the mean and the standard deviation of the distribution of each of the following random variables (having binomial distributions).

(a) The number of heads in 555 flips of a balanced coin.

(b) The number of 6's in 300 rolls of a balanced die.

(c) The number of defectives in a sample of 700 parts made by a machine, when the probability is 0.03 that any one of the parts is defective.

4.91 Use the Poisson distribution to approximate the binomial probability $b(2; 100, 0.02)$.

4.92 With reference to Exercise 4.87, find the mean and the variance of the distribution of the number of microelectrodes made from glass tubing using

(a) the probabilities obtained in that exercise;

(b) the special formulas for the mean and the variance of a hypergeometric distribution.

4.93 The daily number of orders filled by the parts department of a repair shop is a random variable with $\mu = 142$ and $\sigma = 12$. According to Chebyshev's theorem, with what probability can we assert that on any one day it will fill between 82 and 202 orders?

4.94 Records show that the probability is 0.00004 that a car will have a flat tire while driving through a certain tunnel. Use the formula for the Poisson distribution to approximate the probability that at least 2 of 10,000 cars passing through the tunnel will have a flat tire.

4.95 The number of weekly breakdowns of a computer is a random variable having a Poisson distribution with $\lambda = 0.3$. What is the probability that the computer will operate without a breakdown for 2 consecutive weeks?

4.96 A manufacturer determines that a big screen TV set had probabilities of 0.8, 0.15, 0.05, respectively, of being placed in the categories acceptable, minor defect, or major defect. If three TVs are inspected,

(a) find the probability that 2 are acceptable and 1 is a minor defect;

(b) find the marginal distribution of the number in minor defect;

(c) Compare your answer in (b) with the binomial probabilities $b(x; 3, 0.15)$. Comment.

4.97 Suppose that the probabilities are 0.2466, 0.3452, 0.2417, 0.1128, 0.0395, 0.0111, 0.0026, and 0.0005 that there will be 0, 1, 2, 3, 4, 5, 6, or 7 polluting spills in the Great Lakes on any one day.

(a) Distribute the four-digit random numbers from 0000 to 9999 to the 8 values of this random variable, so that the corresponding random numbers can be used to simulate daily polluting spills in the Great Lakes.

(b) Use the result of part (a) to simulate the numbers of polluting spills in the Great Lakes in 30 days.

KEY TERMS

(with page references)

Probability Densities

Continuous sample spaces and continuous random variables arise when we deal with quantities that are measured on a continuous scale—for instance, when we measure the speed of a car, the amount of alcohol in a person's blood, the efficiency of a solar collector, or the tensile strength of a new alloy.

In this chapter we shall learn how to determine, and work with, probabilities relating to continuous sample spaces and continuous random variables. The introduction to probability densities in Section 5.1 is followed by a discussion of the normal distribution in Sections 5.2 and 5.3, and various other special probability densities in Sections 5.4 through 5.9. Problems involving more than one random variable are discussed in Section 5.10. A method for checking whether a data set appears to be generated by a normal distribution is introduced in Section 5.11.

5.1 Continuous Random Variables

When we first introduced the concept of a random variable in Chapter 4, we presented it as a real-valued function defined over the sample space of an experiment, and we illustrated this idea with the random variable giving the number of preferred ratings which a lawn mower received, assigning the numbers 0, 1, 2, or 3 (whichever was appropriate) to the 18 possible outcomes of the experiment. In the continuous case, where random variables can assume values on a continuous scale, the procedure is very much the same. The outcomes of an experiment are represented by the points on a line segment or a line, and the value of a random variable is a number appropriately assigned to each point by means of some rule or equation. When the value of a random variable is given directly by a measurement or observation, we usually do not bother to differentiate between the value of the random variable, the measurement which we obtain, and the outcome of the experiment, which is the corresponding point on the real axis. If an experiment consists of determining what force is required to break a given tensile-test specimen, the result itself, say, 138.4 pounds, is the value of the random variable, X, with which we are concerned. There is no real need in that case to add that the sample space of the experiment consists of all (or part of) the points on the positive real axis. In general, we shall write $P(a \leq X \leq b)$ for the probability associated with the points of the sample space for which the value of a random variable falls on the interval from a to b.

The problem of defining probabilities in connection with continuous sample spaces and continuous random variables involves some complications. To illustrate the nature of these complications, let us consider the following situation: Suppose we want to know the probability that if an accident occurs on a freeway whose length is 200 miles, it will happen at some given location or, perhaps, some particular stretch of the road. The outcomes of this experiment can be looked upon as a continuum of points, namely, those on the continuous interval from 0 to 200. Suppose the probability that the accident occurs on any interval of length L is $L/200$, with L measured in miles. Note that this arbitrary assignment of probability is consistent with Axioms 1 and 2 on page 67, since the probabilities are all nonnegative and less than or equal to 1, and $P(S) = \frac{200}{200} = 1$. Of course, we are considering so far only events represented by intervals which form part of the line segment from 0 to 200. Using Axiom 3′ on page 124, we can also obtain probabilities of events which are not intervals but which can be represented by the union of finitely many or countably many intervals. Thus, for two nonoverlapping intervals of length L_1 and L_2 we have a probability of

$$\frac{L_1 + L_2}{200}$$

and for an infinite sequence of nonoverlapping intervals of length $L_1, L_2, L_3, \ldots$, we have a probability of

$$\frac{L_1 + L_2 + L_3 + \cdots}{200}$$

Note that the probability that the accident occurs at any given point is equal to zero because we can look upon a point as an interval of zero length. However, the probability that the accident occurs in a very short interval is positive; for instance, for an interval of length 1 foot the probability is $(5280 \times 200)^{-1} = 9.5 \times 10^{-7}$.

Thus, in extending the concept of probability to the continuous case, we again use Axioms 1, 2, and 3′, but we shall have to restrict the meaning of the term *event*. So far as practical considerations are concerned, this restriction is of no consequence; we simply do not assign probabilities to some rather abstruse point sets, which cannot be expressed as the unions or intersections of finitely many or countably many intervals.

The way in which we assigned probabilities in the preceding example is, of course, very special; it is similar in nature to the way in which we assign equal probabilities to the six faces of a die, heads and tails, the 52 cards in a standard deck, and so forth. To treat the problem of associating probabilities with continuous random variables generally, suppose we are interested in the probability that a given random variable will take on a value on the interval from a to b, where a and b are constants with $a \leq b$. Suppose, furthermore, that we divide the interval from a to b into n equal subintervals of width Δx containing, respectively, the points x_1, $x_2, \ldots, x_n$, and that the probability that the random variable will take on a value in the subinterval containing x_i is given by $f(x_i) \cdot \Delta x$. Then, the probability that the random variable with which we are concerned will take on a value in the interval from a to b is given by

$$P(a \leq X \leq b) = \sum_{i=1}^{n} f(x_i) \cdot \Delta x$$

Now, if f is an integrable function defined for all values of the random variable with which we are concerned, we shall define the probability that the value of the random variable falls between a and b by letting $\Delta x \to 0$, namely, as

$$P(a \leq X \leq b) = \int_{a}^{b} f(x)dx$$

This definition of probability in the continuous case presupposes the existence of an appropriate function f which, integrated from any constant a to any constant b (with $a \leq b$), gives the probability that the corresponding random variable takes on a value on the interval from a to b. Note that the value $f(x)$ does not give the probability that the corresponding random variable takes on the value x; in the continuous case, probabilities are given by integrals and not by the values $f(x)$.

To obtain the probability that a random variable will actually take on a given value x, we might first determine the probability that it will take on a value on the interval from $x - \Delta x$ to $x + \Delta x$, and then let $\Delta x \to 0$. However, if we did this it would become apparent that the result is always zero. The fact that the probability is always zero that a continuous random variable will take on any given value x should not be disturbing. Indeed, our definition of probability for the continuous case provides a remarkably good model for dealing with measurements or observations. Owing to the limits of our ability to measure, experimental data never seem to come from a continuous sample space. Thus, while temperatures are fruitfully thought of as points on a continuous scale, any temperature measurement actually represents an interval on this scale. If we report a temperature measurement of 74.8 degrees centigrade, we really mean that the temperature lies in the interval from 74.75 to 74.85 degrees centigrade, and not that it is exactly $74.800 \cdots$.

It is important to add that when we say that there is a zero probability that a random variable will take on any given value x, this does not mean that it is impossible that the random variable will take on the value x. In the continuous case, a zero probability does not imply logical impossibility, but the whole matter is largely academic since, owing to the limitations of our ability to measure and observe, we are always interested in probabilities connected with intervals and not with isolated points.

As an immediate consequence of the fact that in the continuous case probabilities associated with individual points are always zero, we find that if we speak of the probability associated with the interval from a to b, it does not matter whether either endpoint is included. Symbolically,

$$P(a \leq X \leq b) = P(a \leq X < b) = P(a < X \leq b) = P(a < X < b)$$

Drawing an analogy with the concept of a density function in physics, we call the functions f, whose existence we stipulated in extending our definition of probability to the continuous cases, **probability density functions,** or simply **probability densities.** Whereas density functions are integrated to obtain weights, probability density functions are integrated to obtain probabilities. We will follow the common practice of also calling $f(x)$ the probability density function with the understanding that we are referring to the function f which assigns the value $f(x)$ to x, for each x that is a possible value for the random variable X.

Since a probability density, integrated between any two constants a and b, gives the probability that a random variable assumes a value between these limits, f cannot be just any real-valued integrable function. However, if we impose the conditions that

$$f(x) \geq 0 \qquad \text{for all } x$$

and

$$\int_{-\infty}^{\infty} f(x)dx = 1$$

it can be shown that the axioms of probability (with the modification about events discussed on page 144) are satisfied. Note the similarity between these conditions and those for probability distributions given on page 101.

As in the discrete case, we shall write as $F(x)$ the probability that a random variable with the probability density $f(x)$ takes on a value less than or equal to x, and we shall again refer to the corresponding function F as the **distribution function** of the random variable. Thus, for any value x, $F(x) = P(X \leq x)$ is the area under the probability density function over the interval $-\infty$ to x. In the usual calculus notation for the integral,

$$F(x) = \int_{-\infty}^{x} f(t)dt$$

Consequently, the probability that the random variable will take on a value on the interval from a to b is $F(b) - F(a)$, and according to the fundamental theorem of integral calculus it follows that

$$\frac{dF(x)}{dx} = f(x)$$

wherever this derivative exists.

EXAMPLE

Calculating probabilities from the probability density function
If a random variable has the probability density

$$f(x) = \begin{cases} 2e^{-2x} & \text{for } x > 0 \\ 0 & \text{for } x \leq 0 \end{cases}$$

find the probabilities that it will take on a value

(a) between 1 and 3;

(b) greater than 0.5.

Solution   Evaluating the necessary integrals, we get

$$\int_1^3 2e^{-2x}dx = e^{-2} - e^{-6} = 0.133$$

for part (a) and

$$\int_{0.5}^{\infty} 2e^{-2x}dx = e^{-1} = 0.368$$

for part (b).

Note that in the preceding example we made the domain of f include all the real numbers even though the probability is zero that x will be negative. This is a practice we shall follow throughout the book. It is also apparent from the graph of this function in Figure 5.1 that it has a discontinuity at $x = 0$; indeed, a probability density need not be everywhere continuous, as long as it is integrable between any two limits a and b (with $a \leq b$.)

EXAMPLE

Determining a distribution function from its density function
With reference to the preceding example, find the distribution function and use it to determine the probability that the random variable will take on a value less than or equal to 1.

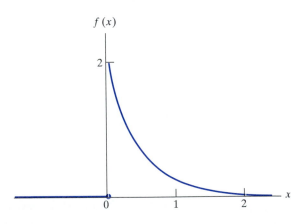

FIGURE 5.1 Graph of probability density.

Solution Performing the necessary integrations, we get

$$F(x) = \begin{cases} 0 & \text{for } x \leq 0 \\ \int_0^x 2e^{-2t}dt = 1 - e^{-2x} & \text{for } x > 0 \end{cases}$$

and substitution of $x = 1$ yields

$$F(1) = 1 - e^{-2} = 0.865 \qquad \checkmark$$

Note that the distribution function of this example is nondecreasing and that $F(-\infty) = 0$ and $F(\infty) = 1$. Indeed, it follows by definition that these properties are shared by all distribution functions.

EXAMPLE **A probability density function assigns probability one to $(-\infty, \infty)$**
Find k so that the following can serve as the probability density of a random variable:

$$f(x) = \begin{cases} 0 & \text{for } x \leq 0 \\ kxe^{-4x^2} & \text{for } x > 0 \end{cases}$$

Solution To satisfy the first of the two conditions on page 145, k must be nonnegative, and to satisfy the second condition we must have

$$\int_{-\infty}^{\infty} f(x)dx = \int_0^{\infty} kxe^{-4x^2}dx = \int_0^{\infty} \frac{k}{8} \cdot e^{-u}du = \frac{k}{8} = 1$$

so that $k = 8$. $\qquad \checkmark$

The statistical measures that are used to describe probability densities are very similar to the ones which we used to describe probability distributions. Replacing summations with integrals, we define the **kth moment about the origin** as

$$\mu_k' = \int_{-\infty}^{\infty} x^k \cdot f(x)dx$$

analogous to the definition we gave on page 118. The first moment about the origin is again referred to as the **mean,** and it is denoted by μ. It is also called the expected value of a random variable having the probability density $f(x)$.

Mean of a probability density

$$\mu = \int_{-\infty}^{\infty} xf(x)dx$$

We also define the **kth moment about the mean** as

$$\mu_k = \int_{-\infty}^{\infty} (x - \mu)^k \cdot f(x)dx$$

In particular, the second moment about the mean is again referred to as the **variance** and it is written as σ^2; as before, it measures the spread of a probability density in the sense that it gives the expected value of the squared deviation from the mean.

Variance of a probability density

$$\sigma^2 = \int_{-\infty}^{\infty} (x - \mu)^2 f(x) dx = \int_{-\infty}^{\infty} x^2 f(x) dx - \mu^2$$

Also, σ is again referred to as the **standard deviation.**

EXAMPLE

Determining the mean and variance using the probability density function
With reference to the example on page 146, find the mean and the variance of the given probability density.

Solution   Performing the necessary integrations, using integrations by parts, we get

$$\mu = \int_{-\infty}^{\infty} x f(x) dx = \int_{0}^{\infty} x \cdot 2e^{-2x} dx = \frac{1}{2}$$

and

$$\sigma^2 = \int_{-\infty}^{\infty} (x - \mu)^2 f(x) dx = \int_{0}^{\infty} \left(x - \frac{1}{2} \right)^2 \cdot 2e^{-2x} dx = \frac{1}{4}$$

EXERCISES

5.1   Verify that the function of the example on page 146 is, in fact, a probability density.

5.2   If the probability density of a random variable is given by

$$f(x) = \begin{cases} kx^3 & 0 < x < 1 \\ 0 & \text{elsewhere} \end{cases}$$

find the value k and the probability that the random variable takes on a value

(a)   between $\frac{1}{4}$ and $\frac{3}{4}$;

(b)   greater than $\frac{2}{3}$.

5.3   With reference to the preceding exercise, find the corresponding distribution function and use it to determine the probabilities that a random variable having this distribution function will take on a value

(a)   greater than 0.8;

(b)   between 0.2 and 0.4.

5.4   If the probability density of a random variable is given by

$$f(x) = \begin{cases} x & \text{for } 0 < x < 1 \\ 2 - x & \text{for } 1 \le x < 2 \\ 0 & \text{elsewhere} \end{cases}$$

find the probabilities that a random variable having this probability density will take on a value

(a) between 0.2 and 0.8;

(b) between 0.6 and 1.2.

5.5 With reference to the preceding exercise, find the corresponding distribution function, and use it to determine the probabilities that a random variable having this distribution function will take on a value

(a) greater than 1.8;

(b) between 0.4 and 1.6.

5.6 Given the probability density $f(x) = \dfrac{k}{1 + x^2}$ for $-\infty < x < \infty$, find k.

5.7 If the distribution function of a random variable is given by

$$F(x) = \begin{cases} 1 - \dfrac{4}{x^2} & \text{for } x > 2 \\ 0 & \text{for } x \le 2 \end{cases}$$

find the probabilities that this random variable will take on a value

(a) less than 3;

(b) between 4 and 5.

5.8 Find the probability density that corresponds to the distribution function of Exercise 5.7. Are there any points at which it is undefined? Also sketch the graphs of the distribution function and the probability density.

5.9 Let the phase error in a tracking device have probability density

$$f(x) = \begin{cases} \cos x & 0 < x < \pi/2 \\ 0 & \text{elsewhere} \end{cases}$$

Find the probability that the phase error is

(a) between 0 and $\pi/4$;

(b) greater than $\pi/3$.

5.10 The mileage (in thousands of miles) that car owners get with a certain kind of tire is a random variable having the probability density

$$f(x) = \begin{cases} \frac{1}{20}e^{-x/20} & \text{for } x > 0 \\ 0 & \text{for } x \le 0 \end{cases}$$

Find the probabilities that one of these tires will last

(a) at most 10,000 miles;

(b) anywhere from 16,000 to 24,000 miles;

(c) at least 30,000 miles.

5.11 In a certain city, the daily consumption of electric power (in millions of kilowatt-hours) is a random variable having the probability density

$$f(x) = \begin{cases} \frac{1}{9}xe^{-x/3} & \text{for } x > 0 \\ 0 & \text{for } x \le 0 \end{cases}$$

If the city's power plant has a daily capacity of 12 million kilowatt-hours, what is the probability that this power supply will be inadequate on any given day?

5.12 Prove that the identity $\sigma^2 = \mu_2' - \mu^2$ holds for any probability density for which these moments exist.

5.13 Find μ and σ^2 for the probability density of Exercise 5.2.

5.14 Find μ and σ^2 for the probability density of Exercise 5.4.

5.15 Find μ and σ for the probability density obtained in Exercise 5.8.

5.16 Find μ and σ for the distribution of the phase error of Exercise 5.9.

5.17 Find μ for the distribution of the mileages of Exercise 5.10.

5.18 Show that μ_2' and, hence, σ^2 do not exist for the probability density of Exercise 5.6.

5.2 The Normal Distribution

Among the special probability densities we shall study in this chapter, the **normal probability density,** usually referred to simply as the **normal distribution,** is by far the most important.[†] It was studied first in the eighteenth century when scientists observed an astonishing degree of regularity in errors of measurement. They found that the patterns (distributions) they observed were closely approximated by a continuous distribution which they referred to as the "normal curve of errors" and attributed to the laws of chance. The equation of the normal probability density, whose graph (shaped like the cross section of a bell) is shown in Figure 5.2, is

Normal distribution

$$f(x; \mu, \sigma^2) = \frac{1}{\sqrt{2\pi}\,\sigma} e^{-(x-\mu)^2/2\sigma^2} \qquad -\infty < x < \infty$$

and in Exercises 5.42 and 5.43, the reader will be asked to verify that its parameters μ and σ are indeed its mean and its standard deviation.

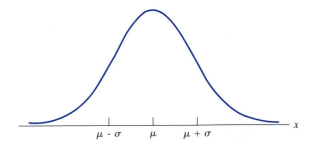

FIGURE 5.2 Graph of normal probability density.

Since the normal probability density cannot be integrated in closed form between every pair of limits a and b, probabilities relating to normal distributions are usually obtained from special tables, such as Table 3 at the end of this book. This table pertains to the **standard normal distribution,** namely, the normal distribution with $\mu = 0$ and $\sigma = 1$, and its entries are the values of

[†]The words *density* and *distribution* are often used interchangeably in the literature of applied statistics.

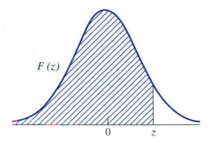

FIGURE 5.3 The standard normal probabilities $F(z) = P(Z \le z)$.

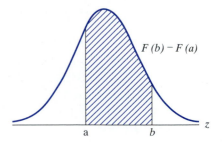

FIGURE 5.4 The standard normal probability $F(b) - F(a) = P(a < Z \le b)$.

$$F(z) = \frac{1}{\sqrt{2\pi}} \int_{-\infty}^{z} e^{-t^2/2} dt = P(Z \le z)$$

for positive or negative $z = 0.00, 0.01, 0.02, \ldots, 3.49$, and also $z = 3.50$, $z = 4.00$, and $z = 5.00$. The cumulative probabilities $F(z)$ correspond to the area under the standard normal density to the left of z, as shown by the shaded area in Figure 5.3.

To find the probability that a random variable having the standard normal distribution will take on a value between a and b, we use the equation $P(a < Z \le b) = F(b) - F(a)$, as shown by the shaded area in Figure 5.4.

We also sometimes make use of the identity $F(-z) = 1 - F(z)$, which the reader will be asked to verify in Exercise 5.41 on page 160.

EXAMPLE

Calculating some standard normal probabilities
Find the probabilities that a random variable having the standard normal distribution will take on a value

(a) between 0.87 and 1.28;
(b) between −0.34 and 0.62;
(c) greater than 0.85;
(d) greater than −0.65.

Solution   It is helpful to first indicate the area in a graph as in Figure 5.5. Looking up the necessary values in Table 3, we get

$$F(1.28) - F(0.87) = 0.8997 - 0.8078$$
$$= 0.0919$$

for part (a),

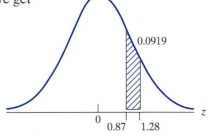

FIGURE 5.5 $P(0.87 < Z < 1.28)$.

As indicated in Figure 5.6 for part (b),

$$F(0.62) - F(-0.34) = 0.7324 - 0.3669$$
$$= 0.3655$$

FIGURE 5.6 $P(-0.34 < Z < 0.62)$.

As indicated in Figure 5.7 for part (c),

$$1 - F(0.85) = 1 - 0.8023$$
$$= 0.1977$$

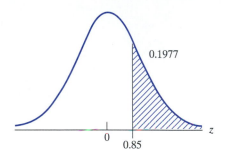

FIGURE 5.7 $P(Z > 0.85)$.

As indicated in Figure 5.8 for part (d),

$$1 - F(-0.65) = 1 - 0.2578 = 0.7422$$

or, alternatively, $1 - F(-0.65) = 1 - [1 - F(0.65)]$

$$= F(0.65)$$
$$= 0.7422$$

FIGURE 5.8 $P(Z > -0.65)$.

There are also problems in which we are given probabilities relating to standard normal distributions and asked to find the corresponding values of z.

Let z_α be such that the probability is α that it will be exceeded by a random variable having the standard normal distribution. That is, $\alpha = P(Z > z_\alpha)$ as illustrated in Figure 5.9.

The results of the example that follows will be used extensively in subsequent chapters.

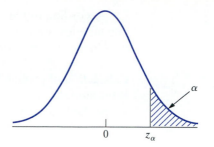

FIGURE 5.9 The z_α
notation for a standard
normal distribution.

EXAMPLE

Two important values for z_α
Find

(a) $z_{0.01}$;
(b) $z_{0.05}$.

Solution   (a) Since $F(z_{0.01}) = 0.99$, we look for the entry in Table 3 which is closest
to 0.99 and get 0.9901 corresponding to $z = 2.33$. Thus $z_{0.01} = 2.33$.
(b) Since $F(z_{0.05}) = 0.95$, we look for the entry in Table 3 which is closest to 0.95
and get 0.9495 and 0.9505 corresponding to $z = 1.64$ and $z = 1.65$. Thus, by interpolation, $z_{0.05} = 1.645$. ✔

To use Table 3 in connection with a random variable X which has a normal distribution with the mean μ and the variance σ^2, we refer to the corresponding **standardized random variable,**

$$Z = \frac{X - \mu}{\sigma}$$

which has the standard normal distribution. Thus, to find the probability that the
original random variable will take on a value less than or equal to a, we look up
$F\left(\dfrac{a - \mu}{\sigma}\right)$ in Table 3.

Also, if we want to find the probability that a random variable having the normal distribution with the mean μ and the variance σ^2 will take on a value between
a and b, we have only to calculate the probability that a random variable having
the standard normal distribution will take on a value between $\dfrac{a - \mu}{\sigma}$ and $\dfrac{b - \mu}{\sigma}$.

Normal probabilities

When X has the normal distribution with mean μ and standard deviation σ

$$P(a < X \le b) = F\left(\frac{b - \mu}{\sigma}\right) - F\left(\frac{a - \mu}{\sigma}\right)$$

According to Figure 2.8, page 21, the observations on the strength of an aluminum alloy appear to be normally distributed. The normal distribution is often used to model variation when the distribution is symmetric and has a single mode.

EXAMPLE

Calculation of probabilities using a normal distribution
If the amount of cosmic radiation to which a person is exposed while flying by jet across the United States is a random variable having the normal distribution with $\mu = 4.35$ mrem and $\sigma = 0.59$ mrem, find the probabilities that the amount of cosmic radiation to which a person will be exposed on such a flight is

(a) between 4.00 and 5.00 mrem;

(b) at least 5.50 mrem.

Solution   Looking up the necessary values in Table 3, we get

$$F\left(\frac{5.00 - 4.35}{0.59}\right) - F\left(\frac{4.00 - 4.35}{0.59}\right) = F(1.10) - F(-0.59)$$
$$= 0.8643 - 0.2776$$
$$= 0.5867$$

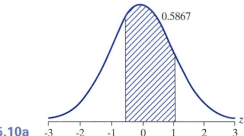

FIGURE 5.10a

corresponding to the shaded area in Figure 5.10a, for part (a), and

$$1 - F\left(\frac{5.50 - 4.35}{0.59}\right) = 1 - F(1.95)$$
$$= 1 - 0.9744$$
$$= 0.0256$$

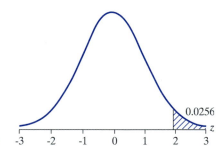

FIGURE 5.10b

corresponding to the shaded area in Figure 5.10b, for part (b).

EXAMPLE

Using normal probabilities to determine the mean fill of jars
The actual amount of instant coffee that a filling machine puts into "4-ounce" jars may be looked upon as a random variable having a normal distribution with $\sigma = 0.04$ ounces. If only 2% of the jars are to contain less than 4 ounces, what should be the mean fill of these jars?

Solution   To find μ such that $F\left(\dfrac{4 - \mu}{0.04}\right) = 0.02$, we look for the entry in Table 3 closest to 0.02 and get 0.0202 corresponding to $z = -2.05$.

As indicated in Figure 5.11,

$$\frac{4 - \mu}{0.04} = -2.05$$

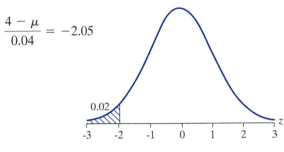

FIGURE 5.11

and, solving for μ, we find that $\mu = 4.082$ ounces.   ✔

EXAMPLE

Calculating probabilities when ln X has a normal distribution
After a large number of assays of gold content in rocks collected from an open pit mine, a mining engineer postulates that the natural log of the gold content (oz/st gold) follows a normal distribution with mean -4.6 and variance 1.21. Under this distribution, would it be unusual to get .0015 oz/st gold or less in an assay?

Solution   Because it is $\ln(X)$ that has a normal distribution, the question concerns the standardized value

$$\frac{\ln(.0015) - (-4.6)}{\sqrt{1.21}} = -1.729$$

The standard normal probability of obtaining this value or smaller (see Figure 5.12) is

$$F\left(\frac{\ln(.0015) - (-4.6)}{\sqrt{1.21}}\right) = F(-1.73) = .0419$$

FIGURE 5.12

This probability is small, so we suspect that the postulated normal distribution with mean −4.6 does not apply. An assay with this small amount of gold content could suggest that the specimen was collected outside of the vein.   ✔

Although the normal distribution applies to continuous random variables, it is often used to approximate distributions of discrete random variables. Quite often, this yields satisfactory results, provided that we make the **continuity correction** illustrated in the following example.

EXAMPLE   **A continuity correction to improve the normal approximation to a count variable**
In a certain city, the number of power outages per month is a random variable having a distribution with $\mu = 11.6$ and $\sigma = 3.3$. If this distribution can be approximated closely with a normal distribution, what is the probability that there will be at least 8 outages in any one month?

Solution   The answer is given by the area of the light region of Figure 5.13—the area to the right of 7.5, not 8. The reason for this is that the number of outages is a discrete random variable, and if we want to approximate its distribution with a normal distribution, we must "spread" its values over a continuous scale. We do this by representing each integer k by the interval from $k - \frac{1}{2}$ to $k + \frac{1}{2}$. For instance, 3 is represented by the interval from 2.5 to 3.5, 10 is represented by the interval from 9.5 to 10.5, and "at least 8" is represented by the interval to the right of 7.5. Thus, the desired probability is approximated by

$$1 - F\left(\frac{7.5 - 11.6}{3.3}\right) = 1 - F(-1.24)$$
$$= F(1.24)$$
$$= 0.8925$$

FIGURE 5.13 Diagram for example dealing with power outages.

5.3   The Normal Approximation to the Binomial Distribution

The normal distribution can be used to approximate the binomial distribution when n is large and p, the probability of a success, is close to 0.50 and, hence, not small enough to use the Poisson approximation. Thus, let us state, without proof, the following theorem:

> **Theorem 5.1** If X is a random variable having the binomial distribution with the parameters n and p, and if
>
> $$Z = \frac{X - np}{\sqrt{np(1 - p)}}$$
>
> then the limiting form of the distribution function of this standardized random variable as $n \to \infty$ is given by
>
> $$F(z) = \int_{-\infty}^{z} \frac{1}{\sqrt{2\pi}} e^{-t^2/2} dt \qquad -\infty < z < \infty$$

Normal approximation to binomial distribution

Note that although X takes on only the values $0, 1, 2, \ldots, n$, in the limit as $n \to \infty$ the distribution of the corresponding standardized random variable is continuous, and the corresponding probability density is the standard normal density. Note that in the following example, which is an application of Theorem 5.1, we use again the continuity correction given on page 156.

EXAMPLE

A normal approximation to binomial probabilities
If 20% of the memory chips made in a certain plant are defective, what are the probabilities that in a lot of 100 randomly chosen for inspection

(a) at most 15 will be defective;

(b) exactly 15 will be defective?

Solution Since $\mu = 100(0.20) = 20$ and $\sigma = \sqrt{100(0.20)(0.80)} = 4$ for the binomial distribution with $n = 100$ and $p = 0.20$, we find that the normal approximation to the binomial distribution yields

$$F\left(\frac{15.5 - 20}{4}\right) = F(-1.13)$$
$$= 0.1292$$

as indicated in Figure 5.14 for part (a) and

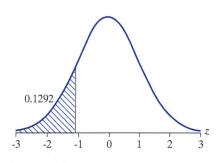

0.1292

FIGURE 5.14

$$F\left(\frac{15.5 - 20}{4}\right) - F\left(\frac{14.5 - 20}{4}\right) = F(-1.13) - F(-1.38)$$

$$= 0.1292 - 0.0838$$

$$= 0.0454$$

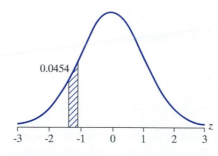

0.0454

FIGURE 5.15

as indicated in Figure 5.15 for part (b). ✔

Had we done the exact binomial calculation on a computer or used the Romig table (referred to in the bibliography) instead of using normal approximation in the preceding example, we would have obtained 0.1285 instead of 0.1292 for part (a) and 0.0481 instead of 0.0454 for part (b). Thus, it can be seen that both approximations are very close.

A good rule of thumb for the normal approximation

Use the normal approximation to the binomial distribution only when np and $n(1 - p)$ are both greater than 15.

EXERCISES

5.19 If a random variable has the standard normal distribution, find the probability that it will take on a value

(a) less than 1.50;

(b) less than −1.20;

(c) greater than 2.16;

(d) greater than −1.75.

5.20 If a random variable has the standard normal distribution, find the probability that it will take on a value

(a) between 0 and 2.7;

(b) between 1.22 and 2.43;

(c) between −1.35 and −0.35;

(d) between −1.70 and 1.35.

5.21 Find z if the probability that a random variable having the standard normal distribution will take on a value

(a) less than z is 0.9911;

(b) greater than z is 0.1093;

(c) greater than z is 0.6443;

(d) less than z is 0.0217;

(e) between $-z$ and z is 0.9298.

5.22 If a random variable has a normal distribution, what are the probabilities that it will take on a value within

(a) 1 standard deviation of the mean;

(b) 2 standard deviations of the mean;

(c) 3 standard deviations of the mean;

(d) 4 standard deviations of the mean?

5.23 Verify that

(a) $z_{0.005} = 2.575$;

(b) $z_{0.025} = 1.96$.

5.24 Given a random variable having the normal distribution with $\mu = 16.2$ and $\sigma^2 = 1.5625$, find the probabilities that it will take on a value

(a) greater than 16.8;

(b) less than 14.9;

(c) between 13.6 and 18.8;

(d) between 16.5 and 16.7.

5.25 A random variable has a normal distribution with $\mu = 62.4$. Find its standard deviation if the probability is 0.20 that it will take on a value greater than 79.2.

5.26 A random variable has a normal distribution with $\sigma = 10$. If the probability is 0.8212 that it will take on a value less than 82.5, what is the probability that it will take on a value greater than 58.3?

5.27 The time required to assemble a piece of machinery is a random variable having approximately a normal distribution with $\mu = 12.9$ minutes and $\sigma = 2.0$ minutes. What are the probabilities that the assembly of a piece of machinery of this kind will take

(a) at least 11.5 minutes;

(b) anywhere from 11.0 to 14.8 minutes?

5.28 Find the *quartiles*

$$-z_{0.25}, z_{0.50}, z_{0.25}$$

of the standard normal distribution.

5.29 In a photographic process, the developing time of prints may be looked upon as a random variable having the normal distribution with a mean of 16.28 seconds and a standard deviation of 0.12 second. Find the probability that it will take

(a) anywhere from 16.00 to 16.50 seconds to develop one of the prints;

(b) at least 16.20 seconds to develop one of the prints;

(c) at most 16.35 seconds to develop one of the prints.

5.30 With reference to the preceding exercise, for which value is the probability 0.95 that it will be exceeded by the time it takes to develop one of the prints?

5.31 Specifications for a certain job call for washers with an inside diameter of 0.300 ± 0.005 inch. If the inside diameters of the washers supplied by a given manufacturer may be looked upon as a random variable having the normal distribution with $\mu = 0.302$ inch and $\sigma = 0.003$ inch, what percentage of these washers will meet specifications?

5.32 With reference to the example on page 155, verify that if the variability of the filling machine is reduced to $\sigma = 0.025$ ounce, this will lower the required average amount of coffee to 4.05 ounces, yet keep 98% of the jars above 4 ounces.

5.33 A stamping machine produces can tops whose diameters are normally distributed with a standard deviation of 0.01 inch. At what "nominal" (mean) diameter should the machine be set so that no more than 5% of the can tops produced have diameters exceeding 3 inches?

5.34 Extruded plastic rods are automatically cut into nominal lengths of 6 inches. Actual lengths are normally distributed about a mean of 6 inches and their standard deviation is 0.06 inch.

(a) What proportion of the rods exceeds tolerance limits of 5.9 inches to 6.1 inches?

(b) To what value does the standard deviation need to be reduced if 99% of the rods must be within tolerance?

5.35 If a random variable has the binomial distribution with $n = 30$ and $p = 0.60$, use the normal approximation to determine the probabilities that it will take on

(a) the value 14;

(b) a value less than 12.

5.36 A manufacturer knows that on the average 2% of the electric toasters that he makes will require repairs within 90 days after they are sold. Use the normal approximation to the binomial distribution to determine the probability that among 1,200 of these toasters at least 30 will require repairs within the first 90 days after they are sold.

5.37 The probability that an electronic component will fail in less than 1,000 hours of continuous use is 0.25. Use the normal approximation to find the probability that among 200 such components fewer than 45 will fail in less than 1,000 hours of continuous use.

5.38 A safety engineer feels that 30% of all industrial accidents in her plant are caused by failure of employees to follow instructions. If this figure is correct, find, approximately, the probability that among 84 industrialized accidents in this plant anywhere from 20 to 30 (inclusive) will be due to failure of employees to follow instructions.

5.39 If 62% of all clouds seeded with silver iodide show spectacular growth, what is the probability that among 40 clouds seeded with silver iodide at most 20 will show spectacular growth?

5.40 To illustrate the law of large numbers mentioned on page 122, find the probabilities that the proportion of heads will be anywhere from 0.49 to 0.51 when a balanced coin is flipped

(a) 1,000 times;

(b) 10,000 times.

5.41 Verify the identity $F(-z) = 1 - F(z)$ given on page 151.

5.42 Verify that the parameter μ in the expression for the normal density on page 150 is, in fact, its mean.

5.43 Verify that the parameter σ^2 in the expression for the normal density on page 150 is, in fact, its variance.

5.44 Normal probabilities can be calculated using MINITAB. Let X have a normal distribution with mean 11.3 and standard deviation 5.7. The following steps yield the cumulative probability of 9.31 or smaller, or $P(X \leq 9.31)$.

Dialog box:	**Session command**
Calc>Probability Distribution>Normal	MTB>CDF 9.31;
Choose **Cumulative Distribution.**	MTB>NORMAL MU = 11.3 SIGMA = 5.7.
Choose **Input constant** and enter 9.31.	
Type 11.3 in **Mean** and	
5.7 in **Standard deviation.**	
Click **OK.**	

Output:
Normal with mean =11.3000 and standard deviation =5.70000

$$
\begin{array}{cc}
x & P(X<=x) \\
9.3100 & 0.3635
\end{array}
$$

For this same normal distribution, find the probability

   (a) of 8.493 or smaller.

   (b) of 16.074 or smaller.

5.4   Other Probability Densities

In the application of statistics to problems in engineering and physical science, we shall encounter many probability densities other than the normal distribution. Among these are the t, F, and chi-square distributions, the fundamental sampling distributions that we introduce in Chapter 6, and the exponential and Weibull distributions, which we apply to problems of reliability and life testing in Chapter 15.

In the remainder of this chapter we shall discuss five continuous distributions, the **uniform distribution,** the **log-normal distribution,** the **gamma distribution,** the **beta distribution,** and the **Weibull distribution,** for the twofold purpose of giving further examples of probability densities and of laying the foundation for future applications.

5.5   The Uniform Distribution

The **uniform distribution,** with the parameters α and β, has probability density function

Uniform distribution

$$
f(x) = \begin{cases} \dfrac{1}{\beta - \alpha} & \text{for } \alpha < x < \beta \\[2mm] 0 & \text{elsewhere} \end{cases}
$$

FIGURE 5.16 Graph of uniform probability density.

whose graph is shown in Figure 5.16. Note that all values of x from α to β are "equally likely" in the sense that the probability that x lies in an interval of width Δx entirely contained in the interval from α to β is equal to $\Delta x / (\beta - \alpha)$, regardless of the exact location of the interval.

To illustrate how a physical situation might give rise to a uniform distribution, suppose that a wheel of a locomotive has the radius r and that x is the location of a point on its circumference measured along the circumference from some reference point 0. When the brakes are applied, some point will make sliding contact with the rail, and heavy wear will occur at that point. For repeated application of the brakes, it would seem reasonable to assume that x is a value of a random variable having the uniform distribution with $\alpha = 0$ and $\beta = 2\pi r$. If this assumption were incorrect, that is, if some set of points on the wheel made contact more often than others, the wheel would eventually exhibit "flat spots" or wear out of round.

To determine the mean and the variance of the uniform distribution, we first evaluate the two integrals

$$\mu = \int_{\alpha}^{\beta} x \cdot \frac{1}{\beta - \alpha} dx = \frac{\alpha + \beta}{2}$$

and

$$\mu_2' = \int_{\alpha}^{\beta} x^2 \cdot \frac{1}{\beta - \alpha} dx = \frac{\alpha^2 + \alpha\beta + \beta^2}{3}$$

Thus,

Mean of uniform distribution

$$\mu = \frac{\alpha + \beta}{2}$$

and, making use of the formula $\sigma^2 = \mu_2' - \mu^2$, we find that

Variance of uniform distribution

$$\sigma^2 = \tfrac{1}{12}(\beta - \alpha)^2$$

5.6   The Log-Normal Distribution

The **log-normal distribution** occurs in practice whenever we encounter a random variable which is such that its logarithm has a normal distribution. Its probability density is given by

Log-normal distribution

$$f(x) = \begin{cases} \dfrac{1}{\sqrt{2\pi}\beta}x^{-1}e^{-(\ln x - \alpha)^2/2\beta^2} & \text{for } x > 0, \beta > 0 \\ 0 & \text{elsewhere} \end{cases}$$

where $\ln x$ is the natural logarithm of x. A graph of the log-normal distribution with $\alpha = 0$ and $\beta = 1$ is shown in Figure 5.17. It can be seen from the figure that this distribution is positively skewed or has a long right-hand tail.

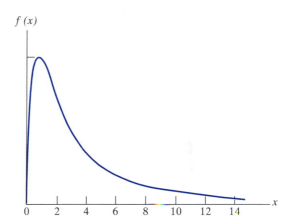

FIGURE 5.17 Graph of log-normal probability density.

To find the probability that a random variable having the log-normal distribution will take on a value between a and $b(0 < a < b)$, we must evaluate the integral

$$\int_a^b \frac{1}{\sqrt{2\pi}\beta}x^{-1}e^{-(\ln x - \alpha)^2/2\beta^2}\,dx$$

Changing variable by letting $y = \ln x$ and identifying the integrand as the normal density with $\mu = \alpha$ and $\sigma = \beta$, we find that the desired probability is given by

$$\int_{\ln a}^{\ln b} \frac{1}{\sqrt{2\pi}\beta}e^{-(y-\alpha)^2/2\beta^2}\,dy = F\left(\frac{\ln b - \alpha}{\beta}\right) - F\left(\frac{\ln a - \alpha}{\beta}\right)$$

where F is the distribution function of the standard normal distribution.

EXAMPLE

Calculating a log-normal probability

The current gain of certain transistors is measured in units which make it equal to the logarithm of I_o/I_i, the ratio of the output to the input current. If this logarithm is normally distributed with $\mu = 2$ and $\sigma^2 = 0.01$, find the probability that I_o/I_i will take on a value between 6.1 and 8.2.

Solution   Since $\alpha = 2$ and $\beta = 0.1$, we get

$$F\left(\frac{\ln 8.2 - 2}{0.1}\right) - F\left(\frac{\ln 6.1 - 2}{0.1}\right) = F(1.0) - F(-1.92)$$

$$= 0.8139 \qquad ✔$$

EXAMPLE

Graphing a probability density function on top of a density histogram to help assess fit

Make a density histogram of the logarithm of the interrequest times on page 20 and relate it to a log-normal distribution.

Solution   Figure 5.18 gives the density histogram. We have also plotted the log-normal density with $\alpha = 8.85$ and $\beta = 1.03$. The log-normal fit is explored further in Section 5.11 (see also Exercise 5.97).   ✔

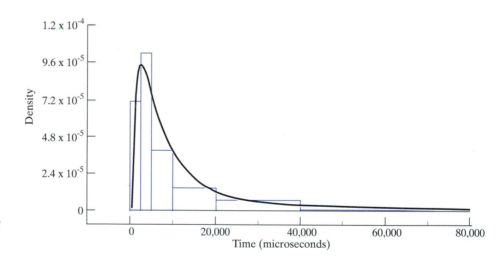

FIGURE 5.18
Density histogram of
Interrequest time.

EXAMPLE

A log-normal probability calculation for a risk analysis

As part of a risk analysis concerning a nuclear power plant, engineers must model the strength of steam generator supports in terms of their ability to withstand the peak acceleration caused by earthquakes. Expert opinion suggests that the ln(strength) is normally distributed with $\mu = 4.0$ and $\sigma^2 = 0.09$. Find the probability that the supports will survive a peak acceleration of 33.

Solution   Since $\alpha = 4.0$ and $\beta = 0.30$, we find

$$1 - F\left(\frac{\ln(33) - 4.0}{0.30}\right) = 1 - F(-1.68) = 0.9535 \qquad \checkmark$$

To find a formula for the mean of the log-normal distribution, we write

$$\mu = \frac{1}{\sqrt{2\pi}\beta} \int_0^\infty x \cdot x^{-1} e^{-(\ln x - \alpha)^2/2\beta^2} dx$$

and upon letting $y = \ln x$, this becomes

$$\mu = \frac{1}{\sqrt{2\pi}\beta} \int_{-\infty}^\infty e^y e^{-(y-\alpha)^2/2\beta^2} dy$$

This integral can be evaluated by completing the square on the exponent $y - (y - \alpha)^2/2\beta^2$, thus obtaining an integrand which has the form of a normal density. The final result, which the reader will be asked to verify in Exercise 5.48 on page 172, is

Mean of log-normal distribution

$$\mu = e^{\alpha + \beta^2/2}$$

Similar, but more lengthy, calculations yield

Variance of log-normal distribution

$$\sigma^2 = e^{2\alpha + \beta^2}(e^{\beta^2} - 1)$$

EXAMPLE

Calculating the mean and variance for a log-normal distribution
With reference to the example on page 164, find the mean and the variance of the distribution of the ratio of the output to the input current.

Solution   Substituting $\alpha = 2$ and $\beta = 0.1$ into the above formulas, we get

$$\mu = e^{2 + (0.1)^2/2} = 7.43$$

and

$$\sigma^2 = e^{4 + (0.1)^2}(e^{(0.1)^2} - 1) = 0.55 \qquad \checkmark$$

5.7 The Gamma Distribution

Several important probability densities whose applications will be discussed later are special cases of the **gamma distribution.** This distribution has probability density

Gamma distribution

$$f(x) = \begin{cases} \dfrac{1}{\beta^\alpha \Gamma(\alpha)} x^{\alpha-1} e^{-x/\beta} & \text{for } x > 0, \alpha > 0, \beta > 0 \\ 0 & \text{elsewhere} \end{cases}$$

where $\Gamma(\alpha)$ is a value of the **gamma function,** defined by

$$\Gamma(\alpha) = \int_0^\infty x^{\alpha-1} e^{-x} dx$$

Integration by parts shows that

$$\Gamma(\alpha) = (\alpha - 1)\Gamma(\alpha - 1)$$

for any $\alpha > 1$ and, hence, that $\Gamma(\alpha) = (\alpha - 1)!$ when α is a positive integer. Graphs of several gamma distributions are shown in Figure 5.19 and they exhibit the fact that these distributions are positively skewed. In fact, the skewness decreases as α increases for any fixed value of β.

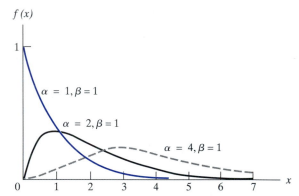

FIGURE 5.19 Graph of some gamma probability density functions.

The mean and the variance of the gamma distribution may be obtained by making use of the gamma function and its special properties mentioned above. For the mean we have

$$\mu = \frac{1}{\beta^\alpha \Gamma(\alpha)} \int_0^\infty x \cdot x^{\alpha-1} e^{-x/\beta} dx$$

and, after letting $y = x/\beta$, we get

$$\mu = \frac{\beta}{\Gamma(\alpha)} \int_0^\infty y^\alpha e^{-y} dy = \frac{\beta \Gamma(\alpha + 1)}{\Gamma(\alpha)}$$

Then, making use of the identity $\Gamma(\alpha + 1) = \alpha \cdot \Gamma(\alpha)$, we arrive at the result that

Mean of gamma distribution

$$\mu = \alpha\beta$$

Using similar methods, it can also be shown that the variance of the gamma distribution is given by

Variance of gamma
distribution

$$\sigma^2 = \alpha\beta^2$$

In the special case where $\alpha = 1$, we get the **exponential distribution,** whose probability density is thus

Exponential
distribution

$$f(x) = \begin{cases} \dfrac{1}{\beta}e^{-x/\beta} & \text{for } x > 0, \beta > 0 \\ 0 & \text{elsewhere} \end{cases}$$

and whose mean and variance are $\mu = \beta$ and $\sigma^2 = \beta^2$. Note that the distribution of the example on page 146 is an exponential distribution with $\beta = \frac{1}{2}$.

EXAMPLE

An exponential density function on top of a density histogram

An engineer, observing a nuclear reaction, measures the time intervals between the emissions of beta particles.

0.894	0.991	0.061	0.186	0.311	0.817	2.267	0.091	0.139	0.083
0.235	0.424	0.216	0.579	0.429	0.612	0.143	0.055	0.752	0.188
0.071	0.159	0.082	1.653	2.010	0.158	0.527	1.033	2.863	0.365
0.459	0.431	0.092	0.830	1.718	0.099	0.162	0.076	0.107	0.278
0.100	0.919	0.900	0.093	0.041	0.712	0.994	0.149	0.866	0.054

Make a density histogram.

Solution   These decay times (in milliseconds) are presented as a density histogram in Figure 5.20. The smooth curve is the exponential density with $\beta = 0.25$. Fit to an exponential density is further explored in Section 15.4. The exponential density has mean $\beta = .25$ and standard deviation .25.

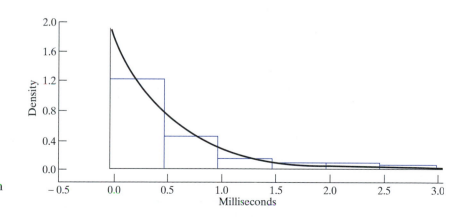

FIGURE 5.20
Density histogram
of decay times.

The exponential distribution has many important applications; for instance, it can be shown that in connection with Poisson processes (see Section 4.7) the **waiting time** between successive arrivals (successes) has an exponential distribution. More specifically, it can be shown that if in a Poisson process the mean arrival rate (average number of arrivals per unit time) is α, the time until the first arrival, or the waiting time between successive arrivals, has an exponential distribution with $\beta = \dfrac{1}{\alpha}$ (see Exercise 5.62 on page 173).

EXAMPLE

Probability calculations using an exponential distribution

With reference to the example on page 129, where on the average three trucks arrived per hour to be unloaded at a warehouse, what are the probabilities that the time between the arrival of successive trucks will be

(a) less than 5 minutes;
(b) at least 45 minutes.

Solution Assuming the arrivals follow a Poisson process with $\alpha = 3$, then $\beta = \frac{1}{3}$ and we get

$$\int_0^{1/12} 3e^{-3x}dx = 1 - e^{-1/4} = 0.221$$

for part (a), and

$$\int_{3/4}^{\infty} 3e^{-3x}dx = e^{-9/4} = 0.105$$

for part (b).   ✔

5.8 The Beta Distribution

A probability density for a random variable which takes on values on the interval from 0 to 1, is the **beta distribution,** whose probability density is

Beta distribution

$$f(x) = \begin{cases} \dfrac{\Gamma(\alpha + \beta)}{\Gamma(\alpha) \cdot \Gamma(\beta)} x^{\alpha-1}(1 - x)^{\beta-1} & \text{for } 0 < x < 1, \alpha > 0, \beta > 0 \\ 0 & \text{elsewhere} \end{cases}$$

The mean and the variance of this distribution are given by

Mean and variance of beta distribution

$$\mu = \frac{\alpha}{\alpha + \beta} \quad \text{and} \quad \sigma^2 = \frac{\alpha\beta}{(\alpha + \beta)^2(\alpha + \beta + 1)}$$

Note that for $\alpha = 1$ and $\beta = 1$ we obtain as a special case the uniform distribution of Section 5.5 defined on the interval from 0 to 1. The following example, pertaining to a proportion, illustrates a typical application of the beta distribution.

EXAMPLE

Probability calculations using a beta distribution
In a certain county, the proportion of highway sections requiring repairs in any given year is a random variable having the beta distribution with $\alpha = 3$ and $\beta = 2$ (shown in Figure 5.21).

(a) On the average what percentage of the highway sections require repairs in any given year?

(b) Find the probability that at most half of the highway sections will require repairs in any given year?

Solution (a) $\mu = \dfrac{3}{3 + 2} = 0.60$, which means that on the average 60% of the highway sections require repairs in any given year. (b) Substituting $\alpha = 3$ and $\beta = 2$ into the formula for the beta distribution and making use of the fact that $\Gamma(5) = 4! = 24$, $\Gamma(3) = 2! = 2$, and $\Gamma(2) = 1! = 1$, we get

$$f(x) = \begin{cases} 12x^2(1 - x) & \text{for } 0 < x < 1 \\ 0 & \text{elsewhere} \end{cases}$$

Thus, the desired probability is given by

$$\int_0^{1/2} 12x^2(1 - x)dx = \frac{5}{16} \qquad \checkmark$$

In most realistically complex situations, probabilities relating to gamma and beta distributions are obtained from special tables or from computer packages.

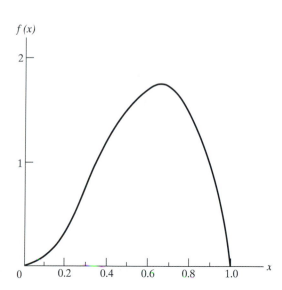

FIGURE 5.21 Graph of the beta density with $\alpha = 3$ and $\beta = 2$.

5.9   The Weibull Distribution

Closely related to the exponential distribution is the **Weibull distribution,** whose probability density is given by

Weibull distribution

$$
f(x) = \begin{cases} \alpha\beta x^{\beta-1}e^{-\alpha x^{\beta}} & \text{for } x > 0, \alpha > 0, \beta > 0 \\ 0 & \text{elsewhere} \end{cases}
$$

To demonstrate this relationship, we evaluate the probability that a random variable having the Weibull distribution will take on a value less than a, namely, the integral

$$
\int_0^a \alpha\beta x^{\beta-1}e^{-\alpha x^{\beta}}dx
$$

Making the change of variable $y = x^{\beta}$, we get

$$
\int_0^{a^{\beta}} \alpha e^{-\alpha y}dy = 1 - e^{-\alpha a^{\beta}}
$$

and it can be seen that y is a value of a random variable having an exponential distribution. The graphs of several Weibull distributions with $\alpha = 1$ and $\beta = \frac{1}{2}, 1,$ and 2 are shown in Figure 5.22.

The mean of the Weibull distribution having the parameters α and β may be obtained by evaluating the integral

$$
\mu = \int_0^{\infty} x \cdot \alpha\beta x^{\beta-1}e^{-\alpha x^{\beta}}dx
$$

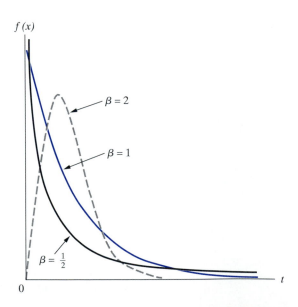

FIGURE 5.22 Graphs of Weibull densities with $\alpha = 1$ and $\beta = \frac{1}{2}, 1,$ and 2.

Making the change of variable $u = \alpha x^\beta$, we get

$$\mu = \alpha^{-1/\beta} \int_0^\infty u^{1/\beta} e^{-u} du$$

and recognizing the integral as $\Gamma\left(1 + \dfrac{1}{\beta}\right)$, namely, as a value of the gamma function which we defined on page 166, we find that the mean of the Weibull distribution is given by

Mean of Weibull distribution

$$\mu = \alpha^{-1/\beta} \Gamma\left(1 + \frac{1}{\beta}\right)$$

Using a similar method to determine first μ_2', the reader will be asked to show in Exercise 5.70 on page 173 that the variance of this distribution is given by

Variance of Weibull distribution

$$\sigma^2 = \alpha^{-2/\beta}\left\{\Gamma\left(1 + \frac{2}{\beta}\right) - \left[\Gamma\left(1 + \frac{1}{\beta}\right)\right]^2\right\}$$

EXAMPLE

Probability calculations using a Weibull distribution

Suppose that the lifetime of a certain kind of an emergency backup battery (in hours) is a random variable X having the Weibull distribution with $\alpha = 0.1$ and $\beta = 0.5$. Find

(a) the mean lifetime of these batteries;

(b) the probability that such a battery will last more than 300 hours.

Solution

(a) Substitution into the formula for the mean yields

$$\mu = (0.1)^{-2}\Gamma(3) = 200 \text{ hours}$$

(b) Performing the necessary integration, we get

$$\int_{300}^\infty (0.05)x^{-0.5} e^{-0.1x^{0.5}} dx = e^{-0.1(300)^{0.5}}$$

$$= 0.177 \qquad ✔$$

EXERCISES

5.45 Find the distribution function of a random variable which has the uniform distribution.

5.46 In certain experiments, the error made in determining the solubility of a substance is a random variable having the uniform density with $\alpha = -0.025$ and $\beta = 0.025$. What are the probabilities that such an error will be

(a) between 0.010 and 0.015;

(b) between −0.012 and 0.012?

5.47 From experience Mr. Harris has found that the low bid on a construction job can be regarded as a random variable having the uniform density

$$f(x) = \begin{cases} \dfrac{3}{4C} & \text{for } \dfrac{2C}{3} < x < 2C \\ 0 & \text{elsewhere} \end{cases}$$

where C is his own estimate of the cost of the job. What percentage should Mr. Harris add to his cost estimate when submitting bids to maximize his expected profit?

5.48 Verify the expression given on page 165 for the mean of the log-normal distribution.

5.49 With reference to the example on page 164, find the probability that I_o/I_i will take on a value between 7.0 and 7.5.

5.50 If a random variable has the log-normal distribution with $\alpha = -1$ and $\beta = 2$, find its mean and its standard deviation.

5.51 With reference to the preceding exercise, find the probabilities that the random variable will take on a value

(a) between 3.2 and 8.4;

(b) greater than 5.0.

5.52 If a random variable has the gamma distribution with $\alpha = 2$ and $\beta = 2$, find the mean and the standard deviation of this distribution.

5.53 With reference to Exercise 5.52, find the probability that the random variable will take on a value less than 4.

5.54 In a certain city, the daily consumption of electric power (in millions of kilowatt-hours) can be treated as a random variable having a gamma distribution with $\alpha = 3$ and $\beta = 2$. If the power plant of this city has a daily capacity of 12 million kilowatt-hours, what is the probability that this power supply will be inadequate on any given day?

5.55 With reference to the example on page 164, suppose the expert opinion is in error. Calculate the probability that the supports will survive if

(a) $\mu = 3.0$ and $\sigma^2 = 0.09$;

(b) $\mu = 4.0$ and $\sigma^2 = 0.36$.

5.56 Verify the expression for the variance of the gamma distribution given on page 167.

5.57 Show that when $\alpha > 1$, the graph of the gamma density has a relative maximum at $x = \beta(\alpha - 1)$. What happens when $0 < \alpha < 1$ and when $\alpha = 1$?

5.58 The amount of time that a surveillance camera will run without having to be reset is a random variable having the exponential distribution with $\beta = 50$ days. Find the probabilities that such a camera will

(a) have to be reset in less than 20 days;

(b) not have to be reset in at least 60 days.

5.59 With reference to Exercise 4.95, find the percent of the time that the interval between breakdowns of the computer will be

(a) less than 1 week;

(b) at least 5 weeks.

5.60 With reference to Exercise 4.56, find the probabilities that the time between successive calls arriving at the switchboard of the consulting firm will be

  (a) less than $\frac{1}{2}$ minute;

  (b) more than 3 minutes.

5.61 Given a Poisson process with on the average α arrivals per unit time, find the probability that there will be no arrivals during a time interval of length t, namely, the probability that the waiting times between successive arrivals will be at least of length t.

5.62 Use the result of Exercise 5.61 to find an expression for the probability density of the waiting time between successive arrivals.

5.63 Verify for $\alpha = 3$ and $\beta = 3$ that the integral of the beta density, from 0 to 1, is equal to 1.

5.64 If the annual proportion of erroneous income tax returns filed with the IRS can be looked upon as a random variable having a beta distribution with $\alpha = 2$ and $\beta = 9$, what is the probability that in any given year there will be fewer than 10% erroneous returns?

5.65 Suppose that the proportion of defectives shipped by a vendor, which varies somewhat from shipment to shipment, may be looked upon as a random variable having the beta distribution with $\alpha = 1$ and $\beta = 4$.

  (a) Find the mean of this beta distribution, namely, the average proportion of defectives in a shipment from this vendor.

  (b) Find the probability that a shipment from this vendor will contain 25% or more defectives.

5.66 Show that when $\alpha > 1$ and $\beta > 1$, the beta density has a relative maximum at

$$x = \frac{\alpha - 1}{\alpha + \beta - 2}$$

5.67 With reference to the example on page 171, find the probability that such a battery will not last 100 hours.

5.68 Suppose that the time to failure (in minutes) of certain electronic components subjected to continuous vibrations may be looked upon as a random variable having the Weibull distribution with $\alpha = \frac{1}{5}$ and $\beta = \frac{1}{3}$.

  (a) How long can such a component be expected to last?

  (b) What is the probability that such a component will fail in less than 5 hours?

5.69 Suppose that the service life (in hours) of a semiconductor is a random variable having the Weibull distribution with $\alpha = 0.025$ and $\beta = 0.500$. What is the probability that such a semiconductor will still be in operating condition after 4,000 hours?

5.70 Verify the formula for the variance of the Weibull distribution given on page 171.

5.10   Joint Distributions—Discrete and Continuous

Discrete Variables

Often, experiments are conducted where two random variables are observed simultaneously in order to determine not only their individual behavior but also the degree of relationship between them.

For two discrete random variables X_1 and X_2, we write the probability that X_1 will take the value x_1 and X_2 will take the value x_2 as $P(X_1 = x_1, X_2 = x_2)$. Consequently, $P(X_1 = x_1, X_2 = x_2)$ is the probability of the intersection of the events $X_1 = x_1$ and $X_2 = x_2$. The distribution of probability is specified by listing the probabilities associated with all possible pairs of values x_1 and x_2, either by formula or in a table. We refer to the function $f(x_1, x_2) = P(X_1 = x_1, X_2 = x_2)$ and the corresponding possible values (x_1, x_2) as the **joint probability distribution** of X_1 and X_2.

EXAMPLE

Calculating probabilities from a discrete joint probability distribution
Let X_1 and X_2 have the joint probability distribution

Joint Probability Distribution $f(x_1, x_2)$ of X_1 and X_2

		x_1		
		0	1	2
x_2	0	.1	.4	.1
	1	.2	.2	0

(a) Find $P(X_1 + X_2 > 1)$.

(b) Find the probability distribution $f_1(x_1) = P(X_1 = x_1)$ of the individual random variable X_1.

Solution (a) The event $X_1 + X_2 > 1$ is composed of the pairs of values $(1, 1), (2, 0)$, and $(2, 1)$. Adding their corresponding probabilities

$$P(X_1 + X_2 > 1) = f(1, 1) + f(2, 0) + f(2, 1) = .2 + .1 + 0 = .3$$

(b) Since the event $X_1 = 0$ is composed of the two pairs of values $(0, 0)$ and $(0, 1)$, we add their corresponding probabilities to obtain

$$P(X_1 = 0) = f(0, 0) + f(0, 1) = .1 + .2 = .3$$

Continuing, we obtain $P(X_1 = 1) = .6$ and $P(X_1 = 2) = .1$. In summary, $f_1(0) = .3, f_1(1) = .6$, and $f_1(2) = .1$ is the probability distribution of X_1.
Rewriting the frequency table but including the row and column totals,

Joint Probability Distribution $f(x_1, x_2)$ of X_1
and X_2 with Marginal Distributions

		x_1			Total
		0	1	2	$f_2(x_2)$
x_2	0	.1	.4	.1	.6
	1	.2	.2	0	.4
Total	$f_1(x_1)$	.3	.6	.1	1.0

Note that the probability distribution $f_1(x_1)$ of X_1 appears in the lower margin of this enlarged table. The probability distribution $f_2(x_2)$ of X_2 appears in the right-hand margin of the table. Consequently, the individual distributions are called **marginal distributions.** ✔

From the example, we see that for each fixed value of x_1, the marginal probability distribution is obtained as

$$P(X_1 = x_1) = f_1(x_1) = \sum_{\text{values } x_2} f(x_1, x_2)$$

where the sum is over all possible values of the second variable.

Consistent with the definition of conditional probability of events when A is the event $X_1 = x_1$ and B is the event $X_2 = x_2$, the **conditional probability distribution** of X_1 given $X_2 = x_2$ is defined as

$$f_1(x_1|x_2) = \frac{f(x_1, x_2)}{f_2(x_2)} \quad \text{for all } x_1 \text{ provided } f_2(x_2) \neq 0$$

If $f_1(x_1|x_2) = f_1(x_1)$ for all x_1 and x_2, so the conditional probability distribution is free of x_2, or equivalently, if

$$f(x_1, x_2) = f_1(x_1)f_2(x_2) \quad \text{for all } x_1, x_2$$

the two random variables are **independent.**

EXAMPLE

A conditional probability distribution
With reference to the previous example, find the conditional probability distribution of X_1 given $X_2 = 1$. Are X_1 and X_2 independent?

Solution $\quad f_1(0|1) = \dfrac{f(0, 1)}{f_2(1)} = \dfrac{.2}{.4} = .5, \qquad f_1(1|1) = \dfrac{f(1, 1)}{f_2(1)} = \dfrac{.2}{.4} = .5,$

$$\text{and } f_1(2|1) = \frac{f(2, 1)}{f_2(1)} = \frac{0}{.4} = 0$$

Since $f_1(0|1) = .5 \neq .3 = f_1(0)$ the conditional probability distribution is not free of the value x_2. Equivalently, $f(0, 1) = .2 \neq (.3)(.4) = f_1(0)f_2(1)$. So X_1 and X_2 are *dependent.* ✔

Let x_1 be a possible value for the first random variable X_1, x_2 be a possible value for the second random variable X_2, and so on with x_k a possible value for the kth random variable. Then the probabilities $P(X_1 = x_1, X_2 = x_2, \ldots, X_k = x_k) = f(x_1, x_2, \ldots, x_k)$ need to be specified. We refer to the function f and the corresponding k-tuples of possible values $(x_1, x_2, \ldots, x_k)$ as the **joint probability distribution** of these random variables.

The probability distribution $f_i(x_i)$ of the individual variable X_i is called the **marginal probability distribution** of the ith random variable.

$$f_i(x_i) = \sum_{x_1} \cdots \sum_{x_{i-1}} \sum_{x_{i+1}} \cdots \sum_{x_k} f(x_1, x_2, \ldots, x_k)$$

where the summation is over all possible k-tuples where the ith component is held fixed at the specified value x_i.

Continuous Variables

There are many situations in which we describe an outcome by giving the values of several continuous random variables. For instance, we may measure the weight and the hardness of a rock, the volume, pressure, and temperature of a gas, or the thickness, color, compressive strength, and potassium content of a piece of glass. If $X_1, X_2, \ldots, X_k$ are k random variables, we shall refer to $f(x_1, x_2, \ldots, x_k)$ as the **joint probability density** of these random variables, if the probability that $a_1 \leq X_1 \leq b_1, a_2 \leq X_2 \leq b_2, \ldots,$ and $a_k \leq X_k \leq b_k$ is given by the multiple integral

$$\int_{a_1}^{b_1} \int_{a_2}^{b_2} \cdots \int_{a_k}^{b_k} f(x_1, x_2, \ldots, x_k) dx_1 dx_2 \cdots dx_k$$

Thus, not every function $f(x_1, x_2, \ldots, x_k)$ can serve as a joint probability density, but if

$$f(x_1, x_2, \ldots, x_k) \geq 0$$

for all values of $x_1, x_2, \ldots, x_k$, and

$$\int_{-\infty}^{\infty} \int_{-\infty}^{\infty} \cdots \int_{-\infty}^{\infty} f(x_1, x_2, \ldots, x_k) dx_1 dx_2 \cdots dx_k = 1$$

it can be shown that the axioms of probability (with the modification of the definition of "event" discussed in Section 5.1) are satisfied.

To extend the concept of a cumulative distribution function to the k-variable case, we write as $F(x_1, x_2, \ldots, x_k)$ the probability that the first random variable will take on a value less than or equal to x_1, the second random variable will take on a value less than or equal to $x_2, \ldots,$ and the kth random variable will take on a value less than or equal to x_k, and we refer to the corresponding function F as the **joint cumulative distribution function** of the k random variables.

EXAMPLE

Calculating probabilities from a joint probability density function
If the joint probability density of two random variables is given by

$$f(x_1, x_2) = \begin{cases} 6e^{-2x_1 - 3x_2} & \text{for } x_1 > 0, x_2 > 0 \\ 0 & \text{elsewhere} \end{cases}$$

find the probabilities that

(a) the first random variable will take on a value between 1 and 2 and the second random variable will take on a value between 2 and 3;

(b) the first random variable will take on a value less than 2 and the second random variable will take on a value greater than 2.

Solution   Performing the necessary integrations, we get

$$\int_1^2 \int_2^3 6e^{-2x_1 - 3x_2} dx_1 dx_2 = (e^{-2} - e^{-4})(e^{-6} - e^{-9})$$

$$= 0.0003$$

for part (a), and

$$\int_0^2 \int_2^\infty 6e^{-2x_1 - 3x_2} dx_1 dx_2 = (1 - e^{-4}) e^{-6}$$

$$= 0.0025$$

for part (b). ✔

EXAMPLE

Determining a joint cumulative distribution function

Find the joint distribution function of the two random variables of the preceding exercise, and use it to find the probability that both random variables will take on values less than 1.

Solution By definition,

$$F(x_1, x_2) = \begin{cases} \displaystyle\int_0^{x_1} \int_0^{x_2} 6e^{-2u - 3v} du\, dv & \text{for } x_1 > 0, x_2 > 0 \\ 0 & \text{elsewhere} \end{cases}$$

so that

$$F(x_1, x_2) = \begin{cases} (1 - e^{-2x_1})(1 - e^{-3x_2}) & \text{for } x_1 > 0, x_2 > 0 \\ 0 & \text{elsewhere} \end{cases}$$

and, hence,

$$F(1, 1) = (1 - e^{-2})(1 - e^{-3})$$

$$= 0.8216$$ ✔

Given the joint probability density of k random variables, the probability density of the ith random variable can be obtained by integrating out the other variables; symbolically,

Marginal density

$$f_i(x_i) = \int_{-\infty}^{\infty} \cdots \int_{-\infty}^{\infty} f(x_1, x_2, \dots, x_k) dx_1 \cdots dx_{i-1} dx_{i+1} \cdots dx_k$$

and, in this context, the function f_i is called the **marginal density** of the ith random variable. Integrating out only some of the k random variables, we can similarly define **joint marginal densities** of any two, three, or more of the k random variables.

EXAMPLE

Determining a marginal density from a joint density

With reference to the example on page 176, find the marginal density of the first random variable.

Solution   Integrating out x_2, we get

$$f_1(x_1) = \begin{cases} \displaystyle\int_0^\infty 6e^{-2x_1-3x_2}dx_2 & \text{for } x_1 > 0 \\ 0 & \text{elsewhere} \end{cases}$$

or

$$f_1(x_1) = \begin{cases} 2e^{-2x_1} & \text{for } x_1 > 0 \\ 0 & \text{elsewhere} \end{cases} \qquad ✔$$

To explain what we mean by the **independence** of continuous random variables, we could proceed as with discrete random variables in Section 3.6 and define **conditional densities** first; however, it will be easier to say that

Independent random variables

> k random variables $X_1, \ldots, X_k$ are independent if and only if
>
> $$F(x_1, x_2, \ldots, x_k) = F_1(x_1) \cdot F_2(x_2) \cdots F_k(x_k)$$
>
> for all values of these random variables for which the respective functions are defined.

In this notation, $F(x_1, x_2, \ldots, x_k)$ is, as before, the joint distribution function of the k random variables, while $F_i(x_i)$ for $i = 1, 2, \ldots, k$ are the corresponding individual distribution functions of the respective random variables. The same condition applies for discrete random variables.

EXAMPLE   **Checking independence via the joint cumulative distribution**
With reference to the example on page 176, check whether the two random variables are independent.

Solution   As we already saw on page 177, the joint distribution function of the two random variables is given by

$$F(x_1, x_2) = \begin{cases} (1 - e^{-2x_1})(1 - e^{-3x_2}) & \text{for } x_1 > 0 \text{ and } x_2 > 0 \\ 0 & \text{elsewhere} \end{cases}$$

Now, since $F_1(x_1) = F(x_1, \infty)$ and $F_2(x_2) = F(\infty, x_2)$, it follows that

$$F_1(x_1) = \begin{cases} 1 - e^{-2x_1} & \text{for } x_1 > 0 \\ 0 & \text{elsewhere} \end{cases}$$

and

$$F_2(x_2) = \begin{cases} 1 - e^{-3x_2} & \text{for } x_2 > 0 \\ 0 & \text{elsewhere} \end{cases}$$

Thus, $F(x_1, x_2) = F_1(x_1) \cdot F_2(x_2)$ and the two random variables are independent.   ✔

When k random variables have a joint probability density, the **k random variables are independent,** if and only if their joint probability density equals the product of the corresponding values of the marginal densities of the k random variables; symbolically,

$$f(x_1, x_2, \ldots, x_k) = f_1(x_1) \cdot f_2(x_2) \cdots f_k(x_k) \qquad \text{for all } (x_1, \ldots, x_k)$$

EXAMPLE

Establishing independence by factoring the joint probability density
With reference to the example on page 176, verify that $f(x_1, x_2) = f_1(x_1) \cdot f_2(x_2)$.

Solution On page 178 we showed that

$$f_1(x_1) = \begin{cases} 2e^{-2x_1} & \text{for } x_1 > 0 \\ 0 & \text{elsewhere} \end{cases}$$

and in the same way it can be shown that

$$f_2(x_2) = \begin{cases} 3e^{-3x_2} & \text{for } x_2 > 0 \\ 0 & \text{elsewhere} \end{cases}$$

Thus

$$f_1(x_1) \cdot f_2(x_2) = \begin{cases} 6e^{-2x_1 - 3x_2} & \text{for } x_1 > 0 \text{ and } x_2 > 0 \\ 0 & \text{elsewhere} \end{cases}$$

and it can be seen that $f_1(x_1) \cdot f_2(x_2) = f(x_1, x_2)$ for all (x_1, x_2). ✔

Given two continuous random variables X_1 and X_2, we shall define the **conditional probability density** of the first given that the second takes on the value x_2 as

Conditional probability density

$$f_1(x_1|x_2) = \frac{f(x_1, x_2)}{f_2(x_2)} \quad \text{provided } f_2(x_2) \neq 0$$

where $f(x_1, x_2)$ and $f_2(x_2)$ are, as before, the joint density of the two random variables and the marginal density of the second. Note that this definition parallels that of conditional probability on page 79.

EXAMPLE

Determining a conditional probability density
If two random variables have the joint probability density

$$f(x_1, x_2) = \begin{cases} \frac{2}{3}(x_1 + 2x_2) & \text{for } 0 < x_1 < 1, 0 < x_2 < 1 \\ 0 & \text{elsewhere} \end{cases}$$

find the conditional density of the first given that the second takes on the value x_2.

Solution   First we find the marginal density of the second random variable by integrating out x_1, and we get

$$f_2(x_2) = \int_0^1 \tfrac{2}{3}(x_1 + 2x_2)dx_1 = \tfrac{1}{3}(1 + 4x_2) \quad \text{for } 0 < x_2 < 1$$

and $f_2(x_2) = 0$ elsewhere. Hence, by definition, the conditional density of the first random variable given that the second takes on the value x_2 is given by

$$f_1(x_1|x_2) = \frac{\tfrac{2}{3}(x_1 + 2x_2)}{\tfrac{1}{3}(1 + 4x_2)} = \frac{2x_1 + 4x_2}{1 + 4x_2} \quad \text{for } 0 < x_1 < 1, 0 < x_2 < 1$$

and $f_1(x_1|x_2) = 0$ for $x_1 \le 0$ or $x_1 \ge 1$ and $0 < x_2 < 1$.   ✔

Properties of Expectation

Consider a function $g(X)$ of a single random variable X. For instance, if X is an oven temperature in degrees centigrade, then $g(X) = \tfrac{9}{5}X + 32$ is the same temperature in degrees Fahrenheit. If X has probability density function f, then the mean or **expectation** of $g(X)$ is given by

$$E[g(X)] = \int_{-\infty}^{\infty} g(x)f(x)dx$$

In the discrete case, where X has probability distribution f,

$$E[g(X)] = \sum_{x_i} g(x_i)f(x_i)$$

where x_i is a possible value for X. If X has mean $\mu = E(X)$, then taking $g(x) = (x - \mu)^2$, we have $E[g(X)] = E(X - \mu)^2$, which is just the variance σ^2 of X.

For any random variable Y, let $E(Y)$ denote its expectation which is also its mean μ_Y. Its variance is $Var(Y)$ which is also written as σ_Y^2.

When $g(x) = ax + b$, for given constants a and b, the random variable $g(X)$ has expectation

$$E(aX + b) = \int_{-\infty}^{\infty} (ax + b)f(x)dx = a\int_{-\infty}^{\infty} xf(x)dx + b\int_{-\infty}^{\infty} f(x)dx = aE(X) + b$$

and variance

$$Var(aX + b) = \int_{-\infty}^{\infty} (ax + b - a\mu_X - b)^2 f(x)dx = a^2 \int_{-\infty}^{\infty} (x - \mu_X)^2 f(x)dx$$

$$= a^2 Var(X)$$

To summarize

For given constants a and b

$$E(aX + b) = aE(X) + b \quad \text{and} \quad Var(aX + b) = a^2 Var(X)$$

EXAMPLE

The mean and standard deviation of a standardized random variable
Let X have mean μ and standard deviation σ. Use the properties of expectation to show that the standardized random variable

$$Z = \frac{X - \mu}{\sigma}$$

has mean 0 and standard deviation 1.

Solution   Since Z is of the form

$$Z = \frac{X - \mu}{\sigma} = \frac{1}{\sigma}X - \frac{\mu}{\sigma} = aX + b$$

where $a = 1/\sigma$ and $b = -\mu/\sigma$,

$$E(Z) = \frac{1}{\sigma}E(X) - \frac{\mu}{\sigma} = \frac{\mu}{\sigma} - \frac{\mu}{\sigma} = 0$$

and the variance of Z is

$$\left(\frac{1}{\sigma}\right)^2 Var(X) = \frac{\sigma^2}{\sigma^2} = 1$$

because $E(X) = \mu$ and $Var(X) = \sigma^2$.   ✔

EXAMPLE

Determining the mean and variance of $20X$
Suppose the daily amount of electricity X required for a plating process has mean 10 and standard deviation 3 kilowatt hours. If the cost of electricity is 20 dollars per kilowatt-hour, find the mean, variance, and standard deviation of the daily cost of electricity.

Solution   The daily cost of electricity, $g(X) = 20X$, has mean $20E(X) = 20 \times 10 = 200$ dollars and variance $(20)^2 Var(X) = (20)^2 3^2 = 3,600$. Its standard deviation is $\sqrt{3,600} = 60$ dollars.   ✔

Given any collection of k random variables, the function $Y = g(X_1, X_2, \ldots, X_k)$ is also a random variable. Examples include $Y = X_1 - X_2$ when $g(x_1, x_2) = x_1 - x_2$ and $Y = 2X_1 + 3X_2$ when $g(x_1, x_2) = 2x_1 + 3x_2$. The random variable $g(X_1, X_2, \ldots, X_k)$ has expected value, or mean, given by

$$\int_{-\infty}^{\infty}\int_{-\infty}^{\infty} \cdots \int_{-\infty}^{\infty} g(x_1, x_2, \ldots, x_k)f(x_1, x_2, \ldots, x_k)dx_1 \cdots dx_k$$

or, in the discrete case,

$$\sum_{x_1}\sum_{x_2} \cdots \sum_{x_k} g(x_1, x_2, \ldots, x_k)f(x_1, x_2, \ldots, x_k)$$

where the summation is over all k-tuples $(x_1, x_2, \ldots, x_k)$ of possible values.
Several important properties of expectation can be deduced from this definition. Taking $g(x_1, x_2) = (x_1 - \mu_1)(x_2 - \mu_2)$, we see that the product $(x_1 - \mu_1)(x_2 - \mu_2)$

will be positive if both values x_1 and x_2 are above their respective means or both are below their respective means. Otherwise it will be negative. The expected value $E[(X_1 - \mu_1)(X_2 - \mu_2)]$ will tend to be positive when large X_1 and X_2 tend to occur together and small X_1 and X_2 tend to occur together, with high probability. This measure $E[(X_1 - \mu_1)(X_2 - \mu_2)]$ of joint variation is called the population **covariance** of X_1 and X_2.

If X_1 and X_2 are independent so $f(x_1, x_2) = f_1(x_1)f_2(x_2)$,

$$\int_{-\infty}^{\infty} \int_{-\infty}^{\infty} (x_1 - \mu_1)(x_2 - \mu_2)f(x_1, x_2)dx_1dx_2$$

$$= \int_{-\infty}^{\infty} (x_1 - \mu_1)f_1(x_1)dx_1 \cdot \int_{-\infty}^{\infty} (x_2 - \mu_2)f_2(x_2)dx_2 = 0$$

This result concerning zero covariance can be stated as

When X_1 and X_2 are independent, their covariance
$$E[(X_1 - \mu_1)(X_2 - \mu_2)] = 0$$

Further, the expectation of a linear combination of two independent random variables $Y = a_1X_1 + a_2X_2$ is

$$\mu_Y = E(Y) = E(a_1X_1 + a_2X_2)$$

$$= \int_{-\infty}^{\infty} \int_{-\infty}^{\infty} (a_1x_1 + a_2x_2)f_1(x_1)f_2(x_2)dx_1dx_2$$

$$= a_1 \int_{-\infty}^{\infty} x_1f_1(x_1)dx_1 \int_{-\infty}^{\infty} f_2(x_2)dx_2 + a_2 \int_{-\infty}^{\infty} f_1(x_1)dx_1 \int_{-\infty}^{\infty} x_2f_2(x_2)dx_2$$

$$= a_1E(X_1) + a_2E(X_2)$$

This result holds even if the two random variables are not independent. Also

$$\begin{aligned} Var(Y) &= E(Y - \mu_Y)^2 = E[(a_1X_1 + a_2X_2 - a_1\mu_1 - a_2\mu_2)^2] \\ &= E[(a_1(X_1 - \mu_1) + a_2(X_2 - \mu_2))^2] \\ &= E[a_1^2(X_1 - \mu_1)^2 + a_2^2(X_2 - \mu_2)^2 + 2a_1a_2(X_1 - \mu_1)(X_2 - \mu_2)] \\ &= a_1^2E[(X_1 - \mu_1)^2] + a_2^2E[(X_2 - \mu_2)^2] + 2a_1a_2E[(X_1 - \mu_1)(X_2 - \mu_2)] \\ &= a_1^2Var(X_1) + a_2^2Var(X_2) \end{aligned}$$

since the third term is zero because X_1 and X_2 are independent.

These properties hold for any number of random variables whether they are continuous or discrete.

Let X_i have mean μ_i and variance σ_i^2 for $i = 1, 2, \ldots, k$. The linear combination $Y = a_1X_1 + a_2X_2 + \cdots + a_kX_k$ has

$$E(a_1X_1 + a_2X_2 + \cdots + a_kX_k) = a_1E(X_1) + a_2E(X_2)$$
$$+ \cdots + a_kE(X_k)$$

or

The mean and variance of linear combinations

$$\mu_Y = \sum_{i=1}^{k} a_i\mu_i$$

When the random variables are independent

$$Var(a_1X_1 + a_2X_2 + \cdots + a_kX_k) = a_1^2Var(X_1) + a_2^2Var(X_2)$$
$$+ \cdots + a_k^2Var(X_k)$$

or

$$\sigma_Y^2 = \sum_{i=1}^{k} a_i^2\sigma_i^2$$

EXAMPLE

Variances of $X_1 - X_2$ and $X_1 + X_2$ when X_1 and X_2 are independent
Let X_1 have mean μ_1 and variance σ_1^2 and let X_2 have mean μ_2 and variance σ_2^2. Find the mean and variance of

(a) $X_1 - X_2$ and
(b) $X_1 + X_2$

if X_1 and X_2 are independent.

Solution (a) Note that $X_1 - X_2$ is of the form $a_1X_1 + a_2X_2$ with $a_1 = -a_2 = 1$ so it has mean

$$1 \cdot \mu_1 + (-1)\mu_2 = \mu_1 - \mu_2$$

and variance

$$(1)^2 \cdot \sigma_1^2 + (-1)^2\sigma_2^2 = \sigma_1^2 + \sigma_2^2$$

(b) Since $X_1 + X_2$ corresponds to the case with $a_1 = a_2 = 1$, it has mean

$$1 \cdot \mu_1 + 1 \cdot \mu_2 = \mu_1 + \mu_2$$

and variance

$$1^2 \cdot \sigma_1^2 + 1^2 \cdot \sigma_2^2 = \sigma_1^2 + \sigma_2^2 \qquad ✔$$

EXAMPLE

Finding the mean and variance of $2X_1 + X_2 - 5$
If X_1 has mean 4 and variance 9 while X_2 has mean -2 and variance 5, and the two are independent, find

(a) $E(2X_1 + X_2 - 5)$
(b) $Var(2X_1 + X_2 - 5)$

Solution   According to the properties of expectation, the constant -5 is added to the expectation of $2X_1 + X_2$ but leaves the variance unchanged.

(a) $E(2X_1 + X_2 - 5) = E(2X_1 + X_2) - 5$

$$= 2E(X_1) + E(X_2) - 5 = 2(4) + (-2) - 5 = 1$$

(b) $Var(2X_1 + X_2 - 5) = Var(2X_1 + X_2)$

$$= 2^2 Var(X_1) + Var(X_2) = 2^2(9) + 5 = 41 \qquad \checkmark$$

EXAMPLE

The mean and variance of total time to coat and rinse
The time to complete a coating process, X_1, has mean 35 minutes and variance 11, while the time to rinse, X_2, has mean 8 minutes and variance 5. Find the mean and standard deviation of the total time to coat and rinse.

Solution   According to properties of expectation, the total time $X_1 + X_2$ has mean $35 + 8 = 43$ minutes. Treating the coating and rinsing times as independent, the variance is $11 + 5 = 16$, so that the standard deviation is 4. $\checkmark$

EXAMPLE

The mean and variance of the sample mean $\overline{X}$
Let the n random variables $X_1, X_2, \ldots, X_n$ be independent and each have the same distribution with mean μ and variance σ^2. Use the properties of expectation to show that the sample mean $\overline{X}$ has

(a) mean: $\mu_{\overline{X}} = E(\overline{X}) = \mu$

(b) variance: $\sigma^2_{\overline{X}} = Var(\overline{X}) = \dfrac{\sigma^2}{n}$.

Solution   (a) The sample mean

$$\overline{X} = \frac{X_1 + X_2 + \cdots + X_n}{n} = \frac{1}{n}X_1 + \frac{1}{n}X_2 + \cdots + \frac{1}{n}X_n$$

is a linear combination with constants $a_i = 1/n$ for $i = 1, 2, \ldots, n$. Consequently,

$$E(\overline{X}) = \frac{1}{n}E(X_1) + \frac{1}{n}E(X_2) + \cdots + \frac{1}{n}E(X_n) = \sum_{i=1}^{n} \frac{1}{n}\mu = \frac{1}{n}n\mu = \mu$$

so the expected value or mean of $\overline{X}$ is the same as the mean of each observation.

(b) The variance of $\overline{X}$ is

$$Var(\overline{X}) = \left(\frac{1}{n}\right)^2 Var(X_1) + \left(\frac{1}{n}\right)^2 Var(X_2) + \cdots + \left(\frac{1}{n}\right)^2 Var(X_n)$$

$$= \sum_{i=1}^{n} \left(\frac{1}{n}\right)^2 \sigma^2 = \left(\frac{1}{n}\right)^2 n\sigma^2 = \frac{\sigma^2}{n}$$

so the variance of $\overline{X}$ equals the variance of a single observation divided by n. $\checkmark$

EXAMPLE

The expected value of the sample variance
Let the n random variables $X_1, X_2, \ldots, X_n$ be independent and each have the same distribution with mean μ and variance σ^2. Use the properties of expectation to show that σ^2 is the mean, or expectation, of the sample variance $\sum_{i=1}^{n}(X_i - \overline{X})^2/(n-1)$.

Solution   We write $(X_i - \overline{X})^2 = (X_i - \mu + \mu - \overline{X})^2 = (X_i - \mu)^2 + (\mu - \overline{X})^2 + 2(X_i - \mu)(\mu - \overline{X})$ so the numerator of the sample variance is

$$\sum_{i=1}^{n}(X_i - \overline{X})^2 = \sum_{i=1}^{n}(X_i - \mu)^2 + \sum_{i=1}^{n}(\mu - \overline{X})^2 + 2\sum_{i=1}^{n}(X_i - \mu)(\mu - \overline{X})$$

and the last term equals $-2(\overline{X} - \mu)\sum_{i=1}^{n}(X_i - \mu) = -2n(\overline{X} - \mu)^2$. Consequently,

$$\sum_{i=1}^{n}(X_i - \overline{X})^2 = \sum_{i=1}^{n}(X_i - \mu)^2 - n(\overline{X} - \mu)^2$$

Since $E(X_i - \mu)^2 = Var(X_i) = \sigma^2$ and, by the previous example, $E(\overline{X}) = \mu$ so $E(\overline{X} - \mu)^2 = Var(\overline{X}) = \sigma^2/n$, taking expectation term by term and summing

$$E\left[\sum_{i=1}^{n}(X_i - \overline{X})^2\right] = \sum_{i=1}^{n}\sigma^2 - n\frac{\sigma^2}{n} = (n-1)\sigma^2$$

Dividing both sides by $n - 1$, we conclude that σ^2 is the expected value of the sample variance.   ✔

EXERCISES

5.71 Two scanners are needed for an experiment. Of the five available, two have electronic defects, another one has a defect in the memory, and two are in good working order. Two units are selected at random.

(a) Find the joint probability distribution of $X_1 =$ the number with electronic defects, and $X_2 =$ the number with a defect in memory.

(b) Find the probability of 0 or 1 total defects among the two selected.

(c) Find the marginal probability distribution of X_1.

(d) Find the conditional probability distribution of X_1 given $X_2 = 0$.

5.72 Two random variables are independent and each has a binomial distribution with success probability .3 and 2 trials.

(a) Find the joint probability distribution.

(b) Find the probability that the second random variable is greater than the first.

5.73 If two random variables have the joint density

$$f(x_1, x_2) = \begin{cases} x_1 x_2 & \text{for } 0 < x_1 < 1, 0 < x_2 < 2 \\ 0 & \text{elsewhere} \end{cases}$$

find the probabilities that

(a) both random variables will take on values less than 1;

(b) the sum of the values taken on by the two random variables will be less than 1.

5.74 With reference to the preceding exercise, find the marginal densities of the two random variables.

5.75 With reference to Exercise 5.73, find the joint distribution function of the two random variables, the distribution functions of the individual random variables, and check whether the two random variables are independent.

5.76 If two random variables have the joint density

$$f(x, y) = \begin{cases} \frac{6}{5}(x + y^2) & \text{for } 0 < x < 1, 0 < y < 1 \\ 0 & \text{elsewhere} \end{cases}$$

find the probability that $0.2 < X < 0.5$ and $0.4 < Y < 0.6$.

5.77 With reference to the preceding exercise, find the joint distribution function of the two random variables and use it to verify the value obtained for the probability.

5.78 With reference to Exercise 5.76 find both marginal densities and use them to find the probabilities that

(a) $X > 0.8$;

(b) $Y < 0.5$.

5.79 With reference to Exercise 5.76 find

(a) an expression for $f_1(x|y)$ for $0 < y < 1$;

(b) an expression for $f_1(x|\frac{1}{2})$;

(c) the mean of the conditional density of the first random variable when the second takes on the value $\frac{1}{2}$.

5.80 With reference to the second example on page 179, find expressions for

(a) the conditional density of the first random variable when the second takes on the value $x_2 = 0.25$;

(b) the conditional density of the second random variable when the first takes on the value x_1.

5.81 If three random variables have the joint density

$$f(x, y, z) = \begin{cases} k(x + y)e^{-z} & \text{for } 0 < x < 1, 0 < y < 2, z > 0 \\ 0 & \text{elsewhere} \end{cases}$$

find

(a) the value of k;

(b) the probability that $X < Y$ and $Z > 1$.

5.82 With reference to the preceding exercise, check whether

(a) the three random variables are independent;

(b) any two of the three random variables are pairwise independent.

5.83 A pair of random variables has the **circular normal distribution** if their joint density is given by

$$f(x_1, x_2) = \frac{1}{2\pi\sigma^2}e^{-[(x_1-\mu_1)^2+(x_2-\mu_2)^2]/2\sigma^2}$$

for $-\infty < x_1 < \infty$ and $-\infty < x_2 < \infty$.

(a) If $\mu_1 = 2$ and $\mu_2 = -2$, and $\sigma = 10$, use Table 3 to find the probability that $-8 < X_1 < 14$ and $-9 < X_2 < 3$.

(b) If $\mu_1 = \mu_2 = 0$ and $\sigma = 3$, find the probability that (X_1, X_2) is contained in the region between the two circles $x_1^2 + x_2^2 = 9$ and $x_1^2 + x_2^2 = 36$.

5.84 A precision drill, positioned over a target point, will make an acceptable hole if it is within 5 microns of the target. Using the target as the origin of a rectangular system of coordinates, assume that the coordinates (x, y) of the point of contact are values of a pair of random variables having the circular normal distribution (see Exercise 5.83) with $\mu_1 = \mu_2 = 0$ and $\sigma = 2$. What is the probability that the hole will be acceptable?

5.85 With reference to Exercise 5.73, find the expected value of the random variable whose values are given by $g(x_1, x_2) = x_1 + x_2$.

5.86 With reference to Exercise 5.76, find the expected value of the random variable whose values are given by $g(x, y) = x^2 y$.

5.87 If measurements of the length and the width of a rectangle have the joint density

$$f(x, y) = \begin{cases} \dfrac{1}{ab} & \text{for } L - \dfrac{a}{2} < x < L + \dfrac{a}{2}, W - \dfrac{b}{2} < y < W + \dfrac{b}{2} \\ 0 & \text{elsewhere} \end{cases}$$

find the mean and the variance of the corresponding distribution of the area of the rectangle.

5.88 Establish a relationship between $f_1(x_1|x_2)$, $f_2(x_2|x_1)$, $f_1(x_1)$, and $f_2(x_2)$.

5.89 If X_1 has mean 1 and variance 5 while X_2 has mean -1 and variance 5, and the two are independent, find

(a) $E(X_1 + X_2)$;

(b) $Var(X_1 + X_2)$.

5.90 If X_1 has mean -2 and variance 2 while X_2 has mean 5 and variance 5, and the two are independent, find

(a) $E(X_1 - X_2)$;

(b) $Var(X_1 - X_2)$.

5.91 If X_1 has mean 1 and variance 5 while X_2 has mean -2 and variance 5, and the two are independent, find

(a) $E(X_1 + 2X_2 - 3)$;

(b) $Var(X_1 + 2X_2 - 3)$.

5.92 The time for an older machine to complete a check on a computer chip, X_1, has mean 65 milliseconds and variance 16, while the time for a newer model, X_2, has mean 54 milliseconds and variance 9. Find the expected time savings using the newer model when

(a) checking a single chip;

(b) checking 200 chips.

(c) Find the standard deviations in parts (a) and (b) assuming all of the checking times are independent.

5.93 Let $X_1, X_2, \cdots, X_{20}$ be independent and let each have the same marginal distribution with mean 10 and variance 3. Find

(a) $E(X_1 + X_2 + \cdots + X_{20})$;

(b) $Var(X_1 + X_2 + \cdots + X_{20})$.

5.11 Checking if the Data Are Normal

In many instances, an experimenter needs to check whether a data set appears to be generated by a normally distributed random variable. As indicated in Figure 2.8 the normal distribution can serve to model variation in some quantities. Further, many commonly used statistical procedures, which we describe in later chapters, require that the probability distribution be nearly normal. Consequently, in a great number of applications, it is prudent to check the assumption that the data are normal.

Although they involve an element of subjective judgment, graphical procedures are the most helpful for detecting serious departures from normality. Histograms can be checked for lack of symmetry. A single long tail certainly contradicts the assumption of a normal distribution. However, another special graph, called a **normal-scores plot,** is even more effective in detecting departures from normality. To introduce such a plot, we consider a sample of size 4. In practice, we need a minimum of 15–20 observations in order to evaluate the agreement with normality.

The term **normal scores** refers to an idealized sample from the standard normal distribution. It consists of the values of z that divide the axes into equal probability intervals. For sample size $n = 4$, the normal scores are

$$m_1 = -z_{0.20} = -0.84$$
$$m_2 = -z_{0.40} = -0.25$$
$$m_3 = z_{0.40} = 0.25$$
$$m_4 = z_{0.20} = 0.84$$

and these are illustrated in Figure 5.23.

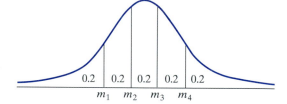

FIGURE 5.23 The standard normal distribution and the normal-scores for $n = 4$.

To construct a normal-scores plot

1. Order the data from smallest to largest;
2. Obtain the normal scores;
3. Plot the ith largest observation, versus the ith normal score m_i, for all i.

EXAMPLE

A simple normal-scores plot
Suppose the four observations are 67, 48, 76, 81. Construct a normal-scores plot.

Solution   The ordered observations are 48, 67, 76, 81. Earlier, we found that $m_1 = -z_{0.20} = -0.84$, so we plot the pair $(48, -0.84)$. Continuing, we obtain Figure 5.24.

FIGURE 5.24 The normal-scores plot.

If the data were from a standard normal distribution, we would expect the ith largest observation to approximate the ith normal score so that the normal-scores plot would resemble a 45° line through the origin. When the distribution is normal with an unspecified μ and σ, $z = \dfrac{(x - \mu)}{\sigma}$; so the idealized z values can be converted to idealized x values through the relation $x = \mu + \sigma z$. Because the idealized values have this linear relation, it is sufficient to plot the ordered observations versus the normal scores obtained from the standard normal distribution. If the normal distribution prevails, the pattern should still be a straight line. But, the line need not pass through the origin or have slope 1.

The construction of normal-scores plots by hand is a difficult task at best. Fortunately, they can be created easily with most statistical packages. (See Exercise 5.96, page 192.) Many slight variants are used in the calculation of the normal scores but the plots are very similar if more than 20 observations are plotted. Whichever computer package you use, if a normal distribution is plausible, the plot will have a straight-line appearance.

Figure 5.25 shows the normal-scores plot for the interrequest times given on page 20. The bending shows that the largest values are larger than would be expected under a normal distribution. On the other hand, Figure 5.26 exhibits a plot of the sulfur emissions data (see the example on page 15) and a normal distribution appears to be plausible.

5.12   Transforming Observations to Near Normality

When the histogram and normal-scores plot indicate that the assumption of a normal distribution is invalid, transformations can often improve the agreement with normality. Scientists regularly express their observations in natural logs. We consider a few other transformations, as indicated in Table 5.1. If the distribution has a long tail or a few stragglers on the right, the $\ln x$ or $\sqrt{x}$ transformations will pull the large values down further than they pull the central or small values. If the transformed observations have a nearly straight line normal-scores plot, it is usually advantageous to use the normality of this new scale to perform any statistical

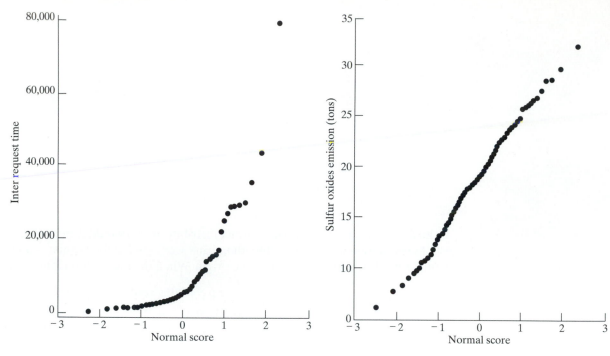

FIGURE 5.25 The normal-scores plot of the interrequest times.

FIGURE 5.26 The normal-scores plot of the sulfur emission data.

TABLE 5.1 Some Useful Transformations

Make large values smaller:	*Make large values larger:*
$-\dfrac{1}{x}, \quad \ln x, \quad x^{1/4}, \sqrt{x}$	x^2, x^3

analysis. Further, the validity of many of the powerful statistical methods described in later chapters rests on the assumption that the probability distribution is nearly normal. By choosing a transformation that leads to nearly normal data, the investigator can greatly extend the range of validity of these techniques.

EXAMPLE

A transformation to better approximate a normal distribution

Transform the interrequest times in the example on page 20 to better approximate a normal distribution.

Solution

On a computer, we calculate $\sqrt{x}$, take the square root again to obtain $x^{1/4}$, and take the natural logarithm $\ln x$ of all 50 values. The transformation $\ln x$ appears to work best. The histogram and normal-scores plot are shown in Figure 5.27 for both the original and transformed data. The quality of the fit further confirms the lognormal model.

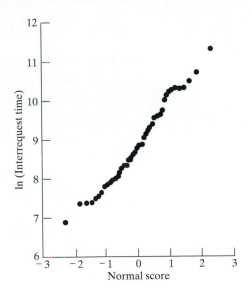

FIGURE 5.27a The normal-scores plot of interrequest time.

FIGURE 5.27b The normal-scores plot of ln (interrequest time).

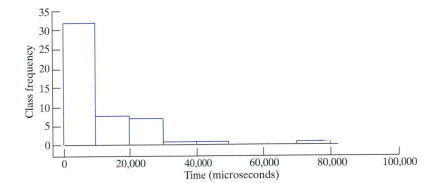

FIGURE 5.27c Histogram of interrequest time.

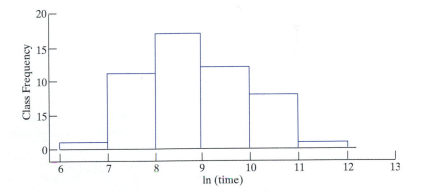

FIGURE 5.27d Histogram of ln (interrequest time).

EXERCISES

5.94 For any seven observations,

(a) use Table 3 to verify that the normal scores are

$$-1.15 \quad -0.67 \quad -0.32 \quad 0 \quad 0.32 \quad 0.67 \quad 1.15$$

(b) construct a normal-scores plot using the observations

16 10 18 27 29 19 17

5.95 For any 11 observations,

(a) use Table 3 to verify that the normal scores are

$$-1.38 \quad -0.97 \quad -0.67 \quad -0.43 \quad -0.21 \quad 0 \quad 0.21 \quad 0.43 \quad 0.67 \quad 0.97 \quad 1.38$$

(b) construct a normal-scores plot using the observations on the times between neutrinos on page 14.

5.96 (Normal-scores plots) The *MINITAB* commands

```
NSCORE  C1  PUT  IN  C2
PLOT  C1  VS  C2
```

will create a normal-scores plot from observations that were set in C1. (*MINITAB* uses a variant of the normal scores, m_i, that we defined.) Construct a normal-scores plot of

(a) the aluminum alloy strength data on page 20;

(b) the decay time data on page 167.

5.97 (Transformations) The *MINITAB* commands

```
LET C2= LOGE(C1)
LET C3= SQRT(C1)
LET C4= SQRT(C3)
```

will place ln x in C2, $\sqrt{x}$ in C3, and $x^{1/4}$ in C4 for observations that are set in C1. Normal-scores plots can then be constructed as in Exercise 5.96. Try these three transformations and construct the corresponding normal-scores plots for

(a) the decay time data on page 167;

(b) the interrequest time data on page 20.

5.13   Simulation

Simulation techniques have grown up with computers. They are ideally suited for doing the repetitious calculations required. To **simulate** the observation of continuous random variables we usually start with uniform random numbers and relate these to the distribution function of interest. We could use two- or three-digit random integers, perhaps selected from Table 7, but most software packages have a continuous uniform random-number generator. That is, they produce approximations to random numbers from the uniform distribution

$$f(x) = \begin{cases} 1 & 0 < x < 1 \\ 0 & \text{elsewhere} \end{cases}$$

Suppose we wish to simulate an observation from the exponential distribution

$$F(x) = 1 - e^{-0.3x}, \qquad 0 < x < \infty$$

The computer would first produce the value u from the uniform distribution. Then we solve (see Exercise 5.101)

$$u = F(x) = 1 - e^{-0.3x}$$

so $x = [-\ln(1 - u)]/0.3$ is the corresponding value of an exponential random variable. For instance, if $u = 0.45$, then $x = [-\ln(1 - 0.45)]/0.3 = 1.993$. This is illustrated graphically in Figure 5.28, where u is located on the vertical scale and the corresponding x-value is read from the horizontal scale. (The theory on which this method is based involves the so-called probability integral transformation, which is treated in all the textbooks on mathematical statistics referred to in the bibliography). If we wish to simulate a sample from F, the preceding process is repeated with a different u for each new observation x.

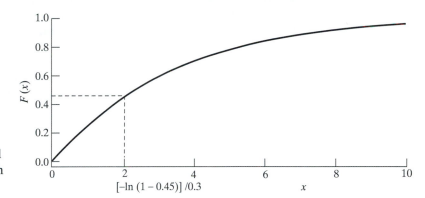

FIGURE 5.28 Exponential cumulative distribution with mean $\frac{10}{3}$.

A similar procedure applies to the simulation of observations from a Weibull distribution. Starting with the value of a uniform variable u, we now solve (see Exercise 5.102)

$$u = F(x) = 1 - e^{-\alpha x^{\beta}}$$

for $x = \left[-\dfrac{1}{\alpha} \ln(1 - u) \right]^{1/\beta}$, which is the corresponding value of a Weibull random variable.

EXAMPLE

Simulating five values from a Weibull distribution
Simulate five observations of a random variable having the Weibull distribution with $\alpha = 0.05$ and $\beta = 2.0$.

Solution   A computer generates the five values $0.57, 0.74, 0.26, 0.77, 0.12$. (Alternatively, they could have been obtained by reading two digits at a time from Table 7.) We calculate

$$x = [-20.0 \ln(1 - 0.57)]^{1/2} = 4.108$$
$$x = [-20.0 \ln(1 - 0.74)]^{1/2} = 5.191$$

In Exercise 5.98 the reader will be asked to show that the last three uniform numbers yield $x = 2.454, 5.422, 1.599$. ✔

Suppose we need to simulate values from the normal distribution with a specified μ and σ^2. By the relation $z = \dfrac{x - \mu}{\sigma}$ (page 153), it follows that $x = \mu + \sigma z$, so a value x can be calculated from the value of a standard normal variable z. Although z can be obtained from the value for a uniform variable u by numerically solving $u = F(z)$, another approach called the Box-Muller-Marsaglia method is almost universally preferred. It starts with a pair of independent uniform variables (u_1, u_2) and produces two standard normal variables

$$z_1 = \sqrt{-2\ln(u_2)}\,\cos(2\pi u_1)$$
$$z_2 = \sqrt{-2\ln(u_2)}\,\sin(2\pi u_1)$$

where the angle is expressed in radians. Then $x_1 = \mu + \sigma z_1$ and $x_2 = \mu + \sigma z_2$ are treated as two independent observations of normal random variables (see Exercise 5.103). Most statistical packages include a normal generator (see Exercise 5.106).

EXAMPLE

Simulating two values from a normal distribution
Simulate two observations of a random variable having the normal distribution with $\mu = 50$ and $\sigma = 5$.

Solution   A computer generates the two values 0.253 and 0.531 from a uniform distribution. (Alternatively, they could have been obtained by reading three digits at a time from Table 7.) We first calculate the standard normal values

$$z_1 = \sqrt{-2\ln(0.531)}\cos(2\pi \cdot 0.253) = -0.021$$
$$z_2 = \sqrt{-2\ln(0.531)}\sin(2\pi \cdot 0.253) = 1.125$$

and then the normal values

$$x_1 = 50 + 5z_1 = 50 + 5(-0.021) = 49.895$$
$$x_2 = 50 + 5z_2 = 50 + 5(1.125) \;\;= 55.625$$
✔

EXERCISES

5.98 Continue the example in the text, that is, find the simulated values of the Weibull random variable corresponding to the values 0.26, 0.77, 0.12 of a uniform random variable.

5.99 Suppose the number of hours it takes a person to learn how to operate a certain machine is a random variable having a normal distribution with $\mu = 5.8$ and $\sigma = 1.2$. Suppose it takes two persons to operate the machine. Simulate the time it takes four pairs of persons to learn how to operate the machine. That is, for each pair, calculate the maximum of the two learning times.

5.100 Suppose that the durability of paint (in years) is a random variable having an exponential distribution (see page 167) with mean $\beta = 2$. Simulating an experiment in which five houses are painted,

(a) find the time of the first failure;

(b) find the time of the fifth failure.

5.101 Verify that

(a) the exponential density $0.3e^{-0.3x}$, $x > 0$ corresponds to the distribution function $F(x) = 1 - e^{-0.3x}$, $x > 0$;

(b) the solution of $u = F(x)$ is given by $x = [-\ln(1 - u)]/0.3$.

5.102 Verify that

(a) the Weibull density $\alpha\beta x^{\beta-1}e^{-\alpha x^{\beta}}$, $x > 0$, corresponds to the distribution function $F(x) = 1 - e^{-\alpha x^{\beta}}$, $x > 0$;

(b) the solution of $u = F(x)$ is given by $x = \left[-\dfrac{1}{\alpha}\ln(1 - u) \right]^{1/\beta}$.

5.103 Consider two independent standard normal variables whose joint probability density is

$$\frac{1}{2\pi}e^{-(z^2_1+z^2_2)/2}$$

Under a change to polar coordinates, $z_1 = r\cos(\theta)$, $z_2 = r\sin(\theta)$, we have $r^2 = z^2_1 + z^2_2$ and $dz_1 dz_2 = r\,dr\,d\theta$, so the joint density of r and θ is

$$re^{-r^2/2}\frac{1}{2\pi}, \qquad 0 < \theta < 2\pi, r > 0$$

Show that

(a) r and θ are independent and that θ has a uniform distribution on the interval from 0 to 2π;

(b) $u_1 = \theta/2\pi$ and $u_2 = 1 - e^{-r^2/2}$ have independent uniform distributions;

(c) the relations between (u_1, u_2) and (z_1, z_2) on page 194 hold [note that $1 - u_2$ also has a uniform distribution, so $\ln(u_2)$ can be used in place of $\ln(1 - u_2)$].

5.104 The statistical package *MINITAB* has a random number generator. To simulate 5 values from an exponential distribution having mean $\beta = .05$, choose

---

Dialog Box:
Calc> Random Sample> Exponential
Type 5 after **Generate,** C1 in **Column** and .05 in **Mean.**
Then click **OK.**

Output:
One call produced the output

0.031949   0.004643   0.030029   0.112834   0.064642

Generate 8 values from the exponential distribution with $\beta = .2$.

5.105 Repeat the simulation in Exercise 5.100 100 times and make a histogram of the values from parts (a) and (b).

5.106 The statistical package *MINITAB* has a normal random number generator. To simulate 5 values from a normal distribution having mean 7 and standard deviation 4, and place them in C1, use the commands

Dialog Box:	**Session command**
Calc> Random Sample > Normal	RANDOM 5 observations in C1;
Type 5 after **Generate**, C1 in **Column**, 7 in **Mean**,	NORMAL MU = 7 SIGMA = 4.
and 4 in **standard deviation.** Then click OK.	

Output:

One call produced the output

5.42137	6.98061	9.41352	7.05932	5.87297

Generate 8 values for a normal variable with $\mu = 123$ and $\sigma^2 = 23.5$.

5.107 Repeat the simulation in Exercise 5.99 100 times and make a histogram of (a) the 400 learning times for the pairs of operators and (b) the 100 values representing the time to train four pairs of operators.

REVIEW EXERCISES

5.108 If the probability density of a random variable is given by

$$f(x) = \begin{cases} k(1 - x^2) & \text{for } 0 < x < 1 \\ 0 & \text{elsewhere} \end{cases}$$

find the value of k and the probabilities that a random variable having this probability density will take on a value

(a) between 0.1 and 0.2;

(b) greater than 0.5.

5.109 With reference to the preceding exercise, find the corresponding distribution function and use it to determine the probabilities that a random variable having this distribution function will take on a value

(a) less than 0.3;

(b) between 0.4 and 0.6.

5.110 In certain experiments, the error made in determining the density of a silicon compound is a random variable having the probability density

$$f(x) = \begin{cases} 25 & \text{for } -0.02 < x < 0.02 \\ 0 & \text{elsewhere} \end{cases}$$

Find the probabilities that such an error will be

(a) between −0.03 and 0.04;

(b) between −0.005 and 0.005.

5.111 Find μ and σ^2 for the probability density of Exercise 5.108.

5.112 If a random variable has the standard normal distribution, find the probability that it will take on a value

(a) between 0 and 2.50;

(b) between 1.22 and 2.35;

(c) between -1.33 and -0.33;

(d) between -1.60 and 1.80.

5.113 The burning time of an experimental rocket is a random variable having the normal distribution with $\mu = 4.76$ seconds and $\sigma = 0.04$ second. What is the probability that this kind of rocket will burn

(a) less than 4.66 seconds;

(b) more than 4.80 seconds;

(c) anywhere from 4.70 to 4.82 seconds?

5.114 Verify that

(a) $z_{0.10} = 1.28$;

(b) $z_{0.001} = 3.09$.

5.115 Referring to Exercise 5.28, find the *quartiles* of the normal distribution with $\mu = 102$ and $\sigma = 27$.

5.116 The probability density shown in Figure 5.6 is the log-normal distribution with $\alpha = 8.85$ and $\beta = 1.03$. Find the probability that

(a) the interrequest time is more than 200 microseconds;

(b) the interrequest time is less than 300 microseconds.

5.117 The probability density shown in Figure 5.8 is the exponential distribution

$$f(x) = \begin{cases} 0.25e^{-0.25x} & 0 < x \\ 0 & \text{elsewhere} \end{cases}$$

Find the probability that

(a) the time to observe a particle is more than 200 microseconds;

(b) the time to observe a particle is less than 10 microseconds.

5.118 Referring to the normal scores in Exercise 5.95, construct a normal-scores plot of the suspended solids data in Exercise 2.64.

5.119 Referring to the normal scores in Exercise 5.95, construct a normal-scores plot of the velocity of light data in Exercise 2.62.

5.120 If n salespeople are employed in a door-to-door selling campaign, the gross sales volume in thousands of dollars may be regarded as a random variable having the gamma distribution with $\alpha = 100\sqrt{n}$ and $\beta = \frac{1}{2}$. If the sales costs are $5,000 per salesperson, how many salespeople should be employed to maximize the profit?

5.121 A mechanical engineer models the bending strength of a support beam in a transmission tower as a random variable having the Weibull distribution with $\alpha = 0.02$ and $\beta = 3.0$. What is the probability that the beam can support a load of 4.5?

5.122 Let the times to breakdown for the processors of a parallel processing machine have joint density

$$f(x, y) = \begin{cases} 0.04e^{-0.2x - 0.2y} & \text{for } x > 0, y > 0 \\ 0 & \text{elsewhere} \end{cases}$$

where x is the time for the first processor and y is the time for the second. Find

(a) the marginal distributions and their means;

(b) the expected value of the random variable whose values are given by $g(x, y) = x + y$.

(c) Verify, in this example, that the mean of a sum is the sum of the means.

5.123 Two random variables are independent and each has a binomial distribution with success probability .7 and 2 trials.

   (a) Find the joint probability distribution.

   (b) Find the probability that the second random variable is greater than the first.

5.124 If X_1 has mean -5 and variance 3 while X_2 has mean 1 and variance 4, and the two are independent, find

   (a) $E(3X_1 + 5X_2 + 2)$;

   (b) $Var(3X_1 + 5X_2 + 2)$.

5.125 Let $X_1, X_2, \ldots, X_{30}$ be independent and let each have the same marginal distribution with mean -5 and variance 2. Find

   (a) $E(X_1 + X_2 + \cdots + X_{30})$;

   (b) $Var(X_1 + X_2 + \cdots + X_{30})$.

KEY TERMS

(with page references)

Beta distribution 168	Log-normal distribution 163
Circular normal distribution 186	Marginal density 177
Conditional probability density 179	Marginal probability distribution 175
Conditional probability distribution 175	Mean 147
Continuity correction 156	Normal distribution 150
Covariance 182	Normal probability density 150
Distribution function 145	Normal scores 188
Expectation 180	Normal-scores plot 188
Exponential distribution 167	Probability density 145
Gamma distribution 165	Probability density function 145
Gamma function 166	Simulation 192
Independence 178	Standard deviation 148
Joint cumulative distribution function 176	Standard normal distribution 150
Joint marginal density 177	Standardized random variable 153
Joint probability density 176	Uniform distribution 161
Joint probability distribution 174	Variance 148
kth moment about the mean 147	Waiting time 168
kth moment about the origin 147	Weibull distribution 170

Sampling Distributions

In most of the inference methods we shall study in this book, it will be assumed that we are dealing with a particular kind of sample called a random sample. This attention to random samples, which we discuss in Section 6.1, is due to their permitting valid, or logical, generalizations from sample data. Then, in Sections 6.2 through 6.4, we see how certain statistics (that is, certain quantities determined from samples) can be expected to vary from sample to sample. The concept of a sampling distribution—the distribution of a statistic calculated on the basis of a random sample—is basic to all of statistical inference. ■

6.1 Populations and Samples

Usage of the term **population** in statistics is a carry-over from the days when statistics was applied mainly to sociological and economic phenomena. Recall from Chapter 1 that today, it is applied to sets or collections of objects, actual or conceptual, and mainly to sets of numbers, measurements, or observations which are under investigation. For example, if we are interested in determining the average number of television sets per household in the United States, the totality of these figures, one for each household, constitutes the population for this study. Similarly, the population from which inspectors draw a sample to determine some quality characteristic of a manufactured product may be the corresponding measurements for all units in a given lot; depending on the objectives of the inspection, it may also consist of the corresponding measurements for all units that may conceivably be manufactured.

In some cases, such as the above example concerning the number of television sets per household, the population is **finite;** in other cases, such as the determination of some characteristic of all units past, present, and future, that might conceivably be manufactured by a given process, it is convenient to think of the population as **infinite.** Similarly, we look upon the results obtained in a series of flips of a coin as a sample from the hypothetically infinite population consisting of all conceivably possible flips of the coin.

Populations are often described by the distributions of their values, and it is common practice to refer to a population in terms of this distribution. (For finite populations, we are referring here to the actual distribution of its values; for infinite populations, we are referring to the corresponding probability distribution or probability density.) For example, we may refer to a number of flips of a coin as a sample from a "binomial population" or to certain measurements as a sample from a "normal population." Hereafter, when referring to a "population $f(x)$" we shall mean a population described by a frequency distribution, a probability distribution, or a density $f(x)$.

If a population is infinite it is impossible to observe all its values, and even if it is finite it may be impractical or uneconomical to observe it in its entirety. Thus, it is usually necessary to use a **sample,** a part of a population, and infer from it results pertaining to the entire population. Clearly, such results can be useful only if the sample is in some way "representative" of the population. It would be unreasonable, for instance, to expect useful generalizations about the population of family incomes in the United States in the year 2000 on the basis of data pertaining to home owners only. Similarly, we can hardly expect reasonable generalizations about the performance of a tire if it is tested only on smooth roads. To assure that a sample is representative of the population from which it is obtained, and to provide a framework for the application of probability theory to problems of sampling, we shall limit our discussion to **random samples.** Before a random sample of size n is selected, the observations are modeled as the random variables $X_1, X_2, \ldots, X_n$. For sampling from finite populations, random samples are defined as follows:

Random sample (finite population)

A set of observations $X_1, X_2, \ldots, X_n$ constitutes a random sample of size n from a finite population of size N, if its values are chosen so that each subset of n of the N elements of the population has the same probability of being selected.

Note that this definition of randomness pertains essentially to the manner in which the sample values are selected. This holds also for the following definition of a random sample from an infinite population:

Random sample (infinite population)

A set of observations $X_1, X_2, \ldots, X_n$ constitutes a random sample of size n from the infinite population $f(x)$ if:

1. Each X_i is a random variable whose distribution is given by $f(x)$.
2. These n random variables are independent.

We also apply the term random sample to the set of observed values $x_1, x_2, \ldots, x_n$ of the random variables.

There are several ways of assuring the selection of a sample that is at least approximately random. When dealing with a finite population, we can serially number the elements of the population and then select a sample with the aid of a table of random digits (see discussion on page 8). For instance, if a population has $N = 500$ elements and we wish to select a random sample of size $n = 10$, we can use three arbitrarily selected columns of Table 7 to obtain 10 different three-digit numbers less than or equal to 500, which will then serve as the serial numbers of the elements to be included in the sample.

When the population size is large, the use of random numbers can become very laborious and at times practically impossible. For instance, if a sample of five cartons of canned peaches is to be chosen for inspection from among the many thousands stored in a warehouse, one can hardly expect to number all the cartons, make a selection with the use of random numbers, and then pull out the ones that were chosen. In a situation like this, one really has very little choice but to make the selection relatively haphazard, hoping that this will not seriously violate the assumption of randomness which is basic to most statistical theory.

When dealing with infinite populations, the situation is somewhat different since we cannot physically number the elements of the population; but efforts should be made to approach conditions of randomness by the use of artificial devices. For example, in selecting a sample from a production line we may be able to approximate conditions of randomness by choosing one unit each half hour; when tossing a coin we can try to flip it in such a way that neither side is intentionally favored, and so forth. The proper use of artificial or mechanical devices for selecting random samples is always preferable to human judgement, as it is extremely difficult to avoid unconscious biases when making almost any kind of selection.

Even with the careful choice of artificial devices, it is all too easy to commit gross errors in the selection of a random sample. To illustrate some of these pitfalls, suppose we have the task of selecting logs being fed into a sawmill by a constant-speed conveyor belt, for the purpose of obtaining a random sample of their lengths. One sampling device, which at first sight would seem to assure randomness, consists of measuring the logs which pass a given point at the end of a certain number of 10-minute intervals. However, further thought reveals that this method of selection favors the longer logs, since they require more time to pass the given point. Thus, the sample is not random since the longer logs have a better chance of being included. Another common mistake in selecting a sample is that of sampling from the wrong population or from a poorly specified population. As we have pointed out earlier, we would hardly get a sample from which we could generalize about family incomes in the United States if we limited our sample to home owners. Similarly, if we wanted to determine the effect of vibrations on a structural member, we should be careful to delineate the frequency band of vibrations that is of relevance, and to vibrate test specimens only at frequencies selected randomly from this band.

EXAMPLE

Selecting where to sample in an area that may be contaminated

In many environmental cleanup studies, engineers are faced with the problem of evaluating the status of land areas or bodies of water. It is not always easy to collect a representative sample where the observations can be treated as independent

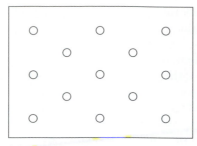

(a) Regular Grid for Homogeneous land.

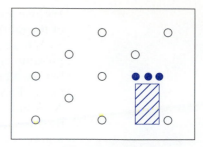

(b) Sample smelter runoff hot spot separately, 3 sites.

FIGURE 6.1 Choosing where to sample.

and from the same distribution. To illustrate some of the key issues consider sampling from a contaminated area in City C that covers a city block. Locations must be selected for taking the soil samples that will then be analyzed for the presence of heavy metals.

Solution   One recommended approach, for homogeneous land areas, is to sample according to a rectangular grid as shown in Figure 6.1(a). This grid could even be randomly placed over the area.

However, more was known about this area. At the time the pollution occurred, a smelter was located in the position indicated by the shaded area in Figure 6.1(b). That is, the soil contamination by heavy metals is definitely not homogeneous! Materials from the smelter flowed towards the north side of the smelter. This area is definitely a "hot spot." The average amount of heavy metals, obtained by averaging the measurements from all locations, is not representative of the contamination problem. Using the average from the whole area as a summary description downplays the seriousness of the contamination around the smelter.

The smelter runoff area should be treated as a separate population. Soil should be collected from at least two locations within the area of this suspected hot spot. We suggest three sites indicated by blue circles. The corresponding measurements of heavy metals should be used to describe just that area.

While sampling the "hot spot" separately might seem like the obvious approach, in the situation on which the example is based, the owners of the site wanted to collect data from more locations throughout the whole block. This, they hoped, would lower the average amount of heavy metals enough so that only simple clean-up tactics would be required rather than resorting to the expensive solution of trucking out the soil.   ✔

EXAMPLE   **Always replicate at least one key measurement**
Refer to the environmental cleanup study in the previous example. Explain why soil samples should be taken in at least two locations rather just doing two chemical analyses on essentially a single soil sample.

Solution   One major aspect of understanding the contamination problem is to evaluate the condition of the known hot spot. Even within the hot spot, the amount of contamination could vary considerably because, for instance, of any particular location's position relative to the old stream of run-off from the smelter. We strongly recommend that soil be collected from at least two soil samples—not just that two chemical analyses be performed on soil from a single location. This approach will provide measurements that can also be used to estimate the total amount of variability in the measurements from the "hot spot."

By repeating the chemical analysis on soil from a single location, we could estimate the variability in the chemical analysis and possibly identify an outlier that might suggest a faulty chemical analysis. However, no matter how many times we repeated the chemical analysis, we would not know how much variation to expect if we sampled soil from the same hot spot but several feet from the first sample. That is, nearby locations are likely to be very much alike but those further apart are less alike. We need to sample from at least two locations to determine the degree of homogeneity within the hot spot.   ✔

The purpose of most statistical investigations is to generalize from information contained in random samples about the population from which the samples were obtained. In particular, we are usually concerned with the problem of making inferences about the **parameters** of populations, such as the mean μ or the standard deviation σ. In making such inferences, we use **statistics** such as $\bar{x}$ and s, namely, quantities calculated on the basis of sample observations. In practice, the term *statistic* is also applied to the corresponding random variables.

EXAMPLE

Sample to sample variation must be understood to accurately assess total water quality
The quality of water leaving a plant must be maintained. It is monitored by taking a tiny volume of water called a test specimen. If the quality of the specimen is bad, action may be taken. The action could range from taking more specimens, making a phone call to alert the plant operators, preparing a written report, or changing how the plant is run, even to shutting down the plant. If the specimen is of good quality, we often infer that the total volume of discharge is satisfactory. Discuss sampling.

Solution   Besides sound laboratory practice, judgements depend crucially on getting test specimens which are representative of the total volume of effluent discharged. Because the quality of water will vary over the total effluent at any one time, the actual test specimens selected may or may not correctly convey the water quality.

The key idea in this discussion is that of sampling variability. Not all choices of actual test specimens will produce the same values for water quality or even a correct appraisal of quality. This variability can be overcome, to a greater or lesser extent, by taking a large enough number of test specimens. The results from examining enough test specimens should then quite accurately reflect water quality most of the time.   ✔

Since the selection of a random sample is controlled largely by chance, so are the values we obtain for statistics, and the remainder of this chapter will be devoted to sampling distributions, namely, to distributions which describe the chance fluctuations of statistics calculated on the basis of random samples.

6.2 The Sampling Distribution of the Mean (σ Known)

Suppose that a random sample of n observations has been taken from some population and that $\bar{x}$ has been computed, say, to estimate the mean of the population. It should be clear that if we took a second random sample of size n from this population, it would be quite unreasonable to expect the identical value for $\bar{x}$, and if we took several more samples, probably no two of the $\bar{x}$'s would be alike. The differences among such $\bar{x}$'s are generally attributed to chance, and this raises important questions concerning their distribution, specifically concerning the extent of their chance fluctuations.

To approach this question experimentally, suppose that 50 random samples of size $n = 10$ are to be taken from a population having the **discrete uniform distribution**

$$f(x) = \begin{cases} \frac{1}{10} & \text{for } x = 0, 1, 2, \ldots, 9 \\ 0 & \text{elsewhere} \end{cases}$$

Sampling is **with replacement,** so to speak, so that we are sampling from an infinite population. A convenient way of obtaining these samples is to use a table of random digits, like Table 7, letting each sample consist of 10 consecutive digits in arbitrarily chosen rows or columns. Actually proceeding in this way, we got 50 samples whose means are

4.4	3.2	5.0	3.5	4.1	4.4	3.6	6.5	5.3	4.4
3.1	5.3	3.8	4.3	3.3	5.0	4.9	4.8	3.1	5.3
3.0	3.0	4.6	5.8	4.6	4.0	3.7	5.2	3.7	3.8
5.3	5.5	4.8	6.4	4.9	6.5	3.5	4.5	4.9	5.3
3.6	2.7	4.0	5.0	2.6	4.2	4.4	5.6	4.7	4.3

Grouping these means into a distribution with the classes 2.0–2.9, 3.0–3.9, ..., and 6.0–6.9, we get

$\bar{x}$	Frequency
2.0–2.9	2
3.0–3.9	14
4.0–4.9	19
5.0–5.9	12
6.0–6.9	3
	50

and it is apparent from this distribution as well as its histogram shown in Figure 6.2 that the distribution of the means is fairly **bell-shaped,** even though the population itself has a uniform distribution. This raises the question whether our result is typical of what we might expect; that is, whether we would get similar distributions if we repeated the experiment again and again.

To answer this kind of question, we shall have to investigate the **theoretical sampling distribution** of the mean which, for the given example, provides us with

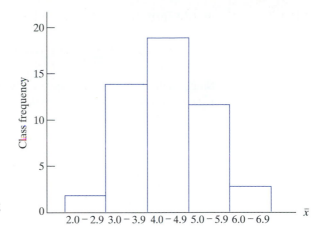

FIGURE 6.2 Experimental sampling distribution of the mean.

the probabilities of getting means from 2.0 to 2.9, from 3.0 to 3.9, . . . , from 6.0 to 6.9, and perhaps values less than 2.0 or greater than 6.9. Although we could evaluate these probabilities for this particular example, it is usually sufficient to refer to some general theorems concerning sampling distributions. The first of these gives expressions for the mean $\mu_{\overline{X}}$ and the variance $\sigma_{\overline{X}}^2$ of sampling distributions of the mean $\overline{X}$.

Formulas for $\mu_{\overline{X}}$ and $\sigma_{\overline{X}}^2$

> **Theorem 6.1**   If a random sample of size n is taken from a population having the mean μ and the variance σ^2, then $\overline{X}$ is a random variable whose distribution has the mean μ.
>
> For samples from infinite populations the variance of this distribution is $\dfrac{\sigma^2}{n}$.
>
> For samples from a finite population of size N the variance is $\dfrac{\sigma^2}{n} \cdot \dfrac{N-n}{N-1}$.

The result for infinite populations was established in the example on page 184 using the properties of expectation. Alternatively, we now prove that $\mu_{\overline{X}} = \mu$ for the continuous case directly starting from the definition on page 181.

$$\mu_{\overline{X}} = \int_{-\infty}^{\infty} \int_{-\infty}^{\infty} \cdots \int_{-\infty}^{\infty} \sum_{i=1}^{n} \frac{x_i}{n} f(x_1, x_2, \ldots, x_n) \, dx_1 \, dx_2 \cdots dx_n$$

$$= \frac{1}{n} \sum_{i=1}^{n} \int_{-\infty}^{\infty} \int_{-\infty}^{\infty} \cdots \int_{-\infty}^{\infty} x_i f(x_1, x_2, \ldots, x_n) \, dx_1 \, dx_2 \cdots dx_n$$

where $f(x_1, x_2, \ldots, x_n)$ is the joint density of the random variables which constitute the random sample. Using the assumption of a random sample, we can write

$$f(x_1, x_2, \ldots, x_n) = f(x_1)f(x_2) \cdots f(x_n)$$

and we now have

$$\mu_{\overline{X}} = \frac{1}{n} \sum_{i=1}^{n} \int_{-\infty}^{\infty} f(x_1) \, dx_1 \cdots \int_{-\infty}^{\infty} x_i f(x_i) \, dx_i \cdots \int_{-\infty}^{\infty} f(x_n) \, dx_n$$

Since each integral except the one with the integrand $x_i f(x_i)$ equals 1, and the one with the integrand $x_i f(x_i)$ equals μ, we finally obtain

$$\mu_{\overline{X}} = \frac{1}{n} \sum_{i=1}^{n} \mu = \mu$$

and this completes the proof. (For the discrete case the proof follows the same steps, with integral signs replaced by $\sum$'s.)

To prove that $\sigma_{\overline{X}}^2 = \sigma^2/n$ for the continuous case, we shall make the simplifying assumption that $\mu = 0$, which does not involve any loss of generality, as the reader will be asked to show in Exercise 6.18 on page 212. Using the definition on page 181, we thus have

$$\sigma_{\overline{X}}^2 = \int_{-\infty}^{\infty} \int_{-\infty}^{\infty} \cdots \int_{-\infty}^{\infty} \overline{x}^2 f(x_1, x_2, \ldots, x_n) \, dx_1 \, dx_2 \cdots dx_n$$

and making use of the fact that

$$\overline{x}^2 = \frac{1}{n^2} \left(\sum_{i=1}^{n} x_i \right)^2 = \frac{1}{n^2} \left(\sum_{i=1}^{n} x_i^2 + \sum\sum_{i \neq j} x_i x_j \right)$$

we obtain

$$\sigma_{\overline{X}}^2 = \frac{1}{n^2} \sum_{i=1}^{n} \int_{-\infty}^{\infty} \int_{-\infty}^{\infty} \cdots \int_{-\infty}^{\infty} x_i^2 f(x_1, x_2, \ldots, x_n) \, dx_1 \, dx_2 \cdots dx_n$$

$$+ \frac{1}{n^2} \sum\sum_{i \neq j} \int_{-\infty}^{\infty} \int_{-\infty}^{\infty} \cdots \int_{-\infty}^{\infty} x_i x_j f(x_1, x_2, \ldots, x_n) \, dx_1 \, dx_2 \cdots dx_n$$

where $\sum\sum_{i \neq j}$ extends over all i and j from 1 to n, not including the terms where $i = j$. Again using the fact that

$$f(x_1, x_2, \ldots, x_n) = f(x_1) f(x_2) \cdots f(x_n)$$

we can write each of the preceding multiple integrals as a product of simple integrals, where each integral with integrand $f(x)$ equals 1. We thus obtain

$$\sigma_{\overline{X}}^2 = \frac{1}{n^2} \sum_{i=1}^{n} \int_{-\infty}^{\infty} x_i^2 f(x_i) \, dx_i + \frac{1}{n^2} \sum\sum_{i \neq j} \int_{-\infty}^{\infty} x_i f(x_i) \, dx_i \cdot \int_{-\infty}^{\infty} x_j f(x_j) \, dx_j$$

and since each integral in the first sum equals σ^2 while each integral in the second sum equals 0, we finally have

$$\sigma_{\overline{X}}^2 = \frac{1}{n^2} \sum_{i=1}^{n} \sigma^2 = \frac{\sigma^2}{n}$$

This completes the proof of the second part of the theorem. We shall not prove the corresponding result for random samples from finite populations. But, it should be noted that in the resulting formula for $\sigma_{\overline{X}}^2$ the factor $\dfrac{N-n}{N-1}$, often called the **finite population correction factor,** is close to 1 (and can be omitted for most practical purposes) unless the sample constitutes a substantial portion of the population.

EXAMPLE

Calculating a finite population correction factor
Find the value of the finite population correction factor for $n = 10$ and $N = 1,000$.

Solution

$$\frac{1,000 - 10}{1,000 - 1} = 0.991$$

Although it should not come as a surprise that $\mu_{\overline{X}} = \mu$, the fact that $\sigma_{\overline{X}}^2 = \sigma^2/n$ for random samples from infinite populations is interesting and important. To point out its implications, let us apply Chebyshev's theorem to the sampling distribution of the mean, substituting $\overline{X}$ for X and $\sigma/\sqrt{n}$ for σ in the formula for the alternate form of the theorem (see page 121). We thus obtain

$$P(|\overline{X} - \mu| < \frac{k\sigma}{\sqrt{n}}) \geq 1 - \frac{1}{k^2}$$

and letting $k\sigma/\sqrt{n} = \varepsilon$, we get

$$P(|\overline{X} - \mu| < \varepsilon) \geq 1 - \frac{\sigma^2}{n\varepsilon^2}$$

Thus, for any given $\varepsilon > 0$, the probability that $\overline{X}$ differs from μ by less than ε can be made arbitrarily close to 1 by choosing n sufficiently large. In less rigorous language, the larger the sample size, the closer we can expect $\overline{X}$ to be to the mean of the population. In this sense we can say that the mean becomes more and more reliable as an estimate of μ as the sample size is increased. This result—that $\overline{X}$ becomes arbitrarily close to μ with arbitrarily high probability—is called the **law of large numbers.**

The reliability of the mean as an estimate of μ is often measured by $\sigma_{\overline{X}} = \sigma/\sqrt{n}$, also called the **standard error of the mean.** Note that this measure of the reliability of the mean decreases in proportion to the square root of n; for instance, it is necessary to quadruple the size of the sample in order to halve the standard deviation of the sampling distribution of the mean. This also indicates what might be called a "law of diminishing returns" so far as increasing the sample size is concerned. Usually it does not pay to take excessively large samples since the extra labor and expense is not accompanied by a proportional gain in reliability. For instance, if we increase the size of a sample from 25 to 2,500, the errors to which we are exposed are reduced only by a factor of 10.

Let us now return to the experimental sampling distribution on page 204, and let us check how closely its mean and variance correspond to the values we should expect in accordance with Theorem 6.1 Since the population from which the 50 samples of size $n = 10$ were obtained has the mean

$$\mu = \sum_{x=0}^{9} x \cdot \frac{1}{10} = 4.5$$

and the variance

$$\sigma^2 = \sum_{x=0}^{9} (x - 4.5)^2 \frac{1}{10} = 8.25$$

Theorem 6.1 leads us to expect a mean of $\mu_{\overline{X}} = 4.5$ and a variance of $\sigma_{\overline{X}}^2 = 8.25/10 = 0.825$. Calculating the mean and the variance from the 50 sample means on page 204, we get $\overline{x}_{\overline{x}} = 4.43$ and $s_{\overline{x}}^2 = 0.930$, which are reasonably close to the theoretical values.

Theorem 6.1 provides only partial information about the theoretical sampling distribution of the mean. In general, it is impossible to determine such a distribution exactly without knowledge of the actual form of the population. But it is possible to find the limiting distribution as $n \to \infty$ of a random variable whose values are closely related to $\overline{X}$, assuming only that the population has a finite variance σ^2. The random variable we are referring to here is the **standardized sample mean**

$$Z = \frac{\overline{X} - \mu}{\sigma/\sqrt{n}}$$

whose values are given by the difference between $\overline{x}$ and μ divided by the standard error of the mean. With reference to this random variable, we can now state the following theorem, called the **central limit theorem:**

Central limit theorem

> **Theorem 6.2**   If $\overline{X}$ is the mean of a sample of size n taken from a population having the mean μ and the finite variance σ^2, then
>
> $$Z = \frac{\overline{X} - \mu}{\sigma/\sqrt{n}}$$
>
> is a random variable whose distribution function approaches that of the standard normal distributions as $n \to \infty$.

The central limit theorem provides a normal distribution that allows us to assign probabilities to intervals of values for $\overline{X}$. Regardless of the form of the population distribution, the distribution of $\overline{X}$ is approximately normal with mean μ and variance σ^2/n whenever n is large. This tendency towards normality is illustrated in Figure 6.3 for a uniform population distribution and an exponential population distribution.

Although proving the central limit theorem is beyond the scope of this text, we can obtain experimental verification by constructing a normal-scores plot of the 50 sample means on page 204, which were obtained by sampling with replacement from a discrete uniform population (Figure 6.4). As can be seen, the points fall close to a straight line, and it seems that even for $n = 10$ the sampling distribution of the mean for this example follows the overall pattern of a normal distribution.

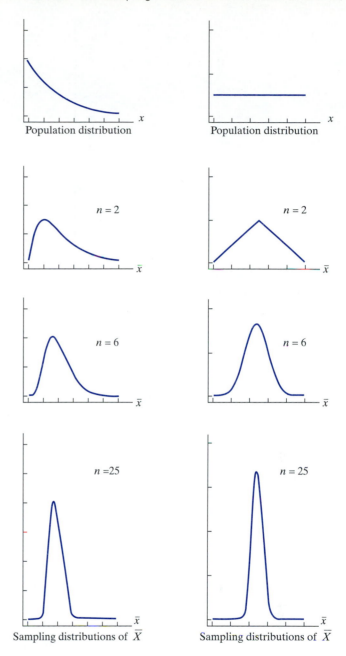

FIGURE 6.3 An illustration of the approach toward normality for the sampling distribution of $\overline{X}$ as sample size increases.

In practice, **the normal distribution provides an excellent approximation to the sampling distribution of the mean $\overline{X}$ for *n* as small as 25 or 30,** with hardly any restrictions on the shape of the population. As we saw in our example, the sampling distribution of the mean has the general shape of a normal distribution even for samples of size $n = 10$ from a discrete uniform distribution. **If the random samples**

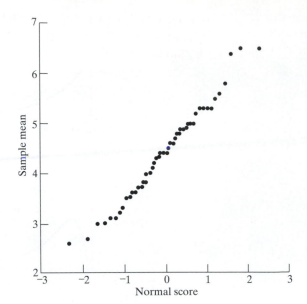

FIGURE 6.4 Experimental verification of the central limit theorem.

come from a normal population, the sampling distribution of the mean is normal regardless of the size of the sample.

EXAMPLE **Using the central limit theorem to calculate the probability of paint coverage**
If a 1-gallon can of paint covers on the average 513.3 square feet with a standard deviation of 31.5 square feet, what is the probability that the sample mean area covered by a sample of 40 of these 1-gallon cans will be anywhere from 510.0 to 520.0 square feet?

Solution By Theorem 6.2 we shall have to find the normal curve area between

$$z = \frac{510.0 - 513.3}{31.5/\sqrt{40}} = -0.66 \quad \text{and} \quad z = \frac{520.0 - 513.3}{31.5/\sqrt{40}} = 1.34$$

and checking these values in Table 3 we obtain a probability of 0.6553. Note that if $\bar{x}$ turned out to be much less than 513.3, say, less than 500.0, this might cause serious doubt whether the sample actually came from a population having $\mu = 513.3$ and $\sigma = 31.5$; the probability of obtaining such a small value (a z-value less than -2.67) is only 0.0038. ✔

E X E R C I S E S

6.1 An inspector examines every twentieth piece coming off an assembly line. List some of the conditions under which this method of sampling might not yield a random sample.

6.2 In 1932 the *Literary Digest* predicted the presidential election by random sampling from telephone directories and from its list of subscribers. The prediction was grossly incorrect; explain why.

6.3 Explain why the following will not lead to random samples from the desired populations.

(a) To determine what the average person spends on a vacation, a researcher interviews passengers on a luxury cruise.

(b) To determine the average income of its graduates 10 years after graduation, the alumni office of a university sent questionnaires in 2001 to all the members of the class of 1991 and based its estimate on the questionnaires returned.

(c) To determine public sentiment about certain import restrictions, an interviewer asks voters: "Do you feel that this unfair practice should be stopped?"

6.4 A market research organization wants to try a new product in 8 of 50 states. Use Table 7 to make this selection.

6.5 How many different samples of size $n = 2$ can be chosen from a finite population of size

(a) $N = 6$;

(b) $N = 25$?

6.6 With reference to Exercise 6.5, what is the probability of each sample in part (a) and the probability of each sample in part (b), if the samples are to be random?

6.7 Take 30 slips of paper and label five each -4 and 4, four each -3 and 3, three each -2 and 2, and two each -1, 0, and 1.

(a) If each slip of paper has the same probability of being drawn, find the probability of getting $-4, -3, -2, -1, 0, 1, 2, 3, 4$, and find the mean and the variance of this distribution.

(b) Draw 50 samples of size 10 from this population, each sample being drawn without replacement, and calculate their means.

(c) Calculate the mean and the variance of the 50 means obtained in part (b).

(d) Compare the results obtained in part (c) with the corresponding values expected according to Theorem 6.1 [Note that μ and σ^2 were obtained in part (a)].

6.8 Repeat Exercise 6.7, but select each sample with replacement; that is, replace each slip of paper and reshuffle before the next one is drawn.

6.9 Given the infinite population whose distribution is given by

x	$f(x)$
1	0.25
2	0.25
3	0.25
4	0.25

list the 16 possible samples of size 2 and use this list to construct the distribution of $\overline{X}$ for random samples of size 2 from the given population. Verify that the mean and the variance of this sampling distribution are identical with corresponding values expected according to Theorem 6.1.

6.10 Suppose that we convert the 50 samples referred to on page 204 into 25 samples of size $n = 20$ by combining the first two, the next two, and so on. Find the means of these samples and calculate their mean and their standard deviation. Compare this mean and this standard deviation with the corresponding values expected in accordance with Theorem 6.1.

6.11 When we sample from an infinite population, what happens to the standard error of the mean if the sample size is

(a) increased from 50 to 200;

(b) increased from 400 to 900;

(c) decreased from 225 to 25;

(d) decreased from 640 to 40?

6.12 What is the value of the finite population correction factor in the formula for $\sigma_{\overline{X}}^2$ when

(a) $n = 5$ and $N = 200$;

(b) $n = 10$ and $N = 400$;

(c) $n = 100$ and $N = 5{,}000$?

6.13 For large sample size n, verify that there is a 50-50 chance that the mean of a random sample from an infinite population with the standard deviation σ will differ from μ by less than $0.6745 \cdot \dfrac{\sigma}{\sqrt{n}}$. It has been the custom to refer to this quantity as the **probable error of the mean.**

6.14 The mean of a random sample of size $n = 25$ is used to estimate the mean of an infinite population with the standard deviation $\sigma = 2.4$. What can we assert about the probability that the error will be less than 1.2, if we use

(a) Chebyshev's theorem;

(b) the central limit theorem?

6.15 A random sample of size 100 is taken from an infinite population having the mean $\mu = 76$ and the variance of $\sigma^2 = 256$. What is the probability that $\overline{X}$ will be between 75 and 78?

6.16 A wire-bonding process is said to be in control if the mean pull strength is 10 pounds. It is known that the pull-strength measurements are normally distributed with a standard deviation of 1.5 pounds. Periodic random samples of size 4 are taken from this process and the process is said to be "out of control" if a sample mean is less than 7.75 pounds. Comment.

6.17 If the distribution of the weights of all men traveling by air between Dallas and El Paso has a mean of 163 pounds and a standard deviation of 18 pounds, what is the probability that the combined gross weight of 36 men traveling on a plane between these two cities is more than 6,000 pounds?

6.18 If X is a continuous random variable and $Y = X - \mu$, show that $\sigma_Y^2 = \sigma_X^2$.

6.19 Prove that $\mu_{\overline{X}} = \mu$ for random samples from discrete (finite or countably infinite) populations.

6.3 The Sampling Distribution of the Mean (σ Unknown)

Application of the theory of the preceding section requires knowledge of the population standard deviation σ. If n is large, this does not pose any problems even when σ is unknown, as it is reasonable in that case to substitute for it the sample standard deviation s. However, when it comes to the random variable whose values are given by $\dfrac{\overline{x} - \mu}{s/\sqrt{n}}$, very little is known about its exact sampling distribution for small values of n unless we make the assumption that the sample comes from a normal population. Under this assumption, one can prove the following.

A random variable having the *t* distribution

> **Theorem 6.3**   If $\overline{X}$ is the mean of a random sample of size n taken from a normal population having the mean μ and the variance σ^2, and
>
> $$S^2 = \sum_{i=1}^{n} \frac{(X_i - \overline{X})^2}{n - 1}, \text{ then}$$
>
> $$t = \frac{\overline{X} - \mu}{S/\sqrt{n}}$$
>
> is a random variable having the *t* distribution with the parameter $\nu = n - 1$.

The lower case *t* notation helps differentiate this important statistic from others. This theorem is more general than Theorem 6.2 in the sense that it does not require knowledge of σ; on the other hand, it is less general than Theorem 6.2 in the sense that it requires the assumption of a normal population.

As can be seen from Figure 6.5 the overall shape of a **t distribution** is similar to that of a normal distribution—both are bell-shaped and symmetrical about the mean. Like the standard normal distribution, the *t* distribution has the mean 0, but its variance depends on the parameter ν (*nu*), called the number of **degrees of freedom.** The variance of the *t* distribution exceeds 1, but it approaches 1 as $n \to \infty$. In fact, it can be shown that the *t* distribution with ν degrees of freedom approaches the standard normal distribution as $\nu \to \infty$.

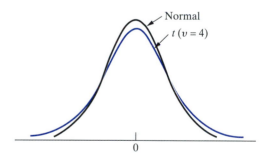

FIGURE 6.5 *t* distribution and standard normal distribution.

Table 4 at the end of the book contains selected values of t_α for various values of ν, where t_α is such that the area under the *t* distribution to its right is equal to α. In this table the left-hand column contains values of ν, the column headings are areas α in the right-hand tail of the *t* distribution, and the entries are values of t_α (see also Figure 6.6). It is not necessary to tabulate values of t_α for $\alpha > 0.50$, as it follows from the symmetry of the *t* distribution that $t_{1-\alpha} = -t_\alpha$; thus, the value of *t* that corresponds to a left-hand tail area of α is $-t_\alpha$.

Note that in the bottom row of Table 4 the entries correspond to the values of *z* that cut off right-hand tails of area α under the standard normal curve. Using

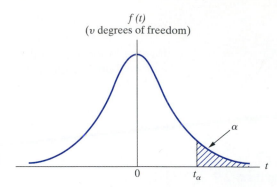

Figure 6.6 Tabulated values of t_α.

the notation z_α for such a value of z, it can be seen, for example, that $z_{0.025} = 1.96 = t_{0.025}$ for $\nu = \infty$. This result should really have been expected, since the t distribution approaches the standard normal distribution as $\nu \to \infty$. In fact, observing that the values of t_α for 29 or more degrees of freedom are close to the corresponding values of z_α, we conclude that **the standard normal distribution provides a good approximation to the t distribution for samples of size 30 or more.**

EXAMPLE

Using a probability calculation from the t distribution to refute a claim
A manufacturer of fuses claims that with a 20% overload, the fuses will blow in 12.40 minutes on the average. To test this claim, a sample of 20 of the fuses was subjected to a 20% overload, and the times it took them to blow had a mean of 10.63 minutes and a standard deviation of 2.48 minutes. If it can be assumed that the data constitute a random sample from a normal population, do they tend to support or refute the manufacturer's claim?

Solution

First we calculate

$$t = \frac{10.63 - 12.40}{2.48/\sqrt{20}} = -3.19$$

which is a value of a random variable having the t distribution with $\nu = 20 - 1 = 19$ degrees of freedom. Now, from Table 4 we find that for $\nu = 19$ the probability that t will exceed 2.861 is 0.005, and hence that the probability that t will be less than -2.861 is also 0.005. Since $t = -3.19$ is less than -2.861 and 0.005 is a very small probability, we conclude that the data tend to refute the manufacturer's claim. In all likelihood, the mean blowing time of his fuses with a 20% overload is less than 12.40 minutes. ✔

The assumption that the sample must come from a normal population is not so severe a restriction as it may seem. Studies have shown that the distribution of random variable $\dfrac{\overline{X} - \mu}{S/\sqrt{n}}$ is fairly close to a t distribution even for samples from certain nonnormal populations. In practice, it is necessary to make sure primarily that the population from which we are sampling is approximately bell-shaped and not too skewed. A practical way of checking this assumption is to construct a normal-scores plot, as described on page 188. (If such a plot shows a distinct curve rather than a straight line, it may be possible to "straighten it out" by transforming the data—say, by taking their logarithms or their square roots, as discussed in Section 5.12.)

6.4 The Sampling Distribution of the Variance

So far we have discussed only the sampling distribution of the mean, but if we had taken the medians or the standard deviations of the 50 samples mentioned in the example on page 204, we would similarly have obtained experimental sampling distributions of these statistics. In this section we shall be concerned with the theoretical sampling distribution of the sample variance for random samples from normal populations. Since S^2 cannot be negative, we should suspect that this sampling distribution is not a normal curve; in fact, it is related to the gamma distribution (see page 166) with $\alpha = \nu/2$ and $\beta = 2$, called the **chi-square distribution.** Specifically, we have the following theorem.

A random variable having the chi-square distribution

> **Theorem 6.4**   If S^2 is the variance of a random sample of size n taken from a normal population having the variance σ^2, then
>
> $$\chi^2 = \frac{(n-1)S^2}{\sigma^2} = \frac{\sum_{i=1}^{n}(X_i - \overline{X})^2}{\sigma^2}$$
>
> is a random variable having the chi-square distribution with the parameter $\nu = n - 1$.

Table 5 at the end of the book contains selected values of χ^2_α for various values of ν, again called the number of **degrees of freedom,** where χ^2_α is such that the area under the chi-square distribution to its right is equal to α. In this table the left-hand column contains values of ν, the column headings are areas α in the right-hand tail of the chi-square distribution, and the entries are values of χ^2_α (see also Figure 6.7). Unlike the t distribution, it is necessary to tabulate values of χ^2_α for $\alpha > 0.50$, because the chi-square distribution is not symmetrical.

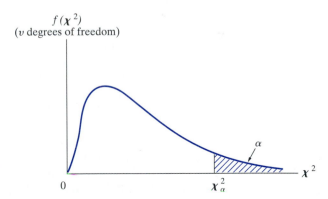

FIGURE 6.7 Tabulated values of chi-square.

EXAMPLE

A probability calculation based on the χ^2 distribution helps monitor variability
An optical firm purchases glass to be ground into lenses, and it is known from past experience that the variance of the refractive index of this kind of glass is $1.26 \cdot 10^{-4}$. As it is important that the various pieces of glass have nearly the same index of refraction, the firm rejects such a shipment if the sample variance of 20 pieces selected at random exceeds $2.00 \cdot 10^{-4}$. Assuming that the sample values may be looked upon as a random sample from a normal population, what is the probability that a shipment will be rejected even though $\sigma^2 = 1.26 \cdot 10^{-4}$?

Solution

Substituting into the formula for the chi-square statistic, we get

$$\chi^2 = \frac{19(2.00 \cdot 10^{-4})}{1.26 \cdot 10^{-4}} = 30.2$$

and then we find from Table 5 that for 19 degrees of freedom $\chi^2_{0.05} = 30.1$. Thus, the probability that a good shipment will erroneously be rejected is less than 0.05. ✔

A problem closely related to that of finding the distribution of the sample variance is that a finding the distribution of the ratio of the variances of two independent random samples. This problem is important because it arises in tests in which we want to determine whether two samples come from populations having equal variances. If they do, the two sample variances should be nearly the same; that is, their ratio should be close to 1. To determine whether the ratio of two sample variances is too small or too large, we use the theory given in the following theorem.

A random variable having the *F* distribution

> Theorem 6.5   If S_1^2 and S_2^2 are the variances of independent random samples of size n_1 and n_2, respectively, taken from two normal populations having the same variance, then
>
> $$F = \frac{S_1^2}{S_2^2}$$
>
> is a random variable having the *F* distribution with the parameters $\nu_1 = n_1 - 1$ and $\nu_2 = n_2 - 1$.

The **F distribution** is related to the beta distribution (page 168), and its two parameters, ν_1 and ν_2, are called the **numerator** and **denominator degrees of freedom.** As it would require too large a table to give values of F_α corresponding to many different right-hand tail probabilities α, and since $\alpha = 0.05$ and $\alpha = 0.01$ are most commonly used in practice, Table 6 contains only values $F_{0.05}$ and $F_{0.01}$ for various combinations of values of ν_1 and ν_2 (see also Figure 6.8).

EXAMPLE

Using Table 6 to evaluate a probability
If two independent random samples of size $n_1 = 7$ and $n_2 = 13$ are taken from a normal population, what is the probability that the variance of the first sample will be at least three times as large as that of the second sample?

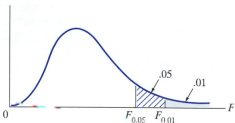

FIGURE 6.8 Tabulated values of F.

Solution From Table 6 we find that $F_{0.05} = 3.00$ for $v_1 = 7 - 1 = 6$ and $v_2 = 13 - 1 = 12$; thus, the desired probability is 0.05. ✔

It is possible to use Table 6 also to find values of F corresponding to left-hand tail probabilities of 0.05 or 0.01. Writing $F_\alpha(v_1, v_2)$ for F_α with v_1 and v_2 degrees of freedom, we simply use the identity

$$F_{1-\alpha}(v_1, v_2) = \frac{1}{F_\alpha(v_2, v_1)}$$

EXAMPLE **Using Table 6 to find a left-hand tail probability**
Find the value of $F_{0.95}$ (corresponding to a left-hand tail probability of 0.05) for $v_1 = 10$ and $v_2 = 20$ degrees of freedom.

Solution Making use of the identity and Table 6, we get

$$F_{0.95}(10, 20) = \frac{1}{F_{0.05}(20, 10)} = \frac{1}{2.77} = 0.36$$ ✔

Note that Theorems 6.4 and 6.5 require the assumption that we are sampling from normal populations. Unlike the situation with the t distribution, deviations from an underlying normal distribution, such as a long tail, may have a serious effect on these sampling distributions. Consequently, it is best to transform to near normality using the approach in Section 5.12 before invoking the sampling distributions in this section.

EXERCISES

6.20 A random sample of size 25 from a normal population has the mean $\bar{x} = 47.5$ and the standard deviation $s = 8.4$. Does this information tend to support or refute the claim that the mean of the population is $\mu = 42.1$?

6.21 The following are the times between 6 calls for an ambulance (in a certain city) and the patient's arrival at the hospital: 27, 15, 20, 32, 18, and 26 minutes. Use these figures to judge the reasonableness of the ambulance service's claim that it takes on the average of 20 minutes between the call for an ambulance and the patient's arrival at the hospital.

6.22 A process for making certain bearings is under control if the diameters of the bearings have a mean of 0.5000 cm. What can we say about this process if a sample of 10 of these bearings has a mean diameter of 0.5060 cm and a standard deviation of 0.0040 cm?

6.23 The claim that the variance of a normal population is $\sigma^2 = 21.3$ is rejected if the variance of a random sample of size 15 exceeds 39.74. What is the probability that the claim will be rejected even though $\sigma^2 = 21.3$?

6.24 A random sample of 10 observations is taken from a normal population having the variance $\sigma^2 = 42.5$. Find the approximate probability of obtaining a sample standard deviation between 3.14 and 8.94.

6.25 If independent random samples of size $n_1 = n_2 = 8$ come from normal populations having the same variance, what is the probability that either sample variance will be at least 7 times as large as the other?

6.26 Find the values of

(a) $F_{0.95}$ for 12 and 15 degrees of freedom;

(b) $F_{0.99}$ for 6 and 20 degrees of freedom.

6.27 The chi-square distribution with 4 degrees of freedom is given by

$$f(x) = \begin{cases} \frac{1}{4} \cdot x \cdot e^{-x/2} & x > 0 \\ 0 & x \leq 0 \end{cases}$$

Find the probability that the variance of a random sample of size 5 from a normal population with $\sigma = 12$ will exceed 180.

6.28 The t distribution with 1 degree of freedom is given by

$$f(t) = \frac{1}{\pi}(1 + t^2)^{-1} \qquad -\infty < t < \infty$$

Verify the value given for $t_{0.05}$ for $\nu = 1$ in Table 4.

6.29 The F distribution with 4 and 4 degrees of freedom is given by

$$f(F) = \begin{cases} 6F(1 + F)^{-4} & F > 0 \\ 0 & F \leq 0 \end{cases}$$

If random samples of size 5 are taken from two normal populations having the same variance, find the probability that the ratio of the larger to the smaller sample variance will exceed 3.

R E V I E W   E X E R C I S E S

6.30 The panel for a national science fair wishes to select 10 states to send a student representative who will be chosen at random from the students participating in the state science fair.

(a) Use Table 7 to select the 10 states.

(b) Does the total selection process give each student who participates in a state science fair an equal chance of being selected to be a representative at the national science fair?

6.31 How many different samples of size $n = 2$ can be chosen from a finite population of size

    (a) $N = 8$;

    (b) $N = 20$?

6.32 With reference to Exercise 6.31, what is the probability of choosing each sample in part (a) and the probability of choosing each sample in part (b), if the samples are to be random?

6.33 Referring to Exercise 6.31, find the value of the finite population correction factor in the formula for $\sigma_{\bar{X}}^2$ for part (a) and part (b).

6.34 A random sample of size $n = 36$ is taken from an infinite population with the mean $\mu = 63$ and the variance $\sigma^2 = 81$. What can we assert about the probability of getting a sample mean greater than 66.75, if we use

    (a) Chebyshev's theorem;

    (b) the central limit theorem?

6.35 The number of pieces of mail that a department receives each day can be modeled by a distribution having mean 44 and standard deviation 8. For a random sample of 25 days, what can be said about the probability that the sample mean will be less than 40 or greater than 48 using

    (a) Chebyshev's theorem;

    (b) the central limit theorem?

6.36 If measurements of the specific gravity of a metal can be looked upon as a sample from a normal population having a standard deviation of 0.04, what is the probability that the mean of a random sample of size 25 will be "off" by at most 0.02?

6.37 Adding graphite to iron can improve its ductile qualities. If measurements of the diameter of graphite spheres within an iron matrix can be modeled as a normal distribution having standard deviation .16, what is the probability that the mean of a sample of size 36 will differ from the population mean by more than .06?

6.38 If 2 independent random samples of size $n_1 = 9$ and $n_2 = 16$ are taken from a normal population, what is the probability that the variance of the first sample will be at least 4 times as large as the variance of the second sample?

6.39 If 2 independent samples of sizes $n_1 = 26$ and $n_2 = 8$ are taken from a normal population, what is the probability that the variance of the second sample will be at least 2.4 times the variance of the first sample?

6.40 When we sample from an infinite population, what happens to the standard error of the mean if the sample size is

    (a) increased from 100 to 200;

    (b) increased from 200 to 300;

    (c) decreased from 360 to 90?

6.41 A traffic engineer collects data on traffic flow at a busy intersection during the rush hour by recording the number of westbound cars that are waiting for a green light. The observations are made for each light change. Explain why this sampling technique will not lead to a random sample.

6.42 Explain why the following may not lead to random samples from the desired populations:

    (a) To determine the smoothness of shafts, a manufacturer measures the roughness of the first piece made each morning.

    (b) To determine the mix of cars, trucks, and buses in the rush hour, an engineer records the type of vehicle passing a fixed point at 1-minute intervals.

KEY TERMS

(with page references)

Central limit theorem 208

Chi-square distribution 215

Degrees of freedom 213, 215

Discrete uniform distribution 204

F distribution 216

Finite population 200

Finite population correction factor 207

Infinite population 200

Law of large numbers 207

Parameter 203

Population 199

Probable error of the mean 212

Random sample 200, 201

Sample 200

Sampling distribution 204

Standard error of the mean 207

Standardized mean 208

Statistic 203

t distribution 213

Inferences Concerning Means

I n the beginning of Chapter 6, we stated that the purpose of most statistical investigations is to generalize from information contained in random samples about the populations from which the samples were obtained. In the classical approach the methods of statistical inference are divided into two major areas—estimation and tests of hypotheses. In Sections 7.1 and 7.2 we shall present some theory and some methods which pertain to the estimation of means. Sections 7.3 and 7.4 deal with the basic concepts of hypothesis testing, and Sections 7.5, 7.6, and 7.8 deal with tests of hypotheses concerning means. Randomization, a procedure to help meet the assumptions, is presented in Section 7.9. ■

7.1 Point Estimation

Basically, **point estimation** concerns the choosing of a statistic, that is, a single number calculated from sample data (and perhaps other information) for which we have some expectation, or assurance, that it is "reasonably close" to the parameter it is supposed to estimate. To explain what we mean here by reasonably close is not an easy task; first, the value of the parameter is unknown, and second, the value of the statistic is unknown until after the sample has been obtained. Thus, we can only ask whether, upon repeated sampling, the distribution of the statistic has certain desirable properties akin to "closeness."

CHAPTER 7

EXAMPLE

Two components of closeness: variance and bias
Scientists need to be able to detect small amounts of contaminants in the environment. As a check on the current capabilities, the following measurements were made on test specimens spiked with a known concentration 1.25 $\mu g/l$ of lead. That is, the readings should average 1.25 if there is no background lead in the samples.

$$2.4 \quad 2.9 \quad 2.7 \quad 2.6 \quad 2.9 \quad 2.0 \quad 2.8 \quad 2.2 \quad 2.4 \quad 2.4 \quad 2.0 \quad 2.5$$

(a) Make a dot diagram;

(b) Compute the point estimator $\overline{X}$ and estimate its standard deviation. This latter quantity is called the **estimated standard error** of $\overline{X}$.

Solution   (a)

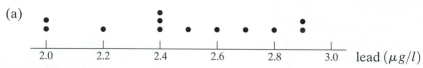

(b) We calculate

$$\overline{x} = \frac{29.8}{12} = 2.483 \quad \text{and} \quad s^2 = \frac{75.08 - (29.8)^2/12}{12 - 1} = 0.09788$$

From Theorem 6.1 $\overline{X}$ has standard deviation $\sigma/\sqrt{n}$, so the estimated standard error is $s/\sqrt{n} = \sqrt{.09788/12} = .090$.

There appears to be either a bias due to the laboratory procedure or some lead already in the samples before they were spiked. All 12 measurements are above the known concentration 1.25 $\mu g/l$.   ✔

Closeness can be expressed as two components: (1) the bias, which is the expected value of the estimator minus the parameter; and (2) the standard deviation or variance of the estimator.

Point Estimation of a Mean

> **Parameter:** Population mean μ
> **Data:** A random sample $X_1, \ldots, X_n$
> **Estimator:** $\overline{X}$
>
> **Estimate of standard error:** $\dfrac{S}{\sqrt{n}}$

We know from Theorem 6.1 that the sampling distribution of the mean has the same mean as the population from which the sample is obtained; hence, we can expect that the means of repeated random samples from a given population will center on the mean of this population and not about some other value.

To formulate this property more generally, let θ be the parameter of interest and $\hat{\theta}$ be a statistic. The **hat notation** distinguishes the sample-based quantity from the parameter. We now make the following definition:

Unbiased estimator

> A statistic $\hat{\theta}$ is said to be an **unbiased estimator,** or its value an unbiased estimate, if and only if the mean of the sampling distribution of the estimator equals θ.

Thus, we call a statistic unbiased if "on the average" its values will equal the parameter it is supposed to estimate. Note that we have distinguished here between an estimator, a random variable, and an estimate, which is one of its values; also, it is customary to apply the term "statistic" to both estimates and estimators.

It is a mathematical fact that $\overline{X}$ is an unbiased estimator of the population mean μ provided the observations are a random sample. However, the particular engineering application may contain unknown biases as in the spiked water sample example.

Generally speaking, the property of unbiasedness is one of the more desirable properties in point estimation, although it is by no means essential and it is sometimes outweighed by other factors. One shortcoming of the criterion of unbiasedness is that it will generally not provide a unique statistic for a given problem of estimation. For instance, it can be shown that for a random sample of size $n = 2$ the mean $\dfrac{X_1 + X_2}{2}$ as well as the weighted mean $\dfrac{aX_1 + bX_2}{a + b}$, where a and b are positive constants, are unbiased estimates of the mean of the population. If we further assume that the population is symmetric, so are the median and the midrange (the mean of the largest value and the smallest) for random samples of any size.

This suggests that we must seek a further criterion for deciding which of several unbiased estimators is "best" for estimating a given parameter. Such a criterion becomes evident when we compare the sampling distributions of the median and the mean for random samples of size n from the same normal population. Although these two sampling distributions have the same mean, the population mean μ, and although they are both symmetrical and bell-shaped, their variances differ. From Theorem 6.1, the variance of the sampling distribution of the mean for random samples from infinite populations is $\dfrac{\sigma^2}{n}$, and it can be shown that for random samples of the same size from normal populations the variance of the sampling distribution of the median is approximately $1.5708 \cdot \dfrac{\sigma^2}{n}$. Thus, it is more likely that the mean will be closer to μ than the median is to μ. Despite this long-run average property, given a particular sample we have no way of knowing which of the two is closest.

We formalize this important comparison of sampling distributions of statistics on the basis of their variances.

More efficient unbiased estimator

A statistic $\hat{\theta}_1$ is said to be a more efficient unbiased estimator of the parameter θ than the statistic $\hat{\theta}_2$ if

1. $\hat{\theta}_1$ and $\hat{\theta}_2$ are both unbiased estimators of θ;
2. the variance of the sampling distribution of the first estimator is less than that of the second.

We have thus seen that for random samples from normal populations the mean $\overline{X}$ is more efficient than the median as an estimator of μ; in fact, it can be shown that in most practical situations where we estimate a population mean μ, the variance of the sampling distribution of no other statistic is less than that of the sampling distribution of the mean. In other words, in most practical situations the sample mean is an acceptable statistic for estimating a population mean μ. (There exist several other criteria for assessing the "goodness" of methods of point estimation, but we shall not discuss them in this book.)

When we use a sample mean to estimate the mean of a population, we know that although we are using a method of estimation which has certain desirable properties, the chances are slim, virtually nonexistent, that the estimate will actually equal μ. Hence, it would seem desirable to accompany such a point estimate of μ with some statement as to how close we might reasonably expect the estimate to be. The error, $\overline{X} - \mu$, is the difference between the estimator and the quantity it is supposed to estimate.

To examine this error, let us make use of the fact that for large n

$$\frac{\overline{X} - \mu}{\sigma/\sqrt{n}}$$

is a random variable having approximately the standard normal distribution.

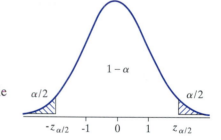

FIGURE 7.1 The large sample distribution of $\dfrac{\overline{X} - \mu}{\sigma/\sqrt{n}}$.

As shown in Figure 7.1, we can assert with probability $1 - \alpha$ that the inequality

$$-z_{\alpha/2} \le \frac{\overline{X} - \mu}{\sigma/\sqrt{n}} \le z_{\alpha/2}$$

will be satisfied or that

$$\frac{|\overline{X} - \mu|}{\sigma/\sqrt{n}} \le z_{\alpha/2}$$

where $z_{\alpha/2}$ is such that the normal curve area to its right equals $\alpha/2$. If we now let E stand for the maximum of these values of $|\overline{X} - \mu|$, the maximum error of estimate, we have that the error $|\overline{X} - \mu|$, will be less than

Maximum error of estimate

$$E = z_{\alpha/2} \cdot \frac{\sigma}{\sqrt{n}}$$

with probability $1 - \alpha$. In other words, if we intend to estimate μ with the mean of a large ($n \ge 30$) random sample, we can assert with probability $1 - \alpha$ that the error, $|\overline{X} - \mu|$, will be at most $z_{\alpha/2} \cdot \dfrac{\sigma}{\sqrt{n}}$. The most widely used values for $1 - \alpha$ are 0.95 and 0.99, and the corresponding values of $z_{\alpha/2}$ are $z_{0.025} = 1.96$ and $z_{0.005} = 2.575$ (see Exercise 5.23 on page 159).

EXAMPLE

Specifying a high probability for the maximum error—σ known
An industrial engineer intends to use the mean of a random sample of size $n = 150$ to estimate the average mechanical aptitude (as measured by a certain test) of assembly line workers in a large industry. If, on the basis of experience, the engineer can assume that $\sigma = 6.2$ for such data, what can he assert with probability 0.99 about the maximum size of his error?

Solution Substituting $n = 150$, $\sigma = 6.2$, and $z_{0.005} = 2.575$ into the preceding formula for E, we get

$$E = 2.575 \cdot \frac{6.2}{\sqrt{150}} = 1.30$$

Thus, the engineer can assert with probability 0.99 that his error will be at most 1.30. ✔

Suppose now that the engineer of this example collects his data and gets $\overline{x} = 69.5$. Can he still assert with probability 0.99 that the error is at most 1.30? First of all, $\overline{x} = 69.5$ either differs from the true average by at most 1.30 or it does not, and he does not know which. Consequently, it must be understood that the 0.99 probability applies to the method he used to determine the maximum error (getting the sample data and using the formula for E) and not directly to the parameter he is trying to estimate. To make this distinction, it has become the custom to use the word **confidence** here instead of *probability*. **In general, we make probability statements about future values of random variables (say, the potential error of an estimate) and confidence statements once the data have been obtained.** Accordingly, we would say in our example that the engineer can be 99% confident that the error of his estimate, $\overline{x} = 69.5$, is at most 1.30.

Determination of sample size. The formula for E on page 224 can also be used to determine the sample size that is needed to attain a desired degree of precision. Suppose that we want to use the mean of a large random sample to estimate the mean of a population, and we want to be able to assert with probability $1 - \alpha$ that the error will be at most some prescribed quantity E [or assert later with $(1 - \alpha)100\%$ confidence that the error is at most E]. As before, we write

$$E = z_{\alpha/2} \cdot \frac{\sigma}{\sqrt{n}}$$

and upon solving this equation for n we get

Sample size determination

$$n = \left[\frac{z_{\alpha/2} \cdot \sigma}{E} \right]^2$$

To be able to use this formula we must know $1 - \alpha$, E, and σ, and for the latter we often substitute an estimate based on prior data of a similar kind (or, if necessary, a good guess).

EXAMPLE

Selecting the sample size

A research worker wants to determine the average time it takes a mechanic to rotate the tires of a car, and she wants to be able to assert with 95% confidence that the mean of her sample is off by at most 0.50 minute. If she can presume from past experience that $\sigma = 1.6$ minutes, how large a sample will she have to take?

Solution

Substituting $E = 0.50$, $\sigma = 1.6$, and $z_{0.025} = 1.96$ into the formula for n, we get

$$n = \left[\frac{1.96 \cdot 1.6}{0.50}\right]^2 = 39.3$$

or 40 rounded up to the nearest integer. Thus, the research worker will have to time 40 mechanics performing the task of rotating the tires of a car. ✔

The methods discussed so far in this section require that σ be known or that it can be approximated with the sample standard deviation s, thus requiring that n be large. However, if it is reasonable to assume that we are sampling from a normal population, we can base our argument on Theorem 6.3 instead of Theorem 6.2, namely on the fact that

$$t = \frac{\overline{X} - \mu}{S/\sqrt{n}}$$

is a random variable having the t distribution with $n - 1$ degrees of freedom. Duplicating the steps on page 224, we thus arrive at the result that with probability $1 - \alpha$ the error we make in using $\overline{X}$ to estimate μ will be at most $t_{\alpha/2} S/\sqrt{n}$. When $\overline{X}$ and S become available, we assert with $(1 - \alpha) 100\%$ confidence that the error made in using $\overline{x}$ to estimate μ is at most

Maximum error of estimate, normal population $-\sigma$ unknown

$$E = t_{\alpha/2} \cdot \frac{s}{\sqrt{n}}$$

EXAMPLE

A 98% confidence bound on the maximum error

In six determinations of the melting point of tin, a chemist obtained a mean of 232.26 degrees Celsius with a standard deviation of 0.14 degrees. If he uses this mean to estimate the actual melting point of tin, what can the chemist assert with 98% confidence about the maximum error?

Solution

Substituting $n = 6$, $s = 0.14$, and $t_{0.01} = 3.365$ (for $n - 1 = 5$ degrees of freedom) into the formula for E, we get

$$E = 3.365 \cdot \frac{0.14}{\sqrt{6}} = 0.19$$

Thus the chemist can assert with 98% confidence that his figure for the melting point of tin is off by at most 0.19 degree. ✔

7.2 Interval Estimation

Since point estimates cannot really be expected to coincide with the quantities they are intended to estimate, it is sometimes preferable to replace them with **interval estimates,** that is, with intervals for which we can assert with a reasonable degree of certainty that they will contain the parameter under consideration. To illustrate the construction of such an interval, suppose that we have a large ($n \geq 30$) random sample from a population with the unknown mean μ and the known variance σ^2. Referring to the inequality

$$-z_{\alpha/2} < \frac{\overline{X} - \mu}{\sigma/\sqrt{n}} < z_{\alpha/2}$$

which, as shown on page 224, will be satisfied with probability $1 - \alpha$, we now apply simple algebra and rewrite it as $\overline{X} - z_{\alpha/2} \cdot \sigma/\sqrt{n} < \mu < \overline{X} + z_{\alpha/2} \cdot \sigma/\sqrt{n}$. When the observed value $\overline{x}$ becomes available, we obtain

Large sample confidence interval for $\mu - \sigma$ known

$$\overline{x} - z_{\alpha/2} \cdot \frac{\sigma}{\sqrt{n}} < \mu < \overline{x} + z_{\alpha/2} \cdot \frac{\sigma}{\sqrt{n}}$$

Thus, when a sample has been obtained and the value of $\overline{x}$ has been calculated, we can claim with $(1 - \alpha)\,100\%$ confidence that the interval from $\overline{x} - z_{\alpha/2} \cdot \dfrac{\sigma}{\sqrt{n}}$ to $\overline{x} + z_{\alpha/2} \cdot \dfrac{\sigma}{\sqrt{n}}$ contains μ. It is customary to refer to an interval of this kind as a **confidence interval** for μ having the **degree of confidence** $1 - \alpha$ or $(1 - \alpha)\,100\%$ and to its endpoints as the **confidence limits.**

EXAMPLE

Calculating and intepretating a large sample confidence interval
A random sample of size $n = 100$ is taken from a population with $\sigma = 5.1$. Given that the sample mean is $\overline{x} = 21.6$, construct a 95% confidence interval for the population mean μ.

Solution Substituting the given values of n, $\overline{x}$, σ, and $z_{0.025} = 1.96$ into the confidence interval formula, we get

$$21.6 - 1.96 \cdot \frac{5.1}{\sqrt{100}} < \mu < 21.6 + 1.96 \cdot \frac{5.1}{\sqrt{100}}$$

or $20.6 < \mu < 22.6$. Of course, either the interval from 20.6 to 22.6 contains the population mean μ, or it does not, but we are 95% confident that it does. As was explained on page 225, this means that the method by which the interval was obtained "works" 95% of the time. In other words, in repeated applications of the confidence interval formula, 95% of the intervals can be expected to contain the means of the respective populations. ✔

The preceding confidence interval formula is exact only for random samples from normal populations, but for large samples it will generally provide good approximations. Since σ is unknown in most applications, we may have to make the further approximation of substituting for σ the sample standard deviation s.

Large sample confidence interval for μ

$$\bar{x} - z_{\alpha/2} \cdot \frac{s}{\sqrt{n}} < \mu < \bar{x} + z_{\alpha/2} \cdot \frac{s}{\sqrt{n}}$$

EXAMPLE

A 99% confidence interval for the mean daily sulfur emissions
With reference to the sulfur oxides emission data on page 15, for which we had $n = 80$, $\bar{x} = 18.85$, and $s^2 = 30.77$ (hence, $s = 5.55$), construct a 99% confidence interval for the plant's true average daily emission of sulfur oxides.

Solution   Substituting into the confidence interval formula with $s = 5.55$ we get

$$18.85 - 2.575 \cdot \frac{5.55}{\sqrt{80}} < \mu < 18.85 + 2.575 \cdot \frac{5.55}{\sqrt{80}}$$

or $17.25 < \mu < 20.45$. We are 99% confident that the interval from 17.25 tons to 20.45 tons contains the true average daily emission. ✔

For small samples ($n < 30$), we proceed as on page 226, provided it is reasonable to assume that we are sampling from a normal population. Thus, with $t_{\alpha/2}$ defined as on page 213, we get the $(1 - \alpha)\,100\%$ confidence interval formula

Small sample confidence interval for μ

$$\bar{x} - t_{\alpha/2} \cdot \frac{s}{\sqrt{n}} < \mu < \bar{x} + t_{\alpha/2} \cdot \frac{s}{\sqrt{n}}$$

This formula applies to samples from normal populations, but in accordance with the discussion on page 214, it may be used as long as the sample does not exhibit any pronounced departures from normality.

EXAMPLE

A 99% confidence interval for the mean of a normal population
The mean weight loss of $n = 16$ grinding balls after a certain length of time in mill slurry is 3.42 grams with a standard deviation of 0.68 gram. Construct a 99% confidence interval for the true mean weight loss of such grinding balls under the stated conditions.

Solution   Substituting $n = 16$, $\bar{x} = 3.42$, $s = 0.68$, and $t_{0.005} = 2.947$ for $n - 1 = 15$ degrees of freedom into the small sample confidence interval formula for μ, we get

$$3.42 - 2.947 \cdot \frac{0.68}{\sqrt{16}} < \mu < 3.42 + 2.947 \cdot \frac{0.68}{\sqrt{16}}$$

or $2.92 < \mu < 3.92$. We are 99% confident that the interval from 2.92 grams to 3.92 grams contains the mean weight loss.   ✔

Because confidence intervals are an important way of making inferences, we review their interpretation in the context of 95% confidence intervals for μ.
Before the observations are made, $\overline{X}$ and S are random variables, so:

1. The interval from $\overline{X} - t_{0.025} \dfrac{S}{\sqrt{n}}$ to $\overline{X} + t_{0.025} \dfrac{S}{\sqrt{n}}$ is a random interval. It is centered at $\overline{X}$ and its length is proportional to S.

2. The interval from $\overline{X} - t_{0.025} \dfrac{S}{\sqrt{n}}$ to $\overline{X} + t_{0.025} \dfrac{S}{\sqrt{n}}$ will cover the true (fixed) μ with probability 0.95.

Once the observations are made and we have the numerical values $\overline{x}$ and s.

3. The calculated interval from $\overline{x} - t_{0.025} \dfrac{s}{\sqrt{n}}$ to $\overline{x} + t_{0.025} \dfrac{s}{\sqrt{n}}$ is fixed. It is no longer possible to talk about the probability of covering μ. The interval either covers μ or it does not. Further, in any particular application, we have no way of knowing if μ is covered or not.

However, because 0.95 is the probability that we cover μ in each application, the long-run relative frequency interpretation of probability promises that

$$\frac{\text{number of intervals that cover the true mean}}{\text{number of intervals calculated}} \rightarrow 0.95$$

when the intervals are calculated for a large number of different problems. This is what gives us 95% confidence! The proportion of intervals that cover μ should be nearly 0.95.

To emphasize these points, we simulated a sample of size $n = 10$ from a normal distribution with $\mu = 20$ and $\sigma = 5$. The 95% confidence interval was then calculated and graphed in Figure 7.2. This procedure was repeated 20 times. The different samples produce different values for $\overline{x}$ and, consequently, the intervals are centered at different points. The different values of s gave rise to intervals of different lengths. Unlike a real application, here we know that the true fixed mean is $\mu = 20$. The proportion of intervals that cover the true value of $\mu = 20$ should be near 0.95 and, in this instance, we happen to have exactly that proportion $19/20 = 0.95$.

E X E R C I S E S

7.1   To illustrate that the mean of a random sample is an unbiased estimate of the mean of the population, consider five slips of paper numbered 3, 6, 9, 15, and 27.

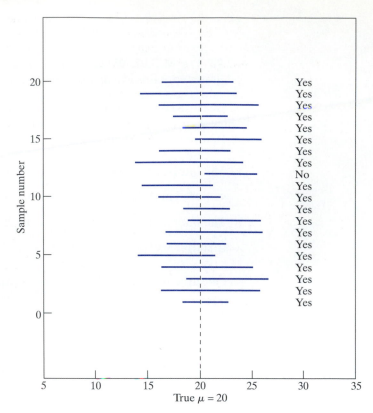

FIGURE 7.2 Interpretation of the confidence interval for population mean, true mean = 20.

(a) List all possible samples of size 3 that can be taken *without* replacement from this finite population.

(b) Calculate the mean of each of the samples listed in (a), and, assigning each sample a probability of $\frac{1}{10}$, verify that the mean of these $\bar{x}$'s equals 12, namely, the mean of the population.

7.2 Suppose that we observe a random variable having the binomial distribution. Let X be the number of successes in n trials.

(a) Show that $\dfrac{X}{n}$ is an unbiased estimate of the binomial parameter p.

(b) Show that $\dfrac{X+1}{n+2}$ is not an unbiased estimate of the binomial parameter p.

7.3 To verify the claim that the mean is generally more efficient than the median (that it is subject to smaller chance fluctuations), a student conducted an experiment consisting of 12 tosses of three dice. The following are his results: 2, 4, and 6; 5, 3, and 5; 4, 5, and 3; 5, 2, and 3; 6, 1, and 5; 2, 3, and 1; 3, 1, and 4; 5, 5, and 2; 3, 3, and 4; 1, 6, and 2; 3, 3, and 3; and 4, 5, and 3.

(a) Calculate the 12 medians and the 12 means.

(b) Plot the medians and the means obtained in part (a) into separate stem-and-leaf displays.

(c) Draw dot diagrams of the two distributions obtained in part (b) and explain how they illustrate the claim that the mean is generally more efficient than the median.

7.4 With reference to the $n = 50$ interrequest time observations on page 20, which have mean 11,795 and standard deviation 14,054, what can one assert with 95% confidence about the maximum error if $\bar{x} = 11,795$ is used as a point estimate of the true population mean interrequest time?

7.5 With reference to the previous exercise, construct a 95% confidence interval for the true mean interrequest time.

7.6 To estimate the average time it takes to assemble a certain computer component, the industrial engineer at an electronics firm timed 40 technicians in the performance of this task, getting a mean of 12.73 minutes and a standard deviation of 2.06 minutes.

  (a) What can we say with 99% confidence about the maximum error if $\bar{x} = 12.73$ is used as a point estimate of the actual average time required to do the job?

  (b) Use the given data to construct a 98% confidence interval for the true average time it takes to assemble the computer component.

7.7 With reference to Exercise 7.6, with what confidence can we assert that the sample mean does not differ from the true mean by more than 30 seconds?

7.8 What is the maximum error one can expect to make with probability 0.90 when using the mean of a random sample of size $n = 64$ to estimate the mean of a population with $\sigma^2 = 2.56$?

7.9 In a study of automobile collision insurance costs, a random sample of 80 body repair costs for a particular kind of damage had a mean of $472.36 and a standard deviation of $62.35. If $\bar{x} = \$472.36$ is used as a point estimate of the true average repair cost of this kind of damage, with what confidence can one assert that the error does not exceed $10?

7.10 If we want to determine the average mechanical aptitude of a large group of workers, how large a random sample will we need to be able to assert with probability 0.95 that the sample mean will not differ from the true mean by more than 3.0 points? Assume that it is known from past experience that $\sigma = 20.0$.

7.11 The dean of a college wants to use the mean of a random sample to estimate the average amount of time students take to get from one class to the next, and she wants to be able to assert with 99% confidence that the error is at most 0.25 minute. If it can be presumed from experience that $\sigma = 1.40$ minutes, how large a sample will she have to take?

7.12 An estimate of the mean time of continuous use until an answering machine will first require service is desired. If it can be assumed that $\sigma = 60$ days, how large a sample is needed so that one will be able to assert with 90% confidence that the sample mean is off by at most 10 days?

7.13 Modify the formula for E on page 224 so that it applies to large samples which constitute substantial portions of finite populations, and use the resulting formula for the following problems:

  (a) A sample of 50 scores on the admission test for a school of engineering is drawn at random from the scores of the 420 persons who applied to the school in 2001. If the sample mean and the standard deviation are $\bar{x} = 546$ and $s = 85$, what can we assert with 95% confidence about the maximum error if $\bar{x} = 546$ is used as an estimate of the mean score of all the applicants?

  (b) A random sample of 40 drums of a chemical, drawn from among 200 such drums whose weights can be expected to have the standard deviation

$\sigma = 12.2$ pounds, has a mean weight of 240.8 pounds. If we estimate the mean weight of all 200 drums as 240.8 pounds, what can we assert with 99% confidence about the maximum error?

7.14 Modify the large sample confidence interval formula for μ on page 227 so that it applies to large samples which constitute substantial portions of finite populations, and use the resulting formula for the following problems:

(a) With reference to part (a) of Exercise 7.13, construct a 99% confidence interval for the mean score of 420 persons who applied to the school of engineering in 2001.

(b) In a random sample of 100 of 500 experimental batteries produced by a firm, the lifetimes have a mean of 148.2 hours with a standard deviation of 24.9 hours. Find a 76.60% confidence interval for the mean life of the 500 batteries.

7.15 A random sample of 100 teachers in a large metropolitan area revealed a mean weekly salary of $487 with a standard deviation of $48. With what degree of confidence can we assert that the average weekly salary of all teachers in the metropolitan area is between $472 and $502?

7.16. Instead of the large sample confidence interval formula for μ on page 227, we could have given the alternative formula

$$\bar{x} - z_{\alpha/3} \cdot \frac{\sigma}{\sqrt{n}} < \mu < \bar{x} + z_{2\alpha/3} \cdot \frac{\sigma}{\sqrt{n}}$$

Explain why the one on page 227 is narrower, and hence preferable, to the one given here.

7.17 Refer to Exercise 2.30, page 39, concerning material costs for rebuilding $n = 35$ traction motors. A computer calculation gives $\bar{x} = 1.4707$ and $s = 0.5235$ thousand dollars. Obtain a 90% confidence interval for the mean material cost to rebuild a motor.

7.18 Refer to the 2×4 lumber strength data in Exercise 2.54, page 43. According to the computer output, a sample of $n = 30$ specimens had $\bar{x} = 1908.8$ and $s = 327.1$. Find a 95% confidence interval for the population mean strength.

7.19 Refer to the data, on page 45, on the number of defects per board for Product B. Obtain a 95% confidence interval for the population mean number of defects per board.

7.20 With reference to the thickness measurements in Exercise 2.37, obtain a 95% confidence interval for the mean thickness.

7.21 Ten bearings made by a certain process have a mean diameter of 0.5060 cm with a standard deviation of 0.0040 cm. Assuming that the data may be looked upon as a random sample from a normal population, construct a 95% confidence interval for the actual average diameter of bearings made by this process.

7.22 Inspecting ceramic tiles prior to their shipment, a quality-control engineer detects 2, 3, 6, 0, 4, and 9 defectives in six cartons, each containing 144 tiles. Assuming that the data can be looked upon as a random sample from a population which can be approximated closely by a normal distribution, what can he assert with 99% confidence about the maximum error, if he uses the mean of the sample as a point estimate of the true average number of defectives per carton?

7.23 With reference to Exercise 7.22 construct a 98% confidence interval for the true average number of defectives per carton.

7.24 In an air-pollution study performed at an experiment station, the following amounts of suspended benzene-soluble organic matter (in micrograms per cubic meter) were obtained for eight different samples of air: 2.2, 1.8, 3.1, 2.0, 2.4, 2.0, 2.1, and 1.2. Assuming that the population sampled is normal, construct a 95% confidence interval for the corresponding true mean.

7.25   (Maximum likelihood estimation) Consider a random sample of size n from a discrete population $f(x; \theta)$ that depends on a parameter θ. The joint distribution is

$$f(x_1; \theta)\, f(x_2; \theta) \cdots f(x_n; \theta)$$

Once the observations become available, we could substitute their actual values $x_1, x_2, \ldots, x_n$ into the joint density. After the substitution, the resulting function of θ

$$L(\theta) = f(x_1; \theta) f(x_2; \theta) \cdots f(x_n; \theta)$$

is called the **likelihood function.** The **maximum likelihood estimator** of θ is the random variable which equals the value for θ that maximizes the probability of the observed sample. Because this is an after-the-fact calculation, we say it maximizes the likelihood.

Find the maximum likelihood estimator

(a) for λ when $f(x; \lambda)$ is the Poisson distribution;

(b) for p when $f(x; p) = p^x(1 - p)^{1-x}$ for $x = 0, 1$.

7.26   Refer to Exercise 7.25. The same procedure for obtaining the maximum likelihood estimator applies also in the continuous case.

Find the maximum likelihood estimator

(a) for β when $f(x; \beta)$ is the exponential distribution;

(b) for μ when $f(x; \mu)$ is a normal distribution with $\sigma^2 = 1$.

7.3   Tests of Hypotheses

There are many problems in which, rather than estimate the value of a parameter, we must decide whether a statement concerning a parameter is true or false; that is, we must test a hypothesis about a parameter. For example, in quality control work a random sample may serve to determine whether the "process mean" (for a given kind of measurement) has remained unchanged or whether it has changed to such an extent that the process has gone "out of control" and adjustments have to be made.

EXAMPLE   **Not all samples will lead to a correct assessment of water quality**
Refer to the example on page 203 of monitoring the quality of water leaving a plant. Why does evaluating a sample of specimens not always lead to correct conclusions regarding water quality?

Solution   The observed values of water quality will depend on the particular specimens in the sample. Because these values can vary from sample to sample, particular samples can produce misleading values and hence incorrect decisions. The possibility of making a mistake about water quality, on the basis of test specimens, cannot be completely eliminated unless the entire discharge could be accurately measured for the entire reporting period. This is, of course, technologically and economically infeasible.

To illustrate the general concepts involved in deciding whether or not a statement about the population is true or false, suppose that a consumer protection agency wants to test a paint manufacturer's claim that the average drying time of his new "fast-drying" paint is 20 minutes. It instructs a member of its research staff to take 36 boards and paint them with paint from 36 different 1-gallon cans of the paint, with the intention of rejecting the claim if the mean of the drying times exceeds 20.75 minutes; otherwise, it will accept the claim, and in either case it will take whatever action is called for in its plans.

This provides a clear-cut criterion for accepting or rejecting the claim, but unfortunately it is not infallible. Since the decision is based on a sample, there is the possibility that the sample mean may exceed 20.75 minutes even though the true mean drying time is $\mu = 20$ minutes, and there is also the possibility that the sample mean may be 20.75 minutes or less even though the true mean drying time is, say, $\mu = 21$ minutes. Thus, before adopting the criterion, it would seem wise to investigate the chances that the criterion may lead to a wrong decision.

Assuming that it is known from past experience that the standard deviation of such drying times can be expected to equal $\sigma = 2.4$ minutes, let us first investigate the possibility that the sample mean may exceed 20.75 minutes even though the true mean drying time is $\mu = 20$. The probability that this will happen purely due to chance is given by the area of the ruled region of Figure 7.3, and it can easily be determined by approximating the sampling distribution of the mean with a normal curve. Assuming that the population is large enough to be treated as an infinite, we have $\sigma_{\bar{X}} = \dfrac{2.4}{\sqrt{36}} = 0.4$, and the dividing line of the criterion in standard units is

$$z = \frac{20.75 - 20}{0.4} = 1.875$$

It follows from Table 3 that the area of the ruled region of Figure 7.3 is $1 - 0.9696 = 0.0304$ (by interpolation). Hence the probability of erroneously rejecting the hypothesis $\mu = 20$ minutes is approximately 0.03.

Let us now consider the other possibility, where the procedure fails to detect that $\mu > 20$ minutes. Suppose again, for the sake of argument, that the true mean drying time is $\mu = 21$ minutes, so that the probability of getting a sample mean less than or equal to 20.75 minutes (and, hence, erroneously accepting the claim that

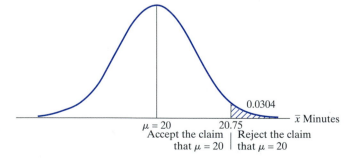

FIGURE 7.3 Probability of falsely rejecting claim.

FIGURE 7.4 Probability
of failing to reject claim.

$\mu = 20$ minutes) is given by the area of the ruled region of Figure 7.4. As before,
$\sigma_{\bar{X}} = 0.4$, so that the dividing line of the criterion, in standard units, is now

$$z = \frac{20.75 - 21}{0.4} = -0.625$$

It follows from Table 3 that the area of the ruled region of Figure 7.4 is 0.2660 (by
interpolation), and hence that the probability of erroneously accepting, or failing
to reject, the hypothesis $\mu = 20$ is approximately 0.27.

The situation described in this example is typical of testing a statistical hypothesis, and it may be summarized in the following table, where we refer to the
hypothesis being tested as hypothesis H:

	Accept H	*Reject H*
H is true	Correct decision	Type I error
H is false	Type II error	Correct decision

If hypothesis H is true and not rejected or false and rejected, the decision is in either case correct. If hypothesis H is true but rejected, it is rejected in error, and if
hypothesis H is false but not rejected, this is an error. The first of these errors is
called a **Type I error** and the probability of committing it is designated by the Greek
letter α (alpha); the second is called a **Type II error** and the probability of committing it is designated by the Greek letter β (beta). Thus, in our example we showed
that for the given test criterion $\alpha = 0.03$ and $\beta = 0.27$ when $\mu = 21$ minutes.

In calculating the probability of a Type II error in our example, we arbitrarily chose the alternative value $\mu = 21$ minutes. However, in this problem, as in most
others, there are infinitely many other alternatives, and for each one of them there
is a positive probability β of erroneously accepting the hypotheses H. What to do
about this will be discussed further in Section 7.8.

7.4   Null Hypotheses and Tests of Hypotheses

In the drying-time example of the preceding section we were able to calculate
the probability of a Type I error because we formulated the hypothesis H as a
single value for the parameter μ; that is, we formulated the hypothesis H so that

μ was completely specified. Had we formulated instead, $\mu \leq 20$ minutes, where μ can take on more than one possible value, we would not have been able to calculate the probability of a Type I error without specifying by how much μ is less than 20 minutes.

We often formulate hypotheses to be tested as a single value for a parameter; at least, we do this whenever possible. This usually requires that we hypothesize the opposite of what we hope to prove. For instance, if we want to show that one method of teaching computer programming is more efficient than another, we hypothesize that the two methods are equally effective. Similarly, if we want to show that one method of irrigating the soil is more expensive than another, we hypothesize that the two methods are equally expensive; and if we want to show that a new copper-bearing steel has a higher yield strength than ordinary steel, we hypothesize that the two yield strengths are the same. Since we hypothesize that there is no difference in the effectiveness of the two teaching methods, no difference in the cost of the two methods of irrigation, and no difference in the yield strength of the two kinds of steel, we call hypotheses like these **null hypotheses** and denote them H_0. Nowadays, the term "null hypothesis" is used for any hypothesis set up primarily to see whether it can be rejected.

The idea of setting up a null hypothesis is not an uncommon one, even in non-statistical thinking. In fact, this is exactly what is done in an American court of law, where an accused person is assumed to be innocent unless he is proven guilty "beyond a reasonable doubt." The null hypothesis states that the accused is not guilty, and the probability expressed subjectively by the phrase "beyond a reasonable doubt" reflects the probability α of risking a Type I error. Note that the "burden of proof" is always on the prosecution in the sense that the accused is found not guilty unless the null hypothesis of innocence is clearly disproved. This does not imply that the defendant has been proved innocent if found not guilty; it implies only that he has not been proved guilty. Of course, since we cannot legally "reserve judgment" if proof of guilt is not established, the accused is freed and we act as if the null hypothesis of innocence were accepted. Note that this is precisely what we may have to do in tests of statistical hypotheses, when we cannot afford the luxury of reserving judgment.

We will develop the procedures for hypothesis testing in the context of the drying-time example. When the goal is to refute the "fast drying" claim, the alternative hypothesis should be $\mu > 20$ minutes.

To approach problems of hypothesis testing systematically, it will help to proceed as outlined in the following five steps.

1. **We formulate a null hypothesis and an appropriate alternative hypothesis which we accept when the null hypothesis must be rejected.**[†]

In the drying-time example the null hypothesis is $\mu = 20$ minutes and the alternative hypothesis is $\mu > 20$ minutes. This kind of alternative, which is called a **one-sided alternative,** may also have the inequality going the other way. For instance, if we hope to be able to show that the average time required to do a cer-

[†]See also the discussion on page 239.

tain job is less than 15 minutes, we would test the null hypothesis $\mu = 15$ against the alternative hypothesis $\mu < 15$.

The following is an example in which we would use the **two-sided alternative** $\mu \neq \mu_0$, where μ_0 is the value assumed under the null hypothesis: A food processor wants to check whether the average amount of coffee that goes into his 4-ounce jars is indeed 4 ounces. Since the food processor cannot afford to put much less than 4 ounces into each jar for fear of losing customer acceptance, nor can he afford to put much more than 4 ounces into each jar for fear of losing part of his profit, the appropriate alternative hypothesis is $\mu \neq 4$.

As in the examples of the two preceding paragraphs, **alternative hypotheses** usually specify that the population mean (or whatever other parameter may be of concern) is not equal to, greater than, or less than the value assumed under the null hypothesis. For any given problem, the choice of an appropriate alternative depends mostly on what we hope to be able to show, or better, where we want to put the burden of proof.

EXAMPLE

Formulating the alternative hypothesis

An appliance manufacturer is considering the purchase of a new machine for stamping out sheet metal parts. If μ_0 is the average number of good parts stamped out per hour by her old machine and μ is the corresponding average for the new machine, the manufacturer wants to test the null hypothesis $\mu = \mu_0$ against a suitable alternative. What should the alternative be if she does not want to buy the new machine unless it is more productive than the old one?

Solution

The manufacturer should use the alternative hypothesis $\mu > \mu_0$ and purchase the new machine only if the null hypothesis can be rejected. ✔

Having formulated the null hypothesis and an alternative hypothesis, we proceed with the following step:

2. **We specify the probability of a Type I error; if possible, desired, or necessary, we may also specify the probabilities of Type II errors for particular alternatives.**

The probability of a Type I error is also called the **level of significance,** and it is usually set at $\alpha = 0.05$ or $\alpha = 0.01$. Which value we choose in any given problem will have to depend on the risks, or consequences, of committing a Type I error. Observe, however, that we should not make the probability of a Type I error too small, because this will have the tendency to make the probabilities of serious Type II errors too large.

Step 2 can often be performed even when the null hypothesis specifies a range of values for the parameter. To illustrate, let us investigate briefly what might be done in the drying time example if we wanted to allow for the possibility that the paint may be better (faster drying) than claimed, and hence test the null hypothesis $\mu \leq 20$ minutes against the alternative hypothesis $\mu > 20$ minutes. Observe that if μ is less than 20 minutes, the normal curve of Figure 7.3 on page 234 is shifted to the left, and the area under the curve to the right of 20.75 becomes less than 0.0304. Thus, if the null hypothesis is $\mu \leq 20$ minutes, we can say that the probability of a Type I error is at most 0.0304, and we write $\alpha \leq 0.0304$. In general, if the null hypothesis is of the form $\mu \leq \mu_0$ or $\mu \geq \mu_0$, we can only specify the maximum probability of a Type I error, and by performing the test as if the null hypothesis were $\mu = \mu_0$, we protect ourselves against the worst possibility (see the example on page 245).

After the null hypothesis, the alternative hypothesis, and the level of significance have been specified, the remaining steps are:

3. **Based on the sampling distribution of an appropriate statistic, we construct a criterion for testing the null hypothesis against the given alternative.**

4. **We calculate from the data the value of the statistic on which the decision is to be based.**

5. **We decide whether to reject the null hypothesis or whether to fail to reject it.**

In the drying-time example we studied the criterion using the normal-curve approximation to the sampling distribution of the mean; in general, step 3 depends not only on the statistic on which we want to base the decision and on its sampling distribution, but also on the alternative hypothesis we happen to choose. In the drying time example we used a **one-sided criterion (one-sided test** or **one-tailed test)** with the one-sided alternative $\mu > 20$ minutes, rejecting the null hypothesis only for large values of the mean. In the example dealing with the food processor and his 4-ounce jars of coffee, we would use a **two-sided criterion (two-sided test** or **two-tailed test)** to go with the two-sided alternative $\mu \neq 4$ ounces. In general, a test is said to be two-sided if the null hypothesis is rejected for values of the test statistic falling into either tail of its sampling distribution.

The purpose of the discussion of this and the preceding section has been to introduce some of the basic problems connected with the testing of statistical hypotheses. Although the methods we have presented are objective—that is, two experimenters analyzing the same data under the same conditions would arrive at the identical results—their use does entail some arbitrary, or subjective, considerations. For instance, in the example on page 234 it was partially a subjective decision to "draw the line" between satisfactory and unsatisfactory values of μ at 21 minutes. It was also partially a subjective decision to use a sample of 36 one-gallon cans of the paint, and to reject the manufacturer's claim for values of $\bar{X}$ exceeding 20.75 minutes. Approaching the problem differently, the government agency investigating the paint manufacturer's claim could have specified values of α and β, thus controlling the risks to which they are willing to be exposed. The choice of α, the probability of a Type I error, could have been based on the consequences of making that kind of error, namely, the manufacturer's cost of having a good product condemned, the possible cost of subsequent litigation, the manufacturer's cost of unnecessarily adjusting his machinery, the cost to the public of not having the product available when needed, and so forth. The choice of β, the probability of a Type II error, could similarly have been based on the consequences of making that kind of error, namely, the cost to the public of buying an inferior product, the manufacturer's savings in using inferior ingredients but loss in good will, again the cost of possible litigation, and so forth. It should be obvious that it would be extremely difficult to put "cash values" on all these eventualities, but they must nevertheless be considered, at least indirectly, in choosing suitable criteria for testing statistical hypotheses.

In this text we shall discuss mainly the **Neyman-Pearson theory,** also called the **classical theory** of testing hypotheses. This means that we shall consider cost factors and other considerations that are partly arbitrary and partly subjective only insofar as they will affect the choice of a sample size, the choice of an alternative hypothesis, the choice of α and β, and so forth.

In this approach, the maximum value of α is controlled over the null hypothesis. For instance, if the null hypothesis is $\mu \le \mu_0$, then μ as well as σ is unspecified. This is a **composite hypothesis.** Otherwise, if all the parameters are completely specified, the hypothesis is **simple.** Even with a composite null hypothesis, we set the critical region so that the error probability is α on the boundary $\mu = \mu_0$. Then, the error probabilities will be even smaller under values of μ that are less than μ_0.

Because the probability of falsely rejecting the null hypothesis is controlled, the null hypothesis is retained unless the observations strongly contradict it. Consequently, if the goal of an experiment is to establish an assertion or hypothesis, that hypothesis must be taken as the alternative hypothesis.

Guideline for selecting the null hypothesis

> When the goal of an experiment is to establish an assertion, the negation of the assertion should be taken as the null hypothesis. The assertion becomes the alternative hypothesis.

Similar reasoning suggests that even when costs are difficult to determine but the consequences of one error are much more serious than for the other, the hypotheses should be labeled so that the most serious error is the Type I error.

The alternative hypothesis is often denoted by H_1. In the paint drying example $H_1 : \mu > 20$. Recalling the notation H_0 for the null hypothesis, we summarize the concepts and notation for hypotheses, types of error and the probability of error.

Notation for the hypotheses

> H_1: The **alternative hypothesis** is the claim we wish to establish.
> H_0: The **null hypothesis** is the negation of the claim.

The two kinds of error and their probabilities are

The errors and their probabilities

> **Type I error:** Rejection of H_0 when H_0 is true.
> **Type II error:** Non-rejection of H_0 when H_1 is true.
> α = probability of making a Type I error (also called the **level of significance**)
> β = probability of making a Type II error

Before we discuss various special tests about means in the remainder of this chapter, let us point out that the concepts we have introduced here apply equally well to hypotheses concerning proportions, standard deviations, the randomness of samples, and relationships among several variables.

EXERCISES

7.27 Suppose that an engineering firm is asked to check the safety of a dam. What type of error would it commit if it erroneously rejects the null hypothesis that the dam is safe? What type of error would it commit if it erroneously accepts the null hypothesis that the dam is safe?

7.28 Suppose that we want to test the null hypothesis that an antipollution device for cars is effective. Explain under what conditions we would commit a Type I error and under what conditions we would commit a Type II error.

7.29 If the criterion on page 234 is modified so that the paint manufacturer's claim is rejected for $\overline{X} > 20.50$ minutes, find

    (a) the probability of a Type I error;

    (b) the probability of a Type II error when $\mu = 21$ minutes.

7.30 A process for making steel pipe is under control if the diameter of the pipe has a mean of 3.0000 inches with a standard deviation of 0.0250 inch. To check whether the process is under control, a random sample of size $n = 30$ is taken each day and the null hypothesis $\mu = 3.0000$ is rejected if $\overline{X}$ is less than 2.9960 or greater than 3.0040. Find

    (a) the probability of a Type I error;

    (b) the probability of a Type II error when $\mu = 3.0050$ inches.

7.31 Suppose that in the drying-time example on page 234, n is changed from 36 to 50 while everything else remains the same. Find

    (a) the probability of a Type I error;

    (b) the probability of a Type II error when $\mu = 21$ minutes.

7.32 It is desired to test the null hypothesis $\mu = 100$ pounds against the alternative hypothesis $\mu < 100$ pounds on the basis of a random sample of size $n = 40$ from a population with $\sigma = 12$. For what values of $\overline{X}$ must the null hypothesis be rejected if the probability of a Type I error is to be $\alpha = 0.01$?

7.33 Suppose that for a given population with $\sigma = 8.4 \text{ in}^2$ we want to test the null hypothesis $\mu = 80.0 \text{ in}^2$ against the alternative hypothesis $\mu < 80.0 \text{ in}^2$ on the basis of a random sample of size $n = 100$.

    (a) If the null hypothesis is rejected for $\overline{X} < 78.0 \text{ in}^2$ and otherwise it is accepted, what is the probability of a Type I error?

    (b) What is the answer to part (a) if the null hypothesis is $\mu \geq 80.0$ square inches instead of $\mu = 80.0$ square inches?

7.34 If the null hypothesis $\mu = \mu_0$ is to be tested on the basis of a large random sample against the alternative hypothesis $\mu < \mu_0$ (or $\mu > \mu_0$), the probability of a Type I error is to be α and the probability of a Type II error is to be β for $\mu = \mu_1$, it can be shown that the required sample size is

$$n = \frac{\sigma^2(z_\alpha + z_\beta)^2}{(\mu_1 - \mu_0)^2}$$

where σ^2 is the variance of the population.

    (a) It is desired to test the null hypothesis $\mu = 40$ against the alternative hypothesis $\mu < 40$ on the basis of a large random sample from a population with $\sigma = 4$. If the probability of a Type I error is to be 0.05 and the probability of a Type II error is to be 0.12 for $\mu = 38$, find the required size of the sample.

(b) Suppose that we want to test the null hypothesis $\mu = 64$ against the alternative hypothesis $\mu < 64$ for a population whose standard deviation is $\sigma = 7.2$. How large a sample must we take if α is to be 0.05 and β is to be 0.01 for $\mu = 61$? Also, for what values of $\overline{X}$ will the null hypothesis have to be rejected?

7.35 If the alternative hypothesis is two-sided, the formula of Exercise 7.34 must be modified by substituting $z_{\alpha/2}$ for z_α. How large a sample must we take if it is desired to test the null hypothesis $\mu = 100$ against the alternative hypothesis $\mu \neq 100$ on the basis of a random sample from a population with $\sigma = 16$, the probability of a Type I error is to be 0.01, and the probability of a Type II error is to be 0.20 for $\mu = 92$?

7.36 A city's police department is considering replacing the tires on its cars with a new type of tires. If μ_1 is the average number of miles they get out of their old tires and μ_2 is the average number of miles they will get out of the new tires, the null hypothesis they shall want to test is $\mu_1 - \mu_2 = 0$.

(a) What alternative hypothesis should they use if they do not want to buy the new tires unless they are definitely proven to give a better mileage? In other words, the burden of proof is put on the new tires and the old tires are to be kept unless the null hypothesis can be rejected.

(b) What alternative hypothesis should they use if they are anxious to get the new tires (which have some other nice features) unless they actually give a poorer mileage than the old tires? Note that now the burden of proof is on the old tires, which will be kept only if the null hypothesis can be rejected.

7.37 A producer of extruded plastic products finds that his mean daily inventory is 1,250 pieces. A new marketing policy has been put into effect and it is desired to test the null hypothesis that the mean daily inventory is still the same. What alternative hypothesis should be used if

(a) it is desired to know whether or not the new policy changes the mean daily inventory;

(b) it is desired to demonstrate that the new policy actually reduces the mean daily inventory;

(c) the new policy will be retained so long as it cannot be shown that it actually increases the mean daily inventory?

7.38 Specify the null hypothesis and the alternative hypothesis in each of the following cases.

(a) An automobile manufacturer wants to confirm a supplier's claim that the maximum resistance in a wiring harness is less than 50 ohms.

(b) An investigator wants to establish the research department's claim that a new filament will increase mean bulb life to more than 3,000 hours.

7.5   Hypotheses Concerning One Mean

Having used tests concerning means to illustrate the basic principles of hypothesis testing, let us now see how we proceed in actual practice. Suppose, for instance, that we want to test on the basis of $n = 35$ determinations and at the 0.05 level of significance whether the thermal conductivity of a certain kind of cement brick is

0.340, as has been claimed. From information gathered in similar studies, we can expect that the variability of such determinations is given by $\sigma = 0.010$.

Following the outline of the preceding section, we begin with Steps 1 and 2 by writing

1. *Null hypothesis:* $\mu = 0.340$
   Alternative hypothesis: $\mu \neq 0.340$
2. *Level of significance:* $\alpha = 0.05$

The alternative hypothesis is two-sided because we shall want to reject the null hypothesis if the mean of the determinations is significantly less than or significantly greater than 0.340.

Next, in Step 3, we depart from the procedure used in the example of the preceding section and base the test on the statistic

Statistic for test concerning mean—σ known

$$Z = \frac{\overline{X} - \mu_0}{\sigma/\sqrt{n}}$$

instead of $\overline{X}$. The reason for working with standard units, or Z values, is that it enables us to formulate criteria which are applicable to a great variety of problems, not just one.

If z_α is, as before, such that the area under the standard normal curve to its right equals α, the **critical regions,** namely, the sets of values of Z for which we reject the null hypothesis $\mu = \mu_0$, can be expressed as in the following table:

Critical Regions for Testing $\mu = \mu_0$
(Normal population and σ known)

Alternative hypothesis	Reject null hypothesis if:
$\mu < \mu_0$	$Z < -z_\alpha$
$\mu > \mu_0$	$Z > z_\alpha$
$\mu \neq \mu_0$	$Z < -z_{\alpha/2}$ or $Z > z_{\alpha/2}$

If $\alpha = 0.05$, the dividing lines, or **critical values,** of the criteria are -1.645 and 1.645 for the one-sided alternatives, and -1.96 and 1.96 for the two-sided alternative. If $\alpha = 0.01$, the dividing lines of the criteria are -2.33 and 2.33 for the one-sided alternatives, and -2.575 and 2.575 for the two-sided alternative. These results come from the example on page 153 and Exercise 5.23.

Returning now to the example dealing with the thermal conductivity of the cement bricks, suppose that the mean of the 35 determinations is 0.343. So we continue by writing

3. *Criterion:* Reject the null hypothesis if $Z < -1.96$ or $Z > 1.96$, where

$$Z = \frac{\overline{X} - \mu_0}{\sigma/\sqrt{n}}$$

4. *Calculations:*

$$Z = \frac{0.343 - 0.340}{0.010/\sqrt{35}} = 1.77$$

5. *Decision:* Since $Z = 1.77$ falls on the interval from -1.96 to 1.96, the null hypothesis cannot be rejected; to put it another way, the difference between $\bar{x} = 0.343$ and $\mu = 0.340$ can be attributed to chance. We actually never establish that the null hypothesis holds. Instead, the conclusion is that we fail to reject the null hypothesis.

In problems like this, many research workers accompany the calculated value of Z with a corresponding **tail probability,** or ***P* value,** which is the probability of getting a difference between $\bar{x}$ and μ_0 greater than or equal to that actually observed. For instance, in the above example, it is given by the total area under the standard normal curve to the left of -1.77 and to the right of 1.77, and it equals $2(1 - 0.9616) = 0.0768$. This *P* value exceeds 0.05, which agrees with our earlier result. Figure 7.5 shows the rejection region, the value of Z and the two tail areas.

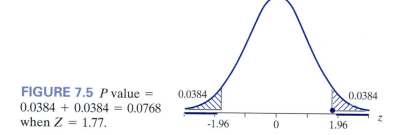

FIGURE 7.5 *P* value = $0.0384 + 0.0384 = 0.0768$ when $Z = 1.77$.

EXAMPLE

Calculating the *P* value
A process for producing vinyl floor covering has been stabilized for a long period of time and the surface hardness measurement has a normal distribution with mean 4.5 and standard deviation $\sigma = 1.5$. A second shift has been hired and trained and their production needs to be monitored. Consider testing the hypothesis $H_0: \mu = 4.5$ versus $H_1: \mu \neq 4.5$. A random sample of hardness measurements is made of $n = 25$ vinyl specimens produced by the second shift. Calculate the *P* value when using the test statistic

$$Z = \frac{\overline{X} - 4.5}{1.5/\sqrt{25}}$$

if $\bar{x} = 3.9$.

FIGURE 7.6 The P value $0.0228 + 0.0228 = 0.0456$ for $Z = -2.00$.

Solution The observed value of the test statistic is

$$z = \frac{3.9 - 4.5}{1.5/\sqrt{25}} = -2.00$$

Since the alternative hypothesis is two-sided, we must consider large negative values for Z as well as large positive values (see Figure 7.6).

From the normal table, $P(Z > 2.00) = .0228$. The probability that Z is smaller than -2.00 is also $.0228$. Consequently, the P value is $.0228 + .0028 = .0456$. This is the probability, under the null hypothesis, of getting the same or a more extreme value of the test statistic than was observed. The small P value suggests that the mean of the second shift is not at the target value of 4.5.

Observe that giving a tail probability does not relieve us of the responsibility of specifying the level of significance before the test is actually performed.

The test we have described in this section is essentially an approximate large sample test; it is exact only when the population we are sampling is normal and σ is known. In many practical situations where σ is unknown, but the sample size is large, we must make the further approximation of substituting for it the sample standard deviation S.

Statistic for large sample test concerning mean

$$Z = \frac{\overline{X} - \mu_0}{S/\sqrt{n}}$$

Critical Regions for Testing $\mu = \mu_0$
(large sample)

Alternative hypothesis	Reject null hypothesis if:
$\mu < \mu_0$	$Z < -z_\alpha$
$\mu > \mu_0$	$Z > z_\alpha$
$\mu \neq \mu_0$	$Z < -z_{\alpha/2}$ or $Z > z_{\alpha/2}$

EXAMPLE

A large sample test of mean tire life

A trucking firm is suspicious of the claim that the average lifetime of certain tires is at least 28,000 miles. To check the claim, the firm puts 40 of these tires on its trucks and gets a mean lifetime of 27,463 miles with a standard deviation of 1,348 miles. What can it conclude if the probability of a Type I error is to be at most 0.01?

Solution

1. *Null hypothesis:* $\mu \geq 28,000$ miles
   Alternative hypothesis: $\mu < 28,000$ miles
2. *Level of significance:* $\alpha \leq 0.01$
3. *Criterion:* Since the probability of a Type I error is greatest when $\mu = 28,000$ miles, we proceed as if we were testing the null hypothesis $\mu = 28,000$ miles against the alternative hypothesis $\mu < 28,000$ miles at the 0.01 level of significance. Thus, the null hypothesis must be rejected if $Z < -2.33$, where

$$ Z = \frac{\overline{X} - \mu_0}{S/\sqrt{n}} $$

4. *Calculations:*

$$ Z = \frac{27,463 - 28,000}{1,348/\sqrt{40}} = -2.52 $$

5. *Decision:* Since $Z = -2.52$ is less than -2.33, the null hypothesis must be rejected at level of significance 0.01. In other words, the trucking firm's suspicion that $\mu < 28,000$ miles is confirmed.

The small P value 0.0059, as shown in Figure 7.7, strengthens the conclusion.

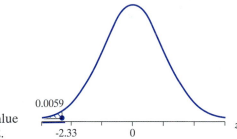

0.0059

-2.33   0 z

FIGURE 7.7 The P value = .0059 for $Z = -2.52$.

If the sample size is small and σ is unknown, the tests just described cannot be used. However, if the sample comes from a normal population (to within a reasonable degree of approximation), we can make use of the theory discussed in Section 6.3 and base the test of the null hypothesis $\mu = \mu_0$ on the statistic

Statistic for small sample test concerning mean—normal population

$$ t = \frac{\overline{X} - \mu_0}{S/\sqrt{n}} $$

which is a random variable having the t distribution with $n - 1$ degrees of freedom. The criteria for the **one-sample t test** are like those for Z but are based on the t distribution.

Critical Regions for Testing $\mu = \mu_0$
(Normal population and σ unknown)
one sample t-test

Alternative hypothesis	*Reject null: hypothesis if:*
$\mu < \mu_0$	$t < -t_\alpha$
$\mu > \mu_0$	$t > t_\alpha$
$\mu \neq \mu_0$	$t < -t_{\alpha/2}$ or $t > t_{\alpha/2}$

t_α and $t_{\alpha/2}$ are based on $n - 1$ degrees of freedom

EXAMPLE

A t test of a normal population mean
The specifications for a certain kind of ribbon call for a mean breaking strength of 180 pounds. If five pieces of the ribbon (randomly selected from different rolls) have a mean breaking strength of 169.5 pounds with a standard deviation of 5.7 pounds, test the null hypothesis $\mu = 180$ pounds against the alternative hypothesis $\mu < 180$ pounds at the 0.01 level of significance. Assume that the population distribution is normal.

Solution

1. *Null hypothesis:* $\mu = 180$ pounds
   Alternative hypothesis: $\mu < 180$ pounds
2. *Level of significance:* $\alpha = 0.01$
3. *Criterion:* Reject the null hypothesis if $t < -3.747$, where 3.747 is the value of $t_{0.01}$ for $5 - 1 = 4$ degrees of freedom and

$$t = \frac{\overline{X} - \mu_0}{S/\sqrt{n}}$$

4. *Calculations:*

$$t = \frac{169.5 - 180}{5.7/\sqrt{5}} = -4.12$$

5. *Decision:* Since $t = -4.12$ is less than -3.747, the null hypothesis must be rejected at level $\alpha = 0.01$. In other words, the breaking strength is below specifications. The exact tail probability, or P value, cannot be determined from Table 4, but it is 0.0073 (see Figure 7.8). The evidence against the mean breaking strength being 180 pounds is even stronger than 0.01. Only about 7 in 1,000 times would we observe a value of t that is -4.12 or smaller, if the mean really were 180 pounds. ✔

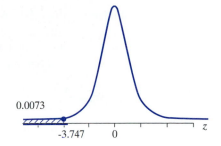

FIGURE 7.8 *P* value
= .0073 for *t* = −4.12.

7.6   The Relation Between Tests and Confidence Intervals

We now describe an important connection between tests for two-sided alternatives and confidence intervals. This relation provides the reason that most statisticians prefer the information available in a confidence interval statement as opposed to the information that the null hypothesis $\mu = \mu_0$ was or was not rejected.

To develop the relation, we consider the $(1 - \alpha)100\%$ confidence interval for μ given on page 228:

$$\bar{x} - t_{\alpha/2}\frac{s}{\sqrt{n}} < \mu < \bar{x} + t_{\alpha/2}\frac{s}{\sqrt{n}}$$

This interval is closely connected to a level α test of $H_0 : \mu = \mu_0$ versus the two-sided alternative $H_1: \mu \neq \mu_0$. In terms of the values of $\bar{x}$ and s, this test has critical region

$$\left|\frac{\bar{x} - \mu_0}{s/\sqrt{n}}\right| = |t| \geq t_{\alpha/2}$$

The acceptance region of this test is obtained by reversing the inequality to obtain all the values of $\bar{x}$ and s that do not lead to the rejection of $H_0: \mu = \mu_0$.

$$acceptance \; region: \left|\frac{\bar{x} - \mu_0}{s/\sqrt{n}}\right| < t_{\alpha/2}$$

The acceptance region can also be expressed as

$$acceptance \; region: \bar{x} - t_{\alpha/2}\frac{s}{\sqrt{n}} < \mu_0 < \bar{x} + t_{\alpha/2}\frac{s}{\sqrt{n}}$$

where the limits of the interval are identical to the preceding confidence interval. That is, the null hypothesis will not be rejected at level α if μ_0 lies within the $(1 - \alpha)$ 100% confidence interval for μ.

The set of plausible values for μ, as determined by the confidence interval, tells us at once about the outcome of all possible two-sided tests of hypothesis that specify a single value for μ.

| EXAMPLE | **Illustrating the relation between tests and confidence intervals** |

Referring to the example on page 228, $n = 16$ measurements of weight loss yielded $\bar{x} = 3.42$ and $s = 0.68$. Since $t_{0.025} = 2.131$ with 15 degrees of freedom, the 95% confidence interval becomes

$$\bar{x} - t_{\alpha/2}\frac{s}{\sqrt{n}} < \mu < \bar{x} + t_{\alpha/2}\frac{s}{\sqrt{n}}, \qquad \text{or } 3.06 < \mu < 3.78$$

Use the relation between 95% confidence intervals and $\alpha = 0.05$ level tests to test the null hypothesis $\mu = 3.7$ versus the alternative hypothesis $\mu \neq 3.7$. Also test the null hypothesis $\mu = 3.0$ versus the alternative hypothesis $\mu \neq 3.0$.

Solution   In view of the relation just established, a test of $\mu = 3.7$ versus $\mu \neq 3.7$ would not reject H_0: $\mu = 3.7$, at the 5% level, since $\mu = 3.7$ falls within the confidence interval.

On the other hand $\mu = 3.0$ does not fall within the 95% confidence interval and hence that null hypothesis would be rejected at level $\alpha = 0.05$.   ✔

The relation holds quite generally. Suppose, for any value θ_0 of a parameter θ, we have a level α test of the null hypothesis $\theta = \theta_0$ versus the alternative $\theta \neq \theta_0$. Collect all the values θ_0 that would not be rejected. These form a $(1 - \alpha)100\%$ confidence interval for θ.

A confidence interval statement provides a more comprehensive inference than a statement concerning a two-sided test of a single null hypothesis. Consequently, we favor a confidence interval approach when one is available.

7.7 Operating Characteristic Curves

So far we have not paid much attention to Type II errors; in the drying-time example of Section 7.4 we calculated one probability of a Type II error, and all the tests of the previous sections were looked upon as tests of significance. Since the choice of the alternative hypothesis $\mu = 21$ minutes in the drying-time example was essentially arbitrary, it may be of interest to see how the testing procedure will perform when other values of μ prevail. The actual mean drying time depends on the chemical reactions governing the paint and the environmental conditions. Lacking a total scientific explanation, we do not know precisely what value to expect for this population mean. Consequently, we must investigate the probability of accepting the null hypothesis under a range of possible values for μ. To this end, let

$$L(\mu) = \text{probability of accepting the null hypothesis when } \mu \text{ prevails}$$

The function $L(\mu)$ completely characterizes the testing procedure whatever the value of population mean μ. If μ equals a value where the null hypothesis is true, then $1 - L(\mu)$ is the probability of the Type I error. When μ has a value where the alternative hypothesis is true, then $L(\mu)$ is the probability of a Type II error. That is, the function $L(\mu)$ carries complete information about the probabilities of both types of error.

To illustrate the calculation of $L(\mu)$, we continue with the drying-time example on page 234, where we had $\mu_0 = 20$, $\sigma = 2.4$, $n = 36$, and the dividing line of the criterion was $\bar{x} = 20.75$. If the prevailing population mean is $\mu = 20.5$, then $Z = \sqrt{n}(\bar{X} - 20.5)/\sigma = 6(\bar{X} - 20.5)/2.4$ is a standard normal variable. We reason that $L(20.5)$ is the probability of observing

$$\bar{X} < 20.75, \quad \text{or} \quad \frac{6(\bar{X} - 20.5)}{2.4} < \frac{6(20.75 - 20.5)}{2.4} = 0.625$$

or $Z < 0.625$. Therefore, from Table 3, $L(20.5) = 0.73$. Continuing with other possible values for μ, we obtain the results shown in the following table and also in Figure 7.9 (see Exercise 7.50):

Value of μ	Probability of accepting null hypothesis
19.50	0.999
19.75	0.99
20.00	0.97
20.25	0.89
20.50	0.73
20.75	0.50
21.00	0.27
21.25	0.11
21.50	0.03
21.75	0.01
22.00	0.001

Note that the probability of committing a Type II error diminishes when μ is increased, and that the probability of not committing a Type I error approaches 1 when μ becomes much smaller than 20 (and the paint is even better than claimed).

The graph of $L(\mu)$ for various values of μ, shown in Figure 7.9, is called the **operating characteristic curve,** or simply the **OC curve,** of the test.

In the context of sampling in order to decide whether or not to accept a shipment of paint on the basis of drying time, we would like to accept the shipment if the mean drying time is low and reject it if it is high. Based on the operating characteristic curve in Figure 7.9, the engineer can decide if the proposed procedure has small enough error probabilities at values of μ she deems important. Ideally, we should want to reject the null hypothesis $\mu = \mu_0$ when actually μ exceeds μ_0, and to accept it when μ is less than or equal to μ_0. Thus, the ideal OC curve for our example would be given by the black and blue horizontal lines of Figure 7.9. In actual practice, OC curves can only approximate such ideal curves, with the approximation becoming better as the sample size is increased. To illustrate this point, the reader will be asked in Exercise 7.91 to recalculate the probabilities in the table above when the sample size is increased from 36 to 50.

Figure 7.9 presents the picture of a typical OC curve for the case where the alternative hypothesis is $\mu > \mu_0$. When the alternative hypothesis is $\mu < \mu_0$, the

FIGURE 7.9 Operating characteristic curve.

OC curve becomes the mirror image of that of Figure 7.9, reflected about the dashed vertical line through μ_0.

When the alternative hypothesis is two-sided, $H_1: \mu < \mu_0$ or $\mu > \mu_0$, then a typical OC curve will have a maximum at $\mu = \mu_0$ and it will fall off as the value for μ moves away from μ_0 in either direction. An OC curve for a two-tailed test is shown in Figure 7.10. It should be observed that $L(\mu)$ now is the probability of a Type II error for all values of μ except μ_0; at μ_0 it is still the probability of not committing a Type I error. Due to the symmetry of this kind of OC curve about the dashed vertical line through μ_0, all problems relating to Type II errors can be answered on the basis of the values of $L(\mu)$ for $\mu > \mu_0$.

In many practical situations, the probabilities of Type II errors can be determined directly from charts like those given in Table 8 at the end of the book. They

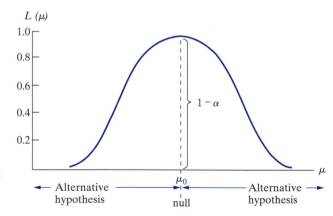

FIGURE 7.10 Operating characteristic curve for two-tailed test.

enable us to read the values of β that correspond to given values of μ_0, μ_1, σ, n, and α, and they are based on the assumption that the sampling distribution of the mean is a normal distribution; hence, they can be used when n is large or the population we are sampling has roughly the shape of a normal distribution. Charts (a) and (b) apply to one-tailed tests with $\alpha = 0.05$ or $\alpha = 0.01$, and they apply regardless of whether the alternative hypothesis is $\mu > \mu_0$ or $\mu < \mu_0$, since the quantity that we plot on the horizontal scale is not μ but

Quantity needed for use of Table 8

$$d = \frac{|\mu - \mu_0|}{\sigma}$$

namely, the absolute value of the difference between μ and μ_0 divided by σ. The following examples illustrate this technique.

EXAMPLE   **Using Table 8(a) to determine the probability of a Type II error**
We want to investigate a claim about the average sound intensity of certain vacuum cleaners. Suppose the sound is a random variable having a normal distribution with a standard deviation of 3.6 dB. Specifically, we shall want to test the null hypothesis $\mu = 75.20$ against the alternative hypothesis $\mu > 75.20$ on the basis of measurements of the sound intensity of $n = 15$ of these machines. If the probability of a Type I error is to be $\alpha = 0.05$, what is the probability of a Type II error for $\mu = 77.00$ dB?

Solution   Since $d = \dfrac{|77.0 - 75.20|}{3.6} = 0.50$, we mark this point on the horizontal scale of chart (a) of Table 8, and going up vertically until we come to the point where the line is crossed by the OC curve for $n = 15$, we find that the corresponding probability of a Type II error is about 0.38.   ✔

EXAMPLE   **Using Table 8(b) to determine the probability of a Type II error**
We want to check a claim concerning the mileage a person will get per tankful with a certain kind of car in city traffic. Suppose the milage may be looked upon as a random variable having a normal distribution with a standard deviation of 0.8 mile per gallon. Specifically, we shall want to test the null hypothesis $\mu = 25.0$ against the alternative hypothesis $\mu < 25.0$ on the basis of the mileage obtained in city traffic with a tankful of gas by 10 of these cars. If the probability of a Type I error is to be $\alpha = 0.01$, what is the probability of a Type II error for $\mu = 24.0$ miles per gallon?

Solution   Since $d = \dfrac{|24.0 - 25.0|}{0.8} = 1.25$, we mark this point on the horizontal scale of chart (b) of Table 8, and going up vertically until we come to the point where the line is crossed by the OC curve for $n = 10$, we find that the corresponding probability of a Type II error is about 0.06.   ✔

For two-tailed tests, that is, for tests of the null hypothesis $\mu = \mu_0$ against the alternative hypothesis $\mu \neq \mu_0$, the procedure is the same as before, with the exception that we must now refer to charts (c) and (d) of Table 8. Note that these charts contain only the right-hand halves of the respective OC curves (as shown in Figure 7.10), and that is all we need, since these OC curves are symmetrical about μ_0.

EXAMPLE

Determining the probability of a Type II error
Suppose that the length of certain machine parts may be looked upon as a random variable having a normal distribution with a mean of 2.000 cm and a standard deviation of 0.050 cm. Specifically, we shall want to test the null hypothesis $\mu = 2.000$ against the alternative hypothesis $\mu \neq 2.000$ on the basis of the mean of a random sample of size $n = 30$. If the probability of a Type I error is to be $\alpha = 0.05$, what is the probability of a Type II error for $\mu = 2.010$?

Solution Since $d = \dfrac{|2.010 - 2.000|}{0.050} = 0.20$, we mark this point on the horizontal scale of chart (c) of Table 8, and going up vertically until we come to the point where the line is crossed by the OC curve for $n = 30$, we find that the corresponding probability of a Type II error is about 0.80. ✔

Table 8 can also be used to solve problems similar to the one of Exercise 7.34 on page 240, in which we are asked to determine the sample size that is required by given values of μ_0, μ_1, α, and β.

EXAMPLE

Determining a sample size
With reference to the drying-time example on page 234, where we had $\mu_0 = 20$, $\sigma = 2.4$, and $\alpha = 0.05$, how large a sample would we need so that $\beta = 0.10$ for $\mu = 21$?

Solution Since $d = \dfrac{|21 - 20|}{2.4} = 0.42$, we locate the point corresponding to $d = 0.42$ and $\beta = 0.10$ on chart (c) of Table 8, and we find that it lies barely above the OC curve for $n = 50$. Thus, a sample of size $n = 50$ will serve the stated purpose. ✔

EXERCISES

7.39 According to the norms established for a mechanical aptitude test, persons who are 18 years old should average 73.2 with a standard deviation of 8.6. If 45 randomly selected persons of that age averaged 76.7, test the null hypothesis $\mu = 73.2$ against the alternative hypothesis $\mu > 73.2$ at the 0.01 level of significance.

7.40 Refer to Exercise 2.30, page 39, concerning material costs for rebuilding $n = 35$ traction motors. A computer calculation gives $\bar{x} = 1.4707$ and $s = 0.5235$ thousand dollars. At the .05 level of significance, conduct a test of hypotheses with the intent of showing the mean is greater than 1.3 thousand dollars.

7.41 In 64 randomly selected hours of production, the mean and the standard deviation of the number of acceptable pieces produced by an automatic stamping machine are $\bar{x} = 1{,}038$ and $s = 146$. At the 0.05 level of significance does this enable us to reject the null hypothesis $\mu = 1{,}000$ against the alternative hypothesis $\mu > 1{,}000$?

7.42 With reference to the thickness measurements in Exercise 2.37, test the null hypothesis that $\mu = 30.0$ versus a two-sided alternative. Take $\alpha = .05$.

7.43 In a labor-management discussion it was brought up that workers at a certain large plant take on the average 32.6 minutes to get to work. If a random sample of 60 workers took on the average 33.8 minutes with a standard deviation of 6.1 minutes, can we reject the null hypothesis $\mu = 32.6$ in favor of the alternative hypothesis $\mu > 32.6$ at the 0.05 level of significance?

7.44 A random sample of 6 steel beams has a mean compressive strength of 58,392 psi (pounds per square inch) with a standard deviation of 648 psi. Use this information and the level of significance $\alpha = 0.05$ to test whether the true average compressive strength of the steel from which this sample came is 58,000 psi. Assume normality.

7.45 Given a random sample of 5 pints from different production lots, we want to test whether the fat content of a certain kind of ice cream exceeds 14%. What can we conclude at the 0.01 level of significance about the null hypothesis $\mu = 14\%$ if the sample has the mean $\bar{x} = 14.9\%$ and the standard deviation $\sigma = 0.42\%$?

7.46 Test runs with 6 models of an experimental engine showed that they operated for 24, 28, 21, 23, 32, and 22 minutes with a gallon of a certain kind of fuel. If the probability of a Type I error is to be at most 0.01, is this evidence against a hypothesis that on the average this kind of engine will operate for at least 29 minutes per gallon with this kind of fuel? Assume normality.

7.47 A random sample from a company's very extensive files shows that orders for a certain piece of machinery were filled, respectively, in 10, 12, 19, 14, 15, 18, 11, and 13 days. Use the level of significance $\alpha = 0.01$ to test the claim that on the average such orders are filled in 10.5 days. Choose the alternative hypothesis so that rejection of the null hypothesis $\mu = 10.5$ implies that it takes longer than indicated. Assume normality.

7.48 Five measurements of the tar content of a certain kind of cigarette yielded 14.5, 14.2, 14.4, 14.3, and 14.6 mg per cigarette. Show that the difference between the mean of this sample, $\bar{x} = 14.4$, and the average tar claimed by the manufacturer, $\mu = 14.0$, is significant at $\alpha = 0.05$. Assume normality.

7.49 Suppose that in the preceding exercise the first measurement is recorded incorrectly as 16.0 instead of 14.5. Show that now the difference between the mean of the sample, $\bar{x} = 14.7$, and the average tar content claimed by the cigarette manufacturer, $\mu = 14.0$, is not significant at $\alpha = 0.05$. Explain the apparent paradox that even though the difference between $\bar{x}$ and μ has increased, it is no longer significant.

7.50 Use the method by which we calculated the probability of a Type II error on page 235 to verify the probabilities given in the table on page 249.

7.51 With reference to the vacuum cleaner example on page 251, use Table 8 to find the probabilities of Type II errors for

    (a) $\mu = 76.00$;

    (b) $\mu = 78.00$.

7.52 With reference to the car mileage example on page 251, use Table 8 to find the probability of a Type II error for $\mu = 24.5$.

7.53 With reference to the machine parts example on page 252, use Table 8 to find the probabilities of Type II errors for

    (a) $\mu = 2.020$;

    (b) $\mu = 2.030$;

    (c) $\mu = 2.040$.

7.54 If a random sample of size $n = 6$ is used to test the hypothesis that the mean of a normal population with $\sigma = 4$ is $\mu_0 = 50$ against the alternative hypothesis that $\mu > 50$, and $\alpha = 0.01$, use Table 8 to determine the probability of committing a Type II error when

    (a) $\mu = 52$;

    (b) $\mu = 53$;

    (c) $\mu = 54$;

    (d) $\mu = 55$;

    (e) $\mu = 56$;

    (f) $\mu = 57$.

7.55 Rework Exercise 7.54, using the alternative hypothesis $\mu \neq 50$ instead of the alternative hypothesis $\mu > 50$.

7.56 If a random sample of size $n = 8$ is used to test the hypothesis that the mean of a normal population with $\sigma = 20$ is $\mu_0 = 200$ against the alternative hypothesis $\mu \neq 200$, and $\alpha = 0.05$, use Table 8 to determine the probability of committing a Type II error when

    (a) $\mu = 190$;

    (b) $\mu = 185$;

    (c) $\mu = 180$;

    (d) $\mu = 175$;

    (e) $\mu = 170$.

7.57 Rework Exercise 7.56, using the alternative hypothesis $\mu < 200$ instead of the alternative hypothesis $\mu \neq 200$.

7.58 Use Table 8 to rework part (b) of Exercise 7.31 on page 240.

7.59 Use Table 8 to rework Exercise 7.35 on page 241.

7.60 The statistical package *MINITAB* will calculate t tests. With the sulfur emission data in C1,

---

Dialog box:	**Session command**
Calc > Stat > Basic Statistics > 1-Sample t	MTB > TTEST 20.0 C1
Type *C1* in **variables.** Choose **Test mean**	
and enter 20.0. Click **OK.**	

---

produces the output

TEST OF MU=20.000 VS MU N.E. 20.000

	N	MEAN	STDEV	SE MEAN	T	P VALUE
C1	80	18.896	5.656	0.632	−1.75	0.085

You must compare your preselected α with the printed P value in order to obtain the conclusion of your test. Here we would reject $H_0 : \mu = 20.0$ at level 0.10.

    (a) Test $H_0 : \mu = 21.5$ with $\alpha = 0.05$.

    (b) Test $H_0 : \mu = 16.0$ for the data in Exercise 2.62 with $\alpha = 0.05$.

7.61 The statistical package *MINITAB* will calculate the small sample confidence interval for μ. With the sulfur emissions data in C1,

Dialog box:	Session command
Calc > Stat > Basic Statistics > 1-Sample t	MTB > TINTERVAL 95 PERCENT C1
Type *C1* in **variables.** Choose **confidence interval,** and in **level,** enter 95. Click **OK.**	

produces the output.

	N	MEAN	STDEV	SE MEAN	95.0 PERCENT C.I.
C1	80	18.896	5.656	0.632	(17.637, 20.155)

    (a) Is the test in Exercise 7.60 consistent with this interval?

    (b) Obtain a 90% confidence interval for μ.

    (c) Obtain a 95% confidence interval for μ with the aluminum alloy data on page 20.

7.62 You can simulate the coverage of the small sample confidence intervals for μ by generating 20 samples of size 10 from a normal distribution with $\mu = 20$ and $\sigma = 5$ and computing the 95% confidence intervals according to the formula on page 228. The *MINITAB* commands are

RANDOM 10 C1-C20;
NORMAL MU = 20 SIGMA = 5.
TINTERVAL 95 PERCENT C1-C20

    (a) From your output, determine the proportion of the 20 intervals that cover the true mean $\mu = 20$.

    (b) Repeat with 20 samples of size 5.

7.8 Inferences Concerning Two Means

There are many statistical problems in which we are faced with decisions about the relative size of the means of two or more populations. Leaving the general problem until Chapter 12, we shall devote this section to tests concerning the difference between two means. For example, if two methods of welding are being considered for use with railroad rails, we may take samples and decide which is better by comparing their mean strengths; also, if a licensing examination is given to engineers who graduated from two different colleges, we may want to decide whether any observed difference between the means of the scores of the students from the two colleges is significant or whether it may be attributed to chance.

    Formulating the problem more generally, we shall consider two populations having the means μ_1 and μ_2 and the variances of σ_1^2 and σ_2^2, and we shall want to test the null hypothesis $\mu_1 - \mu_2 = \delta$, where δ is a specified constant, on the basis of independent random samples of size n_1 and n_2. Analogous to the tests concerning one mean, we shall consider tests of this null hypothesis against each of the alternatives $\mu_1 - \mu_2 < \delta$, $\mu_1 - \mu_2 > \delta$, and $\mu_1 - \mu_2 \neq \delta$. The test itself will depend on the difference between the sample means, $\overline{X}_1 - \overline{X}_2$, and if both samples come from normal populations with known variances, it can be based on the statistic

$$Z = \frac{(\overline{X}_1 - \overline{X}_2) - \delta}{\sigma_{\overline{X}_1 - \overline{X}_2}}$$

which is a random variable having the standard normal distribution. Here $\sigma_{\overline{X}_1 - \overline{X}_2}$ is the standard deviation of the sampling distribution of the difference between the sample means, and its value for random samples from infinite populations may be obtained with the use of the following theorem. (See the example on page 183.)

Mean and variance of sum (or difference) of two random variables

Theorem 7.1 If the distributions of two independent random variables have the means μ_1 and μ_2 and the variances σ_1^2 and σ_2^2, then the distribution of their sum (or difference) has the mean $\mu_1 + \mu_2$ (or $\mu_1 - \mu_2$) and the variance $\sigma_1^2 + \sigma_2^2$.

To find the variance of the difference between the means of two independent random samples of size n_1 and n_2 from infinite populations, note first that the variances of the two means, themselves, are

$$\sigma_{\overline{X}_1}^2 = \frac{\sigma_1^2}{n_1} \quad \text{and} \quad \sigma_{\overline{X}_2}^2 = \frac{\sigma_2^2}{n_2}$$

where σ_1^2 and σ_2^2 are the variances of the respective populations. Thus, by Theorem 7.1 we have

$$\sigma_{\overline{X}_1 - \overline{X}_2}^2 = \frac{\sigma_1^2}{n_1} + \frac{\sigma_2^2}{n_2}$$

and the test statistic can be written as

Statistic for test concerning difference between two means

$$Z = \frac{(\overline{X}_1 - \overline{X}_2) - \delta}{\sqrt{\dfrac{\sigma_1^2}{n_1} + \dfrac{\sigma_2^2}{n_2}}}$$

which is a random variable having the standard normal distribution. In deriving this result we assumed that we are sampling from normal populations. However, the above statistic can also be used when our samples are large enough so that we can apply the central limit theorem and approximate σ_1 and σ_2 with S_1 and S_2, namely, when n_1 and n_2 are both greater than or equal to 30.

Statistic for large samples test concerning difference between two means

$$Z = \frac{(\overline{X}_1 - \overline{X}_2) - \delta}{\sqrt{\dfrac{S_1^2}{n_1} + \dfrac{S_2^2}{n_2}}}$$

Analogous to the table on page 244, the critical regions for testing the null hypothesis $\mu_1 - \mu_2 = \delta$ are as follows:

Critical Regions for Testing $\mu_1 - \mu_2 = \delta$
(Normal populations with σ_1 and σ_2
known, or large samples $n_1, n_2 \geq 30$)

Alternative hypothesis	*Reject null hypothesis if:*
$\mu_1 - \mu_2 < \delta$	$Z < -z_\alpha$
$\mu_1 - \mu_2 > \delta$	$Z > z_\alpha$
$\mu_1 - \mu_2 \neq \delta$	$Z < -z_{\alpha/2}$ or $Z > z_{\alpha/2}$

Although δ can be any constant, it is worth noting that in the great majority of problems its value is zero and we test the null hypothesis of "no difference," namely, the null hypothesis $\mu_1 = \mu_2$.

EXAMPLE

Testing a difference in means with two large samples
To test the claim that the resistance of electric wire can be reduced by more than 0.050 ohm by alloying, 32 values obtained for standard wire yielded $\overline{x}_1 = 0.136$ ohm and $s_1 = 0.004$ ohm, and 32 values obtained for alloyed wire yielded $\overline{x}_2 = 0.083$ ohm and $s_2 = 0.005$ ohm. At the 0.05 level of significance, does this support the claim?

Solution

1. *Null hypothesis:* $\mu_1 - \mu_2 = 0.050$
   Alternative hypothesis: $\mu_1 - \mu_2 > 0.050$
2. *Level of significance:* $\alpha = 0.05$
3. *Criterion:* Reject the null hypothesis if $Z > 1.645$, where Z is given by the large samples formula above.
4. *Calculations:*

$$z = \frac{0.136 - 0.083 - 0.050}{\sqrt{\dfrac{(0.004)^2}{32} + \dfrac{(0.005)^2}{32}}} = 2.65$$

5. *Decision:* Since $z = 2.65$ exceeds 1.645, the null hypothesis must be rejected; that is, the data substantiate the claim. From Table 3, the P value is 0.004

FIGURE 7.11 Large samples
P value $= .004$ for $Z = 2.65$.

(see Figure 7.11), so the evidence for alloying is very strong. Only 4 in 1,000 times would Z be at least 2.65, if the mean difference was 0.05. ✔

EXAMPLE   **Large samples test of the null hypothesis of the equality of two means**
A company claims that its light bulbs are superior to those of its main competitor. If a study showed that a sample of $n_1 = 40$ of its bulbs has a mean lifetime of 647 hours of continuous use with a standard deviation of 27 hours, while a sample of $n_2 = 40$ bulbs made by its main competitor had a mean lifetime of 638 hours of continuous use with a standard deviation of 31 hours, does this substantiate the claim at the 0.05 level of significance?

Solution

1. *Null hypothesis:* $\mu_1 - \mu_2 = 0$
   Alternative hypothesis: $\mu_1 - \mu_2 > 0$
2. *Level of significance:* $\alpha = 0.05$
3. *Criterion:* Reject the null hypothesis if $Z > 1.645$, where Z is given by the large samples formula on page 257.
4. *Calculations:*

$$z = \frac{647 - 638}{\sqrt{\dfrac{27^2}{40} + \dfrac{31^2}{40}}} = 1.38$$

5. *Decision:* Since $z = 1.38$ does not exceed 1.645, the null hypothesis cannot be rejected; that is, the observed difference between the two sample means is not significant.

The P value $= 0.0838$ (see Figure 7.12) so the evidence against equal means is not very strong. ✔

   To judge the strength of support for the null hypothesis when it is not rejected, we consider Type II errors, for which the probabilities depend on the actual alternative differences $\delta' = \mu_1 - \mu_2$. Fortunately, these can be determined with the use of Table 8 (so long as we are sampling from normal populations with known standard deviations or both samples are large). The quantity that we mark on the horizontal scale is

0.0838

FIGURE 7.12 Large samples
P value .0838 for $Z = 1.38$.

0   1.645 z

Quantity needed for
use of Table 8

$$d = \frac{|\delta - \delta'|}{\sqrt{\sigma_1^2 + \sigma_2^2}}$$

where δ is the value of $\mu_1 - \mu_2$ assumed under the null hypothesis and δ' is the alternative value of $\mu_1 - \mu_2$ with which we are concerned. If $n_1 = n_2 = n$, the probability of a Type II error is read off the OC curve corresponding to this value of n; if $n_1 \neq n_2$, it is read off the OC curve corresponding to

$$n = \frac{\sigma_1^2 + \sigma_2^2}{\dfrac{\sigma_1^2}{n_1} + \dfrac{\sigma_2^2}{n_2}}$$

EXAMPLE

Using Table 8 to approximate the probability of a Type II error
With reference to the preceding example, what is the probability of a Type II error for $\delta' = 16$ hours?

Solution   Since $d = \dfrac{|0 - 16|}{\sqrt{27^2 + 31^2}} = 0.39$, we mark this point on the horizontal scale of chart (a) of Table 8, and, going up vertically until we come to the OC curve for $n = 40$, we find that the probability of a Type II error is approximately 0.20.   ✔

When n_1, n_2, or both are small and the population variances are unknown, we can base tests of the null hypothesis $\mu_1 - \mu_2 = \delta$ on a suitable t statistic, provided we can assume that both populations are normal with $\sigma_1 = \sigma_2(= \sigma)$. Under these conditions, it can be shown that

$$t = \frac{(\overline{X}_1 - \overline{X}_2) - \delta}{\hat{\sigma}_{\overline{X}_1 - \overline{X}_2}}$$

is a random variable having the t distribution with $n_1 + n_2 - 2$ degrees of freedom, where $\hat{\sigma}_{\overline{X}_1 - \overline{X}_2}$ is the square root of an estimate of

$$\sigma_{\overline{X}_1 - \overline{X}_2}^2 = \frac{\sigma_1^2}{n_1} + \frac{\sigma_2^2}{n_2} = \sigma^2\left(\frac{1}{n_1} + \frac{1}{n_2}\right)$$

with σ^2 estimated by **pooling** the sums of the squared deviations from the respective sample means. That is, we estimate σ^2 as S_p^2, the pooled estimate

$$S_p^2 = \frac{\sum(X_1 - \overline{X}_1)^2 + \sum(X_2 - \overline{X}_2)^2}{n_1 + n_2 - 2} = \frac{(n_1 - 1)S_1^2 + (n_2 - 1)S_2^2}{n_1 + n_2 - 2}$$

where $\sum(X_1 - \overline{X}_1)^2$ is the sum of the squared deviations from the mean for the first sample, while $\sum(X_2 - \overline{X}_2)^2$ is the sum of the squared deviations from the mean for the second sample. We divide by $n_1 + n_2 - 2$, since there are $n_1 - 1$ independent deviations from the mean in the first sample, $n_2 - 1$ in the second, and we thus have $n_1 + n_2 - 2$ independent deviations from the mean to estimate the population variance. Substituting this estimate of σ^2 into the above expression for $\sigma^2_{\overline{X}_1 - \overline{X}_2}$ and then substituting the square root of the result into the denominator of the formula for t above, we finally obtain

Statistic for small sample test concerning difference between two means

$$t = \frac{\overline{X}_1 - \overline{X}_2 - \delta}{S_p\sqrt{\dfrac{1}{n_1} + \dfrac{1}{n_2}}} \quad \text{where} \quad S_p^2 = \frac{(n_1 - 1)S_1^2 + (n_2 - 1)S_2^2}{n_1 + n_2 - 2}$$

which is a random variable having the t distribution with $n_1 + n_2 - 2$ degrees of freedom. The criteria for the **two-sample t test** based on this statistic are like those for Z.

Critical Regions for Testing $\mu_1 - \mu_2 = \delta$
(Normal populations with $\sigma_1 = \sigma_2$)
two-sample t test

Alternative hypothesis	Reject null hypothesis if:
$\mu_1 - \mu_2 < \delta$	$t < -t_\alpha$
$\mu_1 - \mu_2 > \delta$	$t > t_\alpha$
$\mu_1 - \mu_2 \neq \delta$	$t < -t_{\alpha/2}$ or $t > t_{\alpha/2}$

In the application of this test, n_1 and n_2 may be small, yet $n_1 + n_2 - 2$ may be 30 or more; in that case we use the critical values given in the bottom line of Table 4.

EXAMPLE

A two-sample t test
The following random samples are measurements of the heat-producing capacity (in millions of calories per ton) of specimens of coal from two mines:

Mine 1:	8,260	8,130	8,350	8,070	8,340	
Mine 2:	7,950	7,890	7,900	8,140	7,920	7,840

Use the 0.01 level of significance to test whether the difference between the means of these two samples is significant.

Solution

1. *Null hypothesis:* $\mu_1 - \mu_2 = 0$
   Alternative hypothesis: $\mu_1 - \mu_2 \neq 0$

2. *Level of significance:* $\alpha = 0.01$

3. *Criterion:* Reject the null hypothesis if $t < -3.250$ or $t > 3.250$, where 3.250 is the value of $t_{0.005}$ for $5 + 6 - 2 = 9$ degrees of freedom and t is given by the formula on page 260.

4. *Calculations:* The means and the variances of the two samples are

   $$\bar{x}_1 = 8{,}230, \ \bar{x}_2 = 7{,}940, \ s_1^2 = \frac{63{,}000}{4} = 15{,}750, \text{ and } s_2^2 = \frac{54{,}600}{5} = 10{,}920,$$

   so that $s_p^2 = (64{,}000 + 54{,}600)/(5 + 4) = 13{,}066.7$ so $s_p = 114.31$ and

   $$t = \frac{(8{,}230 - 7{,}940)}{114.31\sqrt{\dfrac{1}{5} + \dfrac{1}{6}}} = 4.19$$

5. *Decision:* Since $t = 4.19$ exceeds 3.250, the null hypothesis must be rejected at level $\alpha = 0.01$. We conclude that the average heat-producing capacity of the coal from the two mines is not the same. The very small P value 0.0024 (see Figure 7.13) strengthens this conclusion. ✓

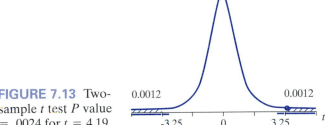

FIGURE 7.13 Two-sample t test P value $= .0024$ for $t = 4.19$.

0.0012   0.0012

-3.25   0   3.25 t

In the preceding example we went ahead and performed the two-sample t test, tacitly assuming that the population variances are equal. Fortunately, the test is not overly sensitive to small differences between the population variances, and the procedure used in this instance is justifiable. As a rule of thumb, if one variance is four times the other, we should be concerned. A transformation will often improve the situation. As another alternative there is the Smith-Satterthwaite test mentioned in Exercise 7.70.

Confidence intervals follow directly from the acceptance region for the tests. For two normal populations with equal variances,

Small sample confidence interval concerning difference between two means

> The $(1 - \alpha)100\%$ confidence interval for $\delta = \mu_1 - \mu_2$ has limits
>
> $$\bar{x}_1 - \bar{x}_2 \pm t_{\alpha/2}\sqrt{\frac{(n_1 - 1)s_1^2 + (n_2 - 1)s_2^2}{n_1 + n_2 - 2}}\sqrt{\frac{1}{n_1} + \frac{1}{n_2}}$$
>
> where $t_{\alpha/2}$ is based on $v = n_1 + n_2 - 2$ degrees of freedom.

EXAMPLE

Graphics to accompany a two-sample *t* test
Strength measurements on an aluminum alloy were introduced on page 20. A second alloy yielded measurements given in the following stem-and-leaf display. Find a 95% confidence interval for the difference in mean strength δ.

Solution

We first place the observations on the two alloys in stem-and-leaf displays. Note that the observations from the first alloy appear normal, but those on the second alloy may deviate from a normal distribution. Since the sample sizes are relatively large, this will not cause any difficulty.

Alloy 1, $N = 58$
Leaf unit $= 0.10$

Alloy 2, $N = 27$
Leaf unit $= 0.10$

	Alloy 1													Alloy 2					
66	4												66						
67	7												67						
68	0	0	3	4	6	8	9						68						
69	0	1	2	3	3	5	5	6	7	8	8	9	69						
70	0	0	1	2	3	3	4	5	6	6	8	9	70						
71	0	1	2	3	3	5	6	6	7	8	8	9	71	2	8				
72	1	2	3	4	6	7	9						72	6	8				
73	1	3	5										73	4	7	9			
74	2	5											74	4	9				
75	3												75	5	9				
76													76	3	5	7	9		
77													77	1	3	6	7	8	
78													78	1	2	4	6		
79													79	0	3	8			

A computer calculation gives the sample means and standard deviations

	N	MEAN	STDEV
ALLOY 1	58	70.70	1.80
ALLOY 2	27	76.13	2.42

From another computer calculation (or by interpolation in Table 4), we find $t_{0.025} = 1.99$, so the 95% confidence interval is

$$\bar{x}_1 - \bar{x} \pm t_{\alpha/2} \sqrt{\frac{(n_1 - 1)s_1^2 + (n_2 - 1)s_2^2}{n_1 + n_2 - 2}} \sqrt{\frac{1}{n_1} + \frac{1}{n_2}}$$

$$= 70.70 - 76.13 \pm 1.99 \sqrt{\frac{57(1.80)^2 + 26(2.42)^2}{83}} \sqrt{\frac{1}{58} + \frac{1}{27}}$$

or

$$-6.4 < \mu_1 - \mu_2 < -4.5$$

We are 95% confident that the mean strength of alloy 2 is 4.5 to 6.4 thousand pounds per square inch higher than the mean strength of alloy 1.   ✔

It is good practice to show stem-and-leaf displays, boxplots, or histograms. Often they reveal more than a mean difference.

The large sample confidence interval follows from the test on page 257.

Large sample
confidence interval
for $\mu_1 - \mu_2$

$$\bar{x}_1 - \bar{x}_2 \pm z_{\alpha/2}\sqrt{\frac{s_1^2}{n_1} + \frac{s_2^2}{n_2}}$$

EXAMPLE

Comparing the two confidence intervals
Referring to the previous example, find the 95% large sample confidence interval.

Solution

$$\bar{x}_1 - \bar{x}_2 \pm z_{\alpha/2}\sqrt{\frac{s_1^2}{n_1} + \frac{s_2^2}{n_2}} = 70.70 - 76.13 \pm 1.96\sqrt{\frac{(1.80)^2}{58} + \frac{(2.42)^2}{27}}$$

or

$$-6.5 < \mu_1 - \mu_2 < -4.4$$

There is not much difference between this 95% confidence interval and the one in the previous example, where the variances were pooled. ✔

Matched Pairs Comparisons

In the application of the two-sample t test we need to watch that the samples are independent. For instance, the test cannot be used when we deal with "before and after" data, the IQ's of husbands and wives, and numerous other kinds of situations where the data are naturally paired.

A manufacturer is concerned about the loss of weight of ceramic parts during a baking step. The readings before and after baking, on the same specimen, are naturally paired. It would make no sense to compare the before-baking weight of one speciman with the after-baking weight of another specimen. Let the pair of random variables (X_i, Y_i) denote the weight before and weight after baking for the i-th specimen, for $i = 1, 2, ... n$. A statistical analysis proceeds by considering the differences

$$D_i = X_i - Y_i \text{ for } i = 1, 2, \ldots, n$$

This collection of (signed) differences is then treated as a random sample of size n from a population having mean μ_D. We interpret $\mu_D = 0$ as indicating the means of the two responses are the same and $\mu_D > 0$ as indicating the mean response of the first is higher than that of the second.

Tests of the null hypothesis $H_0:\mu_D = \mu_{D,0}$ are based on the ratio

$$\frac{\bar{D} - \mu_{D,0}}{S_D/\sqrt{n}} \quad \text{where} \quad \bar{D} = \frac{\sum_{i=1}^{n} D_i}{n} \quad S_D^2 = \frac{\sum_{i=1}^{n}(D_i - \bar{D})^2}{n-1}$$

If n is small, we treat this ratio as the one-sample t statistic on page 245. Otherwise, we treat this ratio as the large-sample statistic on page 244.

EXAMPLE

Conducting a paired t test
The following are the average weekly losses of worker-hours due to accidents in 10 industrial plants before and after a certain safety program was put into operation:

| Before: | 45 | 73 | 46 | 124 | 33 | 57 | 83 | 34 | 26 | 17 |
| After: | 36 | 60 | 44 | 119 | 35 | 51 | 77 | 29 | 24 | 11 |

Use the 0.05 level of significance to test whether the safety program is effective.

Solution

1. *Null hypothesis:* $\mu_D = 0$
   Alternative hypothesis: $\mu_D > 0$
2. *Level of significance:* $\alpha = 0.05$
3. *Criterion:* Reject the null hypothesis if $t > 1.833$, the value of $t_{0.05}$ for $10 - 1 = 9$ degrees of freedom, where

$$t = \frac{\overline{D} - 0}{S_D/\sqrt{n}}$$

and $\overline{D}$ and S_D are the mean and the standard deviation of the differences.

4. *Calculations:* The differences are 9, 13, 2, 5, −2, 6, 6, 5, 2, and 6, their mean is $\overline{d} = 5.2$, their standard deviation is $s_D = 4.08$, so that

$$t = \frac{5.2 - 0}{4.08/\sqrt{10}} = 4.03$$

5. *Decision:* Since $t = 4.03$ exceeds 1.833, the null hypothesis must be rejected at level $\alpha = 0.05$. We conclude that the industrial safety program is effective. The evidence is very strong, since a computer calculation gives the P value 0.0015 (see Figure 7.14). If $\mu_D = 0$, only in 15 out of 10,000 times would we observe t greater than or equal to 4.03. ✔

In connection with this kind of problem, the one-sample t test is referred to as a **matched pairs t test** or just the **paired t test**.

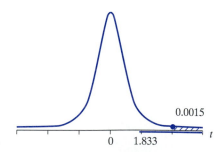

Figure 7.14 The paired-t
P value $= .0015$ for $t = 4.03$.

EXAMPLE

A 90% confidence interval for the mean of a paired difference
Referring to the previous example, find a 90% confidence interval for the mean improvement in lost worker-hours.

Solution   The $n = 10$ differences have $\bar{d} = 5.2$ and $s_D = 4.08$. Since $t_{0.05} = 1.833$, the 90% confidence interval for μ_D, the mean improvement, is

$$5.2 - 1.833\,\frac{4.08}{\sqrt{10}} < \mu_D < 5.2 + 1.833\,\frac{4.08}{\sqrt{10}}, \qquad \text{or } 4.0 < \mu_D < 6.4$$

worker-hours per week. We are 90% confident that between 4.0 and 6.4 fewer worker-hours per week are lost, on average, after the safety program.   ✔

EXERCISES

7.63 The diameters of rotor shafts in a lot have a mean of 0.249 inch and a standard deviation of 0.003 inch. The inner diameters of bearings in another lot have a mean of 0.255 inch and a standard deviation of 0.002 inch.

(a) What are the mean and the standard deviation of the clearances between shafts and bearings selected from these lots?

(b) If a shaft and a bearing are selected at random, what is the probability that the shaft will not fit inside the bearing? (Assume that both dimensions are normally distributed.)

7.64 An investigation of two kinds of photocopying equipment showed that 71 failures of the first kind of equipment took on the average 83.2 minutes to repair with a standard deviation of 19.3 minutes, while 75 failures of the second kind of equipment took on the average 90.8 minutes to repair with a standard deviation of 21.4 minutes.

(a) Test the null hypothesis $\mu_1 - \mu_2 = 0$ (namely, the hypothesis that on the average it takes an equal amount of time to repair either kind of equipment) against the alternative hypothesis $\mu_1 - \mu_2 \neq 0$ at the level of significance $\alpha = 0.05$.

(b) Using 19.3 and 21.4 as estimates of σ_1 and σ_2 and referring to Table 8, find the probability of failing to reject the null hypothesis $\mu_1 - \mu_2 = 0$ with the criterion of part (a) when actually $\mu_1 - \mu_2 = -12$.

7.65 Suppose that we want to investigate whether on the average men earn more than $20 per week more than women in a certain industry. If sample data show that 60 men earn on the average $\bar{x}_1 = \$292.50$ per week with a standard deviation of $s_1 = \$15.60$, while 60 women earn on the average $\bar{x}_2 = \$266.10$ per week with a standard deviation of $s_2 = \$18.20$, what can we conclude at the 0.01 level of significance?

7.66 Studying the flow of traffic at two busy intersections between 4 P.M. and 6 P.M. (to determine the possible need for turn signals), it was found that on 40 weekdays there were on the average 247.3 cars approaching the first intersection from the south which made left turns, while on 30 weekdays there were on the average 254.1 cars approaching the second intersection from the south which made left turns. The corresponding sample standard deviations are $s_1 = 15.2$ and $s_2 = 18.7$.

(a) Test the null hypothesis $\mu_1 - \mu_2 = 0$ against the alternative hypothesis $\mu_1 - \mu_2 \neq 0$ at the level of significance $\alpha = 0.01$.

(b) Using 15.2 and 18.7 as estimates of σ_1 and σ_2 and referring to Table 8, find the probability of accepting the null hypothesis $\mu_1 - \mu_2 = 0$ when actually $|\mu_1 - \mu_2| = 15.6$.

7.67 Measuring specimens of nylon yarn taken from two spinning machines, it was found that 8 specimens from the first machine had a mean denier of 9.67 with a standard deviation of 1.81 while 10 specimens from the second machine had a mean denier of 7.43 with a standard deviation of 1.48. Assuming that the populations sampled are normal and have the same variance, test the null hypothesis $\mu_1 - \mu_2 = 1.5$ against the alternative hypothesis $\mu_1 - \mu_2 > 1.5$ at the 0.05 level of significance.

7.68 As part of an industrial training program, some trainees are instructed by Method A, which is straight teaching-machine instruction, and some are instructed by Method B, which also involves the personal attention of an instructor. If random samples of size 10 are taken from large groups of trainees instructed by each of these two methods, and the scores which they obtained in an appropriate achievement test are

Method A:	71	75	65	69	73	66	68	71	74	68
Method B:	72	77	84	78	69	70	77	73	65	75

use the 0.05 level of significance to test the claim that Method B is more effective. Assume that the populations sampled can be approximated closely with normal distributions having the same variance.

7.69 The following are the number of sales which a sample of 9 salespeople of industrial chemicals in California and a sample of 6 salespeople of industrial chemicals in Oregon made over a certain fixed period of time:

California:	59	68	44	71	63	46	69	54	48
Oregon:	50	36	62	52	70	41			

Assuming that the populations sampled can be approximated closely with normal distributions having the same variance, test the null hypothesis $\mu_1 - \mu_2 = 0$ against the alternative hypothesis $\mu_1 - \mu_2 \neq 0$ at the 0.01 level of significance.

7.70 When we deal with two independent random samples from normal populations whose variances seem to be unequal, the following test, called the **Smith-Satterthwaite test,** can be used instead of the two-sample t test. The test statistic

$$t' = \frac{(\overline{X}_1 - \overline{X}_2) - \delta}{\sqrt{\dfrac{S_1^2}{n_1} + \dfrac{S_2^2}{n_2}}}$$

is a random variable having approximately the t distribution with degrees of freedom estimated from the observed values of the sample variances s_1^2 and s_2^2 as

$$\frac{\left(\dfrac{s_1^2}{n_1} + \dfrac{s_2^2}{n_2}\right)^2}{\dfrac{(s_1^2/n_1)^2}{n_1 - 1} + \dfrac{(s_2^2/n_2)^2}{n_2 - 1}}$$

Use this test in the following problems:

(a) The following are the Brinell hardness values obtained for samples of two magnesium alloys:

Alloy 1:	66.3	63.5	64.9	61.8	64.3	64.7	65.1	64.5	68.4	63.2
Alloy 2:	71.3	60.4	62.6	63.9	68.8	70.1	64.8	68.9	65.8	66.2

Use the 0.05 level of significance to test the null hypothesis $\mu_1 - \mu_2 = 0$ against the alternative hypothesis $\mu_1 - \mu_2 < 0$.

(b) To compare two kinds of bumper guards, 6 of each kind were mounted on a certain kind of compact car. Then each car was run into a concrete wall at 5 miles per hour, and the following are the costs of the repairs (in dollars):

Bumper guard 1: 107   148   123   165   102   119

Bumper guard 2: 134   115   112   151   133   129

Use the 0.01 level of significance to test whether the difference between the two sample means is significant.

7.71 The following data were obtained in an experiment designed to check whether there is a systematic difference in the weights obtained with two different scales:

	Weight in grams	
	Scale I	*Scale II*
Rock specimen 1	11.23	11.27
Rock specimen 2	14.36	14.41
Rock specimen 3	8.33	8.35
Rock specimen 4	10.50	10.52
Rock specimen 5	23.42	23.41
Rock specimen 6	9.15	9.17
Rock specimen 7	13.47	13.52
Rock specimen 8	6.47	6.46
Rock specimen 9	12.40	12.45
Rock specimen 10	19.38	19.35

Use the paired t test at the 0.05 level of significance to test whether the difference of the means of the weights obtained with the two scales is significant.

7.72 In a study of the effectiveness of physical exercise in weight reduction, a group of 16 persons engaged in a prescribed program of physical exercise for one month showed the following results:

Weight before (pounds)	Weight after (pounds)	Weight before (pounds)	Weight after (pounds)
209	196	170	164
178	171	153	152
169	170	183	179
212	207	165	162
180	177	201	199
192	190	179	173
158	159	243	231
180	180	144	140

Use the 0.01 level of significance to test whether the prescribed program of exercise is effective.

7.73 With reference to the example on page 257, construct a 95% confidence interval for the true difference between the average resistance of the two kinds of wire.

7.9 Design Issues—Randomization and Pairing

Often, the experimenter can make the choice of which of the two treatments is applied to an individual unit. Then it is possible to conduct either an independent samples or a matched pairs comparison of means. The method of assignment of units to two groups or pairs can be crucial to the validity of the statistical procedures for comparing the means of two populations. We first emphasize the importance of randomization in the context of the independent samples design of a comparative experiment.

Independent Samples Design: Randomization

In many comparative studies, the investigator applies one or the other treatment to an object we call an experimental unit. The method of assigning the treatments to the experimental units can be crucial to the validity of the statistical procedures for comparing the two population means. Suppose a chemist has a new formula for waterproofing that she applies to several pairs of shoes that are almost like new. She also applies the old formula to several pairs of scuffed shoes. At the end of a month, she will measure the ability of each pair of shoes to withstand water. It doesn't take a statistician to see that this is not a good experimental design. The persons with scuffed shoes probably walk a lot more and do so in all kinds of weather. These sources of variation could very well lead to systematic biases that make the new formula seem better than the old even when this is not the case. The pairs of shoes need to be assigned to the treatments, old and new waterproofing formula, in a random manner.

When possible, the $n = n_1 + n_2$ experimental units should be assigned at random to the two treatments. This means that all $\binom{n}{n_1}$ possible selections of n_1 units to receive the first treatment are equally likely. Practically, the assignment is accomplished by selecting n_1 random integers between 1 and n. The corresponding experimental units are assigned to the first treatment. Generally, a test will have more power if the two sample sizes are equal.

In summary, we must actively assign treatments at random to experimental units. This process is called **randomization.**

Purpose of randomization

> **Randomization** of treatments prevents uncontrolled sources of variation from exerting a systematic influence on the responses.

Matched-Pairs Design: Pairing and Randomization

The object of **pairing** experimental units, according to a characteristic that is likely to influence the response, is to eliminate this source of variation from the comparison. In the context of waterproofing for shoes, each person could have the old formula on one shoe and the new formula on the other. Since the paired t analysis only uses differences from the same pair, this experimental strategy should eliminate most of the variation in response due to different terrain, distance covered and weather conditions.

> **Pairing** according to some variable(s) thought to influence the response will remove the effect of that variable from analysis.

Even after units are paired, there is a need for randomization. For each pair, a fair coin should be flipped to assign the treatments. In the context of the waterproofing example, the old formula could be applied to the right shoe if heads and the left shoe if tails. The new formula is applied to the other shoe. This randomization, restricted to be within pairs, would prevent systematic influences such as those caused by the fact that a majority of persons would tend to kick things with their right shoe.

> **Randomizing** the assignment of treatments within a pair helps prevent any other uncontrolled variables from influencing the responses in a systematic manner.

Notice that in the example on page 264, the experimenter had no control over the before and after. Many uncontrolled variables may also have changed over the course of the experiment: fewer working hours due to strikes, phasing out of an old type of equipment, etc. One of these could have been the cause for the improvement rather than the safety program.

We pursue the ideas of randomization and blocking in Chapter 12. Our purpose here was to show what practical steps can be taken to meet the idealistic assumptions of random samples.

EXERCISES

7.74 An investigator wants to compare two busy network protocols by recording the number of messages that are successfully passed by the network in a day. Describe how to select 5 of the next 10 working days for trying Protocol 1. Protocol 2 would be tried on the other 5 days.

7.75 An electrical engineer has developed a modified power source for reducing noise in either one of the two channels of a stereo amplifier. If 6 modified power sources and 6 stereo amplifiers are available for a comparative test of the old versus the modified power source,

   (a) Describe how you would select the 3 amplifiers in which to insert 2 modified power sources in each.

   (b) Describe how you would conduct a paired comparison and then randomize within the pair.

7.76 It takes an average of 10 weeks to train a typical employee to run a computer-aided machine. The instructor has a new approach that she feels will lead to faster learning. She intends to teach 5 persons by the new method and then compare the results with the 10-week average for the old method. In order to obtain 5 students from the 25 available candidates, she asks for volunteers. Why is this a bad idea?

7.77 How would you randomize, for a two-sample test, if 50 cars are available for an emissions study and you want to compare a modified air pollution device with the current production?

REVIEW EXERCISES

7.78 Specify the null hypothesis and the alternative hypothesis in each of the following cases.

    (a) An engineer hopes to establish that an additive will increase the viscosity of an oil.

    (b) An electrical engineer hopes to establish that a modified circuit board will give a computer a higher average operating speed.

7.79 With reference to the example on page 262, find a 95% confidence interval for the mean strength of aluminum alloy 1.

7.80 While performing a certain task under simulated weightlessness, the pulse rate of 32 astronaut trainees increased on the average by 26.4 beats per minute with a standard deviation of 4.28 beats per minute. What can one assert with 95% confidence about the maximum error if $\bar{x} = 26.4$ is used as a point estimate of the true average increase in the pulse rate of astronaut trainees performing the given task?

7.81 With reference to the preceding exercise, construct a 95% confidence interval for the true average increase in the pulse rate of astronaut trainees performing the given task.

7.82 It is desired to estimate the mean number of hours of continuous use until a certain kind of computer will first require repairs. If it can be assumed that $\sigma = 48$ hours, how large a sample is needed so that one will be able to assert with 90% confidence that the sample mean is off by at most 10 hours?

7.83 A sample of 12 cam shafts intended for use in gasoline engines has an average eccentricity of 1.02 and a standard deviation of 0.044 inch. Assuming the data may be treated as a random sample from a normal population, determine a 95% confidence interval for the actual mean eccentricity of the cam shaft.

7.84 In order to test the durability of a new paint, a highway department had test strips painted across heavily traveled roads in 15 different locations. If on the average the test strips disappeared after they had been crossed by 146,692 cars with standard deviation of 14,380 cars, construct a 99% confidence interval for the true average number of cars it takes to wear off the paint. Assume a normal population.

7.85 Referring to Exercise 7.84 and using 14,380 as an estimate of σ, find the sample size that would have been needed to be able to assert with 95% confidence that the sample mean is off by at most 10,000. [*Hint*: First estimate n_1 by using $z = 1.96$, then use $t_{0.025}$ for $n_1 - 1$ degrees of freedom to obtain a second estimate n_2, and repeat this procedure until the last two values of n thus obtained are equal.]

7.86 With reference to Exercise 2.60 test that the mean charge of the electron is the same for both tubes. Use $\alpha = 0.05$.

7.87 With reference to the previous exercise, find a 90% confidence interval for the difference of the two means.

7.88 With reference to the example on page 14, test that the mean copper content is the same for both heats.

7.89 With reference to the previous exercise, find a 90% confidence interval for the difference of the two means.

7.90 A laboratory technician is timed 20 times in the performance of a task, getting $\bar{x} = 7.9$ and $s = 1.2$. If the probability of a Type I error is to be at most 0.05, does this constitute evidence against the hypothesis that the average time is less than 7.5 minutes?

7.91 Suppose that in the drying-time example on page 234, n is changed from 36 to 50, while the other quantities remain $\mu_0 = 20$, $\sigma = 2.4$, and $\alpha = 0.03$. Find

(a) the new dividing line of the test criterion;

(b) the probability of Type II errors for the same values of μ as shown in the table on page 249.

Also plot the OC curve and compare it with the one shown in Figure 7.9.

7.92 Use Table 8 to rework part (a) of Exercise 7.34 on page 240.

7.93 Use Table 8 to rework part (b) of Exercise 7.34 on page 241.

7.94 In an air-pollution study, ozone measurements were taken in a large California city at 5:00 P.M. The eight readings (in parts per million) were: 7.9, 11.3, 6.9, 12.7, 13.2, 8.8, 9.3, 10.6. Assuming the population sampled is normal, construct a 95% confidence interval for the corresponding true mean.

7.95 Random samples are taken from two normal populations with $\sigma_1 = 10.8$ and $\sigma_2 = 14.4$ to test the null hypothesis $\mu_1 - \mu_2 = 53.2$ against the alternative hypothesis $\mu_1 - \mu_2 > 53.2$ at the level of significance $\alpha = 0.01$. Use Table 8 to determine the common sample size $n = n_1 = n_2$ that is required if the probability of not rejecting the null hypothesis is to be 0.09 when $\mu_1 - \mu_2 = 66.7$.

7.96 With reference to the example on page 262, find a 90% confidence interval for the difference of mean strengths of the alloys

(a) using the pooled procedure;

(b) using the large sample procedure.

7.97 How would you randomize, for a two-sample test, in each of the following cases?

(a) Twenty cars are available for a mileage study and you want to compare a modified spark plug with the regular.

(b) A new oven will be compared with the old. Fifteen ceramic specimens are available for baking.

7.98 With reference to part (a) of Exercise 7.97, how would you pair and then randomize for a paired test?

7.99 Two samples in C1 and C2 can be analyzed using the *MINITAB* commands

Dialog box:	Session command
Calc > Stat > Basic Statistics > 2-Sample t	MTB>TWOSAMPLE TEST 95 C1 C2;
Click **Samples in different columns.**	SUBC>POOLED.
Type *C1* in **First** *C2* in **Second.**	
Click **OK.**	
Click **Assume equal variances.**	

The output relating to the example on page 262 is

TWOSAMPLE T FOR ALLOY1 VS ALLOY2

	N	MEAN	STDEV	SE MEAN
ALLOY1	58	70.70	1.80	0.24
ALLOY2	27	76.13	2.42	0.47

95 PCT CI FOR MU ALLOY1 − MU ALLOY2: (−6.36, −4.50)
TTEST MU ALLOY1 = MU ALLOY2 (VS NE): T = −11.58 P = 0.000 DF = 83.0

Perform the test for the data in Exercise 7.68.

KEY TERMS

(with page references)

Alternative hypothesis 237
Classical theory 239
Composite hypothesis 239
Confidence 225
Confidence interval 227
Confidence limits 227
Critical regions 242
Critical values 242
Degree of confidence 227
Estimated standard error 222
Hat notation 222
Interval estimate 227
Level of significance 237
Likelihood function 233
Matched pairs t test 264
Maximum likelihood estimator 233
Neyman-Pearson theory 239
Null hypothesis 236
One-sample t test 246
One-sided alternative 236
One-sided criterion 238
One-sided test 238

One-tailed test 238
Operating characteristic curve 249
Paired-t test 264
Pairing 268
Point estimation 221
Pooling 260
P value 243
Randomization 268
Simple hypothesis 239
Smith-Satterthwaite test 266
Tail probability 243
Two-sample t test 260
Two-sided alternative 237
Two-sided criterion 238
Two-sided test 238
Two-tailed test 238
Type I error 235
Type II error 235
Unbiased estimator 222

Table 7.1 Summary of the Formulas for Inferences about a Mean (μ), or a Difference of Two Means ($\mu_1 - \mu_2$)

Confidence interval = Point estimator $\pm$ (Tabled value)(Estimated or true std. dev.)

$$\text{Test statistic} = \frac{\text{Point estimator} - \text{Parameter value at } H_0 \text{ (null hypothesis)}}{(\text{Estimated or true}) \text{ std. dev of point estimator}}$$

	Single Sample		Independent Samples			Matched Pairs
	General	Normal with unknown σ	Normal $\sigma_1 = \sigma_2 = \sigma$	Normal $\sigma_1 \neq \sigma_2$	General	Normal for the difference $D_i = X_i - Y_i$
Population(s)	Mean μ	Mean μ	$\mu_1 - \mu_2 = \delta$	$\mu_1 - \mu_2 = \delta$	$\mu_1 - \mu_2 = \delta$	μ_D
Inference on						
Sample(s)	$X_1,\dots,X_n$	$X_1,\dots,X_n$	$X_1,\dots,X_{n_1}$ $Y_1,\dots,Y_{n_2}$	$X_1,\dots,X_{n_1}$ $Y_1,\dots,Y_{n_2}$	$X_1,\dots,X_{n_1}$ $Y_1,\dots,Y_{n_2}$	$D_1 = X_1 - Y_1$ $\vdots$ $D_n = X_n - Y_n$
Sample size n	Large $n \geq 30$	$n \geq 2$	$n_1 \geq 2$ $n_2 \geq 2$	$n_1 \geq 2$ $n_2 \geq 2$	$n_1 \geq 30$ $n_2 \geq 30$	$n \geq 2$
Point estimator	$\overline{X}$	$\overline{X}$	$\overline{X} - \overline{Y}$	$\overline{X} - \overline{Y}$	$\overline{X} - \overline{Y}$	$\overline{D} = \overline{X} - \overline{Y}$
Variance of Point estimator	$\dfrac{\sigma^2}{n}$	$\dfrac{\sigma^2}{n}$	$\sigma^2\left(\dfrac{1}{n_1} + \dfrac{1}{n_2}\right)$	$\dfrac{\sigma_1^2}{n_1} + \dfrac{\sigma_2^2}{n_2}$	$\dfrac{\sigma_1^2}{n_1} + \dfrac{\sigma_2^2}{n_2}$	$\dfrac{\sigma_D^2}{n}$
Estimated std. dev.	$\dfrac{S}{\sqrt{n}}$	$\dfrac{S}{\sqrt{n}}$	$S_p\sqrt{\dfrac{1}{n_1} + \dfrac{1}{n_2}}$	$\sqrt{\dfrac{S_1^2}{n_1} + \dfrac{S_2^2}{n_2}}$	$\sqrt{\dfrac{S_1^2}{n_1} + \dfrac{S_2^2}{n_2}}$	$\dfrac{S_D}{\sqrt{n}}$
Distribution	Normal	t with d.f. $= n - 1$	t with d.f. $= n_1 + n_2 - 2$	t with d.f. estimated†	Normal	t with d.f. $= n - 1$
Test statistic	$\dfrac{\overline{X} - \mu_0}{S/\sqrt{n}}$	$\dfrac{\overline{X} - \mu_0}{S/\sqrt{n}}$	$\dfrac{(\overline{X} - \overline{Y}) - \delta_0}{S_p\sqrt{\dfrac{1}{n_1} + \dfrac{1}{n_2}}}$ $S_p^2 = \dfrac{(n_1 - 1)S_1^2 + (n_2 - 1)S_2^2}{n_1 + n_2 - 2}$	$\dfrac{(\overline{X} - \overline{Y}) - \delta_0}{\sqrt{\dfrac{S_1^2}{n_1} + \dfrac{S_2^2}{n_2}}}$	$\dfrac{(\overline{X} - \overline{Y}) - \delta_0}{\sqrt{\dfrac{S_1^2}{n_1} + \dfrac{S_2^2}{n_2}}}$	$\dfrac{\overline{D} - \mu_{D,0}}{S_D/\sqrt{n}}$ $S_D = $ sample std. dev. of the D_i's

$^\dagger d.f. = [(s_1^2/n_1) + (s_2^2/n_2)]^2 / [(n_1 - 1)^{-1}(s_1^2/n_1)^2 + (n_2 - 1)^{-1}(s_2^2/n_2)^2]$

Inferences Concerning Variances

In Chapter 7 we learned how to judge the size of the error in estimating a population mean, how to construct confidence intervals for means, and how to perform tests of hypotheses about the means of one and of two populations. As we shall see in this and in subsequent chapters, very similar methods apply to inferences about other population parameters.

In this chapter we shall concentrate on population variances, or standard deviations, which are not only important in their own right, but which must sometimes be estimated before inferences about other parameters can be made. Section 8.1 is devoted to the estimation of σ^2 and σ, and Sections 8.2 and 8.3 deal with tests of hypotheses about these parameters. ■

8.1 The Estimation of Variances

In the preceding chapter, there were several instances where we estimated a population standard deviation by means of a sample standard deviation—we substituted s for σ in the large sample confidence interval for μ on page 228, in the large sample test concerning μ on page 244, and in the large sample test concerning the difference between two means on page 257. There are many statistical procedures in which s is thus substituted for σ, or s^2 for σ^2. There are also situations where σ is the primary parameter of interest.

Let $S^2 = \sum_{i=1}^{n}(X_i - \overline{X})^2/(n-1)$ be the sample variance based on a random sample from any population, discrete or continuous, having variance σ^2. It follows from the example on page 185 that the mean of the sampling distribution of S^2 is given by σ^2.

Unbiased estimation
of a population
variance

The sample variance

$$S^2 = \frac{\sum_{i=1}^{n} (X_i - \overline{X})^2}{n - 1} \quad \text{is an unbiased estimator of } \sigma^2$$

Although the sample variance is an unbiased estimator of σ^2, it does not follow that the sample standard deviation is also an unbiased estimator of σ; in fact, it is not. However, for large samples the bias is small and it is common practice to estimate σ with s.

Besides s, population standard deviations are sometimes estimated in terms of the **sample range** R, which we defined in Section 2.6 as the largest value of a sample minus the smallest. Given a random sample of size n from a normal population, it can be shown that the sampling distribution of the range has the mean $d_2\sigma$ and the standard deviation $d_3\sigma$, where d_2 and d_3 are constants which depend on the size of the sample. For $n = 1, 2, \ldots$, and 10, their values are as shown in the following table:

n	2	3	4	5	6	7	8	9	10
d_2	1.128	1.693	2.059	2.326	2.534	2.704	2.847	2.970	3.078
d_3	0.853	0.888	0.880	0.864	0.848	0.833	0.820	0.808	0.797

Thus, R/d_2 is an unbiased estimate of σ, and for very small samples, $n \leq 5$, it provides nearly as good an estimate of σ as does s. As the sample size increases, it becomes more efficient to use s instead of R/d_2. Nowadays, the range is used to estimate σ primarily in problems of industrial quality control, where sample sizes are usually small and computational ease is of prime concern. This application will be discussed in Chapter 14, where we shall need the above values of the constant d_3.

EXAMPLE

Using the sample range to estimate σ

With reference to the example on page 260, use the range of the first sample to estimate σ for the heat-producing capacity of coal from the first mine.

Solution Since the smallest value is 8,070, the largest value is 8,350, and $n = 5$ so that $d_2 = 2.326$, we get

$$\frac{R}{d_2} = \frac{8,350 - 8,070}{2.326} = 120.4$$

Note that this is fairly close to the sample standard deviation $s = 125.5$.

In most practical applications, interval estimates of σ or σ^2 are based on the sample standard deviation or the sample variance. For random samples from normal populations, we make use of Theorem 6.4, according to which

$$\frac{(n-1)S^2}{\sigma^2}$$

is a random variable having the chi-square distribution with $n-1$ degrees of freedom. Thus, with χ^2_α defined as on page 215 for a chi-square distribution with $n-1$ degrees of freedom, we can assert with probability $1-\alpha$ that the inequality

$$\chi^2_{1-\alpha/2} < \frac{(n-1)S^2}{\sigma^2} < \chi^2_{\alpha/2}$$

will be satisfied. Once the data have been obtained, we make the same assertion with $(1-\alpha)100\%$ confidence. Solving this inequality for σ^2, we obtain the following result:

Confidence interval for σ^2

$$\frac{(n-1)s^2}{\chi^2_{\alpha/2}} < \sigma^2 < \frac{(n-1)s^2}{\chi^2_{1-\alpha/2}}$$

If we take the square root of each member of this inequality, we obtain a corresponding $(1-\alpha)100\%$ confidence interval for σ.

Note that confidence intervals for σ or σ^2 obtained by taking "equal tails," as in the above formula, do not actually give the narrowest confidence intervals, because the chi-square distribution is not symmetrical (see Exercise 7.16). Nevertheless, they are used in most applications in order to avoid fairly complicated calculations.

EXAMPLE

Finding a 95% confidence interval for σ

Returning to the example on page 215, suppose that the refractive indices of 20 pieces of glass (randomly selected from a large shipment purchased by the optical firm) have a variance of $1.20 \cdot 10^{-4}$. Construct a 95% confidence interval for σ, the standard deviation of the population sampled.

Solution   For $20-1=19$ degrees of freedom, $\chi^2_{0.975} = 8.907$ and $\chi^2_{0.025} = 32.852$ according to Table 5, so that substitution into the formula yields

$$\frac{(19)(1.20 \cdot 10^{-4})}{32.852} < \sigma^2 < \frac{(19)(1.20 \cdot 10^{-4})}{8.907}$$

$$0.000069 < \sigma^2 < 0.000256$$

and, hence,

$$0.0083 < \sigma < 0.0160$$

This means we are 95% confident that the interval from 0.0083 to 0.0160 contains σ, the true standard deviation of the refractive index.   ✓

The method which we have discussed applies only to random samples from normal populations (or at least to random samples from populations which can be approximated closely with normal distributions).

8.1 Use the data of Exercise 7.46 on page 253 to estimate σ for the length of time the experimental engine will operate with the given fuel in terms of

    (a) the sample standard deviation;

    (b) the sample range.

Compare the two estimates by expressing their difference as a percentage of the first.

8.2 With reference to the example on page 260, use the range of the second sample to estimate σ for the heat-producing capacity of coal from the second mine, and compare the result with the standard deviation of the second sample.

8.3 Use the data of part (a) of Exercise 7.70 to estimate σ for the Brinell hardness of Alloy 1 in terms of

    (a) the sample standard deviation;

    (b) the sample range.

Compare the two estimates by expressing their difference as a percentage of the first.

8.4 With reference to Exercise 7.47, construct a 99% confidence interval for the variance of the amount of time it takes the company to fill an order for a piece of the given kind of machinery.

8.5 With reference to Exercise 7.48, construct a 99% confidence interval for the variance of the population sampled.

8.6 Use the value s obtained in Exercise 8.3 to construct a 98% confidence interval for σ, measuring the actual variability in the hardness of Alloy 1.

8.2 Hypotheses Concerning One Variance

In this section we shall consider the problem of testing the null hypothesis that a population variance equals a specified constant against a suitable one-sided or two-sided alternative; that is, we shall test the null hypothesis $\sigma^2 = \sigma_0^2$ against one of the alternatives $\sigma^2 < \sigma_0^2$, $\sigma^2 > \sigma_0^2$, or $\sigma^2 \neq \sigma_0^2$. Tests like these are important whenever it is desired to control the uniformity of a product or an operation. For example, suppose that a silicon disc, or "wafer," is to be cut into small squares, or "dice," to be used in the manufacture of a semiconductor device. Since certain electrical characteristics of the finished device may depend on the thickness of the die, it is important that all dice cut from a wafer have approximately the same thickness. Thus, not only must the mean thickness of a wafer be kept within specifications, but also the variation in thickness from location to location on the wafer.

Using the same sampling theory as on page 276, we base such tests on the fact that for random samples from a normal population with the variance σ_0^2

Statistic for test concerning variance

$$\chi^2 = \frac{(n-1)S^2}{\sigma_0^2}$$

is a random variable having the chi-square distribution with $n - 1$ degrees of freedom. The critical regions for such tests are as shown in the following table:

Critical Regions for Testing $\sigma^2 = \sigma_0^2$
(Normal population)

Alternative hypothesis	Reject null hypothesis if:
$\sigma^2 < \sigma_0^2$	$\chi^2 < \chi_{1-\alpha}^2$
$\sigma^2 > \sigma_0^2$	$\chi^2 > \chi_\alpha^2$
$\sigma^2 \neq \sigma_0^2$	$\chi^2 < \chi_{1-\alpha/2}^2$ or $\chi^2 > \chi_{\alpha/2}^2$

In this table χ_α^2 is as defined on page 215. Note that "equal tails" are used for the two-sided alternative although this is actually not the best procedure since the chi-square distribution is not symmetrical.

EXAMPLE

Testing hypotheses concerning a standard deviation
The lapping process which is used to grind certain silicon wafers to the proper thickness is acceptable only if σ, the population standard deviation of the thickness of dice cut from the wafers, is at most 0.50 mil. Use the 0.05 level of significance to test the null hypothesis $\sigma = 0.50$ against the alternative hypothesis $\sigma > 0.50$, if the thicknesses of 15 dice cut from such wafers have a standard deviation of 0.64 mil.

Solution

1. *Null hypothesis:* $\sigma = 0.50$
   Alternative hypothesis: $\sigma > 0.50$
2. *Level of significance:* $\alpha = 0.05$
3. *Criterion:* Reject the null hypothesis if $\chi^2 > 23.685$, the value of $\chi_{0.05}^2$ for 14 degrees of freedom, where

$$\chi^2 = \frac{(n-1)S^2}{\sigma_0^2}$$

4. *Calculations:*

$$\chi^2 = \frac{(15-1)(0.64)^2}{(0.50)^2} = 22.94$$

5. *Decision:* Since $\chi^2 = 22.94$ does not exceed 23.685, the null hypothesis cannot be rejected; even though the sample standard deviation exceeds 0.50, there is not sufficient evidence to conclude that the lapping process is unsatisfactory. ✔

There exist tables similar to Table 8, which enable us to read the probabilities of Type II errors connected with this kind of test. As given in the *National Bureau* of *Standards Handbook 91* (see the bibliography), they contain the OC curves for the different one-sided and two-sided alternatives, for $\alpha = 0.05$ and $\alpha = 0.01$, and for various values of n.

8.3 Hypotheses Concerning Two Variances

The two-sample t test, described in Section 7.9, requires that the variances of the two populations sampled are equal. In this section we describe a test of the null hypothesis $\sigma_1^2 = \sigma_2^2$, which applies to independent random samples from two normal populations; it must be used with some discretion as it is very sensitive to departures from this assumption.

If independent random samples of size n_1 and n_2 are taken from normal populations having the same variance, it follows from Theorem 6.5 that

Statistic for test of equality of two variances

$$F = \frac{S_1^2}{S_2^2}$$

is a random variable having the F distribution with $n_1 - 1$ and $n_2 - 1$ degrees of freedom. Thus, if the null hypothesis $\sigma_1^2 = \sigma_2^2$ is true, the ratio of the sample variances S_1^2 and S_2^2 provides a statistic on which tests of the null hypothesis can be based.

The critical region for testing the null hypothesis $\sigma_1^2 = \sigma_2^2$ against the alternative hypothesis $\sigma_1^2 > \sigma_2^2$ is $F > F_\alpha$, where F_α is as defined on page 216. Similarly, the critical region for testing the null hypothesis against the alternative hypothesis $\sigma_1^2 < \sigma_2^2$ is $F < F_{1-\alpha}$, and this causes some difficulties since Table 6 only contains values corresponding to right-hand tails of $\alpha = 0.05$ and $\alpha = 0.01$. As a result, we use the reciprocal of the original test statistic and make use of the relation

$$F_{1-\alpha}(\nu_1, \nu_2) = \frac{1}{F_\alpha(\nu_2, \nu_1)}$$

first given on page 217. Thus, we base the test on the statistic $F = S_2^2/S_1^2$ and the critical region for testing the null hypothesis $\sigma_1^2 = \sigma_2^2$ against the alternative hypothesis $\sigma_1^2 < \sigma_2^2$ becomes $F > F_\alpha$, where F_α is the appropriate critical value of F for $n_2 - 1$ and $n_1 - 1$ degrees of freedom.

For the two-sided alternative $\sigma_1^2 \neq \sigma_2^2$ the critical region is $F < F_{1-\alpha/2}$ or $F > F_{\alpha/2}$, where $F = S_1^2/S_2^2$ and the degrees of freedom are $n_1 - 1$ and $n_2 - 1$. In practice, we modify this test as in the preceding paragraph, so that we can again use the table of F values corresponding to right-hand tails of $\alpha = 0.05$ and $\alpha = 0.01$. To this end we let S_M^2 represent the larger of the two sample variances, S_m^2 the smaller, and we write the corresponding sample sizes as n_M and n_m. Thus, the test statistic becomes $F = S_M^2/S_m^2$ and the critical region is as shown in the following table:

Critical Regions for Testing $\sigma_1^2 = \sigma_2^2$ (Normal populations)

Alternative hypothesis	Test statistic	Reject null hypothesis if:
$\sigma_1^2 < \sigma_2^2$	$F = \dfrac{S_2^2}{S_1^2}$	$F > F_\alpha(n_2 - 1, n_1 - 1)$
$\sigma_1^2 > \sigma_2^2$	$F = \dfrac{S_1^2}{S_2^2}$	$F > F_\alpha(n_1 - 1, n_2 - 1)$
$\sigma_1^2 \neq \sigma_2^2$	$F = \dfrac{S_M^2}{S_m^2}$	$F > F_{\alpha/2}(n_M - 1, n_m - 1)$

The level of significance of these tests is α and the figures indicated in parentheses are the respective degrees of freedom. Note that, as in the chi-square test, "equal tails" are used in the two-tailed test as a matter of mathematical convenience, even though the F distribution is not symmetrical.

EXAMPLE

A one-sided F test of the equality of two variances

It is desired to determine whether there is less variability in the silver plating done by Company 1 than in that done by Company 2. If independent random samples of size 12 of the two companies' work yield $s_1 = 0.035$ mil and $s_2 = 0.062$ mil, test the null hypothesis $\sigma_1^2 = \sigma_2^2$ against the alternative hypothesis $\sigma_1^2 < \sigma_2^2$ at the 0.05 level of significance.

Solution

1. *Null hypothesis: $\sigma_1^2 = \sigma_2^2$*
   Alternative hypothesis: $\sigma_1^2 < \sigma_2^2$

2. *Level of significance: $\alpha = 0.05$*

3. *Criterion:* Reject the null hypothesis if $F > 2.82$, the value of $F_{0.05}$ for 11 and 11 degrees of freedom, where

$$F = \frac{S_2^2}{S_1^2}$$

4. *Calculations:*

$$F = \frac{(0.062)^2}{(0.035)^2} = 3.14$$

5. *Decision:* Since $F = 3.14$ exceeds 2.82, the null hypothesis must be rejected; in other words, the data support the contention that the plating done by Company 1 is less variable than that done by Company 2. ✔

EXAMPLE

A two-sided test for the equality of two variances

With reference to the example dealing with the heat-producing capacity of coal from two mines on page 260, use the 0.02 level of significance to test whether it is reasonable to assume that the variances of the two populations sampled are equal.

Solution
1. *Null hypothesis:* $\sigma_1^2 = \sigma_2^2$
   Alternative hypothesis: $\sigma_1^2 \neq \sigma_2^2$
2. *Level of significance:* $\alpha = 0.02$
3. *Criterion:* Reject the null hypothesis if $F > 11.4$, the value of $F_{0.01}$ for 4 and 5 degrees of freedom, where

$$F = \frac{S_1^2}{S_2^2}$$

since $s_1^2 = 15{,}750$ is greater than $s_2^2 = 10{,}920$.
4. *Calculations:*

$$F = \frac{15{,}750}{10{,}920} = 1.44$$

5. *Decision:* Since $F = 1.44$ does not exceed 11.4, the null hypothesis cannot be rejected; there is no real reason to doubt the equality of the variances of the two populations. ✔

Had we wanted to use the level of significance $\alpha = 0.05$ or $\alpha = 0.01$ in this example, we would have required tables of the values of $F_{0.025}(v_1, v_2)$ or $F_{0.005}(v_1, v_2)$; such tables may be found in the *Biometrika Tables for Statisticians* listed in the bibliography under Pearson and Hartley. Also, OC curves for the one-tailed F tests may be found in the *National Bureau of Standards Handbook 91*.

Caution: In marked contrast to the procedures for making inferences about μ, the validity of the procedures in this chapter depend rather strongly on the assumption that the underlying population is normal. The sampling variance of S^2 can change when the population departs from normality by having, for instance, a single long tail. It can be shown that, when the underlying population is normal, the sampling variance of S^2 is $2\sigma^4/(n-1)$. However, for nonnormal distributions, the sampling variance of S^2 depends not only on σ^2 but also on the population third and fourth moments, μ_3 and μ_4 (see page 118). Consequently, it could be much larger than $2\sigma^4/(n-1)$. This behavior completely invalidates any tests of hypothesis or confidence intervals for σ^2. We say that these procedures for making inferences about σ^2 are not **robust** with respect to deviations from normality.

EXERCISES

8.7 With reference to Exercise 7.44 on page 253, test the null hypothesis $\sigma = 600$ psi for the compressive strength of the given kind of steel against the alternative hypothesis $\sigma > 600$ psi. Use the 0.05 level of significance.

8.8 If 12 determinations of the specific heat of iron have a standard deviation of 0.0086, test the null hypothesis that $\sigma = 0.010$ for such determinations. Use the alternative hypothesis $\sigma \neq 0.010$ and the level of significance $\alpha = 0.01$.

8.9 With reference to Exercise 7.64, test the null hypothesis that $\sigma = 15.0$ minutes for the time that is required for repairs of the first kind of photocopying equipment against the alternative hypothesis that $\sigma > 15.0$ minutes. Use the 0.05 level of significance and assume normality.

8.10   Use the 0.01 level of significance to test the null hypothesis that $\sigma = 0.015$ inch for the diameters of certain bolts against the alternative hypothesis that $\sigma \neq 0.015$ inch, given that a random sample of size 15 yielded $s^2 = 0.00011$.

8.11   Playing 10 rounds of golf on his home course, a golf professional averaged 71.3 with a standard deviation of 1.32. Test the null hypothesis that the consistency of his game on his home course is actually measured by $\sigma = 1.20$, against the alternative hypothesis that he is less consistent. Use the level of significance $\alpha = 0.05$.

8.12   The security department of a large office building wants to test the null hypothesis that $\sigma = 2.0$ minutes for the time it takes a guard to walk his round against the alternative hypothesis that $\sigma \neq 2.0$ minutes. What can it conclude at the 0.01 level of significance if a random sample of size $n = 31$ yields $s = 1.8$ minutes?

8.13   Justify the use of the two-sample t test in Exercise 7.67 on page 266 by testing the null hypothesis that the two populations have equal variances. Use the 0.02 level of significance.

8.14   With reference to Exercise 7.68 on page 266, use the 0.02 level of significance to test the assumption that the two populations have equal variances.

8.15   Two different lighting techniques are compared by measuring the intensity of light at selected locations in areas lighted by the two methods. If 15 measurements in the first area had a standard deviation of 2.7 foot-candles and 21 measurements in the second area had a standard deviation of 4.2 foot-candles, can it be concluded that the lighting in the second area is less uniform? Use a 0.01 level of significance. What assumptions must be made as to how the two samples are obtained?

8.16   With reference to Exercise 7.66, where we had $n_1 = 40$, $n_2 = 30$, $s_1 = 15.2$, and $s_2 = 18.7$, use the 0.05 level of significance to test the claim that there is a greater variability in the number of cars which make left turns approaching from the south between 4 P.M. and 6 P.M. at the second intersection. Assume the distributions are normal.

8.17   Random samples of size $n_1 = 10$ and $n_2 = 15$, respectively, are taken from two lognormal populations, and the resulting sample means are $\bar{x}_1 = 3.74$ and $\bar{x}_2 = 13.91$ and the sample variances are 1.2 and 6.5. You wish to test whether the second population has a standard deviation greater than the first.

(a)   Can you directly use an F test? Why or why not?

(b)   Is there a transformation that can be made on the data that could conceivably allow the use of the F test? Modify the hypotheses to ones that can be tested with the transformed data.

REVIEW   EXERCISES

8.18   With reference to the example on page 246, construct a 95% confidence interval for the true standard deviation of the breaking strength of the given kind of ribbon.

8.19   With reference to the example on page 262, find separate 95% confidence intervals for the standard deviations of the two aluminum alloys.

8.20   While performing a strenuous task, the pulse rate of 25 workers increased on the average by 18.4 beats per minute with a standard deviation of 4.9 beats per minute. Find a 95% confidence interval for the corresponding population standard deviation. What assumption did you make about the population?

8.21 With reference to Exercise 8.20, use the 0.05 level of significance to test the null hypothesis that $\sigma^2 = 30.0$ for such increases in the pulse rate (while performing the given task) against the alternative hypothesis that $\sigma^2 < 30.0$.

8.22 If 31 measurements of the boiling point of sulfur have a standard deviation of 0.83 degree Celsius, construct a 98% confidence interval for the true standard deviation of such measurements. What assumption did you make about the population?

8.23 Past data indicate that the variance of measurements made on sheet metal stampings by experienced quality control inspectors is 0.18 square inch. Such measurements made by an inexperienced inspector could have too large a variance (perhaps because of inability to read instruments properly) or too small a variance (perhaps because unusually high or low measurements are discarded). If a new inspector measures 101 stampings with a variance of 0.13 square inch, test at the 0.05 level of significance whether the inspector is making satisfactory measurements. Assume normality.

8.24 With reference to Exercise 7.69 on page 266, use the 0.02 level of significance to test the assumption that the two populations have equal variances.

8.25 Pull-strength tests on 10 soldered leads for a semiconductor device yield the following results in pounds force required to rupture the bond:

| 15.8 | 12.7 | 13.2 | 16.9 | 10.6 | 18.8 | 11.1 | 14.3 | 17.0 | 12.5 |

Another set of 8 leads was tested after encapsulation to determine whether the pull strength has been increased by encapsulation of the device, with the following results:

| 24.9 | 23.6 | 19.8 | 22.1 | 20.4 | 21.6 | 21.8 | 22.5 |

As a preliminary to the two-sample t test, use the 0.02 level of significance to test whether it is reasonable to assume that the two samples come from populations with equal variances.

8.26 With reference to the example on page 262, test the equality of the variances for the two aluminum alloys. Use the 0.02 level of significance.

KEY TERMS

(with page references)

Robust   281
Sample range   275

Inferences Concerning Proportions

Many engineering problems deal with proportions, percentages, or probabilities. In acceptance sampling we are concerned with the proportion of defectives in a lot, and in life testing we are concerned with the percentage of certain components which will perform satisfactorily during a stated period of time, or the probability that a given component will last at least a given number of hours. It should be clear from these examples that problems concerning proportions, percentages, or probabilities are really equivalent; a percentage is merely a proportion multiplied by 100, and a probability may be interpreted as a proportion in a long series of trials.

Sections 9.1 deals with the estimation of proportions; Section 9.2 deals with tests concerning proportions; Section 9.3 deals with tests concerning two or more proportions; in Section 9.4 we shall learn how to analyze data tallied into a two-way classification; and in Section 9.5 we shall learn how to judge whether differences between an observed frequency distribution and corresponding expectations can be attributed to chance. ■

9.1 Estimation of Proportions

The information that is usually available for the estimation of a proportion is the number of times, X, that an appropriate event occurs in n trials, occasions, or observations. The point estimator, itself, is usually the **sample proportion** $\dfrac{X}{n}$, namely, the proportion of the time that the event actually occurs. If the n trials satisfy the assumptions underlying the binomial distribution listed on page 103, we know that the mean and the standard deviation of the number of successes are given by np and $\sqrt{np(1-p)}$. If we divide both of these quantities by n, we find that the mean and the standard deviation of the proportion of successes (namely, of the sample proportion) are given by

$$\frac{np}{n} = p \quad \text{and} \quad \frac{\sqrt{np(1-p)}}{n} = \sqrt{\frac{p(1-p)}{n}}$$

The first of these results shows that the sample proportion is an unbiased estimator of the binomial parameter p, namely, of the true proportion we are trying to estimate on the basis of a sample.

In the construction of confidence intervals for the binomial parameter p, we meet several obstacles. First, since x and $\frac{x}{n}$ are values of discrete random variables, it may be impossible to get an interval for which the degree of confidence is exactly $(1-\alpha)100\%$. Second, the standard deviation of the sampling distribution of the number of successes, as well as that of the proportion of successes, involves the parameter p that we are trying to estimate.

To construct a confidence interval for p having approximately the degree of confidence $(1-\alpha)100\%$, we first determine for a given set of values of p the corresponding quantities x_0 and x_1, where x_0 is the largest integer for which the binomial probabilities $b(k; n, p) = P[X = k]$ satisfy

$$\sum_{k=0}^{x_0} b(k; n, p) \le \frac{\alpha}{2}$$

while x_1 is the smallest integer for which

$$\sum_{k=x_1}^{n} b(k; n, p) \le \frac{\alpha}{2}$$

To emphasize the point that x_0 and x_1 depend on the value of p, we shall write these quantities as $x_0(p)$ and $x_1(p)$. Thus, we can assert with a probability of approximately $1-\alpha$, and at least $1-\alpha$, that the inequality

$$x_0(p) < x < x_1(p)$$

will be satisfied; here x is a value of a random variable and p is a fixed constant. To change inequalities like these into confidence intervals for p, we can use a simple graphical method which is illustrated by the following example: Suppose, for instance, that we want to find approximate 95% confidence intervals for p for samples of size $n = 20$. Using Table 1 at the end of the book, we first determine x_0 and x_1 for selected values of p such that x_0 is the largest integer for which

$$B(x_0; 20, p) \le 0.025$$

while x_1 is the smallest integer for which

$$1 - B(x_1 - 1; 20, p) \le 0.025$$

Letting p equal $0.1, 0.2, \ldots$, and 0.9, we thus obtain the values shown in the following table:

p	0.1	0.2	0.3	0.4	0.5	0.6	0.7	0.8	0.9
x_0	—	0	1	3	5	7	9	11	14
x_1	6	9	11	13	15	17	19	20	—

Plotting the points with coordinates p and $x(p)$ as in Figure 9.1, and drawing smooth curves, one through the x_0 points and one through the x_1 points, we can now "solve" for p. For any given value of x we can obtain approximate 95% confidence limits for p by going horizontally to the two curves and marking off the corresponding values of p (see Figure 9.1). Thus, for $x = 4$ we obtain the approximate 95% confidence interval

$$0.06 < p < 0.45$$

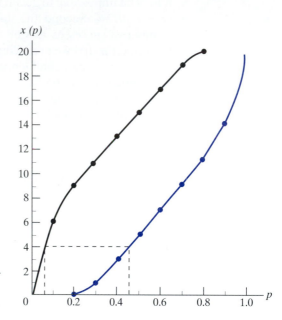

Figure 9.1 95% confidence intervals for proportions ($n = 20$).

Graphs similar to the one shown in Figure 9.1 are given in Tables 9(a) and 9(b) at the end of the book for various values of n and for the 95% and 99% degrees of confidence. These tables differ from the one of Figure 9.1 in that the sample proportion $\frac{x}{n}$ is used instead of x, thus making it possible to graph curves corresponding to various values of n on the same diagram. Also, for increased accuracy, Tables 9(a) and 9(b) are arranged so that values of $\frac{x}{n}$ from 0.00 to 0.50 are marked on the bottom scale while those from 0.50 to 1.00 are marked on the top scale of the diagram. For values of $\frac{x}{n}$ from 0.00 to 0.50 the confidence limits for p are read off the left-hand scale of the diagram, while for values of $\frac{x}{n}$ from 0.50 to 1.00 they are read off the right-hand scale. Note that for $n = 20$ and $x = 4$,

Table 9(a) yields the 95% confidence interval $0.06 < p < 0.44$, which is very close, indeed, to the results obtained with Figure 9.1.

On page 158 we gave the general rule of thumb that the normal distribution provides a good approximation to the binomial distribution when np and $n(1 - p)$ are both greater than 15. Thus, for $n = 50$ the normal curve approximation may be used if it can be assumed that p lies between 0.30 and 0.70; for $n = 100$ it may be used if it can be assumed that p lies between 0.15 and 0.85; for $n = 200$ it may be used if it can be assumed that p lies between 0.075 and 0.925; and so forth. This is what we shall mean here, and later in this chapter, by "n being large."

When n is large, we can construct approximate confidence intervals for the binomial parameter p by using the normal approximation to the binomial distribution. Accordingly, we can assert with probability $1 - \alpha$ that the inequality

$$-z_{\alpha/2} < \frac{X - np}{\sqrt{np(1 - p)}} < z_{\alpha/2}$$

will be satisfied. Solving this quadratic inequality for p, we can obtain a corresponding set of approximate confidence limits for p in terms of the observed value x (see Exercise 9.14 on page 290), but since the necessary calculations are complex, we shall make the further approximation of substituting $\dfrac{x}{n}$ for p in $\sqrt{np(1 - p)}$. This yields

Large sample confidence interval for p

$$\frac{x}{n} - z_{\alpha/2}\sqrt{\frac{\dfrac{x}{n}\left(1 - \dfrac{x}{n}\right)}{n}} < p < \frac{x}{n} + z_{\alpha/2}\sqrt{\frac{\dfrac{x}{n}\left(1 - \dfrac{x}{n}\right)}{n}}$$

where the degree of confidence is $(1 - \alpha)100\%$.

EXAMPLE

A large sample 95% confidence interval for p
If $x = 36$ of $n = 100$ persons interviewed are familiar with the tax incentives for installing certain energy-saving devices, construct a 95% confidence interval for the corresponding true proportion.

Solution   Substituting $\dfrac{x}{n} = \dfrac{36}{100} = 0.36$ and $z_{\alpha/2} = 1.96$ into the above formula, we get

$$0.36 - 1.96\sqrt{\frac{(0.36)(0.64)}{100}} < p < 0.36 + 1.96\sqrt{\frac{(0.36)(0.64)}{100}}$$

or

$$0.266 < p < 0.454$$

We are 95% confident that the population proportion of persons familiar with the tax incentives, p, is contained in the interval from 0.266 to 0.454. Note that if we had used Table 9(a), we would have obtained

$$0.27 < p < 0.46$$

✔

The magnitude of the error we make when we use $\dfrac{X}{n}$ as an estimator of p is given by $\left|\dfrac{X}{n} - p\right|$. Again using the normal approximation, we can thus assert with probability $1 - \alpha$ that the inequality

$$\left|\frac{X}{n} - p\right| \leq z_{\alpha/2}\sqrt{\frac{p(1 - p)}{n}}$$

will be satisfied, namely, that the error will be at most $z_{\alpha/2}\sqrt{\dfrac{p(1 - p)}{n}}$.

Maximum error of estimate

$$E = z_{\alpha/2}\sqrt{\frac{p(1 - p)}{n}}$$

With the observed value $\dfrac{x}{n}$ substituted for p we obtain an estimate of E.

EXAMPLE

An estimate of the maximum error
In a sample survey conducted in a large city, 136 of 400 persons answered yes to the question whether their city's public transportation is adequate. With 99% confidence, what can we say about the maximum error, if $\dfrac{x}{n} = \dfrac{136}{400} = 0.34$ is used as an estimate of the corresponding true proportion?

Solution   Substituting $\dfrac{x}{n} = 0.34$ and $z_{\alpha/2} = 2.575$ into the above formula, we find that the error is at most

$$E = 2.575\sqrt{\frac{(0.34)(0.66)}{400}} = 0.061 \qquad ✔$$

The preceding formula for E can also be used to determine the sample size that is needed to attain a desired degree of precision. Solving for n, we get

Sample size determination

$$n = p(1 - p)\left[\frac{z_{\alpha/2}}{E}\right]^2$$

but this formula cannot be used as it stands unless we have some information about the possible size of p (on the basis of collateral data, say, a pilot sample). If no such information is available, we can make use of the fact that $p(1 - p)$ is at most $\frac{1}{4}$, corresponding to $p = \frac{1}{2}$, as can be shown by the methods of elementary calculus. Thus, if

Sample size— p unknown

$$n = \frac{1}{4}\left[\frac{z_{\alpha/2}}{E}\right]^2$$

we can assert with a probability of at least $1 - \alpha$ that the error in using $\dfrac{X}{n}$ as an estimate of p will not exceed E; once the data have been obtained, we will be able to assert with at least $(1 - \alpha)100\%$ confidence that the error does not exceed E.

EXAMPLE

Selecting a sample size for estimating a proportion

Suppose that we want to estimate the true proportion of defectives in a very large shipment of adobe bricks, and that we want to be at least 95% confident that the error is at most 0.04. How large a sample will we need if

(a) we have no idea what the true proportion might be;

(b) we know that the true proportion does not exceed 0.12?

Solution

(a) Using the second of the two formulas for the sample size, we get

$$n = \frac{1}{4}\left[\frac{1.96}{0.04}\right]^2 = 600.25$$

or $n = 601$ rounded up to the nearest integer.

(b) Using the first of the two formulas for the sample size with $p = 0.12$ (the possible value closest to $p = \frac{1}{2}$), we get

$$n = (0.12)(0.88)\left[\frac{1.96}{0.04}\right]^2 = 253.55$$

or $n = 254$ rounded up to the nearest integer. This serves to illustrate how some collateral information about the possible size of p can substantially reduce the size of the required sample. ✔

EXERCISES

9.1 In a random sample of 200 claims filed against an insurance company writing collision insurance on cars, 84 exceeded $1,200. Construct a 95% confidence interval for the true proportion of claims filed against this insurance company that exceed $1,200, using

(a) Table 9;

(b) the large sample confidence interval formula.

9.2 With reference to Exercise 9.1, what can we say with 99% confidence about the maximum error, if we use the sample proportion as an estimate of the true proportion of claims filed against this insurance company that exceed $1,200?

9.3 In a random sample of 400 industrial accidents, it was found that 231 were due at least partially to unsafe working conditions. Construct a 99% confidence interval for the corresponding true proportion using

(a) Table 9;

(b) the large sample confidence interval formula.

9.4 With reference to Exercise 9.3, what can we say with 95% confidence about the maximum error if we use the sample proportion to estimate the corresponding true proportion?

9.5 In a sample survey of the "safety explosives" used in certain mining operations, explosives containing potassium nitrate were found to be used in 95 of 250 cases.

    (a) Use Table 9 to construct a 95% confidence interval for the corresponding true proportion.

    (b) If $\frac{95}{250} = 0.38$ is used as an estimate of the corresponding true proportion, what can we say with 95% confidence about the maximum error?

9.6 In a random sample of 60 sections of pipe in a chemical plant, 8 showed signs of serious corrosion. Construct a 95% confidence interval for the true proportion of pipe sections showing signs of serious corrosion, using

    (a) Table 9;

    (b) the large sample confidence interval formula.

9.7 In a recent study, 69 of 120 meteorites were observed to enter the earth's atmosphere with a velocity of less than 26 miles per second. If we estimate the corresponding true proportion as $\frac{69}{120} = 0.575$, what can we say with 95% confidence about the maximum error?

9.8 Among 100 fish caught in a large lake, 18 were inedible due to the pollution of the environment. If we use $\frac{18}{100} = 0.18$ as an estimate of the corresponding true proportion, with what confidence can we assert that the error of this estimate is at most 0.065?

9.9 A random sample of 300 shoppers at a supermarket includes 204 who regularly use cents-off coupons. Construct a 98% confidence interval for the probability that any one shopper at the supermarket, selected at random, will regularly use cents-off coupons.

9.10 What is the size of the smallest sample required to estimate an unknown proportion to within a maximum error of 0.06 with at least 95% confidence?

9.11 With reference to Exercise 9.10, how would the required sample size be affected if it is known that the proportion to be estimated is at least 0.75?

9.12 Suppose that we want to estimate what percentage of all drivers exceed the 55-mile-per-hour speed limit on a certain stretch of road. How large a sample will we need to be at least 99% confident that the error of our estimate, the sample percentage, is at most 3.5%?

9.13 With reference to Exercise 9.12, how would the required sample size be affected if it is known that the percentage to be estimated is at most 40%?

9.14 Show that the inequality on page 287 leads to the following $(1 - \alpha)100\%$ confidence limits:

$$\frac{x + \frac{1}{2}z_{\alpha/2}^2 \pm z_{\alpha/2}\sqrt{\frac{x(n - x)}{n} + \frac{1}{4}z_{\alpha/2}^2}}{n + z_{\alpha/2}^2}$$

9.15 Use the formula of Exercise 9.14 to rework Exercise 9.3.

9.16 Use the formula of Exercise 9.14 to rework Exercise 9.6.

9.17 A major automobile company was having trouble with the quality of paint on their grey cars. The first step was to collect data on the magnitude of the problem. Of 4063 recently painted grey automobiles, 533 had paint problems that could easily be detected by visual inspection. Obtain a 95% confidence interval for the population proportion of defective grey paint jobs.

9.18 An international corporation needed several millions of words, from thousands of documents and manuals, translated. The work was contracted to a company that used computer-assisted translation along with some human checks. The corporation conducted its own quality check by sampling the translation. Among the 2,037 mistakes they found, 834 were an incorrect word. Obtain a 99% confidence interval for the population proportion of mistakes that are incorrect words.

9.2 Hypotheses Concerning One Proportion

Many of the methods used in sampling inspection, quality control, and reliability verification are based on tests of the null hypothesis that a proportion (percentage, or probability) equals some specified constant. The details of the application of such tests to quality control will be discussed in Chapter 14, where we shall also go into some problems of sampling inspection; applications to reliability and life testing will be taken up in Chapter 15.

Although there are exact tests based on the binomial distribution that can be performed with the use of Table 1, we shall consider here only approximate large sample tests based on the normal approximation to the binomial distribution. In other words, we shall test the null hypothesis $p = p_0$ against one of the alternatives $p < p_0$, $p > p_0$, or $p \neq p_0$ with the use of the statistic

Statistic for large sample test concerning p

$$Z = \frac{X - np_0}{\sqrt{np_0(1 - p_0)}}$$

which is a random variable having approximately the standard normal distribution.[†] The critical regions are like those shown in the table on page 242 with p and p_0 substituted for μ and μ_0.

Critical Regions for Testing $p = p_0$
(large sample)

Alternative hypothesis	Reject null hypothesis if:
$p < p_0$	$Z < -z_\alpha$
$p > p_0$	$Z > z_\alpha$
$p \neq p_0$	$Z < -z_{\alpha/2}$ or $Z > z_{\alpha/2}$

EXAMPLE

A one-sided test concerning a population proportion
In a study designed to investigate whether certain detonators used with explosives in coal mining meet the requirement that at least 90% will ignite the explosive when charged, it is found that 174 of 200 detonators function properly. Test the

[†]Some authors write the numerator of this formula for Z as $X \pm \frac{1}{2} - np_0$, whichever is numerically smaller, but there is generally no need for this continuity correction so long as n is large.

null hypothesis $p = 0.90$ against the alternative hypothesis $p < 0.90$ at the 0.05 level of significance.

Solution

1. *Null hypothesis:* $p = 0.90$
   Alternative hypothesis: $p < 0.90$
2. *Level of significance:* $\alpha = 0.05$
3. *Criterion:* Reject the null hypothesis if $Z < -1.645$, where

$$Z = \frac{X - np_0}{\sqrt{np_0(1 - p_0)}}$$

4. *Calculations:* Substituting $x = 174$, $n = 200$, and $p_0 = 0.90$ into the formula above, we get

$$z = \frac{174 - 200(0.90)}{\sqrt{200(0.90)(0.10)}} = -1.41$$

5. *Decision:* Since $z = -1.41$ is not less than -1.645, the null hypothesis cannot be rejected; in other words, there is not sufficient evidence to say that the given kind of detonator fails to meet the required standard. ✔

9.3 Hypotheses Concerning Several Proportions

When we compare the consumer response (percentage favorable and percentage unfavorable) to two different products, when we decide whether the proportion of defectives of a given process remains constant from day to day, when we judge whether there is a difference in political persuasion among several nationality groups, and in many similar situations, we are interested in testing whether two or more binomial populations have the same parameter p. Referring to these parameters as $p_1, p_2, \ldots,$ and p_k, we are, in fact, interested in testing the null hypothesis

$$p_1 = p_2 = \cdots = p_k = p$$

against the alternative hypothesis that these population proportions are not all equal. To perform a suitable large sample test of this hypothesis, we require independent random samples of size $n_1, n_2, \ldots,$ and n_k from the k populations; then, if the corresponding numbers of "successes" are $X_1, X_2, \ldots,$ and X_k, the test we shall use is based on the fact that (1) for large samples the sampling distribution of

$$Z_i = \frac{X_i - n_i p_i}{\sqrt{n_i p_i(1 - p_i)}}$$

is approximately the standard normal distribution, (2) the square of a random variable having the standard normal distribution is a random variable having the chi-square distribution with 1 degree of freedom, and (3) the sum of k independent random variables having chi-square distributions with 1 degree of freedom is a random variable having the chi-square distribution with k degrees of freedom. (Proofs of these last two results may be found in the book by John E. Freund mentioned in the bibliography.) Thus,

$$\chi^2 = \sum_{i=1}^{k} \frac{(x_i - n_i p_i)^2}{n_i p_i (1 - p_i)}$$

is a value of a random variable having approximately the chi-square distribution with k degrees of freedom. In practice we substitute for the p_i, which under the null hypothesis are all equal, the pooled estimate

$$\hat{p} = \frac{x_1 + x_2 + \cdots + x_k}{n_1 + n_2 + \cdots + n_k}$$

Since the null hypothesis should be rejected if the differences between the x_i and the $n_i \hat{p}$ are large, the critical region is $\chi^2 > \chi_\alpha^2$, where χ_α^2 is as defined on page 215 and the number of degrees of freedom is $k - 1$. The loss of one degree of freedom results from substituting for p the estimate $\hat{p}$.

In actual practice, when we compare two or more sample proportions it is convenient to determine the value of the χ^2 statistic by looking at the data as arranged in the following way:

	Sample 1	*Sample 2*	$\cdots$	*Sample k*	*Total*
Successes	x_1	x_2	$\cdots$	x_k	x
Failures	$n_1 - x_1$	$n_2 - x_2$	$\cdots$	$n_k - x_k$	$n - x$
Total	n_1	n_2	$\cdots$	n_k	n

The notation is the same as before, except for x and n, which represent, respectively, the total number of successes and the total number of trials for all samples combined. With reference to this table, the entry in the cell belonging to the ith row and jth column is called the **observed cell frequency** o_{ij} with $i = 1, 2$ and $j = 1, 2, \ldots, k$.

Under the null hypothesis $p_1 = p_2 = \cdots = p_k = p$, we estimate p, as before, as the total number of successes divided by the total number of trials, which we now write as $\hat{p} = \frac{x}{n}$. Hence, the expected number of successes and failures for the jth sample are estimated by

$$e_{1j} = n_j \cdot \hat{p} = \frac{n_j \cdot x}{n}$$

and

$$e_{2j} = n_j (1 - \hat{p}) = \frac{n_j \cdot (n - x)}{n}$$

The quantities e_{1j} and e_{2j} are called the **expected cell frequencies** for $j = 1, 2, \ldots, k$. Note that **the expected frequency for any given cell may be obtained by multiplying** the totals of the column and the row to which it belongs and then dividing by the grand total n.

In this notation, the x^2 statistic on page 293, with $\hat{p}$ substituted for the p_i, can be written in the form

Statistic for test
concerning difference
among proportions

$$x^2 = \sum_{i=1}^{2} \sum_{j=1}^{k} \frac{(o_{ij} - e_{ij})^2}{e_{ij}}$$

as the reader will be asked to verify in Exercise 9.36 on page 300. This formula has the advantage that it can easily be extended to the more general case, to be treated in Section 9.4, where each trial permits more than two possible outcomes, and there are, thus, more than two rows in the tabular presentation of the various frequencies.

EXAMPLE

Testing the equality of three proportions using the x^2 statistic
Samples of three kinds of materials, subjected to extreme temperature changes, produced the results shown in the following table:

	Material A	Material B	Material C	Total
Crumbled	41	27	22	90
Remained intact	79	53	78	210
Total	120	80	100	300

Use the 0.05 level of significance to test whether, under the stated conditions, the probability of crumbling is the same for the three kinds of materials.

Solution

1. *Null hypothesis:* $p_1 = p_2 = p_3$
   Alternative hypothesis: $p_1, p_2,$ and p_3 are not all equal.
2. *Level of significance:* $\alpha = 0.05$
3. *Criterion:* Reject the null hypothesis if $x^2 > 5.991$, the value of $x^2_{0.05}$ for $3 - 1 = 2$ degrees of freedom, where x^2 is given by the formula above.
4. *Calculations:* The expected frequencies for the first two cells of the first row are

$$e_{11} = \frac{90 \cdot 120}{300} = 36 \quad \text{and} \quad e_{12} = \frac{90 \cdot 80}{300} = 24$$

and, as it can be shown that **the sum of the expected frequencies for any row or column equals that of the corresponding observed frequencies** (see Exercise 9.37 on page 300), we find by subtraction that $e_{13} = 90 - (36 + 24) = 30$, and that the expected frequencies for the second row are $e_{21} = 120 - 36 = 84$,

$e_{22} = 80 - 24 = 56$, and $e_{23} = 100 - 30 = 70$. Then, substituting these values together with the observed frequencies into the formula for x^2, we get

$$x^2 = \frac{(41 - 36)^2}{36} + \frac{(27 - 24)^2}{24} + \frac{(22 - 30)^2}{30}$$
$$+ \frac{(79 - 84)^2}{84} + \frac{(53 - 56)^2}{56} + \frac{(78 - 70)^2}{70}$$
$$= 4.575$$

5. *Decision:* Since $x^2 = 4.575$ does not exceed 5.991, the null hypothesis cannot be rejected; in other words, the data do not refute the hypothesis that, under the stated conditions, the probability of crumbling is the same for the three kinds of material. ✔

   Most of the entries of Table 5 are given to three decimal places, but, since rounding errors tend to average out, there is seldom any need to give more than two decimal places in the final value of the x^2 statistic. The test we have been discussing here is only an approximate test since the sampling distribution of the x^2 statistic is only approximately the chi-square distribution, and it should not be used when one or more of the expected frequencies is less than 5. If this is the case, we can sometimes combine two or more of the samples in such a way that none of the e's is less than 5.

   If the null hypothesis of equal proportions is rejected, it is a good practice to graph the confidence intervals (see page 287) for the individual proportions p_i. The graph helps illuminate differences between the proportions.

Graphical display of confidence intervals
Four methods are under development for making discs of a superconducting material. Fifty discs are made by each method and they are checked for superconductivity when cooled with liquid nitrogen.

	Method 1	Method 2	Method 3	Method 4	Total
Superconductors	31	42	22	25	120
Failures	19	8	28	25	80
Total	50	50	50	50	200

Perform a chi-square test with $\alpha = 0.05$. If there is a significant difference between the proportions of superconductors produced, plot the individual confidence intervals.

Solution

1. *Null hypothesis:* $p_1 = p_2 = p_3 = p_4$
   Alternative hypothesis: $p_1, p_2, p_3,$ and p_4 are not all equal.
2. *Level of significance:* $\alpha = 0.05$
3. *Criterion:* Reject the null hypothesis if $x^2 > 7.815$, the value of $x^2_{0.05}$ for $4 - 1 = 3$ degrees of freedom.

4. *Calculations:* Each cell in the first row has expected frequency $120 \cdot \dfrac{50}{200} = 30$, and each cell in the second row has expected frequency $80 \cdot \dfrac{50}{200} = 20$.

The chi-square statistic is

$$\chi^2 = \frac{1}{30} + \frac{144}{30} + \frac{64}{30} + \frac{25}{30}$$
$$+ \frac{1}{20} + \frac{144}{20} + \frac{64}{20} + \frac{25}{20}$$
$$= 19.50$$

5. *Decision:* Since 19.50 greatly exceeds 7.815, we reject the null hypothesis of equal proportions at the 5% level of significance.

The confidence intervals obtained from the large sample formula on page 287 are

$$0.62 \pm 0.13, \, 0.84 \pm 0.14, \, 0.44 \pm 0.14, \, 0.50 \pm 0.14$$

These are plotted in Figure 9.2. Note how Method 2 stands out as being better. ✔

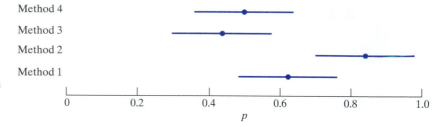

Figure 9.2 Confidence intervals for several proportions.

Although there has been no mention of randomization in the development of the χ^2 statistic, wherever possible the experimental units should be randomly assigned to methods. In the example above, the discs could be numbered from 1 to 200 and random numbers selected from 1 to 200 without replacement. The discs corresponding to the first fifty numbers drawn would be assigned to method 1 and so on. This will prevent uncontrolled sources of variation from systematically influencing the test concerning the four methods.

So far, the alternative hypothesis has been that $p_1, p_2, \ldots,$ and p_k are not all equal, and for $k = 2$ this reduces to the alternative hypothesis $p_1 \neq p_2$. In problems where the alternative hypothesis may also be $p_1 < p_2$ or $p_1 > p_2$, we can base the test on the statistic

Statistic for test concerning difference between two proportions

$$Z = \frac{\dfrac{X_1}{n_1} - \dfrac{X_2}{n_2}}{\sqrt{\hat{p}(1 - \hat{p})\left(\dfrac{1}{n_1} + \dfrac{1}{n_2}\right)}} \quad \text{with} \quad \hat{p} = \frac{X_1 + X_2}{n_1 + n_2}$$

which, for large samples, is a random variable having approximately the standard normal distribution. The test based on this statistic is equivalent to the one based on the χ^2 statistic on page 294 with $k = 2$, in the sense that the square of this Z statistic actually equals the χ^2 statistic (see Exercise 9.38 on page 301). The critical regions for this alternative test of the null hypothesis $p_1 = p_2$ are like those shown in the table on page 257 with p_1 and p_2 substituted for μ and μ_0.

EXAMPLE

A large sample test concerning two proportions
A study shows that 16 of 200 tractors produced on one assembly line required extensive adjustments before they could be shipped, while the same was true for 14 of 400 tractors produced on another assembly line. At the 0.01 level of significance, does this support the claim that the second production line does superior work?

Solution

1. *Null hypothesis:* $p_1 = p_2$
   Alternative hypothesis: $p_1 > p_2$
2. *Level of significance:* $\alpha = 0.01$
3. *Criterion:* Reject the null hypothesis if $Z > 2.33$, where Z is given by the formula on page 296.
4. *Calculations:* Substituting $x_1 = 16, n_1 = 200, x_2 = 14, n_2 = 400$, and

$$\hat{p} = \frac{16 + 14}{200 + 400} = 0.05$$

into the formula for Z, we get

$$Z = \frac{\dfrac{16}{200} - \dfrac{14}{400}}{\sqrt{(0.05)(0.95)\left(\dfrac{1}{200} + \dfrac{1}{400}\right)}} = 2.38$$

5. *Decision:* Since $Z = 2.38$ exceeds 2.33, the null hypothesis must be rejected; we conclude that the true proportion of tractors requiring extensive adjustments is greater for the first assembly line than for the second.

The P value is 0.0087 as shown in Figure 9.3.

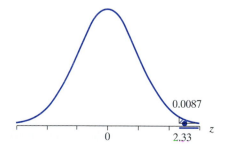

Figure 9.3 The
P value 0.0087.

The test we have described here applies to the null hypothesis $p_1 = p_2$, but it can easily be modified (see Exercise 9.34 on page 300) so that it applies also to the null hypothesis $p_1 - p_2 = \delta$.

The statistic for testing $p_1 = p_2$ leads to a confidence interval which provides the set of plausible values for $p_1 - p_2$.

Large sample confidence interval for the difference of two proportions

$$\frac{x_1}{n_1} - \frac{x_2}{n_2} \pm z_{\alpha/2}\sqrt{\frac{\frac{x_1}{n_1}\left(1 - \frac{x_1}{n_1}\right)}{n_1} + \frac{\frac{x_2}{n_2}\left(1 - \frac{x_2}{n_2}\right)}{n_2}}$$

EXAMPLE

A large sample confidence interval for the difference of two proportions
With reference to the preceding example, find the large sample 95% confidence interval for $p_1 - p_2$.

Solution   Since $x_1/n_1 = \hat{p}_1 = \frac{16}{200} = 0.08$ and $x_2/n_2 = \hat{p}_2 = \frac{14}{400} = 0.035$

$$\frac{x_1}{n_1} - \frac{x_2}{n_2} \pm z_{\alpha/2}\sqrt{\frac{\frac{x_1}{n_1}\left(1 - \frac{x_1}{n_1}\right)}{n_1} + \frac{\frac{x_2}{n_2}\left(1 - \frac{x_2}{n_2}\right)}{n_2}}$$

$$= 0.08 - 0.035 \pm 1.96\sqrt{\frac{(0.08)(0.92)}{200} + \frac{(0.035)(0.965)}{400}},$$

or $0.003 < p_1 - p_2 < 0.087$

The first shift has a rate of extensive adjustment between 3 out of 1,000 and 87 out of 1,000, higher than the rate for the second shift.   ✔

EXERCISES

9.19 A manufacturer of submersible pumps claims that at most 30% of the pumps require repairs within the first 5 years of operation. If a random sample of 120 of these pumps includes 47 which required repairs within the first 5 years, test the null hypothesis $p = 0.30$ against the alternative hypothesis $p > 0.30$ at the 0.05 level of significance.

9.20 The performance of a computer is observed over a period of 2 years to check the claim that the probability is 0.20 that its downtime will exceed 5 hours in any given week. Testing the null hypothesis $p = 0.20$ against the alternative hypothesis $p \neq 0.20$, what can we conclude at the level of significance $\alpha = 0.05$, if there were only 11 weeks in which the downtime of the computer exceeded 5 hours?

9.21 To check on an ambulance service's claim that at least 40% of its calls are life-threatening emergencies, a random sample was taken from its files, and it was found that only 49 of 150 calls were life-threatening emergencies. Can the null hypothesis $p \geq 0.40$ be rejected against the alternative hypothesis $p < 0.40$ if the probability of a Type I error is to be at most 0.01?

9.22 In a random sample of 600 cars making a right turn at a certain intersection, 157 pulled into the wrong lane. Test the null hypothesis that actually 30% of all drivers make this mistake at the given intersection, using the alternative hypothesis $p \neq 0.30$ and the level of significance

(a) $\alpha = 0.05$;

(b) $\alpha = 0.01$.

9.23 An airline claims that only 6% of all lost luggage is never found. If, in a random sample, 17 of 200 pieces of lost luggage are not found, test the null hypothesis $p = 0.06$ against the alternative hypothesis $p > 0.06$ at the 0.05 level of significance.

9.24 Suppose that 4 of 13 undergraduate engineering students state that they will go on to graduate school. Test the dean's claim that 60% of the undergraduate students will go on to graduate school, using the alternative hypothesis $p < 0.60$ and the level of significance $\alpha = 0.05$. [*Hint:* Use Table 1 to determine the probability of getting "at most 4 successes in 13 trials" when $p = 0.60$.]

9.25 Suppose that we want to test the "honesty" of a coin on the basis of the number of heads we will get in 15 flips. Using Table 1, determine how few or how many heads we would have to get so that we could reject the null hypothesis $p = 0.50$ against the alternative hypothesis $p \neq 0.50$ at the level of significance no larger than 0.05. What is the *actual* level of significance we would be using with this criterion?

9.26 It costs more to test a certain type of ammunition than to manufacture it, and, hence, only 3 rounds are tested from each large lot. If the lot is rejected unless all 3 rounds function according to specifications,

(a) sketch the OC curve for this test;

(b) find the actual proportion of defectives for which the test procedure will cause a lot to be rejected with a probability of 0.10.

9.27 Tests are made on the proportion of defective castings produced by 5 different molds. If there were 14 defectives among 100 castings made with Mold I, 33 defectives among 200 castings made with Mold II, 21 defectives among 180 castings made with Mold III, 17 defectives among 120 castings made with Mold IV, and 25 defectives among 150 castings made with Mold V, use the 0.01 level of significance to test whether the true proportion of defectives is the same for each mold.

9.28 A study showed that 64 of 180 persons who saw a photocopying machine advertised during the telecast of a baseball game and 75 of 180 other persons who saw it advertised on a variety show remembered the brand name 2 hours later. Use the χ^2 statistic to test at the 0.05 level of significance whether the difference between the corresponding sample proportions is significant.

9.29 The following data come from a study in which random samples of the employees of three government agencies were asked questions about their pension plan:

	Agency 1	Agency 2	Agency 3
For the pension plan	67	84	109
Against the pension plan	33	66	41

Use the 0.01 level of significance to test the null hypothesis that the actual proportions of employees favoring the pension plan are the same.

9.30 The owner of a machine shop must decide which of two snack-vending machines to install in his shop. If each machine is tested 250 times, the first machine fails to work (neither delivers the snack nor returns the money) 13 times, and the second machine fails to work 7 times, test at the 0.05 level of significance whether the difference between the corresponding sample proportions is significant, using

(a) the χ^2 statistic on page 294,

(b) the Z statistic on page 296.

9.31 With reference to the preceding exercise, verify that the square of the value obtained for Z in part (b) equals the value obtained for χ^2 in part (a).

9.32 Photolithography plays a central role in manufacturing integrated circuits made on thin disks of silicon. Prior to a quality-improvement program, too many rework operations were required. In a sample of 200 units, 26 required reworking of the photolithographic step. Following training in the use of Pareto charts and other approaches to identify significant problems, improvements were made. A new sample of size 200 had only 12 that needed rework.

Is this sufficient evidence to conclude at the 0.01 level of significance that the improvements have been effective in reducing the rework?

9.33 With reference to Exercise 9.32, find a large sample 99% confidence interval for the true difference of the proportions.

9.34 To test the null hypothesis that the difference between two population proportions equals some constant δ, not necessarily 0, we can use the statistic

$$Z = \frac{\frac{X_1}{n_1} - \frac{X_2}{n_2} - \delta}{\sqrt{\frac{\frac{X_1}{n_1}\left(1 - \frac{X_1}{n_1}\right)}{n_1} + \frac{\frac{X_2}{n_2}\left(1 - \frac{X_2}{n_2}\right)}{n_2}}}$$

which, for large samples, is a random variable having the standard normal distribution.

(a) With reference to Exercise 9.32, use this statistic to test at the 0.05 level of significance whether the true proportion of units requiring rework is now at least 4% less than before the improvements were made.

(b) In a true-false test, a test item is considered to be good if it discriminates between well-prepared students and poorly prepared students. If 205 of 250 well-prepared students and 137 of 250 poorly prepared students answer a certain item correctly, test at the 0.01 level of significance whether for the given item the proportion of correct answers can be expected to be at least 15% higher among well-prepared students than among poorly prepared students.

9.35 With reference to part (b) of Exercise 9.34, find a large sample 99% confidence interval for the true difference of the proportions.

9.36 Verify that the formulas for the χ^2 statistic on page 293 (with $\hat{p}$ substituted for the p_i) and on page 294 are equivalent.

9.37 Verify that if the expected frequencies are determined in accordance with the rule on page 293, the sum of the expected frequencies for each row and column equals the sum of the corresponding observed frequencies.

9.38 Verify that the square of the Z statistic on page 296 equals the χ^2 statistic on page 294 for $k = 2$.

9.4 The Analysis of $r \times c$ Tables

As we suggested earlier, the method by which we analyzed the example on page 294 lends itself also to the analysis of **$r \times c$ tables,** or r-by-c tables, that is, tables in which data are tallied into a two-way classification having r rows and c columns. Such tables arise in essentially two kinds of problems. First, we might again have samples from several populations, with the distinction that now each trial permits more than two possible outcomes. This might happen, for example, if persons belonging to different income groups are asked whether they favor a certain political candidate, whether they are against him, or whether they are indifferent or undecided. The other situation giving rise to an $r \times c$ table is one in which we sample from one population but classify each item with respect to two (usually qualitative) categories. This might happen, for example, if a consumer testing service rates cars as excellent, superior, average, or poor with regard to performance and also with regard to appearance. Each car tested would then fall into one of the 16 cells of a 4×4 table, and it is mainly in connection with problems of this kind that $r \times c$ tables are referred to as **contingency tables.**

The essential difference between the two kinds of situations giving rise to $r \times c$ tables is that in the first case the column totals (the sample sizes) are fixed, while in the second case only the **grand total** (the total for the entire table) is fixed. As a result, there are also differences in the null hypotheses we shall want to test. In the first case we want to test whether the probability of obtaining an observation in the ith row is the same for each column; symbolically, we shall want to test the null hypothesis

$$p_{i1} = p_{i2} = \cdots = p_{ic} \quad \text{for } i = 1, 2, \ldots, r$$

where p_{ij} is the probability of obtaining an observation belonging to the ith row and the jth column, and $\sum_{i=1}^{r} p_{ij} = 1$ for each column. The alternative hypothesis is that the p's are not all equal for at least one row. In the second case we shall want to test the null hypothesis that the random variables represented by the two classifications are independent, so that p_{ij} is the product of the probability of getting a value belonging to the ith row and the probability of getting a value belonging to the jth column. The alternative hypothesis is that the two random variables are not independent.

In spite of the differences we have described, the analysis of an $r \times c$ table is the same for both cases. First we calculate the expected cell frequencies.

$$e_{ij} = \frac{(i\text{-th row total}) \times (j\text{-th column total})}{grand\ total}$$

The observed frequencies and the expected frequencies total the same for each row and column, so that only $(r - 1)(c - 1)$ of the e_{ij} have to be calculated directly, while the others can be obtained by subtraction from appropriate row or column totals. We then substitute into the formula

Statistic for analysis
of $r \times c$ table

$$\chi^2 = \sum_{i=1}^{r} \sum_{j=1}^{c} \frac{(o_{ij} - e_{ij})^2}{e_{ij}}$$

and we reject the null hypothesis if the value of this statistic exceeds χ_α^2 for $(r - 1)(c - 1)$ degrees of freedom. This expression for the number of degrees of freedom is justified by the above observation that after we determine $(r - 1)(c - 1)$ of the expected cell frequencies, the others are automatically determined, that is, they may be obtained by subtraction from appropriate row or column totals.

EXAMPLE

The chi-square test of independence

To determine whether there really is a relationship between an employee's performance in the company's training program and his or her ultimate success in the job, the company takes a sample of 400 cases from its very extensive files and obtains the results shown in the following table:

		Performance in training program			
		Below average	*Average*	*Above average*	*Total*
Success in job (employer's rating)	*Poor*	23	60	29	112
	Average	28	79	60	167
	Very good	9	49	63	121
	Total	60	188	152	400

Use the 0.01 level of significance to test the null hypothesis that performance in the training program and success in the job are independent.

Solution

1. *Null hypothesis:* Performance in training program and success in job are independent.

   Alternative hypothesis: Performance in training program and success in job are dependent.

2. *Level of significance:* $\alpha = 0.01$

3. *Criterion:* Reject the null hypothesis if $\chi^2 > 13.277$, the value of $\chi_{0.01}^2$ for $(3 - 1)(3 - 1) = 4$ degrees of freedom, where χ^2 is given by the formula above.

4. *Calculations:* Calculating first the expected cell frequencies for the first two cells of the first two rows, we get

$$e_{11} = \frac{112 \cdot 60}{400} = 16.80 \quad e_{12} = \frac{112 \cdot 188}{400} = 52.64$$

$$e_{21} = \frac{167 \cdot 60}{400} = 25.05 \quad e_{22} = \frac{167 \cdot 188}{400} = 78.49$$

Then, by subtraction, we find that the expected frequencies for the third cell of the first two rows are 42.56 and 63.46, and those for the third row are 18.15, 56.87, and 45.98. Thus,

$$\chi^2 = \frac{(23 - 16.80)^2}{16.80} + \frac{(60 - 52.64)^2}{52.64} + \frac{(29 - 42.56)^2}{42.56}$$
$$+ \frac{(28 - 25.05)^2}{25.05} + \frac{(79 - 78.49)^2}{78.49} + \frac{(60 - 63.46)^2}{63.46}$$
$$+ \frac{(9 - 18.15)^2}{18.15} + \frac{(49 - 56.87)^2}{56.87} + \frac{(63 - 45.98)^2}{45.98}$$
$$= 20.179$$

5. *Decision:* Since $\chi^2 = 20.179$ exceeds 13.277, the null hypothesis must be rejected; we conclude that there is a dependence between an employee's performance in the training program and his or her success in the job. ✔

We pursue this example further in order to determine the form of the dependence.

EXAMPLE

Exploring the form of dependence
With reference to the preceding example, find the individual contributions to the chi-square.

Solution
We display the contingency table, but this time we include the expected frequencies just below the observed frequencies.

Performance in training program

		Below average	Average	Above average	Total
	Poor	23 **16.80**	60 **52.64**	29 **42.56**	112
Success in job *(employer's rating)*	*Average*	28 **25.05**	79 **78.49**	60 **63.46**	167
	Very good	9 **18.15**	49 **56.87**	63 **45.98**	121
	Total	60	188	152	400

Also, we write

$$\chi^2 = 2.288 + 1.029 + 4.320$$
$$+ 0.347 + 0.003 + 0.189$$
$$+ 4.613 + 1.089 + 6.300$$
$$= 20.179$$

From these two displays, it is clear that there is a positive dependence between performance in training and job success. For the three individual cells with the largest contributions to χ^2, the *above average-very good* cell frequency is high, whereas the *above average-poor* and *below average-very good* cell frequencies are low.   ✔

9.5   Goodness of Fit

We speak of **goodness of fit** when we try to compare an observed frequency distribution with the corresponding values of an expected, or theoretical, distribution. To illustrate, suppose that during 400 five-minute intervals the air-traffic control of an airport received $0, 1, 2, \ldots$, or 13 radio messages with respective frequencies of $3, 15, 47, 76, 68, 74, 46, 39, 15, 9, 5, 2, 0$, and 1. Suppose, furthermore, that we want to check whether these data substantiate the claim that the number of radio messages which they receive during a 5-minute interval may be looked upon as a random variable having the Poisson distribution with $\lambda = 4.6$. Looking up the corresponding Poisson probabilities in Table 2 and multiplying them by 400 to get the expected frequencies, we arrive at the result shown in the following table together with the original data:

Number of radio messages	Observed frequencies	Poisson probabilities	Expected frequencies
0	3 ⎫ 18	0.010	4.0 ⎫ 22.4
1	15 ⎭	0.046	18.4 ⎭
2	47	0.107	42.8
3	76	0.163	65.2
4	68	0.187	74.8
5	74	0.173	69.2
6	46	0.132	52.8
7	39	0.087	34.8
8	15	0.050	20.0
9	9	0.025	10.0
10	5 ⎫	0.012	4.8 ⎫
11	2 ⎪ 8	0.005	2.0 ⎪ 8.0
12	0 ⎪	0.002	0.8 ⎪
13	1 ⎭	0.001	0.4 ⎭
	400		400.0

Note that we combined some of the data so that none of the expected frequencies is less than 5.

To test whether the discrepancies between the observed and expected frequencies can be attributed to chance, we use the statistic

Statistic for test of goodness of fit

$$\chi^2 = \sum_{i=1}^{k} \frac{(o_i - e_i)^2}{e_i}$$

where the o_i and e_i are the observed and expected frequencies. The sampling distribution of this statistic is approximately the chi-square distribution with $k - m$ degrees of freedom, where k is the number of terms in the formula for χ^2 and m is the number of quantities, obtained from the observed data, that are needed to calculate the expected frequencies.

EXAMPLE

A chi-square goodness of fit to the Poisson distribution
With reference to the radio message data on page 304, test at the 0.01 level of significance whether the data can be looked upon as values of a random variable having the Poisson distribution with $\lambda = 4.6$.

Solution

1. *Null hypothesis:* Random variable has Poisson distribution with $\lambda = 4.6$.
   Alternative hypothesis: Random variable does not have Poisson distribution with $\lambda = 4.6$.

2. *Level of significance:* $\alpha = 0.01$

3. *Criterion:* Reject the null hypothesis if $\chi^2 > 16.919$, the value of $\chi^2_{0.01}$ for $k - m = 10 - 1 = 9$ degrees of freedom, where χ^2 is given by the formula above. (The number of degrees of freedom is $10 - 1 = 9$, since only one quantity, the total frequency of 400, is needed from the observed data to calculate the expected frequencies.)

4. *Calculations:* Substitution into the formula for χ^2 yields

$$\chi^2 = \frac{(18 - 22.4)^2}{22.4} + \frac{(47 - 42.8)^2}{42.8} + \cdots + \frac{(9 - 10.0)^2}{10.0} + \frac{(8 - 8.0)^2}{8.0}$$
$$= 6.749$$

5. *Decision:* Since $\chi^2 = 6.749$ does not exceed 16.919, the null hypothesis cannot be rejected; we cannot reject that the Poisson distribution with $\lambda = 4.6$ provides a good fit.

EXERCISES

9.39 The results of polls conducted 2 weeks and 4 weeks before a gubernatorial election are shown in the following table:

	Two weeks before election	Four weeks before election
For Republican candidate	79	91
For Democratic candidate	84	66
Undecided	37	43

Use the 0.05 level of significance to test whether there has been a change in opinion during the 2 weeks between the two polls.

9.40 A large electronics firm that hires many workers with disabilities wants to determine whether their disabilities affect such workers' performance. Use the level of significance $\alpha = 0.05$ to decide on the basis of the sample data shown in the following table whether it is reasonable to maintain that the disabilities have no effect on the workers' performance:

	Performance		
	Above average	*Average*	*Below average*
Blind	21	64	17
Deaf	16	49	14
No disability	29	93	28

9.41 Tests of the fidelity and the selectivity of 190 radio receivers produced the results shown in the following table:

		Fidelity		
		Low	*Average*	*High*
Selectivity	*Low*	6	12	32
	Average	33	61	18
	High	13	15	0

Use the 0.01 level of significance to test whether there is a relationship (dependence) between fidelity and selectivity.

9.42 A quality-control engineer takes daily samples of $n = 4$ tractors coming off an assembly line and on 200 consecutive working days the data summarized in the following table are obtained:

Number requiring adjustments	*Number of days*
0	101
1	79
2	19
3	1

To test the claim that 10% of all the tractors coming off this assembly line require adjustments, look up the corresponding probabilities in Table 1, calculate the expected frequencies, and perform the chi-square test at the 0.01 level of significance.

9.43 With reference to Exercise 9.42, verify that the mean of the observed distribution is 0.60, corresponding to 15% of the tractors requiring adjustments. Then look up the probabilities for $n = 4$ and $p = 0.15$ in Table 1, calculate the expected frequencies, and test at the 0.01 level of significance whether the binomial distribution with $n = 4$ and $p = 0.15$ provides a suitable model for this situation.

9.44 Suppose that in the example on page 304 we had shown first that the mean of the distribution, rounded to one decimal, is 4.5, and then tested whether the Poisson distribution with $\lambda = 4.5$ provides a good fit. What would have been the number of degrees of freedom for the appropriate chi-square criterion?

9.45 The following is the distribution of the hourly number of trucks arriving at a company's warehouse:

Trucks arriving per hour	Frequency
0	52
1	151
2	130
3	102
4	45
5	12
6	5
7	1
8	2

Find the mean of this distribution, and using it (rounded to one decimal place) as the parameter λ, fit a Poisson distribution. Test for goodness of fit at the 0.05 level of significance.

9.46 Using any four columns of Table 7 (that is, a total of 200 random digits), construct a table showing how many times each of the digits $0, 1, \ldots,$ and 9 occurred. Comparing the observed frequencies with the corresponding expected frequencies (based on the assumption that the digits are randomly generated), test at the 0.05 level of significance whether the assumption of randomness is tenable.

9.47 The following is the distribution of the sulfur oxides emission data on page 15, for which we showed that $\bar{x} = 18.85$ and $s = \sqrt{30.77} = 5.55$:

Class limits (tons)	Frequency
5.0-8.9	3
9.0-12.9	10
13.0-16.9	14
17.0-20.9	25
21.0-24.9	17
25.0-28.9	9
29.0-32.9	2
Total	80

(a) Find the probabilities that a random variable having a normal distribution with $\mu = 18.85$ and $\sigma = 5.55$ takes on a value less than 8.95, between 8.95 and 12.95, between 12.95 and 16.95, between 16.95 and 20.95, between 20.95 and 24.95, between 24.95 and 28.95, and greater than 28.95.

(b) Multiply the probabilities obtained in part (a) by the total frequency, $n = 80$, thus getting the expected normal curve frequencies corresponding to the 7 classes of the given distribution (with the first one changed to "8.9 or less" and the last one changed to "29.0 or more").

(c) Use the 0.05 level of significance to test the null hypothesis that the given data may be looked upon as a random sample from a normal population. Explain why the number of degrees of freedom for this χ^2 test is $k - 3$, where k is the number of terms in the χ^2 statistic.

9.48 Among 100 purification filters used in an experiment, 46 had a service life of less than 20 hours, 19 had a service life of 20 or more but less than 40 hours, 17 had a service life of 40 or more but less than 60 hours, 12 had a service life of 60 or more but less than 80 hours, and 6 had a service life of 80 hours or more. Using steps similar to those outlined in the preceding exercise, test at the 0.01 level of significance whether the lifetimes may be regarded as a sample from an exponential population with $\mu = 40$ hours.

9.49 A chi-square test is easily implemented on a computer. With the counts

$$
\begin{array}{cccc}
31 & 42 & 22 & 25 \\
19 & 8 & 28 & 25
\end{array}
$$

from the example on page 295 in columns 1– 4, the *MINITAB* commands

Dialog box:	**Session command**
Stat > Tables > Chisquare Test	MTB > CHISQUARE C1–C4
Type *C1–C4* in **columns containing**	
the table. Click **OK.**	

produce the output

Expected counts are printed below observed counts

	Method 1	Method 2	Method 3	Method 4	Total
1	31	42	22	25	120
	30.00	30.00	30.00	30.00	
2	19	8	28	25	80
	20.00	20.00	20.00	20.00	
Total	50	50	50	50	200

ChiSq = 0.033 + 4.800 + 2.133 + 0.833 +
      0.050 + 7.200 + 3.200 + 1.250 = 19.550
      df=3

Repeat the analysis using only the data from the first three methods.

9.50 The procedure in Exercise 9.49 also calculates the chi-square test for independence. Do Exercise 9.40 using the computer.

9.51 In a sample of 100 ceramic pistons made for an experimental diesel engine, 18 were cracked. Construct a 95% confidence interval for the true proportion of cracked pistons, using

  (a) Table 9;

  (b) the large sample confidence interval formula.

9.52 With reference to Exercise 9.51, test the null hypothesis $p = 0.20$ versus the alternative hypothesis $p < 0.20$ at the 0.05 level.

9.53 In a random sample of 160 workers exposed to a certain amount of radiation, 24 experienced some ill effects. Construct a 99% confidence interval for the corresponding true percentage, using

  (a) Table 9;

  (b) the large sample confidence interval formula.

9.54 With reference to Exercise 9.53, test the null hypothesis $p = 0.15$ versus the alternative hypothesis $p \neq 0.15$ at the 0.01 level.

9.55 In a random sample of 100 packages shipped by air freight, 13 had some damage. Construct a 95% confidence interval for the true proportion of damaged packages, using

  (a) Table 9;

  (b) the large sample confidence interval formula.

9.56 With reference to Exercise 9.55, test the hypothesis $p = 0.10$ versus the alternative hypothesis $p > 0.10$ at the 0.01 level.

9.57 In 4,000 firings of a certain kind of rocket there were 20 instances in which a rocket exploded upon ignition. Construct an upper 95% confidence limit for the probability that such a rocket will explode upon ignition.

9.58 If 26 of 200 Brand A tires fail to last 20,000 miles, whereas the corresponding figures for 200 tires each of Brands B, C, and D are 23, 15, and 32, use the 0.05 level of significance to test the null hypothesis that there is no difference in the quality of the four kinds of tires with regard to their durability.

9.59 One method of seeding clouds was successful in 57 of 150 attempts while another method was successful in 33 of 100 attempts. At the 0.05 level of significance, can we conclude that the first method is better than the second?

9.60 With reference to Exercise 9.59, find a large sample 95% confidence interval for the true difference of probabilities.

9.61 Two bonding agents, A and B, are available for making a laminated beam. Of 50 beams made with Agent A, 11 failed a stress test, whereas 19 of the 50 beams made with Agent B failed. At the 0.05 level, can we conclude that Agent A is better than Agent B?

9.62 With reference to Exercise 9.61, find a large sample 95% confidence interval for the true difference of the probabilities of failure.

9.63 Cooling pipes at three nuclear power plants are investigated for deposits that would inhibit the flow of water. From 30 randomly selected spots at each plant, 13 from the first plant, 8 from the second plant, and 19 from the third were clogged.

  (a) Use the 0.05 level to test the null hypothesis of equality.

  (b) Plot the confidence intervals for the three probabilities of being clogged.

9.64 Suppose that in Exercise 9.58 we had been interested also in how many of the tires lasted more than 30,000 miles and obtained the results shown in the following table:

	Brand A	Brand B	Brand C	Brand D
Failed to last 20,000 miles	26	23	15	32
Lasted from 20,000 to 30,000	118	93	116	121
Lasted more than 30,000 miles	56	84	69	47

(a) Use the 0.01 level of significance to test the null hypothesis that there is no difference in the quality of the four kinds of tires with regard to their durability.

(b) Plot the four individual 99% confidence intervals for proportions that last more than 30,000 miles.

9.65 The following is the distribution of the daily number of power failures reported in a western city on 300 days:

Number of power failures	Number of days
0	9
1	43
2	64
3	62
4	42
5	36
6	22
7	14
8	6
9	2

Test at the 0.05 level of significance whether the daily number of power failures in this city is a random variable having the Poisson distribution with $\lambda = 3.2$.

9.66 With reference to the example on page 302, repeat the analysis after combining the categories *below average* and *average* in the training program and the categories *poor* and *average* in success. Comment on the form of the dependence.

9.67 Mechanical engineers, testing a new arc welding technique, classified welds both with respect to appearance and an X-ray inspection.

		Appearance		
		Bad	*Normal*	*Good*	*Total*
	Bad	20	7	3	30
X-ray	*Normal*	13	51	16	80
	Good	7	12	21	40
	Total	40	70	40	150

Test for independence using $\alpha = 0.05$ and find the individual cell contributions to the χ^2 statistic.

KEY TERMS

(with page references)

Nonparametric Tests

Most of the methods of inference that we have studied are based on the assumption that the observations come from normal populations. If this is the case, these methods extract all the information that is available in a sample, and they usually attain the best possible precision. However, since there are many situations where it is doubtful whether the assumption of normality can be met, statisticians have developed alternative techniques based on less stringent assumptions, which have become known as nonparametric tests.

Of the many nonparametric tests that have been developed in recent years, the sign test is presented in Section 10.2; tests based on rank sums are given in Section 10.3; a test of randomness is introduced in Section 10.4; and a goodness-of-fit test is given in Section 10.5 ■

10.1   Introduction

In this chapter, we expand the choice of statistical methods available for inferences concerning one or more populations. The assumption of a normal population underlies most of the "standard methods" discussed in the previous chapters, but it is often difficult to verify this tentative assumption, especially when sample sizes are small. Here we introduce tests that depend only on order relationships among the observations. Consequently, much less has to be assumed about the form of the underlying populations. The main advantage of these **nonparametric tests** is that exact inferences can be made when the assumptions underlying the so-called standard methods cannot be met. When the normal assumption is met, the standard tests will have more power. However, asymmetry or other departures from normality will have no effect on the nonparametric methods. Moreover, their power is usually satisfactory even when the populations deviate from normality.

Also, nonparametric tests apply even when the choice of a particular numerical scale of measurement is arbitrary. Still, their strongest value is the fact that the level of significance is exact even when the populations are quite nonnormal.

10.2 The Sign Test

In this section we shall describe a nonparametric alternative to the one-sample t test, the paired-sample t test, and corresponding large sample tests. As an alternative to the one-sample t test or the corresponding large sample test, the **sign test** applies when we sample a continuous symmetrical population, so that the probability of getting a sample value less than the mean and the probability of getting a sample value greater than the mean are both $\frac{1}{2}$. More generally, because symmetry is often difficult to verify with small or moderate sample sizes, we can formulate the hypotheses in terms of the population median $\tilde{\mu}$. To test the null hypothesis $\tilde{\mu} = \tilde{\mu}_0$ against an appropriate alternative on the basis of a random sample of size n, we replace each sample value greater than $\tilde{\mu}_0$ with a plus sign and each sample value less than $\tilde{\mu}_0$ with a minus sign, and then we test the null hypothesis that these plus and minus signs are the outcomes of binomial trials with $p = \frac{1}{2}$. If a sample value equals $\tilde{\mu}_0$, which may well happen since the values of continuous random variables are virtually always rounded, it is discarded.

To perform this kind of test when the sample is small, we refer directly to a table of binomial probabilities such as Table 1 at the end of the book; when the sample is large we use the test described in Section 9.2.

EXAMPLE

Conducting a sign test
The following data constitute a random sample of 15 measurements of the octane rating of a certain kind of gasoline:

| 99.0 | 102.3 | 99.8 | 100.5 | 99.7 | 96.2 | 99.1 | 102.5 |
| 103.3 | 97.4 | 100.4 | 98.9 | 98.3 | 98.0 | 101.6 | |

Test the null hypothesis $\tilde{\mu} = 98.0$ against the alternative hypothesis $\tilde{\mu} > 98.0$ at the 0.01 level of significance.

Solution Since one of the sample values equals 98.0 and must be discarded, the sample size for the sign test is only $n = 14$.
1. *Null hypothesis:* $\tilde{\mu} = 98.0 \ (p = \frac{1}{2})$
   Alternative hypothesis: $\tilde{\mu} > 98.0 \ (p > \frac{1}{2})$
2. *Level of significance:* $\alpha = 0.01$
3. *Criterion:* The criterion may be based on the number of plus signs or the number of minus signs. Using the number of plus signs, denoted by x, reject the null hypothesis if the probability of getting x or more plus signs is less than or equal to 0.01.

4. *Calculations:* Replacing each value greater than 98.0 with a plus sign and each value less than 98.0 with a minus sign, the 14 sample values yield

$$+ + + + + - + + + - + + + +$$

Thus, $x = 12$ and Table 1 shows that for $n = 14$ and $p = 0.50$ the probability of $X \geq 12$ is $1 - 0.9935 = 0.0065$.

5. *Decision:* Since 0.0065 is less than 0.01, the null hypothesis must be rejected; we conclude that the median octane rating of the given kind of gasoline exceeds 98.0. ✔

The sign test can also be used as a nonparametric alternative to the paired-sample t test or the corresponding large sample test. In such problems, each pair of sample values is replaced with a plus sign if the first is greater than the second, with a minus sign if the first value is smaller than the second, or it is discarded if the two values are equal. The procedure is the same as before. Let $\tilde{\mu}_D$ denote the median of the differences.

EXAMPLE

A sign test of the effectiveness of a safety program
With reference to the example on page 264, which dealt with the effectiveness of an industrial safety program, use the sign test at the 0.05 level of significance to test whether the safety program is effective.

Solution

1. *Null hypothesis:* $\tilde{\mu}_D = 0 \left(p = \frac{1}{2}\right)$
   Alternative hypothesis: $\tilde{\mu}_D > 0 \left(p > \frac{1}{2}\right)$
2. *Level of significance:* $\alpha = 0.05$
3. *Criterion:* If x is the number of plus signs, reject the null hypothesis if the probability of getting x or more plus signs is less than or equal to 0.05.
4. *Calculations:* Replacing each pair of values with a plus sign if the first value is greater than the second or with a minus sign if the first value is smaller than the second, the 10 sample pairs yield

$$+ + + + - + + + + +$$

Thus, $x = 9$ and Table 1 shows that for $n = 10$ and $p = 0.50$ the probability of $X \geq 9$ is $1 - 0.9893 = 0.0107$.

5. *Decision:* Since 0.0107 is less than 0.05, the null hypothesis must be rejected; we conclude that the safety program is effective. ✔

10.3 Rank-Sum Tests

In this section we shall introduce two tests based on **rank sums**—the **U test** will be presented as a nonparametric alternative to the two-sample t test, and the **H test** will be presented as a nonparametric alternative to the one-way analysis of variance, which we shall study in Chapter 12. In other words, the H test serves to test the null hypothesis that k samples come from identical populations against the alternative that the populations are not identical.

To illustrate how the U test (also called the **Wilcoxon test** or the **Mann-Whitney test,** named after the statisticians who contributed to its development) is performed, suppose that in a study of sedimentary rocks, the following diameters (in millimeters) were obtained for two kinds of sand:

Sand *I:*	0.63	0.17	0.35	0.49	0.18	0.43	0.12	0.20
	0.47	1.36	0.51	0.45	0.84	0.32	0.40	
Sand II:	1.13	0.54	0.96	0.26	0.39	0.88	0.92	0.53
	1.01	0.48	0.89	1.07	1.11	0.58		

The problem is to decide whether the two populations are the same or if one is more likely to produce larger observations than the other. Let X_1 be a random variable having the first distribution and X_2 a random variable having the second distribution. If $P(a < X_1) \le P(a < X_2)$ for all a, with strict inequality for some a, we say that the second population (distribution) is **stochastically larger** than the first population (distribution). We formulate one-sided hypotheses in terms of this stochastic order relation.

We begin the U test by ranking the data jointly, as if they comprise one sample, in an increasing order of magnitude, and for our data we get

0.12	0.17	0.18	0.20	0.26	0.32	0.35	0.39	0.40	0.43
I	I	I	I	II	I	I	II	I	I
0.45	0.47	0.48	0.49	0.51	0.53	0.54	0.58	0.63	0.84
I	I	II	I	I	II	II	II	I	I
0.88	0.89	0.92	0.96	1.01	1.07	1.11	1.13	1.36	
II	II	II	II	II	II	II	II	I	

Note that we indicated for each value whether it is a measurement of Sand I or Sand II. Assigning the data in this order the ranks $1, 2, 3, \ldots$, and 29, we find that the values of the first sample (Sand I) occupy ranks 1, 2, 3, 4, 6, 7, 9, 10, 11, 12, 14, 15, 19, 20, and 29, while those of the second sample (Sand II) occupy ranks 5, 8, 13, 16, 17, 18, 21, 22, 23, 24, 25, 26, 27, and 28. There are no ties here among values belonging to different samples, but if there were, we would assign to each of the tied observations the mean of the ranks which they jointly occupy. (For instance, if the third and fourth values are identical we would assign each the rank $\frac{3 + 4}{2} = 3.5$, and if the ninth, tenth, and eleventh values are identical we would assign each the rank $\frac{9 + 10 + 11}{3} = 10$.)

The null hypothesis we want to test is that the two samples come from identical populations, and it stands to reason that in that case the means of the ranks assigned to the values of the two samples should be more or less the same. Instead of the means, we can also compare the sums of the ranks assigned to the values of the two samples, suitably accounting for a possible difference in their size. For our two samples, the sums of the ranks are $W_1 = 162$ and $W_2 = 273$, and it remains to be seen whether their difference is large enough to reject the null hypothesis.

When the use of rank sums was first proposed as a nonparametric alternative to the two-sample t test, the decision was based on W_1 or W_2, but now the decision is based on either of the related statistics

U_1 and U_2 statistics

$$U_1 = W_1 - \frac{n_1(n_1 + 1)}{2}$$

or

$$U_2 = W_2 - \frac{n_2(n_2 + 1)}{2}$$

or on the statistic U, which always equals the smaller of the two. The sizes of the two samples are n_1 and n_2, and as it does not matter how we number the samples, we shall use here the statistic U_1.[†]

Under the null hypothesis that the two samples come from identical populations, it can be shown that the mean and the variance of the sampling distribution of U_1 are

Mean and variance of U_1 statistic

$$\mu_{U_1} = \frac{n_1 n_2}{2}$$

and

$$\sigma_{U_1}^2 = \frac{n_1 n_2 (n_1 + n_2 + 1)}{12}$$

If there are ties in rank, these formulas provide only approximations, but if the number of ties is small, these approximations will generally be good.

Since numerical studies have shown that the sampling distribution of U_1 can be approximated closely by a normal distribution when n_1 and n_2 are both greater than 8, the test of the null hypothesis that the two samples come from identical populations can be based on

Statistic for large sample U test

$$Z = \frac{U_1 - \mu_{U_1}}{\sigma_{U_1}}$$

which is a random variable having approximately the standard normal distribution. For small samples, we can base the test on special tables; for instance, on those in the book by Johnson and Bhattacharyya listed in the bibliography.

Note that when we test the null hypothesis—the two samples come from identical populations—against the alternative hypothesis:

[†]The tests based on U_1 or U_2 are equivalent to those based on W_1 or W_2, but they have the advantage that they lend themselves more readily to the construction of tables of critical values. Not only do U_1 and U_2 take on values on the interval from 0 to $n_1 n_2$—indeed, their sum is always equal to $n_1 n_2$—but their sampling distributions are symmetrical about $\frac{n_1 n_2}{2}$. The use of U, which always equals the smaller of the values of U_1 and U_2, has the added advantage that the resulting test is one-tailed regardless of the alternative hypothesis, and hence easier to tabulate.

population 2 is stochastically larger than population 1

we reject the null hypothesis if $Z < -z_\alpha$ since small values of U_1 correspond to small values of W_1; correspondingly, if the alternative hypothesis is

population 1 is stochastically larger than population 2

we reject the null hypothesis if $Z > z_\alpha$ since large values of U_1 correspond to large values of W_1.

EXAMPLE

Conducting the Wilcoxon test with large samples
With reference to the grain-size data on page 315, use the U test at the 0.01 level of significance to test the null hypothesis that the two samples come from identical populations against the alternative hypothesis that the populations are not identical.

Solution

1. *Null hypothesis:* Populations are identical.
   Alternative hypothesis: The populations are not identical.
2. *Level of significance:* $\alpha = 0.01$
3. *Criterion:* Reject the null hypothesis if $Z < -2.575$ or $Z > 2.575$, where Z is given by the formula on page 316.
4. *Calculations:* Since $n_1 = 15$, $n_2 = 14$, and we have already shown that $W_1 = 162$, we find that

$$U_1 = 162 - \frac{15 \cdot 16}{2} = 42$$

$$\mu_{U_1} = \frac{15 \cdot 14}{2} = 105$$

and

$$\sigma^2_{U_1} = \frac{15 \cdot 14 \cdot 30}{12} = 525$$

and it follows that

$$z = \frac{42 - 105}{\sqrt{525}} = -2.75$$

5. *Decision:* Since $z = -2.75$ is less than -2.575, the null hypothesis must be rejected; we conclude that there is a difference in the populations of grain size. ✔

The **H test**, or **Kruskal-Wallis test,** is a generalization of the U test in that it enables us to test the null hypothesis that k independent random samples come from identical populations. As in the U test, all the observations are ranked jointly, and if R_i is the sum of the ranks occupied by the n_i observations of the ith sample and $n_1 + n_2 + \cdots + n_k = n$, the test is based on the statistic

Statistic for H test

$$H = \frac{12}{n(n+1)} \sum_{i=1}^{k} \frac{R_i^2}{n_i} - 3(n+1)$$

When $n_i > 5$ for all i and the null hypothesis is true, the sampling distribution of the H statistic is well approximated by the chi-square distribution with $k - 1$ degrees of freedom. There exist special tables of critical values for the H test for selected small values of the n_i and k.

EXAMPLE

Conducting an H test to compare three methods
An experiment designed to compare three preventative methods against corrosion yielded the following maximum depths of pits (in thousandths of an inch) in pieces of wire subjected to the respective treatments:

Method A:	77	54	67	74	71	66	
Method B:	60	41	59	65	62	64	52
Method C:	49	52	69	47	56		

Use the 0.05 level of significance to test the null hypothesis that the three samples come from identical populations.

Solution

1. *Null hypothesis:* Populations are identical.
   Alternative hypothesis: Populations are not all equal.
2. *Level of significance:* $\alpha = 0.05$
3. *Criterion:* Reject the null hypothesis if $H > 5.991$, the value of $\chi^2_{0.05}$ for 2 degrees of freedom, where H is given by the formula above.
4. *Calculations:* Ranking these measurements jointly from smallest to largest, we find that those of the first sample occupy ranks 6, 13, 14, 16, 17, and 18; those of the second sample occupy ranks 1, 4.5, 8, 9, 10, 11, and 12; and those of the third sample occupy ranks 2, 3, 4.5, 5, 7, and 15. Thus, $R_1 = 84$, $R_2 = 55.5$, $R_3 = 31.5$, and substitution into the formula for H yields

$$H = \frac{12}{18 \cdot 19}\left(\frac{84^2}{6} + \frac{55.5^2}{7} + \frac{31.5^2}{5}\right) - 3 \cdot 19$$
$$= 6.7$$

5. *Decision:* Since $H = 6.7$ exceeds 5.991, the null hypothesis must be rejected; we conclude that the three preventative methods against corrosion are not equally effective. ✔

EXERCISES

10.1 In a laboratory experiment, 18 determinations of the coefficient of friction between leather and metal yielded the following results: 0.59, 0.56, 0.49, 0.55, 0.65, 0.55, 0.51, 0.60, 0.56, 0.47, 0.58, 0.61, 0.54, 0.68, 0.56, 0.50, 0.57, and 0.53. Use the sign test at the 0.05 level of significance to test the null hypothesis $\tilde{\mu} = 0.55$ against the alternative hypothesis $\tilde{\mu} \neq 0.55$.

10.2 A random sample of 9 women buying new eyeglasses tried on 12, 11, 14, 15, 10, 14, 11, 8, and 12 different frames. Use the sign test at the 0.05 level of significance to test the null hypothesis $\tilde{\mu} = 10$ (that the median number of different frames a woman buying new eyeglasses tries on is 10) against the alternative hypothesis $\tilde{\mu} > 10$.

10.3 With reference to Exercise 2.3, which pertained to the boiling point of a certain silicon compound, use the sign test at the 0.05 level of significance to test the null hypothesis $\tilde{\mu} = 158$ (degrees Celsius) against the alternative hypothesis $\tilde{\mu} \neq 158$.

10.4 The quality-control department of a large manufacturer obtained the following sample data (in pounds) on the breaking strength of a certain kind of 2-inch cotton ribbon: 153, 159, 144, 160, 158, 153, 171, 162, 159, 137, 159, 159, 148, 162, 154, 159, 160, 157, 140, 168, 163, 148, 151, 153, 157, 155, 148, 168, 152, and 149. Use the sign test at the 0.01 level of significance to test the null hypothesis $\tilde{\mu} = 150$ against the alternative hypothesis $\tilde{\mu} > 150$.

10.5 With reference to Exercise 2.12 on page 24, which pertained to the ignition times of certain upholstery materials, use the sign test at the 0.01 level of significance to test the null hypothesis $\tilde{\mu} = 6.50$ seconds against the alternative hypothesis $\tilde{\mu} < 6.50$ seconds.

10.6 The following are the number of speeding tickets issued by 2 police officers on 17 days: 7 and 10, 11 and 13, 14 and 14, 11 and 15, 12 and 9, 6 and 10, 9 and 13, 8 and 11, 10 and 11, 11 and 15, 13 and 11, 7 and 10, 8 and 8, 11 and 12, 9 and 14, 10 and 9, 13 and 16. Use the sign test at the 0.05 level of significance to test the null hypothesis that on the average the 2 police officers issue equally many speeding tickets per day against the alternative hypothesis that the second police officer tends to issue more than the first.

10.7 With reference to Exercise 7.71 on page 267, use the sign test at the 0.10 level of significance to check whether there is a systematic difference between weights obtained with the two scales.

10.8 With reference to Exercise 7.72 on page 267, use the sign test at the 0.01 level of significance to check whether the prescribed program of exercises is effective.

10.9 The following are the number of minutes it took a sample of 15 men and 12 women to complete the application form for a position:

Men:	16.5	20.0	17.0	19.8	18.5	19.2	19.0	18.2	20.8
	18.7	16.7	18.1	17.9	16.4	18.9			
Women:	18.6	17.8	18.3	16.6	20.5	16.3	19.3	18.4	19.7
	18.8	19.9	17.6						

Use the U test at the 0.05 level of significance to test the null hypothesis that the two samples come from identical populations against the alternative that the two populations are not identical.

10.10 With reference to part (a) of Exercise 7.70 on page 266, use the U test at the 0.05 level of significance to test whether the populations of hardness of the 2 alloys are identical.

10.11 Comparing 2 kinds of emergency flares, a consumer testing service obtained the following burning times (rounded to the nearest tenth of a minute):

Brand C:	19.4	21.5	15.3	17.4	16.8	16.6	20.3	22.5	21.3
	23.4	19.7	21.0						
Brand D:	16.5	15.8	24.7	10.2	13.5	15.9	15.7	14.0	12.1
	17.4	15.6	15.8						

Use the U test at the 0.01 level of significance to check whether it is reasonable to say that the populations of burning times of the two kinds of flares are identical.

10.12 The following are the scores which random samples of students from 2 minority groups obtained on a current events test:

Minority Group 1:	73	82	39	68	91	75	89	67	50	86	57	65	70
Minority Group 2:	51	42	36	53	88	59	49	66	25	64	18	76	74

Use the U test at the 0.05 level of significance to test whether or not students from the 2 minority groups can be expected to score equally well on the test.

10.13 The following are data on the breaking strength (in pounds) of 2 kinds of material:

Material 1:	144	181	200	187	169	171	186	194	176	182
	133	183	197	165	180	198				
Material 2:	175	164	172	194	176	198	154	134	169	164
	185	159	161	189	170	164				

Use the U test at the 0.05 level of significance to test the claim that the strength of Material 1 is stochastically larger than the strength of Material 2.

10.14 The following are the numbers of misprints counted on pages selected at random from three Sunday editions of a newspaper:

April 11:	4	10	2	6	4	12
April 18:	8	5	13	8	8	10
April 25:	7	9	11	2	14	7

Use the H test at the 0.05 level of significance to test the null hypothesis that the 3 samples come from identical populations.

10.15 So-called Franklin tests were performed to determine the insulation properties of grain-oriented silicon steel specimens that were annealed in five different atmospheres with the following results:

Atmosphere	Test results (amperes)						
1	0.58	0.61	0.69	0.79	0.61	0.59	
2	0.37	0.37	0.58	0.40	0.28	0.44	0.35
3	0.29	0.19	0.34	0.17	0.29	0.16	
4	0.81	0.69	0.75	0.72	0.68	0.85	0.57	0.77
5	0.26	0.34	0.29	0.47	0.30	0.42	

Use the H test at the 0.05 level of significance to decide whether or not these 5 samples can be assumed to come from identical populations.

10.16 A panel of 7 experts was asked to rate each of 5 industries on the likelihood that technological changes would produce improvement in environmental pollution over the next 10 years. Their ratings (in the form of judgmental probabilities) are as follows:

Industry

Expert	A	B	C	D	E
1	0.15	0.75	0.10	0.00	0.30
2	0.30	0.60	0.20	0.05	0.25
3	0.20	0.80	0.30	0.00	0.50
4	0.00	0.50	0.25	0.10	0.60
5	0.10	0.55	0.15	0.15	0.40
6	0.25	0.70	0.35	0.25	0.45
7	0.40	0.95	0.45	0.20	0.35

(a) Test at the 0.05 level of significance whether or not the ratings given by the experts can be assumed to come from identical populations.

(b) Test at the 0.01 level of significance whether or not the ratings given to the industries can be assumed to come from identical populations. What argument(s) can you make against the validity of this test?

10.4   Tests of Randomness

When we discussed random sampling in Chapter 6, we gave several methods which provide some assurance in advance that a sample taken will be random. Since there are also situations in which we have no control over the way in which the data are selected, it is useful to have a technique for testing whether a sample may be looked upon as random after it has actually been obtained. One such technique is based on the order in which the sample values were obtained; more specifically, it is based on the number of **runs** exhibited in the sample results.

Given a sequence of two symbols, such as H and T (which might represent the occurrence of heads and tails in repeated tosses of a coin), a run is defined as a succession of identical symbols contained between different symbols or none at all. For example, the sequence

$$\underline{T\,T}\ \underline{H\,H}\ \underline{T\,T}\ \underline{H\,H\,H}\ \underline{T}\ \underline{H\,H\,H}\ \underline{T\,T\,T\,T}\ \underline{H\,H\,H}$$

contains 8 runs, as indicated by the underlines. The total number of runs in a sequence of n trials often serves as an indication that the arrangement is not random. For instance, if there had been only two runs consisting of 10 heads followed by 10 tails, we might have suspected that the probability of a success did not remain constant from trial to trial. On the other hand, had the sequence of 20 tosses consisted of alternating heads and tails, we might have suspected that the trials were not independent. In either case, there are grounds to suspect a lack of randomness. Note that our suspicion is not aroused by the numbers of H's and T's, but by the order in which they appeared.

If a sequence contains n_1 symbols of one kind and n_2 of another kind (and neither n_1 nor n_2 is less than 10), the sampling distribution of the **total number of runs,** u, can be approximated closely by a normal distribution with

Mean and standard
deviation of u

$$\mu_u = \frac{2n_1 n_2}{n_1 + n_2} + 1 \quad and \quad \sigma_u = \sqrt{\frac{2n_1 n_2 (2n_1 n_2 - n_1 - n_2)}{(n_1 + n_2)^2 (n_1 + n_2 - 1)}}$$

Thus, the test of the null hypothesis that the arrangement of the symbols (and, hence, the sample) is random can be based on the statistic

Statistic for test of
randomness

$$Z = \frac{u - \mu_u}{\sigma_u}$$

which has approximately the standard normal distribution. Special tables are available for performing the test when n_1, n_2, or both are small.

EXAMPLE

Conducting a test for randomness
The following is the arrangement of defective, d, and nondefective, n, pieces produced in the given order by a certain machine:

$$n\,n\,n\,n\,n\ d\,d\,d\,d\ n\,n\,n\,n\,n\,n\,n\,n\,n\,n\ d\,d\ n\,n\ d\,d\,d\,d$$

Test for randomness at the 0.01 level of significance.

Solution

1. *Null hypothesis:* Arrangement is random.
   Alternative hypothesis: Arrangement is not random.
2. *Level of significance:* $\alpha = 0.01$
3. *Criterion:* Reject the null hypothesis if $Z < -2.575$ or $Z > 2.575$, where Z is given by the above formula.
4. *Calculations:* Since $n_1 = 10$, $n_2 = 17$, and $u = 6$, we get

$$\mu_u = \frac{2 \cdot 10 \cdot 17}{10 + 17} + 1 = 13.59$$

$$\sigma_u = \sqrt{\frac{2 \cdot 10 \cdot 17(2 \cdot 10 \cdot 17 - 10 - 17)}{(10 + 17)^2 (10 + 17 - 1)}} = 2.37$$

and

$$z = \frac{6 - 13.59}{2.37} = -3.20$$

5. *Decision:* Since $z = -3.20$ is less than -2.575, the null hypothesis must be rejected; we conclude that the arrangement is not random. Indeed, the total number of runs is much smaller than expected and there is a strong indication that the defective pieces appear in clusters or groups; the reason for this will have to be uncovered by an engineer who is familiar with the process.   ✔

The run test can be used also to test the randomness of samples consisting of numerical data by counting **runs above and below the median.** Denoting an observation exceeding the median of the sample by the letter *a* and an observation less than the median by the letter *b*, we can use the resulting sequence of *a*'s and *b*'s to test for randomness by the method just indicated. A frequent application of this test is in quality control, where the means of successive small samples are exhibited on a graph in chronological order. The run test can then be used to check whether there might be a trend in the data, so that it is possible to adjust a machine setting or some other process variable before any serious damage occurs.

EXAMPLE

Testing for too many changes
An engineer is concerned about the possibility that too many changes are being made in the settings of an automatic lathe. Given the following mean diameters (in inches) of 40 successive shafts turned on the lathe

0.261	0.258	0.249	0.251	0.247	0.256	0.250	0.247	0.255	0.243
0.252	0.250	0.253	0.247	0.251	0.243	0.258	0.251	0.245	0.250
0.248	0.252	0.254	0.250	0.247	0.253	0.251	0.246	0.249	0.252
0.247	0.250	0.253	0.247	0.249	0.253	0.246	0.251	0.249	0.253

use the 0.01 level of significance to test the null hypothesis of randomness against the alternative that there is a frequently alternating pattern.

Solution

1. *Null hypothesis:* Arrangement of sample values is random.
   Alternative hypothesis: There is a frequently alternating pattern.
2. *Level of significance:* $\alpha = 0.01$
3. *Criterion:* Reject the null hypothesis if $Z > 2.33$, where Z is given by the formula on page 322 for the total number of runs above and below the median.
4. *Calculations:* The median of the 40 measurements is 0.250, so that we get the following arrangement of values above and below 0.250:

   $a\,a\,b\,a\,b\,a\,b\,a\,b\,a\,a\,b\,a\,b\,a\,b\,a\,a\,b\,b\,a\,a\,b\,a\,a\,b\,b\,a\,b\,a\,b\,b\,a\,b\,a\,b\,a$

   Thus, $n_1 = 19$, $n_2 = 16$, and $u = 27$, so that

   $$\mu_u = \frac{2 \cdot 19 \cdot 16}{35} + 1 = 18.37$$

   $$\sigma_u = \sqrt{\frac{2 \cdot 19 \cdot 16(2 \cdot 19 \cdot 16 - 19 - 16)}{(19 + 16)^2(19 + 16 - 1)}} = 2.89$$

   and

   $$z = \frac{27 - 18.37}{2.89} = 2.98$$

5. *Decision:* Since $z = 2.98$ exceeds 2.33, the null hypothesis of randomness must be rejected; since the number of runs is much larger than one might

expect due to chance, it is reasonable to conclude that the lathe is being adjusted too often. ✔

10.5 The Kolmogorov-Smirnov and Anderson-Darling Tests

The **Kolmogorov-Smirnov tests** are nonparametric tests for differences between cumulative distributions. The one-sample test concerns the agreement between an observed, or empirical, cumulative distribution of sample values and a specified continuous distribution function; thus, it is a test of goodness of fit. The two-sample test concerns the agreement between two observed cumulative distributions; it tests the hypothesis whether two independent samples come from identical continuous distributions, and it is sensitive to population differences with respect to location, dispersion, or skewness.

The Kolmogorov-Smirnov one-sample test is generally more efficient than the chi-square test for goodness of fit for small samples, and it can be used for very small samples where the chi-square test does not apply. It must be remembered, however, that the chi-square test of Section 9.6 can be used in connection with discrete distributions, whereas the Kolmogorov-Smirnov test cannot.

The one-sample test is based on the maximum absolute difference D between the values of the empirical cumulative distribution of a random sample of size n and a specified theoretical cumulative distribution. To determine whether this difference is larger than can reasonably be expected for a given level of significance, we look up the critical value of D in Table 10.

EXAMPLE

Using the Kolmogorov-Smirnov test for uniformity
It is desired to check whether pinholes in electrolytic tin plate are uniformly distributed across a plated coil on the basis of the following distances in inches of 10 pinholes from one edge of a long strip of tin plate 30 inches wide:

| 4.8 | 14.8 | 28.2 | 23.1 | 4.4 | 28.7 | 19.5 | 2.4 | 25.0 | 6.2 |

Test the null hypothesis at the 0.05 level of significance.

Solution 1. *Null hypothesis:*

$$F(x) = \begin{cases} 0 & \text{for } x \leq 0 \\ \dfrac{x}{30} & \text{for } 0 < x < 30 \\ 1 & \text{for } x \geq 30 \end{cases}$$

where x is the distance of a pinhole from the edge.
Alternative hypothesis: The pinholes are not uniformly distributed across the tin plate.

2. *Level of Significance:* $\alpha = 0.05$
3. *Criterion:* Reject the null hypothesis if $D > 0.410$, where D is the maximum difference between the empirical cumulative distribution and the cumulative distribution assumed under the null hypothesis. (See Table 10)

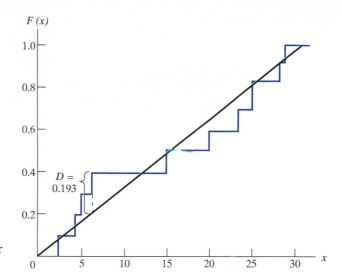

FIGURE 10.1 Diagram for Kolmogorov-Smirnov test.

4. *Calculations:* Plotting the 2 cumulative distributions as in Figure 10.1, we find that the difference is greatest at $x = 6.2$, and that its value is

$$D = 0.40 - \frac{6.2}{30} = 0.193.$$

5. *Decision:* Since $D = 0.193$ does not exceed 0.410, the null hypothesis (that the pinholes are uniformly distributed across the tin plate) cannot be rejected. ✔

Despite their intuitive appeal, the Kolmogorov-Smirnov tests do not have good power. Differences in the tails can be easier to detect if the difference between the empirical cumulative distribution, F_n, and F is divided by $\sqrt{F(x)(1 - F(x))}$. In particular, the **Anderson-Darling test** is based on the large values of the statistic

$$A^2 = \int_{-\infty}^{\infty} [F_n(x) - F(x)]^2 \frac{1}{F(x)(1 - F(x))} f(x)dx$$

At first sight the numerical calculation of this statistic looks difficult. But, it can be shown that

$$A^2 = \left[\sum_{i=1}^{n} (2i - 1)(\ln(u_i) + \ln(1 - u_{n+1-i})) \right]/n - n$$

where $u_i = F(x_{(i)})$ is the value of the theoretical cumulative distribution at the ith largest observation $x_{(i)}$.

The null hypothesis is rejected for large values of the statistic A^2. As a guideline, the large sample 5% point is 2.492 and the 1% point is 3.857. It has been suggested that these critical values are quite accurate even for samples as small as 10.

Evaluating the Anderson-Darling statistic

With reference to the preceding example, evaluate the Anderson-Darling statistic A^2.

Solution

The smallest observation is 2.4 so $u_1 = F(2.4) = 2.4/30 = .08000$. Continuing, the ordered values of the observations and the u_i are

2.4	4.4	4.8	6.2	14.8	19.5	23.1	25.0	28.2	28.7
.08000	.14667	.16000	.20667	.49333	.65000	.77000	.83333	.94000	.95667

Therefore

$$A^2 = -[(2 \times 1 - 1)(\ln(.080000) + \ln(1 - .95667)) + \cdots$$
$$+ (2 \times 10 - 1)(\ln(.95667) + \ln(1 - .08000))]/10 - 10$$
$$= .5267$$

According to the large sample critical value, we fail to reject the null hypothesis that the distribution of pin holes is uniform, with $\alpha = .05$. ✔

EXERCISES

10.17 The following arrangement indicates whether 60 consecutive cars which went by the toll booth of a bridge had local plates, L, or out-of-state plates, O:

$$L\,L\,O\,L\,L\,L\,L\,O\,O\,L\,L\,L\,L\,O\,L\,O\,O\,L\,L\,L\,L\,O\,L\,O\,O\,L\,L\,L\,L\,L$$
$$O\,L\,L\,L\,O\,L\,O\,L\,L\,L\,L\,O\,O\,L\,O\,O\,O\,O\,L\,L\,L\,L\,O\,L\,O\,O\,L\,L\,L\,O$$

Test at the 0.05 level of significance whether this arrangement of L's and O's may be regarded as random.

10.18 The following arrangement indicates whether 50 consecutive persons interviewed by a pollster are for, F, or against, A, an increase in the state gasoline tax to build more roads:

$$A\,A\,F\,A\,F\,A\,A\,A\,A\,F\,F\,A\,A\,F\,A\,A\,A\,A\,A\,F\,A\,A\,F\,F$$
$$A\,A\,F\,A\,A\,A\,A\,F\,A\,F\,F\,A\,A\,A\,A\,A\,F\,A\,A\,F\,A\,A\,A\,A\,F$$

Test at the 0.05 level of significance whether this arrangement of A's and F's may be regarded as random.

10.19 To check the randomness of the digits in Table 7, take those in any five rows, replace the odd digits by the letter O and the even digits by the letter E, and base your decision on the total number of runs in the resulting sequence of O's and E's. Use the 0.01 level of significance.

10.20 The following are the number of defective pieces turned out by a machine during 24 consecutive shifts: 15, 11, 17, 14, 16, 12, 19, 17, 21, 15, 17, 19, 21, 14, 22, 16, 19, 12, 16, 14, 18, 17, 24, and 13. Test for randomness at the 0.01 level of significance.

10.21 The following are 50 consecutive downtimes of a machine (in minutes) which were observed during a certain period of time: 22, 29, 32, 25, 33, 34, 38, 34, 29, 25, 27, 33, 34, 28, 39, 41, 24, 31, 34, 29, 34, 25, 30, 37, 40, 39, 35, 24, 32, 43, 44, 34, 40, 38, 39, 43, 46, 34, 39, 45, 42, 39, 54, 50, 38, 41, 43, 46, 52, and 55. Use the method of runs above and below the median and the 0.05 level of significance to test the null hypothesis of randomness against the alternative that there is a trend.

10.22 Using the result of the illustration given in the example on page 33, namely, that the median of the sulfur oxides emission on page 15, is 19.05, test the original data for randomness at the 0.05 level of significance.

10.23 In a vibration study, certain airplane components were subjected to severe vibrations until they showed structural failures. Given the following failure times (in minutes), test whether they can be looked upon as a sample from an exponential population with the mean $\mu = 10$:

1.5	10.3	3.6	13.4	18.4	7.7	24.3	10.7	8.4
15.4	4.9	2.8	7.9	11.9	12.0	16.2	6.8	14.7

Use the 0.05 level of significance.

10.24 The following are 15 measurements of the boiling point of a silicon compound (in degrees Celsius): 166, 141, 136, 153, 170, 162, 155, 146, 183, 157, 148, 132, 160, 175, and 150. Use the Kolmogorov-Smirnov test at the 0.01 level of significance to test the null hypothesis that the boiling points come from a normal population with $\mu = 160$ degrees Celsius and $\sigma = 10$ degrees Celsius.

REVIEW EXERCISES

10.25 Use the sign test, with level of significance 0.063, to test that the observations in Figure 2.2 on page 14 have median 0 against the alternative $\tilde{\mu} > 0$.

10.26 According to Einstein's theory of relativity, light should bend when it passes through a gravitational field. This was first tested experimentally in 1919 when photographs were taken of stars near the sun during a total eclipse and again when the sun had moved to another part of the sky. These eclipse pictures should show the stars displaced outwards from the position of the sun. The direction, in the first of 2 coordinate axes, predicted by the theory was matched by the observed direction for 6 out of 7 starts. Record $+$ for a match and $-$ for a mismatch. Guessing would give probability $\frac{1}{2}$ of a match. Use the sign test with level 0.063 to support the claim that the theory holds with respect to matching the direction of displacement.

10.27 With reference to Exercise 7.68, use the U statistic at the 0.05 level of significance to test whether Method B is more effective.

10.28 To find the best arrangement of instruments on a control panel of an airplane, 2 different arrangements were compared by simulating an emergency condition and measuring the reaction time required to correct the condition. The reaction times (in tenths of a second) of 20 pilots (randomly assigned to the 2 different arrangements) were as follows:

Arrangement 1:	8	15	10	13	17	10	9	11	12	15
Arrangement 2:	12	7	13	8	14	6	16	7	10	9

Use the U test at the 0.05 level of significance to check the claim that the second arrangement is better than the first.

10.29 The following are the miles per gallon which a test driver got for 10 tankfuls each of 3 brands of gasoline:

Brand 1:	22	25	32	18	23	15	30	27	19	23
Brand 2:	19	22	18	29	28	32	17	33	28	20
Brand 3:	30	29	25	24	15	27	30	27	18	32

Use the H test at the 0.05 level of significance to test whether there is a difference in the performance of the three brands of gasoline.

10.30 To test whether radio signals from deep space contain a message, an interval of time could be subdivided into a number of very short intervals and it could then be determined whether the signal strength exceeded a certain level (background noise) in each short interval. Suppose that the following is part of such a record, where H denotes a high signal strength and L denotes that the signal strength does not exceed a given noise level.

$$L L H L H L H L H L H H H L H H H L H H H L H L H L H L H L L L L$$

Test this sequence for randomness (using the 0.05 level of significance) and ascertain whether it is reasonable to assume that the signal contains a message.

10.31 The total number of retail stores opening for business and also quitting business within the calendar years 1958–1990 in a large city were 108, 103, 109, 107, 125, 142, 147, 122, 116, 153, 144, 162, 143, 126, 145, 129, 134, 137, 143, 150, 148, 152, 125, 106, 112, 139, 132, 122, 138, 148, 155, 146, and 158. Making use of the face that the median is 138, test at the 0.05 level of significance whether there is a significant trend.

10.32 When two populations have the same probability density function, each outcome of n_1 ranks for the first sample, out of the possible values $1, 2, \ldots, n_1 + n_2$, is equally likely.

  (a) Write out all of the possible outcomes when $n_1 = 3 = n_2$.
  (b) Evaluate U_1 at each of the outcomes and construct its probability distribution.

10.33 With reference to the example on page 14, use the U statistic to test the null hypothesis of equality versus the alternative that the distribution of copper content from the first heat is stochastically larger than the distribution for the second heat. Following the approach in Exercise 10.32, it can be shown that the exact distribution gives $P(U_1 \geq 19) = 0.033$. Use this as the level of significance.

10.34 The difference between the observed flux and the theoretical value was observed at 20 points within a reactor. The values were 2, -2, -4, -6, -3, -6, 3, -5, 2, 6, 8, 5, 3, 9, 7, 3, 2, -1, -3, -1. Use a sign test at the 0.036 level to test the null hypothesis $\tilde{\mu} = 0$ versus the alternative hypothesis $\tilde{\mu} \neq 0$.

10.35 With reference to Exercise 10.34, test for randomness with level 0.05.

10.36 Survival times (days) of fuel rods in a nuclear reactor are as follows:

16	11	24	18	31	15	12	21

Test at the 0.01 level of significance whether these data are consistent with the assumption of a log-normal distribution of survival times.

KEY TERMS

(with page references)

Curve Fitting

The main objective of many statistical investigations is to make predictions, preferably on the basis of mathematical equations. For instance, an engineer may wish to predict the amount of oxide that will form on the surface of a metal baked in an oven for one hour at 200 degrees Celsius, or the amount of deformation of a ring subjected to a compressive force of 1,000 pounds, or the number of miles to wear out a tire having a given tread thickness and composition. Usually, such predictions require that a formula be found which relates the dependent variable (whose value one wants to predict) to one or more independent variables.

Problems relating to predictions which are based on the known value of one variable are treated in Sections 11.1 through 11.3 and 11.6; the case where predictions are based on the known values of several variables is treated in Section 11.4. The importance of checking the assumptions concerning the prediction model is considered in Section 11.5. ■

11.1   The Method of Least Squares

In this section we begin our study of the case where a dependent variable is to be predicted in terms of a single independent variable. In many problems of this kind the independent variable is observed without error, or with an error which is negligible when compared with the error (chance variation) in the dependent variable. For example, in measuring the amount of oxide on the surface of a metal specimen, the baking temperature can usually be controlled with good precision, but the oxide-thickness measurement may be subject to considerable chance variation. Thus, even though the independent variable may be fixed at x, repeated measurements of the dependent variable may lead to y-values which differ considerably. Such differences among y-values can be attributed to several causes, chiefly to errors of measurement and to the existence of other, uncontrolled variables which may influence the value of Y when x is fixed. Thus, measurements of the thickness of oxide layers may vary over several specimens baked for the same length of time at the same temperature because of the difficulty in measuring thickness as well as possible differences in the composition of the oven atmosphere, surface conditions of the specimens, and the like.

It should be apparent from this discussion that in this context Y is a random variable whose distribution depends on x. In most situations of this sort we are interested mainly in the relationship between x and the mean of the corresponding distribution of Y, and we refer to this relationship as the **regression curve of Y on x.** (For the time being we shall consider the case where x is fixed, that is, not random; in Section 11.6 we shall consider the case where x and y are both values of random variables.)

Let us first treat the case where the regression curve of Y on x is **linear,** that is, where for any given x, the mean of the distribution of the Y's is given by $\alpha + \beta x$. In general, Y will differ from this mean, and we shall denote this difference by ε, writing

$$Y = \alpha + \beta x + \varepsilon$$

Thus, ε is a random variable and we can always choose α so that the mean of the distribution of this random variable is equal to zero. The value of ε for any given observation will depend on a possible error of measurement and on the values of variables other than x which might have an influence on Y.

To give an example where the regression curve of Y on x can reasonably be assumed to be linear, suppose that a tensile ring is to be calibrated by measuring the deflection at various loads. In the following table, giving the results of 12 measurements, the x's are the load forces in thousands of pounds and the y's are the corresponding deflections in thousandths of an inch:

x	1	2	3	4	5	6	7	8	9	10	11	12
y	16	35	45	64	86	96	106	124	134	156	164	182

It is apparent from Figure 11.1, where these data have been plotted, that it is reasonable to assume that the relationship (regression curve) is linear; that is, a straight line gives a very good approximation over the range of the available data. This kind of diagram, which shows how the data points are scattered, is called a **scattergram** or **scatter plot.**

Now we face the problem of using the observed data to estimate the parameters α and β of the regression line, and this is equivalent to finding the equation of the straight line that somehow provides the best fit. In connection with Figure 11.1, it may well be satisfactory to do this by eye. If different experimenters were to fit a line in this way, they would probably all predict that for a load of 7,500 pounds the deflection should be close to 0.115 inch. However, if we have to deal with data

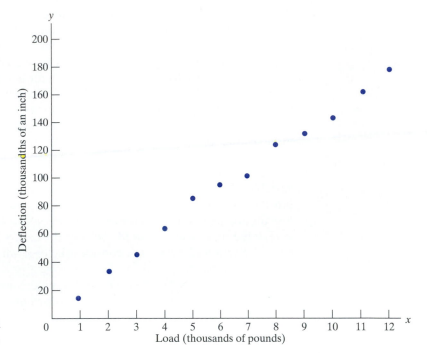

FIGURE 11.1 Scattergram indicating linear regression.

such as those plotted in Figure 11.2, the problem of finding a best-fitting line is not so obvious. To handle problems of this kind, we must seek a nonsubjective method for fitting straight lines which reflects some desirable statistical properties.

To state the problem formally, we have n paired observations (x_i, y_i) for which it is reasonable to assume that the regression of Y on x is linear, and we want to determine the line (that is, the equation of the line) which in some sense provides the best fit. There are several ways in which we interpret the word "best," and the meaning we shall give it here may be explained as follows. If we predict y by means of the equation

$$\hat{y} = a + bx$$

where a and b are constants, then e_i, the error in predicting the value of y corresponding to the given x_i, is

$$e_i = y_i - \hat{y}_i$$

and we shall want to determine a and b so that these errors are in some sense as small as possible.

Since we cannot minimize each of the e_i individually, we might try to make their sum $\sum_{i=1}^{n} e_i$ as close as possible to zero. However, since this sum can be made equal to zero by many choices of totally unsuitable lines for which the positive and negative errors cancel, we shall minimize the sum of the squares of the e_i (for the same reason we worked with the squares of the deviations from the mean in the definition of the standard deviation). In other words, we apply the **principle of least squares** and choose a and b so that

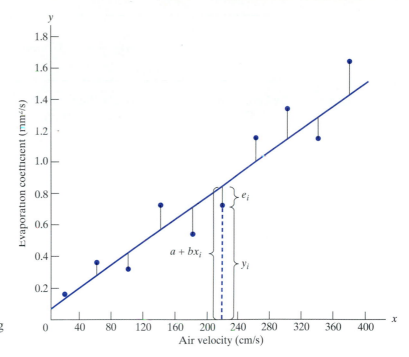

FIGURE 11.2 Diagram for least squares criterion showing the vertical deviations.

$$\sum_{i=1}^{n} [y_i - (a + bx_i)]^2$$

is a minimum. Note from Figure 11.2 that this is equivalent to minimizing the sum of the squares of the vertical distances from the points to the line.

The procedure of finding the equation of the line which best fits a given set of paired data, called the **method of least squares,** yields values for a and b (estimates of α and β) that have many desirable properties; some of these are mentioned on page 337.

Before minimizing the sum of squared deviations to obtain the **least squares estimators,** it is convenient to introduce some notation for the sums of squares and sums of cross-products.

$$S_{xx} = \sum_{i=1}^{n} (x_i - \bar{x})^2 = \sum_{i=1}^{n} x_i^2 - \left(\sum_{i=1}^{n} x_i \right)^2 \Big/ n$$

$$S_{yy} = \sum_{i=1}^{n} (y_i - \bar{y})^2 = \sum_{i=1}^{n} y_i^2 - \left(\sum_{i=1}^{n} y_i \right)^2 \Big/ n$$

$$S_{xy} = \sum_{i=1}^{n} (x_i - \bar{x})(y_i - \bar{y}) = \sum_{i=1}^{n} x_i y_i - \left(\sum_{i=1}^{n} x_i \right) \left(\sum_{i=1}^{n} y_i \right) \Big/ n$$

The first expressions are preferred on conceptual grounds because they highlight deviations from the mean and on computing grounds because they are less susceptible to roundoff error. The second expressions are for hand-held calculators.

Below, we show that the least squares estimates are

Least squares estimates

$$a = \bar{y} - b \cdot \bar{x} \quad \text{and} \quad b = \frac{S_{xy}}{S_{xx}}$$

where $\bar{x}$ and $\bar{y}$ are, respectively, the means of the x's and y's.
The least squares estimates determine the best fitting line

Fitted (or estimated) regression line

$$\hat{y} = a + bx$$

where the $\smallfrown$ on y indicates the estimated value.

The individual deviations of the observations y_i from their fitted values $\hat{y}_i = a + bx_i$ are called the **residuals.**

Residuals

$$\text{observation} - \text{fitted value} = y_i - a - bx_i$$

The minimum value of the sum of squares is called the **residual sum of squares** or **error sum of squares**. Below we show that

$$residual \ sum \ of \ squares = \sum_{i=1}^{n}(y_i - a - bx_i)^2 = S_{yy} - S_{xy}^2/S_{xx}$$

EXAMPLE

A numerical example of fitting a straight line by least squares
The following are measurements of the air velocity and evaporation coefficient of burning fuel droplets in an impulse engine:

Air velocity (cm/sec) x	Evaporation coefficient (mm²/sec) y
20	0.18
60	0.37
100	0.35
140	0.78
180	0.56
220	0.75
260	1.18
300	1.36
340	1.17
380	1.65

Fit a straight line to these data by the method of least squares, and use it to estimate the evaporation coefficient of a droplet when the air velocity is 190 cm/s.

Solution For these $n = 10$ pairs (x_i, y_i) we first calculate

$$\sum_{i=1}^{n} x_i = 2{,}000, \quad \sum_{i=1}^{n} x_i^2 = 532{,}000$$

$$\sum_{i=1}^{n} y_i = 8.35, \quad \sum_{i=1}^{n} x_i y_i = 2{,}175.40$$

$$\sum_{i=1}^{n} y_i^2 = 9.1097$$

and then we obtain

$$S_{xx} = 532{,}000 - (2{,}000)^2/10 = 132{,}000$$

$$S_{xy} = 2{,}175.40 - (2{,}000)(8.35)/10 = 505.40$$

$$S_{yy} = 9.1097 - (8.35)^2/10 = 2.13745$$

Consequently

$$b = \frac{S_{xy}}{S_{xx}} = \frac{505.40}{132{,}000} = 0.00383$$

and then

$$a = \bar{y} - b\bar{x} = \frac{8.35}{10} - 0.00383\frac{2{,}000}{10} = 0.069$$

Thus, the equation of the straight line that best fits the given data in the sense of least squares is

$$\hat{y} = 0.069 + 0.00383x$$

and for $x = 190$ we predict that the evaporation coefficient will be

$$\hat{y} = 0.069 + 0.00383(190) = 0.80 \text{ mm}^2/sec.$$

Finally, the residual sum of squares is

$$S_{yy} - \frac{S_{xy}^2}{S_{xx}} = 2.13745 - \frac{(505.40)^2}{132{,}000} = 0.20238$$ ✔

Determining the Least Squares Estimators

We now show that the choice of estimates

$$b = \frac{S_{xy}}{S_{xx}} \qquad a = \bar{y} - b\bar{x}$$

minimizes the sum of squares, $D(a, b) = \sum_{i=1}^{n}(y_i - a - bx_i)^2$, over all choices of a and b. We first find an alternative expression for the sum of squares for any a and b. Adding and subtracting $b\bar{x} - \bar{y}$, we have

$$y_i - a - bx_i = (y_i - \bar{y}) - b(x_i - \bar{x}) + (\bar{y} - a - b\bar{x})$$

Squaring both sides, we obtain

$$(y_i - a - bx_i)^2 = (y_i - \bar{y})^2 + b^2(x_i - \bar{x})^2 + (\bar{y} - a - b\bar{x})^2$$
$$-2b(y_i - \bar{y})(x_i - \bar{x}) - 2b(\bar{y} - a - b\bar{x})(x_i - \bar{x}) + 2(y_i - \bar{y})(\bar{y} - a - b\bar{x})$$

Now, summing over both sides, the last two terms vanish so we obtain

$$D(a, b) = S_{yy} + b^2 S_{xx} + n(\bar{y} - a - b\bar{x})^2 - 2bS_{xy}$$

$$= n(\bar{y} - a - b\bar{x})^2 + \left(b^2 S_{xx} - 2bS_{xy} + \frac{S_{xy}^2}{S_{xx}} \right) + S_{yy} - \frac{S_{xy}^2}{S_{xx}}$$

$$= n(\bar{y} - a - b\bar{x})^2 + \left(b\sqrt{S_{xx}} - \frac{S_{xy}}{\sqrt{S_{xx}}} \right)^2 + S_{yy} - \frac{S_{xy}^2}{S_{xx}}$$

According to the principle of least squares, we must select values for a and b which will minimize this sum of squares. All three terms on the right hand side are non-negative and the third term does not depend on the choice of a and b. The second term can be made to equal zero, its minimum value, by taking $b = S_{xy}/S_{xx}$. With this choice for b, the first term can be made equal to zero by taking $a = \bar{y} - b\bar{x}$. This confirms the formula for the least squares estimators on page 334.

Further, we have shown that the minimized sum of squares equals the third term. That is, the sum of squares error

$$\text{SSE} = S_{yy} - S_{xy}^2/S_{xx}$$

as stated on the previous page.

The estimate of σ^2 is

$$s_e^2 = \frac{\sum_{i=1}^n (y_i - a - bx_i)^2}{n - 2} \qquad \text{or} \qquad s_e^2 = \frac{S_{yy} - S_{xy}^2/S_{xx}}{n - 2}$$

Normal Equations for the Least Squares Estimators

A necessary condition that the sum of squared deviations, $\sum_{i=1}^n (y_i - a - bx_i)^2$, be a minimum is the vanishing of the partial derivatives with respect to a and b. We thus have

$$2 \sum_{i=1}^n [y_i - (a + bx_i)](-1) = 0$$

$$2 \sum_{i=1}^n [y_i - (a + bx_i)](-x_i) = 0$$

and we can rewrite these two equations as

Normal equations

$$\sum_{i=1}^n y_i = an + b \sum_{i=1}^n x_i$$

$$\sum_{i=1}^n x_i y_i = a \sum_{i=1}^n x_i + b \sum_{i=1}^n x_i^2$$

This set of two linear equations in the unknowns a and b, called the **normal equations,** gives the values of a and b for the line which provides the best fit to a given set of paired data in accordance with the criterion of least squares.

EXAMPLE	**The least square estimates obtained from the normal equations**

Solve the normal equations for the data in the previous example and confirm the values for the least squares estimates.

Solution Using the calculations in the previous example, the normal equations are

$$8.35 = 10a + 2{,}000b$$

$$2{,}175.40 = 2{,}000a + 532{,}000b$$

Solving this system of equations by use of determinants or the method of elimination, we obtain $a = .069$ and $b = 0.00383$.

These values are the same as those obtained in the previous example. ✔

It is impossible to make any exact statements about the "goodness" of an estimate like this unless we make some assumptions about the underlying distributions of the random variables with which we are concerned and about the true nature of the regression. Looking upon the values of a and b as estimates of the actual regression coefficients α and β, the reader will be asked to show in Exercise 11.20 on page 348 that these estimates are linear in the observations y_i and that they are values of unbiased estimators of α and β. With these properties, we can refer to the remarkable **Gauss-Markov theorem,** which states that among all unbiased estimators for α and β which are linear in the Y_i, the least squares estimators have the smallest variance. In other words, the least squares estimators are the most reliable in the sense that they are subject to the smallest chance variations. A proof of the Gauss-Markov theorem may be found in the book by Johnson and Wichern referred to in the bibliography.

11.2 Inferences Based on the Least-Squares Estimators

The method of the preceding section is used when the relationship between x and the mean of Y is linear or close enough to a straight line so that the least-squares line yields reasonably good predictions. In what follows we shall assume that the regression *is* linear and furthermore that the n random variables Y_i are independently normally distributed with the means $\alpha + \beta x_i$ and the common variance σ^2 for $i = 1, 2, \ldots, n$. Equivalently, we write the model as

Statistical model
for straight line
regression

$$Y_i = \alpha + \beta x_i + \varepsilon_i \quad \text{for} \quad i = 1, 2, \ldots, n$$

where it is assumed that the ε_i are independent normally distributed random variables having zero means and the common variance σ^2.

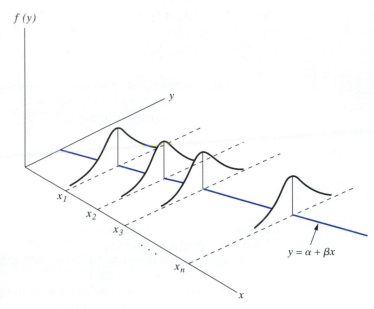

$f(y)$

y

x_1

x_2

x_3

$\cdots$

x_n

$y = \alpha + \beta x$

x

FIGURE 11.3 Diagram
showing assumptions
underlying Theorem 11.1.

The various assumptions we have made here are illustrated in Figure 11.3,
showing the distributions of Y_i for several values of x_i. Note that these additional assumptions are required to discuss the goodness of predictions based on least-
squares equations, the properties of a and b as estimates of α and β, and so on;
they were not required to obtain the original estimates based on the method of
least squares.

Before we state a theorem concerning the distribution of the least squares estimators of α and β, we review the formulas for calculating the least squares estimators and then present an estimate of the error variance σ^2.

Recall from page 334 that the values for the least squares estimators of α and
β are given by

$$a = \overline{y} - b \cdot \overline{x} \qquad\qquad b = \frac{S_{xy}}{S_{xx}}$$

where S_{xx} and S_{xy} are defined on page 333 along with S_{yy}.

Note the close relationship between S_{xx} and S_{yy} and the respective sample
variances of the x's and the y's; in fact, $s_x^2 = S_{xx}/(n-1)$ and $s_y^2 = S_{yy}/(n-1)$, and
we shall sometimes use this alternative notation.

The variance σ^2 defined on page 337 is usually estimated in terms of the vertical deviations of the sample points from the least squares line. The ith such deviation is $y_i - \hat{y}_i = y_i - (a + bx_i)$ and the estimate of σ^2 is

$$s_e^2 = \frac{1}{n-2}\sum_{i=1}^n [y_i - (a + bx_i)]^2$$

where s_e is, traditionally, referred to as the **standard error of estimate.** This estimate is the **residual sum of squares,** or the **error sum of squares,** divided by $n - 2$.
An equivalent formula for this estimate of σ^2, which is more convenient for hand-
held calculators, is given by

Estimate of σ^2

$$s_e^2 = \frac{S_{yy} - (S_{xy})^2/S_{xx}}{n-2}$$

In these formulas the divisor $n-2$ is used to make the resulting estimator for σ^2 unbiased. It can be shown that under the given assumptions $(n-2)s_e^2/\sigma^2$ is a value of a random variable having the chi-square distribution with $n-2$ degrees of freedom. The "loss" of two degrees of freedom is explained by the fact that the two regression coefficients α and β had to be replaced by their least squares estimates.

Based on the assumptions made concerning the distribution of the Y's, one can prove the following theorem concerning the distributions of the least-squares estimators of the regression coefficients α and β.

Statistics for inferences about α and β

Theorem 11.1 Under the assumptions given on page 337, the statistics

$$t = \frac{(a-\alpha)}{s_e}\sqrt{\frac{nS_{xx}}{S_{xx} + n(\bar{x})^2}}$$

and

$$t = \frac{(b-\beta)}{s_e}\sqrt{S_{xx}}$$

are values of random variables having the t distribution with $n-2$ degrees of freedom.

To construct confidence intervals for the regression coefficients α and β, we substitute for the middle term of $-t_{\alpha/2} < t < t_{\alpha/2}$ the appropriate t statistic of Theorem 11.1. Then, simple algebra leads to

Confidence limits for regression coefficients

$$\alpha: \quad a \pm t_{\alpha/2} \cdot s_e \sqrt{\frac{1}{n} + \frac{(\bar{x})^2}{S_{xx}}}$$

and

$$\beta: \quad b \pm t_{\alpha/2} \cdot s_e \frac{1}{\sqrt{S_{xx}}}$$

EXAMPLE

A confidence interval for the intercept
With reference to the example on page 334, construct a 95% confidence interval for the regression coefficient α.

Solution Using the numerical results on page 335, $n = 10, \bar{x} = 200$

$$S_{xx} = 132{,}000$$

$$S_{yy} = 2.13745$$

$$S_{xy} = 505.40$$

$$s_e^2 = \frac{2.13745 - (505.40)^2/132,000}{8} = \frac{.20238}{8} = 0.0253$$

Since $t_{0.025} = 2.306$ for $10 - 2 = 8$ degrees of freedom and $s_e = \sqrt{.0253} = 0.159$, we get the 95% confidence limits

$$0.069 \pm (2.306)(0.159)\sqrt{\frac{1}{10} + \frac{(200)^2}{132,000}}$$

and, hence, the 95% confidence interval

$$-0.164 < \alpha < 0.302$$

Note that 0 is a plausible value for α so the line could pass through the origin. ✔

In connection with tests of hypotheses concerning the regression coefficients α and β, those concerning β are of special importance because β is the **slope of the regression line;** that is, β is the change in the mean of Y corresponding to a unit increase in x. If $\beta = 0$, the regression line is horizontal and the mean of Y does not depend linearly on x. For tests of the null hypothesis $\beta = \beta_0$, we use the second statistic of Theorem 11.1 and the criteria are like those in the table on page 246 with μ replaced by β.

EXAMPLE

A test of hypotheses concerning the slope parameter

With reference to the example on page 334, test the null hypothesis $\beta = 0$ against the alternative hypothesis $\beta \neq 0$ at the 0.05 level of significance.

Solution

1. *Null hypothesis: $\beta = 0$*
   Alternative hypothesis: $\beta \neq 0$

2. *Level of significance: $\alpha = 0.05$*

3. *Criterion:* Reject the null hypothesis if $t < -2.306$ or $t > 2.306$, where 2.306 is the value of $t_{0.025}$ for $10 - 2 = 8$ degrees of freedom, and t is given by the second formula of Theorem 11.1.

4. *Calculations:* Using the quantities obtained above and on page 335 we get

$$t = \frac{0.00383 - 0}{0.159}\sqrt{132,000} = 8.75$$

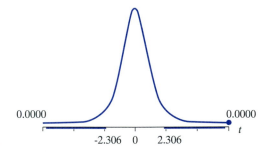

FIGURE 11.4 The extremely small P value.

5. *Decision:* Since $t = 8.75$ exceeds 2.306, the null hypothesis must be rejected; we conclude that there is a relationship between air velocity and the average evaporation coefficient. (The relationship is linear by the scatter plot in Figure 11.2 which confirms the assumptions that underly the test.)

   The evidence for non-zero slope β is extremely strong with P value less than 0.0000 (See Figure 11.4). ✔

Most statistical software packages include a least-squares fit of a straight line. When the number of (x_i, y_i) pairs is moderate to large, a computer should be used. We illustrate with the deflection-strength data on page 331. The first step is to plot the data (see Exercise 11.22), but this was already done on page 332. Typical output from a regression analysis program includes:

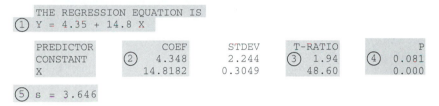

The least-squares line ① is $\hat{y} = 4.35 + 14.8x$ and the estimate of σ^2 is $s_e^2 = (3.646)^2 = 13.29$ using ⑤ $s_e = 3.646$.

Since ③ $t = 48.60$, with $n - 2 = 10$ degrees of freedom, is highly significant, the slope is different from zero. We would expect the deflection to be 0 at 0 load but this is outside of the range of experimentation. Even so, in this case, our least-squares analysis yields $t = 1.94$, which suggests that the constant term α may not be needed in the equation. Further, the large ④ P value $= 0.081$ confirms that the constant term is not needed to fit the data.

In Exercise 11.22, more output is described and the least-squares analysis is modified to treat a possible outlier at $x = 5$.

We will return to this least squares fit in Section 11.5, where we investigate the assumptions of a straight-line model and the normal distribution for errors.

Figure 11.5 gives the *SAS* output for a least squares fit with the deflection-strength data. Notice that more decimal places are given, for instance ⑤ $s_e = RootMSE = 3.64609$, and the ④ P value $0.0001 = Prob > |T|$ is given for testing $\beta = 0$ versus $\beta \neq 0$.

Another problem, closely related to the problem of estimating the regression coefficients α and β, is that of estimating $\alpha + \beta x$, namely, the mean of the distribution of Y for a given value of x. If x is held fixed at x_0, the quantity we want to estimate is $\alpha + \beta x_0$ and it would seem reasonable to use $a + bx_0$, where a and b are again the values obtained by the method of least squares. In fact, it can be shown that this estimator is unbiased, has the variance

$$\sigma^2 \left[\frac{1}{n} + \frac{(x_0 - \bar{x})^2}{S_{xx}} \right]$$

and that $(1 - \alpha) 100\%$ confidence limits for $\alpha + \beta x_0$ are given by

Dependent Variable: Y

Analysis of Variance

Source	DF	Sum of Squares	Mean Square	F Value	Prob > F
Model	1	31399.72727	31399.72727	2361.958	0.001
Error	10	132.93939	13.29394		
C Total	11	31532.66667			

Root MSE	⑤ 3.64609	R-square	0.9958
Dep Mean	100.66667	Adj R-sq	0.9954
C.V.	3.62194		

Parameter Estimates

Variable	DF	Parameter Estimate	Standard Error	T for HO: Parameter = 0	Prob > |T|
INTERCEP	1	② 4.348485	2.24401050	③ 1.938	0.0814 ④
X	1	14.818182	0.30490099	48.600	0.0001

SUM OF RESIDUALS   1.59872E-14
SUM OF SQUARED RESIDUALS   132.9394

FIGURE 11.5
Selected SAS output for a regression analysis using the deflection-strength data on page 331.

Confidence limits for $\alpha + \beta x_0$

$$(a + bx_0) \pm t_{\alpha/2} \cdot s_e \sqrt{\frac{1}{n} + \frac{(x_0 - \bar{x})^2}{S_{xx}}}$$

where the number of degrees of freedom for $t_{\alpha/2}$ is $n - 2$.

EXAMPLE

A confidence interval for the mean response at $x_0 = 190$
With reference to the example on page 334, construct a 95% confidence interval for the mean evaporation coefficient when the air velocity is 190 cm/s.

Solution Substituting the various quantities already calculated on pages 335 and 340 into the above formula, we get

$$0.80 \pm (2.306)(0.159)\sqrt{\frac{1}{10} + \frac{(190 - 200)^2}{132,000}}$$

and, hence, the 95% confidence interval

$$(0.68, 0.92)$$

for the mean evaporation coefficient $\alpha + 190\beta$. ✔

Of even greater importance than the estimation of $\alpha + \beta x_0$ is the prediction of a future value of Y when $x = x_0$, where x_0 is within the range of experimentation. (We added "within the range of experimentation" because, here as elsewhere, extrapolation is risky and a linear relationship we have observed may not continue beyond that range.) Thus, for our example we already showed on page 335 that for an air velocity of 190 cm/s, a value well within the range of experimentation, the predicted evaporation coefficient is 0.79 mm²/s.

To emphasize the danger inherent when extrapolating beyond the range of experimentation, consider the plot of conductivity versus temperature (*Source:* K. Onnes

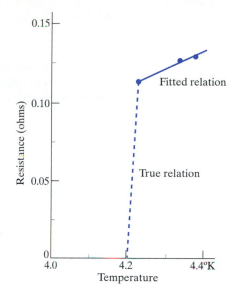

FIGURE 11.6 Resistance versus temperature for a specimen of mercury. A model change invalidates extrapolation.

(1912) *Communications of the Physical Laboratory at the University of Leiden*, no. 124, unnumbered figure) in Figure 11.6. If the line is extended to predict conductivity at 4.10° Kelvin, we would predict 0.10 ohms. This is much greater than the value of 0, which Onnes observed when he discovered superconductivity at 4.19° Kelvin. That is, the physical model changes drastically outside of the experimental range shown.

Now let us indicate a method of constructing an interval in which a future observation , Y, can be expected to lie with a given probability (or confidence) when $x = x_0$. If α and β were known, we could use the fact that Y is a random variable having a normal distribution with the mean $\alpha + \beta x_0$ and the variance σ^2 (or that $Y - \alpha - \beta x_0$ is a random variable having a normal distribution with zero mean and the variance σ^2). However, if α and β are not known, we must consider the quantity $Y - a - bx_0$, where Y, a, and b are all random variables, and the resulting theory leads to the following **limits of prediction** for a future observed value y when $x = x_0$:

Limits of prediction

$$(a + bx_0) \pm t_{\alpha/2} \cdot s_e \sqrt{1 + \frac{1}{n} + \frac{(x_0 - \bar{x})^2}{S_{xx}}}$$

The number of degrees of freedom for $t_{\alpha/2}$ is again $n - 2$.

EXAMPLE

95% prediction limits for a future observation at $x_0 = 190$
With reference to the example on page 334, find 95% limits of prediction for an observation of the evaporation coefficient when the air velocity is 190 cm/s.

Solution   Adding a 1 under the radical in the preceding example, we get

$$0.80 \pm (2.306)(0.159)\sqrt{1 + \frac{1}{10} + \frac{(190 - 200)^2}{132{,}000}}$$

and, hence, the limits of prediction are $0.80 - 0.39 = 0.41$ and $0.80 + 0.39 = 1.19$. ✔

Note that although the mean of the distribution of Y when $x = 190$ can be estimated fairly closely, the value of a single future observation cannot be predicted with much precision. Indeed, even as $n \to \infty$ the difference between the limits of prediction does not approach zero; the limiting width of the interval of prediction depends on s_e, which measures the inherent variability of the data.

Note further that if we do wish to extrapolate, the interval of prediction (and also the confidence interval for $\alpha + \beta x_0$) becomes increasingly wide.

EXAMPLE

The limits of prediction become wider if x_0 is further from $\bar{x}$

With reference to the example on page 334, assume that the linear relationship continues beyond the range of experimentation and find 95% limits of prediction for an observation of the evaporation coefficient when the air velocity is 450 cm/s.

Solution

Substituting the various quantities already calculated on pages 335 and 340 into the formula above, we get

$$1.79 \pm (2.306)(0.159)\sqrt{1 + \frac{1}{10} + \frac{(450 - 200)^2}{132,000}}$$

and, hence, the limits of prediction are $1.79 - 0.46 = 1.33$ and $1.79 + 0.46 = 2.25 \text{ mm}^2/\text{s}$. The width of this interval of prediction is $2(0.46) = 0.92$ compared to the width of $2(0.39) = 0.78$ obtained in the preceding example. ✔

EXERCISES

11.1 A chemical company, wishing to study the effect of extraction time on the efficiency of an extraction operation, obtained the data shown in the following table:

Extraction time (minutes) x	Extraction efficiency (%) y
27	57
45	64
41	80
19	46
35	62
39	72
19	52
49	77
15	57
31	68

(a) Draw a scattergram to verify that a straight line will provide a good fit to the data, draw a straight line by eye, and use it to predict the extraction efficiency one can expect when the extraction time is 35 minutes.

(b) Fit a straight line to the given data by the method of least squares and use it to predict the extraction efficiency one can expect when the extraction time is 35 minutes.

11.2 In the accompanying table, x is the tensile force applied to a steel specimen in thousands of pounds, and y is the resulting elongation in thousandths of an inch:

x	1	2	3	4	5	6
y	14	33	40	63	76	85

(a) Graph the data to verify that it is reasonable to assume that the regression of Y on x is linear.

(b) Find the equation of the least squares line, and use it to predict the elongation when the tensile force is 3.5 thousand pounds.

11.3 With reference to the preceding exercise,

(a) construct a 95% confidence interval for β, the elongation per thousand pounds of tensile stress;

(b) find 95% limits of prediction for the elongation of a specimen with $x = 3.5$ thousand pounds.

11.4 The following table shows how many weeks a sample of 6 persons have worked at an automobile inspection station and the number of cars each one inspected between noon and 2 P.M. on a given day:

Number of weeks employed x	Number of cars inspected y
2	13
7	21
9	23
1	14
5	15
12	21

(a) Find the equation of the least squares line which will enable us to predict y in terms of x.

(b) Use the result of part (a) to estimate how many cars someone who has been working at the inspection station for 8 weeks can be expected to inspect during the given 2-hour period.

11.5 With reference to the preceding exercise, test the null hypothesis $\beta = 1.2$ against the alternative hypothesis $\beta < 1.2$ at the 0.05 level of significance.

11.6 With reference to Exercise 11.4 find

(a) a 95% confidence interval for the average number of cars inspected in the given period of time by a person who has been working at the inspection station for 8 weeks;

    (b) 95% limits of prediction for the number of cars that will be inspected in the given period of time by a person who has worked at the inspection station for 8 weeks.

11.7 The following data pertain to the number of computer jobs per day and the central processing unit (CPU) time required.

Number of jobs x	CPU time y
1	2
2	5
3	4
4	9
5	10

    (a) Use the first set of expressions on page 333, involving the deviations from the mean, to obtain a least squares fit of a line to the observations on CPU time.

    (b) Use the equation of the least squares line to estimate the mean CPU time at $x = 3.5$.

11.8 With reference to Exercise 11.7, construct a 95% confidence interval for α.

11.9 With reference to Exercise 11.7, test the null hypothesis $\beta = 2$ against the alternative hypothesis $\beta > 2$ at the 0.05 level of significance.

11.10 Raw material used in the production of a synthetic fiber is stored in a place which has no humidity control. Measurements of the relative humidity in the storage place and the moisture content of a sample of the raw material (both in percentages) on 12 days yielded the following results:

Humidity x	Moisture content y
42	12
35	8
50	14
43	9
48	11
62	16
31	7
36	9
44	12
39	10
55	13
48	11

    (a) Plot a scattergram to verify that it is reasonable to assume that the regression of Y on x is linear.

    (b) Fit a straight line by the method of least squares.

    (c) Find a 99% confidence interval for the mean moisture content of the raw material when the humidity of the storage place is 40%.

11.11 With reference to the preceding exercise, find 95% limits of prediction for the moisture content of the raw material when the humidity of the storage place is 40%. Also indicate to what extent the width of the interval is affected by the size of the sample and to what extent it is affected by the inherent variability of the data.

11.12 The following show the improvement (gain in reading speed) of 8 students in a speed-reading program, and the number of weeks they have been in the program:

Number of weeks	Speed gain (words per minute)
3	86
5	118
2	49
8	193
6	164
9	232
3	73
4	109

(a) Plot a scattergram to verify that it is reasonable to assume that the regression of speed gain on the number of weeks is linear.

(b) Fit a straight line by the method of least squares.

11.13 With reference to Exercise 11.12, find a 90% confidence interval for β.

11.14 With reference to Exercise 11.1, express 95% limits of prediction for the extraction efficiency in terms of the extraction time x_0. Choosing suitable values of x_0, sketch graphs of the loci of the upper and lower limits of prediction on the diagram of part (a) of Exercise 11.1. Note that since any two sets of limits of prediction obtained from these bands are dependent, they should be used only once for a single extraction time x_0.

11.15 In Exercises 11.2 and 11.12 it would have been entirely reasonable to impose the condition $\alpha = 0$ before fitting a straight line by the method of least squares.

(a) Use the method of least squares to derive a formula for estimating β when the regression line has the form $y = \beta x$.

(b) With reference to Exercise 11.2, use the formula obtained in part (a) to estimate β and compare the result with the estimate previously obtained without the condition that the line must pass through the origin.

(c) With reference to Exercise 11.12, use the formula obtained in part (a) to estimate β and compare the result with the estimate previously obtained without the condition that the line must pass through the origin.

11.16 The cost of manufacturing a lot of a certain product depends on the lot size, as shown by the following sample data:

Cost (dollars)	30	70	140	270	530	1,010	2,500	5,020
Lot size	1	5	10	25	50	100	250	500

(a) Draw a scattergram to verify the assumption that the relationship is linear, letting lot size be x and cost y.

(b) Fit a straight line to these data by the method of least squares, using lot size as the independent variable, and draw its graph on the diagram obtained in part (a).

11.17 With reference to Exercise 11.16, find a 90% confidence interval for α, which can be interpreted here as the fixed overhead cost of manufacturing.

11.18 With reference to Exercise 11.16, fit a straight line to the data by the method of least squares, using cost as the independent variable, and draw its graph on the diagram obtained in part (a) of Exercise 11.16. Note that the two estimated regression lines do not coincide.

11.19 When the sum of the x values is equal to zero, the calculation of the coefficients of the regression line of Y on x is greatly simplified; in fact, their estimates are given by

$$a = \frac{\sum y}{n} \quad \text{and} \quad b = \frac{\sum xy}{\sum x^2}$$

This simplification can also be attained when the x's are equally spaced, that is, when they are in arithmetic progression. We then code the data by substituting for the x's the values $\ldots, -2, -1, 0, 1, 2, \ldots$, when n is odd, or the values $\ldots, -3, -1, 1, 3, \ldots$, when n is even. The preceding formulas are then used in connection with the coded data.

(a) During its first 7 years of operation, a company's gross income from sales was 1.4, 2.1, 2.6, 3.5, 3.7, 4.9, and 5.5 million dollars. Fit a least-squares line and, assuming that the trend continues, predict the company's gross income from sales during the eighth year of operation.

(b) At the ends of years 1992–1999 a manufacturing company had the following net investments in plants and equipment: 1.0, 1.7, 2.3, 3.1, 3.5, 3.4, 3.9, and 4.7 million dollars. Fit a least squares line and, assuming that the trend continues, predict the company's net investment in plant and equipment at the end of 2001.

11.20 Using the formulas on page 334 for a and b, show that

(a) the expression for a is linear in the y_i;

(b) a is an unbiased estimate of α.

(c) the expression for b is linear in the y_i;

(d) b is an unbiased estimate of β.

11.21 The decomposition of the sums of squares into a contribution due to error and a contribution due to regression underlies the least-squares analysis. Consider the identity

$$y_i - \bar{y} - (\hat{y}_i - \bar{y}) = (y_i - \hat{y}_i)$$

Note that $\hat{y}_i = a + bx_i = \bar{y} - b\bar{x} + bx_i = \bar{y} + b(x_i - \bar{x})$ so $\hat{y}_i - \bar{y} = b(x_i - \bar{x})$. Using this last expression, then the definition of b and again the last expression, we see that

$$\sum (y_i - \bar{y})(\hat{y}_i - \bar{y}) = b \sum (y_i - \bar{y})(x_i - \bar{x}) = b^2 \sum (x_i - \bar{x})^2 = \sum (\hat{y}_i - \bar{y})^2$$

and the sum of squares about the mean can be decomposed as

$$\underset{\text{total sum of squares}}{\sum_{i=1}^{n} (y_i - \bar{y})^2} \quad = \quad \underset{\text{error sum of squares}}{\sum_{i=1}^{n} (y_i - \hat{y}_i)^2} \quad + \quad \underset{\text{regression sum of squares}}{\sum_{i=1}^{n} (\hat{y}_i - \bar{y})^2}$$

Generally, we find the straight-line fit acceptable if the ratio

$$r^2 = \frac{\text{regression sum of squares}}{\text{total sum of squares}} = 1 - \frac{\sum_{i=1}^{n} (y_i - \hat{y}_i)^2}{\sum_{i=1}^{n} (y_i - \bar{y})^2}$$

is near 1.

Calculate the decomposition of the sum of squares and calculate r^2 using the observations in Exercise 11.7.

11.22 It is tedious to perform a least squares analysis without using a computer. We illustrate a computer-based analysis using the *MINITAB* package. The observations on page 331 are entered in C1 and C2 of the worksheet.

DATA 11-22.DAT
LOAD: 1   2   3   4   5   6   7   8   9   10   11   12
DEFLECTION: 16   35   45   64   86   96   106   124   134   156   164   182

We first obtain the scatter plot to see if a straight-line pattern is evident.

Dialog box:	**Session command**
Graph>Plot	MTB>PLOT C2 VERSUS C1
Type *C2* in **Y** column and	
Type *C1* in **X** column. Click **OK.**	

Then,

Dialog box:	**Session command**
Stat>Regression>Regression	MTB>REGRESS C2 ON 1 PRED C1
Type *C2* in **Response.**	
Type *C1* in **Predictors.** Click **OK.**	

---

produces the output

```
The regression equation is
y = 4.35 + 14.8 x

Predictor         Coef        Stdev      t-ratio          p
Constant         4.348        2.244         1.94      0.081
x              14.8182       0.3049        48.60      0.000

s  =  3.646    R-square  =  99.6%

Analysis of Variance

SOURCE           DF          SS           MS
Regression        1       31400        31400
Error            10         133           13
Total            11       31533

Unusual Observations
Obs.      x           y         Fit     Residual
  5     5.0       86.00       78.44         7.56
```

(a) The output flags a possible outlier at $x = 5$. Remove that pair of observations and repeat the analysis.

(b) Referring to the previous exercise, identify the decomposition of sums of squares given as the analysis of variance.

11.3 Curvilinear Regression

So far we have studied only the case where the regression curve of Y on x is linear; that is, where for any given x, the mean of the distribution of Y is given by $\alpha + \beta x$. In this section we first investigate cases where the regression curve is nonlinear but where the methods of Section 11.1 can nevertheless be applied; then we take up the problem of polynomial regression, that is, problems where for any given x the mean of the distribution of Y is given by

$$\beta_0 + \beta_1 x + \beta_2 x^2 + \cdots + \beta_p x^p$$

Polynomial curve fitting is also used to obtain approximations when the exact functional form of the regression curve is unknown.

It is common practice for engineers to plot paired data on various kinds of graph paper, in order to determine whether for suitably transformed scales the points will fall close to a straight line. If there is a the transformation that suggests a straight line regression equation, the necessary constants (parameters) can be estimated by applying the method of Section 11.1 to the transformed data. For instance, if a set of paired data consisting of n points (x_i, y_i) "straightens out" when $\log y_i$ is plotted versus x_i, this indicates that the regression curve of Y on x is **exponential,** namely, that for any given x, the mean of the distribution of the Y's is given by $\alpha \cdot \beta^x$. If we take logarithms to the base 10 (or any convenient base), the predicting equation $y = \alpha \cdot \beta^x$ becomes

$$\log y = \log \alpha + x \cdot \log \beta$$

and we can now get estimates of $\log \alpha$ and $\log \beta$, and hence of α and β, by applying the method of Section 11.1 to the n pairs of values $(x_i, \log y_i)$.

EXAMPLE

A plot of log y versus x leads to fitting a straight line
The following are data on the percentage of the high-performance radial tires made by a certain manufacturer that are still usable after having been driven for the given numbers of miles:

Miles driven (thousands) x	Percentage usable y
1	98.2
2	91.7
5	81.3
10	64.0
20	36.4
30	32.6
40	17.1
50	11.3

(a) Plot $\log y_i$ versus x_i to verify that it is reasonable to assume that the relationship is exponential.

(b) Fit an exponential curve by applying the method of least squares to the data points $(x_i, \log y_i)$.

(c) Use the result of part (b) to estimate the percentage of the manufacturer's high-performance radial tires will last at least 25,000 miles.

Solution   (a) As can be seen from Figure 11.7, the overall pattern is linear and this justifies fitting an exponential curve. (b) Determining first the logarithms of the eight y's, we get 1.9921, 1.9624, 1.9101, 1.8062, 1.5611, 1.5132, 1.2330, and 1.0531, and the summations required for substitution into the normal equations are $\sum x = 158$, $\sum x^2 = 5{,}530$, $\sum \log y = 13.0312$, and $\sum x \cdot \log y = 212.1224$, where the subscripts and limits of summation have been omitted for simplicity.

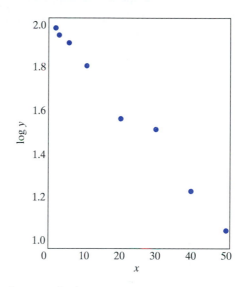

FIGURE 11.7 Plot of transformed data of example.

To fit the line $\log y = c + dx$, we calculate

$$S_{\log y,\,x} = 212.1224 - \frac{(158)(13.0312)}{8} = -45.2438,$$

$$S_{xx} = 5{,}530 - \frac{(158)^2}{8} = 2409.50$$

$$\bar{x} = \frac{158}{8} = 19.750 \qquad \overline{\log y} = \frac{13.0312}{8} = 1.6289$$

so $c = 2.0002$ and $d = -.0188$. Thus, the equation of the estimated regression curve can be written as

$$\log \hat{y} = 2.0002 - 0.0188x$$

in **logarithmic form,** or, since $10^c = 100.0$ and $10^d = 0.96$,

$$\hat{y} = 100.0(0.96)^x$$

in **exponential form.**

(c) Using the logarithmic form, which is more convenient, we get

$$\log \hat{y} = 2.0002 - 0.0188(25)$$
$$= 1.5302$$

and, hence, $\hat{y} = 33.9\%$. ✔

The analysis of transformed relationships is easily implemented on a computer (see Exercise 11.39).

Two other relationships that frequently arise in engineering applications and can be fitted by the method of Section 11.1 after suitable transformations are the **reciprocal function** $y = \dfrac{1}{\alpha + \beta x}$, and the **power function** $y = \alpha \cdot x^{\beta}$. The first of these represents a linear relationship between x and $\dfrac{1}{y}$, namely,

$$\frac{1}{y} = \alpha + \beta x$$

and we obtain estimates of α and β by applying the method of Section 11.1 to the points $\left(x_i, \dfrac{1}{y_i} \right)$. The second represents a linear relationship between $\log x$ and $\log y$, namely,

$$\log y = \log \alpha + \beta \cdot \log x$$

and we obtain estimates of $\log \alpha$ and $\log \beta$, and hence of α and β, by applying the method of Section 11.1 to the points $(\log x_i, \log y_i)$. Another example of a curve that can be fitted by the method of least squares after a suitable transformation is given in Exercise 11.27.

If there is no clear indication about the functional form of the regression of Y on x, we often assume that the underlying relationship is at least "well-behaved" to the extent that it has a Taylor series expansion and that the first few terms of this expansion will yield a fairly good approximation. We thus fit to our data a **polynomial,** that is, a predicting equation of the form

$$y = \beta_0 + \beta_1 x + \beta_2 x^2 + \cdots + \beta_p x^p$$

where the degree is determined by inspection of the data or by a more rigorous method to be discussed below.

Given a set of data consisting of n points (x_i, y_i), we estimate the coefficients $\beta_0, \beta_1, \beta_2, \ldots, \beta_p$ of the pth-degree polynomial by minimizing

$$\sum_{i=1}^{n} [y_i - (\beta_0 + \beta_1 x_i + \beta_2 x_i^2 + \cdots + \beta_p x_i^p)]^2$$

In other words, we are now applying the least squares criterion by minimizing the sum of the squares of the vertical distances from the points to the curve (see Figure 11.8). Taking the partial derivatives with respect to $\beta_0, \beta_1, \beta_2, \ldots, \beta_p$, equating these partial derivatives to zero, rearranging some of the terms, and letting b_i be the estimate of β_i, we obtain the $p + 1$ **normal equations**

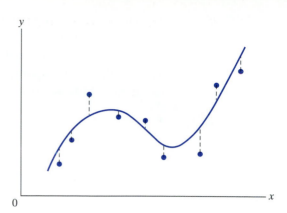

FIGURE 11.8 Least-squares criterion for polynomial curve fitting.

Normal equations for polynomial regression

$$\sum y = nb_0 + b_1 \sum x + \cdots + b_p \sum x^p$$
$$\sum xy = b_0 \sum x + b_1 \sum x^2 + \cdots + b_p \sum x^{p+1}$$
$$\vdots$$
$$\sum x^p y = b_0 \sum x^p + b_1 \sum x^{p+1} + \cdots + b_p \sum x^{2p}$$

where the subscripts and limits of summation are omitted for simplicity. Note that this is a system of $p + 1$ linear equations in the $p + 1$ unknowns $b_0, b_1, b_2, \cdots$, and b_p. Unless the various summations have very unusual values, this system of equations will have a unique solution.

EXAMPLE

Fitting a quadratic function by the method of least squares
The following are data on the drying time of a certain varnish and the amount of an additive that is intended to reduce the drying time:

Amount of varnish additive (grams) x	Drying time (hours) y
0	12.0
1	10.5
2	10.0
3	8.0
4	7.0
5	8.0
6	7.5
7	8.5
8	9.0

(a) Draw a scattergram to verify that it is reasonable to assume that the relationship is parabolic.

(b) Fit a second-degree polynomial by the method of least squares.

(c) Use the result of part (b) to predict the drying time of the varnish when 6.5 grams of the additive is being used.

Solution (a) As can be seen from Figure 11.9, the overall pattern suggests fitting a second-degree polynomial having one relative minimum.

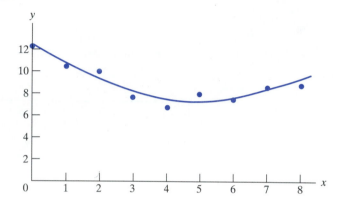

FIGURE 11.9 Parabola fitted to data of example.

(b) The preferred approach is to use computer software (see Exercise 11.40). A partial output includes

Polynomial Regression
Y = 12.1848 − 1.84654X + 0.182900X**2
R-Sq = 92.3%

Alternatively, the summations required for substitution into the normal equations are $\Sigma x = 36$, $\Sigma x^2 = 204$, $\Sigma x^3 = 1{,}296$, $\Sigma x^4 = 8{,}772$, $\Sigma y = 80.5$, $\Sigma xy = 299.0$, and $\Sigma x^2 y = 1{,}697.0$, and we thus have to solve the following system of three linear equations in the unknowns b_0, b_1, and b_2:

$$80.5 = 9b_0 + 36b_1 + 204b_2$$

$$299.0 = 36b_0 + 204b_1 + 1296b_2$$

$$1697.0 = 204b_0 + 1296b_1 + 8772b_2$$

Getting $b_0 = 12.2$, $b_1 = -1.85$, and $b_2 = 0.183$, we find that the equation of the least-squares polynomial is

$$\hat{y} = 12.2 - 1.85x + 0.183x^2$$

(c) Substituting $x = 6.5$ into this equation, we get

$$\hat{y} = 12.2 - 1.85(6.5) + 0.183(6.5)^2$$

$$= 7.9$$

that is, a predicted drying time of 7.9 hours.

Note that it would have been rather dangerous in the preceding example to predict the drying time that corresponds to, say, 24.5 grams of the additive. The risks inherent in extrapolation, discussed on page 343 in connection with fitting straight lines, increase greatly when polynomials are used to approximate unknown regression functions.

In actual practice, it may be difficult to determine the degree of the polynomial to fit to a given set of paired data. As it is always possible to find a polynomial of degree at most $n - 1$ that will pass through each of n points corresponding to n distinct values of x, it should be clear that what we actually seek is a polynomial of lowest possible degree that "adequately" describes the data. As we did in our example, it is often possible to determine the degree of the polynomial by inspection of the data.

There also exists a more rigorous method for determining the degree of the polynomial to be fitted to a given set of data. Essentially, it consists of first fitting a straight line as well as a second-degree polynomial and testing the null hypothesis $\beta_2 = 0$, namely, that nothing is gained by including the quadratic term. If this null hypothesis can be rejected, we then fit a third-degree polynomial and test the hypothesis $\beta_3 = 0$, namely, that nothing is gained by including the cubic term. This procedure is continued until the null hypothesis $\beta_i = 0$ cannot be rejected in two successive steps and there is, thus, no apparent advantage to carrying the extra terms. Note that in order to perform these tests it is necessary to impose the assumptions of normality, independence, and equal variances introduced in Section 11.2. Also, these tests should never be used "blindly," that is, without inspection of the overall pattern of the data.

The use of this technique is fairly tedious and we shall not illustrate it in the text. In Exercise 11.31 on page 363 the reader will be given detailed instructions to apply it to the varnish-additive, drying-time data in order to check whether it was really worthwhile to carry the quadratic term.

11.4   Multiple Regression

Before we extend the methods of the preceding sections to problems involving more than one independent variable, let us point out that the curves obtained (and the surfaces we will obtain) are not used only to make predictions. They are often used also for purposes of optimization—namely, to determine for what values of the independent variable (or variables) the dependent variable is a maximum or minimum. For instance, in the example of page 353 we might use the polynomial fitted to the data to conclude that the drying time is a minimum when the amount of varnish additive used is 5.1 grams (see Exercise 11.32 on page 363).

Statistical methods of prediction and optimization are often referred to under the general heading of **response surface analysis.** Within the scope of this text, we shall be able to introduce two further methods of response surface analysis: **multiple regression** here and related problems of **factorial experimentation** in Chapter 13.

In multiple regression, we deal with data consisting of n $(r + 1)$-tuples $(x_{i1}, x_{i2}, \cdots, x_{ir}, y_i)$, where the x's are again assumed to be known without error while the y's are values of random variables. Data of this kind arise, for example, in studies designed to determine the effect of various climatic conditions on a metal's resistance to corrosion; the effect of kiln temperature, humidity, and iron content on the strength of a ceramic coating; or the effect of factory production, consumption level, and stocks in storage on the price of a product.

As in the case of one independent variable, we shall first treat the problem where the regression equation is linear, namely, where for any given set of values $x_1, x_2, \ldots$, and x_r, for the r independent variables, the mean of the distribution of Y is given by

$$\beta_0 + \beta_1 x_1 + \beta_2 x_2 + \cdots + \beta_r x_r$$

For two independent variables, this is the problem of fitting a plane to a set of n points with coordinates (x_{i1}, x_{i2}, y_i) as is illustrated in Figure 11.10. Applying the method of least squares to obtain estimates of the coefficients β_0, β_1, and β_2, we minimize the sum of the squares of the vertical distances from the observations y_i to the plane (see Figure 11.10); symbolically, we minimize

$$\sum_{i=1}^{n} [y_i - (\beta_0 + \beta_1 x_{i1} + \beta_2 x_{i2})]^2$$

and it will be left to the reader to verify in Exercise 11.33 on page 363 that the resulting normal equations are

Normal equations for multiple regression with $r = 2$

$$\Sigma y = nb_0 + b_1 \Sigma x_1 + b_2 \Sigma x_2$$

$$\Sigma x_1 y = b_0 \Sigma x_1 + b_1 \Sigma x_1^2 + b_2 \Sigma x_1 x_2$$

$$\Sigma x_2 y = b_0 \Sigma x_2 + b_1 \Sigma x_1 x_2 + b_2 \Sigma x_2^2$$

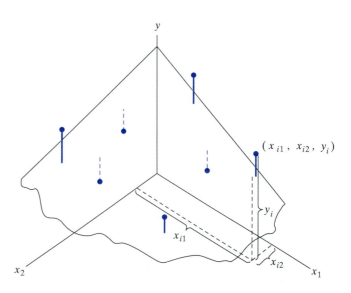

FIGURE 11.10
Regression plane.

As before, we write the least squares estimates of β_0, β_1, and β_2 as b_0, b_1, and b_2. Note that in the abbreviated notation $\sum x_1$ stands for $\sum\limits_{i=1}^{n} x_{i1}$, $\sum x_1 x_2$ stands for $\sum\limits_{i=1}^{n} x_{i1} x_{i2}$, $\sum x_1 y$ stands for $\sum\limits_{i=1}^{n} x_{i1} y_i$, and so forth.

<table>
<tr><td>**EXAMPLE**</td></tr>
</table>

A multiple regression with two predictor variables

The following are data on the number of twists required to break a certain kind of forged alloy bar and the percentages of two alloying elements present in the metal:

Number of twists y	Percent of element A x_1	Percent of element B x_2
41	1	5
49	2	5
69	3	5
65	4	5
40	1	10
50	2	10
58	3	10
57	4	10
31	1	15
36	2	15
44	3	15
57	4	15
19	1	20
31	2	20
33	3	20
43	4	20

Fit a least squares regression plane and use its equation to estimate the number of twists required to break one of the bars when $x_1 = 2.5$ and $x_2 = 12$.

Solution   Substituting $\sum x_1 = 40$, $\sum x_2 = 200$, $\sum x_1^2 = 120$, $\sum x_1 x_2 = 500$, $\sum x_2^2 = 3000$, $\sum y = 723$, $\sum x_1 y = 1963$, and $\sum x_2 y = 8210$ into the normal equations, we get

$$723 = 16b_0 + 40b_1 + 200b_2$$
$$1963 = 40b_0 + 120b_1 + 500b_2$$
$$8210 = 200b_0 + 500b_1 + 3000b_2$$

The unique solution of this system of equations is $b_0 = 46.4$, $b_1 = 7.78$, $b_2 = -1.65$, and the equation of the estimated regression plane is

$$\hat{y} = 46.4 + 7.78x_1 - 1.65x_2$$

Finally, substituting $x_1 = 2.5$ and $x_2 = 12$ into this equation, we get

$$\hat{y} = 46.4 + 7.78(2.5) - 1.65(12)$$
$$= 46.0$$

Note that b_1 and b_2 are estimates of the average change in Y resulting from a unit increase in the corresponding independent variable when the other independent variable is held fixed. ✔

Computers remove the drudgery of calculations from a multiple regression analysis. (See Exercise 11.38.) Typical output includes

```
THE REGRESSION EQUATION IS
Y = 46.4 + 7.78 X1 - 1.65 X2  ①
```

PREDICTOR	COEF	STDEV	T-RATIO	p
CONSTANT	46.438	3.517	13.20 ③	0.000
X1	7.7750 ②	0.9485	8.20	0.000 ⑦
X2	-1.6550	0.1897	-8.72	0.000

```
S = 4.242  ⑥      R-SQ = 91.7%  ⑤
```

ANALYSIS OF VARIANCE

SOURCE	DF	SS ④	MS
REGRESSION	2	2578.5	1289.3
ERROR	13	233.9	18.0
TOTAL	15	2812.4	

We now identify some important parts of the output.

1. The least squares regression plane is

   ① $\hat{y} = 46.4 + 7.78x_1 - 1.65x_2$

   This equation estimates that the average number of twists required to break a bar increases by 7.78 if the percent of element A is increased by 1% and x_2 remains fixed.

2. The least-squares estimates and their corresponding estimated standard errors are:

   $b_0 = 46.438$ with estimated standard error 3.517

   ② $b_1 = 7.7750$ with estimated standard error 0.9485

   $b_2 = -1.6550$ with estimated standard error 0.1897

3. The t ratios 13.20, 8.20, -8.72 are all highly significant, so all the terms are needed in the model. ③

4. In any regression analysis having a β_0 term, the decomposition

   $$y_i - \bar{y} = (y_i - \hat{y}_i) + (\hat{y}_i - \bar{y})$$

   produces the decomposition of the sum of squares

   ④ $$\underbrace{\sum_{i=1}^{n}(y_i - \bar{y})^2}_{\text{total sum of squares}} = \underbrace{\sum_{i=1}^{n}(y_i - \hat{y}_i)^2}_{\text{error sum of squares}} + \underbrace{\sum_{i=1}^{n}(\hat{y}_i - \bar{y})^2}_{\text{regression sum of squares}}$$

or

$$2812.4 = 233.9 + 2578.5$$

Thus, the proportion of variability explained by the regression is (see Exercise 11.57)

$$⑤ \qquad R^2 = \frac{2578.5}{2812.4} = 1 - \frac{233.9}{2812.4} = 0.917$$

5. The estimate of σ^2 is $s_e^2 = 233.9/13 = 18.0$ so $s_e = 4.242$. ⑥
6. The ⑦ P values confirm the significance of the t ratios and thus the fact that all the terms are required in the model.

For comparative purposes, the output from the *SAS* regression program is presented in Figure 11.11.

Dependent Variable: Y

Analysis of Variance

Source	DF	④ Sum of Squares	Mean Square	F Value	Prob>F
Model	2	2578.52500	1289.26250	71.652	0.0001
Error	13	233.91250	17.99327		
C Total	15	2812.43750			

Root MSE	⑥ 4.24185	R-square	0.9168 ⑤
Dep Mean	45.18750	Adj R-sq	0.9040
C.V.	9.38721		

Parameter Estimates

Variable	DF	Parameter Estimate	Standard Error	T for H0: Parameter = 0	Prob > |T|
INTERCEP	1	46.437500	3.51715405	13.203	0.0001
X1	1	7.775000	0.94850591	8.197	0.0001
X2	1	-1.655000	0.18970118	-8.724	0.0001
		②		③	⑦

SUM OF RESIDUALS   -6.21725E-15
SUM OF SQUARED RESIDUALS   233.9125

FIGURE 11.11 Selected *SAS* output for a multiple regression analysis using the data in the example on page 357.

11.5   Checking the Adequacy of the Model

Assuming that the regression model is adequate, we can use the fitted equation to make inferences. Before doing so, it is imperative that we check the assumptions underlying the analysis. In the context of the regression model with two predictors, we question whether Y_i is equal to $\beta_0 + \beta_1 x_{i1} + \beta_2 x_{i2} + \varepsilon_i$, where the errors ε_i are independent and have the same variation σ^2.

All of the information on lack of fit is contained in the residuals

$$e_1 = y_1 - \hat{y}_1 = y_1 - b_0 - b_1 x_{11} - b_2 x_{12}$$
$$e_2 = y_2 - \hat{y}_2 = y_2 - b_0 - b_1 x_{21} - b_2 x_{22}$$
$$\vdots$$
$$e_n = y_n - \hat{y}_n = y_n - b_0 - b_1 x_{n1} - b_2 x_{n2}$$

The residuals should be plotted in various ways to detect systematic departures from the assumptions.

A plot of the residuals versus the predicted values is a major diagnostic tool. Figure 11.12 shows (a) the ideal constant band and two typical violations; (b) variance increases with the response and a transformation is needed; and (c) the model $\beta_0 + \beta_1 x_1 + \beta_2 x_2$ is not adequate. In the latter case, terms with x_1^2 and x_2^2 may be needed.

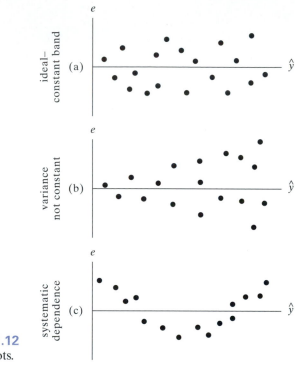

FIGURE 11.12
Residual plots.

We also recommend plotting the residuals versus time in order to detect possible trends over time.

The residual plot for the example on page 331, given in Figure 11.13, has the appearance of a horizontal band so no violations of the model are indicated. The one large residual was already flagged as a possible outlier in Exercise 11.22. It is a good idea to drop this observation and redo the analysis. If there is not much change, then we may wish to leave it in. Otherwise, we must look deeper for reasons before discarding it. This same residual sticks out in the normal-scores plot in Figure 11.14.

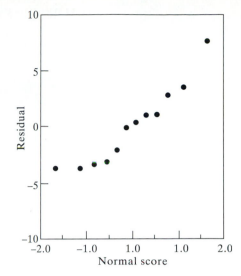

FIGURE 11.13 A plot of the residuals versus predicted values $\hat{y}$.

FIGURE 11.14 A normal-scores plot of the residuals.

Although it is difficult to assess normality with only 12 residuals, the largest and smallest values give the plot in Figure 11.14 a curved appearance and make the normal assumption suspect. Fortunately, the normal assumption is generally not critical for inference so long as serious outliers are not present.

EXERCISES

11.23 The following data pertain to the growth of a colony of bacteria in a culture medium:

Days since inoculation x	Bacteria count y
3	115,000
6	147,000
9	239,000
12	356,000
15	579,000
18	864,000

(a) Plot log y_i versus x_i to verify that it is reasonable to fit an exponential curve.

(b) Fit an exponential curve to the given data.

(c) Use the result obtained in part (b) to estimate the bacteria count at the end of 20 days.

11.24 The following data pertain to the cosmic ray doses measured at various altitudes:

Altitude (feet) x	Dose rate (mrem/year) y
50	28
450	30
780	32
1,200	36
4,400	51
4,800	58
5,300	69

(a) Fit an exponential curve.

(b) Use the result obtained in part (a) to estimate the mean dose at an altitude of 3,000 feet.

11.25 With reference to the preceding exercise, change the equation obtained in part (a) to the form $\hat{y} = a \cdot e^{-cx}$, and use the result to rework part (b).

11.26 The following data pertain to the demand for a product (in thousands of units) and its price (in cents) charged in five different market areas:

Price x	Demand y
20	22
16	41
10	120
11	89
14	56

Fit a power function and use it to estimate the demand when the price of the product is 12 cents.

11.27 Fit a **Gompertz curve** of the form

$$y = e^{e^{\alpha x + \beta}}$$

to the data of Exercise 11.24.

11.28 Plot the curve obtained in the preceding exercise and the one obtained in Exercise 11.24 on one diagram and compare the fit of these two curves.

11.29 The number of inches which a newly built structure is settling into the ground is given by

$$y = 3 - 3e^{-\alpha x}$$

where x is its age in months.

x	2	4	6	12	18	24
y	1.07	1.88	2.26	2.78	2.97	2.99

Use the method of least squares to estimate α. [*Hint:* Note that the relationship between $\ln(3 - y)$ and x is linear.]

11.30 The following data pertain to the amount of hydrogen present (y, in parts per million) in core drillings made at 1-foot intervals along the length of a vacuum-cast ingot (x, core location in feet from base):

x	1	2	3	4	5	6	7	8	9	10
y	1.28	1.53	1.03	0.81	0.74	0.65	0.87	0.81	1.10	1.03

(a) Draw a scattergram to check whether it is reasonable to fit a parabola to the given data.

(b) Fit a parabola by the method of least squares.

(c) Use the equation obtained in part (b) to estimate the amount of hydrogen present at $x = 7.5$.

11.31 When fitting a polynomial to a set of paired data, we usually begin by fitting a straight line and using the method on page 340 to test the null hypothesis $\beta_1 = 0$. Then we fit a second-degree polynomial and test whether it is worthwhile to carry the quadratic term by comparing $\hat{\sigma}_1^2$, the **residual variance** after fitting the straight line, with $\hat{\sigma}_2^2$, the residual variance after fitting the second-degree polynomial. Each of these residual variances is given by the formula

$$\frac{\sum(y - \hat{y})^2}{\text{degrees of freedom}} = \frac{\text{SSE}}{v}$$

with $\hat{y}$ determined, respectively, from the equation of the line and the equation of the second-degree polynomial. The decision whether to carry the quadratic term is based on the statistic

$$F = \frac{\text{SSE}_1 - \text{SSE}_2}{\hat{\sigma}_2^2} = \frac{v_1\hat{\sigma}_1^2 - v_2\hat{\sigma}_2^2}{\hat{\sigma}_2^2}$$

which (under the assumptions of Section 11.2) is a value of a random variable having the F distribution with 1 and $n - 3$ degrees of freedom.

(a) Fit a straight line to the varnish-additive and drying-time data on page 353, test the null hypothesis $\beta_1 = 0$ at the 0.05 level of significance, and calculate $\hat{\sigma}_1^2$.

(b) Using the result on page 354 calculate $\hat{\sigma}_2^2$ for the given data and test at the 0.05 level whether we should carry the quadratic term. (Note that we could continue this procedure and test whether to carry a cubic term by means of a corresponding comparison of residual variances. Then we could test whether to carry a fourth-degree term, and so on. It is customary to terminate this procedure after two successive steps have not produced significant results.)

11.32 With reference to the example on page 353, verify that the drying time is a minimum when the amount of additive used is 5.1 grams.

11.33 Verify that the system of normal equations on page 356 corresponds to the minimization of the sum of squares.

11.34 Twelve specimens of cold-reduced sheet steel, having different copper contents and annealing temperatures, are measured for hardness with the following results:

Hardness (Rockwell 30-T)	Copper content (%)	Annealing temperature (degrees F)
78.9	0.02	1000
65.1	0.02	1100
55.2	0.02	1200
56.4	0.02	1300
80.9	0.10	1000
69.7	0.10	1100
57.4	0.10	1200
55.4	0.10	1300
85.3	0.18	1000
71.8	0.18	1100
60.7	0.18	1200
58.9	0.18	1300

Fit an equation of the form $y = \beta_0 + \beta_1 x_1 + \beta_2 x_2$, where x_1 represents the copper content, x_2 represents the annealing temperature, and y represents the hardness.

11.35 With reference to Exercise 11.34, estimate the hardness of a sheet of steel with a copper content of 0.05% and an annealing temperature of 1150 degrees Fahrenheit.

11.36 The following are data on the ages and incomes of 5 executives working for the same company and the number of years they went to college:

Age x_1	Years college x_2	Income (dollars) y
37	4	71,200
45	0	66,800
38	5	75,000
42	2	70,300
31	4	65,400

Fit an equation of the form $y = \beta_0 = \beta_1 x_1 + \beta_2 x_2$ to the given data, and use it to estimate how much on the average an executive working for this company will make if he is 40 years old and has had 4 years of college.

11.37 The following sample data were collected to determine the relationship between 2 processing variables and the current gain of a transistor in an integrated circuit:

Diffusion time (hours) x_1	Sheet resistance (Ω-cm) x_2	Current gain y
1.5	66	5.3
2.5	87	7.8
0.5	69	7.4
1.2	141	9.8

Diffusion time (hours) x_1	Sheet resistance (Ω-cm) x_2	Current gain y
2.6	93	10.8
0.3	105	9.1
2.4	111	8.1
2.0	78	7.2
0.7	66	6.5
1.6	123	12.6

Fit a regression plane and use its equation to estimate the expected current gain when the diffusion time is 2.2 hours and the sheet resistance is 90 Ω-cm.

11.38 Multiple regression is best implemented on a computer. The following *MINITAB* command fits the y values in C1 to 2 predictor values in C2 and C3.

Dialog box: **Session command**
Stat>Regression>Regression   MTB>REGRESS C1 ON 2 PRED C2 C3
Type *C1* in **Response.**
Type *C2* and *C3* in **Predictors.** Click **OK.**

It produces output like that on page 358. Use a computer to perform the multiple regression analysis in Exercise 11.34.

11.39 Using *MINITAB* we can transform the x values in C1 and/or the y values in C2. For instance, the commands

> LOGTEN C2 SET IN C3
> PLOT C3 VS C1
> REGRESS C3 ON 1 PREDICTOR IN C1

give the plot of log y_i versus x_i and the corresponding least-squares analysis. Use the computer to do Exercise 11.27.

11.40 To fit the quadratic regression model using *MINITAB,* when the x values are in C1 and the y values are in C2, use the session commands

> MULTIPLY C1 BY C1 SET IN C3
> REGRESS C2 ON 2 PREDICTORS IN C1 C3

or

Dialog box:
Stat>Regression>Fitted Line Plot
Enter *C2* in **Response (Y)** and enter *C1* in **Predictor (X).**
Under **Type of Regression Model** choose **Quadratic.** Click **OK.**

Use the computer to repeat the analysis of the example on page 354.

11.41 With reference to Exercise 11.38, in order to plot residuals, you must use the modified session command

> REGRESS C1 ON 2 PREDICTORS IN C2 C3 STORE C4 FIT IN C5;
> RESIDUALS C6.

or

Dialog box:
Stat>Regression>Regression
Enter *C1* in **Response** and enter *C2* and *C3* in **Predictors.**
Click **Storage.** Check **Residuals** and **Fits.**
Click **OK** twice.

The additional steps

Dialog box:	**Session command**
Stat>Regression>Regression	MTB>PLOT C6 VS C5
Click **Graphs.** Check **Normal plot of residuals**	MTB>NSCORE C6 SET C7
and **Residuals versus fits.**	MTB>PLOT C6 VS C7
Click **OK** twice.	

---

will produce a plot of the residuals versus $\hat{y}$ and a normal-scores plot of the residuals.
Use a computer to analyze the residuals from the multiple regression analysis in

   (a) the example on page 357;

   (b) Exercise 11.34.

11.42 With reference to Exercise 11.37, analyze the residuals from the regression plane.

11.43 The following residuals and predicted values were obtained from an experiment
that related yield of a chemical process (y) to the initial concentration (x) of a
component (the time order of the experiments is given in parentheses):

Predicted	Residual	Predicted	Residual
4.1 (5)	−2	3.5 (3)	0
3.2 (9)	−1	4.0 (12)	3
3.5 (13)	3	4.2 (4)	−2
4.3 (1)	−3	3.9 (11)	2
3.3 (7)	−1	4.3 (2)	−5
4.6 (14)	5	3.7 (10)	0
3.6 (8)	0	3.2 (6)	1

Examine the residuals for evidence of a violation of the assumptions.

11.6   Correlation

So far in this chapter, we have studied problems where the independent variable
(or variables) was assumed to be known without error. Although this applies to
many experimental situations, there are also problems where the x's as well as the

y's are values assumed by random variables. This would be the case, for instance, if we studied the relationship between input and output of a wastewater treatment plant, the relationship between the tensile strength and the hardness of aluminum, or the relationship between impurities in the air and the incidence of a certain disease. Problems like these are referred to as problems of **correlation analysis,** where it is assumed that the data points (x_i, y_i) for $i = 1, 2, \cdots, n$ are values of a pair of random variables whose joint density is given by $f(x, y)$.

The scattergram provides a visual impression of the relation between the x and y values in a bivariate data set. Often the points appear to scatter about a straight line. The closeness of the scatter to a straight line can be expressed numerically in terms of the correlation coefficient. The best interpretation of the sample correlation coefficient is in terms of the standardized observations

$$\frac{\text{Observation} - \text{Sample mean}}{\text{Sample standard deviation}} = \frac{x_i - \overline{x}}{s_x}$$

where the subscript x on s distinguishes the sample variance of the x observations, $s_x^2 = \sum_{i=1}^{n}(x_i - \overline{x})^2/(n - 1) = S_{xx}/(n - 1)$, from the sample variance of the y observations.

The **sample correlation coefficient** r is the sum of products of the standardized variables divided by $n - 1$, the same divisor used for sample variance.

Sample correlation coefficient

$$r = \frac{1}{n - 1} \sum_{i=1}^{n} \left(\frac{x_i - \overline{x}}{s_x} \right) \left(\frac{y_i - \overline{y}}{s_y} \right)$$

When most of the pairs of observations are such that either both components are simultaneously above their sample means or both are simultaneously below their sample means, the products of the standardized values will tend to be large and positive so r will be positive. This case corresponds to a southwest to northeast pattern in the scattergram (see Figure 11.15(a)–(e)).

Alternatively, if one component of the pair tends to be large when the other is small, and vice versa, the correlation coefficient r is negative. This case corresponds to a northwest to southeast pattern in the scattergram.

It can be shown that the value of r is always between -1 and 1, inclusive.

1. The magnitude of r describes the strength of a linear relation and its sign indicates the direction.

    $r = +1$ if all pairs (x_i, y_i) lie exactly on a straight line having a positive slope.

    $r > 0$ if the pattern in the scattergram runs from lower left to upper right.

    $r < 0$ if the pattern in the scattergram runs from upper left to lower right.

    $r = -1$ if all pairs (x_i, y_i) lie exactly on a straight line having a negative slope.

    A value of r near -1 or $+1$ describes a strong linear relation.

2. A value of r close to zero implies that the *linear* association is weak. There may still be a strong association along a curve (see Figure 11.15(f)).

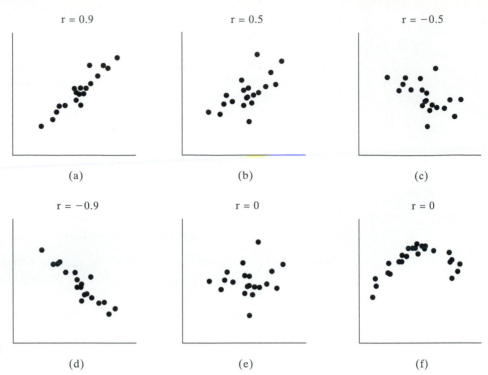

r = 0.9   r = 0.5   r = −0.5

(a)   (b)   (c)

r = −0.9   r = 0   r = 0

(d)   (e)   (f)

FIGURE 11.15 Correspondence between the values of r and the amount of scatter.

From the definitions of S_{xx}, S_{xy}, and S_{yy} we obtain a simpler calculation formula for r.

Alternative calculation for the sample correlation coefficient

$$r = \frac{S_{xy}}{\sqrt{S_{xx} \cdot S_{yy}}}$$

EXAMPLE

Calculating the sample correlation coefficient
The following are the numbers of minutes it took 10 mechanics to assemble a piece of machinery in the morning, x, and in the late afternoon, y:

x	y
11.1	10.9
10.3	14.2
12.0	13.8
15.1	21.5
13.7	13.2
18.5	21.1
17.3	16.4
14.2	19.3
14.8	17.4
15.3	19.0

Calculate r.

Solution The first step is always to plot the data to make sure a linear pattern exists and that there are no outliers. A computer calculation provides the scattergram in Figure 11.16 and the value r = 0.732 (see Exercise 11.63 for details).

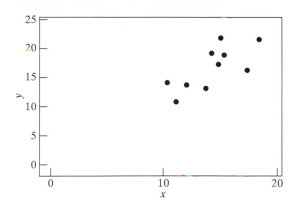

FIGURE 11.16 (Pearson) Correlation of x and y, r = 0.732.

Alternatively, using a calculator, we first determine the summations $\Sigma x = 142.3$, $\Sigma y = 166.8$, $\Sigma x^2 = 2085.31$, $\Sigma xy = 2434.69$, $\Sigma y^2 = 2897.80$. Then, substituting into the formulas on page 333, we get

$$S_{xx} = 2085.31 - (142.3)^2/10 = 60.381$$
$$S_{xy} = 2434.69 - (142.3)(166.8)/10 = 61.126$$
$$S_{yy} = 2897.80 - (166.8)^2/10 = 115.576$$

and, hence,

$$r = \frac{61.126}{\sqrt{(60.381)(115.576)}} = 0.732$$

The positive value for r confirms a positive association where long assembly times tend to pair together and so do short assembly times. Further, it captures the orientation of the pattern in Figure 11.16, which runs from lower left to upper right. Since r = 0.732 is moderately large, the pattern of scatter is moderately narrow. ✔

EXAMPLE

Exploring and interpreting correlation
Heavy metals can inhibit the biological treatment of waste in municipal treatment plants. Monthly measurements were made at a state-of-the-art treatment plant of the amount of chromium ($\mu g/l$) in both the influent and effluent.

influent	250	290	270	100	300	410	110	130	1100
effluent	19	10	17	11	70	60	18	30	180

(a) Make a scattergram.
(b) Make a scattergram after taking ln of both variables.
(c) Calculate the correlation coefficient, r, in Part (a) and Part (b).
(d) Comment on the appropriateness of r in each case.

Solution The scattergrams are shown in Figure 11.17 (a) and (b) respectively.
(c) A computer calculation gives $r = .942$ and $r = .747$ respectively.
(d) r is not really appropriate for the original data since the one large observation in the upper right-hand corner has too much influence. If the pair $(1100, 180)$ is dropped, r drops to 0.578. The situation in (b) is better.

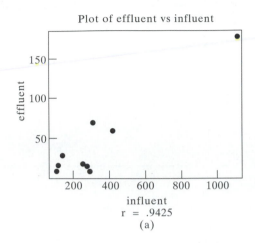

FIGURE 11.17 Scattergrams, original and tansformed data. ✔

Correlation and Regression

There are two important relationships between r and the least squares fit of a straight line. First,

$$r = \frac{S_{xy}}{\sqrt{S_{xx}S_{yy}}} = \frac{\sqrt{S_{xx}}}{\sqrt{S_{yy}}}\frac{S_{xy}}{S_{xx}} = \frac{\sqrt{S_{xx}}}{\sqrt{S_{yy}}}b$$

so the sample correlation coefficient, r, and the least squares estimate of slope, b, have the same sign.

The second relationship concerns the proportion of variability in y explained by x in a least squares fit. The total variation in y is

$$S_{yy} = \sum_{i=1}^{n}(y_i - \bar{y})^2$$

while the unexplained part of the variation is the sum of squares residuals or $S_{yy} - S_{xy}^2/S_{xx}$. This leaves the difference $S_{yy} - (S_{yy} - S_{xy}^2/S_{xx}) = S_{xy}^2/S_{xx}$ as the **sum of squares due to regression.** This decomposes the total variability in y into two components: one due to regression and the other due to error.

Decomposition of Variability

S_{yy}	$=$	S_{xy}^2/S_{xx}	$+$	$S_{yy} - S_{xy}^2/S_{xx}$
Total variability of y		Variability explained by the linear relation		Residual or unexplained variability

For the straight line to provide a good fit to the data, the sum of squares due to regression, S_{xy}^2/S_{xx}, should be a substantial proportion of the total sum of squares S_{yy}.

The **proportion of the y variability explained by the linear relation is**

$$\frac{\text{Sum of squares due to regression}}{\text{Total sum of squares of } y} = \frac{S_{xy}^2/S_{xx}}{S_{yy}} = \frac{S_{xy}^2}{S_{xx}S_{yy}} = r^2$$

where r is the sample correlation coefficient. To summarize, the strength of the linear relationship is measured by the proportion of the y variability explained by the linear relation, the square of the sample correlation coefficient.

The proportion of y variability explained by the linear relation $= r^2$

EXAMPLE

Calculating the proportion of y variation attributed to the linear relation
Refer to the example on page 368 concerning the data on assembly times. Find the proportion of variation in y, the afternoon assembly times, that can be explained by a straight line fit to x, the morning assembly times.

Solution
In the earlier example, we obtained $r = 0.732$. Consequently, the proportion of variation in y attributed to x is $r^2 = (0.732)^2 = 0.536$.

The result we have obtained here implies that $100r^2 = 53.6\%$ of the variation among the afternoon times is explained by (is accounted for or may be attributed to) the corresponding differences among the morning times.   ✔

Correlation and Causation

Scientists have sometimes jumped to unjustified conclusions by mistaking a high observed correlation for a cause-and-effect relationship. The observation that two variables tend to vary simultaneously in the same direction does not imply a direct relationship between them. It would not be surprising, for example, to obtain a high positive correlation between the annual sales of chewing gum and the incidence of crime in cities of various sizes within the United States, but one cannot conclude that crime might be reduced by prohibiting the sale of chewing gum. Both variables depend upon the size of the population, and it is this mutual relationship with a third variable (population size) which produces the positive correlation. This third variable, called a **lurking variable,** is often overlooked when mistaken claims are made about x causing y.

When using the correlation coefficient as a measure of relationship, we must try to avoid the possibility that an important lurking variable is influencing the calculation.

A causal relationship may also exist that is opposite to the observed correlation. During the manufacture of high quality printer paper, the whiteness and amount of metallic particles are measured. The whitest runs of paper have the lowest metal content and vice versa. That is, there is a strong but negative correlation. To someone unacquainted with the paper-making process, this would suggest eliminating the metallic particles. However, the causal relationship is just the opposite.

The metallic particles improve whiteness but they are only added to borderline papers to make sure they pass the standards test.

Inferences About the Correlation Coefficient—Normal Populations

To develop a population measure of association, or correlation, for two random variables X and Y, we begin with the two standardized variables

$$\frac{X - \mu_1}{\sigma_1} \quad \text{and} \quad \frac{Y - \mu_2}{\sigma_2}$$

Each of these two standardized variables is free of its unit of measurement so their product is free of both units of measurement. The expected value of this product, which is also the covariance, is then the measure of association between X and Y called the **population correlation coefficient.** This measure of relationship or association is denoted by ρ (rho).

Population correlation coefficient

$$\rho = E\left[\left(\frac{X - \mu_1}{\sigma_1}\right)\left(\frac{Y - \mu_2}{\sigma_2}\right)\right]$$

The population correlation coefficient ρ is positive when both components (X, Y) are simultaneously large or simultaneously small with high probability. A negative value for ρ prevails when, with high probability, one member of the pair (X, Y) is large and the other is small. The value of ρ is always between -1 and 1, inclusive. The extreme values ± 1 arise only when probability one is assigned to pairs (x, y) where $(y - \mu_2)/\sigma_2 = (\pm 1)(x - \mu_1)/\sigma_1$, respectively. That is, probability one is assigned to a straight line and probability 0 to the rest of the plane.

In summary, when $\rho = \pm 1$ we say that there is a perfect linear correlation (relationship, or association) between the two random variables; when $\rho = 0$, we say there is no correlation (relationship, or association) between the two random variables.

Although the sample correlation coefficient is not an unbiased estimator of ρ, it is widely used as a point estimator whatever the form of the bivariate population.

Test of hypotheses about ρ and confidence intervals require more restrictive assumptions. In the remainder of this section, we assume that the joint distribution of X and Y is, to a reasonable approximation, the **bivariate normal distribution.** This distribution has joint density function

$$f(x, y) = \frac{1}{2\pi \cdot \sigma_1 \sigma_2 \sqrt{1 - \rho^2}} e^{-\left(\left(\frac{x - \mu_1}{\sigma_1}\right)^2 - 2\rho\left(\frac{x - \mu_1}{\sigma_1}\right)\left(\frac{y - \mu_2}{\sigma_2}\right) + \left(\frac{y - \mu_2}{\sigma_2}\right)^2\right)/2(1 - \rho^2)}$$

for $-\infty < x < \infty$ and $-\infty < y < \infty$.

For the bivariate normal distribution, we have a stronger property. When $\rho = 0$, the joint density factors (see Exercise 11.56) so zero correlation also implies that the two random variables are independent.

Inferences about ρ are based on the sample correlation coefficient. Whenever r is based on a random sample from a bivariate normal population, we can perform a test of significance (a test of the null hypothesis $\rho = \rho_0$) or construct a confidence interval for ρ on the basis of the **Fisher $\mathcal{Z}$** transformation:

Fisher $\mathcal{Z}$ transformation

$$\mathcal{Z} = \frac{1}{2}\ln\frac{1+r}{1-r}$$

This statistic is a value of a random variable having approximately a normal distribution with the mean $\mu_{\mathcal{Z}} = \frac{1}{2}\ln\frac{1+\rho}{1-\rho}$ and the variance $\frac{1}{n-3}$. Thus, we can base inferences about ρ on

Statistic for inferences about ρ

$$Z = \frac{\mathcal{Z} - \mu_{\mathcal{Z}}}{1/\sqrt{n-3}} = \frac{\sqrt{n-3}}{2}\cdot\ln\frac{(1+r)(1-\rho)}{(1-r)(1+\rho)}$$

which is a random variable having approximately the standard normal distribution.

In particular, we can test the null hypothesis of no correlation, namely, the null hypothesis $\rho = 0$, with the statistic

Statistic for test of null hypothesis $\rho = 0$

$$Z = \sqrt{n-3}\cdot\mathcal{Z} = \frac{\sqrt{n-3}}{2}\cdot\ln\frac{1+r}{1-r}$$

These tests are facilitated by the use of Table 11, which gives the values of $\mathcal{Z}$ corresponding to $r = 0.00, 0.01, 0.02, \ldots$, and 0.99. When r is negative, we look up the value of $\mathcal{Z}$ corresponding to $-r$, and then take $-\mathcal{Z}$.

EXAMPLE

Testing for non-zero correlation in a normal population
With reference to the example on page 368, where we had $n = 10$ and $r = 0.732$, test the null hypothesis $\rho = 0$ against the null hypothesis $\rho \neq 0$ at the 0.05 level of significance.

Solution

1. *Null hypothesis:* $\rho = 0$
   Alternative hypothesis: $\rho \neq 0$
2. *Level of significance:* $\alpha = 0.05$
3. *Criterion:* Reject the null hypothesis if $Z < -1.96$ or $Z > 1.96$, where $Z = \sqrt{n-3}\cdot\mathcal{Z}$.
4. *Calculations:* The value of $\mathcal{Z}$ corresponding to $r = 0.732$ is $\frac{1}{2}\ln\left(\frac{1+.732}{1-.732}\right) = .933$ so that

$$z = \sqrt{10 - 3} \cdot (0.933) = 2.47$$

5. *Decision:* Since $z = 2.47$ exceeds 1.96, the null hypothesis must be rejected; we conclude that there is a relationship between the morning and late afternoon time it takes a mechanic to assemble the given kind of machinery. ✔

To construct a confidence interval for ρ, we first construct a confidence interval for μ_z, the mean of the sampling distribution of Z, and then convert to r and ρ by means of Table 11. Making use of the theory above, we can write the first of these confidence intervals as

Confidence interval for μ_z—normal population

$$Z - \frac{z_{\alpha/2}}{\sqrt{n-3}} < \mu_z < Z + \frac{z_{\alpha/2}}{\sqrt{n-3}}$$

EXAMPLE

Determining a confidence interval for ρ—normal population
If $r = 0.70$ for the mathematics and physics grades of 30 students, construct a 95% confidence interval for the population correlation coefficient.

Solution

Reading the value of Z that corresponds to $r = 0.70$ from Table 11 and substituting it together with $n = 30$ and $z_{0.025} = 1.96$ into the preceding confidence interval formula for μ_z, we get

$$0.867 - \frac{1.96}{\sqrt{27}} < \mu_z < 0.867 + \frac{1.96}{\sqrt{27}}$$

or

$$0.490 < \mu_z < 1.244$$

Then, looking up the values of r for which Z is closest to 0.490 and 1.244 in Table 11, we get the 95% confidence interval

$$0.45 < \rho < 0.85$$

for the true strength of the linear relationship between grades of students in the two given subjects. ✔

Note that in this example the confidence interval for ρ is fairly wide; this illustrates the fact that correlation coefficients based on relatively small samples are generally not very reliable.

We conclude by reviewing two serious pitfalls in the interpretation of the coefficient of correlation. First, it must be emphasized that r is an estimate of the strength of the linear relationship between the values of two random variables. Thus, as is shown in Figure 11.15(f) r may be close to 0 when there is actually a strong (but nonlinear) relationship. Second, and perhaps of greatest importance, a significant correlation does not necessarily imply a causal relationship between the two random variables.

(Optional) The Bivariate Normal Distribution and the Straight-line Regression Model

Here we develop the bivariate normal joint density function in terms of the conditional density $f_2(y|x)$ and the marginal density $f_1(x)$, as defined in Section 5.10. So far as $f_2(y|x)$ is concerned, the conditions we shall impose are practically identical with the ones we used in connection with the sampling theory of Section 11.2. For any given x, it will be assumed that $f_2(y|x)$ is a normal distribution with the mean $\alpha + \beta x$ and the variance σ^2. Thus, the regression of Y on x is linear and the variance of the conditional density does not depend on x. Furthermore, we shall assume that the marginal density $f_1(x)$ is normal with the mean μ_1 and the variance σ_1^2. Making use of the relationship $f(x, y) = f_1(x) \cdot f_2(y|x)$ given on page 179, we thus obtain

$$f(x, y) = \frac{1}{\sqrt{2\pi}\sigma_1} e^{-\frac{(x-\mu_1)^2}{2\sigma_1^2}} \cdot \frac{1}{\sqrt{2\pi}\sigma} e^{-\frac{[y-(\alpha+\beta x)]^2}{2\sigma^2}}$$

$$= \frac{1}{2\pi \cdot \sigma \cdot \sigma_1} e^{-\left\{\frac{[y-(\alpha+\beta x)]^2}{2\sigma^2} + \frac{(x-\mu_1)^2}{2\sigma_1^2}\right\}}$$

for $-\infty < x < \infty$ and $-\infty < y < \infty$. Note that this joint distribution involves the *five* parameters $\mu_1, \sigma_1, \alpha, \beta$, and σ.

For reasons of symmetry and other considerations to be explained later, it is customary to express the bivariate normal density of the parameters $\mu_1, \sigma_1, \mu_2, \sigma_2$, and ρ. Here μ_2 and σ_2^2 are the mean and the variance of the marginal distribution $f_2(y)$, while ρ, in this notation, is given by

$$\rho^2 = 1 - \frac{\sigma^2}{\sigma_2^2}$$

with ρ taken to be positive when β is positive and negative when β is negative. Leaving it to the reader to show in Exercise 11.55 that

$$\mu_2 = \alpha + \beta\mu_1 \quad \text{and} \quad \sigma_2^2 = \sigma^2 + \beta^2\sigma_1^2$$

we then substitute into the preceding expression for $f(x, y)$ and obtain the following form of the bivariate normal distribution:

$$f(x, y) = \frac{1}{2\pi \cdot \sigma_1\sigma_2\sqrt{1-\rho^2}} e^{-\left[\left(\frac{x-\mu_1}{\sigma_1}\right)^2 - 2\rho\left(\frac{x-\mu_1}{\sigma_1}\right)\left(\frac{y-\mu_2}{\sigma_2}\right) + \left(\frac{y-\mu_2}{\sigma_2}\right)^2\right]/2(1-\rho^2)}$$

for $-\infty < x < \infty$ and $-\infty < y < \infty$ (see Exercise 11.55).

Concerning the correlation coefficient ρ, note that $-1 \leq \rho \leq +1$ since $\sigma_2^2 = \sigma^2 + \beta^2\sigma_1^2$ and, hence, $\sigma_2^2 \geq \sigma^2$. Furthermore, ρ can equal -1 or $+1$ only when $\sigma^2 = 0$, which represents the degenerate case where all the probability is concentrated along the line $y = \alpha + \beta x$ and there is, thus, a perfect linear relationship between the two random variables. (That is, for a given value of x, Y must equal $\alpha + \beta x$.)

EXERCISES

11.44 Use the first set of expressions on page 333, involving the deviations from the mean, to calculate r for the following data.

x	y
8	3
1	4
5	0
4	2
7	1

11.45 Calculate r for the air velocities and evaporation coefficients of the example on page 334. Also, assuming that the necessary assumptions can be met, test the null hypothesis $\rho = 0$ against the alternative hypothesis $\rho \neq 0$ at the 0.05 level of significance.

11.46 The following data pertain to the resistance (ohms) and the failure time (minutes) of certain overloaded resistors:

Resistance	Failure time	Resistance	Failure time
43	32	36	36
29	20	39	33
44	45	36	21
33	35	47	44
33	22	28	26
47	46	40	45
34	28	42	39
31	26	33	25
48	37	46	36
34	33	28	25
46	47	48	45
37	30	45	36

Calculate r.

11.47 With reference to Exercise 11.46, test $\rho = 0$ against $\rho \neq 0$ at $\alpha = 0.01$.

11.48 Calculate r for the extraction times and extraction efficiencies of Exercise 11.1. Assuming that the necessary assumptions can be met, test the null hypothesis $\rho = 0.75$ against the alternative hypothesis $\rho > 0.75$ at the 0.05 level of significance.

11.49 Calculate r for the humidities and moisture contents of Exercise 11.10. Assuming that the necessary assumptions can be met, construct a 95% confidence interval for the population correlation coefficient ρ.

11.50 The following are measurements of the carbon content and the permeability index of 22 sinter mixtures:

Carbon content (%)	Permeability index	Carbon content (%)	Permeability index
4.4	12	4.1	13
5.5	14	4.9	19
4.2	18	4.7	22
3.0	35	5.0	20
4.5	23	4.6	16
4.9	29	3.6	27
4.6	16	4.9	21
5.0	12	5.1	13
4.7	18	4.8	18
5.1	21	5.2	17
4.4	27	5.2	11

    (a) Calculate r.

    (b) Find 99% confidence limits for ρ.

11.51 If $r = 0.83$ for one set of paired data and $r = 0.60$ for another, compare the strengths of the two relationships.

11.52 If data on the ages and prices of 25 pieces of equipment yielded $r = -0.58$, test the null hypothesis $\rho = -0.40$ against the alternative hypothesis $\rho < -0.40$ at the 0.05 level of significance.

11.53 Assuming that the necessary assumptions are met, construct a 95% confidence interval for ρ when

    (a) $r = 0.72$ and $n = 19$;

    (b) $r = 0.35$ and $n = 25$;

    (c) $r = 0.57$ and $n = 40$.

11.54 Assuming that the necessary assumptions are met, construct a 99% confidence interval for ρ when

    (a) $r = -0.87$ and $n = 19$;

    (b) $r = 0.39$ and $n = 24$;

    (c) $r = 0.16$ and $n = 40$.

11.55   (a) Evaluating the necessary integrals, verify the identities

$$\mu_2 = \alpha + \beta\mu_1 \quad \text{and} \quad \sigma_2^2 = \sigma^2 + \beta^2\sigma_1^2$$

    on page 375.

    (b) Substitute $\mu_2 = \alpha + \beta\mu_1$ and $\sigma_2^2 = \sigma^2 + \beta^2\sigma_1^2$ into the formula for the bivariate density given on page 375, and show that this gives the final form shown on page 375.

11.56 Show that for the bivariate normal distribution

    (a) independence implies zero correlation;

    (b) zero correlation implies independence.

11.57 Instead of using the computing formula on page 368, we can obtain the correlation coefficient r with the formula

$$r = \pm \sqrt{1 - \frac{\Sigma(y - \hat{y})^2}{\Sigma(y - \bar{y})^2}}$$

which is analogous to the formula used to define ρ. Although the computations required by the use of this formula are tedious, the formula has the advantage that it can be used also to measure the strength of nonlinear relationships or relationships in several variables. For instance, in the multiple linear regression example on page 357, one could calculate the predicted values by means of the equation

$$\hat{y} = 46.4 + 7.78x_1 - 1.65x_2$$

and then determine r as a measure of how strongly y, the twists required to break one of the forged alloy bars, depends on both percentages of alloying elements present.

(a) Using the data on page 357, find $\Sigma(y - \bar{y})^2$ by means of the formula $\Sigma(y - \bar{y})^2 = \Sigma y^2 - n\bar{y}^2$.

(b) Using the regression equation obtained on page 357, calculate $\hat{y}$ for the 16 points and then determine $\Sigma(y - \hat{y})^2$.

(c) Substitute the results obtained in (a) and (b) into the above formula for r. The result is called the **multiple correlation coefficient.**

11.58 With reference to Exercise 11.37, use the theory of the preceding exercise to calculate the multiple correlation coefficient (which measures how strongly the current gain is related to the two independent variables).

11.59 When we substitute for the actual values of paired data the ranks which the values occupy in the respective samples, the correlation coefficient can be written in the form

$$r_S = 1 - \frac{6 \cdot \Sigma d_i^2}{n(n^2 - 1)}$$

in which it is called the **rank-correlation coefficient** or **Spearman's rank-correlation coefficient.** In this formula, d_i is the difference between the ranks of the paired observations (x_i, y_i) and n is the number of pairs in the sample. The formula for r_S follows from that for r when there are no ties in rank; if there are ties, we substitute for each of the tied observations the mean of the ranks that they jointly occupy, and there may be a small difference between the values of r and r_S obtained for the two sets of ranks.

(a) Calculate r_S for the example on page 368, which deals with the time it takes mechanics to assemble a certain piece of machinery in the morning and in the late afternoon. Compare the result with the value of r obtained for the original data.

(b) Calculate r_S for the data of Exercise 11.46 and compare the result with the value of r obtained from the original data.

(c) Calculate r_S for the air velocities and evaporation coefficients of the example on page 334 and compare the result with the value of r obtained for the original data in Exercise 11.45.

11.60 Since the assumptions underlying the significance test of Section 11.6 are rather stringent, it is often desirable to use a nonparametric alternative based on the rank-correlation coefficient defined in the preceding exercise. It is based on the theory that if there is no relationship between the x's and the y's (in fact, if they are randomly matched), the sampling distribution of r_S can be approximated closely with a normal distribution having zero mean and the standard deviation

$$\sigma_{r_S} = \frac{1}{\sqrt{n-1}}$$

Use the 0.01 level of significance to test the significance of the values of r_S obtained in the three parts of Exercise 11.59.

11.61 If a sample of $n = 18$ pairs of data yielded $r_S = 0.39$, is this rank-correlation coefficient significant at the 0.05 level of significance? [*Hint:* Refer to the two preceding exercises.]

11.62 If a sample of $n = 40$ pairs of data yielded $r_S = 0.48$, is this rank-correlation coefficient significant at the 0.01 level of significance? [*Hint:* Refer to Exercises 11.59 and 11.60.]

11.63 To calculate r using *MINITAB* when the x values are in C1 and the y values are in C2, use

Dialog box:	Session command
Stat>Basic Statistics>Correlation	MTB>CORR C1 C2
Type *C1* and *C2* in **Variables.** Click **OK.**	

Also, you should make a scattergram using the plot procedure in Exercise 11.22. Use the computer to do Exercise 11.46.

11.7 Multiple Linear Regression (Matrix Notation)[†]

The model we are using in multiple linear regression lends itself uniquely to a unified treatment in matrix notation. This notation makes it possible to state general results in compact form and to use to great advantage many of the results of matrix theory.

It is customary to denote matrices by capital letters in boldface type and vectors by lowercase boldface type. To express the normal equations on page 356 in matrix notation, let us define the following three matrices.

$$\mathbf{X} = \begin{bmatrix} 1 & x_{11} & x_{12} \\ 1 & x_{21} & x_{22} \\ \vdots & \vdots & \vdots \\ 1 & x_{n1} & x_{n2} \end{bmatrix}$$

$$\mathbf{y} = \begin{bmatrix} y_1 \\ y_2 \\ \vdots \\ y_n \end{bmatrix} \quad \text{and} \quad \mathbf{b} = \begin{bmatrix} b_0 \\ b_1 \\ b_2 \end{bmatrix}$$

[†]It is assumed for this section that the reader is familiar with the material ordinarily covered in a first course on matrix algebra. Since matrix notation is not used elsewhere in this book, this section may be omitted without loss of continuity.

The first one, $\mathbf{X}$, is an $n \times (2 + 1)$ matrix consisting essentially of the given values of the x's, with the column of 1's appended to accommodate the constant term. $\mathbf{y}$ is an $n \times 1$ matrix (or column vector) consisting of observed values of the response variable and $\mathbf{b}$ is the $(2 + 1) \times 1$ matrix (or column vector) consisting of the least squares estimates of the regression coefficients.

Using these matrices, we can now write the following symbolic solutions of the normal equations on page 356. The least squares estimates of the multiple regression coefficients are given by

$$\mathbf{b} = (\mathbf{X'X})^{-1}\mathbf{X'y}$$

where $\mathbf{X'}$ is the transpose of $\mathbf{X}$ and $(\mathbf{X'X})^{-1}$ is the inverse of $\mathbf{X'X}$.

To verify this relation, we first determine $\mathbf{X'X}, \mathbf{X'Xb}$, and $\mathbf{X'y}$.

$$\mathbf{X'X} = \begin{bmatrix} n & \sum x_1 & \sum x_2 \\ \sum x_1 & \sum x_1^2 & \sum x_1 x_2 \\ \sum x_2 & \sum x_2 x_1 & \sum x_2^2 \end{bmatrix}$$

$$\mathbf{X'Xb} = \begin{bmatrix} b_0 n + b_1 \sum x_1 + b_2 \sum x_2 \\ b_0 \sum x_1 + b_1 \sum x_1^2 + b_2 \sum x_1 x_2 \\ b_0 \sum x_2 + b_1 \sum x_2 x_1 + b_2 \sum x_2^2 \end{bmatrix}$$

$$\mathbf{X'y} = \begin{bmatrix} \sum y \\ \sum x_1 y \\ \sum x_2 y \end{bmatrix}$$

Identifying the elements $\mathbf{X'Xb}$ as the expressions on the right-hand side of the normal equations on page 356 and those of $\mathbf{X'y}$ as the expressions on the left-hand side, we can write

$$\mathbf{X'Xb} = \mathbf{X'y}$$

Multiplying on the left by $(\mathbf{X'X})^{-1}$, we get

$$(\mathbf{X'X})^{-1}\mathbf{X'Xb} = (\mathbf{X'X})^{-1}\mathbf{X'y}$$

and, finally,

$$\mathbf{b} = (\mathbf{X'X})^{-1}\mathbf{X'y}$$

since $(\mathbf{X'X})^{-1}\mathbf{X'X}$ equals the $(2 + 1) \times (2 + 1)$ identity matrix $\mathbf{I}$, and by definition $\mathbf{Ib} = \mathbf{b}$. We have assumed here that $\mathbf{X'X}$ is nonsingular, so that its inverse exists.

EXAMPLE

Calculating the least-squares estimates using $(\mathbf{X'X})^{-1}\mathbf{X'y}$
With reference to the example on page 357, use the matrix expressions to determine the least squares estimates of the multiple regression coefficients.

Solution   Substituting $\Sigma x_1 = 40$, $\Sigma x_2 = 200$, $\Sigma x_1^2 = 120$, $\Sigma x_1 x_2 = 500$, $\Sigma x_2^2 = 3,000$, and $n = 16$ into the expression for $\mathbf{X'X}$ on page 380, we get

$$\mathbf{X'X} = \begin{bmatrix} 16 & 40 & 200 \\ 40 & 120 & 500 \\ 200 & 500 & 3,000 \end{bmatrix}$$

Then, the inverse of this matrix can be obtained by any one of a number of different techniques; using the one based on cofactors, we find that

$$(\mathbf{X'X})^{-1} = \frac{1}{160,000} \begin{bmatrix} 110,000 & -20,000 & -4,000 \\ -20,000 & 8,000 & 0 \\ -4,000 & 0 & 320 \end{bmatrix}$$

where 160,000 is the value of $|\mathbf{X'X}|$, the determinant of $\mathbf{X'X}$.

Substituting $\Sigma y = 723$, $\Sigma x_1 y = 1963$, and $\Sigma x_2 y = 8210$ into the expression for $\mathbf{X'y}$ on page 380, we then get

$$\mathbf{X'y} = \begin{bmatrix} 723 \\ 1,963 \\ 8,210 \end{bmatrix}$$

and finally,

$$\mathbf{b} = (\mathbf{X'X})^{-1}\mathbf{X'y} = \frac{1}{160,000} \begin{bmatrix} 110,000 & -20,000 & -4,000 \\ -20,000 & 8,000 & 0 \\ -4,000 & 0 & 320 \end{bmatrix} \begin{bmatrix} 723 \\ 1,963 \\ 8,210 \end{bmatrix}$$

$$= \frac{1}{160,000} \begin{bmatrix} 7,430,000 \\ 1,244,000 \\ -264,800 \end{bmatrix}$$

$$= \begin{bmatrix} 46.4375 \\ 7.7750 \\ -1.6550 \end{bmatrix}$$

Note that the results obtained here are identical with those shown in the computer printout on page 358.   ✓

The residual sum of squares also has a convenient matrix expression. The predicted values $\hat{y}_i = b_0 + b_1 x_{i1} + b_2 x_{i2}$ can be collected as a matrix (column vector).

$$\hat{\mathbf{y}} = \begin{bmatrix} \hat{y}_1 \\ \hat{y}_2 \\ \vdots \\ \hat{y}_n \end{bmatrix} = \begin{bmatrix} 1 & x_{11} & x_{12} \\ 1 & x_{21} & x_{22} \\ \vdots & \vdots & \vdots \\ 1 & x_{n1} & x_{n2} \end{bmatrix} \begin{bmatrix} b_0 \\ b_1 \\ b_2 \end{bmatrix} = \mathbf{Xb}$$

Then, the residual sum of squares

$$\sum_{i=1}^{n} (y_i - \hat{y}_i)^2 = (\mathbf{y} - \hat{\mathbf{y}})'(\mathbf{y} - \hat{\mathbf{y}}) = (\mathbf{y} - \mathbf{Xb})'(\mathbf{y} - \mathbf{Xb})$$

Consequently, the estimate s_e^2 of σ^2 can be expressed as

$$s_e^2 = \frac{1}{n-3}(\mathbf{y} - \mathbf{Xb})'(\mathbf{y} - \mathbf{Xb})$$

The same matrix expressions for $\mathbf{b}$ and the residual sum of squares hold for any number of predictor variables. If the mean of Y has the form $\beta_0 + \beta_1 x_1 + \beta_2 x_2 + \cdots + \beta_k x_k$, we define the matrices

$$\mathbf{X} = \begin{bmatrix} 1 & x_{11} & x_{12} & \cdots & x_{1k} \\ 1 & x_{21} & x_{22} & \cdots & x_{2k} \\ \vdots & \vdots & \vdots & \ddots & \vdots \\ 1 & x_{n1} & x_{n2} & \cdots & x_{nk} \end{bmatrix}, \quad \mathbf{b} = \begin{bmatrix} b_0 \\ b_1 \\ b_2 \\ \vdots \\ b_k \end{bmatrix}, \quad \mathbf{y} = \begin{bmatrix} y_1 \\ y_2 \\ \vdots \\ y_n \end{bmatrix}$$

Then,

$$\mathbf{b} = (\mathbf{X'X})^{-1}\mathbf{X'y} \quad \text{and} \quad s_e^2 = \frac{1}{n-k-1}(\mathbf{y} - \mathbf{Xb})'(\mathbf{y} - \mathbf{Xb})$$

EXAMPLE

Fitting a straight line using the matrix formulas
Use the matrix relations to fit a straight line to the data

x	0	1	2	3	4
y	8	9	4	3	1

Solution   Here $k = 1$ and dropping the subscript 1 we have

$\mathbf{X'}$	$\mathbf{y}$	$\mathbf{X'X}$	$(\mathbf{X'X})^{-1}$	$\mathbf{X'y}$

$$\begin{bmatrix} 1 & 1 & 1 & 1 & 1 \\ 0 & 1 & 2 & 3 & 4 \end{bmatrix} \quad \begin{bmatrix} 8 \\ 9 \\ 4 \\ 3 \\ 1 \end{bmatrix} \quad \begin{bmatrix} 5 & 10 \\ 10 & 30 \end{bmatrix} \quad \begin{bmatrix} 0.6 & -0.2 \\ -0.2 & 0.1 \end{bmatrix} \quad \begin{bmatrix} 25 \\ 30 \end{bmatrix}$$

Consequently

$$\mathbf{b} = (\mathbf{X'X})^{-1}\mathbf{X'y} = \begin{bmatrix} 0.6 & -0.2 \\ -0.2 & 0.1 \end{bmatrix} \begin{bmatrix} 25 \\ 30 \end{bmatrix} = \begin{bmatrix} 9 \\ -2 \end{bmatrix}$$

and the fitted equation is

$$\hat{y} = 9 - 2x$$

The vector of fitted values is

$$\hat{\mathbf{y}} = \mathbf{Xb} = \begin{bmatrix} 1 & 0 \\ 1 & 1 \\ 1 & 2 \\ 1 & 3 \\ 1 & 4 \end{bmatrix} \begin{bmatrix} 9 \\ -2 \end{bmatrix} = \begin{bmatrix} 9 \\ 7 \\ 5 \\ 3 \\ 1 \end{bmatrix}$$

so the vector of residuals

$$\mathbf{y} - \hat{\mathbf{y}} = \begin{bmatrix} 8 \\ 9 \\ 4 \\ 3 \\ 1 \end{bmatrix} - \begin{bmatrix} 9 \\ 7 \\ 5 \\ 3 \\ 1 \end{bmatrix} = \begin{bmatrix} -1 \\ 2 \\ -1 \\ 0 \\ 0 \end{bmatrix}$$

and the residual sum of squares is

$$\begin{bmatrix} -1 & 2 & -1 & 0 & 0 \end{bmatrix} \begin{bmatrix} -1 \\ 2 \\ -1 \\ 0 \\ 0 \end{bmatrix} = 6$$

Finally,

$$s_e^2 = \frac{1}{n-k-1}(\mathbf{y} - \hat{\mathbf{y}}')(\mathbf{y} - \hat{\mathbf{y}}) = \frac{1}{5-2}(6) = 2.00. \qquad \checkmark$$

The elegance of the expressions using matrices goes one step further. We can express the estimated variances and covariances of the least squares estimators as

$$\begin{bmatrix} \hat{var}(b_0) & \hat{cov}(b_0, b_1) & \cdots & \hat{cov}(b_0, b_k) \\ \hat{cov}(b_1, b_0) & \hat{var}(b_1) & \cdots & \hat{cov}(b_1, b_k) \\ \vdots & \vdots & \ddots & \vdots \\ \hat{cov}(b_k, b_0) & \hat{cov}(b_k, b_1) & \cdots & \hat{var}(b_k) \end{bmatrix} = s_e^2(\mathbf{X'X})^{-1}$$

That is, to obtain the estimated variance, $\hat{var}(b_i)$, of b_i, we multiply the corresponding diagonal entry of $(\mathbf{X'X})^{-1}$ by s_e^2, which is the estimate of σ^2.

EXAMPLE

Estimating the variance of the least squares estimators
With reference to the preceding example, use the matrix relations to obtain the estimated variances $\hat{var}(b_0)$ and $\hat{var}(b_1)$.

Solution   We have

$$\begin{bmatrix} \hat{var}(b_0) & \hat{cov}(b_0, b_1) \\ \hat{cov}(b_1, b_0) & \hat{var}(b_1) \end{bmatrix} = s_e^2(\mathbf{X'X})^{-1}$$

$$= (2.00)\begin{bmatrix} 0.6 & -0.2 \\ -0.2 & 0.1 \end{bmatrix} = \begin{bmatrix} 1.2 & -0.4 \\ -0.4 & 0.2 \end{bmatrix}$$

where the values for $(\mathbf{X'X})^{-1}$ and s_e^2 are those obtained in the preceding example. Therefore the estimates are $\hat{var}(b_0) = 1.2$ and $\hat{var}(b_1) = 0.2$. Note also that the estimated covariance of b_0 and b_1 is $\hat{cov}(b_0, b_1) = -0.4$.   ✔

REVIEW EXERCISES

11.64 The following data pertain to the number of hours jet aircraft engines have been used and the number of hours required for repair.

Number of hours (hundreds)	Repair time (hours)
1	10
2	40
3	30
4	80
5	90

(a) Use the first set of expressions on page 333, involving the deviations from the mean, to fit a least squares line to the observations.

(b) Use the equation of the least squares line to estimate mean repair time at $x = 4.5$.

(c) What difficulty might you encounter if you use the least squares line to predict the mean repair time for a jet aircraft engine with 700 hours?

11.65 With reference to Exercise 11.64, construct a 95% confidence interval for α.

11.66 With reference to Exercise 11.64, test the null hypothesis $\beta = 15$ against the alternative hypothesis $\beta > 15$ at the 0.05 level of significance.

11.67 With reference to Exercise 11.64

(a) find a 95% confidence interval for the mean repair time at $x = 4.5$;

(b) find a 95% limits of prediction for the time to repair an engine that will be run for $x = 4.5$ hundred hours.

11.68 To determine how well existing chemical analyses can detect lead in test specimens in water, a civil engineer submits specimens spiked with known concentrations of lead to a laboratory. The chemists are only told that all samples were from a study about measurements on "low" concentrations, but they were not told the range of values to expect. This is sometimes called a calibration problem because the goal is to relate the measured concentration (y) to the known concentration (x). Given the data

x	0.00	0.00	1.25	1.25	2.50	2.50	2.50	5.00	10.00	10.00
y	0.7	0.5	1.1	2.0	2.8	3.5	2.3	5.3	9.1	9.4

(a) plot measured concentration versus known concentration; comment on the pattern;

(b) fit a straight line by least squares;

(c) if the chemical test is correct, on average, we would expect a straight line that has slope 1. Obtain a 95% confidence interval for β;

(d) test $H_0: \beta = 1$ versus $H_1: \beta \neq 1$ at level $\alpha = 0.05$

11.69 With reference to the preceding exercise, construct a 95% confidence interval for α.

11.70 With reference to the example on page 369,

(a) find the least squares line for predicting the chromium in the effluent from that in the influent after taking natural logarithms of each variable;

(b) predict the mean ln (effluent) when the influent has 500 μg/l chromium.

11.71 In an experiment designed to determine the specific heat ratio γ for a certain gas, the gas was compressed adiabatically to several predetermined volumes V, and the corresponding pressure p was measured with the following results:

$p(lb/in.^2)$	16.6	39.7	78.5	115.5	195.3	546.1
V ($in.^3$)	50	30	20	15	10	5

Assuming the ideal gas law $p \cdot V^\gamma = C$, use these data to estimate γ for this gas.

11.72 With reference to Exercise 11.71, use the method of Section 11.2 to construct a 95% confidence interval for γ. State what assumptions will have to be made.

11.73 The rise of current in an inductive circuit having the time constant τ is given by

$$I = 1 - e^{-t/\tau}$$

where t is the time measured from the instant the switch is closed, and I is the ratio of the current at time t to the full value of the current given by Ohm's law. Given the measurements

I	0.073	0.220	0.301	0.370	0.418	0.467	0.517	0.578
$t(sec)$	0.1	0.2	0.3	0.4	0.5	0.6	0.7	0.8

estimate the time constant of this circuit from the experimental results given. [*Hint:* Note that the relationship between $\ln(1 - I)$ and t is linear.]

11.74 The following are sample data provided by a moving company on the weights of six shipments, the distances they are moved, and the damage that was incurred:

Weight (1,000 pounds) x_1	Distance (1,000 miles) x_2	Damage (dollars) y
4.0	1.5	160
3.0	2.2	112
1.6	1.0	69
1.2	2.0	90
3.4	0.8	123
4.8	1.6	186

(a) Fit an equation of the form $y = \beta_0 + \beta_1 x_1 + \beta_2 x_2$.

(b) Use the equation obtained in part (a) to estimate the damage when a shipment weighing 2,400 pounds is moved 1,200 miles.

11.75 With reference to Exercise 11.7,

(a) find a 95% confidence interval for the mean CPU time required for $x = 3.0$ jobs;

(b) find 95% limits of prediction for the CPU time required on a future day when $x = 3.0$ jobs must be run.

11.76 Use the first set of expressions on page 333, involving the deviations from the mean, to calculate r for the following data.

x	y
8	4
5	5
6	1
2	3
9	2

11.77 If $r = 0.41$ for one set of paired data and $r = 0.29$ for another, compare the strengths of the two relationships.

11.78 If for certain paired data $n = 18$ and $r = 0.44$, test the null hypothesis $\rho = 0.30$ against the alternative hypothesis $\rho > 0.30$ at the 0.01 level of significance.

11.79 Assuming that the necessary assumptions are met, construct a 95% confidence interval for ρ when

(a) $r = 0.78$ and $n = 15$;

(b) $r = -0.62$ and $n = 32$;

(c) $r = 0.17$ and $n = 35$.

11.80 With reference to Exercise 11.74, use the theory of Exercise 11.57 to calculate the multiple correlation coefficient (which measures how strongly the damage is related to both weight and distance).

11.81 Robert A. Millikan (1865–1953) produced the first accurate measurements on the charge e of an electron. He devised a method to observe a single drop of water or oil under the influence of both electric and gravitational fields. Usually, a droplet carried multiple electrons and direct calculations based on voltage, time of fall, etc. provided an estimate of the total charge. (Source: *Philosophical Magazine* 19 (1910); 209–228.)

x (No. of e's)	Observations ($10^9 \times$ charge)
3	1.392 1.392 1.398 1.368 1.368 1.368 1.345
4	1.768 1.768 1.910 1.768 1.746 1.746 1.886 1.768 1.768 1.768
5	2.471 2.471 2.256 2.256 2.471
2	0.944 0.992
6	2.981 2.688

(a) Find the equation of the least squares line for Millikan's data.

(b) Find a 95% confidence interval for the slope β, the charge e on a single electron.

(c) Test the null hypothesis $\alpha = 0$ against the alternative hypothesis $\alpha \neq 0$.

(d) Examine the residuals.

11.82 Robert Boyle (1627–1691) established the law that (pressure $\times$ volume) = constant for a gas at a constant temperature. By pouring mercury into the open top of the long side of a J-shaped tube, he increased the pressure on the air trapped in the short leg. The volume of trapped air $= h \times$ cross section, where h is the height of the air in the short leg. If $y =$ height of mercury, adjusted for the pressure of the atmosphere on the open end, then y and $x = 1/h$ should obey a straight-line relationship. (Source: *The Laws of Gases*, edited by Carl Barus (1899), New York: Harper and Brothers Publishers.)

h	48	46	44	42	40	38	36	34	32	30	28	26	24
y	$29\frac{2}{16}$	$30\frac{9}{16}$	$31\frac{15}{16}$	$33\frac{8}{16}$	$35\frac{5}{16}$	37	$39\frac{5}{16}$	$41\frac{10}{16}$	$44\frac{3}{16}$	$47\frac{1}{16}$	$50\frac{5}{16}$	$54\frac{5}{16}$	$58\frac{13}{16}$

h	23	22	21	20	19	18	17	16	15	14	13	12
y	$61\frac{5}{16}$	$64\frac{1}{16}$	$67\frac{1}{16}$	$70\frac{11}{16}$	$74\frac{2}{16}$	$77\frac{14}{16}$	$82\frac{12}{16}$	$87\frac{14}{16}$	$93\frac{1}{16}$	$100\frac{7}{16}$	$107\frac{13}{16}$	$117\frac{9}{16}$

(a) Fit a straight line by least squares to Boyle's data.

(b) Check the residuals for a possible violation of the assumptions.

KEY TERMS

(with page references)

Analysis of Variance

Some of the examples of Chapter 11 have already taught us that considerable economies in calculation can result by appropriately planning an experiment in advance. What is even more important, proper experimental planning can give a reasonable assurance that the results of an experiment will provide clear-cut answers to questions under investigation. While it is impossible to give in this chapter a complete discussion of experimental design, including the many pitfalls to which the experimenter is exposed, we shall begin by presenting some of the general principles of experimental design. Several of the designs most frequently used in engineering and other applied research will be given in subsequent sections.

In Sections 12.2 and 12.3 we shall discuss the often used one- and two-way classification designs, in Section 12.5 we introduce Latin-square and Graeco-Latin-square designs, and in the remainder of the chapter we introduce tests for comparing several means as well as the analysis of a balanced experiment in the presence of a concomitant variable, or covariate. ■

12.1 Some General Principles

Many of the most important aspects of **experimental design** can be illustrated by means of an example drawn from the important field of engineering measurement.

Suppose that a steel mill supplies tin plate to 3 can manufacturers, the major specification being that the tin-coating weight should be at least 0.25 pound per base box. The mill and each can manufacturer has a laboratory where measurements are made of the tin-coating weights of samples taken from each shipment. Suppose, also, that some disagreement has arisen about the actual tin-coating weights of the tin plate being shipped, and it is decided to plan an experiment to determine whether the 4 laboratories are making consistent measurements. A complicating factor is that part of the measuring process consists of the chemical removal of the tin from the surface of the base metal; thus, it is impossible to have the identical sample measured by each laboratory to determine how closely the measurements correspond.

One possibility is to send several samples (in the form of circular discs having equal areas) to each of the laboratories. Although these discs may not actually have identical tin-coating weights, it is hoped that such differences will be small and that they will more or less "average out." In other words, it will be assumed that whatever differences there will be among the means of the 4 samples can be attributed to no other causes but systematic differences in measuring techniques and chance variability. This would make it possible to determine whether the results produced by the laboratories are consistent by comparing the variability of the 4 sample means with an appropriate measure of chance variation.

Now there remains the problem of deciding how many discs are to be sent to each laboratory and how the discs are actually to be selected. The question of sample size can be answered in many different ways, one of which is to use the formula on page 256 for the standard deviation of the difference between two means. Substituting known values of σ_1 and σ_2 and specifying what differences between the true means of any 2 of the laboratories should be detected with a probability of the least 0.95 (or 0.98, or 0.99), it is possible to determine $n_1 = n_2 = n$ (see Exercise 12.12 on page 405). Suppose that this method and, perhaps, also considerations of cost and availability of the necessary specimens lead to the decision to send a sample of 12 discs to each laboratory.

The problem of selecting the required 48 discs and allocating 12 to each laboratory is not as straightforward as it may seem at first. To begin with, suppose that a sheet of tin plate, sufficiently long and sufficiently wide, is selected and that the 48 discs are cut as shown in Figure 12.1. The 12 discs cut from strip 1 are sent to the first laboratory, the 12 discs from strip 2 are sent to the second laboratory, and so forth. If the 4 mean coating weights subsequently obtained were then found to differ significantly, would this allow us to conclude that these differences can be attributed to lack of consistency in the measuring techniques? Suppose, for instance,

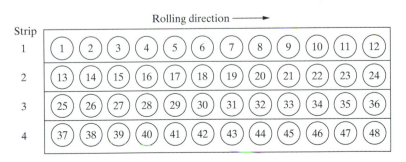

FIGURE 12.1 Numbering of tin-plate samples.

that additional investigation shows that the amount of tin deposited electrolytically on a long sheet of steel has a distinct and repeated pattern of variation perpendicular to the direction in which it is rolled. (Such a pattern might be caused by the placement of electrodes, "edge effects," and so forth.) Thus, even if all 4 laboratories measured the amount of tin consistently and without error, there could be cause for differences in the tin-coating weight determinations. The allocation of an entire strip of discs to each laboratory is such that the inconsistencies among the laboratories' measuring techniques are inseparable from (or **confounded** with) whatever differences there may be in the actual amount of tin deposited perpendicular to the direction in which the sheet of steel is rolled.

One way to avoid that kind of confounding is to number the discs and allocate them to the four laboratories at random, such as in the following arrangement, which was obtained with the aid of a table of random numbers:

Laboratory A:	3	38	17	32	24	30	48	19	11	31	22	41
Laboratory B:	44	20	15	25	45	4	14	5	39	7	40	34
Laboratory C:	12	21	42	8	27	16	47	46	18	43	35	26
Laboratory D:	9	2	28	23	37	1	10	6	29	36	33	13

If there were any actual pattern of tin-coating thickness on the sheet of tin plate, it would be "broken up" by the **randomization.**

Although we have identified and counteracted one possible systematic pattern of variation, there is no assurance that there can be no others. For instance, there may be systematic differences in the areas of the discs caused by progressive wear of the cutting instrument, or there may be scratches or other imperfections on one part of the sheet that could affect the measurements. Thus, there is always the possibility that differences in means attributed to inconsistencies among the laboratories are actually caused by some other uncontrolled variable. **It is the purpose of randomization to avoid confounding the variable under investigation with other uncontrolled variables.**

By distributing the 48 discs among the 4 laboratories entirely at random, we have no choice but to include whatever variation may be attributable to extraneous causes under the heading of "chance variation." This may give us an excessively large estimate of chance variation which, in turn, may make it difficult to detect differences between the true laboratory means. In order to avoid this, we could, perhaps, use only discs cut from the same strip (or from an otherwise homogeneous region). Unfortunately, this kind of **controlled experimentation** presents us with new complications. Of what use would it be, for example, to perform an experiment that allows us to conclude that the laboratories are consistent (or inconsistent), *if such a conclusion is limited to measurements made at a fixed distance from one edge of a sheet?* To consider a more poignant example, suppose that a manufacturer of plumbing materials wishes to compare the performance of several kinds of material to be used in underground water pipes. If such conditions as soil acidity, depth of pipe, and mineral content of water were all held fixed, any conclusions as to which material is best would be valid only for the given set of conditions. What the manufacturer really wants to know is which material is best over a fairly wide variety of conditions, and in designing a suitable experiment it would be advisable (indeed, necessary) to specify that pipe of each material be buried at each of several depths in each of several kinds of soil, and in locations where the water varies in hardness.

This example serves to illustrate that it is seldom desirable to hold all or most extraneous factors fixed throughout an experiment in order to obtain an estimate of chance variation that is not "inflated" by variations due to other causes. (In fact, it is rarely, if ever, possible to exercise such strict control, that is, to hold *all* extraneous variables fixed.) In actual practice, experiments should be planned so that known sources of variability are deliberately varied over as wide a range as necessary; furthermore, they should be varied in such a way that their variability can be eliminated from the estimate of chance variation. One way to accomplish this is to repeat the experiment in several **blocks,** where known sources of variability (that is, extraneous variables) are held fixed in each block, but vary from block to block.

In the tin-plating problem we might thus account for variations across the sheet of steel by randomly allocating 3 discs from each strip to each of the laboratories as in the following arrangement:

	Strip 1	*Strip 2*	*Strip 3*	*Strip 4*
Laboratory A	8, 4, 10	23, 24, 19	26, 29, 35	37, 44, 48
Laboratory B	2, 6, 12	21, 15, 22	34, 33, 32	45, 43, 46
Laboratory C	1, 5, 11	16, 20, 13	36, 27, 30	41, 38, 47
Laboratory D	7, 3, 9	17, 18, 14	28, 31, 25	39, 40, 42

In this experimental layout, the strips form the blocks, and if we base our estimate of chance variation on the variability *within* each of the 16 sets of 3 discs, this estimate will not be inflated by the extraneous variable, that is, differences among the strips. (Note also that, with this arrangement, differences among the means obtained for the 4 laboratories cannot be attributed to differences among the strips. The arrangement on page 390 does not have this property, since, for instance, 5 discs from strip 1 are allocated to Laboratory D.)

The analysis of experiments in which **blocking** is used to eliminate one source of variability is discussed in Section 12.3. The analysis of experiments in which two or three sources of variability are thus eliminated is treated in Section 12.5.

12.2 Completely Randomized Designs

In this section we consider the statistical analysis of the **completely randomized design,** or **one-way classification.** We shall suppose that the experimenter has available the results of k independent random samples, from k different populations (that is, data concerning k treatments, k groups, k methods of production, etc.); and he or she is concerned with testing the hypothesis that the means of these k populations are all equal.

In general, we denote the jth observation in the ith sample by y_{ij} and the schema for a one-way classification is as follows:

	Observations	Means	Sum of Squares
Sample 1:	$y_{11}, y_{12}, \ldots, y_{1j}, \ldots, y_{1n_1}$	$\bar{y}_1$	$\sum_{j=1}^{n_1}(y_{1j} - \bar{y}_1)^2$
Sample 2:	$y_{21}, y_{22}, \ldots, y_{2j}, \ldots, y_{2n_2}$	$\bar{y}_2$	$\sum_{j=1}^{n_2}(y_{2j} - \bar{y}_2)^2$
$\vdots$	$\vdots$	$\vdots$	$\vdots$
Sample i:	$y_{i1}, y_{i2}, \ldots, y_{ij}, \ldots, y_{in_i}$	$\bar{y}_i$	$\sum_{j=1}^{n_i}(y_{ij} - \bar{y}_i)^2$
$\vdots$	$\vdots$	$\vdots$	$\vdots$
Sample k:	$y_{k1}, y_{k2}, \ldots, y_{kj}, \ldots, y_{kn_k}$	$\bar{y}_k$	$\sum_{j=1}^{n_k}(y_{kj} - \bar{y}_k)^2$

To simply the calculations below, we use the notation $T.$ for the sum of all the observations and N for the total sample size.

$$T. = \sum_{i=1}^{k}\sum_{j=1}^{n_i} y_{ij} \quad N = \sum_{i=1}^{k} n_i$$

The overall sample mean $\bar{y}$ is

$$\bar{y} = \frac{\sum_{i=1}^{k}\sum_{j=1}^{n_i} y_{ij}}{\sum_{i=1}^{k} n_i} = \frac{\sum_{i=1}^{k} n_i\bar{y}_i}{\sum_{i=1}^{k} n_i} = \frac{T.}{N}$$

An example of such an experiment with $k = 4$ treatments and equal sample sizes $n_i = 12$ is given on page 390 where y_{ij} is the jth tin-coating weight measured by the ith laboratory, $\bar{y}_i$ is the mean of the measurements obtained by the ith laboratory, and $\bar{y}$ is the overall mean (or **grand mean**) of all $N = 48$ observations.

The statistical analysis leading to a comparison of the k different population means essentially consists of splitting the sum of squares about the overall grand mean $\bar{y}$ into a component due to treatment differences and a component due to error or variation within a sample. It is instructive to see how this analysis emanates from a decomposition of the individual observations.

Suppose 3 drying formulas for curing a glue are studied and the following times observed.

Formula A:	13	10	8	11	8	
Formula B:	13	11	14	14		
Formula C:	4	1	3	4	2	4

There are $N = 5 + 4 + 6 = 15$ observations in all and these total $T. = 120$.

Let the grand mean $\bar{y} = T./N = \sum_{i=1}^{k}\sum_{j=1}^{n_i} y_{ij}/N$. Each observation y_{ij} will be decomposed as

$$y_{ij} = \bar{y} + (\bar{y}_i - \bar{y}) + (y_{ij} - \bar{y}_i)$$

observation grand mean deviation due to treatment error

For instance, $13 = 8 + (10 - 8) + (13 - 10) = 8 + 2 + 3$. Repeating this decomposition for each observation, we obtain the arrays

$$
\begin{array}{cc}
\text{observation} & \text{grand mean} \\
y_{ij} & \bar{y}
\end{array}
$$

$$
\begin{bmatrix}
13 & 10 & 8 & 11 & 8 \\
13 & 11 & 14 & 14 \\
4 & 1 & 3 & 4 & 2 & 4
\end{bmatrix}
=
\begin{bmatrix}
8 & 8 & 8 & 8 & 8 \\
8 & 8 & 8 & 8 \\
8 & 8 & 8 & 8 & 8 & 8
\end{bmatrix}
$$

$$
\begin{array}{cc}
\text{treatment effects} & \text{error} \\
\bar{y}_i - \bar{y} & y_{ij} - \bar{y}_i
\end{array}
$$

$$
+
\begin{bmatrix}
2 & 2 & 2 & 2 & 2 \\
5 & 5 & 5 & 5 \\
-5 & -5 & -5 & -5 & -5 & -5
\end{bmatrix}
+
\begin{bmatrix}
3 & 0 & -2 & 1 & -2 \\
0 & -2 & 1 & 1 \\
1 & -2 & 0 & 1 & -1 & 1
\end{bmatrix}
$$

Taking the sum of squares as a measure of variation for the whole array:

$$
\text{treatment sum of squares} = \sum_{i=1}^{k} n_i (\bar{y}_i - \bar{y})^2 = 5(2)^2 + 4(5)^2 + 6(-5)^2 = 270
$$

$$
\text{error sum of squares} = \sum_{i=1}^{k} \sum_{j=1}^{n_i} (y_{ij} - \bar{y}_i)^2
$$

$$
= 3^2 + 0^2 + (-2)^2 + \cdots + (-1)^2 + 1^2 = 32
$$

Their sum, $302 = 270 + 32$, the total sum of squares, also equals the sum of squared entries in the observation array minus the sum of squares of the entries in the grand mean array. That is, the array for total sum of squares has entries $y_{ij} - \bar{y}$ whose sum of squares is 302.

The decomposition also provides us with an interpretation of the degrees of freedom associated with each sum of squares. In this example, the treatment effects array has only 3 possibly distinct entries: $\bar{y}_1 - \bar{y}, \bar{y}_2 - \bar{y}$, and $\bar{y}_3 - \bar{y}$. Further, the sum of entries is always zero so, for instance, the third value is determined by the first two. Consequently, there are $3 - 1 = 2$ degrees of freedom associated with treatments. In the general case, there are $k - 1$ degrees of freedom.

Among the entries of the error array, each row sums to zero, so 1 degree of freedom is lost for each row. The array has $n_1 + n_2 + n_3 - 3 = 5 + 4 + 6 - 3 = 12$ degrees of freedom. In the general case, there are $n_1 + n_2 + \cdots + n_k - k$ degrees of freedom.

The grand mean array has a single value $\bar{y}$ and hence has 1 degree of freedom, whereas the observation array has $n_1 + n_2 + \cdots + n_k$ possible distinct entries and hence that number of degrees of freedom. The total sum of squares, based on the difference of these last two arrays, has

$$
n_1 + n_2 + \cdots + n_k - 1 = 5 + 4 + 6 - 1 = 14
$$

degrees of freedom.

To summarize our calculations for the curing times, we enter the degrees of freedom and sums of squares in a table called an analysis of variance table.

Analysis of Variance Table for Cure Times

Source of variation	Degrees of freedom	Sum of Squares
Treatment	2	270
Error	12	32
Total	14	302

For further reference, we also summarize the decomposition of the degrees of freedom associated with total, treatment, and error sum of squares, for the general one-way analysis of variance.

Decomposition of the degrees of freedom

$$\text{d.f. Total} = \text{d.f. Treatment} + \text{d.f. Error}$$
$$\sum_{i=1}^{k} n_i - 1 = k - 1 \qquad\qquad + \sum_{i=1}^{k} n_i - k$$

With reference to the **total sum of squares**

$$\sum_{i=1}^{k} \sum_{j=1}^{n_i} (y_{ij} - \bar{y})^2$$

we shall now prove the following theorem.

Theorem 12.1

Identity for one-way analysis of variance

$$\sum_{i=1}^{k} \sum_{j=1}^{n_i} (y_{ij} - \bar{y})^2 = \sum_{i=1}^{k} \sum_{j=1}^{n_i} (y_{ij} - \bar{y}_i)^2 + \sum_{i=1}^{k} n_i (\bar{y}_i - \bar{y})^2$$

The proof of this theorem is based on the identity

$$y_{ij} - \bar{y} = (y_{ij} - \bar{y}_i) + (\bar{y}_i - \bar{y})$$

Squaring both sides and summing on i and j, we obtain

$$\sum_{i=1}^{k} \sum_{j=1}^{n_i} (y_{ij} - \bar{y})^2 = \sum_{i=1}^{k} \sum_{j=1}^{n_i} (y_{ij} - \bar{y}_i)^2 + \sum_{i=1}^{k} \sum_{j=1}^{n_i} (\bar{y}_i - \bar{y})^2$$
$$+ 2 \sum_{i=1}^{k} \sum_{j=1}^{n_i} (y_{ij} - \bar{y}_i)(\bar{y}_i - \bar{y})$$

Next, we observe that

$$\sum_{i=1}^{k} \sum_{j=1}^{n_i} (y_{ij} - \bar{y}_i)(\bar{y}_i - \bar{y}) = \sum_{i=1}^{k} (\bar{y}_i - \bar{y}) \sum_{j=1}^{n_i} (y_{ij} - \bar{y}_i) = 0$$

since $\bar{y}_i$ is the mean of the ith sample and, hence, $\sum_{j=1}^{n_i} (y_{ij} - \bar{y}_i) = 0$ for all i. To complete the proof of Theorem 12.1, we have only to observe that the summand of the second sum on the right-hand side of the above identity does not involve the subscript j and that, consequently,

$$\sum_{i=1}^{k}\sum_{j=1}^{n_i}(\bar{y}_i - \bar{y})^2 = \sum_{i=1}^{k} n_i(\bar{y}_i - \bar{y})^2$$

It is customary to denote the total sum of squares, the left-hand member of the identity of Theorem 12.1, by *SST*. We refer to the first term on the right-hand side as the **error sum of squares,** *SSE*. The term "error sum of squares" expresses the idea that the quantity estimates random (or chance) error. The second term on the right-hand side of the identity of Theorem 12.1 we refer to as the **between-samples sum of squares** or the **treatment sum of squares,** *SS(Tr)*. (Most of the early applications of this kind of analysis were in the field of agriculture, where the k populations represented different **treatments,** such as fertilizers, applied to agricultural plots.)

To be able to test the hypothesis that the samples were obtained from k populations with equal means, we shall make several assumptions. Specifically, it will be assumed that we are dealing with *normal populations* having *equal variances*. There exist methods for testing the reasonableness of this last assumption (see the book by A. M. Mood, F. A. Graybill and D. C. Boes mentioned in the bibliography), but the methods we develop in this chapter are fairly **robust;** that is, they are relatively insensitive to violations of the assumption of normality as well as the assumption of equal variances.

If μ_i denotes the mean of the ith population and σ^2 denotes the common variance of the k populations, we can express each observation Y_{ij} as μ_i plus the value of a random component; that is, we can write[†]

$$Y_{ij} = \mu_i + \varepsilon_{ij} \quad \text{for } i = 1, 2, \ldots, k; j = 1, 2, \ldots, n_i$$

In accordance with the preceding assumptions, the ε_{ij} are independent, normally distributed random variables with zero means and the common variance σ^2.

To attain uniformity with corresponding equations for more complicated kinds of designs, it is customary to replace μ_i by $\mu + \alpha_i$, where μ is the mean $\sum_{i=1}^{k} n_i\mu_i/N$ of the μ_i in the experiment and α_i is the **effect** of the ith treatment; hence, $\sum_{i=1}^{k} n_i\alpha_i = 0$. (see Exercise 12.13 on page 405). Using these new parameters, we can write the **model equation** for the one-way classification as

Model equation for one-way classification

$$Y_{ij} = \mu + \alpha_i + \varepsilon_{ij} \quad \text{for } i = 1, 2, \ldots, k; j = 1, 2, \ldots, n_i$$

and the null hypothesis that the k population means are all equal can be replaced by the null hypothesis that $\alpha_1 = \alpha_2 = \cdots = \alpha_k = 0$. The alternative hypothesis

[†]Note that this equation, or model, can be regarded as a multiple regression equation; introducing the variables x_{il} that equal 0 or 1 depending on whether the two subscripts are unequal or equal, we can write

$$Y_{ij} = \mu_1 x_{i1} + \mu_2 x_{i2} + \cdots + \mu_k x_{ik} + \varepsilon_{ij}$$

The parameters μ_i can be interpreted as regression coefficients, and they can be estimated by the least-squares methods of Chapter 11.

that at least two of the population means are unequal is equivalent to the alternative hypothesis that $\alpha_i \neq 0$ for some i.

To test the null hypothesis that the k population means are all equal, we shall compare two estimates of σ^2—one based on the variation among the sample means, and one based on the variation within the samples.

Each sum of squares is first converted to a **mean square** so a test for the equality of treatment means can be performed.

Mean Square

$$\textbf{Mean Square} = \frac{\text{Sum of squares}}{\text{degrees of freedom}}$$

When the population means are equal, both the

$$\text{Treatment Mean Square} = \frac{\sum_{i=1}^{k} n_i (\bar{y}_i - \bar{y})^2}{k - 1}$$

and the

$$\text{Error Mean Square} = \frac{\sum_{i=1}^{k} \sum_{j=1}^{n_i} (y_{ij} - \bar{y})^2}{N - k}$$

are estimates of σ^2. However, when the null hypothesis is *false*, the **treatment** or **between-sample** mean square can be expected to exceed the **error** or **within-sample** mean square. If the null hypothesis is true, it can be shown that the two mean squares are independent and that their ratio

F ratio for treatments

$$F = \frac{\sum_{i=1}^{k} n_i (\bar{Y}_i - \bar{Y})^2 / (k - 1)}{\sum_{i=1}^{k} \sum_{j=1}^{n_i} (Y_{ij} - \bar{Y})^2 / (N - k)} = \frac{SS(Tr)/(k - 1)}{SSE/(N - k)}$$

has an F distribution with $k - 1$ and $N - k$ degrees of freedom.

The null hypothesis will be rejected, at level α, if the value of F exceeds F_α where F_α is obtained from Table 6 with $k - 1$ and $N - k$ degrees of freedom.

To test for the equality of the mean curing times, we complete the **Analysis of Variance (ANOVA)** table by including the mean square errors and value of F.

Analysis of Variance Table for Cure Times

Source of variation	Degrees of freedom	Sum of Squares	Mean Square	F
Treatment	2	270	135	50.6
Error	12	32	2.667	
Total	14	302		

The value of $F_{.05}$ with 2 and 12 degrees of freedom is 3.89 so we reject the null hypothesis of equal means.

In general, the results obtained in analyzing the total sum of squares into its components are conveniently summarized by means of the **analysis of variance table:**

Source of variation	Degrees of freedom	Sum of Squares	Mean Square	F
Treatments	$k - 1$	$SS(Tr)$	$MS(Tr) = SS(Tr)/(k-1)$	$\dfrac{MS(Tr)}{MSE}$
Error	$N - k$	SSE	$MSE = SSE/(N - k)$	
Total	$N - 1$	SST		

where $N = \sum_{i=1}^{k} n_i$. Note that each **mean square** is obtained by dividing the corresponding sum of squares by its degrees of freedom.

The sums of squares required for substitution into this last formula are usually obtained by means of the following shortcut formulas, which the reader will be asked to verify in Exercise 12.14. We first calculate SST and $SS(Tr)$ by means of the formulas

Sums of squares

$$SST = \sum_{i=1}^{k} \sum_{j=1}^{n_i} y_{ij}^2 - C$$

$$SS(Tr) = \sum_{i=1}^{k} \frac{T_i^2}{n_i} - C$$

where C, called the **correction term**, is given by

$$C = \frac{T_{\cdot}^2}{N}$$

with $N = \sum_{i=1}^{k} n_i, \quad T_{\cdot} = \sum_{i=1}^{k} T_i \quad \text{and} \quad T_i = \sum_{j=1}^{n_i} y_{ij}$

That is, in these formulas, T_i is the total of the n_i observations in the ith sample, whereas $T_{\cdot}$ is the grand total of all N observations. The error sum of squares, SSE, is then obtained by subtraction; according to Theorem 12.1, we can write

Error sum of squares

$$SSE = SST - SS(Tr)$$

EXAMPLE

Conducting a one-way analysis of variance

To illustrate the **analysis of variance** (as this technique is appropriately called) for a one-way classification, suppose that in accordance with the layout on page 390 each laboratory measures the tin-coating weights of 12 discs and that the results are as follows:

Laboratory A	Laboratory B	Laboratory C	Laboratory D
0.25	0.18	0.19	0.23
0.27	0.28	0.25	0.30
0.22	0.21	0.27	0.28
0.30	0.23	0.24	0.28
0.27	0.25	0.18	0.24
0.28	0.20	0.26	0.34
0.32	0.27	0.28	0.20
0.24	0.19	0.24	0.18
0.31	0.24	0.25	0.24
0.26	0.22	0.20	0.28
0.21	0.29	0.21	0.22
0.28	0.16	0.19	0.21

Construct an analysis of variance table.

Solution

The totals for the $k = 4$ samples all of sample size $n_i = 12$ are, respectively, 3.21, 2.72, 2.76, and 3.00, the grand total is $T. = 11.69$, and the calculations required to obtain the necessary sums of squares are as follows:

$$N = 12 + 12 + 12 + 12 = 48$$

$$C = \frac{(11.69)^2}{48} = 2.8470$$

$$SST = (0.25)^2 + (0.27)^2 + \cdots + (0.21)^2 - 2.8470 = 0.0809$$

$$SS(Tr) = \frac{(3.21)^2}{12} + \frac{(2.72)^2}{12} + \frac{(2.76)^2}{12} + \frac{(3.00)^2}{12} - 2.8470 = 0.0130$$

$$SSE = 0.0809 - 0.0130 = 0.0679$$

Thus, we get the following analysis of variance table:

Source of variation	Degrees of freedom	Sum of squares	Mean square	F
Laboratories	3	0.0130	0.0043	2.87
Error	44	0.0679	0.0015	
Total	47	0.0809		

Since the value obtained for F exceeds 2.82, the value of $F_{0.05}$ with 3 and 44 degrees of freedom, the null hypothesis can be rejected at the 0.05 level of significance; we conclude that the laboratories are *not* obtaining consistent results. ✔

To estimate the parameters $\mu, \alpha_1, \alpha_2, \alpha_3, \ldots, \alpha_k$ (or $\mu_1, \mu_2, \mu_3, \ldots, \mu_k$), we can use the method of least squares, minimizing

$$\sum_{i=1}^{k} \sum_{j=1}^{n_i} (y_{ij} - \mu - \alpha_i)^2$$

with respect to μ and α_i, subject to the restriction that $\sum_{i=1}^{k} n_i \alpha_i = 0$. This may be done by eliminating one of the α's or, better, by using the method of Lagrange multipliers, which is treated in most texts on advanced calculus. In either case we obtain the "intuitively obvious" estimate $\hat{\mu} = \bar{y}$ and $\hat{\alpha}_i = \bar{y}_i - \bar{y}$ for $i = 1, 2, \ldots, k$, and the corresponding estimates for the μ_i are given by $\hat{\mu}_i = \bar{y}_i$.

EXAMPLE
Estimating the treatment effects
Estimate the parameters of the one-way classification model for the tin-coating weights given in the preceding example.

Solution   For the data from the 4 laboratories we get

$$\hat{\mu} = \frac{11.69}{48} = 0.244, \quad \hat{\alpha}_1 = \frac{3.21}{12} - 0.244 = 0.024$$

$$\hat{\alpha}_2 = \frac{2.72}{12} - 0.244 = -0.017, \quad \hat{\alpha}_3 = \frac{2.76}{12} - 0.244 = -0.014$$

and

$$\hat{\alpha}_4 = \frac{3.00}{12} - 0.244 = 0.006$$

EXAMPLE
Comparing mean shear strength at three roof locations
As part of the investigation of the collapse of the roof of a building, a testing laboratory is given all the available bolts that connected the steel structure at 3 different positions on the roof. The forces required to shear each of these bolts (coded values) are as follows:

Position 1:	90	82	79	98	83	91
Position 2:	105	89	93	104	89	95	86
Position 3:	83	89	80	94			

Perform an analysis of variance to test at the 0.05 level of significance whether the differences among the sample means at the 3 positions are significant.

Solution   Using the same steps as in previous chapters for tests of hypotheses, we get
1. *Null hypothesis:* $\mu_1 = \mu_2 = \mu_3$
   Alternative hypothesis: The μ's are not all equal.
2. *Level of significance:* $\alpha = 0.05$

3. *Criterion:* Reject the null hypothesis if $F > 3.74$, the value of $F_{0.05}$ for $k - 1 = 3 - 1 = 2$ and $N - k = 17 - 3 = 14$ degrees of freedom, where F is to be determined by an analysis of variance.

4. *Calculations:* Substituting $n_1 = 6$, $n_2 = 7$, $n_3 = 4$, $N = 17$, $T_1 = 523$, $T_2 = 661$, $T_3 = 346$, $T. = 1,530$, and $\sum \sum y_{ij}^2 = 138,638$ into the computing formulas for the sums of squares, we get

$$SST = 138638 - \frac{1530^2}{17} = 938$$

$$SS(Tr) = \frac{523^2}{6} + \frac{661^2}{7} + \frac{346^2}{4} - \frac{1530^2}{17} = 234$$

and

$$SSE = 938 - 234 = 704$$

The remainder of the work is shown in the following analysis of variance table:

Source of variation	Degrees of freedom	Sums of squares	Mean square	F
Positions	2	234	117	2.33
Error	14	704	50.3	
Total	16	938		

5. *Decision:* Since $F = 2.33$ does not exceed 3.74, the null hypothesis cannot be rejected. We cannot conclude that there is a difference in the mean shear strengths of the bolts at the three different positions on the roof. ✔

When the null hypothesis of equal treatment effects is rejected, the magnitudes of the differences should be estimated using confidence intervals. The difference of sample means for treatment i and treatment l, $\bar{y}_i - \bar{y}_l$ estimates the difference in mean response $\mu + \alpha_i - \mu - \alpha_l$. Using the mean square error, s^2, from the ANOVA table, the $(1 - \alpha)100\%$ confidence interval for the true difference in mean response is

$$\bar{y}_i - \bar{y}_l \pm t_{\alpha/2} \sqrt{s^2\left(\frac{1}{n_i} + \frac{1}{n_l}\right)}$$

When many means need to be compared, α can be modified to $2\alpha/k(k - 1)$ according to Bonferroni's procedure discussed in Section 12.4.

EXAMPLE

Comparing the mean strengths of different resins
The internal bonding strengths of 3 different resins ED, MD, and PF need to be compared. Five specimens were prepared with each of the resins.

Resin	Strength					Mean
ED	0.99	1.19	0.79	0.95	0.90	.964
MD	1.11	1.53	1.37	1.24	1.42	1.334
PF	0.83	0.68	0.94	0.86	0.57	.776

The analysis of variance table shows that there is a statistically significant difference at level $\alpha = .05$ (see Exercise 12.44).

Source of variation	Degrees of freedom	Sums of squares	Mean square	F	P-value
Resin	2	.8060	.4030	17.2	0.000
Error	12	.2810	.0234		
Total	14	1.0870			

Determine the individual 95% confidence intervals for the 3 differences of means.

Solution   The confidence intervals use the MSE = .0234 as the estimate s^2 and the degrees of freedom = 12, so $t_{.025} = 2.179$. The three confidence intervals become

$$\text{MD} - \text{ED}: 1.334 - .964 \pm 2.179\sqrt{.0234(\tfrac{1}{5} + \tfrac{1}{5})} \text{ or } (.159, .581)$$

$$\text{MD} - \text{PF}: 1.334 - .776 \pm 2.179\sqrt{.0234(\tfrac{1}{5} + \tfrac{1}{5})} \text{ or } (.347, .769)$$

$$\text{ED} - \text{PF}: \; .964 - .776 \pm 2.179\sqrt{.0234(\tfrac{1}{5} + \tfrac{1}{5})} \text{ or } (-.023, .399)$$

The resin MD has a higher internal bond strength than the other two, which cannot be distinguished.   ✔

EXAMPLE   **Confidence intervals quantify the amount of difference**
The old way of testing the strength of paper with a special tearing machine is by testing a single sheet (ply). It has been suggested that measuring 5 sheets together (5 plys) and then adjusting to the single-thickness strength would be a better procedure. The first question is whether or not the two procedures give essentially the same value for strength. There is a strong element of design involved here. Five pieces of paper are cut in half. One-half of each piece is randomly selected and its strength obtained. Next, the 5 remaining halves are tested together as the 5-ply specimen. The scientist then calculates the average of the 5 individual readings minus the adjusted 5-ply reading. This procedure was repeated 3 times for each of 4 different but representative types of paper. The observations of the differences are given in the following table.

Paper type	Rep. 1	Rep. 2	Rep. 3	Mean
No. 1	2.80	0.75	3.70	2.417
No. 2	0.00	−0.10	3.45	1.117
No. 3	1.15	1.75	4.20	2.367
No. 4	1.88	2.65	2.70	2.410

Test, at level .05, the null hypothesis that there is no difference between the two methods of testing paper strength. Also summarize the results using confidence intervals.

Solution   Formally, we test whether the mean difference changes with paper type. Omitting the details, a computer calculation gives the ANOVA table

Source of variation	Degrees of freedom	Sum of squares	Mean square	F
Type	3	3.70	1.23	.54
Error	8	18.39	2.30	
Total	11	22.08		

Because $F = .54$ is less than 1, we cannot reject H_0: $\alpha_1 = \alpha_2 = \alpha_3 = \alpha_4 = 0$ even at the 50% level. Consequently, it is reasonable to treat all 12 of the differences as coming from the same population. We calculate $\bar{y} = 2.078$ and the standard deviation $= 1.417$. Since, with the degrees of freedom $12 - 1 = 11$, $t_{.025} = 2.201$ and the 95% confidence interval for the mean of the differences is

$$2.078 \pm 2.201 \frac{1.417}{\sqrt{12}} \quad \text{or} \quad (1.18, 2.98)$$

The tearing strength based on the 5-ply reading is about 1 to 3 units lower than that of the individual readings. It is up to the scientist to decide if this discrepancy is of importance in the engineering application.   ✔

EXERCISES

12.1 An experiment is performed to compare the cleansing action of two detergents, Detergent A and Detergent B. Twenty swatches of cloth are soiled with dirt and grease, each is washed with one of the detergents in an agitator-type machine, and then measured for "whiteness." Criticize the following aspects of the experiment:

(a) The entire experiment is performed with soft water.

(b) Fifteen of the swatches are washed with Detergent A and five with Detergent B.

(c) To accelerate the testing procedure, very hot water and 30-second washing times are used in the experiment.

(d) The "whiteness" readings of all swatches with Detergent A are taken first.

12.2 A certain *bon vivant*, wishing to ascertain the cause of his frequent hangovers, conducted the following experiment. On the first night, he drank nothing but whiskey and water; on the second night he drank vodka and water; on the third night he drank gin and water; and on the fourth night he drank rum and water. On each of the following mornings he had a hangover, and he concluded that it was the common factor, the water, that made him ill.

(a) This conclusion is obviously unwarranted, but can you state what principles of sound experimental design are violated?

(b) Give a less obvious example of an experiment having the same shortcoming.

(c) Suppose that our friend had modified his experiment so that each of the 4 alcoholic beverages was used both with and without water, so that the experiment lasted 8 nights. Could the results of this enlarged experiment serve to support or refute the hypothesis that water was the cause of the hangovers? Explain.

12.3 To compare the effectiveness of three methods of teaching the programming of a certain computer—Method A, which is straight teaching-machine instruction, Method B, which involves the personal attention of an instructor and some direct experience working with the computer, and Method C, which involves the personal attention of an instructor but no work with the computer—random samples of size 4 are taken from large groups of persons taught by the methods and the following are the scores which they obtained in an appropriate achievement test:

Method A	Method B	Method C
73	91	72
77	81	77
67	87	76
71	85	79

(a) Without using the shortcut formulas, calculate

$$\sum_{i=1}^{k} \sum_{j=1}^{n_i} (y_{ij} - \bar{y})^2 \quad \sum_{i=1}^{k} \sum_{j=1}^{n_i} (y_{ij} - \bar{y}_i)^2 \quad \text{and} \quad \sum_{i=1}^{k} n_i (\bar{y}_i - \bar{y})^2$$

and verify the identity of Theorem 12.1.

(b) Verify the results obtained for the three sums of squares by using the shortcut formulas on page 397

12.4 Using the sums of squares obtained in Exercise 12.3, test at the level of significance $\alpha = 0.05$ whether the differences among the means obtained for the 3 samples are significant.

12.5 The following are the numbers of mistakes made in 5 successive days for 4 technicians working for a photographic laboratory:

Technician I	Technician II	Technician III	Technician IV
6	14	10	9
14	9	12	12
10	12	7	8
8	10	15	10
11	14	11	11

Test at the level of significance $\alpha = 0.01$ whether the differences among the 4 sample means can be attributed to chance.

12.6 The following are the weight losses of certain machine parts (in milligrams) due to friction, when 3 different lubricants were used under controlled conditions:

Lubricant A:	12.2	11.8	13.1	11.0	3.9	4.1	10.3	8.4
Lubricant B:	10.9	5.7	13.5	9.4	11.4	15.7	10.8	14.0
Lubricant C:	12.7	19.9	13.6	11.7	18.3	14.3	22.8	20.4

(a) Test at the 0.01 level of significance whether the differences among the means can be attributed to chance.

(b) Estimate the parameters of the model used in the analysis of this experiment.

12.7 Given the following observations collected according to the one-way analysis of variance design:

Treatment 1:	6	4	5	
Treatment 2:	13	10	13	12
Treatment 3:	7	9	11	
Treatment 4:	3	6	1	4	1

(a) decompose each observation y_{ij} as
$$y_{ij} = \bar{y} + (\bar{y}_i - \bar{y}) + (y_{ij} - \bar{y}_i)$$
and obtain the sum of squares and degrees of freedom for each component;

(b) construct the analysis of variance table and test the equality of treatments using $\alpha = 0.05$.

12.8 With reference to the example on page 392, suppose one additional observation $y_{25} = 8$ is available using formula B. Construct the analysis of variance table and test the equality of the mean curing times using $\alpha = 0.05$.

12.9 To find the best arrangement of instruments on a control panel of an airplane, 3 different arrangements were tested by simulating an emergency condition and observing the reaction time required to correct the condition. The reaction times (in tenths of a second) of 28 pilots (randomly assigned to the different arrangements) were as follows:

Arrangement 1:	14	13	9	15	11	13	14	11			
Arrangement 2:	10	12	9	7	11	8	12	9	10	13	9	10
Arrangement 3:	11	5	9	10	6	8	8	7			

Test at the level of significance $\alpha = 0.01$ whether we can reject the null hypothesis that the differences among the arrangements have no effect.

12.10 Several different aluminum alloys are under consideration for use in heavy-duty circuit wiring applications. Among the desired properties is low electrical resistance, and specimens of each wire are tested by applying a fixed voltage to a given length of wire and measuring the current passing through the wire. Given the following results, would you conclude that these alloys differ in resistance? (Use the 0.01 level of significance.)

Alloy	Current (amperes)				
1	1.085	1.016	1.009	1.034	
2	1.051	0.993	1.022		
3	0.985	1.001	0.990	0.988	1.011
4	1.101	1.015			

12.11 Two tests are made of the compressive strength of each of 6 samples of poured concrete. The force required to crumble each of 12 cylindrical specimens, measured in kilograms, is as follows:

			Sample			
	A	B	C	D	E	F
Test 1	110	125	98	95	104	115
Test 2	105	130	107	91	96	121

Test at the 0.05 level of significance whether these samples differ in compressive strength.

12.12 Referring to the discussion on page 389, assume that the standard deviations of the tin-coating weights determined by any one of the 4 laboratories have the common value $\sigma = 0.012$, and that it is desired to be 95% confident of detecting a difference in means between any 2 of the laboratories in excess of 0.01 pound per base box. Show that these assumptions lead to the decision to send a sample of 12 discs to each laboratory.

12.13 Show that if $\mu_i = \mu + \alpha_i$ and μ is the mean of the μ_i, it follows that $\sum_{i=1}^{k} n_i \alpha_i = 0$.

12.14 Verify the shortcut formulas for computing SST and $SS(Tr)$ given on page 397.

12.15 With reference to Exercise 12.9, determine individual 99% confidence intervals for the differences of mean reaction times.

12.16 Samples of peanut butter produced by 2 different manufacturers are tested for aflatoxin content, with the following results:

Aflatoxin content (ppb)

Brand A	Brand B
0.5	4.7
0.0	6.2
3.2	0.0
1.4	10.5
0.0	2.1
1.0	0.8
8.6	
2.9	

(a) Use analysis of variance to test whether the two brands differ in aflatoxin content.

(b) Test the same hypothesis using a two-sample t test.

(c) It can be shown that the t statistic with ν degrees of freedom and the F statistic with 1 and ν degrees of freedom are related by the formula

$$F(1, \nu) = t^2(\nu)$$

where $\nu = $ degrees of freedom. Using this result, prove that the analysis of variance and two-sample t-test methods are equivalent in this case.

12.17 The one-way analysis of variance is conveniently implemented using *MINITAB*. With reference to the example on page 392, we first set the observations in columns.

DATA:
```
C1:  13  10   8  11   8
C2:  13  11  14  14
C3:   4   1   3   4   2   4
```

Dialog Box:	**Session command**
Stat > ANOVA > One-way (Unstacked)	MTB > AOVONEWAY C1-C3
Enter *C1-C3* in **Responses.**	
Click **OK**.	

One-way Analysis of Variance

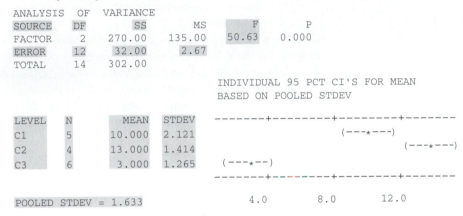

```
ANALYSIS   OF  VARIANCE
SOURCE     DF        SS        MS        F        P
FACTOR      2    270.00    135.00    50.63    0.000
ERROR      12     32.00      2.67
TOTAL      14    302.00

                                    INDIVIDUAL 95 PCT CI'S FOR MEAN
                                    BASED ON POOLED STDEV

LEVEL    N      MEAN    STDEV    -------+--------+--------+-------
C1       5    10.000    2.121                     (---*---)
C2       4    13.000    1.414                            (---*---)
C3       6     3.000    1.265      (---*--)
                                 -------+--------+--------+-------
POOLED STDEV = 1.633               4.0      8.0     12.0
```

Use the computer to perform the analysis of variance suggested in Exercise 12.9.

12.3 Randomized-Block Designs

As we observed in Section 12.1, the estimate of chance variation (the experimental error) can often be reduced, that is, freed of variability due to extraneous causes, by dividing the observations in each classification into blocks. This is accomplished when known sources of variability (that is, extraneous variables) are fixed in each block, but vary from block to block.

In this section we shall suppose that the experimenter has available measurements pertaining to *a* treatments distributed over *b* blocks. First, we shall consider the case where there is exactly one observation from each treatment in each block; with reference to the illustration on page 389, this case would arise if each laboratory tested one disc from each strip. Letting y_{ij} denote the observation pertaining to the *i*th treatment and the *j*th block, $\bar{y}_{i.}$ the mean of the *b* observations for the *i*th treatment, $\bar{y}_{.j}$ the mean of the *a* observations in the *j*th block, and the $\bar{y}_{..}$ the grand mean of all the *ab* observations, we shall use the following layout for this kind of **two-way classification:**

Blocks

	B_1	B_2	$\cdots$	B_j	$\cdots$	B_b	Means
Treatment 1:	y_{11}	y_{12}	$\cdots$	y_{1j}	$\cdots$	y_{1b}	$\bar{y}_{1.}$
Treatment 2:	y_{21}	y_{22}	$\cdots$	y_{2j}	$\cdots$	y_{2b}	$\bar{y}_{2.}$
				$\vdots$			$\vdots$
Treatment i:	y_{i1}	y_{i2}	$\cdots$	y_{ij}	$\cdots$	y_{ib}	$\bar{y}_{i.}$
				$\vdots$			$\vdots$
Treatment a:	y_{a1}	y_{a2}	$\cdots$	y_{aj}	$\cdots$	y_{ab}	$\bar{y}_{a.}$
Means	$\bar{y}_{.1}$	$\bar{y}_{.2}$	$\cdots$	$\bar{y}_{.j}$	$\cdots$	$\bar{y}_{.b}$	$\bar{y}_{..}$

This kind of arrangement is also called a **randomized-block design,** provided the treatments are allocated at random *within* each block. Note that when a dot is used in place of a subscript, this means that the mean is obtained by summing over that subscript.

The underlying model which we shall assume for the analysis of this kind of experiment with one observation per "cell" (that is, there is one observation corresponding to each treatment within each block) is given by

Model equation for randomized-block design

$$Y_{ij} = \mu + \alpha_i + \beta_j + \varepsilon_{ij} \quad \text{for } i = 1, 2, \ldots, a; j = 1, 2, \ldots, b$$

Here μ is the grand mean, α_i is the effect of the ith treatment, β_j is the effect of the jth block, and the ε_{ij} are *independent, normally distributed* random variables having *zero means* and the *common variance* σ^2. Analogous to the model for the one-way classification, we restrict the parameters by imposing the conditions that $\sum_{i=1}^{a} \alpha_i = 0$ and $\sum_{j=1}^{b} \beta_j = 0$ (see Exercise 12.27).

In the analysis of a two-way classification where each treatment is represented once in each block, the major objective is to test the significance of the differences among the $\bar{y}_{i.}$, that is, to test the null hypothesis

$$\alpha_1 = \alpha_2 = \cdots = \alpha_a = 0$$

In addition, it may also be desirable to test whether the blocking has been effective, that is, whether the null hypothesis

$$\beta_1 = \beta_2 = \cdots = \beta_b = 0$$

can be rejected. In either case, the alternative hypothesis is that at least one of the effects is different from zero.

As in the one-way analysis of variance, we shall base these significance tests on comparisons of estimates of σ^2— one based on the variation among treatments, one based on the variation among blocks, and one measuring the experimental error. Note that only the latter is an estimate of σ^2 when either (or both) of the null hypotheses do not hold. The required sums of squares are given by the three components into which the total sum of squares is partitioned by means of the following theorem:

Theorem 12.2

$$\sum_{i=1}^{a} \sum_{j=1}^{b} (y_{ij} - \bar{y}_{..})^2 = \sum_{i=1}^{a} \sum_{j=1}^{b} (y_{ij} - \bar{y}_{i.} - \bar{y}_{.j} + \bar{y}_{..})^2$$

$$+ b \sum_{i=1}^{a} (\bar{y}_{i.} - \bar{y}_{..})^2 + a \sum_{j=1}^{b} (\bar{y}_{.j} - \bar{y}_{..})^2$$

The left-hand side of this identity represents the total sum of squares, SST, and the terms of the right-hand side are, respectively, the error sum of squares, SSE, the treatment sum of squares, $SS(Tr)$, and the **block sum of squares** $SS(Bl)$. To prove this theorem, we would make use of the identity

$$y_{ij} - \bar{y}_{..} = (y_{ij} - \bar{y}_{i.} - \bar{y}_{.j} + \bar{y}_{..}) + (\bar{y}_{i.} - \bar{y}_{..}) + (\bar{y}_{.j} - \bar{y}_{..})$$

and follow essentially the same argument as in the proof of Theorem 12.1.

Convenient formulas are available to calculate SST, $SS(Tr)$, and $SS(Bl)$ using hand-held calculators.

Sums of squares for
two-way analysis of
variance

$$SST = \sum_{i=1}^{a} \sum_{j=1}^{b} y_{ij}^2 - C$$

$$SS(Tr) = \frac{\sum_{i=1}^{a} T_{i.}^2}{b} - C$$

$$SS(Bl) = \frac{\sum_{j=1}^{b} T_{.j}^2}{a} - C$$

where C, the correction term, is given by

$$C = \frac{T_{..}^2}{ab}$$

In these formulas, $T_{i.}$ is the sum of the b observations for the ith treatment, $T_{.j}$ is the sum of the a observations in the jth block, and $T_{..}$ is the grand total of all the observations. Note that the divisors for $SS(Tr)$ and $SS(Bl)$ are the number of observations in the respective totals, $T_{i.}$ and $T_{.j}$. The error sum of squares is then obtained by subtraction; according to Theorem 12.2 we can write

$$SSE = SST - SS(Tr) - SS(Bl)$$

In Exercise 12.28, the reader will be asked to verify that all these computing formulas are, indeed, equivalent to the corresponding terms of the identity of Theorem 12.2.

Using the sums of squares, we can reject the null hypothesis that the α_i are all equal to zero at the level of significance α if

F ratio for treatments

$$F_{Tr} = \frac{MS(Tr)}{MSE} = \frac{SS(Tr)/(a-1)}{SSE/(a-1)(b-1)}$$

exceeds F_α with $a-1$ and $(a-1)(b-1)$ degrees of freedom. The null hypothesis that the β_j are all equal to zero can be rejected at the level of significance α if

F ratio for blocks

$$F_{Bl} = \frac{MS(Bl)}{MSE} = \frac{SS(Bl)/(b-1)}{SSE/(a-1)(b-1)}$$

exceeds F_α with $b-1$ and $(a-1)(b-1)$ degrees of freedom. Note that the mean squares, $MS(Tr)$, $MS(Bl)$, and MSE, are again defined as the corresponding sums of squares divided by their degrees of freedom.

The results obtained in this analysis are summarized in the following analysis of variance table:

Source of variation	Degrees of freedom	Sum of squares	Mean square	F
Treatments	$a-1$	$SS(Tr)$	$MS(Tr) = \dfrac{SS(Tr)}{(a-1)}$	$F_{Tr} = \dfrac{MS(Tr)}{MSE}$
Blocks	$b-1$	$SS(Bl)$	$MS(Bl) = \dfrac{SS(Bl)}{(b-1)}$	$F_{Bl} = \dfrac{MS(Bl)}{MSE}$
Error	$(a-1)(b-1)$	SSE	$MSE = \dfrac{SSE}{(a-1)(b-1)}$	
Total	$ab-1$	SST		

It is instructive to see how the analysis of variance for a randomization block experiment follows from the decomposition of each observation. Given the observations

	Blocks			
Treatment 1	13	7	9	3
Treatment 2	6	6	3	1
Treatment 3	11	5	15	5

Each observation y_{ij} will be decomposed as

$$y_{ij} \;=\; \bar{y}_{..} \;+\; (\bar{y}_{i.} - \bar{y}_{..}) \;+\; (\bar{y}_{.j} - \bar{y}_{..}) \;+\; (y_{ij} - \bar{y}_{i.} - \bar{y}_{.j} + \bar{y}_{..})$$

$$\underset{\substack{\text{observation}}}{} \quad \underset{\substack{\text{grand}\\\text{mean}}}{} \quad \underset{\substack{\text{deviation}\\\text{due to}\\\text{treatment}}}{} \quad \underset{\substack{\text{deviation}\\\text{due to}\\\text{blocks}}}{} \quad \underset{\substack{\text{error}}}{}$$

For instance, $13 = 7 + (8 - 7) + (10 - 7) + (13 - 8 - 10 + 7) = 7 + 1 + 3 + 2$. Repeating this decomposition for each observation, we obtain the arrays

$$\underset{y_{ij}}{\overset{observation}{\begin{bmatrix} 13 & 7 & 9 & 3 \\ 6 & 6 & 3 & 1 \\ 11 & 5 & 15 & 5 \end{bmatrix}}} = \underset{\bar{y}_{..}}{\overset{mean}{\begin{bmatrix} 7 & 7 & 7 & 7 \\ 7 & 7 & 7 & 7 \\ 7 & 7 & 7 & 7 \end{bmatrix}}} + \underset{\bar{y}_{i.} - \bar{y}_{..}}{\overset{treatment}{\begin{bmatrix} 1 & 1 & 1 & 1 \\ -3 & -3 & -3 & -3 \\ 2 & 2 & 2 & 2 \end{bmatrix}}}$$

$$+ \underset{\bar{y}_{.j} - \bar{y}_{..}}{\overset{block}{\begin{bmatrix} 3 & -1 & 2 & -4 \\ 3 & -1 & 2 & -4 \\ 3 & -1 & 2 & -4 \end{bmatrix}}} + \underset{y_{ij} - \bar{y}_{i.} - \bar{y}_{.j} + \bar{y}_{..}}{\overset{error}{\begin{bmatrix} 2 & 0 & -1 & -1 \\ -1 & 3 & -3 & 1 \\ -1 & -3 & 4 & 0 \end{bmatrix}}}$$

Taking the sum of squares for each array,

$$treatment\ sum\ of\ squares = b \sum_{i=1}^{a} (\bar{y}_{i.} - \bar{y}_{..})^2 = 4(1)^2 + 4(-3)^2 + 4(2)^2 = 56$$

$$block\ sum\ of\ squares = a \sum_{j=1}^{b} (\bar{y}_{.j} - \bar{y}_{..})^2$$

$$= 3(3)^2 + 3(-1)^2 + 3(2)^2 + 3(-4)^2 = 90$$

$$error\ sum\ of\ squares = \sum_{i=1}^{a} \sum_{j=1}^{b} (y_{ij} - \bar{y}_{i.} - \bar{y}_{.j} + \bar{y}_{..})^2$$

$$= 2^2 + 0^2 + \cdots + 4^2 + 0^2 = 52$$

we obtain the entries in the body of the analysis of variance table. Their sum, $90 + 56 + 52 = 198$, the total sum of squares, is also equal to the sum of squares of the observations, 786, minus the sum of squares $12 \times 7^2 = 588$ for the grand mean array.

The mean array, which has a single entry $\bar{y}_{..}$, has 1 degree of freedom. The 3 distinct values in the treatment array always sum to zero, so it has $3 - 1 = 2$ degrees of freedom. In general, it has $a - 1$ degrees of freedom when there are a treatments. Similarly, the block array has $4 - 1 = 3$ degrees of freedom in this example and $b - 1$ when there are b blocks.

The number of degrees of freedom associated with the error array is $(a - 1) \cdot (b - 1) = (2)(3) = 6$. Because every row sum is zero, the last column is always determined from the first $b - 1$. Similarly, the last row is always determined by the first $a - 1$. Thus there are $(a - 1)(b - 1)$ unconstrained entries. In summary, the degrees of freedom can be decomposed as

$$ab - 1 = \underset{total}{(a - 1)} + \underset{treatment}{(b - 1)} + \underset{blocks}{\quad} + \underset{error}{(a - 1)(b - 1)}$$

EXAMPLE

Constructing the randomized block analysis of variance table
Construct the analysis of variance from the decomposition of the observations just given.

Solution Using the sums of squares and their associated degrees of freedom, we have

Source of variation	Degrees of freedom	Sum of squares	Mean square	F
Treatments	2	56.0	28.00	3.23
Blocks	3	90.0	30.00	3.46
Error	6	52.0	8.67	
Total	11	198.0		

In practice, with hand-held calculators we calculate the necessary sums of squares using shortcut formulas on page 408.

EXAMPLE

Comparing four detergents using an F test
An experiment was designed to study the performance of 4 different detergents for cleaning fuel injectors. The following "cleanness" readings were obtained with specially designed equipment for 12 tanks of gas distributed over 3 different models of engines:

	Engine 1	Engine 2	Engine 3	Totals
Detergent A	45	43	51	139
Detergent B	47	46	52	145
Detergent C	48	50	55	153
Detergent D	42	37	49	128
Totals	182	176	207	565

Looking on the detergents as treatments and the engines as blocks, obtain the appropriate analysis of variance table and test at the 0.01 level of significance whether there are differences in the detergents or in the engines.

Solution 1. *Null hypotheses:* $\alpha_1 = \alpha_2 = \alpha_3 = \alpha_4 = 0$; $\beta_1 = \beta_2 = \beta_3 = 0$
Alternative hypotheses: The α's are not all equal to zero; the β's are not all equal to zero.

2. *Level of significance:* $\alpha = 0.01$

3. *Criteria:* For treatments, reject the null hypothesis if $F > 9.78$, the value of $F_{0.01}$ with $a - 1 = 4 - 1 = 3$ and $(a - 1)(b - 1) = (4 - 1)(3 - 1) = 6$ degrees of freedom; for blocks, reject the null hypothesis if $F > 10.92$, the value of $F_{0.01}$ for $b - 1 = 3 - 1 = 2$ and $(a - 1)(b - 1) = (4 - 1)(3 - 1) = 6$ degrees of freedom.

4. *Calculations:* Substituting $a = 4$, $b = 3$, $T_{1.} = 139$, $T_{2.} = 145$, $T_{3.} = 153$, $T_{4.} = 128$, $T_{.1} = 182$, $T_{.2} = 176$, $T_{.3} = 207$, $T_{..} = 565$, and $\Sigma\Sigma y_{ij}^2 = 26{,}867$ into the formulas for the sums of squares, we get

$$C = \frac{(565)^2}{12} = 26{,}602$$

$$SST = 45^2 + 43^2 + \cdots + 49^2 = 26{,}867 - 26{,}602 = 265$$

$$SS(Tr) = \frac{139^2 + 145^2 + 153^2 + 128^2}{3} - 26{,}602 = 111$$

$$SS(Bl) = \frac{182^2 + 176^2 + 207^2}{4} - 26{,}602 = 135$$

$$SSE = 265 - 111 - 136 = 19$$

Then dividing the sums of squares by their respective degrees of freedom to obtain the appropriate mean squares, we get the results of the following analysis of variance table:

Source of variation	Degrees of freedom	Sum of squares	Mean square	F
Detergents	3	111	37.0	11.6
Engines	2	135	67.5	21.1
Error	6	19	3.2	
Total	11	265		

5. *Decisions:* Since $F_{Tr} = 11.6$ exceeds 9.78, the value of $F_{0.01}$ with 3 and 6 degrees of freedom, we conclude that there are differences in the effectiveness of the 4 detergents. Also, since $F_{Bl} = 21.1$ exceeds 10.92, the value of $F_{0.01}$ with 2 and 6 degrees of freedom, we conclude that the differences among the results obtained for the 3 engines are significant, namely, that the blocking has been effective. To make the effect of this blocking even more evident, the reader will be asked to verify in Exercise 12.23 that the test for differences among the detergents would *not* yield significant results if we looked upon the data as a one-way classification.   ✔

The effect of the ith detergent can be estimated by means of the formula $\hat{\alpha}_i = \bar{y}_{i.} - \bar{y}_{..}$, which may be obtained by the method of least squares. The resulting estimates are

$$\hat{\alpha}_1 = 46.3 - 47.1 = -0.8 \qquad \hat{\alpha}_2 = 48.3 - 47.1 = 1.2$$

$$\hat{\alpha}_3 = 51.0 - 47.1 = 3.9 \qquad \hat{\alpha}_4 = 42.7 - 47.1 = -4.4$$

Similar calculations lead to $\hat{\beta}_1 = -1.6$, $\hat{\beta}_2 = -3.1$, and $\hat{\beta}_3 = 4.7$ for the estimated effects of the engines.

It should be observed that a two-way classification automatically allows for repetitions of the experimental conditions; for example, in the preceding experiment each detergent was tested 3 times. Further repetitions may be handled in several ways, and care must be taken that the model used appropriately describes the situation. One way to provide further repetition in a two-way classification is to include additional blocks—for example, to test each detergent using several additional engines, randomizing the order of testing for each engine. Note that the model remains essentially the same as before, the only change being an increase in b, and a corresponding increase in the degrees of freedom for blocks and for error. The latter is important, because an increase in the degrees of freedom for error makes the test of the null hypothesis $\alpha_i = 0$ for all i *more sensitive* to small differences among the treatment means. In fact, the real purpose of this kind of repetition is to increase the degrees of freedom for error, thereby increasing the sensitivity of the F tests (see Exercise 12.26).

A second method is to repeat the entire experiment, using a new pattern of randomization to obtain $a \cdot b$ additional observations. This is possible only if the blocks are *identifiable*, that is, if the conditions defining each block can be repeated. For example, in the tin-coating weight experiment described in Section 12.1, the blocks are strips across the rolling direction of a sheet of tin plate, and, given a new sheet, it is possible to identify which is strip 1, which is strip 2, and so forth. In the example of this section, the kind of repetition (usually called **replication**) would require that the conditions of the engines be exactly duplicated. This kind of repetition will be used in connection with Latin-square designs in Section 12.5; see also Exercises 12.24 and 12.25.

A third method of repetition is to include n observations for each treatment in each block. When an experiment is designed in this way, the n observations in each "cell" are regarded as duplicates, and it is to be expected that their variability will be somewhat less than experimental error. To illustrate this point, suppose that the tin-coating weights of 3 discs from adjacent positions in a strip are measured in sequence by one of the laboratories, using the same chemical solutions. The variability of these measurements will probably be considerably less than that of 3 discs from the same strip measured in that laboratory at different times, using different chemical solutions, and perhaps different technicians. The analysis of variance appropriate for this kind of repetition reduces essentially to a two-way analysis of variance applied to the *means* of the n duplicates in the $a \cdot b$ cells; thus, *there would be no gain in degrees of freedom for error*, and, consequently, *no gain in sensitivity of the F tests*. It can be expected, however, that there will be some reduction in the error mean square, since it now measures the residual variance of the *means* of several observations.

12.4 Multiple Comparisons

The F tests used so far in this chapter showed whether differences among several means are significant, but they did not tell us whether a given mean (or groups of means) differs significantly from another given mean (or group of means). In actual practice, the latter is the kind of information an investigator really wants; for instance, having determined on page 398 that the means of the tin-coating weights obtained by the 4 laboratories differ significantly, it may be important to find out which laboratory (or laboratories) differs from which others.

If an experimenter is confronted with k means, it may seem reasonable at first to test for significant differences between all possible pairs, that is, to perform

$$\binom{k}{2} = \frac{k(k-1)}{2}$$

two-sample t tests as described on page 260. Aside from the fact that this would require a large number of tests even if k is relatively small, these tests would not be independent, and it would be virtually impossible to assign an overall level of significance to this procedure.

Several **multiple-comparisons** procedures have been proposed to overcome these difficulties. One method, called the **Bonferroni** procedure, simply modifies this level from α to $2\alpha/k(k-1)$ for each of $k(k-1)/2$ differences. This requires entering the t table with $\alpha/k(k-1)$ rather than $\alpha/2$. The confidence level α then pertains to all of the $k(k-1)/2$ confidence intervals covering their respective differences of population means (see Exercise 12.34). The confidence intervals help to judge if statistically significant differences are large enough to be of practical importance.

EXAMPLE

Calculating Bonferroni simultaneous confidence intervals for mean resin strength
With reference to the resin strength data in the example on page 400, obtain the 94% Bonferroni simultaneous confidence intervals for the three differences of means.

Solution The confidence intervals use the MSE $= .0234$ as the estimate s^2. Since $\alpha = .06$ and $k = 3$, the Bonferroni procedure uses the $\alpha/k(k-1) = .01$ point of the t distribution with 12 degrees of freedom so $t_{.01} = 2.681$. The three confidence intervals become

$$\text{MD} - \text{ED} \quad : \quad 1.334 - .964 \pm 2.681\sqrt{0.234(\tfrac{1}{5} + \tfrac{1}{5})} \quad \text{or } (.111, .629)$$

$$\text{MD} - \text{PF} \quad : \quad 1.334 - .776 \pm 2.681\sqrt{.0234(\tfrac{1}{5} + \tfrac{1}{5})} \quad \text{or } (.299, .817)$$

$$\text{ED} - \text{PF} \quad : \quad .964 - .776 \pm 2.681\sqrt{.0234(\tfrac{1}{5} + \tfrac{1}{5})} \quad \text{or } (-.071, .447)$$

Notice that these are longer than the individual 95% intervals previously calculated. That is because we have 94% confidence that all 3 hold simultaneously. ✔

Another approach to multiple comparisons is to test all of the differences using the **Duncan multiple-range test.** (References to other multiple-comparisons tests are mentioned in the book by H. Scheffe listed in the bibliography.) The assumptions underlying the Duncan multiple-range test are, essentially, those of the one-way analysis of variance for which the sample sizes are equal. The test compares the range of any set of p means with an appropriate **least significant range, R_p,** given by

Least significant range

$$R_p = s_{\bar{y}} \cdot r_p$$

Here $s_{\bar{y}}$ is an estimate of $\sigma_{\bar{y}} = \sigma/\sqrt{n}$, and it is computed by means of the formula

Standard error of the mean

$$s_{\bar{y}} = \sqrt{\frac{MSE}{n}}$$

where MSE is the error mean square in the analysis of variance. The value of r_p depends on the desired level of significance and the number of degrees of freedom corresponding to MSE, and it may be obtained from Tables 12(a) and (b) for $\alpha = 0.05$ and 0.01, for $p = 2, 3, \ldots, 10$, and for various degrees of freedom from 1 to 120.

EXAMPLE

Conducting the Duncan multiple-range test
Referring to the tin-coating weight data on page 398, perform a Duncan multiple-range test to determine which laboratory means differ from which others, using the 0.05 level of significance.

Solution First we arrange the 4 sample means as follows in an increasing order of magnitude:

Laboratory	B	C	D	A
Mean	0.227	0.230	0.250	0.268

Next, we compute $s_{\bar{y}}$, using the error mean square of 0.0015 in the analysis of variance on page 398, and the common sample size $n = 12$. We obtain

$$s_{\bar{y}} = \sqrt{\frac{0.0015}{12}} = 0.011$$

Then, we get (by linear interpolation) from Table 12(a) the following values of r_p for $\alpha = 0.05$ and 44 degrees of freedom:

p	2	3	4
r_p	2.85	3.00	3.09

Multiplying each value of r_p by $s_{\bar{y}} = 0.011$, we finally obtain

p	2	3	4
R_p	0.031	0.033	0.034

The range of *all 4 means* is $0.268 - 0.227 = 0.041$, which exceeds $R_4 = 0.034$, the least significant range. This result should have been expected, since the F test on page 399 showed that the differences among all 4 means are significant at $\alpha = 0.05$. To test for significant differences among *3 adjacent means,* we obtain ranges of 0.038 and 0.023, respectively, for 0.230, 0.250, 0.268, and 0.227, 0.230, 0.250. Since the first of these values exceeds $R_3 = 0.033$, the differences observed in the first set are significant; since the second value does not exceed 0.033, the corresponding differences are not significant. Finally, for *adjacent pairs* of means we find that no adjacent pair has a range greater than the least significant range $R_2 = 0.031$. All these results can be summarized by writing

$$\underline{0.227 \qquad 0.230 \qquad \underline{0.250 \qquad 0.268}}$$

where *a line is drawn under any set of adjacent means for which the range is less than the appropriate value of R_p, that is, under any set of adjacent means for which differences are not significant.* We thus conclude in our example that Laboratory *A* averages higher tin-coating weights than Laboratories *B* and *C*. ✔

If we apply this same method to the example on page 411, where we compared the 4 detergents, we obtain (see also Exercise 12.30)

Detergent

D	A	B	C
42.7	46.3	48.3	51.0

In other words, among triplets of adjacent means both sets of differences are significant. So far as pairs of adjacent means are concerned, we find that only the difference between 42.7 and 46.3 is significant. Interpreting these results, we conclude that detergent *D* is significantly inferior to any of the others, and detergent *A* is significantly inferior to detergent *C*.

EXERCISES

12.18 A laboratory technician measures the breaking strength of each of 5 kinds of linen thread by means of 4 different instruments, and obtains the following results (in ounces):

Measuring instrument

	I_1	I_2	I_3	I_4
Thread 1	20.6	20.7	20.0	21.4
Thread 2	24.7	26.5	27.1	24.3
Thread 3	25.2	23.4	21.6	23.9
Thread 4	24.5	21.5	23.6	25.2
Thread 5	19.3	21.5	22.2	20.6

Looking upon the threads as treatments and the instruments as blocks, perform an analysis of variance at the level of significance $\alpha = 0.01$.

12.19 Looking at the days (rows) as blocks, rework Exercise 12.5 by the method of Section 12.3.

12.20 Four different, though supposedly equivalent, forms of a standardized reading achievement test were given to each of 5 students, and the following are the scores which they obtained:

	Student 1	Student 2	Student 3	Student 4	Student 5
Form A	75	73	59	69	84
Form B	83	72	56	70	92
Form C	86	61	53	72	88
Form D	73	67	62	79	95

Perform a two-way analysis of variance to test at the level of significance $\alpha = 0.01$ whether it is reasonable to treat the 4 forms as equivalent.

12.21 Given the observations

	Blocks				
	1	2	3	4	5
Treatment 1:	14	6	11	0	9
Treatment 2:	14	10	16	9	16
Treatment 3:	12	7	10	9	12
Treatment 4:	12	9	11	6	7

(a) decompose each observation y_{ij} as

$$y_{ij} = \bar{y}_{..} + (\bar{y}_{i.} - \bar{y}_{..}) + (\bar{y}_{.j} - \bar{y}_{..}) + (y_{ij} - \bar{y}_{i.} - \bar{y}_{.j} + \bar{y}_{..})$$

(b) obtain the sums of squares and degrees of freedom for each component;

(c) construct the analysis of variance table and test for differences among the treatments using $\alpha = 0.05$.

12.22 An industrial engineer tests 4 different shop-floor layouts by having each of 6 work crews construct a subassembly and measuring the construction times (minutes) as follows:

	Layout 1	Layout 2	Layout 3	Layout 4
Crew A	48.2	53.1	51.2	58.6
Crew B	49.5	52.9	50.0	60.1
Crew C	50.7	56.8	49.9	62.4
Crew D	48.6	50.6	47.5	57.5
Crew E	47.1	51.8	49.1	55.3
Crew F	52.4	57.2	53.5	61.7

Test at the 0.01 level of significance whether the 4 floor layouts produce different assembly times and whether some of the work crews are consistently faster in constructing this subassembly than the others.

12.23 To emphasize the importance of "blocking" reanalyze the "cleanness" data on page 411 as a one-way classification with the 4 detergents being the different treatments.

12.24 If, in a two-way classification, the entire experiment is repeated r times, the model becomes

$$Y_{ijk} = \mu + \alpha_i + \beta_j + \rho_k + \varepsilon_{ijk}$$

for $i = 1, 2, \ldots, a, j = 1, 2, \ldots, b$, and $k = 1, 2, \ldots, r$, where the sum of the α's, the sum of the β's, and the sum of the ρ's are equal to zero, and where the ρ's represent the effects of the replications. The ε_{ijk} are independent normally distributed random variables with zero means and the common variance σ^2.

(a) Write down (but do not prove) an identity analogous to the one of Theorem 12.2, subdividing the total sum of squares into components attributable to treatments, blocks, replications, and error.

(b) Generalize the computing formulas on page 408 so that they apply to a replicated randomized-block design. Note that the divisor in each case equals the number of observations in the respective totals.

(c) If the number of degrees of freedom for the replicate sum of squares is $r - 1$, how many degrees of freedom are there for the error sum of squares?

12.25 The following are the number of defectives produced by the 4 workers operating, in turn, 3 different machines; in each case, the first figure represents the number of defectives produced on a Friday and the second figure represents the number of defectives produced on the following Monday:

Worker

	B_1	B_2	B_3	B_4
Machine A_1	37, 43	38, 44	38, 40	32, 36
Machine A_2	31, 36	40, 44	43, 41	31, 38
Machine A_3	36, 40	33, 37	41, 39	38, 45

Use the theory developed in Exercise 12.24 to analyze the combined figures for the 2 days as a two-way classification with replication. Use the level of significance $\alpha = 0.05$.

12.26 As was pointed out on page 413, two ways of increasing the size of a two-way classification experiment are (a) to double the number of blocks, and (b) to replicate the entire experiment. Discuss and compare the gain in degrees of freedom for the error sum of squares by the two methods.

12.27 Show that if $\mu_{ij} = \mu + \alpha_i + \beta_j$, the mean of the μ_{ij} (summed on j) is equal to $\mu + \alpha_i$, and the mean of μ_{ij} (summed on i and j) is equal to μ, it follows that $\sum_{i=1}^{a} \alpha_i = \sum_{j=1}^{b} \beta_j = 0$

12.28 Verify that the computing formulas for SST, $SS(Tr)$, $SS(Bl)$, and SSE, given on page 408, are equivalent to the corresponding terms of the identity of Theorem 12.2.

12.29 Use the Duncan test with $\alpha = 0.05$ to test for differences among the treatments in Exercise 12.21.

12.30 Verify the results of Duncan's test for the comparison of the 4 detergents, given on page 416.

12.31 Use the Duncan test with $\alpha = 0.05$ to compare the effectiveness of the 3 methods of teaching the programming of the computer in Exercise 12.3.

12.32 Use the Duncan test with $\alpha = 0.05$ to compare the effectiveness of the 3 lubricants in Exercise 12.6.

12.33 (a) Use the Duncan test with $\alpha = 0.01$ to compare the strength of the 5 linen threads in Exercise 12.18.

      (b) Use the confidence interval approach on page 414, with $\alpha = .10$, to compare the mean linen thread strengths in Exercise 12.18.

12.34 The **Bonferroni** inequality states that

$$P(\cap_i C_i) \geq 1 - \sum_i P(\overline{C}_i)$$

      (a) Show that this holds for 3 events.

      (b) Let C_i be the event that the i th confidence interval will cover the true value of the parameter for $i = 1, \ldots, m$. If $P(\overline{C}_i) \leq \alpha/m$, so the probability of not covering the i th parameter is at most α/m, show that the probability that all of the confidence intervals cover their respective parameters is at least $1 - \alpha$.

12.5   Some Further Experimental Designs

The randomized-block design of Section 12.4 is appropriate when one extraneous source of variability is to be eliminated in comparing a set of sample means. An important feature of this kind of design is its **balance,** achieved by assigning the same number of observations for each treatment to each block. (In this connection, see also the comment on page 391, where we pointed out that differences due to blocks will not affect the means obtained for the different treatments.) The same kind of balance can be attained in more complicated kinds of designs, where it is desired to eliminate the effect of several extraneous sources of variability. In this section we shall introduce two further balanced designs, the Latin-square design and the Graeco-Latin-square design, which are used to eliminate the effects of 2 and 3 extraneous sources of variability, respectively.

To introduce the **Latin-square design,** suppose that it is desired to compare 3 treatments, A, B, and C, in the presence of 2 other sources of variability. For example, the 3 treatments may be 3 methods for soldering copper electrical leads, and the two extraneous sources of variability may be (1) different operators doing the soldering, and (2) the use of different solder fluxes. If 3 operators and 3 fluxes are to be considered, the experiment might be arranged in the following pattern:

	Flux 1	Flux 2	Flux 3
Operator 1	A	B	C
Operator 2	C	A	B
Operator 3	B	C	A

Here each soldering method is applied once by each operator in conjunction with each flux, and if there are systematic effects due to differences among operators or differences among fluxes, these effects are present equally for each treatment, that is, for each method of soldering.

An experimental arrangement such as the one just described is called a **Latin square.** An $n \times n$ Latin square is a square array of n distinct letters, with each letter appearing once and only once in each row and in each column. Examples of Latin squares with $n = 4$ and $n = 5$ are shown in Figure 12.2, and larger ones may be obtained from the book by W. G. Cochran and G. M. Cox mentioned in the bibliography. Note that in a Latin-square experiment involving n treatments, it is necessary to include n^2 observations, n for each treatment.

FIGURE 12.2
Latin squares

As we shall see on page 422, a Latin-square experiment without replication provides only $(n - 1)(n - 2)$ degrees of freedom for estimating the experimental error. Thus, such experiments are rarely run without replication if n is small, that is, without repeating the entire Latin-square pattern several times. If there is a total of r replicates, the analysis of the data presumes the following model, where $y_{ij(k)l}$ is the observation in the ith row and the jth column of the lth replicate, and the subscript k, in parentheses, indicated that is pertains to the kth treatment.

Model equation for Latin square

$$Y_{ij(k)l} = \mu + \alpha_i + \beta_j + \gamma_k + \rho_l + \varepsilon_{ij(k)l}$$

for $i, j, k = 1, 2, \ldots, n$, and $l = 1, 2, \ldots, r$, subject to the restrictions

$$\sum_{i=1}^{n} \alpha_i = 0 \qquad \sum_{j=1}^{n} \beta_j = 0 \qquad \sum_{k=1}^{n} \gamma_k = 0 \qquad \text{and} \qquad \sum_{l=1}^{r} \rho_l = 0$$

Here μ is the grand mean, α_i is the effect of the ith row, β_j is the effect of the jth column, γ_k is the effect of the kth treatment, ρ_l is the effect of the lth replicate, and the $\varepsilon_{ij(k)l}$ are independent, normally distributed random variables with zero means and the common variance σ^2. Note that by "effects of the rows" and "effects of the columns" we mean the effects of the 2 extraneous variables and that we are including replicate effects, since, as we shall see, replication can introduce a third extraneous variable. Note also that the subscript k is in parenthesis in $y_{ij(k)l}$ because, for a given Latin-square design, k is automatically determined when i and j are known.

The main hypothesis we shall want to test is the null hypothesis $\gamma_k = 0$ for all k, namely, the null hypothesis that there is no difference in the effectiveness of the n treatments. However, we can also test whether the "cross blocking" of the Latin-square design has been effective; that is, we can test the two null hypotheses $\alpha_i = 0$ for all i and $\beta_j = 0$ for all j (against suitable alternatives) to see whether the 2 extraneous variables actually have an effect on the phenomenon under consideration. Furthermore, we can test the null hypothesis $\rho_l = 0$ for all l against the alternative that the ρ_l are not all equal to zero, and this test for effects of the replicates may be important if the parts of the experiment representing the individual Latin squares were performed on different days, by different technicians, at different temperatures, and so on.

The sums of squares required to perform these tests are usually obtained by means of the following shortcut formulas, where $T_{i..}$ is the total of the $r \cdot n$ observations in all of the ith rows, $T_{.j.}$ is the total of the $r \cdot n$ observations in all of the jth columns, $T_{..l}$ is the total of the n^2 observations in the lth replicate, $T_{(k)}$ is the total of all the $r \cdot n$ observations pertaining to the kth treatment, and $T_{...}$ is the grand total of all the $r \cdot n^2$ observations:

Sums of squares— Latin square

$$C = \frac{(T_{...})^2}{r \cdot n^2}$$

$$SS(Tr) = \frac{1}{r \cdot n} \sum_{k=1}^{n} T_{(k)}^2 - C$$

$$SSR = \frac{1}{r \cdot n} \sum_{i=1}^{n} T_{i..}^2 - C \quad (for\ rows)$$

$$SSC = \frac{1}{r \cdot n} \sum_{j=1}^{n} T_{.j.}^2 - C \quad (for\ columns)$$

$$SS(Rep) = \frac{1}{n^2} \sum_{l=1}^{r} T_{..l}^2 - C \quad (for\ replicates)$$

$$SST = \sum_{i=1}^{n} \sum_{j=1}^{n} \sum_{l=1}^{r} y_{ij(k)l}^2 - C$$

$$SSE = SST - SS(Tr) - SSR - SSC - SS(Rep)$$

Note that again each divisor equals the number of observations in the corresponding squared totals. Finally, the results of the analysis are as shown in the following analysis of variance table:

Source of variation	Degrees of freedom	Sums of squares	Mean square	F
Treatments	$n-1$	$SS(Tr)$	$MS(Tr) = \dfrac{SS(Tr)}{n-1}$	$\dfrac{MS(Tr)}{MSE}$
Rows	$n-1$	SSR	$MSR = \dfrac{SSR}{n-1}$	$\dfrac{MSR}{MSE}$
Columns	$n-1$	SSC	$MSC = \dfrac{SSC}{n-1}$	$\dfrac{MSC}{MSE}$
Replicates	$r-1$	$SS(Rep)$	$MS(Rep) = \dfrac{SS(Rep)}{r-1}$	$\dfrac{MS(Rep)}{MSE}$
Error	$(n-1)(rn+r-3)$	SSE	$MSE = \dfrac{SSE}{(n-1)(rn+r-3)}$	
Total	$rn^2 - 1$	SST		

As before, the degrees of freedom for the total sum of squares equals the *sum* of the degrees of freedom for the individual components; thus, the degrees of freedom for error are usually found last, by subtraction.

EXAMPLE

Conducting an analysis of variance for a Latin square design

Suppose that 2 replicates of the aforementioned soldering experiment were run, using the following arrangement:

Replicate I
flux

	1	2	3
Operator 1	A	B	C
Operator 2	C	A	B
Operator 3	B	C	A

Replicate II
flux

	1	2	3
Operator 1	C	B	A
Operator 2	A	C	B
Operator 3	B	A	C

The results, showing the number of pounds tensile force required to separate the soldered leads, were as follows:

Replicate I

14.0	16.5	11.0
9.5	17.0	15.0
11.0	12.0	13.5

Replicate II

10.0	16.5	13.0
12.0	12.0	14.0
13.5	18.0	11.5

Analyze this experiment as a Latin square and test at the 0.01 level of significance whether there are differences in the methods, the operators, the fluxes, or the replicates.

Solution

1. *Null hypotheses:* $\alpha_1 = \alpha_2 = \alpha_3 = 0$; $\beta_1 = \beta_2 = \beta_3 = 0$; $\gamma_1 = \gamma_2 = \gamma_3 = 0$; $\rho_1 = \rho_2 = 0$.

   Alternative hypotheses: The α's are not all equal to zero; The β's are not all equal to zero; The γ's are not all equal to zero; The ρ's are not all equal to zero.

2. *Levels of significance:* $\alpha = 0.01$ for each test

3. *Criteria:* For treatments, rows, or columns, reject the null hypothesis if $F > 7.56$, the value of $F_{0.01}$ for $n - 1 = 3 - 1 = 2$ and $(n - 1)(rn + r - 3) = (3 - 1)(2 \times 3 + 2 - 3) = 10$ degrees of freedom. For replicates, reject the null hypothesis if $F > 10.04$, the value of $F_{0.01}$ for $r - 1 = 2 - 1 = 1$ and 10 degrees of freedom.

4. *Calculations:* Substituting $n = 3$, $r = 2$, $T_{1..} = 81.0$, $T_{2..} = 79.5$, $T_{3..} = 79.5$, $T_{.1.} = 70.0$, $T_{.2.} = 92.0$, $T_{.3.} = 78.0$, $T_{..1} = 119.5$, $T_{..2} = 120.5$, $T_{(A)} = 87.5$, $T_{(B)} = 86.5$, $T_{(C)} = 66.0$, $T_{...} = 240.0$ and $\Sigma\Sigma\Sigma y_{ij(k)l}^2 = 3{,}304.5$ into the formulas for the sums of squares, we get

$$C = \frac{(240)^2}{18} = 3200.0$$

$$SS(Tr) = \tfrac{1}{6}[(87.5)^2 + (86.5)^2 + (66.0)^2] - 3200.0 = 49.1$$

$$SSR = \tfrac{1}{6}[(81.0)^2 + (79.5)^2 + (79.5)^2] - 3200.0 = 0.2$$

$$SSC = \tfrac{1}{6}[(70.0)^2 + (92.0)^2 + (78.0)^2] - 3200.0 = 41.3$$

$$SS(Rep) = \tfrac{1}{9}[(119.5)^2 + (120.5)^2] - 3200.0 = 0.1$$

$$SST = (14.0)^2 + (16.5)^2 + \cdots + (11.5)^2 - 3200.0 = 104.5$$

$$SSE = 104.5 - 49.1 - 41.3 - 0.2 - 0.1 = 13.8$$

and the results are as shown in the following analysis of variance table:

Source of variation	Degrees of freedom	Sum of squares	Mean square	F
Treatments (methods)	2	49.1	24.6	17.6
Rows (operators)	2	0.2	0.1	0.1
Columns (fluxes)	2	41.3	20.6	14.7
Replicates	1	0.1	0.1	0.1
Error	10	13.8	1.4	
Total	17	104.5		

5. *Decisions:* For treatments (methods) and columns (fluxes), since $F = 17.6$ and 14.7 exceed 7.56, the corresponding null hypotheses must be rejected; for rows (operators), since $F = 0.1$ does not exceed 7.56, and for replicates,

since $F = 0.1$ does not exceed 10.04, the corresponding null hypotheses cannot be rejected. In other words, we conclude that differences in methods and fluxes, but not differences in operators or replications, affect the solder strengths of the electrical leads. To go one step further, the Duncan multiple-range test of Section 12.4 gives the following *decision pattern* at the 0.01 level of significance:

	Method C	Method B	Method A
Mean	11.0	14.4	14.6

Thus, we conclude that Method *C* definitely yields weaker solder bonds than Methods *A* or *B*.   ✔

The elimination of *3* extraneous sources of variability can be accomplished by means of a design called a **Graeco-Latin square.** This design is a square array of *n* Latin letters and *n* Greek letters, with the Latin and Greek letters each forming a Latin square; furthermore, each Latin letter appears once and only once in conjunction with each Greek letter. The following is an example of a 4 × 4 Graeco-Latin square:

$A\alpha$	$B\beta$	$C\gamma$	$D\delta$
$B\delta$	$A\gamma$	$D\beta$	$C\alpha$
$C\beta$	$D\alpha$	$A\delta$	$B\gamma$
$D\gamma$	$C\delta$	$B\alpha$	$A\beta$

Graeco-Latin squares are also called **orthogonal Latin squares.**

To give an example where the use of a Graeco-Latin square might be appropriate, suppose that in the soldering example an additional source of variability is the temperature of the solder. If 3 solder temperatures, denoted by α, β, and γ, are to be used together with the 3 methods, 3 operators (rows), and 3 solder fluxes (columns), a replicate of a suitable Graeco-Latin-square experiment could be laid out as follows:

	Flux 1	Flux 2	Flux 3
Operator 1	$A\alpha$	$B\gamma$	$C\beta$
Operator 2	$C\gamma$	$A\beta$	$B\alpha$
Operator 3	$B\beta$	$C\alpha$	$A\gamma$

Thus, Method *A* would be used by operator 1 using solder flux 1 and temperature α, by operator 2 using solder flux 2 and temperature β, and by operator 3 using solder flux 3 and temperature γ. Similarly, Method *B* would be used by operator 1 using solder flux 2 and temperature γ, and so forth.

In a Graeco-Latin square each variable (represented by rows, columns, Latin letters, or Greek letters) is "distributed evenly" over the other variables. Thus, in comparing the means obtained for one variable, the effects of the other variables are all averaged out. The analysis of a Graeco-Latin square is similar to that of a Latin square, with the addition of an extra source of variability corresponding to the Greek letters.

There exists a wide variety of experimental designs, other than the ones discussed in this chapter, that are suitable for many diverse purposes. Among the more widely used designs are the **incomplete-block designs,** which are characterized by the feature that each treatment is not represented in each block. If the number of treatments under investigation in an experiment is large, it often happens that it is impossible to find homogeneous blocks such that all of the treatments can be accommodated in each block.

For instance, if n paints are to be compared by applying each paint to a sheet of metal and then baking the sheets in an oven, it may be impossible to put all of the sheets in the oven at one time. Consequently, it would be necessary to use an experimental design in which $k < n$ treatments (paints) are included in each block (oven run). One way of doing this is to assign the treatments to each oven run in such a way that each treatment occurs together with each other treatment in the same number of blocks. For example, for $n = 4$ and $k = 2$ we might use the following scheme:

Oven run	Paints
1	1 and 2
2	3 and 4
3	1 and 3
4	2 and 4
5	1 and 4
6	2 and 3

This kind of design in called a **balanced incomplete-block design,** and it has the important feature that *comparisons between any two treatments can be made with equal precision.*

Since balanced incomplete-block designs may require too many blocks, many other schemes have been developed. Most of these experimental designs arose to meet the specific needs of experimenters, notably in the field of agriculture. As we have pointed out earlier, much of the language of experimental design, including such terms as "treatments," "block," "plots," etc., has been borrowed from agriculture. Only in recent years have the more sophisticated designs been applied to industrial and engineering experimentation, and, with more widespread application, it is to be expected that many new designs will be developed to meet the requirements in these fields.

EXERCISES

12.35 Referring to the problem in which samples of tin plate are to be distributed among 4 laboratories (Section 12.1), suppose that we are concerned with systematic differences in tin-coating weight along the direction of rolling as well as across the rolling direction. To eliminate these 2 sources of variability, each of 2 sheets of tin plate is divided into 16 parts, representing 4 positions across and 4 positions along the rolling direction. Then, 4 samples from each sheet are sent to each of the Laboratories A, B, C, and D, as shown, and the resulting tin-coating weights are determined.

Replicate I

C	A	D	B
0.20	0.24	0.20	0.27
B	C	A	D
0.28	0.19	0.22	0.28
D	B	C	A
0.34	0.23	0.21	0.28
A	D	B	C
0.32	0.22	0.16	0.27

Rolling direction

Replicate II

B	A	C	D
0.29	0.25	0.18	0.28
D	B	A	C
0.28	0.18	0.21	0.25
C	D	B	A
0.28	0.23	0.20	0.28
A	C	D	B
0.30	0.19	0.24	0.25

Determine from these data whether the laboratories were obtaining consistent results. Also determine whether there are actual tin-coating weight differences across and along the rolling direction. (Use the 0.05 level of significance.)

12.36 A Latin-square design was used to compare the bond strengths of gold semiconductor lead wires bonded to the lead terminal by 5 different methods, A, B, C, D, and E. The bonds were made by 5 different operators, and the devices were encapsulated using 5 different plastics, with the following results, expressed as pounds of force required to break the bond.

		Operator				
		O_1	O_2	O_3	O_4	O_5
	P_1	A 3.0	B 2.4	C 1.9	D 2.2	E 1.7
	P_2	B 2.1	C 2.7	D 2.3	E 2.5	A 3.1
Plastic	P_3	C 2.1	D 2.6	E 2.5	A 2.9	B 2.1
	P_4	D 2.0	E 2.5	A 3.2	B 2.5	C 2.2
	P_5	E 2.1	A 3.6	B 2.4	C 2.4	D 2.1

Analyze these results and apply the Duncan multiple-range test with $\alpha = 0.01$ to the mean breaking strengths of the 5 bonding methods.

12.37 To study the effectiveness of 5 different kinds of front-seat passenger restraint systems in automobiles, A, B, C, D, and E, the following Graeco-Latin square experiment was performed. The rows represent different automotive size classes (from subcompact to full size), the columns represent different barrier impact speeds, and the Greek letters α, β, γ, δ, and ε represent different impact angles. The experimental results are given in terms of an index of forces at critical points on the test dummy that relates to the probability of fatal injury.

$A\alpha$	$B\beta$	$C\gamma$	$D\delta$	$E\varepsilon$
0.50	0.21	0.43	0.35	0.46
$B\gamma$	$C\delta$	$D\varepsilon$	$E\alpha$	$A\beta$
0.51	0.20	0.40	0.25	0.39
$C\varepsilon$	$D\alpha$	$E\beta$	$A\gamma$	$B\delta$
0.45	0.07	0.29	0.20	0.31
$D\beta$	$E\gamma$	$A\delta$	$B\varepsilon$	$C\alpha$
0.39	0.10	0.31	0.24	0.27
$E\delta$	$A\varepsilon$	$B\alpha$	$C\beta$	$D\gamma$
0.43	0.17	0.31	0.22	0.32

Analyze this experiment.

12.38 A clothing manufacturer wishes to determine which of 4 different needle designs is best for the sewing machines. The sources of variability that must be eliminated to make this comparison are the actual sewing machine used, the operator, and the type of thread. Using the design shown (the rows represent the operators, the columns represent the machines, the Latin letters represent the needles, and the Greek letters stand for the types of thread), the manufacturer recorded the number of rejected garments at the end of 2 weeks, with the following results:

First week

$D\gamma$	$B\alpha$	$A\beta$	$C\delta$
47	40	23	72
$C\beta$	$A\delta$	$B\gamma$	$D\alpha$
74	37	28	75
$A\alpha$	$C\gamma$	$D\delta$	$B\beta$
52	95	57	15
$B\delta$	$D\beta$	$C\alpha$	$A\gamma$
10	45	93	52

Second week

$C\alpha$	$A\gamma$	$B\delta$	$D\beta$
105	38	15	60
$D\delta$	$B\beta$	$A\alpha$	$C\gamma$
70	20	60	85
$B\gamma$	$D\alpha$	$C\beta$	$A\delta$
13	82	90	28
$A\beta$	$C\delta$	$D\gamma$	$B\alpha$
33	75	53	31

Using the 0.05 level of significance, determine whether there is a difference in the effectiveness of the needles. Also, determine whether there are significant differences attributable to the operators, the machines, and the types of thread.

12.39 Give an example of a balanced incomplete-block design for which

(a) $n = 3$ and $k = 2$;

(b) $n = 4$ and $k = 3$;

(c) $n = 6$ and $k = 4$.

What is the minimum number of times each treatment must be replicated in each of these designs?

12.6   Analysis of Covariance

The purpose of the methods of Sections 12.3 and 12.5 was to free the experimental error from variability due to identifiable and controllable extraneous causes. In this section, we shall introduce a method, called the **analysis of covariance,** which applies when such extraneous, or **concomitant,** variables cannot be held fixed, but can be measured. This would be the case, for example, if we wanted to compare the effectiveness of several industrial training programs and the results depended on the trainees' IQs; if we wanted to compare the durability of several kinds of leather soles and the results depended on the weight of the persons wearing the shoes; or if we wanted to compare the merits of several cleaning agents and the results depended on the original condition of the surfaces cleaned.

The method by which we analyze data of this kind is a combination of the linear regression method of Section 11.1 and the analysis of variance of Section 12.2. The underlying model is given by

Model equation for analysis of covariance

$$Y_{ij} = \mu + \alpha_i + \delta x_{ij} + \varepsilon_{ij}$$

for $i = 1, 2, \ldots, k; j = 1, 2, \ldots, n$. As in the model on page 395, μ is the grand mean, α_i is the effect of the ith treatment, and the ε_{ij} are independent, normally distributed variables with zero means and the common variance σ^2; as in the model on page 337 where we called it β, δ is the slope of the linear regression equation.

In the analysis of such data, the values of the concomitant variable, the x_{ij}, are eliminated by regression methods, namely, by estimating δ by the method of least squares, and then an analysis of variance is performed on the adjusted y's, namely, on the quantities $y'_{ij} = y_{ij} - \hat{\delta} x_{ij}$. This procedure is referred to as an analysis of covariance, as it involves a partitioning of the total **sum of products**

$$SPT = \sum_{i=1}^{k} \sum_{j=1}^{n} (y_{ij} - \bar{y}_{..})(x_{ij} - \bar{x}_{..})$$

in the same way as an ordinary analysis of variance involves the partitioning of the total sum of squares. In actual practice, the calculations are performed as follows:

1. The total, treatment, and error sums of squares are calculated for the x's by means of the formulas for a one-way classification on page 397; they will be denoted by SST_x, $SS(Tr)_x$, and SSE_x.

2. The total, treatment, and error sums of squares are calculated for the y's by means of the formulas for a one-way classification on page 397; they will be denoted by SST_y, $SS(Tr)_y$, and SSE_y.

3. The total, treatment, and error sums are calculated by means of the formulas

Sums of products— analysis of covariance

$$SPT = \sum_{i=1}^{k} \sum_{j=1}^{n} x_{ij} \cdot y_{ij} - C$$

$$SP(Tr) = \frac{\sum_{i=1}^{k} T_{x_i} \cdot T_{y_i}}{n} - C$$

$$SPE = SPT - SP(Tr)$$

where the correction term C, is given by

$$C = \frac{T_x \cdot T_y}{k \cdot n}$$

and where T_{x_i} is the total of the x's for the ith treatment, T_{y_i} is the total of the y's for the ith treatment, T_x is the total of all x's and T_y is the total of all the y's.

4. The total, error, and treatment sums of squares are calculated for the adjusted y's by means of the formulas

Adjusted sums of squares—analysis of covariance

$$SST_{y'} = SST_y - \frac{(SPT)^2}{SST_x}$$

$$SSE_{y'} = SSE_y - \frac{(SPE)^2}{SSE_x}$$

$$SS(Tr)_{y'} = SST_{y'} - SSE_{y'}$$

The results obtained in these calculations are conveniently summarized by means of the following kind of **analysis-of-covariance table:**

Source of variation	Sums of squares for x	Sums of squares for y	Sum of products	Sum of squares for y'	Degrees of freedom	Mean square
Treatments	$SS(Tr)_x$	$SS(Tr)_y$	$SP(Tr)$	$SS(Tr)_{y'}$	$k - 1$	$MS(Tr)_{y'} = \dfrac{SS(Tr)_{y'}}{k - 1}$
Error	SSE_x	SSE_y	SPE	$SSE_{y'}$	$nk - k - 1$	$MSE_{y'} = \dfrac{SSE_{y'}}{nk - k - 1}$
Total	SST_x	SST_y	SPT	$SST_{y'}$	$nk - 2$	

Note that each mean square is obtained by dividing the corresponding sum of squares by its degrees of freedom.

Finally, the null hypothesis $\alpha_1 = \alpha_2 = \cdots = \alpha_k = 0$ is tested against the alternative hypothesis that the α_i are not equal to zero on the basis of the statistic

F ratio for adjusted treatments

$$F = \frac{MS(Tr)_{y'}}{MSE_{y'}}$$

It is rejected at the level of significance α if the value obtained for F exceeds F_α with $k - 1$ and $nk - k - 1$ degrees of freedom.

EXAMPLE

Conducting an analysis of covariance with one covariate

Suppose that a research worker has three different cleaning agents, A_1, A_2, and A_3, and he wishes to select the most efficient agent for cleaning a metallic surface. The cleanliness of a surface is measured by its reflectivity, expressed in arbitrary units as the ratio of the reflectivity observed to that of a standard mirror surface. Analysis of covariance must be used because the effect of a cleaning agent on reflectivity will depend on the original cleanliness, namely, the original reflectivity of the surface. The research worker obtained the following results:

A_1	Original reflectivity, x	0.50	0.55	0.60	0.35
	Final reflectivity, y	1.00	1.20	0.80	1.40
A_2	Original reflectivity, x	0.75	1.65	1.00	1.10
	Final reflectivity, y	0.75	0.60	0.55	0.50
A_3	Original reflectivity, x	0.60	0.90	0.80	0.70
	Final reflectivity, y	1.00	0.70	0.80	0.90

Perform an analysis of covariance to determine (at the 0.05 level of significance) whether there are differences in the reflectivity improvements by the 3 cleaning agents.

Solution

1. *Null hypothesis:* $\alpha_1 = \alpha_2 = \alpha_3 = 0$.
   Alternative hypothesis: The α's are not all equal to zero.
2. *Level of significance:* $\alpha = 0.05$
3. *Criterion:* Reject the null hypothesis if $F > 4.46$, the value of $F_{0.05}$ for $k - 1 = 3 - 1 = 2$ and $nk - k - 1 = 4 \times 3 - 3 - 1 = 8$ degrees of freedom.
4. *Calculations:* The totals are $T_{x_1} = 2.00$, $T_{x_2} = 4.50$, $T_{x_3} = 3.00$, $T_x = 9.50$, $T_{y_1} = 4.40$, $T_{y_2} = 2.40$, $T_{y_3} = 3.40$, and $T_y = 10.20$.

   For the x's, the correction term is $\dfrac{(9.50)^2}{3 \cdot 4} = 7.52$, and the sums of squares are

$$SST_x = 0.50^2 + 0.55^2 + \cdots + 0.70^2 - 7.52 = 1.31$$

$$SS(Tr)_x = \frac{2.00^2 + 4.50^2 + 3.00^2}{4} - 7.52 = 0.79$$

$$SSE_x = 1.31 - 0.79 = 0.52$$

For the y's, the correction term is $\frac{(10.20)^2}{3 \cdot 4} = 8.67$, and the sums of squares are

$$SST_y = 1.00^2 + 1.20^2 + \cdots + 0.90^2 - 8.67 = 0.79$$

$$SS(Tr)_y = \frac{4.40^2 + 2.40^2 + 3.40^2}{4} - 8.67 = 0.50$$

$$SSE_y = 0.79 - 0.50 = 0.29$$

For the sums of products, the correction term is $\frac{(9.50)(10.20)}{3 \cdot 4} = 8.08$, and we get

$$SPT = (0.50)(1.00) + (0.55)(1.20) + \cdots + (0.70)(0.90) - 8.08$$
$$= -0.80$$

$$SP(Tr) = \frac{(2.00)(4.40) + (4.50)(2.40) + (3.00)(3.40)}{4} - 8.08$$
$$= -0.63$$

$$SPE = -0.80 - (-0.63) = -0.17$$

Finally, for the adjusted y's we get

$$SST_{y'} = 0.79 - \frac{(-0.80)^2}{1.31} = 0.30$$

$$SSE_{y'} = 0.29 - \frac{(-0.17)^2}{0.52} = 0.23$$

$$SS(Tr)_{y'} = 0.30 - 0.23 = 0.07$$

All these results are summarized in the following analysis-of-covariance table:

Source of variation	Sum of squares for x	Sum of squares for y	Sum of products	Sum of squares for y'	Degrees of freedom	Mean square
Treatments	0.79	0.50	-0.63	0.07	2	0.035
Error	0.52	0.29	-0.17	0.23	8	0.029
Total	1.31	0.79	-0.80	0.30	10	

5. *Decision:* Since $F = \frac{0.035}{0.029} = 1.21$ does not exceed 4.46, the null hypothesis cannot be rejected. In other words, one cannot conclude that any one of the cleaning agents is more effective than the others. ✓

Although the calculations may at first appear to be formidable, they are routine with many computer statistical packages. The output from the *SAS* program for this example is presented in Figure 12.3. Because only two decimal points are

```
DEPENDENT VARIABLE:   Y

SOURCE      DF     SUM OF SQUARES   MEAN SQUARE    F VALUE      PR>F    R-SQUARE

MODEL       3        0.55421498     0.18473833       6.40     0.0161   0.706006

ERROR       8        0.23078502     0.02884813                ROOT MSE

C TOTAL    11        0.78500000                              0.16984737


SOURCE              DF      TYPE III SS     F VALUE     PR > F

TREATMENTS          2        0.07447755       1.29     0.3267
X                   1        0.05421498       1.88     0.2076
```

FIGURE 12.3
Selected SAS output
for the analysis of
covariance using
the data from the
example on page 430.

retained in the preceding example, the computer calculations for the *F statistic* are more accurate. However, the conclusions are the same. Moreover, the large *P* value .2076 for the covariate shows that it is not needed in the model.

Analysis of covariance methods have not been widely used until recent years, due mainly to the rather extensive calculations that are required. Of course, with the widespread availability of computers and appropriate programs, this is no longer a problem. There are several ways in which the analysis of covariance method presented here can be generalized. First, there can be more than one concomitant variable; then, the method can be applied to more complicated kinds of designs, say, to a randomized block design, where the regression coefficient could even assume a different value for each block.

EXERCISES

12.40 To compare the life expectancy of a transistor under 3 storage conditions and account at the same time for a leakage current (collector to base), a laboratory technician obtained the following results, where the leakage current x, is in microamperes, and the life times, y, are in hours:

Storage condition 1		Storage condition 2		Storage condition 3	
x	y	x	y	x	y
4.8	9,912	6.4	9,952	8.8	9,596
7.2	9,383	8.7	9,482	6.2	9,697
5.5	9,734	7.1	9,435	7.5	9,700
6.0	9,551	5.3	9,915	4.9	9,610
8.3	8,959	4.6	9,492	5.4	10,145
7.6	9,474	6.0	9,565	5.8	10,191
5.9	9,179	7.2	9,704	7.3	9,855
8.0	9,359	8.8	9,636	8.6	9,682
4.3	9,580	5.4	9,608	8.8	10,160
5.1	9,245	7.8	9,548	6.0	9,982

Perform an analysis of covariance, using the level of significance $\alpha = 0.05$. Also, estimate the value of the regression coefficient.

12.41 Four different railroad-track cross-section configurations were tested to determine which is most resistant to breakage under use conditions. Ten miles of each kind of track were laid in each of 5 locations, and the number of cracks and other fracture-related conditions (y) was measured over a two-year usage period. To compare these track designs adequately, however, it is necessary to correct for extent of usage (x), measured in terms of the average number of trains per day that ran over each section of track. Use the following experimental results to test (0.01 level of significance) whether the track designs were equally resistant to breakage and to estimate the effect of usage on breakage resistance.

Track design A		Track design B		Track design C		Track design D	
x	y	x	y	x	y	x	y
10.4	3	16.9	8	17.8	5	19.6	9
19.3	7	23.6	11	24.4	9	25.4	8
13.7	4	14.4	7	13.5	5	35.5	16
7.2	0	17.2	10	20.1	6	16.8	7
16.3	5	9.1	4	11.0	4	31.2	11

REVIEW EXERCISES

12.42 Assume the following data obey the one-way analysis of variance model.

Treatment 1:	13	8	10	11	8	
Treatment 2:	1	0	3	0		
Treatment 3:	8	5	10	3	7	3

(a) Decompose each observation y_{ij} as

$$y_{ij} = \bar{y} + (\bar{y}_i - \bar{y}) + (y_{ij} - \bar{y}_i)$$

(b) Obtain the sums of squares and degrees of freedom for each array.

(c) Construct the analysis of variance table and test for differences among the treatments with $\alpha = 0.05$.

12.43 To determine the effect on exit dust loading in a precipitator, the following measurements were made:

Total flow (ft^3/hr)	Exit dust loading (grains per cubic yard in flue gas)				
200	1.5	1.7	1.6	1.9	1.9
300	1.5	1.8	2.2	1.9	2.2
400	1.4	1.6	1.7	1.5	1.8
500	1.1	1.5	1.4	1.4	2.0

Use the level of significance $\alpha = 0.05$ to test whether the flow through the precipitator has an effect on the exit dust loading.

12.44 Verify the analysis of variance table for the resin example on page 400. What is the conclusion when testing for a treatment effect with $\alpha = 0.05$?

12.45 Given the following data from a randomized block design

	Blocks			
	1	2	3	4
Treatment 1	9	10	2	7
Treatment 2	6	13	1	12
Treatment 3	9	16	9	14

(a) Decompose each observation y_{ij} as

$$y_{ij} = \bar{y}_{..} + (\bar{y}_{i.} - \bar{y}_{..}) + (\bar{y}_{.j} - \bar{y}_{..}) + (y_{ij} - \bar{y}_{i.} - \bar{y}_{.j} + \bar{y}_{..})$$

(b) Obtain the sums of squares and degrees of freedom for each array.

(c) Construct the analysis of variance table and test for differences among the treatments with $\alpha = 0.05$.

12.46 Use the Duncan test with $\alpha = 0.05$ to compare the treatments in Exercise 12.45.

12.47 An experiment was performed to judge the effect of 4 different fuels and 2 different types of launchers on the range of a certain rocket. Test, on the basis of the following data (in nautical miles) whether there are significant differences (a) among the means obtained for the fuels, and (b) between the means obtained for the launchers:

	Fuel I	Fuel II	Fuel III	Fuel IV
Launcher X	62.5	49.3	33.8	43.6
Launcher Y	40.4	39.7	47.4	59.8

Use the level of significance $\alpha = 0.05$.

12.48 Samples of groundwater were taken from 5 different toxic-waste dump sites by each of 3 different agencies: the EPA, the company that owned each site, and an independent consulting engineer. Each sample was analyzed for the presence of a certain contaminant by whatever laboratory method was customarily used by the agency collecting the sample, with the following results:

Concentration (parts per million)				
	Site A	Site B	Site C	Site D	Site E
Agency 1	23.8	7.6	15.4	30.6	4.2
Agency 2	19.2	6.8	13.2	22.5	3.9
Agency 3	20.9	5.9	14.0	27.1	3.0

Is there reason to believe that the agencies are not consistent with one another in their measurements? Do the dump sites differ from one another in their level of contamination? Use the $\alpha = 0.05$ level of significance.

12.49 Referring to Exercise 12.43, suppose that the data in each of the 5 columns were obtained from a different precipitator. Repeat the analysis of variance, treating the experiment as a two-way classification, and observe what change results in the error mean square.

12.50 Does it make sense to use the Duncan test with $\alpha = 0.05$ to compare the results obtained with the 4 fuels in Exercise 12.47? Why?

12.51 Use the Duncan test with $\alpha = 0.05$ to compare the pollution levels of the five sites in Exercise 12.48.

12.52 Is one of the agencies in Exercise 12.48 producing results that are consistently higher (or lower) than those of the other two? (Use $\alpha = 0.05$.)

12.53 A test was made to determine which of 3 different golf-ball designs, A, B, and C, will give the greatest distance. Golf balls were driven by 3 different golf pros, P_1, P_2, and P_3, using 3 different drivers, D_1, D_2, and D_3. The experiment was performed on 3 different fairways, and the distances from the tee to the point where the ball came to rest were measured in yards, as follows:

First fairway

	D_1	D_2	D_3
P_1	B 265	A 311	C 249
P_2	A 350	C 284	B 330
P_3	C 258	B 305	A 351

Second fairway

	D_1	D_2	D_3
P_1	B 220	A 276	C 189
P_2	A 319	C 232	B 264
P_3	C 175	B 254	A 307

Third fairway

	D_1	D_2	D_3
P_1	B 159	A 205	C 142
P_2	A 262	C 168	B 246
P_3	C 198	B 237	A 283

Is any of the golf-ball designs superior to the others with respect to distance?

12.54 Three different instrument-panel configurations were tested by placing airline pilots in flight simulators and testing their reaction time to simulated flight emergencies. Each pilot was faced with 10 emergency conditions in a randomized sequence, and the total time required to take corrective action for all 8 conditions was measured, with the following results:

Instrument panel 1		Instrument panel 2		Instrument panel 3	
x	y	x	y	x	y
8.1	6.55	12.1	5.74	15.2	6.37
19.4	6.40	2.1	5.93	8.7	6.97
11.6	5.93	3.9	6.16	7.2	7.38
24.9	6.79	5.2	5.68	6.1	6.43
6.2	7.16	4.6	5.41	11.8	7.59
3.8	5.64	14.4	6.29	12.1	7.16
18.4	5.87	16.1	5.55	9.5	7.02
9.4	6.32	8.5	4.82	2.6	6.85

In this table, x is the number of years of experience of the pilot, and y is the total reaction time in seconds. Perform an analysis of covariance to test whether the instrument-panel configurations yield significantly different results ($\alpha = 0.05$). Also, perform a one-way analysis of variance (ignoring the covariate, x) and determine in that way what effect experience has on the results.

12.55 Verify the analysis of variance table for the paper-strength example on page 401.

12.56 Benjamin Franklin (1706–1790) conducted an experiment to study the effect of water depth on the amount of drag on a boat being pulled up a canal. He made a 14-foot trough and a model boat 6 inches long. A thread was attached to the bow, put through a pulley, and then a weight was attached. Not having a second hand on his watch, he counted as fast as he could to 10 repeatedly. These times, for the model boat to traverse the trough at the different water depths, are

Water 1.5 inches:	100	104	104	106	100	99	100	100
Water 2.0 inches:	94	93	91	87	88	86	90	88
Water 4.5 inches:	79	78	77	79	79	80	79	81

(Source: Letter to John Pringle, May 10, 1768)

(a) Perform an analysis of variance and test for differences due to water depth using $\alpha = 0.05$.

(b) Use the Duncan test with $\alpha = 0.05$ to investigate differences.

(c) Use the Bonferroni 94% confidence interval approach on page 414 to compare the mean times.

KEY TERMS

(with page references)

Factorial Experimentation

In Chapter 12 we were interested mainly in the effects of one variable, whose values we referred to as "treatments." In this chapter we shall be concerned with the individual and joint effects of several variables, and combinations of the values, or levels, of these variables will now play the roles of the different treatments. Extraneous variables, if any, will be handled as before by means of blocks.

In Sections 13.1 and 13.2 we deal with the analysis of experiments whose treatments can be regarded as combinations of the levels of two or more factors. In Sections 13.3 and 13.4 we study the special case of factors having two levels, and in the remainder of the chapter we take up the analysis of experiments where there are too many combinations of all the factors to be included in the same block or experimental program. ▪

13.1 Two-Factor Experiments

To introduce the idea of a simple **two-factor (two-variable) experiment,** suppose that it is desired to determine the effects of flue temperature and oven width on the time required to make coke. The experimenter will combine 3 oven widths and 2 temperatures as given on the next page. If several blocks (or replicates) were run, each consisting of these 6 "treatments," it would be possible to analyze the data as a two-way classification and test for significant differences among the 6 treatment means. In this instance, however, the experimenter is interested in knowing far more than that—he wishes to know whether variations in oven width or in flue

Oven width (inches)	Flue temperature (degrees F)
4	1,600
4	1,900
8	1,600
8	1,900
12	1,600
12	1,900

temperature affect the coking time, and perhaps also whether any changes in coking time attributable to variations in oven width are the same at different temperatures.

It is possible to answer questions of this kind if the experimental conditions, the treatments, consist of appropriate combinations of the **levels** (or values) of the various **factors.** The factors in the preceding example are oven width and flue temperature; oven width has the 3 levels 4, 8, and 12 inches, while flue temperature has the 2 levels 1,600 and 1,900 degrees Fahrenheit. Note that the 6 treatments were chosen in such a way that each level of oven width is used once in conjunction with each level of flue temperature. In general, if 2 factors A and B are to be investigated at a and b levels, respectively, then there are $a \cdot b$ experimental conditions (treatments) corresponding to all possible combinations of the levels of the 2 factors. The resulting experiment is referred to as a **complete a $\times$ b factorial experiment.** Note that if one or more of the $a \cdot b$ experimental conditions is omitted, the experiment can still be analyzed as a two-way classification, but it cannot readily be analyzed as a factorial experiment. It is customary to omit the word "complete" so that an **a $\times$ b factorial experiment** is understood to contain experimental conditions corresponding to all possible combinations of the levels of the two factors.

In order to obtain an estimate of the experimental error in a two-factor experiment it is necessary to replicate, that is, to repeat the entire set of $a \cdot b$ experimental conditions, say, a total of r times, randomizing the order of applying the condition in each replicate. If y_{ijk} is the observation in the kth replicate, taken at the ith level of factor A and the jth level of factor B, the model assumed for the analysis of this kind of experiment is usually written as

Model equation for two-factor experiment

$$Y_{ijk} = \mu + \alpha_i + \beta_j + (\alpha\beta)_{ij} + \rho_k + \varepsilon_{ijk}$$

for $i = 1, 2, \ldots, a, j = 1, 2, \ldots, b$, and $k = 1, 2, \ldots, r$. Here μ is the grand mean, α_i is the effect of the ith level of factor A, β_j is the effect of the jth level of factor B, $(\alpha\beta)_{ij}$ is the **interaction,** or joint effect, of the ith level of factor A and the jth level of factor B, and ρ_k is the effect of the kth replicate. As in the models used in Chapter 12 we shall assume that the ε_{ijk} are independent random variables having normal distributions with zero means and the common variance σ^2. Also, analogous to the restrictions imposed on the models on pages 395 and 407, we shall assume that

$$\sum_{i=1}^{a} \alpha_i = \sum_{j=1}^{b} \beta_j = \sum_{i=1}^{a} (\alpha\beta)_{ij} = \sum_{j=1}^{b} (\alpha\beta)_{ij} = \sum_{k=1}^{r} \rho_k = 0$$

It can be shown that these restrictions will assure unique definitions of the parameters μ, α_i, β_j, $(\alpha\beta)_{ij}$, and ρ_k.

To illustrate the model underlying a two-factor experiment, let us consider an experiment with two replicates in which factor A occurs at two levels, factor B occurs at two levels, and the replication effects are zero, that is $\rho_1 = \rho_2 = 0$. In view of the restrictions on the parameters we also have

$$\alpha_2 = -\alpha_1, \beta_2 = -\beta_1 \quad \text{and} \quad (\alpha\beta)_{21} = (\alpha\beta)_{12} = -(\alpha\beta)_{22} = -(\alpha\beta)_{11}$$

and the population means corresponding to the four experimental conditions defined by the 2 levels of factor A and the 2 levels of factor B can be written as

$$\mu_{111} = \mu_{112} = \mu + \alpha_1 + \beta_1 + (\alpha\beta)_{11}$$

$$\mu_{121} = \mu_{122} = \mu + \alpha_1 - \beta_1 - (\alpha\beta)_{11}$$

$$\mu_{211} = \mu_{212} = \mu - \alpha_1 + \beta_1 - (\alpha\beta)_{11}$$

$$\mu_{221} = \mu_{222} = \mu - \alpha_1 - \beta_1 + (\alpha\beta)_{11}$$

Substituting for $\mu_{ij1} = \mu_{ij2}$ the mean of all observations obtained for the ith level of factor A and the jth level of factor B, we get 4 simultaneous linear equations which can be solved to yield estimates for the parameters μ, α_1, β_1, and $(\alpha\beta)_{11}$ (see Exercise 13.9).

To continue our illustration, let us now suppose that $\mu = 10$. If all of the other effects equaled zero, each of the μ_{ijk} would equal 10, and the response surface would be the horizontal plane shown in Figure 13.1(a). If we now add an effect of factor A, with $\alpha_1 = -4$, the response surface becomes the tilted plane shown in Figure 13.1(b), and if we add to this an effect of factor B, with $\beta_1 = 5$, we get the plane shown in Figure 13.1(c). Note that, so far, the effects of factors A and B are *additive*, that is, the change in the mean for either factor in going from level 1 to level 2 does not depend on the level of the other factor, and the response surface is a plane. If we now include an interaction, with $(\alpha\beta)_{11} = -2$, the plane becomes twisted as shown in Figure 13.1(d), the effects are no longer additive, and the response surface is no longer a plane. Note, also, that if the replication effects had not equalled zero, we would have obtained a different surface for each replicate; for each replicate the surface of Figure 13.1(d) would have been shifted an appropriate number of units up or down.

Generalizing these ideas from the 2×2 factorial experiment, the analysis of an $a \times b$ factorial experiment is based on the following breakdown of the total sum of squares. First, we partition SST into components attributed to treatments, replicates (or blocks), and error, by means of the identity

$$\sum_{i=1}^{a} \sum_{j=1}^{b} \sum_{k=1}^{r} (y_{ijk} - \bar{y}_{...})^2 = r \sum_{i=1}^{a} \sum_{j=1}^{b} (\bar{y}_{ij.} - \bar{y}_{...})^2 + ab \sum_{k=1}^{r} (\bar{y}_{..k} - \bar{y}_{...})^2$$

$$+ \sum_{i=1}^{a} \sum_{j=1}^{b} \sum_{k=1}^{r} (y_{ijk} - \bar{y}_{ij.} - \bar{y}_{..k} + \bar{y}_{...})^2$$

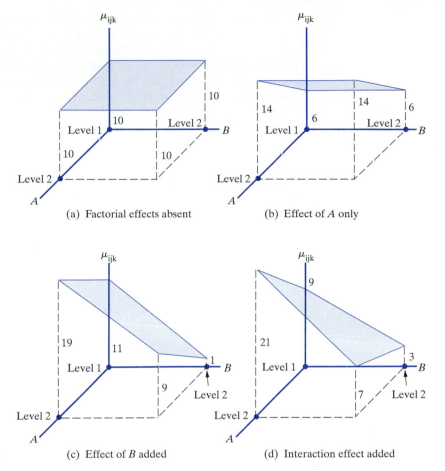

(a) Factorial effects absent

(b) Effect of A only

FIGURE 13.1
Factorials effects.

(c) Effect of B added

(d) Interaction effect added

Except for notation, this identity is equivalent to that of Theorem 12.2. The total sum of squares, on the left-hand side of the identity, has $abr - 1$ degrees of freedom. The terms on the right are, respectively, the treatment sum of squares having $ab - 1$ degrees of freedom, the replicate (block) sum of squares having $r - 1$ degrees of freedom, and the error sum of squares having $(ab - 1)(r - 1)$ degrees of freedom. (Note that the various degrees of freedom are the same as those of the analysis of variance table on page 409 if we substitute ab for a and r for b.)

So far there is nothing new about the analysis of the data; it is the analysis of a two-way classification, *but the distinguishing feature of a factorial experiment is that the treatment sum of squares can be further subdivided into components corresponding to the various factorial effects.* Thus, for a two-factor experiment we have the following partition, or breakdown, of the treatment sum of squares:

$$r \sum_{i=1}^{a} \sum_{j=1}^{b} (\bar{y}_{ij.} - \bar{y}_{...})^2 = rb \sum_{i=1}^{a} (\bar{y}_{i..} - \bar{y}_{...})^2 + ra \sum_{j=1}^{b} (\bar{y}_{.j.} - \bar{y}_{...})^2$$

$$+ r \sum_{i=1}^{a} \sum_{j=1}^{b} (\bar{y}_{ij.} - \bar{y}_{i..} - \bar{y}_{.j.} + \bar{y}_{...})^2$$

The first term on the right measures the variability of the means corresponding to the different levels of factor A, and we refer to it as the **factor A sum of squares, SSA**. Similarly, the second term is the sum of squares for factor B, SSB, and the third term is the **interaction sum of squares** $SS(AB)$ which measures the variability of the means $\bar{y}_{ij}$ that is not attributable to the individual (or separate) effects of factors A and B. The $ab - 1$ degrees of freedom for treatments are, accordingly, subdivided into $a - 1$ degrees of freedom for the effect of factor A, $b - 1$ for the effect of factor B, and

$$ab - 1 - (a - 1) - (b - 1) = (a - 1)(b - 1)$$

degrees of freedom for interaction.

The perceptive reader will notice that the breakdown of total sum of squares corresponds to the breakdown

$$\underset{\substack{observation}}{y_{ijk}} = \underset{\substack{grand \\ mean}}{\bar{y}_{...}} + \underset{\substack{factor\ A \\ effect}}{(\bar{y}_{i..} - \bar{y}_{...})} + \underset{\substack{factor\ B \\ effect}}{(\bar{y}_{.j.} - \bar{y}_{...})}$$

$$+ \underset{\substack{AB\ interaction}}{(\bar{y}_{ij.} - \bar{y}_{i..} - \bar{y}_{.j.} + \bar{y}_{...})} + \underset{\substack{replication}}{(\bar{y}_{..k} - \bar{y}_{...})} + \underset{\substack{error}}{(y_{ijk} - \bar{y}_{ij.} - \bar{y}_{..k} + \bar{y}_{...})}$$

of the individual observations, which, in turn, corresponds to the terms in the population model on page 439. Transposing $\bar{y}_{...}$ to the left-hand side, the breakdown corresponds to the breakdown in variation.

The next example illustrates the successive breakdown of the sum of squares. For the amount of calculation involved, you can appreciate the widespread availability of computer programs for creating an analysis of variance table (see Exercise 13.10).

EXAMPLE

Conducting statistical tests for a 3 × 2 factorial experimental design
Referring to the coking experiment described on page 439, suppose that 3 replicates of this experiment yield the following coking times (in hours):

Factor A Oven width	Factor B Flue temp.	Rep. 1	Rep. 2	Rep. 3	Total
4	1600	3.5	3.0	2.7	9.2
4	1900	2.2	2.3	2.4	6.9
8	1600	7.1	6.9	7.5	21.5
8	1900	5.2	4.6	6.8	16.6
12	1600	10.8	10.6	11.0	32.4
12	1900	7.6	7.1	7.3	22.0
	Total	36.4	34.5	37.7	108.6

Perform an analysis of variance based on this two-factor experiment and test for the significance of the factorial effects, using the 0.01 level of significance.

Solution   Following steps analogous to those used in the analysis of a two-way classification, we get

1. *Null hypotheses:*

$$\alpha_1 = \alpha_2 = \alpha_3 = 0, \qquad \beta_1 = \beta_2 = 0$$

$$(\alpha\beta)_{11} = (\alpha\beta)_{12} = (\alpha\beta)_{21} = (\alpha\beta)_{22} = (\alpha\beta)_{31} = (\alpha\beta)_{32} = 0$$

$$\rho_1 = \rho_2 = \rho_3 = 0$$

Alternative hypotheses: The α's are not all equal to zero; the β's are not all equal to zero; the $(\alpha\beta)$ terms are not all equal to zero; the ρ's are not all equal to zero.

2. *Levels of significance:* $\alpha = 0.01$ for all tests
3. *Criteria:* For replications, reject the null hypotheses if $F > 7.56$, the value of $F_{0.01}$ for $r - 1 = 3 - 1 = 2$ and $(ab - 1)(r - 1) = (3 \times 2 - 1)(3 - 1) = 10$ degrees of freedom; for the main effect of factor A, reject the null hypothesis if $F > 7.56$, the value of $F_{0.01}$ for $a - 1 = 3 - 1 = 2$ and $(ab - 1)(r - 1) = (3 \times 2 - 1)(3 - 1) = 10$ degrees of freedom; for the main effect of factor B, reject if $F > 10.04$, the value of $F_{0.01}$ for $b - 1 = 2 - 1 = 1$ and $(ab - 1)(r - 1) = (3 \times 2 - 1)(3 - 1) = 10$ degrees of freedom; for the interaction effect, reject if $F > 7.56$, the value of $F_{0.01}$ for $(a - 1)(b - 1) = (3 - 1)(2 - 1) = 2$ and $(ab - 1)(r - 1) = (3 \times 2 - 1)(3 - 1) = 10$ degrees of freedom.

4. *Calculations:* Following the procedure used in analyzing a two-way classification, we first compute the correction term

$$C = \frac{(108.6)^2}{18} = 655.22$$

Then, the total sum of squares is given by

$$SST = (3.5)^2 + (2.2)^2 + \cdots + (7.3)^2 - 655.22 = 149.38$$

and the treatment and replicate (instead of blocks) sums of squares are given by

$$SS(Tr) = \tfrac{1}{3}[(9.2)^2 + (6.9)^2 + \cdots + (22.0)^2] - 655.22 = 146.05$$

$$SSR = \tfrac{1}{6}[(36.4)^2 + (34.5)^2 + (37.7)^2] - 655.22 = 0.86$$

Finally, by subtraction, we obtain

$$SSE = 149.38 - 146.05 - 0.86 = 2.47$$

Subdivision of the treatment sum of squares into components for factors A and B, and for interaction, can be facilitated by constructing the following kind of two-way table, where the entries are the totals in the right-hand column of the table giving the original data:

Factor B

Flue temperature

		1600	1900	
	4	9.2	6.9	16.1
Factor A *Oven width*	*8*	21.5	16.6	38.1
	12	32.4	22.0	54.4
		63.1	45.5	108.6

Using formulas analogous to the ones with which we computed the sums of squares for various effects in Chapter 12, we now have for the two main effects

$$SSA = \frac{1}{b \cdot r} \sum_{i=1}^{a} T_{i..}^2 - C$$

$$= \frac{1}{6}[(16.1)^2 + (38.1)^2 + (54.4)^2] - 655.22 = 123.14$$

$$SSB = \frac{1}{a \cdot r} \sum_{j=1}^{b} T_{.j.}^2 - C$$

$$= \frac{1}{9}[(63.1)^2 + (45.5)^2] - 655.22 = 17.21$$

and for the interaction

$$SS(AB) = SS(Tr) - SSA - SSB$$

$$= 146.05 - 123.14 - 17.21 = 5.70$$

Finally, dividing the various sums of squares by their degrees of freedom, and dividing the appropriate means squares by the error mean square, we obtain the results shown in the following analysis of variance table:

Source of variation	Degrees of freedom	Sum of squares	Mean square	F
Replication	2	0.86	0.43	1.72
Main Effects:				
A	2	123.14	61.57	246
B	1	17.21	17.21	68.8
Interaction	2	5.70	2.85	11.4
Error	10	2.47	0.25	
Total	17	149.38		

FIGURE 13.2 Results of coking experiment.

5. *Decisions:* For replications, since $F = 1.72$ does not exceed 7.56, the value of $F_{0.01}$ for 2 and 10 degrees of freedom, we cannot reject the null hypothesis. For the main effect of factor A, since $F = 246$ exceeds 7.56, and for the main effect of factor B, since $F = 68.8$ exceeds 10.04, the null hypotheses must be rejected. For the interaction effect, since $F = 11.4$ exceeds 7.56 we must reject the null hypothesis. As illustrated in Figure 13.2, the trend of mean coking times for changing oven width is different for the two flue temperatures. It is apparent from this figure that the increase in coking time for changing oven width is greater at the lower flue temperature. In view of this interaction, great care must be exercised in stating the results of this experiment. For instance, it would be very misleading to state merely that the effect of increasing flue temperature from 1,600 to 1,900 degrees Fahrenheit is to lower the coking time by $\dfrac{63.1}{9} - \dfrac{45.5}{9} = 1.96$ hours. In fact, the coking time is lowered on the average by as little as 0.77 hour when the oven width is 4 inches, and by as much as 3.47 hours when the oven width is 12 inches.

Alternatively, the summary can take the form of the two-way table of cell means.

Summary Table of Cell Means

		Factor B *Flue temperature*		
		1600	*1900*	
	4	3.07	2.30	2.69
Factor A *Oven width*	8	7.17	5.53	6.35
	12	10.80	7.33	9.07
		7.01	5.05	6.03

DEPENDENT VARIABLE: Y

SOURCE	DF	SUM OF SQUARES	MEAN SQUARE	F VALUE	PR>F	R-SQUARE
MODEL	7	146.91666667	20.98809524	85.20	0.0001	0.983510
ERROR	10	2.46333333	0.24633333		ROOT MSE	
C TOTAL	17	149.38000000			0.49631979	

SOURCE	DF	TYPE 1 SS	F VALUE	PR>F
REP	2	0.86333333	1.75	0.2226
A	2	123.14333333	249.95	0.0001
B	1	17.20888889	69.86	0.0001
A*B	2	5.70111111	11.57	0.0025

Figure 13.3 Selected SAS output for ANOVA using the data in the example on page 442.

Repeating the analysis in the previous example, using the *SAS* statistical package ANOVA program, we obtained the output presented in Figure 13.3. The *P* values less than 0.01 confirm our previous analysis and their very small values strengthen the conclusions. Note that the *F* values in Figure 13.3 differ somewhat from those above because more decimals were retained in the computer calculations.

When replications and interactions are not significant, the influence of factor *A* and the influence of factor *B* can be interpreted separately. Then, when a factor is significant, many statisticians recommend comparing the levels by calculating confidence intervals using the two sample intervals on page 261. The confidence intervals for the difference in mean response at levels i_1 and i_2 of factor *A* is

$$\bar{y}_{i_1..} - \bar{y}_{i_2..} \pm t_{\alpha/2}\sqrt{s^2 \frac{2}{b \cdot r}}$$

where $s^2 = SSE/(ab - 1)(r - 1)$ is the mean square error and the $t_{\alpha/2}$ value is based on $(ab - 1)(r - 1)$ degrees of freedom.

Similarly, for levels j_1 and j_2 of Factor *B*, the confidence interval for the difference in mean response is

$$\bar{y}_{.j_1.} - \bar{y}_{.j_2.} \pm t_{\alpha/2}\sqrt{s^2 \frac{2}{a \cdot r}}$$

EXAMPLE

Using confidence intervals to compare factor levels
Illustrate the calculation of the confidence intervals for the difference in mean response using the means and s^2 from the previous example.

Solution
From the analysis of variance table, $s^2 = 0.25$ is the mean square error based on 10 degrees of freedom. For these degrees of freedom, we find $t_{0.025} = 2.228$. Therefore, the confidence intervals for differences in mean due to the $a = 3$ levels of oven width, Factor *A*, are

$$\bar{y}_{1..} - \bar{y}_{2..} \pm t_{0.025}\sqrt{s^2\frac{2}{b \cdot r}} \qquad \bar{y}_{1..} - \bar{y}_{3..} \pm t_{0.025}\sqrt{s^2\frac{2}{b \cdot r}} \qquad \bar{y}_{2..} - \bar{y}_{3..} \pm t_{0.025}\sqrt{s^2\frac{2}{b \cdot r}}$$

$$2.69 - 6.35 \pm 2.228\sqrt{0.25\frac{2}{2 \cdot 3}} \qquad 2.69 - 9.07 \pm 2.228\sqrt{0.25\frac{2}{2 \cdot 3}} \qquad 6.35 - 9.07 \pm 2.228\sqrt{0.25\frac{2}{2 \cdot 3}}$$

$$-4.30 \text{ to } -3.02 \qquad\qquad -7.02 \text{ to } -5.74 \qquad\qquad -3.35 \text{ to } -2.08$$

Because the interaction was significant, we cannot interpret these intervals on differences of mean coking times as due to changing oven width alone.

Similarly the single difference in mean due to the $b = 2$ flue temperatures is

$$\bar{y}_{.1.} - \bar{y}_{.2.} \pm t_{0.025}\sqrt{s^2\frac{2}{a \cdot r}}$$

$$7.01 - 5.05 \pm 2.228\sqrt{0.25\frac{2}{3 \cdot 3}}$$

or 1.43 to 2.49   ✔

13.2   Multifactor Experiments

Much industrial research and experimentation is conducted to discover the individual and joint effects of several factors on variables which are most relevant to phenomena under investigation. The experimental designs most often used are of the simple randomized-block or two-way classification type, but the distinguishing feature of most of them is the factorial arrangement of the treatments, or experimental conditions. As we observed in the preceding section, r sets of data pertaining to $a \cdot b$ experimental conditions can be analyzed as a factorial experiment in r replicates if the experimental conditions represent all possible combinations of the levels of two or more factors A and B. In this section, we shall extend the discussion to factorial experiments involving more than 2 factors, that is, to experiments where the experimental conditions represent all possible combinations of the levels of 3 or more factors.

To illustrate the analysis of a **multifactor experiment,** let us consider the following situation. A warm sulfuric pickling bath is used to remove oxides from the surface of a metal prior to plating, and it is desired to determine what factors in addition to the concentration of the sulfuric acid might affect the electrical conductivity of the bath. As it is felt that the salt concentration as well as the bath temperature might also affect the electrical conductivity, an experiment is planned to determine the individual and joint effects of these 3 variables on the electrical conductivity of the bath. In order to cover the ranges of concentrations and temperatures normally encountered, it is decided to use the following levels of the 3 factors:

Factor	Level 1	Level 2	Level 3	Level 4
A. Acid concentration (percent)	0	6	12	18
B. Salt concentration (percent)	0	10	20	
C. Bath temperature (degrees F)	80	100		

The resulting factorial experiment requires $4 \cdot 3 \cdot 2 = 24$ experimental conditions in each replicate, where each experimental condition is a pickling bath made up according to specifications. The order in which these pickling baths are made up should be random. Let us suppose that 2 replicates of the experiment have actually been completed, that is, the electrical conductivities of the various pickling baths have been measured, and that the results are as shown in the following table:

Results of Acid-Bath Experiment

Level of Factor			Conductivity ($mhos/cm^3$)		
A	B	C	Rep. 1	Rep. 2	Total
1	1	1	0.99	0.93	1.92
1	1	2	1.15	0.99	2.14
1	2	1	0.97	0.91	1.88
1	2	2	0.87	0.86	1.73
1	3	1	0.95	0.86	1.81
1	3	2	0.91	0.85	1.76
2	1	1	1.00	1.17	2.17
2	1	2	1.12	1.13	2.25
2	2	1	0.99	1.04	2.03
2	2	2	0.96	0.98	1.94
2	3	1	0.97	0.95	1.92
2	3	2	0.94	0.99	1.93
3	1	1	1.24	1.22	2.46
3	1	2	1.12	1.15	2.27
3	2	1	1.15	0.95	2.10
3	2	2	1.11	0.95	2.06
3	3	1	1.03	1.01	2.04
3	3	2	1.12	0.96	2.08
4	1	1	1.24	1.20	2.44
4	1	2	1.32	1.24	2.56

Level of Factor			Conductivity ($mhos/cm^3$)		
A	*B*	*C*	*Rep. 1*	*Rep. 2*	*Total*
4	2	1	1.14	1.10	2.24
4	2	2	1.20	1.19	2.39
4	3	1	1.02	1.01	2.03
4	3	2	1.02	1.00	2.02
		Total	25.53	24.64	50.17

The model we shall assume for the analysis of this experiment (or any similar three-factor experiment) is an immediate extension of the one used in Section 13.1. If y_{ijkl} is the conductivity measurement obtained at the ith level of acid concentration, the jth level of salt concentration, the kth level of bath temperature, in the lth replicate, we write

Model equation for three-factor experiment

$$Y_{ijkl} = \mu + \alpha_i + \beta_j + \gamma_k + (\alpha\beta)_{ij} + (\alpha\gamma)_{ik} + (\beta\gamma)_{jk} + (\alpha\beta\gamma)_{ijk} + \rho_l + \varepsilon_{ijkl}$$

for $i = 1, 2, \ldots, a, j = 1, 2, \ldots, b, k = 1, 2, \ldots, c$, and $l = 1, 2, \ldots, r$. We also assume that the sums of the **main effects** (α's, β's, and γ's) as well as the sum of the replication effects are equal to zero, that the sums of the **two-way interaction effects** summed on either subscript equal zero for any value of the other subscript, and that the sum of the **three-way interaction effects** summed on any one of the subscripts is zero for any values of the other two subscripts. As before, the ε_{ijkl} are assumed to be independent normal random variables having zero means and the common variance σ^2.

We begin the analysis of the data by treating the experiment as a two-way classification with $a \cdot b \cdot c$ treatments and r replicates (blocks), and using the short-cut formulas on page 408, we obtain

$$C = \frac{(50.17)^2}{48} = 52.4381$$

$$SST = (0.99)^2 + (1.15)^2 + \cdots + (1.00)^2 - 52.4381 = 0.6624$$

$$SS(Tr) = \frac{1}{2}[(1.92)^2 + (2.14)^2 + \cdots + (2.02)^2] - 52.4381 = 0.5712$$

$$SSR = \frac{1}{24}[(25.53)^2 + (24.64)^2] - 52.4381 = 0.0165$$

$$SSE = 0.6624 - 0.5712 - 0.0165 = 0.0747$$

The degrees of freedom for these sums of squares are, respectively, 47, 23, 1, and 23.

Next, we shall want to subdivide the treatment sum of squares into the three **main effect sums of squares** SSA, SSB, SSC, and the three **two-way interaction sums of squares**, $SS(AB)$, $SS(AC)$, and $SS(BC)$, and the **three-way interaction sum of squares** $SS(ABC)$. To facilitate the calculation of these sums of squares we first construct the following three tables analogous to the one on page 444:

		B		
	1	*2*	*3*	
1	4.06	3.61	3.57	11.24
2	4.42	3.97	3.85	12.24
3	4.73	4.16	4.12	13.01
4	5.00	4.63	4.05	13.68
	18.21	16.37	15.59	50.17

(*A* labels the rows)

		C	
	1	*2*	
1	5.61	5.63	11.24
2	6.12	6.12	12.24
3	6.60	6.41	13.01
4	6.71	6.97	13.68
	25.04	25.13	50.17

(*A* labels the rows)

		B		
	1	*2*	*3*	
1	8.99	8.25	7.80	25.04
2	9.22	8.12	7.79	25.13
	18.21	16.37	15.59	50.17

(*C* labels the rows)

The entries of these tables are the totals of all measurements obtained at the respective levels of the two variables. Note the self-checking feature of these tables; the same marginal totals appear several times, thus providing a rapid and effective check on the calculations.

To calculate SSA, SSB, and $SS(AB)$ we refer to the first of the preceding tables and an identity analogous to the one on page 441. As a matter of fact, the calculations parallel those for calculating SSA, SSB, and $SS(AB)$ in the two-factor experiment. To take the place of the treatment sum of squares, we first calculate

$$rc \sum_{i-1}^{a} \sum_{j=1}^{b} (\bar{y}_{ij..} - \bar{y}_{....})^2 = \frac{1}{r \cdot c} \sum_{i=1}^{a} \sum_{j=1}^{b} T_{ij..}^2 - C$$

$$= \frac{1}{4}[(4.06)^2 + (4.42)^2 + \cdots + (4.05)^2] - 52.4381$$

$$= 0.5301$$

and we then obtain

$$SSA = \frac{1}{bcr} \sum_{i=1}^{a} T_{i...}^2 - C$$

$$= \frac{1}{12}[(11.24)^2 + \cdots + (13.68)^2] - 52.4381$$

$$= 0.2750$$

$$SSB = \frac{1}{acr} \sum_{j=1}^{b} T_{.j..}^2 - C$$

$$= \frac{1}{16}[(18.21)^2 + (16.37)^2 + (15.59)^2] - 52.4381$$

$$= 0.2262$$

and

$$SS(AB) = 0.5301 - 0.2750 - 0.2262$$

$$= 0.0289$$

Performing the same calculations for the second of the tables on page 450, we obtain similarly,

$$SSC = 0.0002 \quad \text{and} \quad SS(AC) = 0.0085$$

and the analysis of the third table yields

$$SS(BC) = 0.0042$$

For the three-way interaction sum of squares, we finally obtain by subtraction

$$SS(ABC) = SS(Tr) - SSA - SSB - SSC$$

$$- SS(AB) - SS(AC) - SS(BC)$$

$$= 0.5712 - 0.2750 - 0.2262 - 0.0002$$

$$- 0.0289 - 0.0085 - 0.0042$$

$$= 0.0282$$

Note the degrees of freedom for each main effect is one less than the number of levels of the corresponding factor. The degrees of freedom for each interaction is the *product* of the degrees of freedom for those factors appearing in the interaction. Thus, the degrees of freedom for the three main effects are 3, 2, and 1 in this example, while the degrees of freedom for the two-way interactions are 6, 3, and 2, and the degrees of freedom for the three-way interaction is 6.

The following table shows the complete analysis of variance for the acid-bath experiment:

Source of variation	Degrees of freedom	Sum of squares	Mean square	F
Replicates	1	0.0165	0.0165	5.16
Main effects:				
A	3	0.2750	0.0917	28.66
B	2	0.2262	0.1131	35.34
C	1	0.0002	0.0002	< 1
Two-factor interactions:				
AB	6	0.0289	0.0048	1.50
AC	3	0.0085	0.0028	< 1
BC	2	0.0042	0.0021	< 1
Three-factor interaction:				
ABC	6	0.0282	0.0047	1.47
Error	23	0.0747	0.0032	
Total	47	0.6624		

Obtaining the appropriate values of $F_{0.05}$ and $F_{0.01}$ from Table 6, we find that the test for replicates is significant at the 0.05 level (perhaps the two replicates were performed under different atmospheric conditions or the thermometer used to measure bath temperatures went out of calibration, etc.), the tests for the factor A and factor B main effects are significant at the 0.01 level, while none of the other F's is significant at either level. We conclude from this analysis that variations in acid concentration and salt concentration affect the electrical conductivity, variations in bath temperature do not, and that there are no interactions. To go one step further, we might investigate the *magnitudes* of the effects by studying graphs of means like those shown in Figure 13.4 and 13.5. Here we find that the conductivity increases as acid is added and decreases as salt is added; using the methods of Chapter 11 we might even fit lines, curves, or surfaces to describe the response surface relating conductivity to the variables under consideration.

EXAMPLE

Conducting an analysis of variance to improve the safety of an ignitor
A customer requested improvements in the safety of an ignitor. Statistically designed experiments, run at the development stage, can help build quality into this product. It was decided to study 3 initiators (A), 2 booster charges (B), and 4 main charges (C). One response measured was the delay time (milliseconds). From safety considerations, this should remain under 30. Two replicates were run of the factorial design.

FIGURE 13.4 Effect of acid concentration.

FIGURE 13.5 Effect of salt concentration.

A	B	C	Delay time (milliseconds)	
			Rep. 1	*Rep. 2*
Initiator 1	Powder	Mc 1	10.70	9.82
Initiator 1	Pellet	Mc 1	10.02	13.66
Initiator 1	Powder	Mc 2	14.46	20.86
Initiator 1	Pellet	Mc 2	11.44	13.76
Initiator 1	Powder	Mc 3	15.04	16.02
Initiator 1	Pellet	Mc 3	27.26	21.42
Initiator 1	Powder	Mc 4	20.82	14.46
Initiator 1	Pellet	Mc 4	24.56	36.48
Initiator 2	Powder	Mc 1	18.42	18.62
Initiator 2	Pellet	Mc 1	22.80	25.14
Initiator 2	Powder	Mc 2	33.40	20.62
Initiator 2	Pellet	Mc 2	31.86	19.78
Initiator 2	Powder	Mc 3	22.94	31.12
Initiator 2	Pellet	Mc 3	32.92	21.38
Initiator 2	Powder	Mc 4	27.92	59.86
Initiator 2	Pellet	Mc 4	31.94	28.32
Initiator 3	Powder	Mc 1	7.14	7.98
Initiator 3	Pellet	Mc 1	24.32	10.26
Initiator 3	Powder	Mc 2	8.30	7.86
Initiator 3	Pellet	Mc 2	7.00	8.40
Initiator 3	Powder	Mc 3	8.40	10.94
Initiator 3	Pellet	Mc 3	17.82	15.28
Initiator 3	Powder	Mc 4	9.56	19.04
Initiator 3	Pellet	Mc 4	19.98	18.46

Analyze this experiment:

Solution We analyze this experiment without including a replication term in the model. A computer program produced the following ANOVA table:

SOURCE	DF	SS	MS	F	P
A	2	1973.18	986.59	22.22	0.000
B	1	74.90	74.90	1.69	0.206
C	3	864.39	288.13	6.49	0.002
AB	2	141.83	70.91	1.60	0.223
AC	6	200.97	33.50	0.75	0.612
BC	3	122.14	40.71	0.92	0.448
ABC	6	319.57	53.26	1.20	0.340
ERROR	24	1065.86	44.41		
TOTAL	47	4762.84	101.34		

Only the initiators and main charges are significant. They are significant even at $\alpha = .01$. The experiment can therefore be summarized by the two sets of sample means:

initiator 1	$\bar{y}_{1...} = 17.55$	Mc 1	$\bar{y}_{..1.} = 14.91$
initiator 2	$\bar{y}_{2...} = 27.94$	Mc 2	$\bar{y}_{..2.} = 16.48$
initiator 3	$\bar{y}_{3...} = 12.55$	Mc 3	$\bar{y}_{..3.} = 20.05$
		Mc 4	$\bar{y}_{..4.} = 25.95$

According to the estimated model

$$\hat{y}_{i.k.} = \bar{y}_{....} + (\bar{y}_{i...} - \bar{y}_{....}) + (y_{..k.} - \bar{y}_{....})$$

the lowest estimated delay time would come from using initiator 3 with main charge Mc 1. This experiment was successful in identifying better components for the ignitor.

The standard deviation of the delay times is estimated by s, which is the square root of the mean square error. Since $s = 6.66$ milliseconds, there is considerable variation in the individual delay times. The confidence intervals for the difference in mean delay times for two initiators are

$$\bar{y}_{i...} - \bar{y}_{m...} \pm t_{0.025}\sqrt{\frac{s^2}{2 \cdot 4}} = \bar{y}_{i...} - \bar{y}_{m...} \pm 2.064\sqrt{\frac{44.41}{8}}$$

so differences of 4.86 are significant. All three initiator means are different. The confidence intervals for main charges

$$\bar{y}_{..k.} - \bar{y}_{..m.} \pm t_{0.025}\sqrt{\frac{s^2}{3 \cdot 2}}$$

leads to differences of 5.62 being significant. Consequently, these data do not establish any difference between Mc 1, Mc 2, and Mc 3. ✔

The general computational procedure for a multifactor experiment is similar to the method illustrated here for a $4 \times 3 \times 2$ factorial experiment. We first analyze the data as a two-way classification (or whatever other design is being used) and then we analyze the treatment sum of squares into the components attributed to the various main effects and interactions. In general, the sum of squares for each main effect is found by adding the squares of the totals corresponding to the different levels of the factor, dividing by the number of observations comprising each of these totals, and then subtracting the correction term. The sum of squares for any interaction is found by adding the squares of all totals obtained by summing over those subscripts pertaining to factors not involved in the interaction, dividing by the number of observations comprising each of these totals, and then subtracting the correction term *and* all sums of squares corresponding to main effects and fewer-factor interactions involving the factors contained in that interaction.

EXERCISES

13.1 To determine optimum conditions for a plating bath, the effects of sulfone concentration and bath temperature on the reflectivity of the plated metal are studied in a 2×5 factorial experiment. The results of three replicates are as follows:

Concentration (grams/liter)	Temperature (degrees F)	Reflectivity Rep. 1	Rep. 2	Rep. 3
5	75	35	39	36
5	100	31	37	36
5	125	30	31	33
5	150	28	20	23
5	175	19	18	22
10	75	38	46	41
10	100	36	44	39
10	125	39	32	38
10	150	35	47	40
10	175	30	38	31

Analyze these results and determine the bath condition or conditions that produce the highest reflectivity. Also construct a 95% confidence interval for the reflectivity of the plating bath corresponding to these optimum conditions.

13.2 A spoilage-retarding ingredient is added in brewing beer. To determine the extent to which the taste of the beer is affected by the amount of this ingredient added to each batch, and how such taste changes might depend on the age of the beer, a 3×4 factorial experiment in two replications was designed. The taste of the beer was rated on a scale of 0, 1, 2, or 3 (3 being the most desirable) by a panel of trained experts, who reported the following mean ratings:

Amount of ingredient (grams per batch)	Aging period (weeks)	Mean ratings Rep. 1	Rep. 2
2	2	2.1	1.6
2	4	2.6	1.9
2	6	2.9	2.4
3	2	1.4	1.7
3	4	1.9	2.2
3	6	2.3	2.7
4	2	0.5	0.9
4	4	1.2	0.8
4	6	1.7	1.4
5	2	1.0	1.6
5	4	2.2	1.3
5	6	2.3	2.1

(a) Analyze the data first as a two-way classification with 12 treatments and two blocks (replicates).

(b) Calculate the sums of squares corresponding to the main effects and interaction, and present the results in an analysis of variance table.

(c) Interpret the results of the experiment.

13.3 Suppose that in the experiment described on page 411 it is desired to determine also whether there is an interaction between the detergents and the engines, that is, whether one detergent might perform better in Engine 1, another might perform better in Engine 2, and so forth. Combining the data on page 411 with the following replicate of the experiment, test for a significant interaction and discuss the results.

	Engine 1	Engine 2	Engine 3
Detergent A	39	42	58
Detergent B	44	46	48
Detergent C	34	47	45
Detergent D	47	45	57

13.4 Given the two replications of a 2 × 3 factorial experiment, calculate the analysis of variance table using the formulas on pages 440 and 441 rather than the shortcut formulas in the example.

Factor A	Factor B	Rep. 1	Rep. 2
1	1	15	21
1	2	1	3
1	3	10	8
2	1	1	1
2	2	16	14
2	3	5	13

13.5   An experiment was designed to study the effects of melt flow index (rate) and filler content (% of weight) on the strength of resin as measured by the secant modulus.

Melt flow index	Filler content	Rep. 1	Rep. 2
3	32	1.95	2.14
3	37	2.36	2.28
3	42	2.61	2.56
12	32	2.32	2.31
12	37	2.33	2.28
12	42	2.60	2.53
30	32	2.29	2.36
30	37	2.61	2.50
30	42	2.68	2.52

Analyze this experiment.

13.6   The commercial value of softwood species would be increased if the wood could be treated to meet preserver's standards. The response, y, is the amount of retention (lb/ft^3) of the preservative. Two treatments (preservatives) were considered and the samples were either incised or unincised. Further, the conditions of spruce trees were undefoliated, partially defoliated, or totally defoliated.

		Replicate 1		Replicate 2	
		Treatment 1	Treatment 2	Treatment 1	Treatment 2
Undefoliated	Incised	1.28	1.22	.77	1.09
	Unincised	1.28	1.22	1.22	1.17

		Replicate 1		Replicate 2	
		Treatment 1	Treatment 2	Treatment 1	Treatment 2
Partially Defoliated	Incised	.63	.78	.64	.74
	Unincised	.39	.49	.39	.53

		Replicate 1		Replicate 2	
		Treatment 1	Treatment 2	Treatment 1	Treatment 2
Totally Defoliated	Incised	.65	1.09	.38	.63
	Unincised	.40	.82	.40	.60

Perform an appropriate analysis of variance and interpret the results.

13.7   To study the effects of ignot location (A), slab position (B), specimen preparation (C), and twisting temperature (D) on the number of turns required to break a steel specimen by twisting, the following observations were recorded:

A	B	C	D	No. of turns Rep. 1	Rep. 2
Top	1	Turn	2,100°F	24	22
Top	1	Turn	2,200	25	28
Top	1	Turn	2,300	41	39
Top	1	Grind	2,100	18	18
Top	1	Grind	2,200	33	27
Top	1	Grind	2,300	35	41
Top	2	Turn	2,100	22	19
Top	2	Turn	2,200	26	31
Top	2	Turn	2,300	37	43
Top	2	Grind	2,100	23	7
Top	2	Grind	2,200	30	26
Top	2	Grind	2,300	34	30
Mid	1	Turn	2,100	26	19
Mid	1	Turn	2,200	30	31
Mid	1	Turn	2,300	39	42
Mid	1	Grind	2,100	19	19
Mid	1	Grind	2,200	31	31
Mid	1	Grind	2,300	26	35
Mid	2	Turn	2,100	30	26
Mid	2	Turn	2,200	31	34
Mid	2	Turn	2,300	39	42
Mid	2	Grind	2,100	22	20
Mid	2	Grind	2,200	32	26
Mid	2	Grind	2,300	38	22
Bot	1	Turn	2,100	18	21
Bot	1	Turn	2,200	35	32
Bot	1	Turn	2,300	34	37
Bot	1	Grind	2,100	21	19
Bot	1	Grind	2,200	20	29
Bot	1	Grind	2,300	44	31
Bot	2	Turn	2,100	23	22
Bot	2	Turn	2,200	31	26
Bot	2	Turn	2,300	38	41
Bot	2	Grind	2,100	18	19
Bot	2	Grind	2,200	31	24
Bot	2	Grind	2,300	35	41

Analyze this experiment.

13.8 A market test was performed to evaluate shelf position, label color, and package size of a canned food product, with the following results:

Shelf position	Label color	Package size (oz)	Sales (dollars) Day 1	Day 2	Day 3
Low	Red	10	70.10	68.00	69.50
Low	Red	12	72.25	71.90	74.40
Low	Red	16	78.05	74.85	82.60
Low	Red	24	61.50	62.10	59.15
Low	Green	10	65.75	62.35	68.60
Low	Green	12	69.45	71.05	75.45
Low	Green	16	75.15	70.70	71.25
Low	Green	24	64.80	60.85	59.90
Medium	Red	10	94.10	90.20	88.05
Medium	Red	12	104.85	99.55	96.80
Medium	Red	16	109.10	105.80	112.60
Medium	Red	24	59.90	62.50	54.75
Medium	Green	10	88.95	91.10	90.15
Medium	Green	12	100.60	94.05	101.35
Medium	Green	16	98.70	99.90	96.75
Medium	Green	24	62.50	53.85	59.40
High	Red	10	92.60	88.80	85.50
High	Red	12	100.55	102.15	99.10
High	Red	16	111.95	108.25	109.45
High	Red	24	61.40	65.20	59.70
High	Green	10	97.35	98.70	92.60
High	Green	12	120.65	115.45	108.65
High	Green	16	118.10	116.35	121.90
High	Green	24	70.30	65.05	71.40

Analyze this experiment.

13.9 Solve the 4 equations on page 440 for μ, α_1, β_1, and $(\alpha\beta)_{11}$ in terms of the population means μ_{ij1} corresponding to the 4 experimental conditions in the first replicate. Note that these equations serve as a guide for estimating the parameters in terms of the *sample means* corresponding to the various experimental conditions.

13.10 We illustrate computer calculation of the analysis of variance table given on page 444 using *MINITAB*. The 3 levels of A are coded as 1, 2, and 3, and the 2 levels of B are coded as 1 and 2. Notice that the last column contains the replication number.

3.5	1	1	1
3.0	1	1	2
2.7	1	1	3
2.2	1	2	1

. . .

The columns are named Y, A, B, and REPS. The commands and output are

> **Dialog box:**   **Session command**
> **Stat > ANOVA > Balanced ANOVA**   MTB > ANOVA Y=A B A*B REPS
> Type *Y* in **Responses.**
> In **Model,** type *A B A*B REPS.* click **OK.**

```
Analysis of Variance for Y

Source   DF        SS        MS        F        P
A         2   123.143    61.572   249.95    0.000
B         1    17.209    17.209    69.86    0.000
A*B       2     5.701     2.851    11.57    0.003
REPS      2     0.863     0.432     1.75    0.223
Error    10     2.463     0.246
Total    17   149.380
```

Repeat Exercise 13.5 using the computer.

13.3 2^n Factorial Experiments

Factorial experiments provide a powerful tool for understanding complex physical phenomena. Their key ingredient is the systematic variation of all input variables simultaneously. To see how important it is to change more than one variable at a time, suppose two input variables, x_1 and x_2 are varied in an attempt to locate the maximum response. In the situation illustrated in Figure 13.6, moving (x_1, x_2) toward the upper right-hand corner will increase the response from 6 to 10 and even higher. However, if the experimenter fixes x_1 at 1.6 and varies x_2, it will look like a maximum occurs at $x_2 = 1.7$. If x_2 is then fixed at 1.7 and x_1 varied, it will then appear as if a maximum is confirmed. That is, the classical method of varying one variable at a time can lead to a false location for maximum response. Factorial designs are well suited for studying the influence of several factors on a response.

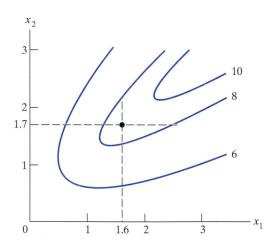

FIGURE 13.6 False location of a maximum response.

There are several reasons why factorial experiments are often performed with each factor taken at only two levels. Primarily, the number of experimental conditions in a factorial experiment increases multiplicatively with the number of levels of each factor; thus, if many factors are to be investigated simultaneously, it may be economically impossible to include more than two levels of each factor. Another important reason for treating **2^n factorial experiments** separately is that the analysis simplifies. Moreover, for $n = 2$ or 3, easily understood graphics can help communicate the main features of the data. Other advantages, such as the ease of confounding higher-order interactions and the adaptability of 2^n factorials to experiments involving fractional replication, will be discussed in succeeding sections.

Before we introduce some of the special notation used in connection with 2^n factorial experiments, let us point out that such experiments do have some drawbacks. Since each factor is measured only at two levels, it is impossible to judge whether the effects produced by variations in a factor are linear or, perhaps, parabolic or exponential. For this reason 2^n factorial experiments are often used in "screening experiments," which are followed up by experiments involving fewer factors (ordinarily those found to be "significant" individually or jointly in the screening experiment) taken at more than two levels.

In the analysis of a 2^n factorial experiment it is convenient to denote the two levels of each factor by 0 and 1 (instead of 1 and 2). Thus, the models used for the analysis of this kind of experiment differ from those of Section 13.2 only inasmuch as we now have $i = 0, 1$ instead of $i = 1, 2, \ldots, a, j = 0, 1$ instead of $j = 1, 2, \ldots, b$, and so forth. For instance, for a 2^3 factorial experiment the model on page 449 becomes

Model equation for 2^3 factorial experiment

$$Y_{ijkl} = \mu + \alpha_i + \beta_j + \gamma_k + (\alpha\beta)_{ij} + (\alpha\gamma)_{ik} + (\beta\gamma)_{jk} + (\alpha\beta\gamma)_{ijk} + \rho_l + \varepsilon_{ijkl}$$

for $i = 0, 1, j = 0, 1, k = 0, 1$, and $l = 1, 2, \ldots, r$. The ε_{ijkl} are defined as before, and the parameters are now subject to the restrictions $\alpha_1 = -\alpha_0, \beta_1 = -\beta_0, \gamma_1 = -\gamma_0, (\alpha\beta)_{10} = (\alpha\beta)_{01} = -(\alpha\beta)_{11} = -(\alpha\beta)_{00}$, and $\sum_{l=1}^{r} \rho_l = 0$. Note that besides the parameters for replicates we need only *one parameter of each kind:* that is, besides the parameters for replicates, we can express the entire model in terms of the parameters $\mu, \alpha_0, \beta_0, \gamma_0, (\alpha\beta)_{00}, (\alpha\gamma)_{00}, (\beta\gamma)_{00}$, and $(\alpha\beta\gamma)_{000}$.

A 2^n factorial experiment requires 2^n experimental conditions; since their number can be fairly large, it will be convenient to represent the experimental conditions by means of a special notation and list them in a so-called standard order. The notation consists of representing each experimental condition by the product of lowercase letters corresponding to the factors which are taken at level 1, called the "higher level." If a lowercase letter corresponding to a factor is missing, this means that the factor is taken at level 0, called the "lower level." Thus, in a three-factor experiment, ac represents the experimental condition where factors A and C are taken at the higher level and factor B is taken at the lower level, c represents the experimental condition where factor C is taken at the higher level and factors A and B are taken at the lower level, and so forth. The symbol "1" is used to denote the experimental condition in which all factors are taken at the lower level.

Although the experimental conditions are applied in a random order during the experiment itself, for the purpose of analyzing the results it is convenient to arrange them in a so-called **standard order.** For $n = 2$, this order is $1, a, b, ab$, and for $n = 3$ it is the order shown in the following table:

Experimental condition	Level of factor		
	A	B	C
1	0	0	0
a	1	0	0
b	0	1	0
ab	1	1	0
c	0	0	1
ac	1	0	1
bc	0	1	1
abc	1	1	1

Note that the symbols for the first 4 experimental conditions are like those for a two-factor experiment, and that the second 4 are obtained by multiplying each of the first 4 symbols by c. Similarly, the arrangement for $n = 4$ on page 464 is obtained by first listing the 8 symbols for a three-factor experiment and then repeating the set with each symbol multiplied by d.

Throughout this and the preceding chapter we referred to the total of all observations corresponding to a given experimental condition as a treatment total, and we represented these totals by means of symbols such as $T_{i.}, T_{ij..}$, and so forth. Having introduced a special notation for the experimental conditions in a 2^n factorial experiment, we extend this notation by letting $(1), (a), (b), (ab), (c), \ldots,$ be the treatment totals corresponding to experimental conditions $1, a, b, ab, c, \ldots.$ Thus, in a three-factor experiment

$$(1) = \sum_{l=1}^{r} y_{000l} \qquad (a) = \sum_{l=1}^{r} y_{100l}$$

$$\vdots \qquad\qquad \vdots$$

$$(bc) = \sum_{l=1}^{r} y_{011l} \qquad (abc) = \sum_{l=1}^{r} y_{111l}$$

The simplification in the analysis referred to on page 461 consists of the fact that estimates of the various main effects and interactions, as well as the corresponding sum of squares, can be expressed in terms of linear combinations of the treatment totals. To illustrate what we mean, let us consider the quantity

$$-(1) + (a) - (b) + (ab) - (c) + (ac) - (bc) + (abc)$$

which is a linear combination, with coefficients $+1$ and -1, of the treatment totals corresponding to the 8 experimental conditions. Referring to the model equation on page 461 and making use of the relationships among the parameters (but leaving all details to the reader in Exercises 13.15, 13.16, and 13.17) it can be shown that

$$-(1) + (a) - (b) + (ab) - (c) + (ac) - (bc) + (abc) = -8r\alpha_0 + \varepsilon_A$$

where ε_A is a corresponding linear combination of sums of the ε_{ijkl}. From Theorem 7.1 on page 256 it follows that ε_A is a value of a random variable whose distribution has zero mean; as a matter of fact, it can be shown that ε_A is a value of a random variable having a normal distribution with zero mean and the variance of $8r\sigma^2$. Referring to the above linear combination as the **effect total** $[A]$ for factor A, we find that $-[A]/8r$ provides an estimate of α_0, the main effect for factor A, and it can be shown that $[A]^2/8r$ actually equals SSA, the sum of squares for the main effect of factor A.

Similarly analyzing the linear combination

$$(1) + (a) - (b) - (ab) - (c) - (ac) + (bc) + (abc)$$

the reader will be asked to show in Exercise 13.17 that it equals $8r(\beta\gamma)_{00} + \varepsilon_{BC}$, where ε_{BC} is a corresponding linear combination of sums of the ε_{ijkl}. Referring to this linear combination of treatment totals as the effect total $[BC]$ for the two-way interaction of factors B and C, we find that $[BC]/8r$ provides an estimate of $(\beta\gamma)_{00}$, the effect of the BC interaction, and it can also be shown that $[BC]^2/8r$ equals $SS(BC)$, the sum of squares for the BC interaction. Proceeding in this fashion, we can present linear combinations of the treatment totals that yield estimates of the various other main effects and interactions, and whose squares, divided by $8r$, yield the corresponding sums of squares. These linear combinations, or effect totals, can easily be obtained with the use of the following **table of signs:**

(1)	(a)	(b)	(ab)	(c)	(ac)	(bc)	(abc)	Effect totals
1	1	1	1	1	1	1	1	$[I]$
−1	1	−1	1	−1	1	−1	1	$[A]$
−1	−1	1	1	−1	−1	1	1	$[B]$
1	−1	−1	1	1	−1	−1	1	$[AB]$
−1	−1	−1	−1	1	1	1	1	$[C]$
1	−1	1	−1	−1	1	−1	1	$[AC]$
1	1	−1	−1	−1	−1	1	1	$[BC]$
−1	1	1	−1	1	−1	−1	1	$[ABC]$

The entries of this table are the coefficients of the linear combinations of the treatment totals for the various main effects and interactions. As an aid for constructing similar tables for $n = 4$, $n = 5$, etc., note that for each main effect there is a "+1" when the factor is at the higher level and a "−1" when the factor is at the lower level. The signs for an interaction effect are obtained by multiplying the corresponding coefficients of all factors contained in the interaction. Thus, for $[AB]$ we multiply each sign for $[A]$ by the corresponding sign for $[B]$, getting

$$(-1)(-1) \quad (1)(-1) \quad (-1)(1) \quad (1)(1) \quad (-1)(-1) \quad (1)(-1) \quad (-1)(1) \quad (1)(1)$$

or

$$1 \quad -1 \quad -1 \quad 1 \quad 1 \quad -1 \quad -1 \quad 1$$

Note also that in the preceding table $[I]$ stands for the grand total of all the observations, so that $[I]^2/8r$ gives the correction term for calculating SST, SSE, SSR, and $SS(Tr)$.

Although we have illustrated the above shortcut method for obtaining the various main-effect and interaction sums of squares with reference to a 2^3 factorial experiment, the only difference in a 2^n factorial experiment with $n > 3$ is that we require a more extensive table of signs and that the respective sums of squares are obtained by dividing the squares of the effect totals by $r \cdot 2^n$.

To illustrate this technique and introduce a further simplification, let us consider the following 2^4 factorial experiment, designed to determine the effects of certain variables on the reliability of a rotary stepping switch. The factors studied were as follows:

Factor	Low level	High level
A. Lubrication	Dry	Lubricated
B. Dust protection	Unprotected	Enclosed in dust cover
C. Spark suppression	No	Yes
D. Current	0	0.5 Amps

Each switch was operated continuously until a malfunction occurred, and the number of hours of operation was recorded. The whole experiment was performed twice, with the following results:

Experimental condition	Hours of operation Rep. 1	Rep. 2	Total
1	828	797	1,625
a	997	948	1,945
b	735	776	1,511
ab	807	1,003	1,810
c	994	949	1,943
ac	1,069	1,094	2,163
bc	989	1,215	2,204
abc	889	1,010	1,899
d	593	813	1,406
ad	773	1,026	1,799
bd	740	922	1,662
abd	936	1,138	2,074

Experimental	Hours of operation		
condition	Rep. 1	Rep. 2	Total
cd	748	970	1,718
acd	1,202	1,182	2,384
bcd	1,103	966	2,069
abcd	985	1,154	2,139
Total	14,388	15,963	30,351

Analyzing these data first as a two-way classification with 16 treatments and 2 replications (blocks), we obtain

$$C = \frac{(30,351)^2}{32} = 28,786,975$$

$$SST = (838)^2 + (977)^2 + \cdots + (1,154)^2 - 28,786,975$$

$$= 744,876$$

$$SS(Tr) = \frac{1}{2}[(1,625)^2 + (1,945)^2 + \cdots + (2,139)^2] - 28,786,975$$

$$= 547,288$$

$$SSR = \frac{1}{16}[(14,388)^2 + (15,963)^2] - 28,786,975$$

$$= 77,520$$

$$SSE = 744,876 - 547,288 - 77,520 = 120,068$$

In order to subdivide the treatment sum of squares into SSA, SSB, ..., and $SS(ABCD)$, we could construct a table of signs like the one on page 463, calculate the effect totals, and then divide the squares of the effect totals by $r \cdot 2^n = 2 \cdot 2^4 = 32$. For the A factor main effect we would thus obtain

$$[A] = -1,625 + 1,945 - 1,511 + 1,810 - 1,943 + 2,163 - 2,204$$

$$+ 1,899 - 1,406 + 1,799 - 1,662 + 2,074 - 1,718 + 2,384$$

$$- 2,069 + 2,139$$

$$= 2,075$$

and

$$SSA = \frac{(2,075)^2}{32} = 134,551$$

These calculations are quite tedious, but they can be simplified considerably by using a further shortcut, called **Yates's method.** This method of calculating the effect totals is illustrated in the following table. The experimental conditions and the corresponding totals are listed in standard order. In the column marked (1), the upper half is obtained by adding successive pairs of treatment totals, and the lower half is obtained by subtracting successive pairs. Thus, in column (1) we obtained

$$1{,}625 + 1{,}945 = 3{,}570$$

$$1{,}511 + 1{,}810 = 3{,}321$$

$$\vdots$$

$$2{,}069 + 2{,}139 = 4{,}208$$

$$1{,}945 - 1{,}625 = \quad 320$$

$$1{,}810 - 1{,}511 = \quad 299$$

$$\vdots$$

$$2{,}139 - 2{,}069 = \quad 70$$

Experimental condition	Treatment total	(1)	(2)	(3)	(4)	Identification	Sum of squares
1	1,625	3,570	6,891	15,100	30,351	$[I]$	28,786,975
a	1,945	3,321	8,209	15,251	2,075	$[A]$	134,551
b	1,511	4,106	6,941	534	385	$[B]$	4,632
ab	1,810	4,103	8,310	1,541	−1,123	$[AB]$	39,410
c	1,943	3,205	619	−252	2,687	$[C]$	225,624
ac	2,163	3,736	−85	637	−773	$[AC]$	18,673
bc	2,204	4,102	805	−546	−179	$[BC]$	1,001
abc	1,899	4,208	736	−577	−1,119	$[ABC]$	39,130
d	1,406	320	−249	1,318	151	$[D]$	713
ad	1,799	299	−3	1,369	1,007	$[AD]$	31,689
bd	1,662	220	531	−704	889	$[BD]$	24,698
abd	2,074	−305	106	−69	−31	$[ABD]$	30
cd	1,718	393	−21	246	51	$[CD]$	81
acd	2,384	412	−525	−425	635	$[ACD]$	12,601
bcd	2,069	666	19	−504	−671	$[BCD]$	14,070
$abcd$	2,139	70	−596	−615	−111	$[ABCD]$	385

Note that, in the lower half of column (1), the first total in each pair is subtracted from the second. Column (2) is then obtained by performing the identical operations on the entries of column (1), and columns (3) and (4) are obtained in the same manner from the entries in columns (2) and (3), respectively. Column (4), and in general column (n), gives the effect totals in standard order, as shown. Each sum of squares is then obtained as before, by squaring the corresponding effect total and then dividing the result by $r \cdot 2^n = 2 \cdot 2^4 = 32$.

Dividing the sums of squares by their degrees of freedom to obtain the mean squares, and dividing the various mean squares by the error mean square, we get the following analysis of variance table for the 2^4 factorial experiment:

Source of variation	Degrees of freedom	Sum of squares	Mean square	F
Replicates	1	77,520	77,520	9.68
Main effects:				
A	1	134,551	134,551	16.81
B	1	4,632	4,632	< 1
C	1	225,624	225,624	28.19
D	1	713	713	< 1
Two-factor interactions:				
AB	1	39,410	39,410	4.92
AC	1	18,673	18,673	2.33
AD	1	31,689	31,689	3.96
BC	1	1,001	1,001	< 1
BD	1	24,698	24,698	3.09
CD	1	81	81	< 1
Three-factor interactions:				
ABC	1	39,130	39,130	4.89
ABD	1	30	30	< 1
ACD	1	12,601	12,601	1.57
BCD	1	14,070	14,070	1.76
Four-factor interactions:				
ABCD	1	385	385	< 1
Error	15	120,068	8,005	
Total	31	744,876		

Since $F_{0.05} = 4.54$ and $F_{0.01} = 8.68$ for 1 and 15 degrees of freedom, we find that the replication effects as well as the effects of lubrication and spark suppression are significant at the 0.01 level, and that there are significant interactions at the 0.05 level between lubrication, dust protection, and spark suppression. The reader will be asked to interpret these results and estimate the magnitude of some of the effects in Exercise 13.18.

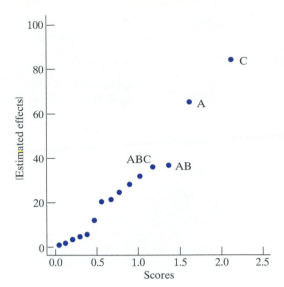

FIGURE 13.7 Half normal plot of | estimate effect |.

A graphical display called a **half normal plot** can also help indicate the most important effects. To illustrate this plot in the context of the previous example, we first divide the entries in the column marked (4), in the table on page 466, by $r2^4 = 32$ to obtain the estimated effects. Their absolute values are ordered and then plotted against the positive normal scores corresponding to a sample of size $2(15) = 30$ or twice the number of effects. This half normal plot is shown in Figure 13.7. In a given experiment, only a few of the effects are likely to be large in magnitude, either positive or negative, and the majority will be nearly zero. In the half normal plot, any large estimated effects should bend upward from the straight line pattern formed by the many small estimated effects. For the half normal plot in Figure 13.7, the A and C main effect estimates are large and clearly stick out above the straight line pattern. Contrary to the significant F tests for interactions, the visual evidence for AB and ABC is not very strong.

The half normal plot procedure can provide insights regarding major effects even when there is only a single replication. However, care must be taken to first check that the residuals are well-behaved. Even so, the half normal plot can be misleading if several rather than a few effects are large.

13.4   The Graphic Presentation of 2^2 and 2^3 Experiments

Both the 2^2 and 2^3 factorial designs have the added advantage that dramatic graphical displays are available to convey the results of the experiment. In spite of its simplicity, even the 2^2 design is a powerful tool to improve products and processes. The key is the decision to perform any designed experiment at all.

2^2 Design

Suppose the yield of a new chemical process for growing crystals needs improvement. Because temperature and pH are thought to influence yield, a 2^2 design is attempted and the following results obtained for yield.

Temperature	pH	Rep. 1	Rep. 2	Total
1	300	2	10	14	24
a	350	2	21	19	40
b	300	3	17	15	32
ab	350	3	20	24	44

The means for each experimental condition are written at the corners of the square, representing the design, in Figure 13.8. For instance, $\bar{y}_{00.} = 24/2 = 12$ is attached to the lower left-hand corner.

FIGURE 13.8 The graphical summary of a 2^2 factorial experiment.

It is clear from Figure 13.8 that changing temperature from low (300°) to high (350°) increases the yield substantially at both levels of pH. Changing pH has little or no effect. This figure is a very effective way to present the information contained in the experiment.

If the interaction is significant, the square in Figure 13.8, with means at the corners, is an alternative display to the table of cell means (see page 445). If the interaction is not significant, we continue the analysis by finding point estimates and confidence intervals for the magnitude of the difference in the mean response that results when a factor is changed from the low to the high level.

Our population model will not include a term for a replication effect. When a replication effect is suspected, the estimate of variance needs to be further refined (see Exercises 13.22 and 13.24). The population model for a 2^2 design, analogous to the 2^3 model on page 461 but without the replication term, is

$$Y_{ijk} = \mu + \alpha_i + \beta_j + (\alpha\beta)_{ij} + \varepsilon_{ijk}$$

with $\alpha_1 = -\alpha_0$. Consequently, the difference in mean response $\alpha_1 - \alpha_0 = 2\alpha_1 = -2\alpha_0$ is twice each factor A effect term. We estimate the difference in mean response $\alpha_1 - \alpha_0$ by

$$\bar{y}_{1..} - \bar{y}_{0..} = \frac{1}{2}(\bar{y}_{11.} + \bar{y}_{10.}) - \frac{1}{2}(\bar{y}_{01.} + \bar{y}_{00.}) = \frac{1}{2}(22 + 20) - \frac{1}{2}(16 + 12) = 7$$

$$+ \tfrac{1}{2}(\bar{y}_{01\bullet} + \bar{y}_{11\bullet})$$

$$- \tfrac{1}{2}(\bar{y}_{01\bullet} + \bar{y}_{00\bullet}) \qquad + \tfrac{1}{2}(\bar{y}_{11\bullet} + \bar{y}_{10\bullet})$$

$$- \tfrac{1}{2}(\bar{y}_{00\bullet} + \bar{y}_{10\bullet})$$

(a) Effect of A   (b) Effect of B

$$+ \tfrac{1}{2}(\bar{y}_{11\bullet} + \bar{y}_{00\bullet})$$

FIGURE 13.9 The signs for the $\bar{y}_{ij\bullet}$ to estimate effects in a 2^2 design.

$$- \tfrac{1}{2}(\bar{y}_{10\bullet} + \bar{y}_{01\bullet})$$

(c) AB interaction

That is, we take the average on the right side and subtract the average on the left side of the square, as indicated in Figure 13.9.

For the second factor, pH, we estimate the difference in mean response between the low and high level by

$$\bar{y}_{\cdot 1\cdot} - \bar{y}_{\cdot 0\cdot} = \frac{1}{2}(\bar{y}_{01\cdot} + \bar{y}_{11\cdot}) - \frac{1}{2}(\bar{y}_{00\cdot} + \bar{y}_{10\cdot}) = \frac{1}{2}(16 + 22) - \frac{1}{2}(12 + 20) = 3$$

To estimate the interaction, we note that $\bar{y}_{10\cdot} - \bar{y}_{00\cdot}$ gives the increase in yield at pH = 2, whereas $\bar{y}_{11\cdot} - \bar{y}_{01\cdot}$ gives the increase in yield at pH = 3. The average of these two differences estimates the interaction

$$\frac{1}{2}(\bar{y}_{11\cdot} - \bar{y}_{01\cdot}) - \frac{1}{2}(\bar{y}_{10\cdot} - \bar{y}_{00\cdot}) = \frac{1}{2}(\bar{y}_{11\cdot} - \bar{y}_{10\cdot} - \bar{y}_{01\cdot} + \bar{y}_{00\cdot})$$

$$= \frac{1}{2}(22 - 20 - 16 + 12) = -1$$

In Exercise 13.21, the reader is asked to verify that the preceding estimates are equal to twice the effects estimated in the analysis of variance model, or $[A]/2r$, $[B]/2r$, and $[AB]/2r$, respectively.

Each estimator of an effect is a linear combination of the four independent $\bar{Y}_{ij\cdot}$'s and so has the same variance. This common variance is estimated by s^2/r where s^2 is the error mean square which is obtained by pooling the estimates from the 4 corners of the square (see Exercise 13.22 for s^2 when a replication term is included in the model).

$$s^2 = \frac{1}{(r-1)2^2} \sum_{i=0}^{1} \sum_{j=0}^{1} \sum_{l=1}^{r} (y_{ijl} - \bar{y}_{ij.})^2$$

$$= \frac{1}{(2-1)2^2}(4 + 4 + 1 + 1 + 1 + 1 + 4 + 4) = 5$$

This mean square error has $(r-1)2^2 = 4$ degrees of freedom. The $t_{0.025} = 2.776$, so the resulting individual 95% confidence intervals are

temperature effect: $\bar{y}_{1..} - \bar{y}_{0..} + t_{0.025}\sqrt{\dfrac{s^2}{r}} = 7 \pm 4.39$,   or   2.61 to 11.39

pH effect: $\bar{y}_{.1.} - \bar{y}_{.0.} \pm t_{0.025}\sqrt{\dfrac{s^2}{r}} = 3 \pm 4.39$,   or -1.39 to 7.39

temperature $\times$ pH interaction:

$$\frac{1}{2}(\bar{y}_{11.} - \bar{y}_{10.} - \bar{y}_{01.} + \bar{y}_{00.}) \pm t_{0.025}\sqrt{\frac{s^2}{r}}$$

$$= -1 \pm 4.39, \quad \text{or} \quad -5.39 \text{ to } 3.39$$

Here the confidence interval for interaction covers 0, so we neglect interaction. The same is true for the pH effect. We are 95% confident that changing temperature from 300 degrees to 350 degrees will increase the mean yield by anywhere from 2.61 to 11.39 units.

An alternative approach to the same analysis begins by coding the input variables. They are coded by assigning -1 to the low level and $+1$ to the high level of each factor. When the factors are quantitative, as in the present discussion, the coded values can be expressed by the formula

$$x_1 = \frac{Temperature - (300 + 350)/2}{(350 - 300)/2} \quad \text{and} \quad x_2 = \frac{pH - (2 + 3)/2}{(3 - 2)/2}$$

The design for the experiment consists of the pair of values for x_1 and x_2, for each run. Augmenting the design by including a column for the product $x_1 x_2$ of the two input variables, we obtain

Design Temperature	pH				
x_1	x_2	$x_1 x_2$	Rep. 1	Rep. 2	Total
-1	-1	1	10	14	24
1	-1	-1	21	19	40
-1	1	-1	17	15	32
1	1	1	20	24	44

The first column alternates between -1 and $+1$ starting with -1, while the second column alternates doubles starting with two -1's. This is the standard order design in the coded variable notation.

Notice that the signs in the x_1, x_2, and x_1x_2 columns in the table above are coefficients for the totals when calculating the respective effects of changing from the low to high values of the input variables. The resulting linear combination is divided by $r2^{2-1}$. For instance, the estimate of the temperature $\times$ pH interaction would be calculated as

$$\frac{1}{r2^{2-1}}(24 - 40 - 32 + 44) = -1$$

In the coded variable notation, the lower left-hand corner of the square corresponding to temperature 300 and pH 2 is located at $x_1 = -1$ and $x_2 = -1$.

2^3 Design

We now turn to graphic displays for the 2^3 factorial design. In order to help expand the company's market for a plastic wrapping material, engineers were asked to improve the opacity. They felt that three factors—rate of extrusion, amount of an additive, and nozzle setting—might have an effect. Two levels were selected for each factor and a 2^3 factorial experiment produced the observations:

Factor A Rate	Factor B Amount additive	Factor C Nozzle setting	Rep. 1	Rep. 2
0	0	0	4.5	4.1
1	0	0	3.8	3.4
0	1	0	3.1	4.3
1	1	0	7.2	6.8
0	0	1	5.4	5.0
1	0	1	4.5	4.9
0	1	1	4.2	5.4
1	1	1	7.3	6.9

Assuming no replication effect, a cube representing the factors is shown in Figure 13.10. At the corners of the cube, we have attached the mean response for that set of experimental conditions. For instance, $(7.3 + 6.9)/2 = 7.1$ appears at the upper right corner of the front face. It is clear from Figure 13.10 that the response increases as both Factor A and Factor B are simultaneously changed from their low to high levels. This is an interaction effect since just changing one of the factors does not always increase the response. Factor C, nozzle setting, also seems to have an effect.

We verify these conclusions under the model on page 461 with all $\rho_l = 0$. The difference in mean response between the low and high level of factor A is $\alpha_1 - \alpha_0 = 2\alpha_1 = -2\alpha_0$, or twice the effect term. We estimate this mean difference by

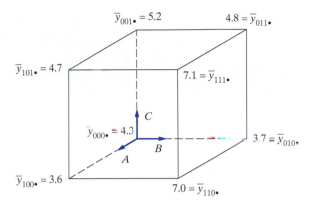

FIGURE 13.10
Graphic summary of a
2^3 design experiment.

$$\bar{y}_{1\ldots} - \bar{y}_{0\ldots} = \frac{1}{4}\left(\bar{y}_{100.} + \bar{y}_{110.} + \bar{y}_{101.} + \bar{y}_{111.}\right) - \frac{1}{4}\left(\bar{y}_{000.} + \bar{y}_{010.} + \bar{y}_{001.} + \bar{y}_{011.}\right)$$

$$= \frac{1}{4}(3.6 + 7.0 + 4.7 + 7.1) - \frac{1}{4}(4.3 + 3.7 + 5.2 + 4.8) = 1.1$$

which is the average of the four $\bar{y}_{ijk.}$ on the front face minus the average of the 4 observations on the back face (see Figure 13.11). Alternatively, it is the average of the 4 increases along each edge. Note that each $\bar{y}_{ijk.}$ in the first set of parentheses is associated with an experimental condition that has a term a in the special notation. Thus the signs are the same as those used with Yates's algorithm.

The estimates of the difference in mean response, when changing from the low to the high level, have a similar interpretation for the other two factors:

$$\bar{y}_{.1..} - \bar{y}_{.0..} = 1.2$$

$$\bar{y}_{..1.} - \bar{y}_{..0.} = 0.8$$

The AB interaction is estimated as the average of the interaction on the top face and the interaction on the bottom face. Figure 13.11 gives the signs for the $\bar{y}_{ijk.}$. For the AB interaction, we estimate

$$\frac{1}{2}\left(\bar{y}_{11..} - \bar{y}_{10..} - \bar{y}_{01..} + \bar{y}_{00..}\right)$$

$$= \frac{1}{4}\left(\bar{y}_{111.} - \bar{y}_{101.} - \bar{y}_{011.} + \bar{y}_{001.}\right) + \frac{1}{4}\left(\bar{y}_{110.} - \bar{y}_{100.} - \bar{y}_{010.} + \bar{y}_{000.}\right)$$

$$= \frac{1}{4}\left(7.1 - 4.7 - 4.8 + 5.2\right) + \frac{1}{4}\left(7.0 - 3.6 - 3.7 + 4.3\right) = 1.7$$

The combination of signs for the 8 means are obtained in a similar manner for the other 2 factor interactions.

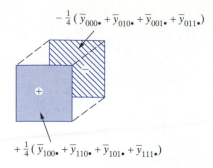

$$-\tfrac{1}{4}\left(\bar{y}_{000\bullet}+\bar{y}_{010\bullet}+\bar{y}_{001\bullet}+\bar{y}_{011\bullet}\right)$$

$$+\tfrac{1}{4}\left(\bar{y}_{100\bullet}+\bar{y}_{110\bullet}+\bar{y}_{101\bullet}+\bar{y}_{111\bullet}\right)$$

(a) Main effect of A

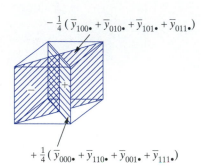

$$-\tfrac{1}{4}\left(\bar{y}_{100\bullet}+\bar{y}_{010\bullet}+\bar{y}_{101\bullet}+\bar{y}_{011\bullet}\right)$$

$$+\tfrac{1}{4}\left(\bar{y}_{000\bullet}+\bar{y}_{110\bullet}+\bar{y}_{001\bullet}+\bar{y}_{111\bullet}\right)$$

(b) AB interaction

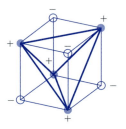

FIGURE 13.11 The signs for estimating effects in a 2^3 design.

(c) ABC interaction

$$\frac{1}{2}\left(\bar{y}_{1.1.}-\bar{y}_{1.0.}-\bar{y}_{0.1.}+\bar{y}_{0.0.}\right)=-0.2$$

$$\frac{1}{2}\left(\bar{y}_{.11.}-\bar{y}_{.10.}-\bar{y}_{.01.}+\bar{y}_{.00.}\right)=-0.2$$

The three-factor interaction ABC is a measure of the difference of the AB interaction on the top face and the interaction on the bottom face (see Figure 13.11). That is, it quantifies the influence of C on the AB interaction. (There is a symmetry here and, up to a minus sign, the same result is obtained starting with any two-factor interaction.)

$$\frac{1}{4}(\bar{y}_{111.} - \bar{y}_{101.} - \bar{y}_{011.} + \bar{y}_{001.}) + \frac{1}{4}(\bar{y}_{110.} - \bar{y}_{100.} - \bar{y}_{010.} + \bar{y}_{000.})$$

$$= \frac{1}{4}(7.1 - 4.7 - 4.8 + 5.2) - \frac{1}{4}(7.0 - 3.6 - 3.7 + 4.3) = -0.3$$

The confidence intervals are obtained by adding and subtracting $t_{\alpha/2}\sqrt{\frac{s^2}{2r}}$ to each estimate, where s^2 is the mean square error. This estimate of variance, when there is no replication term in the model, is obtained by pooling the estimates from the 8 corners of the cube.

$$s^2 = \frac{1}{(r-1)2^3} \sum_{i=0}^{1} \sum_{j=0}^{1} \sum_{k=0}^{1} \sum_{l=1}^{r} (y_{ijkl} - \bar{y}_{ijk.})^2$$

$$= \frac{1}{(2-1)2^3}(.04 + .04 + .04 + .04 + .36 + \cdots + .36 + .36 + .04 + .04)$$

$$= 0.240$$

This mean square error has $(r-1)2^3 = 8$ degrees of freedom, so $t_{0.025} = 2.306$ and the resulting individual 95% confidence intervals are

rate effect: $\quad \bar{y}_{1...} - \bar{y}_{0...} \pm t_{0.025}\sqrt{\dfrac{s^2}{2r}} = 1.1 \pm 0.56, \quad$ or $\quad$ 0.54 to 1.66

additive effect: $\quad \bar{y}_{.1..} - \bar{y}_{.0..} \pm t_{0.025}\sqrt{\dfrac{s^2}{2r}} = 1.2 \pm 0.56, \quad$ or $\quad$ 0.64 to 1.76

nozzle effect: $\quad \bar{y}_{..1.} - \bar{y}_{..0.} \pm t_{0.025}\sqrt{\dfrac{s^2}{2r}} = 0.8 \pm 0.56, \quad$ or $\quad$ 0.24 to 1.36

rate $\times$ additive interaction: $\quad \dfrac{1}{2}(\bar{y}_{11..} - \bar{y}_{01..} - \bar{y}_{10..} + \bar{y}_{00..}) \pm t_{0.025}\sqrt{\dfrac{s^2}{2r}}$

$$= 1.7 \pm 0.56, \quad \text{or} \quad 1.14 \text{ to } 2.26$$

rate $\times$ nozzle interaction: $\quad \dfrac{1}{2}(\bar{y}_{1.1.} - \bar{y}_{0.1.} - \bar{y}_{1.0.} + \bar{y}_{0.0.}) \pm t_{0.025}\sqrt{\dfrac{s^2}{2r}}$

$$= -0.2 \pm 0.56, \quad \text{or} \quad -0.76 \text{ to } 0.36$$

additive $\times$ nozzle interaction: $\quad \dfrac{1}{2}(\bar{y}_{.11.} - \bar{y}_{.01.} - \bar{y}_{.10.} + \bar{y}_{.00.}) \pm t_{0.025}\sqrt{\dfrac{s^2}{2r}}$

$$= -0.2 \pm 0.56, \quad \text{or} \quad -0.76 \text{ to } 0.36$$

rate $\times$ *additive* $\times$ *nozzle interaction:*

$$\frac{1}{4}\left(\bar{y}_{111.} - \bar{y}_{101.} - \bar{y}_{011.} + \bar{y}_{001.}\right)$$

$$-\frac{1}{4}\left(\bar{y}_{110.} - \bar{y}_{100.} - \bar{y}_{010.} + \bar{y}_{000.}\right)$$

$$\pm t_{0.025}\sqrt{\frac{s^2}{2r}}$$

$$= -0.3 \pm 0.56, \text{ or } -0.86 \text{ to } 0.26.$$

Here the confidence interval for the three-factor interaction covers 0, so we neglect this interaction. However, we are 95% confident that the interval from 1.14 to 2.26 contains the rate $\times$ additive interaction, so we cannot interpret the rate and additive factors individually. Factor C, nozzle setting, is not involved in any significant interaction. With 95% confidence, we conclude that using the high nozzle setting will increase the opacity of the plastic wrap from between 0.24 to 1.36 units.

Under the alternative approach, the design for the experiment is the collection of values x_1, x_2, and x_3 for each run. Augmenting the design by including additional columns for products of the original columns, we obtain

Design

rate	additive	nozzle							
x_1	x_2	x_3	x_1x_2	x_1x_3	x_2x_3	$x_1x_2x_3$	Rep. 1	Rep. 2	Total
-1	-1	-1	1	1	1	-1	4.5	4.1	8.6
1	-1	-1	-1	-1	1	1	3.8	3.4	7.2
-1	1	-1	-1	1	-1	1	3.1	4.3	7.4
1	1	-1	1	-1	-1	-1	7.2	6.8	14.0
-1	-1	1	1	-1	-1	1	5.4	5.0	10.4
1	-1	1	-1	1	-1	-1	4.5	4.9	9.4
-1	1	1	-1	-1	1	-1	4.2	5.4	9.6
1	1	1	1	1	1	1	7.3	6.9	14.2

Notice that again the signs of the columns are the coefficients of the linear combination of totals. The value of each linear combination, when divided by $r2^{3-1}$, is the estimated effect when changing from the low to high values of the input variables. For the main effect of rate,

$$\frac{1}{r2^{3-1}}\left(-8.6 + 7.2 - 7.4 + 14.0 - 10.4 + 9.4 - 9.6 + 14.2\right) = 1.1$$

The estimates of the other main effects and interactions are similarly obtained using the appropriate column of signs.

Blocking in a 2^3 design

It is always desirable to conduct the 8 runs of a 2^3 factorial design under conditions that are as homogenous as possible except for the settings of the 3 factors. However, limitations of time, space, equipment or available people may make it impossible to perform all 8 runs under homogeneous conditions. For instance, if large ceramic parts need to be baked, the oven may only hold 4 at one time. In our example of a 2^3 design for investigating factors that influence opacity, the time to manufacture the large rolls of plastic could be a limiting condition. Suppose a maximum of 4 runs can be conducted during one day. Consequently, the experiment needs to be divided up so 4 runs can be conducted one day and the other 4 the next day. How should the 4 runs for the first day be selected from among the total of 8 runs?

The answer lies in the fact that the three-factor interaction can often be neglected. Figure 13.12 shows how the 2^3 design can be divided into two groups of runs or **blocks** each consisting of four runs. The 4 runs in each block all have the same sign for the three-factor interaction term $x_1 x_2 x_3$ in the table of signs on page 476.

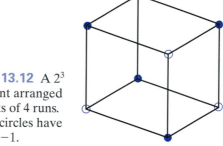

FIGURE 13.12 A 2^3 experiment arranged in 2 blocks of 4 runs. The blue circles have $x_1 x_2 x_3 = -1$.

The 4 runs in the first block, with $x_1 x_2 x_3 = -1$, are

Block I

x_1	x_2	x_3	$x_1 x_2$	$x_1 x_3$	$x_2 x_3$	$x_1 x_2 x_3$
-1	-1	-1	1	1	1	-1
1	1	-1	1	-1	-1	-1
1	-1	1	-1	1	-1	-1
-1	1	1	-1	-1	1	-1

Those in the second block are

Block II

x_1	x_2	x_3	$x_1 x_2$	$x_1 x_3$	$x_2 x_3$	$x_1 x_2 x_3$
1	-1	-1	-1	-1	1	1
-1	1	-1	-1	1	-1	1
-1	-1	1	1	-1	-1	1
1	1	1	1	1	1	1

This division of the 8 runs into 2 blocks tends to neutralize the effect of differences in uncontrolled variables between the 2 days on which the experiment is conducted. Suppose that, due to some uncontrollable variable, all the runs on the second day were d units higher than if they were performed on the first day. Whatever the value of d, it will cancel out in the estimation of the 3 main effects and the two-factor interactions. To see this, we inspect the appropriate column in the tables of signs for each of the 2 blocks. The column corresponding to each of these effects, in each block, has 2 plus signs and 2 minus signs so the d term cancels. Alternatively, from the geometric representation, each face of the cube has 2 blue dots and 2 white dots. Consequently, the average over any face is unaffected by the additive effect d and hence the estimates of the main effects are unaffected. The diagonal contrasts for a two-factor interaction have the same property on each face.

To be able to split the experiment into 2 blocks, we did have to give up information about the three-factor interaction. We deliberately confused or **confounded** the three-factor interaction with the day-to-day differences. Where the three-factor interaction is unimportant, this choice ensures that the main effects and the two-factor interactions can be estimated more precisely than would be the case if the 8 runs had to be conducted over a two-day period under less homogeneous conditions.

EXERCISES

13.11 To determine the effect on taste of 3 different factors in manufacturing soft-drink cans, an experiment was performed where the taste of one soft drink was rated by a judge on a scale from 1 to 10. The results are as follows:

A Lubricant	B Heat	C Resin	Ratings Rep. 1	Rep. 2
Fresh	Unheated	A	6	8
Fresh	Unheated	B	8	7
Fresh	Heated	A	9	9
Fresh	Heated	B	1	2
Aged	Unheated	A	6	7
Aged	Unheated	B	6	8
Aged	Heated	A	9	8
Aged	Heated	B	2	3

(a) Analyze the results first as a two-way classification with 7 degrees of freedom for treatments and 1 degree of freedom for blocks (replicates).

(b) Use an appropriate table of signs to calculate the effect totals $[A]$, $[B]$, $[C]$, $[AB]$, $[AC]$, $[BC]$, $[ABC]$.

(c) Using the results obtained in part (b) find the sums of squares corresponding to the main effects and interactions, and check their total against the treatment sum of squares obtained in part (a).

(d) Arrange the data with treatment combinations in standard order, and use the Yates method to find the effect totals. Compare the results obtained in part (b).

(e) Construct an analysis of variance table and analyze the experiment.

13.12 A screening experiment was conducted to determine what factors are influential in controlling the final phosphorus content of steel produced in a converter. The levels of the factors studied and the experimental results are contained in the following table:

E Pouring temp. (°F)	D Lime ratio	C Oxygen	B Original phosphorus	A Original manganese	Final phosphorus Rep. 1	Rep. 2
2,400	3	5%	0.15%	1%	0.003%	0.001%
2,400	3	5	0.15	3	0.004	0.009
2,400	3	5	0.30	1	0.002	0.008
2,400	3	5	0.30	3	0.015	0.007
2,400	3	15	0.15	1	0.002	0.005
2,400	3	15	0.15	3	0.011	0.006
2,400	3	15	0.30	1	0.004	0.001
2,400	3	15	0.30	3	0.002	0.004
2,400	4	5	0.15	1	0.000	0.003
2,400	4	5	0.15	3	0.008	0.002
2,400	4	5	0.30	1	0.003	0.007
2,400	4	5	0.30	3	0.005	0.012
2,400	4	15	0.15	1	0.010	0.006
2,400	4	15	0.15	3	0.006	0.001
2,400	4	15	0.30	1	0.006	0.014
2,400	4	15	0.30	3	0.011	0.015
2,600	3	5	0.15	1	0.003	0.007
2,600	3	5	0.15	3	0.007	0.004
2,600	3	5	0.30	1	0.011	0.005
2,600	3	5	0.30	3	0.010	0.017
2,600	3	15	0.15	1	0.004	0.008
2,600	3	15	0.15	3	0.019	0.013
2,600	3	15	0.30	1	0.004	0.008
2,600	3	15	0.30	3	0.017	0.023
2,600	4	5	0.15	1	0.007	0.004
2,600	4	5	0.15	3	0.015	0.009
2,600	4	5	0.30	1	0.004	0.011
2,600	4	5	0.30	3	0.010	0.006
2,600	4	15	0.15	1	0.017	0.011
2,600	4	15	0.15	3	0.005	0.010
2,600	4	15	0.30	1	0.014	0.009
2,600	4	15	0.30	3	0.016	0.011

Analyze the results of this experiment.

13.13 An experiment was conducted to determine the effects of the following factors on the gain of a semiconductor device:

Factor	Level 0	Level 1
A. Location of assembly	Laboratory	Production line
B. Partial pressure of controlling material	10^{-15}	10^{-4}
C. Relative humidity	1%	30%
D. Aging time	72 hours	144 hours

The results were as follows:

Experimental condition	Gain Rep. 1	Gain Rep. 2
1	39.0	43.2
a	31.8	43.7
b	47.0	51.4
ab	40.9	40.3
c	43.8	40.5
ac	29.3	52.9
bc	34.8	48.2
abc	45.6	58.2
d	40.1	41.9
ad	42.0	40.5
bd	54.9	53.0
abd	39.9	40.2
cd	43.1	40.2
acd	30.1	39.9
bcd	35.6	53.7
abcd	41.4	49.5

Perform an appropriate analysis of variance and interpret the results.

13.14 A study was performed to examine the effect of 5 different factors on the time required for odorants in natural gas to reach the surface once a leak has occurred. The results of the experiment were reported as follows:

A Odorant	B Odorant concentration mg/ml	C Soil moisture	D Flow rate ml/min	E Temperature	Time (hours) Rep. 1	Time (hours) Rep. 2
A	4	8%	20	50°F	20	20
A	4	8	20	70	17	18
A	4	8	80	50	20	19
A	4	8	80	70	18	19

A	4	16	20	50	12	13
A	4	16	20	70	14	16
A	4	16	80	50	15	14
A	4	16	80	70	17	16
A	16	8	20	50	10	9
A	16	8	20	70	9	8
A	16	8	80	50	8	9
A	16	8	80	70	7	8
A	16	16	20	50	7	6
A	16	16	20	70	6	4
A	16	16	80	50	5	6
A	16	16	80	70	4	5
B	4	8	20	50	28	29
B	4	8	20	70	27	26
B	4	8	80	50	25	27
B	4	8	80	70	28	28
B	4	16	20	50	24	25
B	4	16	20	70	26	25
B	4	16	80	50	23	24
B	4	16	80	70	24	25
B	16	8	20	50	26	24
B	16	8	20	70	23	25
B	16	8	80	50	27	26
B	16	8	80	70	25	26
B	16	16	20	50	19	18
B	16	16	20	70	16	17
B	16	16	80	50	20	19
B	16	16	80	70	17	15

Analyze the results of this experiment.

13.15 Writing the treatment total (a) as the sum of the corresponding observations y_{100l} and substituting for these observations the expressions given by the model equation on page 461, it can be shown that

$$(a) = r[\mu + \alpha_1 + \beta_0 + \gamma_0 + (\alpha\beta)_{10} + (\alpha\gamma)_{10} + (\beta\gamma)_{00} + (\alpha\beta\gamma)_{100}] + \sum_{l=1}^{r} \varepsilon_{100l}$$

Making use of the restrictions imposed on the parameters, rewrite this expression for (a) in terms of the parameters μ, α_0, β_0, γ_0, $(\alpha\beta)_{00}$, $(\alpha\gamma)_{00}$, $(\beta\gamma)_{00}$, and $(\alpha\beta\gamma)_{000}$.

13.16 Duplicating the work of Exercise 13.15, express (1), (b), (ab), (c), (ac), (bc), and (abc) in terms of the parameters μ, α_0, β_0, γ_0, $(\alpha\beta)_{00}$, $(\alpha\gamma)_{00}$, $(\beta\gamma)_{00}$, and $(\alpha\beta\gamma)_{000}$.

13.17 Using the results of Exercises 13.15 and 13.16, verify the expressions for $[A]$ and $[BC]$ obtained on page 463. Also express ε_A in terms of the quantities ε_{ijkl}.

13.18 Interpret the results of the analysis of variance given by the table on page 467, and estimate the magnitude of the significant effects.

13.19 A computational check on the sums of squares obtained for the various main effects and interactions is that their sum must equal the treatment sum of squares obtained by analyzing the data first as a two-way classification. Perform this check on the sums of squares given in the table on page 467.

13.20 If it is desired to find an expression for an effect total without constructing a complete table of signs, we can use the following method, illustrated by finding $[ABC]$ for a 2^4 factorial experiment. We take the expression $(a \pm 1)(b \pm 1)(c \pm)(d \pm 1)$ with a "+" if the corresponding letter does not appear in the symbol for the main effect or interaction for which we want to calculate an effect total, and a "−" if the corresponding letter does appear. Thus, for finding $[ABC]$ we write

$$(a - 1)(b - 1)(c - 1)(d + 1) = abcd + abc - abd - acd - bcd$$
$$- ab - ac + ad - bc + bd + cd$$
$$+ a + b + c - d - 1$$

and after arranging the terms in standard order and adding parentheses, we finally obtain

$$[ABC] = -(1) + (a) + (b) - (ab) + (c) - (ac) - (bc) + (abc) - (d)$$
$$+ (ad) + (bd) - (abd) + (cd) - (acd) - (bcd) + (abcd)$$

(a) Use this method to express $[B]$, $[AC]$, and $[ABC]$ in terms of the treatment totals in a 2^3 factorial experiment.

(b) Use this method to express $[AC]$ and $[BCD]$ in terms of the treatment totals in a 2^4 factorial experiment.

13.21 Referring to the 2^2 factorial design example on page 469, use the table of signs

1	a	b	ab	Total
1	1	1	1	$[I]$
−1	1	−1	1	$[A]$
−1	−1	1	1	$[B]$
1	−1	−1	1	$[AB]$

(a) to verify the calculation of the mean square error;

(b) to verify the expression $\bar{y}_{.1.} - \bar{y}_{.0.} = [B]/2r$;

(c) to verify the expression

$$\frac{1}{2}(\bar{y}_{11.} + \bar{y}_{00.}) - \frac{1}{2}(\bar{y}_{10.} + \bar{y}_{01.}) = \frac{[AB]}{2r}$$

13.22 When a replication effect is suspected in a 2^2 design, the replication sum of squares is

$$2^2 \sum_{l=1}^{r} (\bar{y}_{..l} - \bar{y}_{...})^2$$

and the error sum of squares becomes

$$SSE = \sum_{i=0}^{1}\sum_{j=0}^{1}\sum_{l=1}^{r}(y_{ijl} - \bar{y}_{ij.})^2 - 2^2\sum_{l=1}^{r}(\bar{y}_{..l} - \bar{y}_{...})^2$$

Then $s^2 = SSE/(2^2 - 1)(r - 1)$ has $(r - 1)(2^2 - 1)$ degrees of freedom. With reference to the example on page 469,

(a) obtain the estimate of s^2 adjusted for a replication effect;

(b) obtain the 95% confidence intervals for the effects using your estimate from part (a).

13.23 Given the following observations,

Factor A	Factor B	Rep. 1	Rep. 2
0	0	14	6
1	0	15	21
0	1	11	17
1	1	24	16

summarize the experiment according to the graphic procedure given in Section 13.4. Interpret the effects based on the confidence intervals.

13.24 When a replication effect is suspected in a 2^3 design, the replication sum of squares is

$$2^3 \sum_{l=1}^{r} (\bar{y}_{...l} - \bar{y}_{....})^2$$

and the error sum of squares becomes

$$SSE = \sum_{i=0}^{1}\sum_{j=0}^{1}\sum_{k=0}^{1}\sum_{l=1}^{r}(y_{ijkl} - \bar{y}_{ijk.})^2 - 2^3 \sum_{l=1}^{r}(\bar{y}_{...l} - \bar{y}_{....})^2$$

Then $s^2 = SSE/(2^3 - 1)(r - 1)$ has $(r - 1)(2^3 - 1)$ degrees of freedom. With reference to the example on page 472

(a) obtain the estimate of s^2 adjusted for a replication effect;

(b) obtain the 95% confidence intervals for the effects using your estimate from part (a).

13.25 The effect on engine wear of oil viscosity, temperature, and a special additive, were tested using a 2^3 factorial design. Given the following results from the experiment,

Factor A Viscosity	Factor B Temperature	Factor C Additive	Rep. 1	Rep. 2
0	0	0	3.7	4.1
1	0	0	4.6	5.0
0	1	0	3.1	2.7
1	1	0	3.4	3.8
0	0	1	3.4	3.6
1	0	1	5.3	4.9
0	1	1	2.4	3.2
1	1	1	4.7	4.1

summarize the experiment according to the visual procedure given in Section 13.4. Interpret the effects based on the confidence intervals.

13.26 Two analysts A and B grew bacterial cultures using samples of sewage effluent and of clean stream water. The bacterial cultures were grown on two media C and CP.

The design was repeated 3 times. The y values given below are the logarithms of the measured bacterial populations.

Source	Analyst	Medium	Rep. 1	Rep. 2	Rep. 3
Effluent	A	C	3.54	3.79	3.40
Stream	A	C	1.85	1.76	1.72
Effluent	B	C	3.81	3.82	3.79
Stream	B	C	1.72	1.75	1.55
Effluent	A	CP	3.63	3.67	3.71
Stream	A	CP	1.60	1.74	1.72
Effluent	B	CP	3.86	3.86	4.08
Stream	B	CP	2.05	1.51	1.70

Analyze this experiment using the visual procedure and determine if there is a difference between the two analysts.

13.27 Construct the analysis of variance table for the example on page 472. [*Hint:* The sum of squares for any treatment = (estimated effect)$^2 \times r \times 2^{n-2}$ for a 2^n design.]

13.5   Confounding in a 2^n Factorial Experiment

In some experiments it is impossible to run all the required experimental conditions in one block. For example, if a 2^3 factorial experiment involves 8 combinations of paint pigments that are to be applied to a surface and baked in an oven that can accommodate only 4 specimens, it becomes necessary to divide the eight treatments into 2 blocks (oven runs) in each replicate. As we have pointed out earlier, if the block size is too small to accommodate all treatments, this requires special **incomplete-block designs.**

When the experimental conditions are distributed over several blocks, one or more of the effects may become confounded (inseparable) with possible block effects, that is, between-block differences. For example, if in the 2^3 factorial experiment referred to in the preceding paragraph, experimental conditions a, ab, ac, and abc are included in one oven run (Block 1) and experimental conditions 1, b, c, and bc are included in a second oven run, (Block 2), then the block effect, the difference between the two block totals, is given by

$$[(a) + (ab) + (ac) + (abc)] - [(1) + (b) + (c) + (bc)]$$

Referring to the table of signs on page 463, we observe that this quantity is, in fact, the effect total $[A]$, so that the estimate of the main effect of factor A is **confounded** with blocks. Note that all other factorial effects remain unconfounded. For each other effect total there are two $+1$ coefficients and two -1 coefficients in each block, so that the block effects cancel out. This kind of argument can also be used to decide what experimental conditions to put into each block to confound a given main effect or interaction. For instance, had we wanted to confound the ABC interaction with blocks in the above example, we could have put experimental conditions a, b, c, and abc, whose totals have $+1$ coefficients in $[ABC]$, into one block, and experimental conditions 1, ab, ac, and bc, whose totals have -1 coefficients, into another.

In general, confounding in a 2^n factorial experiment can be much more complicated than in the example just given. To avoid serious difficulties, we shall require that the number of blocks used is a power of 2, say 2^p. It turns out that the price paid for running a 2^n factorial experiment in 2^p blocks is that a total of $2^p - 1$ effects are confounded with blocks. To make it clear just which effects are confounded, and to indicate a method that can be used to confound only certain effects and no others, it is helpful to define the term "generalized interaction" as follows: the **generalized interaction** of two effects is the "product" of these effects, with like letters canceled. Thus, the generalized interaction of AB and CD is $ABCD$, and the generalized interaction of ABC and BCD is $AB\cancel{C}\cancel{B}\cancel{C}D$, or AD. To confound a 2^n factorial experiment in 2^p blocks, the following method can be used: one selects any p effects for confounding, making sure that none is the generalized interaction of any of the others selected. Then, it can be shown that a further $2^p - (p + 1)$ effects are automatically confounded with blocks; together with the p effects originally chosen, this gives a total of $2^p - 1$ confounded effects in the experiment. The additional confounded effects are, in fact, the generalized interactions of the p effects originally chosen.

To illustrate the construction of a confounded design, let's divide a 2^4 factorial experiment into 4 blocks so that desired effects are confounded with blocks. In actual practice one ordinarily confounds only the higher-order interactions (in the hope that they are nonexistent anyhow). Since we have decided upon 4 blocks, we have $2^p = 4$ and $p = 2$, we shall arbitrarily select two higher-order interactions for confounding. If we were to select $ABCD$ and BCD, then their generalized interaction, A, would also be confounded. Thus, to avoid confounding any main effects, and to confound as few two-factor interactions as possible, we shall select ABD and ACD, noting that the BC interaction is also confounded. (Observe that it is impossible to avoid confounding at least one main effect or two-factor interaction in this experiment.)

In order to assign the 16 experimental conditions to 4 blocks, we first distribute them into 2 blocks, so that the ABD interaction is confounded with blocks. Referring to an appropriate table of signs, we put all treatments whose totals have a "$+1$" in the row for $[ABD]$ into one block, all those whose totals have a "-1" into a second block, and we get the following blocks:

First block:	a	b	ac	bc	d	abd	cd	$abcd$
Second block:	1	ab	c	abc	ad	bd	acd	bcd

Note that each experimental condition in the first block has an *odd number* of letters in common with ABD, whereas each experimental condition in the second block has an *even number* of letters in common with ABD. This **odd-even rule** provides an alternative way of distributing experimental conditions among 2 blocks to confound a given effect, and it has the advantage that it does not require the construction of a complete table of signs.

So far, we have confounded the *ABD* interaction by dividing the 16 experimental conditions into 2 blocks; now we shall confound the *ACD* interaction by dividing each of these blocks into 2 blocks of 4 conditions each. Using the odd-even rule just described (or a table of signs), we obtain the following four blocks:

Block 1:	*a*	*bc*	*d*	*abcd*
Block 2:	*b*	*ac*	*abd*	*cd*
Block 3:	*ab*	*c*	*bd*	*acd*
Block 4:	1	*abc*	*ad*	*bcd*

By comparing these blocks with a table of signs, or, equivalently, by applying the odd-even rule, the reader will be asked to verify in Exercise 13.32 that the *BC* interaction is also confounded with blocks, whereas all other main effects are left unconfounded.

The analysis of a confounded 2^n factorial experiment is similar to that of an unconfounded experiment, with the exception that the sums of squares for the confounded effects are not computed, and we compute a block sum of squares as if the experiment consisted of *br* blocks rather than *b* blocks in each of *r* replicates.

Referring to our example of a 2^4 factorial experiment with the *ABD*, *ACD*, and *BC* interactions confounded, and using two replicates, we have the following *dummy* analysis of variance table:

Source of variation	Degrees of freedom
Blocks	7
Main effects	4
Unconfounded two-factor interactions	5
Unconfounded three-factor interactions	2
Four-factor interaction	1
Intrablock error	12
Total	31

The sum of squares for blocks is obtained, as usual, by adding the squares of the 8 block totals, dividing the result by 4 (the number of observations in each block), and subtracting the correction term. The total sum of squares and the sums of squares for the unconfounded factorial effects are obtained in the usual way, and the sum of squares for the **intrablock error,** a measure of the variability *within blocks*, is obtained by subtraction.

To illustrate the analysis of a confounded 2^n factorial experiments, let us suppose that each replicate of the stepping-switch experiment described on page 464 was actually run in 4 blocks, because only 4 mountings were available for the 16 switches. (The order of running the blocks is assumed to have been randomized within each replicate, and the assignment of switches is assumed to have been randomized within each block). Assuming also that the ABD, ACD, and BC interactions were confounded with the blocks as shown on page 486, we obtain the following block totals from the data on pages 464 and 465:

	Block 1	Block 2	Block 3	Block 4
Replicate 1	3,564	3,488	3,743	3,593
Replicate 2	4,130	3,978	4,056	3,799

Thus, the sum of squares for blocks is given by

$$SS(Bl) = \frac{(3{,}564)^2 + (3{,}488)^2 + \cdots + (3{,}799)^2}{4} - 28{,}786{,}975$$

$$= 101{,}240$$

where the correction factor is the same as in the analysis on page 465.

Copying the total sum of squares and the sum of squares for the various unconfounded effects from the table on page 467, we obtain the analysis of variance table for the following confounded factorial experiment. In this analysis, the A and C main effects are again significant at the 0.01 level, but none of the other main effects or interactions is significant.

Source of variation	Degrees of freedom	Sum of squares	Mean square	F
Blocks	7	101,240	14,463	1.58
Main effects:				
A	1	134,551	134,551	14.68
B	1	4,632	4,632	< 1
C	1	225,624	225,624	24.62
D	1	713	713	< 1
Unconfounded two-factor interactions:				
AB	1	39,410	39,410	4.30
AC	1	18,673	18,673	2.04
AD	1	31,689	31,689	3.46
BD	1	24,698	24,698	2.69
CD	1	81	81	< 1

Source of variation	Degrees of freedom	Sum of squares	Mean square	F
Unconfounded three-factor interactions:				
ABC	1	39,130	39,130	4.27
BCD	1	14,070	14,070	1.54
Four-factor interaction:				
ABCD	1	385	385	< 1
Intrablock error	12	109,980	9,165	
Total	31	744,876		

If there is replication, some of the lost information about the confounded effects can be recovered by a further breakdown of the above blocks sum of squares. This analysis consists of dividing the sum of squares for blocks into a component for each of the confounded effects, a component for replications, and a residual component called the *interblock error,* which is a measure of the variability *between blocks.* Copying the sum of squares for replicates as well as those for the BC, ABD, and ACD interactions from the analysis of variance table on page 467 and copying the blocks sum of squares from the preceding **intrablock analysis of variance** table, we obtain the following **interblock analysis of variance** table:

Source of variation	Degrees of freedom	Sum of squares	Mean square	F
Replicates	1	77,520	77,520	23.05
Confounded effects:				
BC	1	1,001	1,001	< 1
ABD	1	30	30	< 1
ACD	1	12,601	12,601	3.75
Interblock error	3	10,088	3,363	
Total (blocks)	7	101,240		

Note that the **interblock error** is obtained by subtraction and that the F ratios are obtained by dividing the mean squares for the confounded effects and the mean square for replicates by the mean square for the interblock error. Only the F test for replicates is significant (at the 0.05 level). The small number of degrees of freedom for the interblock error implies that the sensitivity of these significance tests is *very poor;* in fact, it rarely pays to make this kind of interblock analysis unless the number of replications is relatively large.

13.6   Fractional Replication

In studies involving complex production lines, chemical processes such as may be encountered in the petroleum, plastics, or metal industries, physical-chemical processes such as may be encountered in the electronics or space-technology industries, and in many other engineering studies, experimenters are often faced with a large and bewildering array of interrelated variables. The principles of factorial experimentation treated so far in this chapter help them to "sort out" these variables, to discover which of them have the greatest influence on the process under consideration, and to find what important interrelationships may exist.

There are, however, some serious limitations to the simultaneous study of a large number of factors. Even if each factor is assigned only 2 levels, one replicate of a six-factor experiment requires 64 observations; there are 128 observations in one replicate of a seven-factor experiment, and 1,024 observations in one replicate of a ten-factor experiment. The economic and practical limitations of these large numbers make it necessary to seek out ways in which the size of factorial experiments can be kept within manageable bounds. Of course, it must be emphasized that there is no substitute for careful preliminary planning which, coupled with engineering insight, can result in the elimination of many needless factors.

In spite of the most careful preliminary planning, however, it is often difficult to avoid having to include as many as 6 or 10 (or more) factors in a single experiment. One way to reduce the size of such an experiment would be to break it up into several parts, each part involving the deliberate variation of one factor while all others are held fixed. This would have the undesirable consequence that we could not study any of the interactions. Even if we were to include half the factors in one part and the other half in another, such as replacing a ten-factor experiment (requiring 1,024 observations) by two five-factor experiments (each requiring 32 observations), any interaction between factors in the first part and factors in the second part would be irretrievably lost. It is possible to overcome some of these difficulties by observing that most of the time we are not interested in *all* the interactions. For instance, it is possible to perform only a fraction of a 2^n factorial and yet obtain most of the desired information, say, about the main effects and two-factor interactions (but not the higher interactions).

The principles involved in **fractional replication,** that is, in performing only a fraction of a complete 2^n factorial experiment, are similar to those used in confounding. To obtain a **half-replicate** one selects only one of the 2 blocks into which the experimental conditions have been divided by confounding one effect; to obtain a **quarter-replicate** one selects only one of the 4 blocks into which the experimental conditions have been divided by confounding 2 effects, and so forth. In contrast to a confounded experiment as discussed in Section 13.5, we find that in a fractional replicate *the effects are confounded, not with blocks, but with each other.*

To illustrate, suppose that only the experimental conditions a, b, c, and abc are included in a half-replicate of a 2^3 factorial experiment. (This is one block of a 2^3 factorial experiment with the abc interaction confounded.) Considering the table of signs on page 463 with all columns except those corresponding to a, b, c, and abc crossed out, we find that the effect total for factor A is now given by

$$[A] = (a) - (b) - (c) + (abc)$$

If we write $(a) = \sum_{l=1}^{r} y_{100l}, (b) = \sum_{l=1}^{r} y_{010l}, \ldots$, and substitute for the y_{ijkl} the expressions given by the model equation on page 461, we obtain

$$[A] = -4r[\alpha_0 - (\beta\gamma)_{00}] + \varepsilon$$

where ε is the value of a random variable having zero mean (see Exercise 13.39). We thus find that $[A]$ measures the main effect of factor A as well as the BC interaction, so that these two effects have become inseparable, or confounded. Note also that in the reduced table of signs (having columns only corresponding to a, b, c, and abc) the signs for $[A]$ and $[BC]$ are identical, and hence $[A] = [BC]$. In Exercise 13.40, the reader will be asked to show that for the given fractional replicate the main effect for factor B is similarly confounded, or **aliased,** with the AC interaction, while the main effect for factor C is confounded, or aliased, with the AB interaction. The ABC interaction cannot be estimated.

With careful design, it is generally possible to confound all main effects and two-factor interactions *only* with interactions of higher order. This is illustrated in the following example, where we shall construct a half-replicate of a 2^5 factorial. First, we select an effect (usually a higher-order interaction) to split the experiment into two blocks, as in confounding. The effect chosen is called the **defining contrast,** and cannot be estimated at all by the fractional replicate. Every other effect is aliased with another effect, namely, its generalized interaction (see page 485) with the defining contrast. Thus, if the defining contrast is $ABCDE$, the main effect for factor A has the four-factor interaction $BCDE$ as its alias, BC and ADE are an alias pair, and so forth. As we have seen, only the combined effect (the sum or difference of the aliased effects) can be estimated in the experiment. However, if it can be assumed that there are no higher-order interactions, one can attribute the effect of the alias pair BC and ADE entirely to the two-factor interaction BC, one can attribute the effect of the alias pair A and $BCDE$ entirely to the main effect of factor A, and so forth. A complete listing of the aliases in a half-replicate of a 2^5 factorial experiment having the defining contrast $ABCDE$ is as follows:

A and $BCDE$	B and $ACDE$	C and $ABDE$	D and $ABCE$
E and $ABCD$	AB and CDE	AC and BDE	AD and BCE
AE and BCD	BC and ADE	BD and ACE	BE and ACD
CD and ABE	CE and ABD	DE and ABC	

Note that no main effect or two-factor interaction is aliased with another main effect or two-factor interaction.

The 16 experimental conditions to be included in the half-replicate are given by those in either of the 2 blocks obtained by confounding the defining contrast.

Choosing "evens" in the odd-even rule, namely, those conditions which have an even number of letters in common with the defining contrast $ABCDE$, we obtain the following half-replicate:

$$
\begin{array}{llll}
1 & ad & ae & de \\
ab & bd & be & abde \\
ac & cd & ce & acde \\
bc & abcd & abce & bcde
\end{array}
$$

To go one step further, let us illustrate how to construct a quarter-replicate of the given 2^5 factorial. We shall do this by dividing the above half-replicate in half, confounding the three-factor interaction ABC. Again using "evens," we get the following 8 experimental conditions:

$$
\begin{array}{llll}
1 & de & ab & abde \\
ac & acde & bc & bcde
\end{array}
$$

Since DE, the generalized interaction of the two confounded effects, is also confounded, we now have the 3 defining contrasts, $ABCDE$, ABC, and DE. None of these effects can be estimated in the quarter-replicate, and each other effect is aliased with its 3 generalized interactions with the 3 defining contrasts. The complete aliasing is as follows:

Alias sets

A	$BCDE$	BC	ADE
B	$ACDE$	AC	BDE
C	$ABDE$	AB	CDE
D	$ABCE$	$ABCD$	E
AD	BCE	BCD	AE
BD	ACE	ACD	BE
CD	ABE	ABD	CE

We have given this quarter-replicate merely as an illustration; it would hardly seem useful in actual practice because of the hopeless aliasing of main effects and two-factor interactions. Nevertheless, quarter-replicates of six-and seven-factor experiments (and even eighth-replicates of seven- and eight-factor experiments) can often provide much useful information.

The analysis of a fractional factorial is practically the same as that of a fully replicated factorial experiment. Given the fraction $1/2^p$ of a 2^n factorial, there are 2^{n-p} experimental conditions, and the Yates's method can be used as if the experiment were a 2^{n-p} factorial. Some care must be exercised to arrange the experimental conditions in a modified standard order as indicated in Exercise 13.37.

When dealing with fractional factorials, there is the problem of obtaining an estimate of the experimental error. For example, in the half-replicate of a 2^5 factorial described above, the breakdown of the total sum of squares having 15 degrees of freedom yields sums of squares for main effects (5 degrees of freedom), sums of squares for two-factor interactions (10 degrees of freedom), but no component (0 degrees of freedom) for the experimental error. In a situation like this, and in all other cases where the number of degrees of freedom for error is small, it is best to include a limited amount of replication. This may be accomplished by randomly selecting several experimental conditions, and making additional observations corresponding to these conditions. Furthermore, if it can be assumed that there are no higher-order interactions, the total of the sums of squares corresponding to higher-order interactions *which are not aliased with main effects or lower-order interactions* can be attributed to "error," and used in the denominator of the F test (see Exercise 13.38). In this way, use can be made of the "hidden replication" inherent in most large factorial experiments.

To summarize, fractional replication is useful whenever the number of factors to be included in an experiment is large and it is not economically feasible to include all possible experimental conditions. The reduction is size (and, therefore, in cost) of a fractionally replicated experiment is partially offset by the loss of information caused by aliasing, and by the difficulties inherent in estimating the experimental error. A more detailed discussion of fractional replication, including fractional replicates of 3^n experiments and a variety of other designs, can be found in the book by W. G. Cochran and G. M. Cox listed in the bibliography.

EXERCISES

13.28 A 2^5 factorial experiment, having the factors A, B, C, D, and E, is to be run in several blocks. Show which treatments are assigned to each block if

(a) there are to be 2 blocks, with the $ACDE$ interaction confounded;

(b) there are to be 4 blocks, with the BDE and $ABCE$ interactions confounded. What other factorial effect or effects are also confounded?

13.29 List the experimental conditions included in each block if a 2^4 factorial experiment is to be confounded

(a) in two blocks on $ABCD$;

(b) in four blocks on ABC and BCD.

13.30 List the experimental conditions included in each block if a 2^6 factorial experiment is to be confounded in 8 blocks on $ABDE$, $BCDF$, and ABC. What other factorial effects are confounded?

13.31 Four new drugs are to be investigated to determine their effectiveness as tranquilizers, individually and in combination with each other. Each patient was given regular doses of one of the 16 tranquilizers formed from these drugs (including a placebo corresponding to the 0 level for each drug) and, after a two-week period, the effect of these tranquilizers on the emotional stability of each patient was judged (on a scale from 1 to 5) by 5 psychiatrists. To keep the staff work load within reasonable bounds, 2 hospitals were used in this experiment, and 8 patients were selected by the staff of each hospital for each trial (replicate); thus, the experiment involved 2 replicates of 2 blocks each, with the $ABCD$ interaction confounded. The results of the two 2-weeks trials were as follows:

| *First Hospital* | | | *Second Hospital* | | |
Treatment combination	Mean rating Trial 1	Trial 2	Treatment combination	Mean rating Trial 1	Trial 2
1	2.0	2.6	*a*	2.8	2.6
ab	3.8	3.4	*b*	3.6	2.0
ac	4.2	4.8	*c*	2.4	1.8
bc	4.8	4.0	*abc*	4.0	3.8
ad	1.8	2.4	*d*	1.8	2.2
bd	3.4	3.8	*abd*	1.6	2.0
cd	4.6	2.8	*acd*	3.6	2.4
abcd	4.2	4.6	*bcd*	3.4	3.8

If a high rating indicates satisfactory progress, which drug combination (or combinations) seems to be the most promising? Perform an intrablock analysis of variance to test for significant effects.

13.32 Verify that in the example on page 486 all treatment totals having $+1$ as a coefficient in $[BC]$ are in Blocks 1 and 4, that all treatment totals having -1 as a coefficient in $[BC]$ are in Blocks 2 and 3, and hence, that the BC interaction is confounded with blocks.

13.33 Show that the "odd-even" rule for assigning treatments to blocks, given on page 485, is equivalent to the method described in Exercise 13.20.

13.34 Referring to Exercise 13.29, list the alias sets if an experiment consists of

(a) a half-replicate of a 2^4 factorial experiment with $ABCD$ confounded;

(b) a quarter-replicate of a 2^4 factorial experiment with ABC and BCD confounded.

13.35 Construct a half-replicate of a 2^6 factorial having the defining contrast $ABCDEF$. List the 32 treatments in the block containing experimental condition 1, and show the alias pairs.

13.36 Design an experiment consisting of a quarter-replicate of a 2^7 factorial with $ABCDE$, $ABCFG$, and $DEFG$ confounded, if the experimental condition with each factor at the 0 level is to be included. Also exhibit all alias sets.

13.37 Referring to Exercise 13.35, we can define a **modified standard order** for the 32 treatment combinations in the half-replicate as follows. First, we list the 32 treatment combinations corresponding to the five factors A, B, C, D, and E in standard order. Then we append the letter f to 16 of these treatment combinations, so that the list contains the same ones as the block chosen for the half-replicate.

(a) Use this method to list the treatment combinations obtained in Exercise 13.35 in modified standard order.

(b) Generalize the above rule for arranging the treatment combinations in modified standard order so that it applies to a half-replicate of a 2^n factorial experiment. (For a $1/2^p$ fractional replicate of a 2^n factorial, a modified standard order can be obtained by noting that any block chosen contains a subset of $n - p$ letters which form a complete replicate of a 2^{n-p} factorial. The modified standard order is then obtained by using these letters only and later appending the remaining p letters to get the required treatment combinations.)

13.38 The following factors are to be studied in a half-replicate of a 2^6 factorial experiment (defining contrast $ABCDEF$), designed to evaluate several chemicals as insecticides.

Factor	Level 0	Level 1
A. BMC	0%	5%
B. Malathion	3%	6%
C. Tedion	1%	2%
D. Chlordane	2%	5%
E. Lindane	1%	4%
F. Pyrethrum	2%	4%

Each experimental unit consists of 10 insects, and the average lifetimes (in seconds) after application of the respective insecticides are as follows, in the random order in which they are obtained:

ce	181	acdf	162	bd	135	abdf	131
ae	172	1	182	df	171	ab	136
abef	140	bf	171	acef	159	bcde	105
bcdf	165	cf	176	bc	179	abcdef	109
acde	139	be	187	ac	165	af	176
ef	186	abce	131	bcef	181	ad	150
de	164	abcf	125	cdef	163	abde	115
abcd	112	adef	158	bdef	128	cd	166

(a) Write down the alias pairs.

(b) Arrange the results in modified standard order (see Exercise 13.37) and use the Yates's method to find the effect totals.

(c) Identify the effect totals as follows. In the last column of the Yates table, write down the 32 combinations $[I], [A], [B], [AB], \ldots, [ABCDE]$ in standard order. Each of these is aliased with another one; identify the alias pairs by using the main effect or lower-order interaction. (For example, $ABCDE$ is aliased with F—identify the effect total $[ABCDE]$ as that of the main effect F.) Note that 10 of the alias pairs are three-factor interactions aliased with three-factor interactions—label these "error."

(d) Obtain the mean squares and complete the analysis of variance. Note that the error mean square, having 10 degrees of freedom, is the average of the mean squares of the 10 effects labeled "error."

13.39 Verify the expression obtained for $[A]$ on page 490.

13.40 Duplicating the steps indicated in page 490, show that in the given design the main effect for factor B is confounded with the AC interaction. [*Hint*: Express $[B]$ and $[AC]$ in terms of the parameters of the model.]

13.41 In Exercise 13.13 on page 480 suppose that only one-half of the replicates can be performed in the time available. Construct the half-replicate having the defining contrast $ABCD$. Using the appropriate data from Rep. 1, together with replicates of experimental conditions 1, ab, bc, and $abcd$ taken from Rep. 2, perform an analysis of this half-replicate identifying those effects attributable to "error." [*Hint:* Each of the 4 pairs of replicated treatments provides one additional degree of freedom for error, and contributes $(y_1 - y_2)^2/2$ to the error sum of squares, where y_1 is the observation resulting from applying the treatment in the first replicate, and y_2 is the corresponding observation in the second replicate.]

REVIEW EXERCISES

13.42 Referring to Exercise 12.47 on page 434, it can be argued that the rocket-launcher experiment was poorly designed, as it was not replicated, and, thus, it is impossible to test whether there is an interaction between launchers and rocket fuels. Suppose that a second replicate were performed, with the following results:

	Fuel I	*Fuel II*	*Fuel III*	*Fuel IV*
Launcher X	66.8	51.1	40.1	49.2
Launcher Y	47.7	38.2	50.6	64.3

Combining the results of replicates, perform an appropriate analysis of variance, and test for the presence of an interaction.

13.43 A study was conducted to measure the effect of 3 different meat tenderizers on the weight loss of steaks having the same initial (precooked) weights. The effects of cooking temperatures and cooking times also were measured by performing a $3 \times 2 \times 2$ factorial experiment in 3 replicates. The results are as follows:

Tenderizer	*Cooking time (minutes)*	*Cooking temperature (°F)*	*Weight loss (ounces)* Rep. 1	Rep. 2	Rep. 3
A	20	350	1.5	1.3	1.4
A	20	400	1.6	1.4	1.5
A	30	350	1.7	1.8	1.7
A	30	400	1.8	1.9	2.0
B	20	350	1.9	2.1	2.0
B	20	400	2.2	2.4	2.5
B	30	350	2.6	2.3	2.4
B	30	400	2.6	2.7	2.5
C	20	350	0.9	0.8	0.8
C	20	400	1.1	1.0	0.9
C	30	350	0.8	0.9	1.0
C	30	400	1.2	1.0	1.1

(a) Analyze this experiment first as a two-way classification with 12 treatments and 3 replicates (blocks).

(b) Complete the analysis by computing the sums of squares corresponding to the various main effects and interactions.

(c) Present the results in an analysis of variance table and interpret the experiment.

13.44 An experiment was conducted to determine the effects of certain alloying elements on the ductility of a metal, and the following results were obtained:

			Breaking strength (ft-lb)		
Nickel	Carbon	Manganese	Rep. 1	Rep. 2	Rep. 3
0.0%	0.3%	0.5%	36.7	39.6	38.2
0.0	0.3	1.0	47.5	43.5	45.9
0.0	0.6	0.5	40.6	36.8	36.0
0.0	0.6	1.0	41.1	45.8	46.4
4.0	0.3	0.5	37.8	32.7	31.6
4.0	0.3	1.0	34.2	37.2	36.5
4.0	0.6	0.5	39.5	41.7	39.1
4.0	0.6	1.0	46.4	43.7	49.4

Perform an appropriate analysis of variance and interpret the results.

13.45 Given the two replicates of a 2×3 factorial experiment, calculate the analysis of variance tables using the formulas on pages 440 and 441 rather than the shortcut formulas in the example.

Factor A	Factor B	Rep. 1	Rep. 2
1	1	29	35
1	2	15	17
1	3	14	22
2	1	15	13
2	2	27	25
2	3	16	24

13.46 Given the following observations

Factor A	Factor B	Rep. 1	Rep. 2
0	0	11	7
1	0	16	14
0	1	10	12
1	1	19	11

summarize the experiment according to the visual procedure given in Section 13.4. Interpret the effects based on the confidence intervals.

13.47 With reference to the example on page 469, suppose a third replicate

	Temperature	pH	Rep. 3
1	300	2	9
a	350	2	23
b	300	3	16
ab	350	3	25

is run. Analyze the experiment, using all 3 replicates, according to the visual procedure given in Section 13.4. Interpret the effects based on the confidence intervals.

13.48 Given the following results from a 2^3 factorial experiment

Factor A	Factor B	Factor C	Rep. 1	Rep. 2
0	0	0	13.8	14.6
1	0	0	10.8	8.4
0	1	0	9.0	9.8
1	1	0	10.1	10.9
0	0	1	14.4	13.6
1	0	1	6.2	8.6
0	1	1	7.7	7.9
1	1	1	9.0	8.2

summarize the experiment according to the visual procedure given in Section 13.4. Interpret the effects based on the confidence intervals.

13.49 With reference to Exercise 13.47, create the analysis of variance table.

13.50 With reference to Exercise 13.48, create the analysis of variance table.

13.51 What is the largest number of blocks in which one can perform a 2^6 factorial experiment without confounding any main effects?

13.52 Suppose that in Exercise 13.11 on page 478 the judge rates the soft drinks in sets of 4, with a rest period in between, and the experiment was actually performed so that each replicate consisted of 2 blocks with ABC confounded. Perform an intrablock analysis of the data.

13.53 Suppose that in Exercise 13.12 on page 479 only 8 specimens could be tested in any one shift, and that the experiment was actually performed so that each replicate consists of 4 blocks with ABC, ADE and $BCDE$ confounded.

    (a) If for each factor, levels 0 and 1 are the lower and higher values, construct a table showing which experimental conditions go into each of the four blocks.

    (b) Perform an intrablock analysis of the experiment.

13.54 Referring to Exercise 13.28, suppose that in each case the block containing treatment combination 1 was chosen as a fractional replicate of a 2^5 factorial.

    (a) Show the alias pairs in the resulting half-replicate.

    (b) Show the alias sets in the resulting quarter-replicate. (In practice, random selection should be used to choose the block to be included in a fractional replicate.)

13.55 In Exercise 13.14 on page 480 construct and analyze the half-replicate having the defining contrast $ABCDE$, using the appropriate experimental results from Rep. 1.

13.56 With reference to the example on page 452 concerning improvements in the safety of an ignitor, the time to reach maximum pressure was also recorded. Two replicates were run of the factorial design and the times to reach maximum pressure recorded.

Analyze the results of this experiment.

A	B	C	Time (milliseconds) Rep. 1	Rep. 2
Initiator 1	Powder	Mc 1	54.02	49.64
Initiator 1	Pellet	Mc 1	60.74	70.66
Initiator 1	Powder	Mc 2	37.56	43.72
Initiator 1	Pellet	Mc 2	46.40	42.04
Initiator 1	Powder	Mc 3	40.54	41.60
Initiator 1	Pellet	Mc 3	50.56	45.44
Initiator 1	Powder	Mc 4	47.08	44.28
Initiator 1	Pellet	Mc 4	47.68	60.22
Initiator 2	Powder	Mc 1	47.00	58.74
Initiator 2	Pellet	Mc 1	51.30	53.96
Initiator 2	Powder	Mc 2	59.82	45.66
Initiator 2	Pellet	Mc 2	52.20	57.82
Initiator 2	Powder	Mc 3	68.46	59.86
Initiator 2	Pellet	Mc 3	82.78	57.16
Initiator 2	Powder	Mc 4	75.14	90.82
Initiator 2	Pellet	Mc 4	82.38	75.38
Initiator 3	Powder	Mc 1	35.78	30.34
Initiator 3	Pellet	Mc 1	56.06	38.30
Initiator 3	Powder	Mc 2	20.60	22.18
Initiator 3	Pellet	Mc 2	21.38	21.50
Initiator 3	Powder	Mc 3	45.06	43.18
Initiator 3	Pellet	Mc 3	50.24	56.74
Initiator 3	Powder	Mc 4	44.54	69.96
Initiator 3	Pellet	Mc 4	63.42	49.66

KEY TERMS

(with page references)

Alias   490
Complete factorial experiment   439
Confounding   478
Defining contrast   490
Effect total   463
Factorial experiment   439
Factors   439
Fractional replicate   489
Generalized interaction   485
Half normal plot   468
Half-replicate   489
Incomplete block design   484
Interaction   439
Interaction sum of squares   442
Interblock analysis of variance   488
Interblock error   488

Intrablock analysis of variance   488
Intrablock error   486
Levels of factors   439
Main effects   449
Model equation for three-factor experiment   449
Model equation for two-factor experiment   439
Model equation for 2^3 factorial experiment   461
Multifactor experiment   447
Odd-even rule   485
Quarter-replicate   489
Standard order   462
Table of signs   463
Two-factor experiment   438
2^n factorial experiment   461
Yates's method   465

The Statistical Content of Quality-Improvement Programs

Although there is a tendency to think of the subject of quality as a recent development, there is nothing new about the basic idea of making a quality product characterized by a high degree of uniformity. For centuries skilled artisans have striven to make products distinctive through superior quality, and once a standard of quality was achieved, to eliminate insofar as possible all variability between products that were nominally alike.

What is new in **quality improvement** is the idea that a product is never good enough and should be continually improved. This concept, honed to a fine edge in Japan, has created a crisis in the international marketplace for firms that do not follow suit. In quality-improvement programs, the emphasis is on employing designed experiments to improve the product in the design, production, and assembly stages rather than in futile attempts to inspect quality into a product after it is produced. We introduce these ideas in Sections 14.1 through 14.3.

Three special techniques of (statistical) **quality assurance** are also treated in this chapter: quality control is discussed in Sections 14.4 through 14.6, the establishment of tolerance limits in Section 14.7, and acceptance sampling in Section 14.8. Note that the word *quality,* when used technically as in this discussion, refers to some measurable or countable property of a product, such as the outside diameter of a ball bearing, the breaking strength of a yarn, the number of imperfections in a piece of cloth, the potency of a drug, and so forth.

CHAPTER 14

14.1   Quality-Improvement Programs

What is a quality-improvement program? To answer this question, we present a scenario of what happens when action is taken to improve quality. In the context of a machine tooling operation, we first plot the fraction of defective pieces per day [see Figure 14.1(a)] for each day over a 5-week period. This plot reveals stable variation about a value of nearly 15% defective. That is, the process is predictable. We can estimate the mean by the average over days and we can also estimate the amount of variation (see Section 14.4). The fact that the process is stable does not make it good! It is turning out too many defective pieces.

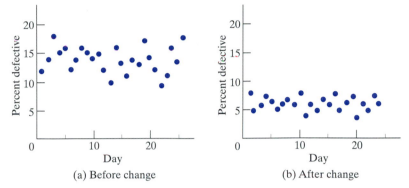

FIGURE 14.1 Fraction defective per day.
 (a) Before change
 (b) After change

Once it is realized the process needs improvement, action can be taken. Data collected on several possible sources of variation are displayed in the Pareto diagram (see Section 2.1) in Figure 14.2. The cumulative percentages are given by the broken line curve and are read from the right-hand scale. Based on these data, it was decided to give the operators more training on the use of the machine. The record for the next 5 weeks of the daily fraction defectives, after the training, is plotted in Figure 14.1(b). The new process also appears stable but this time about a lower mean. Should we be satisfied? No. The central precept of quality improvement calls for the process of improvement to be continual. Maybe the gains will be smaller at each progressive stage, but efforts must be continued to reduce the amount of variation and the proportion of defectives. Further substantial improvements will come only by taking action on the system. However, since the process is stable, the effects of change can be observed. Engineers can make innovations to improve the process. The two-level factorial designs discussed in the previous chapter are particularly relevant.

There is some folklore that high quality and low production costs are incompatible. But time and again it is the cost of reworking bad products that is a major component of production cost. It is really low quality that results in high costs. Besides the high costs of reworking pieces to make them usable, there are also high costs associated with lost customers who were sold inferior products.

The transformation to quality production in Japan, starting in 1950, has created a new economic age and a crisis for American businesses. Briefly, Japanese merchandise of the time was known to be shoddy. Several highly placed engineers in

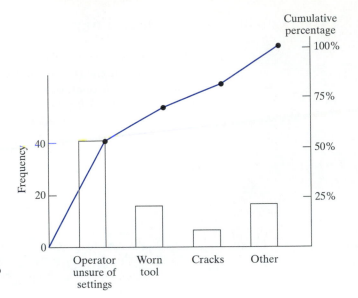

FIGURE 14.2 Pareto diagram of defects.

Japan studied the literature on quality control produced at Bell Laboratories by Walter Shewhart and others. W. Edwards Deming was brought in as a foreign expert. Unlike in America, where the applications of statistical methods to problems of quality fell far below their wartime successes because managers did not fully appreciate them, in Japan the top managers came with their engineers to learn about the techniques. What followed was company- and industry-wide commitments to improve quality through education which included statistical methods. This transformation has taken many Japanese companies to world leadership. In order to compete in the international marketplace, other companies and countries must also stress quality improvement.

A theory of management for product or service improvement has been pioneered by W. Edwards Deming (1900–1993). It contains concise statements of the elements of the transformation that must take place. Deming sums up his ideas on the transformation of American industry in 14 points for management. They apply not only to manufacturing but also service industries and pertain to organizations of all sizes, large and small. We present **Deming's 14 points** as an overview of his philosophy and heartily recommend his book, listed in the bibliography, to all interested readers.

1. Create constancy of purpose toward improvement of the product and service, with the aim to become competitive and to stay in business and to provide jobs.
2. Adopt the new philosophy. We are in the new economic age. Western management must awaken to the challenge, must learn their responsibilities, and take on leadership for change.
3. Cease dependence on inspection to achieve quality. Eliminate the need for inspection on a mass basis by building quality into the product in the first place.

4. End the practice of awarding business on the basis of price tag. Instead, minimize total cost. Move toward a single supplier for any one item, on a long-term relationship of loyalty and trust.

5. Improve constantly and forever the system of production and service, to improve quality and productivity, and thus constantly decrease costs.

6. Institute training on the job.

7. Institute leadership. The aim of supervision should be to help people and machines and gadgets to do a better job.

8. Drive out fear, so that everyone may work effectively for the company.

9. Break down barriers between departments. People in research, design, sales, and production must work as a team, to foresee problems of production and in use that may be encountered with the product or service.

10. Eliminate slogans, exhortations, and targets for the work force asking for zero defects and new levels of productivity. Such exhortations only create adversarial relationships, as the bulk of the causes of low quality and low productivity belong to the system and thus lie beyond the power of the work force.

11. a. Eliminate work standards (quotas) on the factory floor. Substitute leadership.

   b. Eliminate management by objective. Eliminate management by numbers, numerical goals. Substitute leadership.

12. a. Remove barriers that rob the hourly worker of his right to pride of workmanship. The responsibility of supervisors must be changed from sheer number to quality.

   b. Remove barriers that rob people in management and in engineering of their right to pride of workmanship. This means, *inter alia,* abolishment of annual or merit rating and of management by objective.

13. Institute a vigorous program of education and self-improvement.

14. Put everybody in the company to work to accomplish the transformation. The transformation is everybody's job.[†]

It requires a method to achieve quality improvement, not just hopes. A central problem of management is to understand the meaning of variation and to extract the pertinent information from it. It is here that statistics comes into play. Engineers need to understand the basic principles of experimental design to fulfill their roles in points 3 and 5.

The main thrust of the statistical approach is that, in order to improve quality, it is better to work upstream on the processes. That is, build quality into the product by concentrating on the equipment, components, and materials that go into making it.

[†]"Out of the Crisis," W. Edwards Deming (1986), Massachusetts Institute of Technology, Cambridge, Mass. Reprinted by permission of the author.

The consumer also has a role in the new way of quality improvement. It has always been (1) design of a product, (2) make it, and (3) market it. Now, there is a new fourth step, (4) find out the purchasers' reactions to the product. Also find out why others did not purchase. Statistical methods of sampling will provide a way of finding out what the consumer thinks. Changes can then be made in design and production to better match the product to the market. These four steps must be repeated over and over again in the search for continual product improvement.

14.2   Starting a Quality-Improvement Program

It is the prevailing wisdom that top managers must be involved in any quality improvement. Once committed, it must take action and select initial processes to serve as flagship projects. It is good to start with processes that have a large potential for improvement and where the prospect for large financial gains is greatest. Even though that is management's decision, the most successful programs start with committees formed with employees from all levels. More enthusiasm can be generated when there is a consensus regarding the selection of the process. A modified Delphi technique can help groups reach unanimity. Each person writes down his or her top three choices. With 3 points for first place, 2 for second, and 1 for third, the totals for each candidate process are tabulated for all to see. Perhaps after some discussion, each person votes again and the process continues until a unanimous choice is reached.

Suppose the process selected concerns piston rings. The first step is to collect data. We will talk to those who run the process about causes and types of defects, but to start we want fresh data on all of the defectives that occur over a period of two weeks. This information is presented as a Pareto diagram in Figure 14.3.

Defect	Number
Height	30
Diameter	14
Cracks	4
Scratches	2
Other	5

We see that 30 out of 55 defective rings have incorrect heights.

To proceed, we gather the engineers, supervisors, and operators who make the rings for a "brainstorming" session. They construct a list of the possible causes for the variation in height. These may be graphically displayed in a **cause-and-effect diagram.** It arranges causes and causes of causes, as shown in Figure 14.4 (see the book by K. Ishikawa, listed in the bibliography, for more examples). The cause-and-effect diagram, which resembles the skeleton of a fish, starts with a central horizontal line for a major problem such as incorrect height. Major factors that

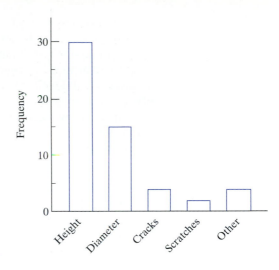

FIGURE 14.3 Pareto diagram for piston rings.

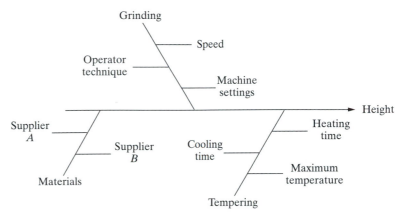

FIGURE 14.4 Cause-and-effect diagram for piston rings.

affect height are listed on diagonal lines attached to the central horizontal line. Factors that affect the major factors, as cooling time affects tempering, are labeled on horizontal lines connected to the diagonal lines. To proceed further, action must be taken on the system.

A two-level factorial design was run with the suppliers as Factor A and two speeds for the grinder as Factor B. The response, the number of defectives out of 200 rings made at each condition, is recorded in Figure 14.5. The results confirm Deming's fourth point. Work with a single supplier.

FIGURE 14.5 Number of defective rings from a 2^2 design.

If the process is stable with the material from supplier 1, then it is time to make another Pareto diagram and continue the cycle of improvement.

One outgrowth of the Japanese way of working together has been the formation of small groups of employees called *quality circles*. These groups, consisting of employees at all levels, meet on a regular basis to discuss ways of continually improving their process.

With all the workers given some statistical training and engineers some training in experimental design, all the processes within the company can receive attention and be improved.

14.3   Experimental Designs for Quality Improvement

The modern emphasis, developed in Japan, has been to build quality into the product rather than waiting until the end of the line and trying to inspect bad quality out. The job of quality becomes a full-time job for everyone in the company, working as a team. They must learn about the process by observing and conducting statistically designed experiments.

In addition to the factorial designs discussed in the previous chapter, the Japanese, and Professor Genichi Taguchi in particular, have introduced good engineering ideas to produce new design procedures. Two of his major contributions involve using designed experiments to

(a) **select one input variable to minimize variation while another input variable holds the response on target;**

(b) **create products that are not sensitive to variations in their components or environmental conditions.**

To illustrate the minimization of variation concept, suppose a 2^3 factorial design is run to study the effects of initial concentration of Acid A, rag content, and digester time on the tear strength of writing paper. Rather than summarize the experiment in terms of the means $\bar{y}_{ijk.}$ at each experimental condition, the statistician G. E. P. Box suggests a chart of the individual values. This graph portrays both the level with respect to the indicated target and the amount of variation. From Figure 14.6 we see that the acid concentration can influence the mean level, whereas rag content can be used to reduce variation. The third factor, digester time, does not seem to have an effect. That is, we can manipulate rag content and initial concentration both to be on target and to reduce variation.

In studying the effect of various factors on variance, it is usually better to consider $\ln(s^2)$ as this is apt to be more nearly normal.

| EXAMPLE | **Estimating the factor effects on both means and variance** |

Investigators replicated a 2^3 experiment three times to study the effects of $x_1 =$ type of solvent, $x_2 =$ time in oven, and $x_3 =$ temperature of oven, on the tensile strength of test specimens of synthetic fiber to be used in carpeting. For each run we have computed the variance of the 3 responses and placed them in the second

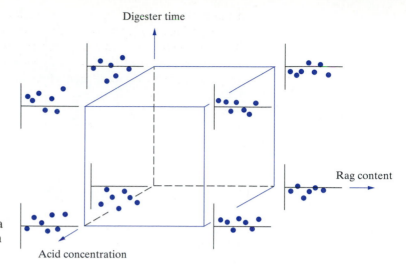

FIGURE 14.6 The summary of a design to study the effect on both mean response and variation.

to last column of the table. The values of their natural logarithms are given in the last column. Determine if any of the factors have an influence on the variance.

Design				
Solvent	*Time*	*Temp.*		
x_1	x_2	x_3	s_i^2	$\ln(s_i^2)$
−1	−1	−1	2048	7.6246
1	−1	−1	2813	7.9420
−1	1	−1	800	6.6846
1	1	−1	1352	7.2093
−1	−1	1	2113	7.6559
1	−1	1	1568	7.3576
−1	1	1	882	6.7822
1	1	1	1013	6.9207

Solution Multiplying the column of ln(variance) by the appropriate column and dividing by 4 we obtain the estimated effects on ln(variance)

$$solvent: \frac{-7.6246 + 7.9420 - 6.6846 + \cdots + 6.9207}{4} = .171$$

$$time: -.746 \quad temp: -.186 \quad solvent \times time: .091$$

$$solvent \times temp: .161 \quad time \times temp: -.250 \quad solvent \times time \times temp: .057$$

Because there is no replication of values for s_i^2, we cannot compute an F statistic. Instead we create a half normal plot as described on page 000. Plotting the absolute values of the estimated effects in Figure 14.7, we see that the second factor, B: time in oven, seems important. It is far above the straight-line pattern formed

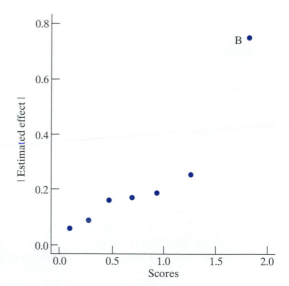

FIGURE 14.7 A half normal plot of the |estimated effect| for $\ln(s_i^2)$.

by the small estimated effects. If the oven time is kept at its higher level, the variance will be reduced.

   We caution that 7 may be too few effects in order to read patterns from the plot, so this tentative conclusion needs to be verified by further experimentation. ✔

   To illustrate the idea of making products that are insensitive to variation, suppose that the output voltage of a circuit is related to the value of a resistor, as in Figure 14.8. It is possible to exploit the *nonlinear* relationship in order to obtain a more stable output. Even if the resistors have a 10% tolerance (the nominal 200-ohm resistor would vary between 180 and 220, whereas the 400-ohm resistor would vary between 360 and 440), it would be better to use the higher-

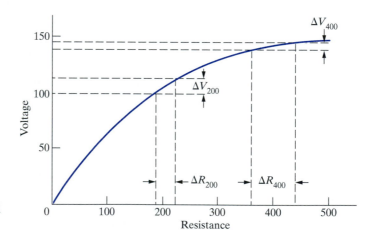

FIGURE 14.8 A non-linear relation between output voltage and a re-sistance can be exploited to reduce variation.

valued resistor because the variation in the response, output voltage, is much smaller. Then, as in Figure 14.6, we could seek a device that would bring the output voltage into the desired range.

G. Taguchi and Y. Wu, in the reference listed in the bibliography, give an example of making a product insensitive to environmental conditions. The Ina Tile company had experienced large amounts of scrap because of temperature variations within their kiln. Rather than immediately buy a new expensive kiln, they experimented with new recipes for making the tiles. After running a fractional factorial design with 7 factors, it was found that only lime content was important. As suggested by the Pareto rule, which postulates a vital few and many trivial elements, only 1 out of 7 variables had an effect. A low-cost solution was found and the problem surmounted by increasing the lime content.

14.4   Quality Control

It may surprise some persons to learn that 2 apparently identical parts made under carefully controlled conditions, from the same batch of raw material, and only seconds apart by the same machine, can nevertheless be different in many respects. Indeed, any manufacturing process, however good, is characterized by a certain amount of variability, which is of a random nature and which cannot be completely eliminated.

Usually manufacturing processes go through several stages of development before actual production begins. Assessments must be made to determine whether the process can produce units that meet engineering specifications. If a characteristic is nearly normally distributed, its natural variation is within plus or minus 3 standard deviations of its mean. A typical baseline assessment is to determine if this interval of length 6σ is within the specification limits. Process capability can be quantified on this basis. Let LSL be the lower specification limit and USL the upper specification limit for the process. Then process potential can be assessed from a **process capability index** which is estimated by

$$\widehat{C}_p = \frac{USL - LSL}{6s}$$

where s is the standard deviation obtained by measuring a sample of units.

Because we must deal with the estimated capability index, $\widehat{C}_p$, practitioners suggest that a value of at least 1.33 is required before an ongoing process is deemed capable.

When the process mean is not centered between the specification limits, the closest specification may be most important. An alternative process capability index having estimated value

$$\widehat{C}_{pk} = \frac{\min(\overline{x} - LSL, USL - \overline{x})}{3s}$$

takes this distance into account.

EXAMPLE

Calculating the process capability index

The specification limits on a valve diameter (mm) are $LSL = 10.98$ and $USL = 11.01$. Measurements on 80 valves gave $\bar{x} = 10.991$ and $s = .0035$. Estimate the process capability indices C_p and C_{pk}.

Solution

$$\hat{C}_p = \frac{USL - LSL}{6s} = \frac{11.01 - 10.98}{6(.0035)} = 1.43$$

so the process would be judged to be capable.

$$\hat{C}_{pk} = \frac{\min(\bar{x} - LSL, USL - \bar{x})}{3s} = \frac{\min(10.991 - 10.98, 11.01 - 10.991)}{3(.0035)} = 1.048$$

This second index is substantially smaller than the first because the mean is off-center. ✔

According to the ideas of quality improvement, getting the six sigma interval within specifications is just a first step. Further improvements can lead to tighter specifications and the production of better units. However, before any assessment of capability can be made, the process must be made stable or in control.

When the variability present in a production process is confined to chance variation, the process is said to be in a state of **statistical control.** Such a state is usually attained by finding and eliminating trouble of the sort causing another kind of variation, called **assignable variation,** which may be due to poorly trained operators, poor-quality raw materials, faulty machine settings, worn parts, and the like. Since manufacturing processes are rarely free from trouble of this kind, it is important to have some systematic method of detecting serious deviations from a state of statistical control when, or if possible *before,* they actually occur. It is to this end that **control charts** are principally used.

In what follows, we shall differentiate between **control charts for measurements** and **control charts for attributes,** depending on whether the observations with which we are concerned are measurements or count data (say, the numbers of defectives in a sample in a given size). In either case, a control chart consists of a **central line** (see Figure 14.9) corresponding to the *average* quality at which the process is to perform, and lines corresponding to the **upper and lower control limits.** These limits are chosen so that values falling between them can be attributed to chance, while values falling beyond them are interpreted as indicating a lack of control. By plotting the results obtained from samples taken periodically at frequent intervals, it is possible to check by means of such a chart whether the process is under control, or whether trouble of the sort indicated above has entered the process. When a sample point falls beyond the control limits, one looks for trouble, but even if the points fall between the control limits, a trend of some other systematic pattern may serve notice that action should be taken to avoid serious trouble.

The ability to "read" control charts and to determine from them just what corrective action should be taken is a matter of experience and highly developed judgement.

FIGURE 14.9
Control chart.

A quality-control engineer must not only understand the statistical foundation of the subject but must also be thoroughly acquainted with the processes themselves. The engineering and managerial aspects of quality control (and quality assurance in general), which nowadays includes incoming raw materials, outgoing products, and in-process control, constitute an extensive subject in themselves. In the following sections we present only the statistical aspects of the subject; more complete discussions of other aspects can be found in the book by A. J. Duncan listed in the bibliography.

14.5 Control Charts for Measurements

When dealing with measurements, it is customary to exercise control over the average quality of a process as well as its variability. The first goal is accomplished by plotting the means of periodic samples on a **control chart for means,** called an **X-bar** or $\bar{x}$ **chart.** Variability is controlled by plotting the sample ranges or standard deviations, respectively, on an **R chart,** or a σ **chart,** depending on which statistic is used to estimate the population standard deviation.

If the process mean and standard deviation, μ and σ, are known, and it is reasonable to treat the measurements as samples from a normal population, we can assert with probability $1 - \alpha$ that the mean of a random sample of size n will fall between

$$\mu - z_{\alpha/2}\frac{\sigma}{\sqrt{n}} \quad \text{and} \quad \mu + z_{\alpha/2}\frac{\sigma}{\sqrt{n}}$$

These two limits on $\bar{x}$ provide upper and lower control limits, and, under the given assumptions, they enable the quality-control engineer to determine whether or not to make an adjustment in the process.

In actual practice, μ and σ are usually unknown and it is necessary to estimate their values from a large sample (or samples) taken while the process is "in control." For this reason and because there may be no assurance that the measurements can be treated as samples from a normal population, the $(1 - \alpha)100\%$ confidence level associated with the control limits is only approximate, and such "probability limits" are seldom used in practice. Instead, it is common industrial practice to use **three-sigma limits** obtained by substituting 3 for $z_{\alpha/2}$. With three-sigma limits one usually is highly confident that the process will not be declared out of control when, in fact, it is actually in control.

If there exists a long history of a process in good control, μ and σ can be estimated from past data practically without error. Thus, the central line of an $\bar{x}$ chart is given by μ, and the upper and lower three-sigma control limits are given by $\mu \pm A\sigma$, where $A = 3/\sqrt{n}$ and n is the size of each sample.[†] For convenience, values of A for $n = 2, 3, \cdots$, and 15 are given in Table 13. The use of a constant sample size n simplifies the maintenance and interpretation of an $\bar{x}$ chart, but as the reader will observe in Exercise 14.4, this restriction is not absolutely necessary.

In the more common case where the population parameters are *unknown*, it is necessary to estimate these parameters on the basis of preliminary samples. For this purpose, it is usually desirable to obtain the results of 20 or 25 consecutive samples taken when the process is in control. If k samples are used, each of size n, we shall denote the mean of the ith sample by $\bar{x}_i$, and the grand mean of the k sample means by $\bar{\bar{x}}$, that is,

Grand mean of sample means

$$\bar{\bar{x}} = \frac{1}{k} \sum_{i=1}^{k} \bar{x}_i$$

The process variability σ can be estimated either from the standard deviations or the ranges of the k samples. Since the sample size commonly used in connection with control charts for measurements is small, there is usually very little loss of efficiency in estimating σ from the sample ranges. (For an example where sample standard deviations are used in this connection, see Exercise 14.5.) Denoting the range of the ith sample by R_i, we shall thus make use of the statistic

Mean sample range

$$\bar{R} = \frac{1}{k} \sum_{i=1}^{k} R_i$$

Since $\bar{\bar{x}}$ provides an unbiased estimate of the population mean μ, the central line for the $\bar{x}$ chart is given by $\bar{\bar{x}}$. The statistic $\bar{R}$ does not provide an unbiased estimate of σ, but multiplying $\bar{R}$ by the constant A_2, we obtain an unbiased estimate of $3\sigma/\sqrt{n}$. The constant multiplier A_2, tabulated in Table 13 for various values of n, depends on the assumption that the measurements constitute a sample from a

---

[†] Throughout this chapter we depart somewhat from the customary quality-control notation in order to be consistent with the more widely accepted statistical notation used elsewhere in this book. (For instance, in quality control it is customary to denote the sample mean and standard deviation by $\bar{x}$ and σ and the corresponding population parameters by $\bar{x}'$ and σ'.)

normal population. Thus, the central line and the upper and lower three-sigma control limits, UCL and LCL, for an $\bar{x}$ chart (with μ and σ estimated from past data) are given by

Control-chart values for and $\bar{x}$ chart

$$central\ line\ =\ \bar{\bar{x}}$$
$$UCL = \bar{\bar{x}} + A_2\bar{R}$$
$$LCL = \bar{\bar{x}} - A_2\bar{R}$$

An example of this kind of control chart for the mean is shown in Figure 14.10.

FIGURE 14.10
$\bar{x}$ chart.

In controlling a process, it may not be enough to monitor the population mean. Although an increase in process variability may become apparent from increased fluctuations of the $\bar{x}$'s, a more sensitive test of shifts in process variability is provided by a separate control chart, an R chart based on the sample ranges or a σ chart based on the sample standard deviations. An example of the latter may be found in Exercise 14.5.

The central line and control limits of an R chart are based on the distribution of the range of samples of size n from a normal population. As we observed on page 275, the mean and the standard deviation of this sampling distribution are given by $d_2\sigma$ and $d_3\sigma$, respectively, when σ is known. Thus, three-sigma control limits for the range are given by $d_2\sigma \pm 3d_3\sigma$, and the complete set of control-chart values for an R chart (with σ known) is given by

Control-chart values for an R chart (σ known)

$$central\ line = d_2\sigma$$
$$UCL = D_2\sigma$$
$$LCL = D_1\sigma$$

Here $D_1 = d_2 - 3d_3$ and $D_2 = d_2 + 3d_3$, and values of these constants can be found in Table 13 for various values of n.

If σ is unknown, it is estimated from past data as previously described, and the control-chart values for R chart (with σ unknown) are as follows:

Control-chart values
for an R chart (σ
unknown)

$$central\ line = \bar{R}$$
$$UCL = D_4\,\bar{R}$$
$$LCL = D_3\,\bar{R}$$

Here $D_3 = D_1/d_2$ and $D_4 = D_2/d_2$, and values of these constants can also be found in Table 13 for various values of n.

To illustrate the construction of an $\bar{x}$ chart and an R chart, suppose a manufacturer of a certain bearing knows from a preliminary record of 20 hourly samples of size 4 that for the diameters of these bearings $\bar{\bar{x}} = 0.9752$ and $\bar{R} = 0.0002$. Coding her data by means of the equation $\dfrac{x - 0.9750}{0.0001}$, that is, expressing each measurement as a deviation from 0.9750 in 0.0001 inch, she obtains

$\bar{x}$ chart (coded)		R chart (coded)	
central line	$\bar{\bar{x}} = 2.0$	central line	$\bar{R} = 2.0$
UCL	$\bar{\bar{x}} + A_2\bar{R} = 3.4$	UCL	$D_4\bar{R} = 4.6$
LCL	$\bar{\bar{x}} - A_2\bar{R} = 0.6$	LCL	$D_3\bar{R} = 0$

The values of $A_2 = 0.729$, $D_3 = 0$, and $D_4 = 2.282$ for samples of size 4 were obtained from Table 13. Graphically, these control charts are shown in Figures 14.10 and 14.11, where we have also indicated the results subsequently obtained in the following 20 samples:

Hour	Coded sample values				$\bar{x}$	R
1	1.7	2.2	1.9	1.2	1.75	1.0
2	0.8	1.5	2.1	0.9	1.32	1.3
3	1.0	1.4	1.0	1.3	1.18	0.4
4	0.4	−0.6	0.7	0.2	0.18	1.3
5	1.4	2.3	2.8	2.7	2.30	1.4
6	1.8	2.0	1.1	0.1	1.25	1.9
7	1.6	1.0	1.5	2.0	1.52	1.0
8	2.5	1.6	1.8	1.2	1.78	1.3
9	2.9	2.0	0.5	2.2	1.90	2.4
10	1.1	1.1	3.1	1.6	1.72	2.0
11	1.7	3.6	2.5	1.8	2.40	1.9

Hour	Coded sample values				$\bar{x}$	R
12	4.6	2.8	3.5	1.9	3.20	2.7
13	2.6	2.8	3.2	1.5	2.52	1.7
14	2.3	2.1	2.1	1.7	2.05	0.6
15	1.9	1.6	1.8	1.4	1.68	0.5
16	1.3	2.0	3.9	0.8	2.00	3.1
17	2.8	1.5	0.6	0.2	1.28	2.6
18	1.7	3.6	0.9	1.5	1.92	2.7
19	1.6	0.6	1.0	0.8	1.00	1.0
20	1.7	1.0	0.5	2.2	1.35	1.7

Inspection of Figure 14.10 shows the only one of the points falls outside of the control limits, but it also shows that there may nevertheless have been a downward shift in the process average. Figure 14.11 shows a definite downward shift in the process variability; note especially that most of the sample ranges fall below the central line of the R chart.

FIGURE 14.11
R chart.

The reader may have observed the close connection between the use of control charts and the testing of hypotheses. A point on an $\bar{x}$ chart that is out of control corresponds to a sample for which the null hypotheses that $\mu = \mu_0$ is rejected. To be more precise, we should say that control-chart techniques provide sequential, *temporally ordered* sets of tests. We are interested not only in the positions of individual points, but also in possible trends or other patterns exhibited by the points representing successive samples.

A different graph, called a **cumulative sum (cusum)** chart, is more effective for detecting small shifts in the mean. Consider the deviations *observation – target value.* In the context of our example, the target value should be 2.00. To construct the cusum chart, plot

$$S_1 = (1.75 - 2.00) = -0.25 \text{ versus } 1$$

$$S_2 = (1.75 - 2.00) + (1.32 - 2.00) = -0.93 \text{ versus } 2$$

$$S_3 = (-0.25) + (-0.68) + (1.18 - 2.00) = -1.75 \text{ versus } 3$$

$$\vdots$$

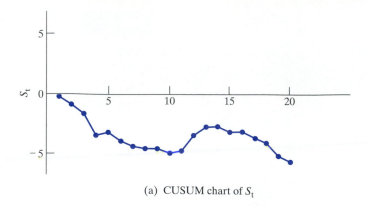

(a) CUSUM chart of S_t

FIGURE 14.12
CUSUM plots.

(b) CUSUM statistic $S_t - \min\limits_{m \leq t} S_m$

In Figure 14.12(a) we see evidence of an initial constant downward trend masked somewhat by random variation. This behavior indicates that the level of the process is a fixed amount below the target value of 2.00. At observation 11 there is a distinct shift up in level, as if a change has been made, but after a few hours a shift to a level below 2.0 appears to occur.

The **cusum statistic** for detecting an increase is

current value of S_t − minimum of S_m over all previous times

This is plotted in Figure 14.12(b). It shows more vividly the temporary increase in level at observation 11.

There are theoretical reasons for creating separate charts to detect an increase and to detect a decrease. Separate centering constants may be used for each chart. If it is deemed important for engineering reasons to detect an increase to 2.50, we could then use the centering value $2.25 = 2.00 + (2.50 - 2.00)/2$ as recommended. (See the entry on cumulative sum control charts in the encyclopedia by S. Kotz and N. L. Johnson, listed in the bibliography, for more details on critical values for cusum statistics.)

14.6 Control Charts for Attributes

Although more complete information can usually be gained from measurements made on a finished product, it is often quicker and cheaper to check the product against specifications on an "attribute" or "go, no-go" basis. For example, in checking the diameter and eccentricity of a ball bearing it is far simpler to determine whether it will pass through circular holes cut in a template than to make several measurements of the diameter with a micrometer. In this section we discuss two fundamental kinds of control charts used in connection with attribute sampling, the **fraction-defective chart,** also called a ***p* chart,** and the **number-of-defects chart,** also called a ***c* chart.** To clarify the distinction between "number defective" and "number of defects," note that a unit tested can have several **defects,** whereas, on the other hand, it is either defective or it is not. In many applications a unit is referred to as **defective** if it has at least one defect.

Control limits for a fraction-defective chart are based on the sampling theory for proportions introduced in Section 9.1 and on the normal curve approximation to the binomial distribution. Thus, if a standard is given—that is, if the fraction defective should take on some preassigned value p—the central line is p and three-sigma control limits for the fraction defective in random samples of size n are given by

$$p \pm 3\sqrt{\frac{p(1 - p)}{n}}$$

If no standard is given, which is more frequently the case in actual practice, p will have to be estimated from past data. If k samples are available, d_i is the number of defectives in the ith sample, and n_i is the number of observations in the ith sample, it is customary to estimate p as the proportion of defectives in the combined sample, namely, as

Proportion of defectives in combined sample

$$\bar{p} = \frac{d_1 + d_2 + \cdots + d_k}{n_1 + n_2 + \cdots + n_k}$$

Control-chart values for a fraction-defective chart

$$central\ line = \bar{p}$$

$$UCL = \bar{p} + 3\sqrt{\frac{\bar{p}(1 - \bar{p})}{n}}$$

$$LCL = \bar{p} - 3\sqrt{\frac{\bar{p}(1 - \bar{p})}{n}}$$

Note that if p is small, as is often the case in practice, substitution in the formula for the lower control limit might yield a negative number. When this occurs, it is customary to regard the lower control limit as if it were zero and, in effect, to use only the upper control limit. Another complication that can arise if p is small is that the binomial distribution may not be adequately approximated by the normal distribution. Generally speaking, the use of the above control limits for p charts is unrealistic whenever n and p are such that the underlying binomial (or hypergeometric) distribution cannot be approximated by a normal curve (see page 158).

In such cases it is best to use an upper control limit obtained directly from a table of binomial probabilities or, perhaps use the Poisson approximation to the binomial distribution.

As an illustration of a p chart, suppose that it is desired to control the output of a certain integrated circuit production line to maintain a "yield" of 60 percent, that is, a proportion defective of 40 percent. To this end, daily samples of 100 units are checked to electrical specifications, with the following results:

Date	Number of defectives	Date	Number of defectives	Date	Number of defectives
3-12	24	3-26	44	4-09	23
3-13	38	3-27	52	4-10	31
3-16	62	3-30	45	4-13	26
3-17	34	3-31	30	4-14	32
3-18	26	4-01	34	4-15	35
3-19	36	4-02	33	4-16	15
3-20	38	4-03	22	4-17	24
3-23	52	4-06	34	4-20	38
3-24	33	4-07	43	4-21	21
3-25	44	4-08	28	4-22	16

Since the standard is given as $p = 0.40$, the control-chart values are

$$central\ line = 0.40$$

$$UCL = 0.40 + 3\sqrt{\frac{(0.40)(0.60)}{100}} = 0.55$$

$$LCL = 0.40 - 3\sqrt{\frac{(0.40)(0.60)}{100}} = 0.25$$

The corresponding control chart with points for the 30 sample fractions defective is shown in Figure 14.13, and it exhibits some interesting characteristics. Note that there is only 1 point out of control on the high side, but there are 7 points out of

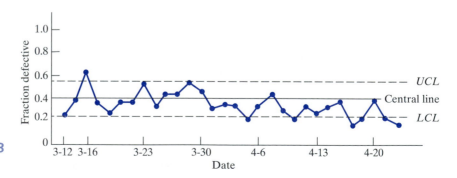

FIGURE 14.13
p chart.

control on the low side. Most of these 7 "low points" occurred after April 1, and there appears to be a general downward trend. In fact, there is an unbroken run of 11 points below the central line after April 7. It would appear from this chart that the yield is not yet stabilized and that the process is potentially capable of maintaining a yield well above the nominal 60% value.

Equivalent to the *p* chart for the fraction defective is the control chart for the number of defectives. Instead of plotting the fraction defective in a sample of size *n*, one plots the number of defectives, and the control-chart values for this kind of chart are obtained by multiplying the above values for the central line and the control-limits by *n*. Thus, if *p* is estimated by $\overline{p}$, the control-chart values for a **number-of-defectives chart** are as follows:

Control-chart values for a number-of-defectives chart

$$central\ line = n\overline{p}$$
$$UCL = n\overline{p} + 3\sqrt{n\overline{p}(1 - \overline{p})}$$
$$LCL = n\overline{p} - 3\sqrt{n\overline{p}(1 - \overline{p})}$$

There are situations where it is necessary to control the number of defects in a unit of product, rather than the fraction defective or the number of defectives. For example, in the production of carpeting it is important to control the number of defects per hundred yards; in the production of newsprint one may wish to control the number of defects per roll. These situations are similar to the one described in Section 4.7, which led to the Poisson distribution. Thus, if *c* is the number of defects per manufactured unit, *c* is taken to be a value of a random variable having the Poisson distribution.

It follows that the center line for a number-of-defects chart is the parameter λ of the corresponding Poisson distribution, and the three-sigma control limits can be based on the fact that the standard deviation of this distribution is $\sqrt{\lambda}$. If λ is unknown, that is, if no standard is given, its value is usually estimated from at least 20 values of *c* observed from past data. If *k* is the number of units of product available for estimating λ, and if c_i is the number of defects in the *i*th unit, then λ is estimated by

Mean number of defects

$$\overline{c} = \frac{1}{k}\sum_{i=1}^{k} c_i$$

and the control-chart values for the **c chart** are

Control-chart values for a number-of-defects chart

$$central\ line = \overline{c}$$
$$UCL = \overline{c} + 3\sqrt{\overline{c}}$$
$$LCL = \overline{c} - 3\sqrt{\overline{c}}$$

To illustrate this kind of control chart, suppose that it is known from past experience that on the average an aircraft assembly made by a certain company has $\bar{c} = 4$ missing rivets. The corresponding control chart for the number of missing rivets is shown in Figure 14.14, on which we have also plotted the results of inspections that revealed 4, 6, 5, 1, 2, 3, 5, 7, 1, 2, 2, 4, 6, 5, 3, 2, 4, 1, 8, 4, 5, 6, 3, 4, and 2 missing rivets in 25 assemblies.

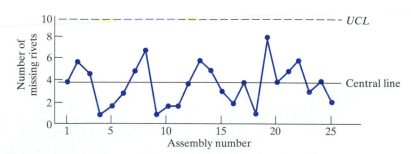

FIGURE 14.14
c chart.

For any control chart, one point outside of the control limits is enough to suggest that a special cause has influenced the process. It is now common practice to increase the sensitivity of the chart to detect special causes by adding other tests for special causes. Two of these extra tests merit special mention. In addition to one point outside of the control limits, a chart will signal a special cause if either

Additional tests for special causes

1. There are 9 points in a row on the same side of the central line.
2. There are 6 points in a row, all increasing or all decreasing.

As mentioned, there is a run of 11 points below the central line in Figure 14.3.

EXERCISES

14.1 A plastics manufacturer extrudes blanks for use in the manufacture of eyeglass temples. Specifications require that the thickness of these blanks have $\mu = 0.150$ inch and $\sigma = 0.002$ inch.

(a) Use the specifications to calculate a central line and three-sigma control limits for an $\bar{x}$ chart with $n = 5$.

(b) Use the specifications to calculate a central line and three-sigma control limits for an R chart with $n = 5$.

(c) Plot the following means and ranges, obtained in 20 successive random samples of size 5, on charts based on the control-chart constants obtained in parts (a) and (b), and discuss the process.

Sample	$\bar{x}$	R	Sample	$\bar{x}$	R
1	0.152	0.004	11	0.149	0.003
2	0.147	0.006	12	0.153	0.004
3	0.153	0.004	13	0.150	0.005
4	0.153	0.002	14	0.152	0.001
5	0.151	0.003	15	0.149	0.003
6	0.148	0.002	16	0.146	0.002
7	0.149	0.006	17	0.154	0.004
8	0.144	0.001	18	0.152	0.005
9	0.149	0.003	19	0.151	0.002
10	0.152	0.005	20	0.149	0.004

14.2 Calculate $\bar{\bar{x}}$ and $\bar{R}$ of the data of part (c) of Exercise 14.1, and use these values to construct the central lines and three-sigma control limits for new $\bar{x}$ and R charts to be used in the control of the thickness of the extruded plastic blanks.

14.3 The following data give the means and ranges of 25 samples, each consisting of 4 compression test results on steel forgings, in thousands of pounds per square inch:

Sample	1	2	3	4	5	6	7	8
$\bar{x}$	45.4	48.1	46.2	45.7	41.9	49.4	52.6	54.5
R	2.7	3.1	5.0	1.6	2.2	5.7	6.5	3.6

Sample	9	10	11	12	13	14	15	16
$\bar{x}$	45.1	47.6	42.8	41.4	43.7	49.2	51.1	42.8
R	2.5	1.0	3.9	5.6	2.7	3.1	1.5	2.2

Sample	17	18	19	20	21	22	23	24	25
$\bar{x}$	51.1	52.4	47.9	48.6	53.3	49.7	48.2	51.6	52.3
R	1.4	4.3	2.2	2.7	3.0	1.1	2.1	1.6	2.4

(a) Use these data to find the central line and control limits for an $\bar{x}$ chart.

(b) Use these data to find the central line and control limits for an R chart.

(c) Plot the given data on $\bar{x}$ and R charts based on the control-chart constants computed in parts (a) and (b), and interpret the results.

(d) Using runs above and below the central line (similar to runs above and below the median discussed on page 323), test at a level of significance of 0.05 whether there is a trend in the $\bar{x}$ values.

(e) Would it be reasonable to use the control limits found in this exercise in connection with subsequent compression test measurements from the same process? Why?

14.4 Reverse-current readings (in nanoamperes) are made on a sample of 10 transistors every half hour. Since some of the units may prove to be "shorts" or "opens," it is not always possible to obtain 10 readings. The following table shows the number of readings made at the end of each half-hour interval during an 8-hour shift, and the mean reverse currents obtained:

Sample	1	2	3	4	5	6	7	8
n	10	6	9	8	8	10	7	9
$\bar{x}$	12.5	11.1	10.2	11.6	21.9	12.3	9.7	15.6

Sample	9	10	11	12	13	14	15	16
n	7	8	10	9	7	8	9	10
$\bar{x}$	16.7	9.8	11.6	17.2	10.1	9.5	13.1	14.2

(a) Find the central line for an $\bar{x}$ chart by taking the weighted mean of the 16 $\bar{x}$'s, weighting each value with the size of the corresponding sample.

(b) Construct a table showing the central line in part (a) and three-sigma control limits corresponding to $n = 6, 7, 8, 9,$ and 10. Use $R = 4.0$, a value based on prior data.

(c) Plot the data on a control chart like the one in Figure 14.15 and interpret the results.

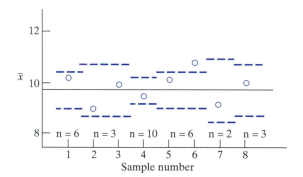

FIGURE 14.15
Exercise 14.4.

14.5 If the sample standard deviations instead of the sample ranges are used to estimate σ, the control limits for the resulting $\bar{x}$ chart are given by $\bar{\bar{x}} \pm A_1 \bar{s}$ where $\bar{s}$ is the mean of the sample standard deviations obtained from given data, and A_1 can be found in Table 13. Note that in connection with problems of quality control the sample standard deviation is defined using the divisor n instead of $n - 1$. The corresponding R chart is replaced by a σ chart, having the central line $c_2 \bar{s}$ and the lower and upper control limits $B_3 \bar{s}$ and $B_4 \bar{s}$, where c_2, B_3, and B_4 can be obtained from Table 13.

(a) Construct an $\bar{x}$ chart and a σ chart for 20 samples of size 3 which had $\bar{x}$ equal to 21.2, 19.4, 20.4, 20.4, 20.4, 19.0, 20.3, 21.1, 21.6, 22.1, 24.4, 23.9, 24.9, 24.1, 21.8, 19.5, 20.3, 22.5, 23.4, 23.3, and s equal to 2.0, 0.8, 1.1, 0.9, 1.0, 0.3, 1.3, 2.0, 0.8, 1.0, 1.5, 1.0, 1.5, 0.8, 1.3, 2.9, 4.3, 1.2, 0.3, 3.1.

(b) Would it be reasonable to use these control limits for subsequent data? Why?

14.6 In order to establish control charts for a boring process, 30 samples of five measurements of the inside diameters are taken, and the results are $\bar{x} = 1.317$ inches and $s = 0.002$ inch. Using the method of Exercise 14.5, construct an $\bar{x}$ chart for $n = 5$ and on it plot the following means obtained in 25 successive samples: 1.328, 1.330, 1.321, 1.325, 1.332, 1.340, 1.327, 1.321, 1.324, 1.325, 1.329, 1.326, 1.330, 1.324, 1.328, 1.322, 1.326, 1.327, 1.329, 1.325, 1.324, 1.329, 1.330, 1.321, and 1.329. Discuss the results.

14.7 Suppose that with the samples of Exercise 14.6, it is desired to establish control also over the variability of the process. Using the method of Exercise 14.5 and the values of $\bar{\bar{x}}$ and $\bar{s}$ given in Exercise 14.6, calculate the central line and control limits for a σ chart with $n = 5$.

14.8 Thirty-five successive samples of 100 castings each, taken from a production line, contained, respectively, 3, 3, 5, 3, 5, 0, 3, 2, 3, 5, 6, 5, 9, 1, 2, 4, 5, 2, 0, 10, 3, 6, 3, 2, 5, 6, 3, 3, 2, 5, 1, 0, 7, 4, and 3 defectives. If the fraction defective is to be maintained at 0.02, construct a p chart for these data and state whether or not this standard is being met.

14.9 The data of Exercise 14.8 may be looked upon as evidence that the standard of 2% defectives is being exceeded.

(a) Use the data of Exercise 14.8 to construct new control limits for the fraction defective.

(b) Using the control limits found in part (a), continue the control of the process by plotting the following data on the number of defectives obtained in 20 subsequent samples of size $n = 100$: 2, 4, 2, 4, 7, 5, 3, 2, 2, 3, 5, 6, 4, 5, 8, 0, 5, 5, 4, and 2.

14.10 The specifications for a certain mass-produced valve prescribe a testing procedure according to which each valve can be classified as satisfactory or unsatisfactory (defective). Past experience has shown that the process can perform so that $\bar{p} = 0.03$. Construct a three-sigma control chart for the number of defectives obtained in samples of size 100, and on it plot the following numbers of defectives obtained in such samples randomly selected from 30 successive half-days of production: 3, 4, 2, 1, 5, 2, 1, 2, 3, 1, 3, 2, 2, 2, 1, 1, 2, 0, 4, 3, 1, 0, 2, 4, 0, 1, 5, 7, 3, and 2.

14.11 The standard for a process producing tin plate in a continuous strip is 5 defects in the form of pinholes or visual blemishes per 100 feet. Based on the following set of 25 observations, giving the number of defects per 100 feet, can it be concluded that the process is in control to this standard?

Inspection number	1	2	3	4	5	6	7	8	9	10	11	12
Number of defects	3	2	2	4	4	4	6	4	1	7	5	5

Inspection number	13	14	15	16	17	18	19	20	21	22	23	24	25
Number of defects	4	6	6	9	5	2	6	5	11	6	6	8	2

14.12 A process for the manufacture of 4-feet-by-8-feet woodgrained panels has performed in the past with an average of 2.7 imperfections per 100 panels. Construct a chart to be used in the inspection of the panels and discuss the control if 25 successive 100-panel lots contained, respectively, 4, 1, 0, 3, 5, 3, 5, 4, 1, 4, 0, 1, 4, 2, 3, 7, 4, 2, 1, 3, 0, 2, 6, 1, and 3 imperfections.

14.7 Tolerance Limits

Inherent in every phase of industrial quality control is the problem of comparing some quality characteristic or measurement of a finished product against given specifications. Sometimes the specifications, or **tolerance limits,** are so stated by the customer or by the design engineer that any appreciable departure will make the product unusable. There remains, however, the problem of producing the part so that an acceptably high proportion of units will fall within tolerance limits specified for the given quality characteristic. Also, if a product is made without prior specifications, or if modifications are made, it is desirable to know within what limits the process can hold a quality characteristic a reasonably high percentage of the time. We, thus, speak of "natural" tolerance limits; that is, we let the process establish its own limits which, according to experience, can be met in actual practice.

If reliable information is available about the distribution underlying the measurement in question, it is a relatively simple matter to find natural tolerance limits. For instance, if long experience with a product enables us to assume that a certain dimension is normally distributed with the mean μ and the standard deviation σ, it is easy to construct limits between which we can expect to find any given proportion P of the population. For $P = 0.90$, we have the tolerance limits $\mu \pm 1.645\sigma$, and for $P = 0.95$ we have $\mu \pm 1.96\,\sigma$, as can easily be verified from a table of normal-curve areas.

In most practical situations the true values of μ and σ are not known, and tolerance limits must be based on the mean $\overline{X}$ and the standard deviation S of a random sample. Whereas $\mu \pm 1.96\,\sigma$ are limits including 95% of a normal population, the same cannot be said for the limits $\overline{X} \pm 1.96\,S$. These limits are random variables and they may or may not include a given proportion of the population. Nevertheless, it is possible to determine a constant K so the *one can assert with* $(1 - \alpha)$ 100% *confidence that the proportion of the population contained between* $\overline{x} - Ks$ *and* $\overline{x} + Ks$ *is at least P.* Such values of K for random samples from normal populations are given in Table 14 for $P = 0.90, 0.95$, and 0.99, with 95% or 99% levels of confidence, and selected values of n from 2 to 1,000.

To illustrate this technique, suppose that a manufacturer takes a sample of size $n = 100$ from a very large lot of mass-produced compression springs and that he obtains $\overline{x} = 1.507$ and $s = 0.004$ inch for the free lengths of the springs. Choosing the 99% level of confidence and a minimum proportion of $P = 0.95$, he obtains the tolerance limits $1.507 \pm (2.355)(0.004)$; in other words, the manufacturer can assert with 99% confidence that at least 95% of the springs in the entire lot have free lengths from 1.497 to 1.517 inches. Note that in problems like these the minimum proportion P as well as the degree of confidence $1 - \alpha$ must be specified; also note that the lower tolerance limit is rounded *down* and the upper tolerance limit is rounded *up*.

To avoid confusion, let us also point out that there is an essential difference between confidence limits and tolerance limits. Whereas confidence limits are used to estimate a parameter of a population, tolerance limits are used to indicate between what limits one can find a certain proportion of a population. This distinction is emphasized by the fact that when n becomes large the length of a confidence interval approaches zero, while the tolerance limits will approach the corresponding values for the population. Thus, for large n, K approaches 1.96 in the columns for $P = 0.95$ in Table 14.

The situation for one-sided tolerance bounds is different. In the context of strength of materials, it is the weaker specimens that break. Consequently, it is important for engineers to have an accurate estimate of the lower tail of the population of strengths. Recently engineers have realized that it is wiser to set specifications for strength in terms of a lower percentile η_β rather than the mean μ. It is the weaker specimens, not those of average strength, which break. The lumber industry and many space-age materials groups specify that a 95% one-sided confidence bound be calculated for the fifth percentile $\eta_{0.05}$. That is, a lower bound $L(x_1, x_2, \ldots, x_n)$ is calculated from the observations and, prior to taking the observations,

$$P[L(X_1, X_2, \ldots, X_n) < \eta_{0.05}] = 0.95$$

But this one-sided confidence bound is just a **one-sided tolerance bound,** since the event *the bound* $L(x_1, x_2, \ldots, x_n)$ *is less than the population 0.05 point* $\eta_{0.05}$ is the same as the event *at least 95% of the population is above* $L(x_1, x_2, \ldots, x_n)$.

For normal populations

$$L(x_1, x_2, \ldots, x_n) = \bar{x} - Ks$$

where K can be obtained from Table 14(b). (A more extensive table appears in the book by I. Guttman listed in the bibliography.)

EXAMPLE

Calculating a lower tolerance bound for the strength of cardboard

The cardboard industry is considering new standards for the cardboard used in boxes. One test involves placing weight on the box until it bursts. The burst strength, in pounds per square inch, for 40 boxes are

210	234	216	232	262
183	227	197	248	218
256	218	244	259	263
185	218	196	235	223
212	237	275	240	217
263	240	247	253	269
231	254	248	261	268
262	247	292	238	215

Obtain a 95% tolerance bound that will be less than proportion 0.95 of the population of burst strengths.

Solution
By computer, we determine that $\bar{x} = 237.32$ and $s = 25.10$. From Table 14(b), $K = 2.126$, so

$$L = \bar{x} - Ks = 237.32 - 2.126(25.10) = 183.96$$

which is rounded down to 183.

We are 95% confident that at least a proportion 0.95 of the population of burst strengths, for cardboard boxes, is above 183 psi.

In Exercise 14.43 you are asked to verify that the strength measurements fail to exhibit departures from normality.   ✔

EXERCISES

14.13 To check the strength of carbon steel for use in chain links, the yield stress of a random sample of 25 pieces was measured, yielding a mean and a standard deviation of 52,800 psi and 4,600 psi, respectively. Establish tolerance limits with $\alpha = 0.05$ and $P = 0.99$, and express *in words* what these tolerance limits mean.

14.14 In a study designed to determine the number of turns required for an artillery-shell fuse to arm, 75 fuses, rotated on a turntable, averaged 38.7 turns with a standard deviation of 4.3 turns. Establish tolerance limits for which one can assert with 99% confidence that *at least 95%* of the fuses will arm within these limits.

14.15 In a random sample of 40 piston rings chosen from a production line, the mean edge width was 0.1063 inch, and the standard deviation was 0.0004 inch.

   (a) Between what limits can it be said with 95% confidence that at least 90% of the edge widths of piston rings produced by this production line will lie?

   (b) Find 95% confidence limits for the true mean edge width, and explain the difference between these limits and the tolerance limits found in part (a).

14.16 *Nonparametric tolerance limits* can be based on the extreme values in a random sample of size n from any continuous population. The following equation relates the quantities n, P, and α, where P is the minimum proportion of the population contained between the smallest and the largest observations with $(1 - \alpha)100\%$ confidence:

$$nP^{n-1} - (n-1)P^n = \alpha$$

An approximate solution for n is given by

$$n \approx \frac{1}{2} + \frac{1+P}{1-P} \cdot \frac{\chi_\alpha^2}{4}$$

where χ_α^2 is the value of chi square for 4 degrees of freedom that corresponds to a right-hand tail area α.

   (a) How large a sample is required to be 95% certain that at least 90% of the population will be included between the extreme values of a sample?

   (b) With 95% confidence, at least what proportion of the population can be expected to be included between the extreme values of a sample of size 100?

14.8 Acceptance Sampling

Manufactured goods are shipped to the purchaser in lots ranging in size from only a few to many thousands of individual items. Ideally, each lot should not contain any defectives, but practically speaking it is rarely possible to meet this goal. Recognizing the fact that some defective goods are bound to be delivered, even if each lot were to be inspected 100%, most consumers require that evidence, based on careful inspection, be given that the proportion of defectives in each lot is not excessive.

We must stress that this philosophy is strictly at odds with the new philosophy of quality improvement. There is no reason, in the long run, to settle for any fixed proportion of defectives. Instead, there must be continual effort to improve the process. However, because many contracts still specify the use of these plans, the engineer should be acquainted with the details of acceptance sampling.

A frequently used and highly effective method for providing such evidence is that of sampling inspection, where items are selected from each lot prior to shipment (or prior to acceptance by the consumer), and a decision is made on the basis of this sample whether to accept or reject the lot. Acceptance of a lot ordinarily implies that it can be shipped (or be accepted by the consumer), even though it may contain some defective items. Arrangements between the producer and the consumer may allow for some form of credit to be given for defectives subsequently discovered by the consumer. Rejection of a lot need not mean that it is to be scrapped; a rejected lot may be subjected to closer inspection with the aim of eliminating all defective items.

Since the cost of inspection is rarely negligible (sometimes it is nearly as high as or higher than the cost of production), it is seldom desirable to inspect each item in a lot. Thus, acceptance inspection usually involves **sampling;** more specifically, a random sample is selected from each lot and the lot is accepted if the number of defectives found in the sample does not exceed a given **acceptance number.** This procedure is equivalent to a test of the null hypothesis that the proportion defective p in the lot equals some specified value p_0 against the alternative that it equals p_1, where $p_1 > p_0$. In acceptance sampling the value p_0 is called the **acceptable quality level,** or **AQL,** and p_1 is called the **lot tolerance percent defective,** or **LTPD.** The probability of a Type I error, α, can be interpreted as an upper limit to the proportion of "good" lots (lots with $p \leq p_0$) that will be rejected, and in this context it is called the **producer's risk.** The probability of a Type II error, β, gives an upper bound to the proportion of "bad" lots (lots with $p \geq p_1$) that will be accepted; it is called the **consumer's risk.**

A **single-sampling plan** is simply a specification of the sample size and the acceptance number to be used, and its choice is usually based on a specified AQL and (or) LTPD in association with given producer's and (or) consumer's risks. A given sampling plan is best described by its operating characteristic or OC curve, which gives the probability of acceptance for each value that can be assumed by the lot proportion defective p. Thus, the OC curve describes the degree of protection offered by the sampling plan against incoming lots of various qualities. If a sample of size n is taken from a lot containing N units, and if the acceptance number is c, the probability of accepting a lot containing the proportion of defectives p (the lot contains Np defectives) can be calculated by using the hypergeometric distribution, as follows:

Probability of lot acceptance

$$L(p) = \sum_{x=0}^{c} h(x; n, Np, N)$$

To illustrate the calculation of points on an OC curve, suppose that the lot size is $N = 100$, the sample size is $n = 10$, and the acceptance number is $c = 1$. We have

$$L(p) = \frac{\binom{100p}{0}\binom{100(1-p)}{10} + \binom{100p}{1}\binom{100(1-p)}{9}}{\binom{100}{10}}$$

Since calculations involving the hypergeometric distribution are fairly tedious, especially when n and N are large, it is customary in acceptance sampling to approximate the hypergeometric distribution with the binomial distribution, as on page 108. For instance, for $p = 0.10$ the exact value of $L(0.10) = 0.739$, as the reader will be asked to verify in Exercise 14.21, while Table 1 with $n = 10$ and $p = 0.10$ yields the binomial approximation

$$L(0.10) \simeq B(1; 10, 0.10) = 0.736$$

A sketch of the OC curve for the sampling plan $n = 10, c = 1$ can be made rapidly with the aid of Table 1, and the result is shown in Figure 14.16. From this curve it can be seen that the producer's risk is approximately 0.05 when the AQL is 0.04, and the consumer's risk is approximately 0.10 when the LPTD is 0.34.

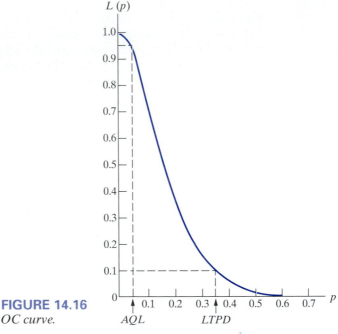

FIGURE 14.16
OC curve.

A sampling plan can also be described by means of its **average outgoing quality** or **AOQ** curve. This curve describes the degree of protection offered by the sampling plan by showing the average quality of outgoing lots corresponding to each quality level of incoming lots (that is, lots prior to inspection). If incoming lots are of good quality, that is, if their proportion defective is smaller than the AQL, very few lots will be rejected and the average outgoing quality of AOQ will be good. If the incoming lots are of poor quality, that is, if their proportion defective is larger than LTPD, most of them will be rejected. If all rejected lots are inspected 100% and all defective units are replaced by good units prior to acceptance of the lot, then the average outgoing quality will be good even though the average incoming quality is poor. It is when the average incoming quality lies between the AQL and the LTPD that the poorest quality of lots will be shipped. In general, there will be a maximum AOQ over all values of incoming quality p, and this value is called the **average outgoing quality limit,** or **AOQL.**

It is not difficult to derive a formula for finding the AOQ corresponding to a given incoming quality p under the assumption that all defectives in rejected lots are replaced by acceptable items prior to their final acceptance. If the incoming quality is p, the probability that a lot will be accepted is $L(p)$, and each such lot contains the proportion p of defectives. The proportion $1 - L(p)$ of lots that are eventually rejected contain no defectives, and it follows that the AOQ is given by $p \cdot L(p) + 0 \cdot [1 - L(p)]$, or

Average outgoing
quality

$$\text{AOQ} = p \cdot L(p)$$

More common practice is to remove or replace defectives found in accepted as well as rejected lots, but the modification thus required in the AOQ is usually minor and it is customary to use the above formula regardless of the inspection procedure.

The AOQ curve for the sampling plan $n = 10, c = 1$ is shown in Figure 14.17 and it is apparent from this figure that the AOQL is approximately 0.081.

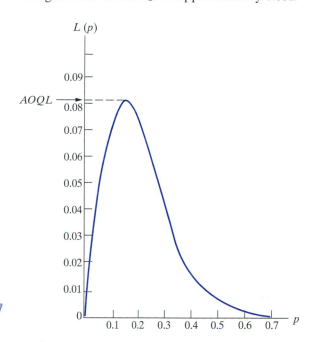

FIGURE 14.17
AOQ curve.

Sometimes, smaller samples (and hence, reductions in cost) can be achieved without sacrifice in the degree of protection by the use of **double** or **multiple sampling.** A double-sampling plan involves the selection of a random sample of size n_1 from a lot; if the sample contains c_1 or fewer defectives, the lot is accepted; if it contains c_1' or more defectives $(c_1' > c_1)$ the lot is rejected; otherwise, a second sample of size n_2 is taken from the lot, and the lot is accepted unless the total number of defectives in the combined sample of size $n_1 + n_2$ exceeds c_2. A multiple-sampling plan is similar in nature to a double-sampling plan, but it involves more than two stages.

An illustration of a multiple-sampling plan is given in the following table:

Sample	Sample size	Combined samples		
		Size	Acceptance number	Rejection number
First	20	20		3
Second	20	40	1	4
Third	20	60	3	5
Fourth	20	80	3	6
Fifth	20	100	5	7
Sixth	20	120	6	8
Seventh	20	140	7	8

This table summarizes a procedure that can be described as follows. In the first step, the lot is rejected if there are 3 or more defectives; otherwise, sampling continues. In the second step, the lot is accepted if the combined sample contains at most 1 defective, it is rejected if there are 4 or more defectives; otherwise, sampling continues. This goes on, if necessary, until in the final step the lot is accepted if there are at most 7 defectives in the combined sample of size 140, and otherwise it is rejected.

By an appropriate choice of the sample sizes and the acceptance and rejection numbers it is possible to match the OC curve of a double- or multiple-sampling plan closely to that of an equivalent single-sampling plan. Thus, the degree of protection offered by a double- or multiple-sampling plan can be made essentially the same as that offered by an equivalent single-sampling plan.

The advantage of double or multiple sampling is that there is a high probability that a very good lot will be accepted or a very poor lot will be rejected on the basis of the first sample, (or, at least, an early sample), thus reducing the required amount of inspection. On the other hand, if the lot quality is "intermediate," the total sample size required may actually be larger than that of the equivalent single-sampling plan.

To observe how a double- or multiple-sampling plan can conserve sampling effort, and to introduce the idea of the **average sample number (ASN) curve,** we consider the following double-sampling plan:

Sample	Sample size	Combined samples		
		Size	Acceptance number	Rejection number
First	15	15	1	5
Second	30	45	5	6

If the incoming lot quality is $p = 0.05$, the probability that a second sample will be required is the same as the probability that there will be 2, 3, or 4 defectives in a sample of size 15. According to Table 1, this probability is equal to

$$B(4; 15, 0.05) - B(1; 15, 0.05) = 0.170$$

Thus, on the average, it will require a sample of size $15 + (0.170)(30) = 20.1$ to decide whether to accept or reject an incoming lot of quality $p = 0.05$. Similar calculations enable us to find the average sample size required to inspect a lot having any given incoming quality p. A graph showing the relation between the average sample size (also called the **average sample number**) and the incoming lot quality is called an ASN curve; the ASN curve for the double-sampling plan described above is shown in Figure 14.18.

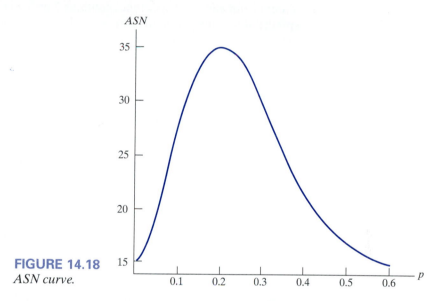

FIGURE 14.18
ASN curve.

Several standard sampling plans have been published to facilitate the use of acceptance sampling (see the book by A. Duncan in the bibliography). Among the most widely used standard plans are those contained in **Military Standard _105D_** (see the bibliography). These plans stress the maintenance of a specified AQL, and they are designed to encourage the producer to offer only good products to the consumer. To accomplish this there are three general levels of inspection corresponding to different consumer's risks. (Inspection level II is normally chosen; level I uses smaller sample sizes and level III uses larger sample sizes than level II.) There are also three types of inspection: normal, tightened, and reduced. The type of inspection depends on whether the average proportion defectives for prior samples has been above or below the AQL, and it may be changed during the course of inspection. Under tightened inspection the producer's risk is increased and the consumer's risk is (slightly) decreased; under reduced inspection the consumer's risk is increased and the producer's risk is (slightly) decreased. Tables are available for single, double, and multiple sampling, and a brief portion of these tables is included in this book in Tables 15 and 16.

The procedure in using MIL-STD-105D for single sampling is first to find the sample size code letter corresponding to the lot size and the desired inspection level and type. Then, using the sample size code letter thus obtained and the appropriate AQL, one finds the sample size and the acceptance number from the master table. A portion of the table for finding sample size code letters is given in Table 15, and a portion of the master table for normal inspection is included in Table 16.

To illustrate the use of MIL-STD-105D, suppose that incoming lots contain 2,000 items, and inspection level II is to be used in conjunction with normal inspection and an AQL of 0.025, or 2.5%. From Table 15 we find that the sample size code letter is K. Then, entering Table 16 in the row labeled K, we find that the sample size to be used is 125. Using the column labeled 2.5, we find the acceptance number is 7 and rejection number is 8. Thus, if a single sample of size 125, selected at random from a lot of 2,000 items, contains 7 or fewer defectives the lot is to be accepted; if the sample contains 8 or more defectives, the sample is to be rejected.

The concept of multiple sampling is carried to its extreme in **sequential sampling.** A sampling procedure is said to be sequential if, after each observation, one of the following decisions is made: accept whatever hypothesis is being tested, reject the hypothesis, or make another observation. Although sequential procedures are used also in connection with other kinds of problems, we shall discuss this kind of sampling only in connection with acceptance sampling, where we shall thus decide after the inspection of each successive item whether to accept a lot, reject it, or continue sampling.

The construction of a sequential sampling plan consists of finding two sequences of numbers a_n and r_n, where n is the number of observations, so that the lot is accepted as soon as the number of defectives is less than or equal to a_n for some n, the lot is rejected as soon as the number of defectives is greater than or equal to r_n for some n, and sampling continues so long as the number of defectives in a sample of size n falls between a_n and r_n. If an acceptance plan is to have p_0 and p_1 as its AQL and LTPD, the producer's risk α, and the consumer's risk β, it can be shown (see the book by A. Wald in the bibliography) that the required values of a_n and r_n can be computed by means of the formulas

Acceptance and rejection numbers for sequential sampling

$$a_n = \frac{\log \dfrac{\beta}{1 - \alpha} + n \cdot \log \dfrac{1 - p_0}{1 - p_1}}{\log \dfrac{p_1}{p_0} - \log \dfrac{1 - p_1}{1 - p_0}}$$

$$r_n = \frac{\log \dfrac{1 - \beta}{\alpha} + n \cdot \log \dfrac{1 - p_0}{1 - p_1}}{\log \dfrac{p_1}{p_0} - \log \dfrac{1 - p_1}{1 - p_0}}$$

If a_n is not an integer, it is replaced by the largest integer less than a_n; if r_n is not an integer, it is replaced by the smallest integer greater than r_n.

To illustrate this procedure, let $p_0 = 0.05$, $p_1 = 0.20$, $\alpha = 0.05$, and $\beta = 0.10$. Substituting these values into the above formulas for a_n and r_n, we obtain

$$a_n = -1.45 + 0.11n$$

$$r_n = 1.86 + 0.11n$$

and, letting $n = 1, 2, 3, \ldots$, and 25, we get the acceptance and rejection numbers shown in the second and fourth columns of the following table:

Number of items inspected n	Acceptance number a_n	Number of defectives d_n	Rejection number r_n
1	—	0	—
2	—	0	—
3	—	0	3
4	—	0	3
5	—	0	3
6	—	0	3
7	—	0	3
8	—	1	3
9	—	1	3
10	—	1	3
11	—	1	4
12	—	1	4
13	—	1	4
14	0	1	4
15	0	1	4
16	0	1	4
17	0	2	4
18	0	2	4
19	0	3	4
20	0	3	5
21	0	3	5
22	0	4	5
23	1	5	5
24	1		5
25	1		5

In the third column we have indicated the results obtained in an inspection where the 8th, 17th, 19th, 22nd, and the 23rd items are defective, and where the inspection terminates with rejection of the lot after inspection of the 23rd item.

The tabular procedure illustrated can be replaced by an equivalent graphical procedure for carrying out sequential sampling inspection. Plotting the values of a_n and r_n obtained from the equations above (without rounding), we obtain

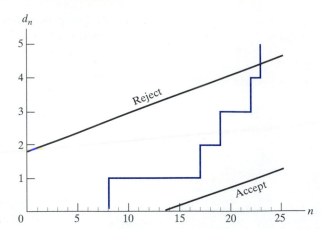

FIGURE 14.19
Graphical procedure for sequential sampling.

two *straight lines* like those of Figure 14.19. Sampling terminates with rejection or acceptance if the number of defectives observed falls above the line for r_n or below the line for a_n, respectively.

The main advantage of sequential sampling is that it can materially reduce the required amount of inspection. Studies have shown that the average decrease in sample size is often near 50% when compared with the sample size of equivalent single-sampling plans. The major disadvantage is that, in a sequential sampling plan, there is no upper limit to the number of items that might have to be inspected in order to reach a decision concerning the acceptance or rejection of a lot. In fact, the sample size is a random variable and its value will occasionally be very large. For this reason it is customary to *truncate* sequential sampling procedures by selecting a number N such that a decision must be made to accept or reject a lot prior to or at $n = N$.

EXERCISES

14.17 A sampling plan, calling for a sample of size $n = 50$, has the acceptance number $c = 3$. Assuming that the lot size is very large, calculate the probability of accepting a lot of incoming quality 15% defective and the probability of rejecting a lot of incoming quality 4% defective

    (a) by calculating the corresponding binomial probabilities;

    (b) by using the Poisson approximation to the binomial distribution.

14.18 A single-sampling plan calls for a sample of size 150.

    (a) Use the normal approximation to find the acceptance number c if the AQL is to be 2.5% and the producer's risk is to be $\alpha = 0.05$.

    (b) Using the acceptance number obtained in part (a), determine the consumer's risk if the LTPD is to be 6%.

14.19 Referring to the sampling plan of Exercise 14.17, use the Poisson approximation to calculate $L(p)$ for $p = 0.01, 0.02,\dots,0.19$, and 0.20. Sketch the OC curve for this sampling plan and read off the consumer's and producer's risks corresponding to an AQL of 4% and an LTPD of 14%.

14.20 A single-sampling plan has $n = 100$ and $c = 5$.

    (a) Find the AQL if the producer's risk is to be 0.025.

    (b) Find the LTPD if the consumer's risk is to be 0.05. [*Hint:* Use the normal approximation and set up equations leading to quadratic equations in p_0 and p_1, respectively.]

14.21 With reference to the example on page 528, verify that

    (a) $L(0.10) = 0.739$, using the exact (hypergeometric) formula;

    (b) $L(0.10) \simeq 0.736$, using the approximate (binomial) formula;

    (c) the OC curve is as given in Figure 14.16;

    (d) the AOQ is as given in Figure 14.17.

14.22 Calculate $L(p)$ for selected values of p and sketch the OC curve for the single-sampling plan $n = 120$, $c = 3$. [*Hint:* Assume a large lot size, and use the normal approximation to the binomial distribution.]

14.23 Sketch the AOQ curve for the sampling plan of Exercise 14.22, and estimate the AOQL.

14.24 Using the values of $L(p)$ obtained in Exercise 14.19, sketch the AOQ curve for the given sampling plan and estimate the AOQL.

14.25 Referring to the double-sampling plan on page 530, use Table 1 and the normal approximation (when necessary) to calculate the producer's risk α when AQL is $p_0 = 0.10$.

14.26 Calculate the average sample size required for selected values of p and sketch the ASN curve for the following double-sampling plan:

		Combined samples		
Sample	Sample size	Size	Acceptance number	Rejection number
First	10	10	0	3
Second	35	45	3	4

14.27 A lot of 200 items is to be inspected at an AQL of 6.5%. If MIL-STD-105D is to be used, with normal inspection at general inspection level II, what single-sampling plan is required?

14.28 An incoming lot of 5,000 items is to be inspected using MIL-STD-105D, with normal inspection at general inspection level II and an AQL of 2.5%. What single-sampling plan is required?

14.29 Find formulas for the acceptance and rejection numbers for the sequential sampling plan having an AQL of 0.10, and LTPD of 0.30, a producer's risk of 0.05, and a consumer's risk of 0.10. If a sample should contain defectives on the third, fifth, seventh, and eighth trials, would this plan accept or reject the corresponding lot prior to the tenth trial? If so, on which trial?

14.30 A sequential sampling plan is to have $p_0 = 0.01$, $p_1 = 0.10$, $\alpha = 0.05$, and $\beta = 0.20$.

(a) Determine the acceptance and rejection numbers for $n = 1, 2, \ldots$, and 50.

(b) Use random numbers and the acceptance and rejection numbers obtained in part (a) to simulate the inspection of a very large lot containing 20% defectives.

R E V I E W   E X E R C I S E S

14.31 The specifications require that the weight of castings have $\mu = 4.1$ ounces and $\sigma = 0.05$ ounces.

(a) Use the specifications to calculate a central line and three-sigma control limits for an $\bar{x}$ chart with $n = 5$.

(b) Use the specifications to calculate a central line and three-sigma control limits for an R chart with $n = 5$.

(c) Plot the following means and ranges, obtained in 20 successive random samples of size 5, on charts based on the control-chart constants obtained in part (a) and (b), and discuss the process.

Sample	$\bar{x}$	R	Sample	$\bar{x}$	R
1	4.24	0.09	11	4.20	0.21
2	4.18	0.12	12	4.25	0.20
3	4.26	0.14	13	4.25	0.17
4	4.21	0.24	14	4.21	0.07
5	4.22	0.15	15	4.19	0.16
6	4.18	0.28	16	4.23	0.16
7	4.23	0.06	17	4.27	0.19
8	4.19	0.15	18	4.22	0.20
9	4.21	0.09	19	4.20	0.12
10	4.18	0.15	20	4.19	0.16

14.32 Calculate $\bar{\bar{x}}$ and $\bar{R}$ for the data of part (c) of Exercise 14.31, and use these values to construct the central lines and three-sigma control limits for new $\bar{x}$ and R charts to be used in the control of the weight of the castings.

14.33 Twenty-five successive samples of 200 switches, each taken from a production line, contained, respectively, 6, 7, 13, 7, 0, 9, 4, 6, 0, 4, 5, 11, 6, 18, 1, 4, 9, 8, 2, 17, 9, 12, 10, 5, and 4 defectives. If the fraction of defectives is to be maintained at 0.02, construct a p chart for these data and state whether or not this standard is being met.

14.34 The data of Exercise 14.33 may be looked upon as evidence that the standard of 2% defectives is being exceeded.

(a) Use the data of Exercise 14.33 to construct new control limits for the fraction defective.

(b) Using the limits found in part (a), continue the control of the process by plotting the following data on the next ten samples of size $n = 200$: 4, 7, 5, 3, 8, 3, 1, 4, 3, 9.

14.35 A process for the manufacture of film has performed in the past with an average of 0.8 imperfections per 10 linear feet.

(a) Construct a chart to be used in the inspection of 10 foot sections.

(b) Discuss the control if 20 successive 10-foot sections contained, respectively, 1, 0, 0, 1, 3, 1, 2, 1, 0, 2, 1, 3, 0, 0, 1, 1, 2, 0, 4, and 1 imperfections.

14.36 With reference to the aluminum alloy strength data on page 20, obtain two-sided 95% tolerance limits on the proportion $P = 0.90$ of the population of strengths.

14.37 With reference to the interrequest time data on page 19, obtain 95% tolerance limits on the proportion $P = 0.90$ of the population of interrequest times. Take logs, use the normal theory approach, and then transform back to the original scale.

14.38 A sampling plan, calling for a sample of size $n = 40$, has the acceptance number $c = 2$. Assuming the lot size is very large, calculate the probability of accepting a lot of incoming quality 15% defective and the probability of rejecting a lot of incoming quality 4% defective

(a) by calculating the corresponding binomial probabilities;

(b) by using the Poisson approximation to the binomial distribution.

14.39 Referring to the sampling plan of Exercise 14.38, use the Poisson approximation to calculate $L(p)$ for $p = 0.01, 0.02, \ldots, 0.19$, and 0.20. Sketch the OC curve for this sampling plan and read off the consumer's and producer's risks corresponding to an AQL of 4% and LTPD of 14%.

14.40 Using the values of $L(p)$ obtained in Exercise 14.39, sketch the AOQ curve for the given sampling plan and estimate the AOQL.

14.41 A lot of 150 items is to be inspected at an AQL of 4.0%. If MIL-STD-105D is to be used, with normal inspection at general inspection level II, what single-sampling plan is required?

14.42 With reference to the discussion on page 516, calculate the cusum using 2.25 in place of 2.00 as the centering value. Also make the cusum chart.

14.43 With reference to the example on page 525,

(a) verify the calculation of the tolerance bound L;

(b) if the confidence is decreased to 90%, calculate the new tolerance bound (use $K = 2.010$);

(c) check the cardboard strength data for departures from normality using a normal-score plot.

14.44 Explain, from the perspective of quality improvement programs, why the $\bar{x}$, R and fraction defective charts should be used to listen to the process and observe its natural variability, at any stage, rather than for the long-run control of the process.

14.45 A critical width dimension on an integrated circuit board was measured on 100 boards. The ordered measurements are:

2.500	2.502	2.502	2.502	2.503	2.503	2.503	2.504	2.504
2.504	2.504	2.504	2.504	2.504	2.504	2.504	2.504	2.504
2.504	2.504	2.504	2.504	2.504	2.505	2.505	2.505	2.505
2.505	2.505	2.505	2.505	2.505	2.505	2.505	2.505	2.505
2.505	2.506	2.506	2.506	2.506	2.506	2.506	2.506	2.506

2.506	2.506	2.506	2.506	2.506	2.506	2.506	2.506	2.507
2.507	2.507	2.507	2.507	2.507	2.507	2.507	2.507	2.507
2.507	2.508	2.508	2.508	2.508	2.508	2.508	2.508	2.508
2.508	2.508	2.508	2.508	2.508	2.508	2.509	2.509	2.509
2.509	2.509	2.509	2.509	2.509	2.509	2.509	2.509	2.509
2.509	2.509	2.509	2.509	2.509	2.509	2.509	2.510	2.511
2.511								

Given the specification limits $LSL = 2.496$ and $USL = 2.516$, evaluate the process capability by determining the estimates (a) $\hat{C}_p$ and (b) $\hat{C}_{pk}$.

14.46 The following are the number of pounds per day shipped by a trucking company.

222415	140670	396868	240678	101786	166217	177900
349900	131100	465800	417700	305600	264500	224400
360400	211600	378200	285400	166100	230900	593300
214200	147800	119510	159200	353200	408300	275100
254100	423500	324800	304500	298600	202200	

It is suggested that the shipments be treated as a process. Because these data are not symmetrically distributed you could try a transformation. For the choice of the fourth root of weight, set the specification limits LSL and USL symmetrically about 22.6 (pounds)$^{1/4}$, so that the estimated capability index $\hat{C}_{pk}$ is 1.5.

14.47 A critical dimension on pieces following a flame cutting operation was measured on 37 pieces. In coded units, the measurements are:

−5	−10	0	−15	0	−10	−10	0	0	0	−10	0	20
10	−15	0	−5	0	0	−20	−10	−25	10	10	10	−10
−10	0	−25	0	−15	−10	0	10	0	5	10		

Given the specification limits $LSL = -50$ and $USL = 50$ in coded units, evaluate the estimates of the process capability indices (a) $\hat{C}_p$ and (b) $\hat{C}_{pk}$.

KEY TERMS

(with page references)

Applications to Reliability and Life Testing

The task of designing and supervising the manufacture of a product has been made increasingly difficult by rapid strides in the sophistication of modern products and the severity of the environmental conditions under which they must perform. No longer can an engineer be satsified if the operation of a product is technically feasible, or if it can be made to "work" under optimum conditions. In addition to such considerations as cost and ease of manufacture, increasing attention must now be paid to size and weight, ease of maintenance, and reliability. The magnitude of the problem of maintainability and reliability is illustrated by surveys which have uncovered the fact that frequently a high percentage of space-age electronic equipment has been in inoperative condition. Military surveys have further shown that maintenance and repair expenses for electronic equipment often exceed the original cost of procurement, even during the first year of operation.

In Section 15.1 we define the concept of reliability; we discuss and apply special probability distributions to the calculation of reliabilities in Sections 15.2 and 15.3. Some theory and applications relating to testing products for useful lifetime are introduced in Sections 15.4 and 15.5.

CHAPTER 15

15.1 Reliability

The problem of assuring and maintaining reliability has many facets, including original equipment design, control of quality during production, acceptance inspection, field trials, life testing, and design modifications. To complicate matters further, reliability competes directly or indirectly with a host of other engineering considerations, chiefly cost, complexity, size and weight, and maintainability. In spite of its complicated engineering aspects, it is possible to give a relatively simple mathematical definition of reliability. To motivate this definition, we call the reader's attention to the fact that a product may function satisfactorily under one set of conditions but not under other conditions, and that satisfactory performance for one purpose does not assure adequate performance for another purpose. For example, a microchip that is perfectly satisfactory for use in a home radio may be entirely unsatisfactory for use in the airborne guidance system of a missile. Accordingly, we shall define the **reliability** of a product as *the probability that it will function within specified limits for at least a specified period of time under specified environmental conditions*. Thus, the reliability of a "standard equipment" automobile tire is close to unity for 10,000 miles of normal operation on a passenger car, but it is virtually zero for use at the Indianapolis "500."

Since reliability has been defined as a probability, the theoretical treatment of this subject is based essentially on the material introduced in the early chapters of this book. Thus, the rules of probability introduced in Chapter 3 can be applied directly to the calculation of the reliability of a complex system, if the reliabilities of the individual components are known. (Estimates of the reliabilities of the individual components are usually obtained from statistical life tests, such as those discussed in Sections 15.4 and 15.5.)

Many systems can be considered to be series or parallel systems, or a combination of both. A **series system** is one in which all components are so interrelated that the entire system will fail if any one of its components fails; a **parallel system** is one that will fail only if all of its components fail.

Let us first discuss a system of n components connected in series, and let us suppose that the components are independent, namely, that the performance of any one part does not affect the reliability of the others. Under these conditions, the probability that the system will function is given by the special rule of multiplication for probabilities, and we have

Product law of reliabilities

$$R_S = \prod_{i=1}^{n} R_i$$

where R_i is the reliability of the ith component and R_S is the reliability of the series system. This simple **product law of reliabilities,** applicable to series systems of independent components, vividly demonstrates the effect of increased complexity on reliability.

EXAMPLE

Calculating the reliability of a series system

A system consists of 5 independent components in series, each having a reliability of 0.970. What is the reliability of the system? What happens to the system reliability if its complexity is increased so that it contains 10 similar components?

Solution The reliability of the five-component series system is

$$(0.970)^5 = 0.859$$

Increasing system complexity to 10 components will decrease the system reliability to

$$(0.970)^{10} = 0.737$$

Looking at the effect of increasing complexity in another way, we find that each of the components in the 10-component system would require a reliability of 0.985, instead of 0.970, for the 10-component system to have a reliability equal to that of the original 5-component system. ✔

One way to increase the reliability of a system is to replace certain components by several similar components connected in parallel. If a system consists of n independent components connected in parallel, it will fail to function only if all n components fail. Thus, if $F_i = 1 - R_i$ is the "unreliability" of the ith component, we can again apply the special rule of multiplication for probabilities to obtain

$$F_P = \prod_{i=1}^{n} F_i$$

where F_P is the unreliability of the parallel system, and $R_P = 1 - F_P$ is the reliability of the parallel system. Thus, for parallel systems we have a **product law of unreliabilities** analogous to the product law of reliabilities for series systems. Writing this law in another way, we get

Product law of
unreliabilities

$$R_P = 1 - \prod_{i=1}^{n} (1 - R_i)$$

for the reliability of a parallel system.

EXAMPLE

Calculating reliability for a complex system

The two basic formulas for the reliability of series and parallel systems can be used in combination to calculate the reliability of a system having both series and parallel parts. To illustrate such a calculation, consider the system diagrammed in Figure 15.1, which consists of eight components having the reliabilities shown in that figure. Find the reliability of this system.

Solution The parallel assembly C, D, E can be replaced by an equivalent component C' having the reliability $1 - (1 - 0.70)^3 = 0.973$, without affecting the overall reliability of the system. Similarly, the parallel assembly F, G can be replaced by a sin-

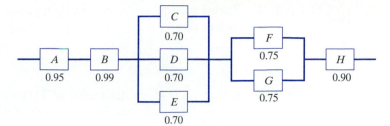

Figure 15.1
System reliability.

gle component F' having the reliability $1 - (1 - 0.75)^2 = 0.9375$. The resulting series system A, B, C', F', H, equivalent to the original system, has the reliability

$$(0.95)(0.99)(0.973)(0.9375)(0.90) = 0.772 \qquad ✔$$

15.2 Failure-time Distributions

According to the definition of reliability given in the preceding section, the reliability of a system or a component will often depend on the length of time it has been in service. Thus, of fundamental importance in reliability studies is the **failure-time distribution,** that is, the distribution of the time to failure of a component under given environmental conditions. A useful way to characterize this distribution is by means of its associated **instantaneous failure rate.** To develop this concept, first let $f(t)$ be the probability density of the time to failure of a given component, that is, the probability that the component will fail between times t and $t + \triangle t$ is given by $f(t) \cdot \triangle t$. Then, the probability that the component will fail on the interval from 0 to t is given by

$$F(t) = \int_0^t f(x)dx$$

and the **reliability function,** expressing the probability that it survives to time t, is given by

$$R(t) = 1 - F(t)$$

Thus, the probability that the component will fail in the interval from t to $t + \triangle t$ is $F(t + \triangle t) - F(t)$, and the conditional probability of failure in this interval, *given that the component survived to time* t, is expressed by

$$\frac{F(t + \triangle t) - F(t)}{R(t)}$$

Dividing by $\triangle t$, we find that the average rate of failure in the interval from t to $t + \triangle t$, given that the component survived to time t, is

$$\frac{F(t + \triangle t) - F(t)}{\triangle t} \cdot \frac{1}{R(t)}$$

Taking the limit as $\triangle t \to 0$, we then get the instantaneous failure rate, or simply the **failure rate**

$$Z(t) = \frac{F'(t)}{R(t)}$$

where $F'(t)$ is the derivative of $F(t)$ with respect to t. Finally, observing that $f(t) = F'(t)$ (see page 145) we get the relation

General equation for failure-rate function

$$Z(t) = \frac{f(t)}{R(t)} = \frac{f(t)}{1 - F(t)}$$

which expresses the failure rate in terms of the failure-time distribution.

A failure-rate curve that is typical of many manufactured items is shown in Figure 15.2. The curve is conveniently divided into three parts. The first part is characterized by a decreasing failure rate and it represents the period during which poorly manufactured items are weeded out. (It is common in the electronics industry to "burn in" components prior to actual use in order to eliminate any early failures.) The second part, which is often characterized by a constant failure rate, is normally regarded as the period of useful life during which only chance failures occur. The third part is characterized by an increasing failure rate, and it is the period during which components fail primarily because they are worn out. Note that the same general failure-rate curve is typical of human mortality, where the first part represents infant mortality, and the third part corresponds to old-age mortality.

Let us now derive an important relationship expressing the failure-time density in terms of the failure-rate function. Making use of the fact that $R(t) = 1 - F(t)$ and, hence, that $F'(t) = -R'(t)$, we can write

$$Z(t) = -\frac{R'(t)}{R(t)} = -\frac{d[\ln R(t)]}{dt}$$

Figure 15.2 Typical failure-rate curve.

Failure rate

Early failures | Chance failures | Wearout failures

0   Time

Solving this differential equation for $R(t)$, we obtain

$$R(t) = e^{-\int_0^t Z(x)\,dx}$$

and, making use of the relation $f(t) = Z(t) \cdot R(t)$, we finally get

General equation for
failure-time
distribution

$$f(t) = Z(t) \cdot e^{-\int_0^t Z(x)\,dx}$$

As illustrated in Figure 15.2, it is often assumed that the failure rate is constant during the period of useful life of a component. Denoting this constant failure rate by α, where $\alpha > 0$, and substituting α for $Z(t)$ in the formula for $f(t)$, we obtain

$$f(t) = \alpha \cdot e^{-\alpha t} \quad t > 0$$

Thus, we have an **exponential failure-time distribution** when it can be assumed that the failure rate is constant. For this reason, the assumption of constant failure rates is sometimes also called the *exponential assumption*. The time to failure also has an interpretation as a waiting time. If a component which fails is immediately replaced with a new one having the same constant failure rate α and the occurrence of failures follows a Poisson process, then the waiting times have this exponential distribution according to results in section 5.7. As we observed on page 168, the mean waiting time between successive failures is $1/\alpha$, or the reciprocal of the failure rate. Thus, the constant $1/\alpha$ is often referred to as the **mean time between failures,** abbreviated MTBF.

There are situations in which the assumption of a constant failure rate is not realistic, and in many of these situations one assumes instead that the failure rate function increases or decreases "smoothly" with time. In other words, it is assumed that there are no discontinuities or turning points. This assumption would be consistent with either the initial or the last stage of the failure-rate curve shown in Figure 15.2.

A useful function that is often used to approximate such failure-rate curves is given by

$$Z(t) = \alpha\beta t^{\beta-1} \quad t > 0$$

where α and β are positive constants. Note the generality of this function: If $\beta < 1$ the failure rate *decreases* with time, if $\beta > 1$ it *increases* with time, and if $\beta = 1$ the failure rate equals α. Note that the assumption of a constant failure rate, the exponential assumption, is thus included as a special case.

If we substitute the above expression for $Z(t)$ into the formula for $f(t)$ above, we obtain

$$f(t) = \alpha\beta t^{\beta-1} e^{-\alpha t^{\beta}} \quad t > 0$$

where α and β are positive constants. This density, or distribution, is the Weibull distribution, introduced in Section 5.9, and we discuss its application to problems of life testing in Section 15.5.

15.3   The Exponential Model in Reliability

If we make the exponential assumption about the distribution of failure times, some very useful results can be derived concerning the MTBF, the mean time between failures, of series and parallel systems. In order to use the product laws of Section 15.1, we shall first have to obtain a relation expressing the reliability of a component in terms of its service time $T = t$. Making use of the fact that

$$R(t) = 1 - F(t) = 1 - \int_0^t f(x)dx$$

we obtain

$$R(t) = 1 - \int_0^t \alpha e^{-\alpha x}dx = e^{-\alpha t}$$

for the reliability function of the exponential model. Thus, if a component has a failure rate of 0.05 per thousand hours, the probability that it will survive at least 10,000 hours of operation is $e^{-(0.05)10} = 0.607$.

Suppose now that a system consists of n components connected in *series*, and that these components have the respective failure rates $\alpha_1, \alpha_2, \ldots,$ and α_n. The product law of reliabilities can be written as

Product law of reliabilities—exponential case

$$R_S(t) = \prod_{i=1}^{n} e^{-\alpha_i t} = e^{-t \sum_{i=1}^{n} \alpha_i}$$

and it can be seen that the reliability function of the series system also satisfies the exponential assumption. The failure rate of the entire series system is readily identified as $\sum_{i=1}^{n} \alpha_i$, the *sum* of the failure rates of its components. Since the MTBF is the reciprocal of the failure rate when each component which fails is replaced immediately with another having the identical failure rate, we obtain the formula

Mean time between failures—series system

$$\mu_S = \frac{1}{\dfrac{1}{\mu_1} + \dfrac{1}{\mu_2} + \cdots + \dfrac{1}{\mu_n}}$$

expressing the MTBF μ_S of a series system in terms of the MTBF's μ_i of its components. In the special case where all n components have the same failure rate α and hence the same MTBF μ, the system failure rate is $n\alpha$, and the system MTBF is $1/n\alpha = \mu/n$.

For parallel systems the results are not quite so simple. If a system consists of n components in parallel, having the respective failure rates $\alpha_1, \alpha_2, \ldots, \alpha_n$, the system "unreliability" to time t is given by

$$F_P(t) = \prod_{i=1}^{n}(1 - e^{-\alpha_i t})$$

Thus, the failure-time distribution of a parallel system is not exponential even when each of its components satisfies the exponential assumption. The system failure-rate function can be obtained by means of the formula $Z_P(t) = F'_P(t)/R_P(t)$, but the result is fairly complicated. Note, however, that the system failure rate is not constant, but depends on t, the "age" of the system.

The mean time to failure of a parallel system is also difficult to obtain in general, but in the special case where all components have the same failure rate α, an interesting and useful result can be obtained. In this special case the system reliability function becomes

$$R_P(t) = 1 - (1 - e^{-\alpha t})^n$$

$$= \binom{n}{1}e^{-\alpha t} - \binom{n}{2}e^{-2\alpha t} + \cdots + (-1)^{n-1}e^{-n\alpha t}$$

after using the binomial theorem to expand $(1 - e^{-\alpha t})^n$. Then, making use of the fact that $f_P(t) = -R'_P(t)$, we obtain

$$f_P(t) = \alpha\binom{n}{1}e^{-\alpha t} - 2\alpha\binom{n}{2}e^{-2\alpha t} + \cdots + (-1)^{n-1}n\alpha e^{-n\alpha t}$$

and the mean of the failure-time distribution is given by

$$\mu_P = \int_0^\infty t \cdot f_P(t)dt$$

$$= \alpha\binom{n}{1}\int_0^\infty te^{-\alpha t}dt - 2\alpha\binom{n}{2}\int_0^\infty te^{-2\alpha t}dt + \cdots + (-1)^{n-1}n\alpha\int_0^\infty te^{-n\alpha t}dt$$

$$= \frac{1}{\alpha}\binom{n}{1} - \frac{1}{2\alpha}\binom{n}{2} + \cdots + (-1)^{n-1}\frac{1}{n\alpha}$$

It can be proved by induction that this expression is equivalent to

Mean time between
failures—parallel
system

$$\mu_P = \frac{1}{\alpha}\left(1 + \frac{1}{2} + \cdots + \frac{1}{n}\right)$$

Thus, if a parallel system consists of n components having the identical failure rate α, the mean time between failures of the system equals $\left(1 + \dfrac{1}{2} + \cdots + \dfrac{1}{n}\right)$ times the common MTBF of its components, provided each defective component is replaced whenever the whole parallel system fails. Thus, if we use two parallel components rather than one, the mean time to failure of the pair exceeds that of the single component by 50 percent, rather than doubling it. In general, the above formula for μ_P expresses a rather severe law of diminishing returns for parallel redundancy.

The formulas derived in this section can be used in system design. To illustrate, we again consider the system diagrammed in Figure 15.1 on page 543. Assuming the exponential model and that the reliabilities are given for 10 hours of operation, we can calculate the failure rate of component A by solving the equation $0.95 = e^{-10\alpha}$ for α, and we obtain $\alpha = 5.1 \cdot 10^{-3}$ failures per hour, or 5.1 failures per thousand hours. The failure rates of all 8 components (in failures per thousand hours) are as shown in the following table:

Component	A	B	C	D	E	F	G	H
Failure rate	5.1	1.0	35.7	35.7	35.7	28.8	28.8	10.5

To compute the mean time to failure for the entire system, we first obtain the mean failure times for the parallel assemblies C, D, E, and F, G, respectively. For C, D, E we have $\mu_{CDE} = \dfrac{1}{35.7}\left(1 + \dfrac{1}{2} + \dfrac{1}{3}\right) = 0.051$ thousand hours, or 51 hours;

for F, G we have $\mu_{FG} = \dfrac{1}{28.8}\left(1 + \dfrac{1}{2}\right) = 0.052$ thousand hours, or 52 hours.

Although the two parallel assemblies do not have constant failure rates, we shall approximate their respective failure rates by $1/0.051 = 19.6$ and $1/0.052 = 19.2$ failures per thousand hours, and treat the entire system as a series system. Thus, the system failure rate is given approximately by $5.1 + 1.0 + 19.6 + 19.2 + 10.5 = 55.4$ failures per thousand hours, and the mean time to failure of the system is approximately $1/55.4 = 0.018$, or 18 hours.

EXERCISES

15.1 An old-fashioned string of holiday lights has 8 bulbs connected in series. What would have to be the reliability of each bulb if there is to be a 95% chance of the string's lighting after a year's storage?

15.2 A system consists of 5 identical components connected in parallel. What must be the reliability of each component if the overall reliability of the system is to be 0.96?

15.3 A system consists of 6 components connected as in Figure 15.3. Find the overall reliability of the system, given that the reliabilities of A, B, C, D, E, and F are, respectively, 0.95, 0.80, 0.90, 0.99, 0.90, and 0.85.

15.4 Suppose that the flight of an aircraft is regarded as a system having the three main components A (aircraft), B (pilot), and C (airport). Suppose, furthermore, that component B can be regarded as a parallel subsystem consisting of B_1 (captain), B_2 (first officer), and B_3 (flight engineer); and C is a parallel subsystem consisting of C_1 (scheduled airport) and C_2 (alternate airport). Under given flight conditions, the reliabilities of components A, B_1, B_2, B_3, C_1, and C_2 (defined as the probabilities that they can contribute to the successful completion of the scheduled flight) are, respectively, 0.9999, 0.9995, 0.999, 0.20, 0.95, and 0.85.

(a) What is the reliability of the system?

(b) What is the effect on system reliability of having a flight engineer who is also a trained pilot, so that the reliability of B_3 is increased from 0.20 to 0.99?

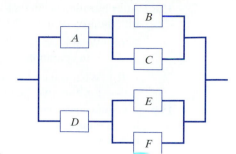

Figure 15.3
Exercise 15.3.

(c) If the flight crew did not have a first officer, what then would be the effect of increasing the reliability of B_3 from 0.20 to 0.99?

(d) What is the effect of adding a second alternate landing point, C_3, with reliability 0.80?

15.5 In some reliability problems we are concerned only with initial failures, treating a component as if (for all practical purposes) it never fails, once it has survived past a certain time $t = \alpha$. In a problem like this, it may be reasonable to use the failure rate

$$Z(t) = \begin{cases} \beta\left(1 - \dfrac{t}{\alpha}\right) & \text{for } 0 < t < \alpha \\ 0 & \text{elsewhere} \end{cases}$$

(a) Find expressions for $f(t)$ and $F(t)$.

(b) Show that the probability of an initial failure is given by

$$1 - e^{-\alpha\beta/2}$$

15.6 As has been indicated in the text, one often distinguishes between initial failures, random failures during the useful life of the product, and wear-out failures. Thus, suppose that for a given product the probability of an initial failure (a failure prior to time $t = \alpha$) is θ_1, the probability of a wear-out failure (a failure beyond time $t = \beta$) is θ_2, and that for the interval $\alpha \leq t \leq \beta$ the failure-time density is given by

$$f(t) = \frac{1 - \theta_1 - \theta_2}{\beta - \alpha}$$

(a) Find an expression for $F(t)$ for the interval $\alpha \leq t \leq \beta$.

(b) Show that for the interval $\alpha \leq t \leq \beta$. the failure rate is given by

$$Z(t) = \frac{1 - \theta_1 - \theta_2}{(\beta - \alpha)(1 - \theta_1) - (1 - \theta_1 - \theta_2)(t - \alpha)}$$

(c) Suppose that the failure of a digital television set is considered to be an initial failure if it occurs during the first 100 hours of usage and a wear-out failure if it occurs after 15,000 hours. Assuming that the model given in this exercise holds and that θ_1 and θ_2 equal 0.05 and 0.75, respectively, sketch the graph of the failure-rate function from $t = 100$ to $t = 15,000$ hours.

15.7 An integrated-circuit chip has a constant failure rate of 0.02 per thousand hours.

(a) What is the probability that it will operate satisfactorily for at least 20,000 hours?

(b) What is the 5,000-hour reliability of a component consisting of 4 such chips connected in series?

15.8   After burn-in, the lifetime of a solar cell is modeled as an exponential distribution with failure rate $\alpha = 0.0005$ failures per day.

(a) What is the probability that the cell will fail within the first 365 days that it is in operation?

(b) What is the probability that two such cells, operating independently, will both survive the first 365 days they are in operation?

15.9   A system consisting of several identical components connected in parallel is to have a failure rate of at most 4×10^{-4} per hour. What is the least number of components that must be used if each has a constant failure rate of 9×10^{-4}?

15.10   A system consists of 4 different components connected in series. Find the MTBF of the system if the 4 components have exponential time-to-failure distributions with failure rates 1.9, 3.1, 1.4, and 2.2 per 10,000 hours, respectively.

15.11   A certain part has an exponential life distribution with a mean life, that is an MTBF, of 1,000 hours.

(a) What is the probability that such a part will last at least 500 hours?

(b) What is the probability that among 3 such parts at least 1 will fail during the first 1,000 hours?

(c) What is the probability that among 4 such parts exactly 2 will fail during the first 600 hours?

15.12   If a component has the Weibull failure-time distribution with the parameters $\alpha = 0.005$ per hour and $\beta = 0.80$, find the probability that it will operate successfully for at least 5,000 hours.

15.13   Throughout Sections 15.2 and 15.3 we assumed that the products with which we were concerned were in continuous operation. Consequently, the models discussed in these sections do not apply if we want to investigate the ability of light bulbs to withstand successive voltage overloads, the performance of switches which are repeatedly turned on and off, etc. In each of these cases failure can occur on the xth trial ($x = 1, 2, 3, \ldots$), and it is often assumed that the probability of failure on the xth trial equals some constant p, provided the item has not failed prior to that trial.

(a) Show that the probability of failure on the xth trial is given by

$$f(x) = p(1 - p)^{x-1}$$

for $x = 1, 2, 3, \ldots$. This probability distribution is the *geometric distribution* introduced in Section 4.8.

(b) Find $F(x)$ for the probability distribution obtained in part (a).

(c) What is the probability that a switch will survive 2,000 cycles of operation if the preceding model holds and the constant probability of failure as the result of any one of the switching cycles is $p = 6 \times 10^{-4}$?

15.4   The Exponential Model in Life Testing

An effective and widely used method of handling problems of reliability is that of **life testing.** For the purpose of such tests, a random sample of n components is selected from a lot, put on test under specified environmental conditions, and the times to failure of the individual components are observed. If each component that fails is immediately replaced by a new one, the resulting life test is called a **re-**

placement test; otherwise, the life test is called a **nonreplacement test.** Whenever the mean lifetime of the components is so large that it is not practical, or economically feasible, to test each component to failure, the life test may be **truncated,** that is, it may be terminated after the first r failures have occurred ($r \leq n$), or after a fixed period of time has elapsed.

A special method that is often used when early results are required in connection with very-high-reliability components is that of **accelerated life testing.** In an accelerated life test the components are put on test under environmental conditions that are far more severe than those normally encountered in practice. This causes the components to fail more quickly, and it can drastically reduce both the time required for the test and the number of components that must be placed on test. Accelerated life testing can be used to compare two or more types of components for the purpose of obtaining a rapid assessment of which is the most reliable. Sometimes, preliminary experimentation is carried out to determine the relationship between the proportion of failures that can be expected under nominal conditions and under various levels of accelerated environmental conditions. The methods of Sections 11.4 and 13.2 can be applied in this connection to determine "derating curves," relating the reliability of the component to the severity of the environmental conditions under which it is to operate.

In the remainder of this section we shall assume that the exponential model holds, namely, that the failure-time distribution of each component is given by

$$f(t) = \alpha \cdot e^{-\alpha t} \quad t > 0, \alpha > 0$$

In what follows, we shall assume that n components are put on test, life testing is discontinued after a fixed number, $r (r \leq n)$, of components have failed, and that the observed failure times are $t_1 \leq t_2 \leq \cdots \leq t_r$. We shall be concerned with estimating and testing hypotheses about the mean life of the component, namely, $\mu = 1/\alpha$.

Using theory developed in the article by B. Epstein mentioned in the bibliography, it can be shown that unbiased estimates of the mean life of the component are given by

Estimate of mean life

$$\hat{\mu} = \frac{T_r}{r}$$

where T_r is the accumulated life on test until the rth failure occurs, and hence

Accumulated life to r failures— nonreplacement test

$$T_r = \sum_{i=1}^{r} t_i + (n - r)t_r$$

for nonreplacement tests and

Accumulated life to r failures—replacement test

$$T_r = nt_r$$

if the test is with replacement. Note that if the test is without replacement and $r = n$, $\hat{\mu}$ is simply the mean of the observed times to failure.

To make inferences concerning the mean life μ of the component, we use the fact that $2T_r/\mu$ is a value of a random variable having the chi-square distribution with $2r$ degrees of freedom (see reference to B. Epstein in the bibliography). With the appropriate expression substituted for T_r, this is true regardless of whether the test is conducted with or without replacement. Thus, in either case a two-sided $(1 - \alpha)100\%$ confidence interval for μ is given by

Confidence interval for mean life

$$\frac{2T_r}{\chi^2_{\alpha/2}} < \mu < \frac{2T_r}{\chi^2_{1-\alpha/2}}$$

where $\chi^2_{1-\alpha/2}$ and $\chi^2_{\alpha/2}$ cut off left- and right-hand tails of area $\alpha/2$ under the chi-square distribution with $2r$ degrees of freedom. (See Exercise 15.19.)

Tests of the null hypothesis that $\mu = \mu_0$ can also be based on the sampling distribution of $2T_r/\mu$, using the appropriate expression for T_r depending on whether the test is with or without replacement. Thus, if the alternative hypothesis is $\mu > \mu_0$, we reject the null hypothesis at the level of significance α when $2T_r/\mu_0$ exceeds χ^2_α, or

Critical region for testing $H_0: \mu = \mu_0$ against $H_1: \mu > \mu_0$

$$T_r > \frac{1}{2}\mu_0\chi^2_\alpha$$

where χ^2_α, to be determined for $2r$ degrees of freedom, is as defined on page 215. In Exercises 15.14 and 15.17 the reader is asked to construct and perform similar tests corresponding to the alternative hypotheses $\mu < \mu_0$ and $\mu \neq \mu_0$.

An alternate life-testing procedure consists of discontinuing the test after a fixed accumulated amount of lifetime T has elapsed and treating the observed number of failures k as the value of a random variable. In the important special case where n items are tested with replacement for a length of time t^*, we have $T = nt^*$. Regardless of whether the test is with or without replacement, an *approximate* $(1 - \alpha)100\%$ confidence interval for the mean life of the component is given by

$$\frac{2T}{\chi^2_2} < \mu < \frac{2T}{\chi^2_1}$$

Here χ^2_2 cuts off a right-hand tail of area $\alpha/2$ under the chi-square distribution with $2k + 2$ degrees of freedom, while χ^2_1 cuts off a left-hand tail of area $\alpha/2$ under the chi-square distribution with $2k$ degrees of freedom.

EXAMPLE

Obtaining a confidence interval for mean life

Suppose that 50 units are placed on life test (without replacement) and the test is to be truncated after $r = 10$ of them have failed. We shall suppose, furthermore, that the first 10 failure times are 65, 110, 380, 420, 505, 580, 650, 840, 910, and 950 hours. Estimate the mean life of the component, and its failure rate, and calculate a 90% confidence interval for μ.

Solution   Since $n = 50, r = 10$,

$$T_{10} = (65 + 110 + \cdots + 950) + (50 - 10)950$$

$$= 43,410 \text{ hours}$$

We estimate the mean life of the component as $\hat{\mu} = \dfrac{43,410}{10} = 4,341$ hours. The failure rate α is estimated by $1/\hat{\mu} = 0.00023$ failure per hour, or 0.23 failure per thousand hours. Using $\chi^2_{0.05} = 31.410$ and $\chi^2_{0.95} = 10.851$ for $2(10) = 20$ degrees of freedom, a 90% confidence interval for μ is given by

$$\frac{2(43,410)}{31.410} < \mu < \frac{2(43,410)}{10.851}$$

or

$$2,764 < \mu < 8,001 \qquad\qquad ✔$$

EXAMPLE   **Testing hypotheses concerning mean life**
Using the data of the preceding example, test whether the failure rate is 0.40 failure per thousand hours against the alternative that the failure rate is less. Use the 0.05 level of significance.

Solution

1. *Null hypothesis:* $\mu = \dfrac{1,000}{0.40} = 2,500$ hours

   Alternative hypothesis: $\mu > 2,500$ hours

2. *Level of significance:* $\alpha = 0.05$

3. *Criterion:* Reject the null hypothesis if $T_r > \frac{1}{2}\mu_0\chi^2_{0.05}$ where $\chi^2_{0.05} = 31.410$ is the value of $\chi^2_{0.05}$ having $2r = 20$ degrees of freedom.

4. *Calculations:* Substituting $\chi^2_{0.05} = 31.410$ and $\mu_0 = 2,500$, we find the critical value for this test to be

$$\tfrac{1}{2}\mu_0\chi^2_{0.05} = \tfrac{1}{2}(2,500)(31.410) = 39,263$$

5. *Decision:* Since $T_{10} = 43,410$ exceeds the critical value, we must reject the null hypothesis, concluding that the mean life-time exceeds 2,500 hours, or, equivalently, that the failure rate is less than 0.40 failure per thousand hours. ✔

Because of the simplicity of the statistical procedures, the exponential model is frequently considered. Before making inferences, it is imperative that this model be checked for adequacy. We recommend making a **total time on test plot.** Plot the total time on test until the ith failure, T_i, divided by the total time on test through the last (rth) observed failure, against i/r. If the population is exponential, we would expect to see a straight line along the 45-degree line. When this straight-line pattern occurs, we conclude that no violations of the exponential model are evident over the range of failure times. If the plot is a curve above the 45-degree line, the evidence favors an increasing hazard rate model.

We illustrate the total time on test plot using the data of the example on page 552. For $t_1 = 65$, we calculate the total time on test

$$T_1 = 65 + (50 - 1)65 = 3{,}250$$

Next, for $t_2 = 110$,

$$T_2 = 65 + 110 + (50 - 2)110 = 5{,}455$$

Continuing, we obtain all the values

3,250	5,455	18,415	20,295	24,205
27,580	30,660	38,830	41,770	43,410

so the total time on test until the last, $r = 10$, failure is $T_r = 43{,}410$. The first ratio $T_1/T_{10} = 3{,}250/43{,}410 = 0.0749$ is plotted against $1/10 = 0.10$. The ratios for all 10 failures are plotted in Figure 15.4. Over the range of failure times observed, the plot does not exhibit any marked departures from the assumed exponential model.

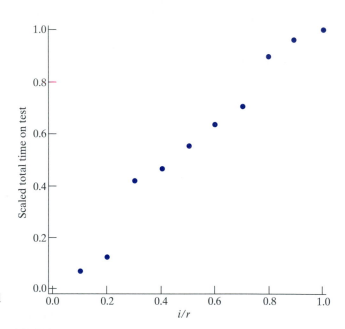

Figure 15.4 The total time on test plot.

15.5 The Weibull Model in Life Testing

Although life testing of components during the period of useful life is generally based on the exponential model, we have already pointed out that the failure rate of a component may not be constant throughout a period under investigation. In some instances the period of initial failure may be so long that the component's main use is during this period. However, the main purpose of most life testing is to determine the time to wear-out failure rather than chance failure of a critical component in a complex system. In such cases the exponential model generally does not apply, and it is necessary to substitute a more general assumption for that of a constant failure rate.

As we observed earlier, the Weibull distribution may adequately describe the failure times of components when their failure rate either increases or decreases with time. It has the parameters α and β and its formula is given by

Weibull distribution

$$f(t) = \alpha\beta t^{\beta-1}e^{-\alpha t^{\beta}} \qquad t > 0, \alpha > 0, \beta > 0$$

and it follows (see Exercise 15.24) that the reliability function associated with the **Weibull failure-time distribution** is given by

Weibull reliability function

$$R(t) = e^{-\alpha t^{\beta}}$$

We already showed on page 545 that the failure rate leading to the Weibull distribution is given by

Weibull failure-rate function

$$Z(t) = \alpha\beta t^{\beta-1}$$

The range of shapes a graph of the Weibull density can take on is very broad, depending primarily on the value of the parameter β. As illustrated in Figure 15.5, the Weibull curve is asymptotic to both axes and highly skewed to the right for

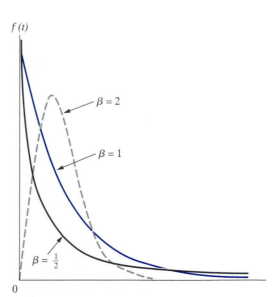

Figure 15.5 Weibull density functions ($\alpha = 1$).

values of β less than 1; it is identical to that of the exponential density for $\beta = 1$, and it is "bell-shaped" but skewed for values of β greater than 1.

The mean of the Weibull distribution having the parameters α and β may be obtained by evaluating the integral

$$\mu = \int_0^\infty t \cdot \alpha\beta t^{\beta-1} e^{-\alpha t^\beta} dt$$

Making the change of variable $u = \alpha t^\beta$, we get

$$\mu = \alpha^{-1/\beta} \int_0^\infty u^{1/\beta} e^{-u} du$$

Recognizing the integral as $\Gamma\left(1 + \dfrac{1}{\beta}\right)$, we find that the mean time to failure for the Weibull model is

Mean time to failure—Weibull model

$$\mu = \alpha^{-1/\beta} \Gamma\left(1 + \frac{1}{\beta}\right)$$

The reader will be asked to show in Exercise 15.25 that the variance of this distribution is given by

Variance of Weibull model

$$\sigma^2 = \alpha^{-2/\beta} \left\{ \Gamma\left(1 + \frac{2}{\beta}\right) - \left[\Gamma\left(1 + \frac{1}{\beta}\right)\right]^2 \right\}$$

Estimates of the parameters α and β of the Weibull distribution are somewhat difficult to obtain. The most widely accepted approach, the *maximum likelihood* method (see Exercise 7.25), maximizes the likelihood. Because the partial derivatives with respect to α and β must vanish at the maximum, the method selects the solution to these two equations as the estimates of α and β. If the lifetimes are **censored** at the rth failure, or uncensored so $r = n$, the equations are

$$\frac{\sum_{i=1}^r t_i^\beta \ln t_i + (n-r)t_r^\beta \ln t_r}{\sum_{i=1}^r t_i^\beta + (n-r)t_r^\beta} - \frac{1}{\beta} - \frac{1}{r}\sum_{i=1}^r \ln t_i = 0$$

$$\alpha = \frac{1}{\frac{1}{r}\left[\sum_{i=1}^r t_i^\beta + (n-r)t_r^\beta\right]}$$

The first equation is solved for $\hat{\beta}$ by numerical techniques. Then the second yields the estimate of $\hat{\alpha}$. These are easy computer calculations.

If the lifetimes are time censored at time T_0, the terms with a factor $n - r$ are modified by replacing each t_r by T_0.

A graphical method provides a check on the adequacy of the Weibull model. This method is based on the fact that the reliability function of the Weibull distribution can be transformed into a linear function of $\ln t$ by means of a double-logarithmic transformation. Taking the natural logarithm of $R(t)$, we obtain

$$\ln R(t) = -\alpha t^{\beta} \quad \text{or} \quad \ln \frac{1}{R(t)} = \alpha t^{\beta}$$

Again taking logarithms, we have

$$\ln \ln \frac{1}{R(t)} = \ln \alpha + \beta \, \ln t$$

and it can be seen that the right-hand side is linear in $\ln t$.

The usual experimental procedure is to place n units on life test and observe their failure times. If the ith unit fails at time t_i, we estimate $F(t_i) = 1 - R(t_i)$ by the same method used for the normal-scores plot on page 188, namely,

$$\widehat{F(t_i)} = \frac{i}{n+1}$$

To construct a **Weibull plot,** we plot $\ln \ln \dfrac{1}{1 - \widehat{F(t_1)}}$ versus $\ln t_i$. If the points fall reasonably close to a straight line, it can reasonably be assumed that the underlying failure-time distribution is of the Weibull type.

A sample of 100 components is put on life test for 500 hours and the times to failure of the 12 components that failed during the test are as follows: 6, 21, 50, 84, 95, 130, 205, 260, 270, 370, 440, and 480 hours. Setting

$$x_i = \ln t_i$$

$$y_i = \ln \ln \frac{1}{1 - \widehat{F(t_i)}}$$

we obtain

$\widehat{F(t_i)}$	t_i	x_i	y_i
0.010	6	1.79	−4.61
0.020	21	3.04	−3.91
0.030	50	3.91	−3.50
0.040	84	4.43	−3.21
0.050	95	4.55	−2.98
0.059	130	4.87	−2.79
0.069	205	5.32	−2.63
0.079	260	5.56	−2.49
0.089	270	5.60	−2.37
0.099	370	5.91	−2.26
0.109	440	6.09	−2.16
0.119	480	6.17	−2.07

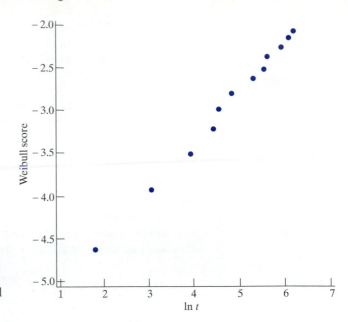

Figure 15.6 A Weibull plot of failure times.

The points (x_i, y_i) are plotted in Figure 15.6, and it can be seen that they fall fairly close to a straight line. After checking the adequacy of the Weibull distribution, we obtain the maximum likelihood estimators defined on page 556. Our computer calculations yield $\hat{\alpha} = 0.001505$ and $\hat{\beta} = 0.7148$. It follows that the mean time to failure is estimated as

$$\hat{\mu} = (0.001505)^{-1/0.7148}\,\Gamma\!\left(1 + \frac{1}{0.7148}\right)$$

which equals approximately 11,000 hours. Also, values of the failure-rate function may be obtained by substituting for t into

$$\widehat{Z(t)} = (0.001505)(0.7148)\,t^{0.7148-1} = 0.00108t^{-0.2852}$$

Since $\hat{\beta} < 1$, the failure rate is decreasing with time. After 1 hour ($t = 1$), units are failing at the rate of 0.00108 unit per hour, and after 1,000 hours the failure rate has decreased to $0.00108(1000)^{-0.2852} = 0.00015$ unit per hour.

EXERCISES

15.14 Suppose that 50 units are put on life test, each unit that fails is immediately replaced, and the test is discontinued after 8 units have failed. If the eighth failure occurred at 760 hours, assuming an exponential model,

(a) construct a 95% confidence interval for the mean life of such units;

(b) test at the 0.05 level of significance whether or not the mean life is less than 10,000 hours.

15.15 In a life test with replacement, 35 space heaters were put into continuous operation, and the first 5 failures occurred after 250, 380, 610, 980, and 1,250 hours.

    (a) Assuming the exponential model, construct a 99% confidence interval for the mean life of this kind of space heater.

    (b) To check the manufacturer's claim that the mean life of these heaters is at least 5,000 hours, test the null hypothesis $\mu = 5,000$ against an appropriate alternative, so that the burden of proof is put on the manufacturer. Use $\alpha = 0.05$.

15.16 With reference to the data in Exercise 15.15, make a total time on test plot.

15.17 To investigate the average time to failure of a certain weld subjected to continuous vibration, 7 welded pieces were subjected to specified frequencies and amplitudes of vibration and their times to failure were 211, 350, 384, 510, 539, 620, and 715 thousand cycles.

    (a) Assuming the exponential model, construct a 95% confidence interval for the mean life (in thousands of cycles) of such a weld under the given vibration conditions.

    (b) Assuming the exponential model, test the null hypothesis that the mean life of the weld under the given vibration conditions is 500,000 cycles against the two-sided alternative $\mu \neq 500,000$. Use the level of significance 0.10.

15.18 In life testing we are sometimes interested in establishing tolerance limits for the life of a component (see Section 14.7); in particular, we may be interested in a one-sided tolerance limit t^*, for which we can assert with a $(1 - \alpha)100\%$ confidence that at least $100 \cdot P$ percent of the components have a life exceeding t^*. Using the exponential model, it can be shown that a good approximation is given by

$$t^* = \frac{-2T_r(\ln P)}{\chi_\alpha^2}$$

where T_r is as defined on page 551 and the value of χ_α^2 is to be obtained from Table 5 with $2r$ degrees of freedom.

    (a) Using the data of Exercise 15.15, establish a lower tolerance limit for which one can assert with 95% confidence that it is exceeded by at least 80% of the lifetimes of the heaters.

    (b) Using the data of Exercise 15.17, establish a lower tolerance limit for which one can assert with 99% confidence that it is exceeded by at least 90% of the lifetimes of the given welds.

15.19 Using the fact that $2T_r/\mu$ is a value of a random variable having the chi-square distribution with $2r$ degrees of freedom, derive the confidence interval for μ given on page 552.

15.20 One hundred devices are put on life test and the times to failure (in hours) of the first 10 that fail are as follows: 7.0, 14.1, 18.9, 31.6, 52.8, 80.0, 164.5, 355.4, 451.0, and 795.1. Assuming a Weibull failure-time distribution, estimate the parameters α and β as well as the failure rate at 1,000 hours. How does this value of the failure rate compare with the value we would obtain if we assumed the exponential model?

15.21 A sample of 200 switches was placed on life test for 3000 on-off cycles and there were no failures; the test was then terminated. Find a 95% *lower* confidence limit for the mean life, in number of cycles, of the switches. Use the exponential model.

15.22 A sample of 60 diaphragm valves, used in the control system of a chemical process, are placed on life test (without replacement). The first 9 failures are observed after

3.6, 6.9, 9.5, 15.7, 27.3, 41.2, 81.7, 178.3, and 227.1 hours. Using the Weibull model, estimate the mean life of this valve. How does this value compare with the mean life that would have been obtained under the exponential assumption?

15.23 Using the estimates of the parameters of the Weibull model obtained in Exercise 15.22, estimate the probability that this kind of diaphragm valve will perform satisfactorily for at least 150 hours.

15.24 Show that the reliability function associated with the Weibull failure-time distribution is given by

$$R(t) = e^{-\alpha t^\beta}$$

15.25 Derive the formula for the variance of the Weibull distribution given on page 556.

REVIEW EXERCISES

15.26 A system consists of 7 identical components connected in parallel. What must be the reliability of each component if the overall reliability of the system is to be 0.90?

15.27 A certain component has an exponential life distribution with a failure rate of $\alpha = 0.0045$ failures per hour.

(a) What is the probability that the component will fail during the first 250 hours it is in operation?

(b) What is the probability that two such components will both survive the first 100 hours of operation?

15.28 A system containing several identical components in parallel is to have a failure rate of at most $5 \cdot 10^{-5}$ per hour. What is the least number of components that must be used if each has a constant failure rate of $2.0 \cdot 10^{-4}$ per hour?

15.29 A system consists of 6 different components connected in series. Find the MTBF of the system if the 6 components have exponential time-to-failure distributions with failure rates of 1.8, 2.4, 2.0, 1.3, 3.0, and 1.5 per 1,000 hours, respectively.

15.30 Fifteen assemblies are put on accelerated life test without replacement, and the test is truncated after 4 failures. If the first 4 failures occurred at 16.5, 19.2, 20.8, and 37.3 hours, assuming an exponential model,

(a) find a 90% confidence interval for the failure rate of such assemblies under these accelerated conditions;

(b) test the null hypothesis that the failure rate is 0.004 failure per hour against the alternative that it is less than 0.004, using the 0.01 level of significance.

15.31 A sample of 300 high-reliability capacitors was placed on life test for 2,000 hours and there were no failures; the test was then terminated. Find a 95% *lower* confidence limit for the mean life of the capacitors assuming an exponential model.

15.32 To investigate the performance of a logic circuit for a small electronic calculator, a laboratory puts 75 of the circuits on life test (without replacement) under specified environmental conditions, and the first 10 failures are observed after 28, 46, 50, 63, 81, 101, 116, 137, 159, and 175 hours. Using the Weibull model, estimate the mean life of such a circuit. How does this value compare with the mean life that would have been obtained under the exponential assumption?

15.33 Using the estimates of the parameters of the Weibull model obtained in Exercise 15.32, estimate the probability that this kind of circuit will perform satisfactorily for at least 100 hours.

15.34 With reference to Exercise 15.32, make

(a) a total time on test plot;

(b) a Weibull plot.

15.35 (*Stress-strength models for reliability*) An alternative model used in reliability treats the environmental stress as a random variable X and the strength of the component to withstand this stress as an independent random variable Y. Then, the reliability is defined as

$$R = P[Y > X] = \int_{-\infty}^{\infty} \int_{-\infty}^{y} f(x, y)dxdy = \int_{-\infty}^{\infty} F(y)g(y)dy$$

where $F(x)$ is the distribution function of X and $g(y)$ is the probability density of Y. Evaluate this reliability when

(a) X has an exponential distribution with $\alpha = 0.01$ and Y has an exponential distribution with failure rate 0.005;

(b) X has an exponential distribution with $\alpha = 0.005$ and Y has an exponential distribution with failure rate 0.005;

(c) $\ln X$ has a normal distribution with $\mu = 60$ and $\sigma = 5$ and $\ln Y$ has a normal distribution with $\mu = 80$ and $\sigma = 5$.

KEY TERMS

(with page references)

Bibliography

1. Engineering Statistics

GUTTMAN, I., WILKS, S. S., AND HUNTER, J.S., *Introductory Engineering Statistics*, 3d ed. New York: John Wiley & Sons, Inc., 1982.

WALPOLE, R.E., AND MYERS, R.H., *Probability and Statistics for Engineers and Scientists*, 3d ed. New York: Macmillian Publishing Company, 1985.

2. Theoretical Statistics

FREUND, J. E., *Mathematical Statistics*, 5th ed. Englewood Cliffs, N.J.: Prentice-Hall, Inc., 1992

HOGG, R.V., AND CRAIG, A.T., *Introduction to Mathematical Statistics*, 4th ed. New York: Macmillian Publishing Company, 1978.

MOOD, A. M., GRAYBILL, F.A., AND BOES, D.C., *Introduction to the Theory of Statistics*, 3d ed. New York: McGraw-Hill Book Company, 1973.

3. Experimental Design and Analysis of Variance

BOX, G. E. P., HUNTER, W.G., AND HUNTER, J.S., *Statistics for Experimenters*. New York: John Wiley & Sons, Inc., 1978.

COCHRAN, W. G., AND COX, G. M., *Experimental Designs*, 2d ed. New York: John Wiley & Sons, Inc., 1957.

SCHEFFE, H., *The Analysis of Variance*. New York: John Wiley & Sons, Inc., 1959.

4. Quality Improvement and Assurance

DEMING, W. E., *Out of the Crisis.* Cambridge, Mass.: MIT, 1986.

DUNCAN, A. J., *Quality Control and Industrial Statistics*, 5th ed. Homewood, Ill.: Richard D. Irwin, Inc., 1986.

ISHIKAWA, K., *Guide to Quaility Control*. Tokyo: Asian Productivity Organization, 1976.

TAGUCHI, G., AND WU, Y., *Introduction to Off-Line Quality Control*. Nagoya, Japan: Central Japan Quality Control Association.

5. Special Topics

BARLOW, R. E., AND PROSCHAN, F., S*tatistical Theory of Reliability and Life Testing: Probability Models*. New York: Holt, Rinehart and Winston, 1975.

BOX, G. E. P., AND DRAPER, N.R., *Empirical Model-Building and Response Surfaces*. New York: John Wiley & Sons, Inc., 1987.

GUTTMAN, I., *Statistical Tolerance Regions: Classical and Bayesian.* Darien, Conn.: Hafner, 1970.

JOHNSON, R. A., AND WICHERN, D. W., *Applied Multivariate Statistical Analysis*, 4th ed. Engelwood Cliffs, NJ: Prentice-Hall, Inc., 1998.

KALBFLEISCH, J. D., AND PRENTICE, R. L., *The Statistical Analysis of Failure Time Data.* New York: John Wiley & Sons, Inc., 1980.

LAWLESS, J. F., *Statistical Models and Methods for Lifetime Data.* New York: John Wiley & Sons, Inc., 1981.

MILLER, R. G., JR., *Survival Analysis.* New York: John Wiley & Sons, Inc., 1981.

NELSON, W., *Applied Life Data Analysis.* New York: John Wiley & Sons, Inc., 1981.

WALD, A., *Sequential Analysis.* New York: John Wiley & Sons, Inc., 1947.

6. General Reference Works and Tables

JOHNSON, R. A., AND BHATTACHARYYA, G. K., *Statistics: Principles and Methods*, 3rd ed. New York: John Wiley & Sons, Inc., 1996.

KOTZ, S., AND JOHNSON, N. L., *Encyclopedia of Statistical Sciences,* Vol. 2. New York: John Wiley & Sons, Inc., 1982.

Military Standard 105D. Washington, D.C.: U.S. Government Printing Office, 1963.

National Bureau of Standards Handbook 91: Experimental Statistics. Washington, D.C.: U.S. Government Printing Office, 1950.

PEARSON, E. S., AND HARTLEY, H. O., *Biometrika Tables for Statisticians*, 3d ed. Cambridge: Cambridge University Press, 1966.

RAND CORPORATION, *A Million Random Digits with 100,000 Normal Deviates.* New York: Macmillian Publishing Company, third printing 1966.

ROMIG, H. G., *50–100 Binomial Tables.* New York: John Wiley & Sons, Inc., 1953.

Statistical Tables

APPENDIX B

TABLE 1 Binomial Distribution Function

$$B(x; n, p) = \sum_{k=0}^{x} \binom{n}{k} p^k (1 - p)^{n-k}$$

n	x	p																		
		0.05	0.10	0.15	0.20	0.25	0.30	0.35	0.40	0.45	0.50	0.55	0.60	0.65	0.70	0.75	0.80	0.85	0.90	0.95
2	0	0.9025	0.8100	0.7225	0.6400	0.5625	0.4900	0.4225	0.3600	0.3025	0.2500	0.2025	0.1600	0.1225	0.0900	0.0625	0.0400	0.0225	0.0100	0.0025
	1	0.9975	0.9900	0.9775	0.9600	0.9375	0.9100	0.8775	0.8400	0.7975	0.7500	0.6975	0.6400	0.5775	0.5100	0.4375	0.3600	0.2775	0.1900	0.0975
3	0	0.8574	0.7290	0.6141	0.5120	0.4219	0.3430	0.2746	0.2160	0.1664	0.1250	0.0911	0.0640	0.0429	0.0270	0.0156	0.0080	0.0034	0.0010	0.0001
	1	0.9927	0.9720	0.9393	0.8960	0.8438	0.7840	0.7183	0.6480	0.5748	0.5000	0.4252	0.3520	0.2818	0.2160	0.1563	0.1040	0.0607	0.0280	0.0073
	2	0.9999	0.9990	0.9966	0.9920	0.9844	0.9730	0.9571	0.9360	0.9089	0.8750	0.8336	0.7840	0.7254	0.6570	0.5781	0.4880	0.3859	0.2710	0.1426
4	0	0.8145	0.6561	0.5220	0.4096	0.3164	0.2401	0.1785	0.1296	0.0915	0.0625	0.0410	0.0256	0.0150	0.0081	0.0039	0.0016	0.0005	0.0001	0.0000
	1	0.9860	0.9477	0.8905	0.8192	0.7383	0.6517	0.5630	0.4752	0.3910	0.3125	0.2415	0.1792	0.1265	0.0837	0.0508	0.0272	0.0120	0.0037	0.0005
	2	0.9995	0.9963	0.9880	0.9728	0.9492	0.9163	0.8735	0.8208	0.7585	0.6875	0.6090	0.5248	0.4370	0.3483	0.2617	0.1808	0.1095	0.0523	0.0140
	3	1.0000	0.9999	0.9995	0.9984	0.9961	0.9919	0.9850	0.9744	0.9590	0.9375	0.9085	0.8704	0.8215	0.7599	0.6836	0.5904	0.4780	0.3439	0.1855
5	0	0.7738	0.5905	0.4437	0.3277	0.2373	0.1681	0.1160	0.0778	0.0503	0.0313	0.0185	0.0102	0.0053	0.0024	0.0010	0.0003	0.0001	0.0000	0.0000
	1	0.9774	0.9185	0.8352	0.7373	0.6328	0.5282	0.4284	0.3370	0.2562	0.1875	0.1312	0.0870	0.0540	0.0308	0.0156	0.0067	0.0022	0.0005	0.0000
	2	0.9988	0.9914	0.9734	0.9421	0.8965	0.8369	0.7648	0.6826	0.5931	0.5000	0.4069	0.3174	0.2352	0.1631	0.1035	0.0579	0.0266	0.0086	0.0012
	3	1.0000	0.9995	0.9978	0.9933	0.9844	0.9692	0.9460	0.9130	0.8688	0.8125	0.7438	0.6630	0.5716	0.4718	0.3672	0.2627	0.1648	0.0815	0.0226
	4	1.0000	1.0000	0.9999	0.9997	0.9990	0.9976	0.9947	0.9898	0.9815	0.9688	0.9497	0.9222	0.8840	0.8319	0.7627	0.6723	0.5563	0.4095	0.2262
6	0	0.7351	0.5314	0.3771	0.2621	0.1780	0.1176	0.0754	0.0467	0.0277	0.0156	0.0083	0.0041	0.0018	0.0007	0.0002	0.0001	0.0000	0.0000	0.0000
	1	0.9672	0.8857	0.7765	0.6554	0.5339	0.4202	0.3191	0.2333	0.1636	0.1094	0.0692	0.0410	0.0223	0.0109	0.0046	0.0016	0.0004	0.0001	0.0000
	2	0.9978	0.9841	0.9527	0.9011	0.8306	0.7443	0.6471	0.5443	0.4415	0.3438	0.2553	0.1792	0.1174	0.0705	0.0376	0.0170	0.0059	0.0013	0.0001
	3	0.9999	0.9987	0.9941	0.9830	0.9624	0.9295	0.8826	0.8208	0.7447	0.6563	0.5585	0.4557	0.3529	0.2557	0.1694	0.0989	0.0473	0.0158	0.0022
	4	1.0000	0.9999	0.9996	0.9984	0.9954	0.9891	0.9777	0.9590	0.9308	0.8906	0.8364	0.7667	0.6809	0.5798	0.4661	0.3446	0.2235	0.1143	0.0328
	5	1.0000	1.0000	1.0000	0.9999	0.9998	0.9993	0.9982	0.9959	0.9917	0.9844	0.9723	0.9533	0.9246	0.8824	0.8220	0.7379	0.6229	0.4686	0.2649
7	0	0.6983	0.4783	0.3206	0.2097	0.1335	0.0824	0.0490	0.0280	0.0152	0.0078	0.0037	0.0016	0.0006	0.0002	0.0001	0.0000	0.0000	0.0000	0.0000
	1	0.9556	0.8503	0.7166	0.5767	0.4449	0.3294	0.2338	0.1586	0.1024	0.0625	0.0357	0.0188	0.0090	0.0038	0.0013	0.0004	0.0001	0.0000	0.0000
	2	0.9962	0.9743	0.9262	0.8520	0.7564	0.6471	0.5323	0.4199	0.3164	0.2266	0.1529	0.0963	0.0556	0.0288	0.0129	0.0047	0.0012	0.0002	0.0000
	3	0.9998	0.9973	0.9879	0.9667	0.9294	0.8740	0.8002	0.7102	0.6083	0.5000	0.3917	0.2898	0.1998	0.1260	0.0706	0.0333	0.0121	0.0027	0.0002
	4	1.0000	0.9998	0.9988	0.9953	0.9871	0.9712	0.9444	0.9037	0.8471	0.7734	0.6836	0.5801	0.4677	0.3529	0.2436	0.1480	0.0738	0.0257	0.0038
	5	1.0000	1.0000	0.9999	0.9996	0.9987	0.9962	0.9910	0.9812	0.9643	0.9375	0.8976	0.8414	0.7662	0.6706	0.5551	0.4233	0.2834	0.1497	0.0444
	6	1.0000	1.0000	1.0000	1.0000	0.9999	0.9998	0.9994	0.9984	0.9963	0.9922	0.9848	0.9720	0.9510	0.9176	0.8665	0.7903	0.6794	0.5217	0.3017
8	0	0.6634	0.4305	0.2725	0.1678	0.1001	0.0576	0.0319	0.0168	0.0084	0.0039	0.0017	0.0007	0.0002	0.0001	0.0000	0.0000	0.0000	0.0000	0.0000
	1	0.9428	0.8131	0.6572	0.5033	0.3671	0.2553	0.1691	0.1064	0.0632	0.0352	0.0181	0.0085	0.0036	0.0013	0.0004	0.0001	0.0000	0.0000	0.0000
	2	0.9942	0.9619	0.8948	0.7969	0.6785	0.5518	0.4278	0.3154	0.2201	0.1445	0.0885	0.0498	0.0253	0.0113	0.0042	0.0012	0.0002	0.0000	0.0000
	3	0.9996	0.9950	0.9786	0.9437	0.8862	0.8059	0.7064	0.5941	0.4770	0.3633	0.2604	0.1737	0.1061	0.0580	0.0273	0.0104	0.0029	0.0004	0.0000
	4	1.0000	0.9996	0.9971	0.9896	0.9727	0.9420	0.8939	0.8263	0.7396	0.6367	0.5230	0.4059	0.2936	0.1941	0.1138	0.0563	0.0214	0.0050	0.0004
	5	1.0000	1.0000	0.9998	0.9988	0.9958	0.9887	0.9747	0.9502	0.9115	0.8555	0.7799	0.6846	0.5722	0.4482	0.3215	0.2031	0.1052	0.0381	0.0058
	6	1.0000	1.0000	1.0000	0.9999	0.9996	0.9987	0.9964	0.9915	0.9819	0.9648	0.9368	0.8936	0.8309	0.7447	0.6329	0.4967	0.3428	0.1869	0.0572
	7	1.0000	1.0000	1.0000	1.0000	1.0000	0.9999	0.9998	0.9993	0.9983	0.9961	0.9916	0.9832	0.9681	0.9424	0.8999	0.8322	0.7275	0.5695	0.3366

n	x	0.05	0.10	0.15	0.20	0.25	0.30	0.35	0.40	0.45	p 0.50	0.55	0.60	0.65	0.70	0.75	0.80	0.85	0.90	0.95
9	0	0.6302	0.3874	0.2316	0.1342	0.0751	0.0404	0.0207	0.0101	0.0046	0.0020	0.0008	0.0003	0.0001	0.0000	0.0000	0.0000	0.0000	0.0000	0.0000
	1	0.9288	0.7748	0.5995	0.4362	0.3003	0.1960	0.1211	0.0705	0.0385	0.0195	0.0091	0.0038	0.0014	0.0004	0.0001	0.0000	0.0000	0.0000	0.0000
	2	0.9916	0.9470	0.8591	0.7382	0.6007	0.4628	0.3373	0.2318	0.1495	0.0898	0.0498	0.0250	0.0112	0.0043	0.0013	0.0003	0.0000	0.0000	0.0000
	3	0.9994	0.9917	0.9661	0.9144	0.8343	0.7297	0.6089	0.4826	0.3614	0.2539	0.1658	0.0994	0.0536	0.0253	0.0100	0.0031	0.0006	0.0001	0.0000
	4	1.0000	0.9991	0.9944	0.9804	0.9511	0.9012	0.8283	0.7334	0.6214	0.5000	0.3786	0.2666	0.1717	0.0988	0.0489	0.0196	0.0056	0.0009	0.0000
	5	1.0000	0.9999	0.9994	0.9969	0.9900	0.9747	0.9464	0.9006	0.8342	0.7461	0.6386	0.5174	0.3911	0.2703	0.1657	0.0856	0.0339	0.0083	0.0006
	6	1.0000	1.0000	1.0000	0.9997	0.9987	0.9957	0.9888	0.9750	0.9502	0.9102	0.8505	0.7682	0.6627	0.5372	0.3993	0.2618	0.1409	0.0530	0.0084
	7	1.0000	1.0000	1.0000	1.0000	0.9999	0.9996	0.9986	0.9962	0.9909	0.9805	0.9615	0.9295	0.8789	0.8040	0.6997	0.5638	0.4005	0.2252	0.0712
	8	1.0000	1.0000	1.0000	1.0000	1.0000	1.0000	0.9999	0.9997	0.9992	0.9980	0.9954	0.9899	0.9793	0.9596	0.9249	0.8658	0.7684	0.6126	0.3698
10	0	0.5987	0.3487	0.1969	0.1074	0.0563	0.0282	0.0135	0.0060	0.0025	0.0010	0.0003	0.0001	0.0000	0.0000	0.0000	0.0000	0.0000	0.0000	0.0000
	1	0.9139	0.7361	0.5443	0.3758	0.2440	0.1493	0.0860	0.0464	0.0233	0.0107	0.0045	0.0017	0.0005	0.0001	0.0000	0.0000	0.0000	0.0000	0.0000
	2	0.9885	0.9298	0.8202	0.6778	0.5256	0.3828	0.2616	0.1673	0.0996	0.0547	0.0274	0.0123	0.0048	0.0016	0.0004	0.0001	0.0000	0.0000	0.0000
	3	0.9990	0.9872	0.9500	0.8791	0.7759	0.6496	0.5138	0.3823	0.2660	0.1719	0.1020	0.0548	0.0260	0.0106	0.0035	0.0009	0.0001	0.0000	0.0000
	4	0.9999	0.9984	0.9901	0.9672	0.9219	0.8497	0.7515	0.6331	0.5044	0.3770	0.2616	0.1662	0.0949	0.0473	0.0197	0.0064	0.0014	0.0001	0.0000
	5	1.0000	0.9999	0.9986	0.9936	0.9803	0.9527	0.9051	0.8338	0.7384	0.6230	0.4956	0.3669	0.2485	0.1503	0.0781	0.0328	0.0099	0.0016	0.0001
	6	1.0000	1.0000	0.9999	0.9991	0.9965	0.9894	0.9740	0.9452	0.8980	0.8281	0.7340	0.6177	0.4862	0.3504	0.2241	0.1209	0.0500	0.0128	0.0010
	7	1.0000	1.0000	1.0000	0.9999	0.9996	0.9984	0.9952	0.9877	0.9726	0.9453	0.9004	0.8327	0.7384	0.6172	0.4744	0.3222	0.1798	0.0702	0.0115
	8	1.0000	1.0000	1.0000	1.0000	1.0000	0.9999	0.9995	0.9983	0.9955	0.9893	0.9767	0.9536	0.9140	0.8507	0.7560	0.6242	0.4557	0.2639	0.0861
	9	1.0000	1.0000	1.0000	1.0000	1.0000	1.0000	1.0000	0.9999	0.9997	0.9990	0.9975	0.9940	0.9865	0.9718	0.9437	0.8926	0.8031	0.6513	0.4013
11	0	0.5688	0.3138	0.1673	0.0859	0.0422	0.0198	0.0088	0.0036	0.0014	0.0005	0.0002	0.0000	0.0000	0.0000	0.0000	0.0000	0.0000	0.0000	0.0000
	1	0.8981	0.6974	0.4922	0.3221	0.1971	0.1130	0.0606	0.0302	0.0139	0.0059	0.0022	0.0007	0.0002	0.0000	0.0000	0.0000	0.0000	0.0000	0.0000
	2	0.9848	0.9104	0.7788	0.6174	0.4552	0.3127	0.2001	0.1189	0.0652	0.0327	0.0148	0.0059	0.0020	0.0006	0.0001	0.0000	0.0000	0.0000	0.0000
	3	0.9984	0.9815	0.9306	0.8389	0.7133	0.5696	0.4256	0.2963	0.1911	0.1133	0.0610	0.0293	0.0122	0.0043	0.0012	0.0002	0.0000	0.0000	0.0000
	4	0.9999	0.9972	0.9841	0.9496	0.8854	0.7897	0.6683	0.5328	0.3971	0.2744	0.1738	0.0994	0.0501	0.0216	0.0076	0.0020	0.0003	0.0000	0.0000
	5	1.0000	0.9997	0.9973	0.9883	0.9657	0.9218	0.8513	0.7535	0.6331	0.5000	0.3669	0.2465	0.1487	0.0782	0.0343	0.0117	0.0027	0.0003	0.0000
	6	1.0000	1.0000	0.9997	0.9980	0.9924	0.9784	0.9499	0.9006	0.8262	0.7256	0.6029	0.4672	0.3317	0.2103	0.1146	0.0504	0.0159	0.0028	0.0001
	7	1.0000	1.0000	1.0000	0.9998	0.9988	0.9957	0.9878	0.9707	0.9390	0.8867	0.8089	0.7037	0.5744	0.4304	0.2867	0.1611	0.0694	0.0185	0.0016
	8	1.0000	1.0000	1.0000	1.0000	0.9999	0.9994	0.9980	0.9941	0.9852	0.9673	0.9348	0.8811	0.7999	0.6873	0.5448	0.3826	0.2212	0.0896	0.0152
	9	1.0000	1.0000	1.0000	1.0000	1.0000	1.0000	0.9998	0.9993	0.9978	0.9941	0.9861	0.9698	0.9394	0.8870	0.8029	0.6779	0.5078	0.3026	0.1019
	10	1.0000	1.0000	1.0000	1.0000	1.0000	1.0000	1.0000	1.0000	0.9998	0.9995	0.9986	0.9964	0.9912	0.9802	0.9578	0.9141	0.8327	0.6862	0.4312
12	0	0.5404	0.2824	0.1422	0.0687	0.0317	0.0138	0.0057	0.0022	0.0008	0.0002	0.0001	0.0000	0.0000	0.0000	0.0000	0.0000	0.0000	0.0000	0.0000
	1	0.8816	0.6590	0.4435	0.2749	0.1584	0.0850	0.0424	0.0196	0.0083	0.0032	0.0011	0.0003	0.0001	0.0000	0.0000	0.0000	0.0000	0.0000	0.0000
	2	0.9804	0.8891	0.7358	0.5583	0.3907	0.2528	0.1513	0.0834	0.0421	0.0193	0.0079	0.0028	0.0008	0.0002	0.0000	0.0000	0.0000	0.0000	0.0000
	3	0.9978	0.9744	0.9078	0.7946	0.6488	0.4925	0.3467	0.2253	0.1345	0.0730	0.0356	0.0153	0.0056	0.0017	0.0004	0.0001	0.0000	0.0000	0.0000
	4	0.9998	0.9957	0.9761	0.9274	0.8424	0.7237	0.5833	0.4382	0.3044	0.1938	0.1117	0.0573	0.0255	0.0095	0.0028	0.0006	0.0001	0.0000	0.0000
	5	1.0000	0.9995	0.9954	0.9806	0.9456	0.8822	0.7873	0.6652	0.5269	0.3872	0.2607	0.1582	0.0846	0.0386	0.0143	0.0039	0.0007	0.0001	0.0000
	6	1.0000	0.9999	0.9993	0.9961	0.9857	0.9614	0.9154	0.8418	0.7393	0.6128	0.4731	0.3348	0.2127	0.1178	0.0544	0.0194	0.0046	0.0005	0.0000
	7	1.0000	1.0000	0.9999	0.9994	0.9972	0.9905	0.9745	0.9427	0.8883	0.8062	0.6956	0.5618	0.4167	0.2763	0.1576	0.0726	0.0239	0.0043	0.0002
	8	1.0000	1.0000	1.0000	0.9999	0.9996	0.9983	0.9944	0.9847	0.9644	0.9270	0.8655	0.7747	0.6533	0.5075	0.3512	0.2054	0.0922	0.0256	0.0022
	9	1.0000	1.0000	1.0000	1.0000	1.0000	0.9998	0.9992	0.9972	0.9921	0.9807	0.9579	0.9166	0.8487	0.7472	0.6093	0.4417	0.2642	0.1109	0.0196
	10	1.0000	1.0000	1.0000	1.0000	1.0000	1.0000	0.9999	0.9997	0.9989	0.9968	0.9917	0.9804	0.9576	0.9150	0.8416	0.7251	0.5565	0.3410	0.1184
	11	1.0000	1.0000	1.0000	1.0000	1.0000	1.0000	1.0000	1.0000	0.9999	0.9998	0.9992	0.9978	0.9943	0.9862	0.9683	0.9313	0.8578	0.7176	0.4596

p

n	x	0.05	0.10	0.15	0.20	0.25	0.30	0.35	0.40	0.45	0.50	0.55	0.60	0.65	0.70	0.75	0.80	0.85	0.90	0.95
13	0	0.5133	0.2542	0.1209	0.0550	0.0238	0.0097	0.0037	0.0013	0.0004	0.0001	0.0000	0.0000	0.0000	0.0000	0.0000	0.0000	0.0000	0.0000	0.0000
	1	0.8646	0.6213	0.3983	0.2336	0.1267	0.0637	0.0296	0.0126	0.0049	0.0017	0.0005	0.0001	0.0000	0.0000	0.0000	0.0000	0.0000	0.0000	0.0000
	2	0.9755	0.8661	0.6920	0.5017	0.3326	0.2025	0.1132	0.0579	0.0269	0.0112	0.0041	0.0013	0.0003	0.0001	0.0000	0.0000	0.0000	0.0000	0.0000
	3	0.9969	0.9658	0.8820	0.7473	0.5843	0.4206	0.2783	0.1686	0.0929	0.0461	0.0203	0.0078	0.0025	0.0007	0.0001	0.0000	0.0000	0.0000	0.0000
	4	0.9997	0.9935	0.9658	0.9009	0.7940	0.6543	0.5005	0.3530	0.2279	0.1334	0.0698	0.0321	0.0126	0.0040	0.0010	0.0002	0.0000	0.0000	0.0000
	5	1.0000	0.9991	0.9925	0.9700	0.9198	0.8346	0.7159	0.5744	0.4268	0.2905	0.1788	0.0977	0.0462	0.0182	0.0056	0.0012	0.0002	0.0000	0.0000
	6	1.0000	0.9999	0.9987	0.9930	0.9757	0.9376	0.8705	0.7712	0.6437	0.5000	0.3563	0.2288	0.1295	0.0624	0.0243	0.0070	0.0013	0.0001	0.0000
	7	1.0000	1.0000	0.9998	0.9988	0.9944	0.9818	0.9538	0.9023	0.8212	0.7095	0.5732	0.4256	0.2841	0.1654	0.0802	0.0300	0.0075	0.0009	0.0000
	8	1.0000	1.0000	1.0000	0.9998	0.9990	0.9960	0.9874	0.9679	0.9302	0.8666	0.7721	0.6470	0.4995	0.3457	0.2060	0.0991	0.0342	0.0065	0.0003
	9	1.0000	1.0000	1.0000	1.0000	0.9999	0.9993	0.9975	0.9922	0.9797	0.9539	0.9071	0.8314	0.7217	0.5794	0.4157	0.2527	0.1180	0.0342	0.0031
	10	1.0000	1.0000	1.0000	1.0000	1.0000	0.9999	0.9997	0.9987	0.9959	0.9888	0.9731	0.9421	0.8868	0.7975	0.6674	0.4983	0.3080	0.1339	0.0245
	11	1.0000	1.0000	1.0000	1.0000	1.0000	1.0000	1.0000	0.9999	0.9995	0.9983	0.9951	0.9874	0.9704	0.9363	0.8733	0.7664	0.6017	0.3787	0.1354
	12	1.0000	1.0000	1.0000	1.0000	1.0000	1.0000	1.0000	1.0000	1.0000	0.9999	0.9996	0.9987	0.9963	0.9903	0.9762	0.9450	0.8791	0.7458	0.4867
14	0	0.4877	0.2288	0.1028	0.0440	0.0178	0.0068	0.0024	0.0008	0.0002	0.0001	0.0000	0.0000	0.0000	0.0000	0.0000	0.0000	0.0000	0.0000	0.0000
	1	0.8470	0.5846	0.3567	0.1979	0.1010	0.0475	0.0205	0.0081	0.0029	0.0009	0.0003	0.0001	0.0000	0.0000	0.0000	0.0000	0.0000	0.0000	0.0000
	2	0.9699	0.8416	0.6479	0.4481	0.2811	0.1608	0.0839	0.0398	0.0170	0.0065	0.0022	0.0006	0.0001	0.0000	0.0000	0.0000	0.0000	0.0000	0.0000
	3	0.9958	0.9559	0.8535	0.6982	0.5213	0.3552	0.2205	0.1243	0.0632	0.0287	0.0114	0.0039	0.0011	0.0002	0.0000	0.0000	0.0000	0.0000	0.0000
	4	0.9996	0.9908	0.9533	0.8702	0.7415	0.5842	0.4227	0.2793	0.1672	0.0898	0.0426	0.0175	0.0060	0.0017	0.0003	0.0000	0.0000	0.0000	0.0000
	5	1.0000	0.9985	0.9885	0.9561	0.8883	0.7805	0.6405	0.4859	0.3373	0.2120	0.1189	0.0583	0.0243	0.0083	0.0022	0.0004	0.0000	0.0000	0.0000
	6	1.0000	0.9998	0.9978	0.9884	0.9617	0.9067	0.8164	0.6925	0.5461	0.3953	0.2586	0.1501	0.0753	0.0315	0.0103	0.0024	0.0003	0.0000	0.0000
	7	1.0000	1.0000	0.9997	0.9976	0.9897	0.9685	0.9247	0.8499	0.7414	0.6047	0.4539	0.3075	0.1836	0.0933	0.0383	0.0116	0.0022	0.0002	0.0000
	8	1.0000	1.0000	1.0000	0.9996	0.9978	0.9917	0.9757	0.9417	0.8811	0.7880	0.6627	0.5141	0.3595	0.2195	0.1117	0.0439	0.0115	0.0015	0.0000
	9	1.0000	1.0000	1.0000	1.0000	0.9997	0.9983	0.9940	0.9825	0.9574	0.9102	0.8328	0.7207	0.5773	0.4158	0.2585	0.1298	0.0467	0.0092	0.0004
	10	1.0000	1.0000	1.0000	1.0000	1.0000	0.9998	0.9989	0.9961	0.9886	0.9713	0.9368	0.8757	0.7795	0.6448	0.4787	0.3018	0.1465	0.0441	0.0042
	11	1.0000	1.0000	1.0000	1.0000	1.0000	1.0000	0.9999	0.9994	0.9978	0.9935	0.9830	0.9602	0.9161	0.8392	0.7189	0.5519	0.3521	0.1584	0.0301
	12	1.0000	1.0000	1.0000	1.0000	1.0000	1.0000	1.0000	0.9999	0.9997	0.9991	0.9971	0.9919	0.9795	0.9525	0.8990	0.8021	0.6433	0.4154	0.1530
	13	1.0000	1.0000	1.0000	1.0000	1.0000	1.0000	1.0000	1.0000	1.0000	0.9999	0.9998	0.9992	0.9976	0.9932	0.9822	0.9560	0.8972	0.7712	0.5123
15	0	0.4633	0.2059	0.0874	0.0352	0.0134	0.0047	0.0016	0.0005	0.0001	0.0000	0.0000	0.0000	0.0000	0.0000	0.0000	0.0000	0.0000	0.0000	0.0000
	1	0.8290	0.5490	0.3186	0.1671	0.0802	0.0353	0.0142	0.0052	0.0017	0.0005	0.0001	0.0000	0.0000	0.0000	0.0000	0.0000	0.0000	0.0000	0.0000
	2	0.9638	0.8159	0.6042	0.3980	0.2361	0.1268	0.0617	0.0271	0.0107	0.0037	0.0011	0.0003	0.0001	0.0000	0.0000	0.0000	0.0000	0.0000	0.0000
	3	0.9945	0.9444	0.8227	0.6482	0.4613	0.2969	0.1727	0.0905	0.0424	0.0176	0.0063	0.0019	0.0005	0.0001	0.0000	0.0000	0.0000	0.0000	0.0000
	4	0.9994	0.9873	0.9383	0.8358	0.6865	0.5155	0.3519	0.2173	0.1204	0.0592	0.0255	0.0093	0.0028	0.0007	0.0001	0.0000	0.0000	0.0000	0.0000
	5	0.9999	0.9977	0.9832	0.9389	0.8516	0.7216	0.5643	0.4032	0.2608	0.1509	0.0769	0.0338	0.0124	0.0037	0.0008	0.0001	0.0000	0.0000	0.0000
	6	1.0000	0.9997	0.9964	0.9819	0.9434	0.8689	0.7548	0.6098	0.4522	0.3036	0.1818	0.0950	0.0422	0.0152	0.0042	0.0008	0.0001	0.0000	0.0000
	7	1.0000	1.0000	0.9994	0.9958	0.9827	0.9500	0.8868	0.7869	0.6535	0.5000	0.3465	0.2131	0.1132	0.0500	0.0173	0.0042	0.0006	0.0000	0.0000
	8	1.0000	1.0000	0.9999	0.9992	0.9958	0.9848	0.9578	0.9050	0.8182	0.6964	0.5478	0.3902	0.2452	0.1311	0.0566	0.0181	0.0036	0.0003	0.0000
	9	1.0000	1.0000	1.0000	0.9999	0.9992	0.9963	0.9876	0.9662	0.9231	0.8491	0.7392	0.5968	0.4357	0.2784	0.1484	0.0611	0.0168	0.0022	0.0001
	10	1.0000	1.0000	1.0000	1.0000	0.9999	0.9993	0.9972	0.9907	0.9745	0.9408	0.8796	0.7827	0.6481	0.4845	0.3135	0.1642	0.0617	0.0127	0.0006
	11	1.0000	1.0000	1.0000	1.0000	1.0000	0.9999	0.9995	0.9981	0.9937	0.9824	0.9576	0.9095	0.8273	0.7031	0.5387	0.3518	0.1773	0.0556	0.0055
	12	1.0000	1.0000	1.0000	1.0000	1.0000	1.0000	0.9999	0.9997	0.9989	0.9963	0.9893	0.9729	0.9383	0.8732	0.7639	0.6020	0.3958	0.1841	0.0362
	13	1.0000	1.0000	1.0000	1.0000	1.0000	1.0000	1.0000	1.0000	0.9999	0.9995	0.9983	0.9948	0.9858	0.9647	0.9198	0.8329	0.6814	0.4510	0.1710
	14	1.0000	1.0000	1.0000	1.0000	1.0000	1.0000	1.0000	1.0000	1.0000	1.0000	0.9999	0.9995	0.9984	0.9953	0.9866	0.9648	0.9126	0.7941	0.5367

n	x	0.95	0.90	0.85	0.80	0.75	0.70	0.65	0.60	0.55	0.50	0.45	0.40	0.35	0.30	0.25	0.20	0.15	0.10	0.05
16	0	0.0000	0.0000	0.0000	0.0000	0.0000	0.0000	0.0000	0.0000	0.0000	0.0000	0.0001	0.0003	0.0010	0.0033	0.0100	0.0281	0.0743	0.1853	0.4401
	1	0.0000	0.0000	0.0000	0.0000	0.0000	0.0000	0.0000	0.0000	0.0001	0.0003	0.0010	0.0033	0.0098	0.0261	0.0635	0.1407	0.2839	0.5147	0.8108
	2	0.0000	0.0000	0.0000	0.0000	0.0000	0.0000	0.0000	0.0001	0.0006	0.0021	0.0066	0.0183	0.0451	0.0994	0.1971	0.3518	0.5614	0.7892	0.9571
	3	0.0000	0.0000	0.0000	0.0000	0.0000	0.0000	0.0002	0.0009	0.0035	0.0106	0.0281	0.0651	0.1339	0.2459	0.4050	0.5981	0.7899	0.9316	0.9930
	4	0.0000	0.0000	0.0000	0.0000	0.0000	0.0003	0.0013	0.0049	0.0149	0.0384	0.0853	0.1666	0.2892	0.4499	0.6302	0.7982	0.9209	0.9830	0.9991
	5	0.0000	0.0000	0.0000	0.0000	0.0003	0.0016	0.0062	0.0191	0.0486	0.1051	0.1976	0.3288	0.4900	0.6598	0.8103	0.9183	0.9765	0.9967	0.9999
	6	0.0000	0.0000	0.0000	0.0002	0.0016	0.0071	0.0229	0.0583	0.1241	0.2272	0.3660	0.5272	0.6881	0.8247	0.9204	0.9733	0.9944	0.9995	1.0000
	7	0.0000	0.0000	0.0002	0.0015	0.0075	0.0257	0.0671	0.1423	0.2559	0.4018	0.5629	0.7161	0.8406	0.9256	0.9729	0.9930	0.9989	0.9999	1.0000
	8	0.0000	0.0001	0.0011	0.0070	0.0271	0.0744	0.1594	0.2839	0.4371	0.5982	0.7441	0.8577	0.9329	0.9743	0.9925	0.9985	0.9998	1.0000	1.0000
	9	0.0000	0.0005	0.0056	0.0267	0.0796	0.1753	0.3119	0.4728	0.6340	0.7728	0.8759	0.9417	0.9771	0.9929	0.9984	0.9998	1.0000	1.0000	1.0000
	10	0.0001	0.0033	0.0235	0.0817	0.1897	0.3402	0.5100	0.6712	0.8024	0.8949	0.9514	0.9809	0.9938	0.9984	0.9997	1.0000	1.0000	1.0000	1.0000
	11	0.0009	0.0170	0.0791	0.2018	0.3698	0.5501	0.7108	0.8334	0.9147	0.9616	0.9851	0.9951	0.9987	0.9997	1.0000	1.0000	1.0000	1.0000	1.0000
	12	0.0070	0.0684	0.2101	0.4019	0.5950	0.7541	0.8661	0.9349	0.9719	0.9894	0.9965	0.9991	0.9998	1.0000	1.0000	1.0000	1.0000	1.0000	1.0000
	13	0.0429	0.2108	0.4386	0.6482	0.8029	0.9006	0.9549	0.9817	0.9934	0.9979	0.9994	0.9999	1.0000	1.0000	1.0000	1.0000	1.0000	1.0000	1.0000
	14	0.1892	0.4853	0.7161	0.8593	0.9365	0.9739	0.9902	0.9967	0.9990	0.9997	0.9999	1.0000	1.0000	1.0000	1.0000	1.0000	1.0000	1.0000	1.0000
	15	0.5599	0.8147	0.9257	0.9719	0.9900	0.9967	0.9990	0.9997	0.9999	1.0000	1.0000	1.0000	1.0000	1.0000	1.0000	1.0000	1.0000	1.0000	1.0000
17	0	0.0000	0.0000	0.0000	0.0000	0.0000	0.0000	0.0000	0.0000	0.0000	0.0000	0.0000	0.0002	0.0007	0.0023	0.0075	0.0225	0.0631	0.1668	0.4181
	1	0.0000	0.0000	0.0000	0.0000	0.0000	0.0000	0.0000	0.0000	0.0000	0.0001	0.0006	0.0021	0.0067	0.0193	0.0501	0.1182	0.2525	0.4818	0.7922
	2	0.0000	0.0000	0.0000	0.0000	0.0000	0.0000	0.0000	0.0001	0.0003	0.0012	0.0041	0.0123	0.0327	0.0774	0.1637	0.3096	0.5198	0.7618	0.9497
	3	0.0000	0.0000	0.0000	0.0000	0.0000	0.0000	0.0001	0.0005	0.0019	0.0064	0.0184	0.0464	0.1028	0.2019	0.3530	0.5489	0.7556	0.9174	0.9912
	4	0.0000	0.0000	0.0000	0.0000	0.0000	0.0001	0.0006	0.0025	0.0086	0.0245	0.0596	0.1260	0.2348	0.3887	0.5739	0.7582	0.9013	0.9779	0.9988
	5	0.0000	0.0000	0.0000	0.0000	0.0001	0.0007	0.0030	0.0106	0.0301	0.0717	0.1471	0.2639	0.4197	0.5968	0.7653	0.8943	0.9681	0.9953	0.9999
	6	0.0000	0.0000	0.0000	0.0001	0.0006	0.0032	0.0120	0.0348	0.0826	0.1662	0.2902	0.4478	0.6188	0.7752	0.8929	0.9623	0.9917	0.9992	1.0000
	7	0.0000	0.0000	0.0000	0.0005	0.0031	0.0127	0.0383	0.0919	0.1834	0.3145	0.4743	0.6405	0.7872	0.8954	0.9598	0.9891	0.9983	0.9999	1.0000
	8	0.0000	0.0000	0.0003	0.0026	0.0124	0.0403	0.0994	0.1989	0.3374	0.5000	0.6626	0.8011	0.9006	0.9597	0.9876	0.9974	0.9997	1.0000	1.0000
	9	0.0000	0.0001	0.0017	0.0109	0.0402	0.1046	0.2128	0.3595	0.5257	0.6855	0.8166	0.9081	0.9617	0.9873	0.9969	0.9995	1.0000	1.0000	1.0000
	10	0.0000	0.0008	0.0083	0.0377	0.1071	0.2248	0.3812	0.5522	0.7098	0.8338	0.9174	0.9652	0.9880	0.9968	0.9994	0.9999	1.0000	1.0000	1.0000
	11	0.0001	0.0047	0.0319	0.1057	0.2347	0.4032	0.5803	0.7361	0.8529	0.9283	0.9699	0.9894	0.9970	0.9993	0.9999	1.0000	1.0000	1.0000	1.0000
	12	0.0012	0.0221	0.0987	0.2418	0.4261	0.6113	0.7652	0.8740	0.9404	0.9755	0.9914	0.9975	0.9994	0.9999	1.0000	1.0000	1.0000	1.0000	1.0000
	13	0.0088	0.0826	0.2444	0.4511	0.6470	0.7981	0.8972	0.9536	0.9816	0.9936	0.9981	0.9995	0.9999	1.0000	1.0000	1.0000	1.0000	1.0000	1.0000
	14	0.0503	0.2382	0.4802	0.6904	0.8363	0.9226	0.9673	0.9877	0.9959	0.9988	0.9997	0.9999	1.0000	1.0000	1.0000	1.0000	1.0000	1.0000	1.0000
	15	0.2078	0.5182	0.7475	0.8818	0.9499	0.9807	0.9933	0.9979	0.9994	0.9999	1.0000	1.0000	1.0000	1.0000	1.0000	1.0000	1.0000	1.0000	1.0000
	16	0.5819	0.8332	0.9369	0.9775	0.9925	0.9977	0.9993	0.9998	1.0000	1.0000	1.0000	1.0000	1.0000	1.0000	1.0000	1.0000	1.0000	1.0000	1.0000
18	0	0.0000	0.0000	0.0000	0.0000	0.0000	0.0000	0.0000	0.0000	0.0000	0.0000	0.0000	0.0001	0.0004	0.0016	0.0056	0.0180	0.0536	0.1501	0.3972
	1	0.0000	0.0000	0.0000	0.0000	0.0000	0.0000	0.0000	0.0000	0.0000	0.0001	0.0003	0.0013	0.0046	0.0142	0.0395	0.0991	0.2241	0.4503	0.7735
	2	0.0000	0.0000	0.0000	0.0000	0.0000	0.0000	0.0000	0.0000	0.0000	0.0007	0.0025	0.0082	0.0236	0.0600	0.1353	0.2713	0.4797	0.7338	0.9419
	3	0.0000	0.0000	0.0000	0.0000	0.0000	0.0000	0.0000	0.0002	0.0010	0.0038	0.0120	0.0328	0.0783	0.1646	0.3057	0.5010	0.7202	0.9018	0.9891
	4	0.0000	0.0000	0.0000	0.0000	0.0000	0.0000	0.0003	0.0013	0.0049	0.0154	0.0411	0.0942	0.1886	0.3327	0.5187	0.7164	0.8794	0.9718	0.9985
	5	0.0000	0.0000	0.0000	0.0000	0.0000	0.0003	0.0014	0.0058	0.0183	0.0481	0.1077	0.2088	0.3550	0.5344	0.7175	0.8671	0.9581	0.9936	0.9998
	6	0.0000	0.0000	0.0000	0.0000	0.0002	0.0014	0.0062	0.0203	0.0537	0.1189	0.2258	0.3743	0.5491	0.7217	0.8610	0.9487	0.9882	0.9988	1.0000
	7	0.0000	0.0000	0.0000	0.0002	0.0012	0.0061	0.0212	0.0576	0.1280	0.2403	0.3915	0.5634	0.7283	0.8593	0.9431	0.9837	0.9973	0.9998	1.0000
	8	0.0000	0.0000	0.0001	0.0009	0.0054	0.0210	0.0597	0.1347	0.2527	0.4073	0.5778	0.7368	0.8609	0.9404	0.9807	0.9957	0.9995	1.0000	1.0000
	9	0.0000	0.0000	0.0005	0.0043	0.0193	0.0596	0.1391	0.2632	0.4222	0.5927	0.7473	0.8653	0.9403	0.9790	0.9946	0.9991	0.9999	1.0000	1.0000
	10	0.0000	0.0002	0.0027	0.0163	0.0569	0.1407	0.2717	0.4366	0.6085	0.7597	0.8720	0.9424	0.9788	0.9939	0.9988	0.9998	1.0000	1.0000	1.0000

n	x	0.05	0.10	0.15	0.20	0.25	0.30	0.35	0.40	0.45	0.50	0.55	0.60	0.65	0.70	0.75	0.80	0.85	0.90	0.95
	11	1.0000	1.0000	1.0000	1.0000	0.9998	0.9986	0.9938	0.9797	0.9463	0.8811	0.7742	0.6257	0.4509	0.2783	0.1390	0.0513	0.0118	0.0012	0.0000
	12	1.0000	1.0000	1.0000	1.0000	1.0000	0.9997	0.9986	0.9942	0.9817	0.9519	0.8923	0.7912	0.6450	0.4656	0.2825	0.1329	0.0419	0.0064	0.0002
	13	1.0000	1.0000	1.0000	1.0000	1.0000	1.0000	0.9997	0.9987	0.9951	0.9846	0.9589	0.9058	0.8114	0.6673	0.4813	0.2836	0.1206	0.0282	0.0015
	14	1.0000	1.0000	1.0000	1.0000	1.0000	1.0000	1.0000	0.9998	0.9990	0.9962	0.9880	0.9672	0.9217	0.8354	0.6943	0.4990	0.2798	0.0982	0.0109
	15	1.0000	1.0000	1.0000	1.0000	1.0000	1.0000	1.0000	1.0000	0.9999	0.9993	0.9975	0.9918	0.9764	0.9400	0.8647	0.7287	0.5203	0.2662	0.0581
	16	1.0000	1.0000	1.0000	1.0000	1.0000	1.0000	1.0000	1.0000	1.0000	0.9999	0.9997	0.9987	0.9954	0.9858	0.9605	0.9009	0.7759	0.5497	0.2265
	17	1.0000	1.0000	1.0000	1.0000	1.0000	1.0000	1.0000	1.0000	1.0000	1.0000	1.0000	0.9999	0.9996	0.9984	0.9944	0.9820	0.9464	0.8499	0.6028
19	0	0.3774	0.1351	0.0456	0.0144	0.0042	0.0011	0.0003	0.0001	0.0000	0.0000	0.0000	0.0000	0.0000	0.0000	0.0000	0.0000	0.0000	0.0000	0.0000
	1	0.7547	0.4203	0.1985	0.0829	0.0310	0.0104	0.0031	0.0008	0.0002	0.0000	0.0000	0.0000	0.0000	0.0000	0.0000	0.0000	0.0000	0.0000	0.0000
	2	0.9335	0.7054	0.4413	0.2369	0.1113	0.0462	0.0170	0.0055	0.0015	0.0004	0.0001	0.0000	0.0000	0.0000	0.0000	0.0000	0.0000	0.0000	0.0000
	3	0.9868	0.8850	0.6841	0.4551	0.2631	0.1332	0.0591	0.0230	0.0077	0.0022	0.0005	0.0001	0.0001	0.0000	0.0000	0.0000	0.0000	0.0000	0.0000
	4	0.9980	0.9648	0.8556	0.6733	0.4654	0.2822	0.1500	0.0696	0.0280	0.0096	0.0028	0.0006	0.0001	0.0000	0.0000	0.0000	0.0000	0.0000	0.0000
	5	0.9998	0.9914	0.9463	0.8369	0.6678	0.4739	0.2968	0.1629	0.0777	0.0318	0.0109	0.0031	0.0007	0.0001	0.0000	0.0000	0.0000	0.0000	0.0000
	6	1.0000	0.9983	0.9837	0.9324	0.8251	0.6655	0.4812	0.3081	0.1727	0.0835	0.0342	0.0116	0.0031	0.0006	0.0001	0.0000	0.0000	0.0000	0.0000
	7	1.0000	0.9997	0.9959	0.9767	0.9225	0.8180	0.6656	0.4878	0.3169	0.1796	0.0871	0.0352	0.0114	0.0028	0.0005	0.0000	0.0000	0.0000	0.0000
	8	1.0000	1.0000	0.9992	0.9933	0.9713	0.9161	0.8145	0.6675	0.4940	0.3238	0.1841	0.0885	0.0347	0.0105	0.0023	0.0003	0.0000	0.0000	0.0000
	9	1.0000	1.0000	0.9999	0.9984	0.9911	0.9674	0.9125	0.8139	0.6710	0.5000	0.3290	0.1861	0.0875	0.0326	0.0089	0.0016	0.0001	0.0000	0.0000
	10	1.0000	1.0000	1.0000	0.9997	0.9977	0.9895	0.9653	0.9115	0.8159	0.6762	0.5060	0.3325	0.1855	0.0839	0.0287	0.0067	0.0008	0.0000	0.0000
	11	1.0000	1.0000	1.0000	1.0000	0.9995	0.9972	0.9886	0.9648	0.9129	0.8204	0.6831	0.5122	0.3344	0.1820	0.0775	0.0233	0.0041	0.0003	0.0000
	12	1.0000	1.0000	1.0000	1.0000	0.9999	0.9994	0.9969	0.9884	0.9658	0.9165	0.8273	0.6919	0.5188	0.3345	0.1749	0.0676	0.0163	0.0017	0.0000
	13	1.0000	1.0000	1.0000	1.0000	1.0000	0.9999	0.9993	0.9969	0.9891	0.9682	0.9223	0.8371	0.7032	0.5261	0.3322	0.1631	0.0537	0.0086	0.0002
	14	1.0000	1.0000	1.0000	1.0000	1.0000	1.0000	0.9999	0.9994	0.9972	0.9904	0.9720	0.9304	0.8500	0.7178	0.5346	0.3267	0.1444	0.0352	0.0020
	15	1.0000	1.0000	1.0000	1.0000	1.0000	1.0000	1.0000	0.9999	0.9995	0.9978	0.9923	0.9770	0.9409	0.8668	0.7369	0.5449	0.3159	0.1150	0.0132
	16	1.0000	1.0000	1.0000	1.0000	1.0000	1.0000	1.0000	1.0000	0.9999	0.9996	0.9985	0.9945	0.9830	0.9538	0.8887	0.7631	0.5587	0.2946	0.0665
	17	1.0000	1.0000	1.0000	1.0000	1.0000	1.0000	1.0000	1.0000	1.0000	1.0000	0.9998	0.9992	0.9969	0.9896	0.9690	0.9171	0.8015	0.5797	0.2453
	18	1.0000	1.0000	1.0000	1.0000	1.0000	1.0000	1.0000	1.0000	1.0000	1.0000	1.0000	0.9999	0.9997	0.9989	0.9958	0.9856	0.9544	0.8649	0.6226
20	0	0.3585	0.1216	0.0388	0.0115	0.0032	0.0008	0.0002	0.0000	0.0000	0.0000	0.0000	0.0000	0.0000	0.0000	0.0000	0.0000	0.0000	0.0000	0.0000
	1	0.7358	0.3917	0.1756	0.0692	0.0243	0.0076	0.0021	0.0005	0.0001	0.0000	0.0000	0.0000	0.0000	0.0000	0.0000	0.0000	0.0000	0.0000	0.0000
	2	0.9245	0.6769	0.4049	0.2061	0.0913	0.0355	0.0121	0.0036	0.0009	0.0002	0.0000	0.0000	0.0000	0.0000	0.0000	0.0000	0.0000	0.0000	0.0000
	3	0.9841	0.8670	0.6477	0.4114	0.2252	0.1071	0.0444	0.0160	0.0049	0.0013	0.0003	0.0000	0.0000	0.0000	0.0000	0.0000	0.0000	0.0000	0.0000
	4	0.9974	0.9568	0.8298	0.6296	0.4148	0.2375	0.1182	0.0510	0.0189	0.0059	0.0015	0.0003	0.0000	0.0000	0.0000	0.0000	0.0000	0.0000	0.0000
	5	0.9997	0.9887	0.9327	0.8042	0.6172	0.4164	0.2454	0.1256	0.0553	0.0207	0.0064	0.0016	0.0003	0.0000	0.0000	0.0000	0.0000	0.0000	0.0000
	6	1.0000	0.9976	0.9781	0.9133	0.7858	0.6080	0.4166	0.2500	0.1299	0.0577	0.0214	0.0065	0.0015	0.0003	0.0000	0.0000	0.0000	0.0000	0.0000
	7	1.0000	0.9996	0.9941	0.9679	0.8982	0.7723	0.6010	0.4159	0.2520	0.1316	0.0580	0.0210	0.0060	0.0013	0.0002	0.0000	0.0000	0.0000	0.0000
	8	1.0000	0.9999	0.9987	0.9900	0.9591	0.8867	0.7624	0.5956	0.4143	0.2517	0.1308	0.0565	0.0196	0.0051	0.0009	0.0001	0.0000	0.0000	0.0000
	9	1.0000	1.0000	0.9998	0.9974	0.9861	0.9520	0.8782	0.7553	0.5914	0.4119	0.2493	0.1275	0.0532	0.0171	0.0039	0.0006	0.0000	0.0000	0.0000
	10	1.0000	1.0000	1.0000	0.9994	0.9961	0.9829	0.9468	0.8725	0.7507	0.5881	0.4086	0.2447	0.1218	0.0480	0.0139	0.0026	0.0002	0.0000	0.0000
	11	1.0000	1.0000	1.0000	0.9999	0.9991	0.9949	0.9804	0.9435	0.8692	0.7483	0.5857	0.4044	0.2376	0.1133	0.0409	0.0100	0.0013	0.0001	0.0000
	12	1.0000	1.0000	1.0000	1.0000	0.9998	0.9987	0.9940	0.9790	0.9420	0.8684	0.7480	0.5841	0.3990	0.2277	0.1018	0.0321	0.0059	0.0004	0.0000
	13	1.0000	1.0000	1.0000	1.0000	1.0000	0.9997	0.9985	0.9935	0.9786	0.9423	0.8701	0.7500	0.5834	0.3920	0.2142	0.0867	0.0219	0.0024	0.0000
	14	1.0000	1.0000	1.0000	1.0000	1.0000	1.0000	0.9997	0.9984	0.9936	0.9793	0.9447	0.8744	0.7546	0.5836	0.3828	0.1958	0.0673	0.0113	0.0003
	15	1.0000	1.0000	1.0000	1.0000	1.0000	1.0000	1.0000	0.9997	0.9985	0.9941	0.9811	0.9490	0.8818	0.7625	0.5852	0.3704	0.1702	0.0432	0.0026
	16	1.0000	1.0000	1.0000	1.0000	1.0000	1.0000	1.0000	1.0000	0.9997	0.9987	0.9951	0.9840	0.9556	0.8929	0.7748	0.5886	0.3523	0.1330	0.0159
	17	1.0000	1.0000	1.0000	1.0000	1.0000	1.0000	1.0000	1.0000	1.0000	0.9998	0.9991	0.9964	0.9879	0.9645	0.9087	0.7939	0.5951	0.3231	0.0755
	18	1.0000	1.0000	1.0000	1.0000	1.0000	1.0000	1.0000	1.0000	1.0000	1.0000	0.9999	0.9995	0.9979	0.9924	0.9757	0.9308	0.8244	0.6083	0.2642
	19	1.0000	1.0000	1.0000	1.0000	1.0000	1.0000	1.0000	1.0000	1.0000	1.0000	1.0000	1.0000	0.9998	0.9992	0.9968	0.9885	0.9612	0.8784	0.6415

TABLE 2 Poisson Distribution Function

$$F(x; \lambda) = \sum_{k=0}^{x} e^{-\lambda}\frac{\lambda^k}{k!}$$

λ \ x	0	1	2	3	4	5	6	7	8	9
0.02	0.980	1.000								
0.04	0.961	0.999	1.000							
0.06	0.942	0.998	1.000							
0.08	0.923	0.997	1.000							
0.10	0.905	0.995	1.000							
0.15	0.861	0.990	0.999	1.000						
0.20	0.819	0.982	0.999	1.000						
0.25	0.779	0.974	0.998	1.000						
0.30	0.741	0.963	0.996	1.000						
0.35	0.705	0.951	0.994	1.000						
0.40	0.670	0.938	0.992	0.999	1.000					
0.45	0.638	0.925	0.989	0.999	1.000					
0.50	0.607	0.910	0.986	0.998	1.000					
0.55	0.577	0.894	0.982	0.998	1.000					
0.60	0.549	0.878	0.977	0.997	1.000					
0.65	0.522	0.861	0.972	0.996	0.999	1.000				
0.70	0.497	0.844	0.966	0.994	0.999	1.000				
0.75	0.472	0.827	0.959	0.993	0.999	1.000				
0.80	0.449	0.809	0.953	0.991	0.999	1.000				
0.85	0.427	0.791	0.945	0.989	0.998	1.000				
0.90	0.407	0.772	0.937	0.987	0.998	1.000				
0.95	0.387	0.754	0.929	0.984	0.997	1.000				
1.00	0.368	0.736	0.920	0.981	0.996	0.999	1.000			
1.1	0.333	0.699	0.900	0.974	0.995	0.999	1.000			
1.2	0.301	0.663	0.879	0.966	0.992	0.998	1.000			
1.3	0.273	0.627	0.857	0.957	0.989	0.998	1.000			
1.4	0.247	0.592	0.833	0.946	0.986	0.997	0.999	1.000		
1.5	0.223	0.558	0.809	0.934	0.981	0.996	0.999	1.000		
1.6	0.202	0.525	0.783	0.921	0.976	0.994	0.999	1.000		
1.7	0.183	0.493	0.757	0.907	0.970	0.992	0.998	1.000		
1.8	0.165	0.463	0.731	0.891	0.964	0.990	0.997	0.999	1.000	
1.9	0.150	0.434	0.704	0.875	0.956	0.987	0.997	0.999	1.000	
2.0	0.135	0.406	0.677	0.857	0.947	0.983	0.995	0.999	1.000	

TABLE 2 Poisson Distribution Function (continued)

λ \ x	0	1	2	3	4	5	6	7	8	9
2.2	0.111	0.355	0.623	0.819	0.928	0.975	0.993	0.998	1.000	
2.4	0.091	0.308	0.570	0.779	0.904	0.964	0.988	0.997	0.999	1.000
2.6	0.074	0.267	0.518	0.736	0.877	0.951	0.983	0.995	0.999	1.000
2.8	0.061	0.231	0.469	0.692	0.848	0.935	0.976	0.992	0.998	0.999
3.0	0.050	0.199	0.423	0.647	0.815	0.916	0.966	0.988	0.996	0.999
3.2	0.041	0.171	0.380	0.603	0.781	0.895	0.955	0.983	0.994	0.998
3.4	0.033	0.147	0.340	0.558	0.744	0.871	0.942	0.977	0.992	0.997
3.6	0.027	0.126	0.303	0.515	0.706	0.844	0.927	0.969	0.988	0.996
3.8	0.022	0.107	0.269	0.473	0.668	0.816	0.909	0.960	0.984	0.994
4.0	0.018	0.092	0.238	0.433	0.629	0.785	0.889	0.949	0.979	0.992
4.2	0.015	0.078	0.210	0.395	0.590	0.753	0.867	0.936	0.972	0.989
4.4	0.012	0.066	0.185	0.359	0.551	0.720	0.844	0.921	0.964	0.985
4.6	0.010	0.056	0.163	0.326	0.513	0.686	0.818	0.905	0.955	0.980
4.8	0.008	0.048	0.143	0.294	0.476	0.651	0.791	0.887	0.944	0.975
5.0	0.007	0.040	0.125	0.265	0.440	0.616	0.762	0.867	0.932	0.968
5.2	0.006	0.034	0.109	0.238	0.406	0.581	0.732	0.845	0.918	0.960
5.4	0.005	0.029	0.095	0.213	0.373	0.546	0.702	0.822	0.903	0.951
5.6	0.004	0.024	0.082	0.191	0.342	0.512	0.670	0.797	0.886	0.941
5.8	0.003	0.021	0.072	0.170	0.313	0.478	0.638	0.771	0.867	0.929
6.0	0.002	0.017	0.062	0.151	0.285	0.446	0.606	0.744	0.847	0.916

λ \ x	10	11	12	13	14	15	16
2.8	1.000						
3.0	1.000						
3.2	1.000						
3.4	0.999	1.000					
3.6	0.999	1.000					
3.8	0.998	0.999	1.000				
4.0	0.997	0.999	1.000				
4.2	0.996	0.999	1.000				
4.4	0.994	0.998	0.999	1.000			
4.6	0.992	0.997	0.999	1.000			
4.8	0.990	0.996	0.999	1.000			
5.0	0.986	0.995	0.998	0.999	1.000		
5.2	0.982	0.993	0.997	0.999	1.000		
5.4	0.977	0.990	0.996	0.999	1.000		
5.6	0.972	0.988	0.995	0.998	0.999	1.000	
5.8	0.965	0.984	0.993	0.997	0.999	1.000	
6.0	0.957	0.980	0.991	0.996	0.999	0.999	1.000

TABLE 2 Poisson Distribution Function (continued)

λ\x	0	1	2	3	4	5	6	7	8	9
6.2	0.002	0.015	0.054	0.134	0.259	0.414	0.574	0.716	0.826	0.902
6.4	0.002	0.012	0.046	0.119	0.235	0.384	0.542	0.687	0.803	0.886
6.6	0.001	0.010	0.040	0.105	0.213	0.355	0.511	0.658	0.780	0.869
6.8	0.001	0.009	0.034	0.093	0.192	0.327	0.480	0.628	0.755	0.850
7.0	0.001	0.007	0.030	0.082	0.173	0.301	0.450	0.599	0.729	0.830
7.2	0.001	0.006	0.025	0.072	0.156	0.276	0.420	0.569	0.703	0.810
7.4	0.001	0.005	0.022	0.063	0.140	0.253	0.392	0.539	0.676	0.788
7.6	0.001	0.004	0.019	0.055	0.125	0.231	0.365	0.510	0.648	0.765
7.8	0.000	0.004	0.016	0.048	0.112	0.210	0.338	0.481	0.620	0.741
8.0	0.000	0.003	0.014	0.042	0.100	0.191	0.313	0.453	0.593	0.717
8.5	0.000	0.002	0.009	0.030	0.074	0.150	0.256	0.386	0.523	0.653
9.0	0.000	0.001	0.006	0.021	0.055	0.116	0.207	0.324	0.456	0.587
9.5	0.000	0.001	0.004	0.015	0.040	0.089	0.165	0.269	0.392	0.522
10.0	0.000	0.000	0.003	0.010	0.029	0.067	0.130	0.220	0.333	0.458

	10	11	12	13	14	15	16	17	18	19
6.2	0.949	0.975	0.989	0.995	0.998	0.999	1.000			
6.4	0.939	0.969	0.986	0.994	0.997	0.999	1.000			
6.6	0.927	0.963	0.982	0.992	0.997	0.999	0.999	1.000		
6.8	0.915	0.955	0.978	0.990	0.996	0.998	0.999	1.000		
7.0	0.901	0.947	0.973	0.987	0.994	0.998	0.999	1.000		
7.2	0.887	0.937	0.967	0.984	0.993	0.997	0.999	1.000	1.000	
7.4	0.871	0.926	0.961	0.980	0.991	0.996	0.998	0.999	1.000	
7.6	0.854	0.915	0.954	0.976	0.989	0.995	0.998	0.999	1.000	
7.8	0.835	0.902	0.945	0.971	0.986	0.993	0.997	0.999	1.000	
8.0	0.816	0.888	0.936	0.966	0.983	0.992	0.996	0.998	0.999	1.000
8.5	0.763	0.849	0.909	0.949	0.973	0.986	0.993	0.997	0.999	0.999
9.0	0.706	0.803	0.876	0.926	0.959	0.978	0.989	0.995	0.998	0.999
9.5	0.645	0.752	0.836	0.898	0.940	0.967	0.982	0.991	0.996	0.998
10.0	0.583	0.697	0.792	0.864	0.917	0.951	0.973	0.986	0.993	0.997

	20	21	22
8.5	1.000		
9.0	1.000		
9.5	0.999	1.000	
10.0	0.998	0.999	1.000

TABLE 2 Poisson Distribution Function (continued)

λ \ x	0	1	2	3	4	5	6	7	8	9
10.5	0.000	0.000	0.002	0.007	0.021	0.050	0.102	0.179	0.279	0.397
11.0	0.000	0.000	0.001	0.005	0.015	0.038	0.079	0.143	0.232	0.341
11.5	0.000	0.000	0.001	0.003	0.011	0.028	0.060	0.114	0.191	0.289
12.0	0.000	0.000	0.001	0.002	0.008	0.020	0.046	0.090	0.155	0.242
12.5	0.000	0.000	0.000	0.002	0.005	0.015	0.035	0.070	0.125	0.201
13.0	0.000	0.000	0.000	0.001	0.004	0.011	0.026	0.054	0.100	0.166
13.5	0.000	0.000	0.000	0.001	0.003	0.008	0.019	0.041	0.079	0.135
14.0	0.000	0.000	0.000	0.000	0.002	0.006	0.014	0.032	0.062	0.109
14.5	0.000	0.000	0.000	0.000	0.001	0.004	0.010	0.024	0.048	0.088
15.0	0.000	0.000	0.000	0.000	0.001	0.003	0.008	0.018	0.037	0.070

	10	11	12	13	14	15	16	17	18	19
10.5	0.521	0.639	0.742	0.825	0.888	0.932	0.960	0.978	0.988	0.994
11.0	0.460	0.579	0.689	0.781	0.854	0.907	0.944	0.968	0.982	0.991
11.5	0.402	0.520	0.633	0.733	0.815	0.878	0.924	0.954	0.974	0.986
12.0	0.347	0.462	0.576	0.682	0.772	0.844	0.899	0.937	0.963	0.979
12.5	0.297	0.406	0.519	0.628	0.725	0.806	0.869	0.916	0.948	0.969
13.0	0.252	0.353	0.463	0.573	0.675	0.764	0.835	0.890	0.930	0.957
13.5	0.211	0.304	0.409	0.518	0.623	0.718	0.798	0.861	0.908	0.942
14.0	0.176	0.260	0.358	0.464	0.570	0.669	0.756	0.827	0.883	0.923
14.5	0.145	0.220	0.311	0.413	0.518	0.619	0.711	0.790	0.853	0.901
15.0	0.118	0.185	0.268	0.363	0.466	0.568	0.664	0.749	0.819	0.875

	20	21	22	23	24	25	26	27	28	29
10.5	0.997	0.999	0.999	1.000						
11.0	0.995	0.998	0.999	1.000						
11.5	0.992	0.996	0.998	0.999	1.000					
12.0	0.988	0.994	0.997	0.999	0.999	1.000				
12.5	0.983	0.991	0.995	0.998	0.999	0.999	1.000			
13.0	0.975	0.986	0.992	0.996	0.998	0.999	1.000			
13.5	0.965	0.980	0.989	0.994	0.997	0.998	0.999	1.000		
14.0	0.952	0.971	0.983	0.991	0.995	0.997	0.999	0.999	1.000	
14.5	0.936	0.960	0.976	0.986	0.992	0.996	0.998	0.999	0.999	1.000
15.0	0.917	0.947	0.967	0.981	0.989	0.994	0.997	0.998	0.999	1.000

TABLE 3 Standard Normal Distribution Function

$$F(z) = \frac{1}{\sqrt{2\pi}} \int_{-\infty}^{z} e^{-t^2/2}\,dt$$

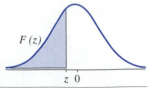

z	0.00	0.01	0.02	0.03	0.04	0.05	0.06	0.07	0.08	0.09
−5.0	0.0000003									
−4.0	0.00003									
−3.5	0.0002									
−3.4	0.0003	0.0003	0.0003	0.0003	0.0003	0.0003	0.0003	0.0003	0.0003	0.0002
−3.3	0.0005	0.0005	0.0005	0.0004	0.0004	0.0004	0.0004	0.0004	0.0004	0.0003
−3.2	0.0007	0.0007	0.0006	0.0006	0.0006	0.0006	0.0006	0.0005	0.0005	0.0005
−3.1	0.0010	0.0009	0.0009	0.0009	0.0008	0.0008	0.0008	0.0008	0.0007	0.0007
−3.0	0.0013	0.0013	0.0013	0.0012	0.0012	0.0011	0.0011	0.0011	0.0010	0.0010
−2.9	0.0019	0.0018	0.0018	0.0017	0.0016	0.0016	0.0015	0.0015	0.0014	0.0014
−2.8	0.0026	0.0025	0.0024	0.0023	0.0023	0.0022	0.0021	0.0021	0.0020	0.0019
−2.7	0.0035	0.0034	0.0033	0.0032	0.0031	0.0030	0.0029	0.0028	0.0027	0.0026
−2.6	0.0047	0.0045	0.0044	0.0043	0.0041	0.0040	0.0039	0.0038	0.0037	0.0036
−2.5	0.0062	0.0060	0.0059	0.0057	0.0055	0.0054	0.0052	0.0051	0.0049	0.0048
−2.4	0.0082	0.0080	0.0078	0.0075	0.0073	0.0071	0.0069	0.0068	0.0066	0.0064
−2.3	0.0107	0.0104	0.0102	0.0099	0.0096	0.0094	0.0091	0.0089	0.0087	0.0084
−2.2	0.0139	0.0136	0.0132	0.0129	0.0125	0.0122	0.0119	0.0116	0.0113	0.0110
−2.1	0.0179	0.0174	0.0170	0.0166	0.0162	0.0158	0.0154	0.0150	0.0146	0.0143
−2.0	0.0228	0.0222	0.0217	0.0212	0.0207	0.0202	0.0197	0.0192	0.0188	0.0183
−1.9	0.0287	0.0281	0.0274	0.0268	0.0262	0.0256	0.0250	0.0244	0.0239	0.0233
−1.8	0.0359	0.0351	0.0344	0.0336	0.0329	0.0322	0.0314	0.0307	0.0301	0.0294
−1.7	0.0446	0.0436	0.0427	0.0418	0.0409	0.0401	0.0392	0.0384	0.0375	0.0367
−1.6	0.0548	0.0537	0.0526	0.0516	0.0505	0.0495	0.0485	0.0475	0.0465	0.0455
−1.5	0.0668	0.0655	0.0643	0.0630	0.0618	0.0606	0.0594	0.0582	0.0571	0.0559
−1.4	0.0808	0.0793	0.0778	0.0764	0.0749	0.0735	0.0721	0.0708	0.0694	0.0681
−1.3	0.0968	0.0951	0.0934	0.0918	0.0901	0.0885	0.0869	0.0853	0.0838	0.0823
−1.2	0.1151	0.1131	0.1112	0.1093	0.1075	0.1056	0.1038	0.1020	0.1003	0.0985
−1.1	0.1357	0.1335	0.1314	0.1292	0.1271	0.1251	0.1230	0.1210	0.1190	0.1170
−1.0	0.1587	0.1562	0.1539	0.1515	0.1492	0.1469	0.1446	0.1423	0.1401	0.1379
−0.9	0.1841	0.1814	0.1788	0.1762	0.1736	0.1711	0.1685	0.1660	0.1635	0.1611
−0.8	0.2119	0.2090	0.2061	0.2033	0.2005	0.1977	0.1949	0.1922	0.1894	0.1867
−0.7	0.2420	0.2389	0.2358	0.2327	0.2296	0.2266	0.2236	0.2206	0.2177	0.2148
−0.6	0.2743	0.2709	0.2676	0.2643	0.2611	0.2578	0.2546	0.2514	0.2483	0.2451
−0.5	0.3085	0.3050	0.3015	0.2981	0.2946	0.2912	0.2877	0.2843	0.2810	0.2776
−0.4	0.3446	0.3409	0.3372	0.3336	0.3300	0.3264	0.3228	0.3192	0.3156	0.3121
−0.3	0.3821	0.3783	0.3745	0.3707	0.3669	0.3632	0.3594	0.3557	0.3520	0.3483
−0.2	0.4207	0.4168	0.4129	0.4090	0.4052	0.4013	0.3974	0.3936	0.3897	0.3859
−0.1	0.4602	0.4562	0.4522	0.4483	0.4443	0.4404	0.4364	0.4325	0.4286	0.4247
−0.0	0.5000	0.4960	0.4920	0.4880	0.4840	0.4801	0.4761	0.4721	0.4681	0.4641

TABLE 3 Standard Normal Distribution Function

$$F(z) = \frac{1}{\sqrt{2\pi}} \int_{-\infty}^{z} e^{-t^2/2} dt$$

$F(z)$

$0\ z$

z	0.00	0.01	0.02	0.03	0.04	0.05	0.06	0.07	0.08	0.09
0.0	0.5000	0.5040	0.5080	0.5120	0.5160	0.5199	0.5239	0.5279	0.5319	0.5359
0.1	0.5398	0.5438	0.5478	0.5517	0.5557	0.5596	0.5636	0.5675	0.5714	0.5753
0.2	0.5793	0.5832	0.5871	0.5910	0.5948	0.5987	0.6026	0.6064	0.6103	0.6141
0.3	0.6179	0.6217	0.6255	0.6293	0.6331	0.6368	0.6406	0.6443	0.6480	0.6517
0.4	0.6554	0.6591	0.6628	0.6664	0.6700	0.6736	0.6772	0.6808	0.6844	0.6879
0.5	0.6915	0.6950	0.6985	0.7019	0.7054	0.7088	0.7123	0.7157	0.7190	0.7224
0.6	0.7257	0.7291	0.7324	0.7357	0.7389	0.7422	0.7454	0.7486	0.7517	0.7549
0.7	0.7580	0.7611	0.7642	0.7673	0.7704	0.7734	0.7764	0.7794	0.7823	0.7852
0.8	0.7881	0.7910	0.7939	0.7967	0.7995	0.8023	0.8051	0.8078	0.8106	0.8133
0.9	0.8159	0.8186	0.8212	0.8238	0.8264	0.8289	0.8315	0.8340	0.8365	0.8389
1.0	0.8413	0.8438	0.8461	0.8485	0.8508	0.8531	0.8554	0.8577	0.8599	0.8621
1.1	0.8643	0.8665	0.8686	0.8708	0.8729	0.8749	0.8770	0.8790	0.8810	0.8830
1.2	0.8849	0.8869	0.8888	0.8907	0.8925	0.8944	0.8962	0.8980	0.8997	0.9015
1.3	0.9032	0.9049	0.9066	0.9082	0.9099	0.9115	0.9131	0.9147	0.9162	0.9177
1.4	0.9192	0.9207	0.9222	0.9236	0.9251	0.9265	0.9279	0.9292	0.9306	0.9319
1.5	0.9332	0.9345	0.9357	0.9370	0.9382	0.9394	0.9406	0.9418	0.9429	0.9441
1.6	0.9452	0.9463	0.9474	0.9484	0.9495	0.9505	0.9515	0.9525	0.9535	0.9545
1.7	0.9554	0.9564	0.9573	0.9582	0.9591	0.9599	0.9608	0.9616	0.9625	0.9633
1.8	0.9641	0.9649	0.9656	0.9664	0.9671	0.9678	0.9686	0.9693	0.9699	0.9706
1.9	0.9713	0.9719	0.9726	0.9732	0.9738	0.9744	0.9750	0.9756	0.9761	0.9767
2.0	0.9772	0.9778	0.9783	0.9788	0.9793	0.9798	0.9803	0.9808	0.9812	0.9817
2.1	0.9821	0.9826	0.9830	0.9834	0.9838	0.9842	0.9846	0.9850	0.9854	0.9857
2.2	0.9861	0.9864	0.9868	0.9871	0.9875	0.9878	0.9881	0.9884	0.9887	0.9890
2.3	0.9893	0.9896	0.9898	0.9901	0.9904	0.9906	0.9909	0.9911	0.9913	0.9916
2.4	0.9918	0.9920	0.9922	0.9925	0.9927	0.9929	0.9931	0.9932	0.9934	0.9936
2.5	0.9938	0.9940	0.9941	0.9943	0.9945	0.9946	0.9948	0.9949	0.9951	0.9952
2.6	0.9953	0.9955	0.9956	0.9957	0.9959	0.9960	0.9961	0.9962	0.9963	0.9964
2.7	0.9965	0.9966	0.9967	0.9968	0.9969	0.9970	0.9971	0.9972	0.9973	0.9974
2.8	0.9974	0.9975	0.9976	0.9977	0.9977	0.9978	0.9979	0.9979	0.9980	0.9981
2.9	0.9981	0.9982	0.9982	0.9983	0.9984	0.9984	0.9985	0.9985	0.9986	0.9986
3.0	0.9987	0.9987	0.9987	0.9988	0.9988	0.9989	0.9989	0.9989	0.9990	0.9990
3.1	0.9990	0.9991	0.9991	0.9991	0.9992	0.9992	0.9992	0.9992	0.9993	0.9993
3.2	0.9993	0.9993	0.9994	0.9994	0.9994	0.9994	0.9994	0.9995	0.9995	0.9995
3.3	0.9995	0.9995	0.9995	0.9996	0.9996	0.9996	0.9996	0.9996	0.9996	0.9997
3.4	0.9997	0.9997	0.9997	0.9997	0.9997	0.9997	0.9997	0.9997	0.9997	0.9998
3.5	0.9998									
4.0	0.99997									
5.0	0.9999997									

TABLE 4 Values of t_α

v	$\alpha = 0.10$	$\alpha = 0.05$	$\alpha = 0.025$	$\alpha = 0.01$	$\alpha = 0.00833$	$\alpha = 0.00625$	$\alpha = 0.005$	v
1	3.078	6.314	12.706	31.821	38.204	50.923	63.657	1
2	1.886	2.920	4.303	6.965	7.650	8.860	9.925	2
3	1.638	2.353	3.182	4.541	4.857	5.392	5.841	3
4	1.533	2.132	2.776	3.747	3.961	4.315	4.604	4
5	1.476	2.015	2.571	3.365	3.534	3.810	4.032	5
6	1.440	1.943	2.447	3.143	3.288	3.521	3.707	6
7	1.415	1.895	2.365	2.998	3.128	3.335	3.499	7
8	1.397	1.860	2.306	2.896	3.016	3.206	3.355	8
9	1.383	1.833	2.262	2.821	2.934	3.111	3.250	9
10	1.372	1.812	2.228	2.764	2.870	3.038	3.169	10
11	1.363	1.796	2.201	2.718	2.820	2.981	3.106	11
12	1.356	1.782	2.179	2.681	2.780	2.934	3.055	12
13	1.350	1.771	2.160	2.650	2.746	2.896	3.012	13
14	1.345	1.761	2.145	2.624	2.718	2.864	2.977	14
15	1.341	1.753	2.131	2.602	2.694	2.837	2.947	15
16	1.337	1.746	2.120	2.583	2.673	2.813	2.921	16
17	1.333	1.740	2.110	2.567	2.655	2.793	2.898	17
18	1.330	1.734	2.101	2.552	2.639	2.775	2.878	18
19	1.328	1.729	2.093	2.539	2.625	2.759	2.861	19
20	1.325	1.725	2.086	2.528	2.613	2.744	2.845	20
21	1.323	1.721	2.080	2.518	2.602	2.732	2.831	21
22	1.321	1.717	2.074	2.508	2.591	2.720	2.819	22
23	1.319	1.714	2.069	2.500	2.582	2.710	2.807	23
24	1.318	1.711	2.064	2.492	2.574	2.700	2.797	24
25	1.316	1.708	2.060	2.485	2.566	2.692	2.787	25
26	1.315	1.706	2.056	2.479	2.559	2.684	2.779	26
27	1.314	1.703	2.052	2.473	2.553	2.676	2.771	27
28	1.313	1.701	2.048	2.467	2.547	2.669	2.763	28
29	1.311	1.699	2.045	2.462	2.541	2.663	2.756	29
inf.	1.282	1.645	1.960	2.326	2.394	2.498	2.576	inf.

TABLE 5 Values of χ_α^2*

ν	$\alpha = 0.995$	$\alpha = 0.99$	$\alpha = 0.975$	$\alpha = 0.95$	$\alpha = 0.05$	$\alpha = 0.025$	$\alpha = 0.01$	$\alpha = 0.005$	ν
1	0.0000393	0.000157	0.000982	0.00393	3.841	5.024	6.635	7.879	1
2	0.0100	0.0201	0.0506	0.103	5.991	7.378	9.210	10.597	2
3	0.0717	0.115	0.216	0.352	7.815	9.348	11.345	12.838	3
4	0.207	0.297	0.484	0.711	9.488	11.143	13.277	14.860	4
5	0.412	0.554	0.831	1.145	11.070	12.832	15.056	16.750	5
6	0.676	0.872	1.237	1.635	12.592	14.449	16.812	18.548	6
7	0.989	1.239	1.690	2.167	14.067	16.013	18.475	20.278	7
8	1.344	1.646	2.180	2.733	15.507	17.535	20.090	21.955	8
9	1.735	2.088	2.700	3.325	16.919	19.023	21.666	23.589	9
10	2.156	2.558	3.247	3.940	18.307	20.483	23.209	25.188	10
11	2.603	3.053	3.816	4.575	19.675	21.920	24.725	26.757	11
12	3.074	3.571	4.404	5.226	21.026	23.337	26.217	28.300	12
13	3.565	4.107	5.009	5.892	22.362	24.736	27.688	29.819	13
14	4.075	4.660	5.629	6.571	23.685	26.119	29.141	31.319	14
15	4.601	5.229	6.262	7.261	24.996	27.488	30.578	32.801	15
16	5.142	5.812	6.908	7.962	26.296	28.845	32.000	34.267	16
17	5.697	6.408	7.564	8.672	27.587	30.191	33.409	35.718	17
18	6.265	7.015	8.231	9.390	28.869	31.526	34.805	37.156	18
19	6.844	7.633	8.907	10.117	30.144	32.852	36.191	38.582	19
20	7.434	8.260	9.591	10.851	31.410	34.170	37.566	39.997	20
21	8.034	8.897	10.283	11.591	32.671	35.479	38.932	41.401	21
22	8.643	9.542	10.982	12.338	33.924	36.781	40.289	42.796	22
23	9.260	10.196	11.689	13.091	35.172	38.076	41.638	44.181	23
24	9.886	10.856	12.401	13.484	36.415	39.364	42.980	45.558	24
25	10.520	11.524	13.120	14.611	37.652	40.646	44.314	46.928	25
26	11.160	12.198	13.844	15.379	38.885	41.923	45.642	48.290	26
27	11.808	12.879	14.573	16.151	40.113	43.194	46.963	49.645	27
28	12.461	13.565	15.308	16.928	41.337	44.461	48.278	50.993	28
29	13.121	14.256	16.047	17.708	42.557	45.772	49.588	52.336	29
30	13.787	14.953	16.791	18.493	43.773	46.979	50.892	53.672	30
40	20.706	22.164	24.433	26.509	55.758	59.342	63.691	66.766	40
50	27.991	29.707	32.357	34.764	67.505	71.420	76.154	79.490	50
60	35.535	37.485	40.482	43.118	79.082	83.298	88.379	91.952	60
70	43.275	45.442	48.758	51.739	90.531	95.023	100.425	104.215	70
80	51.172	53.540	57.153	60.391	101.879	106.629	112.329	116.321	80
90	59.196	61.754	65.646	69.126	113.145	118.136	124.116	128.299	90
100	67.328	70.065	74.222	77.929	124.342	129.561	135.807	140.169	100

* This table is based on Table 8 of *Biometrika Tables for Statisticians*, Vol. 1, by permission of the *Biometrika* trustees.

TABLE 6(a) Values of $F_{0.05}$

v_1 = Degrees of freedom for numerator

v_2 = Degrees of freedom for denominator	1	2	3	4	5	6	7	8	9	10	12	15	20	25	30	40	60	120	∞
1	161	200	216	225	230	234	237	239	241	242	244	246	248	249	250	251	252	253	254
2	18.51	19.00	19.16	19.25	19.30	19.33	19.35	19.37	19.38	19.40	19.41	19.43	19.45	19.46	19.46	19.47	19.48	19.49	19.50
3	10.13	9.55	9.28	9.12	9.01	8.94	8.89	8.85	8.81	8.79	8.74	8.70	8.66	8.63	8.62	8.59	8.57	8.55	8.53
4	7.71	6.94	6.59	6.39	6.26	6.16	6.09	6.04	6.00	5.96	5.91	5.86	5.80	5.77	5.75	5.72	5.69	5.66	5.63
5	6.61	5.79	5.41	5.19	5.05	4.95	4.88	4.82	4.77	4.74	4.68	4.62	4.56	4.52	4.50	4.46	4.43	4.40	4.37
6	5.99	5.14	4.76	4.53	4.39	4.28	4.21	4.15	4.10	4.06	4.00	3.94	3.87	3.83	3.81	3.77	3.74	3.70	3.67
7	5.59	4.74	4.35	4.12	3.97	3.87	3.79	3.73	3.68	3.64	3.57	3.51	3.44	3.40	3.38	3.34	3.30	3.27	3.23
8	5.32	4.46	4.07	3.84	3.69	3.58	3.50	3.44	3.39	3.35	3.28	3.22	3.15	3.11	3.08	3.04	3.01	2.97	2.93
9	5.12	4.26	3.86	3.63	3.48	3.37	3.29	3.23	3.18	3.14	3.07	3.01	2.94	2.89	2.86	2.83	2.79	2.75	2.71
10	4.96	4.10	3.71	3.48	3.33	3.22	3.14	3.07	3.02	2.98	2.91	2.85	2.77	2.73	2.70	2.66	2.62	2.58	2.54
11	4.84	3.98	3.59	3.36	3.20	3.09	3.01	2.95	2.90	2.85	2.79	2.72	2.65	2.60	2.57	2.53	2.49	2.45	2.40
12	4.75	3.89	3.49	3.26	3.11	3.00	2.91	2.85	2.80	2.75	2.69	2.62	2.54	2.50	2.47	2.43	2.38	2.34	2.30
13	4.67	3.81	3.41	3.18	3.03	2.92	2.83	2.77	2.71	2.67	2.60	2.53	2.46	2.41	2.38	2.34	2.30	2.25	2.21
14	4.60	3.74	3.34	3.11	2.96	2.85	2.76	2.70	2.65	2.60	2.53	2.46	2.39	2.34	2.31	2.27	2.22	2.18	2.13
15	4.54	3.68	3.29	3.06	2.90	2.79	2.71	2.64	2.59	2.54	2.48	2.40	2.33	2.28	2.25	2.20	2.16	2.11	2.07
16	4.49	3.63	3.24	3.01	2.85	2.74	2.66	2.59	2.54	2.49	2.42	2.35	2.28	2.23	2.19	2.15	2.11	2.06	2.01
17	4.45	3.59	3.20	2.96	2.81	2.70	2.61	2.55	2.49	2.45	2.38	2.31	2.23	2.18	2.15	2.10	2.06	2.01	1.96
18	4.41	3.55	3.16	2.93	2.77	2.66	2.58	2.51	2.46	2.41	2.34	2.27	2.19	2.14	2.11	2.06	2.02	1.97	1.92
19	4.38	3.52	3.13	2.90	2.74	2.63	2.54	2.48	2.42	2.38	2.31	2.23	2.16	2.11	2.07	2.03	1.98	1.93	1.88
20	4.35	3.49	3.10	2.87	2.71	2.60	2.51	2.45	2.39	2.35	2.28	2.20	2.12	2.07	2.04	1.99	1.95	1.90	1.84
21	4.32	3.47	3.07	2.84	2.68	2.57	2.49	2.42	2.37	2.32	2.25	2.18	2.10	2.05	2.01	1.96	1.92	1.87	1.81
22	4.30	3.44	3.05	2.82	2.66	2.55	2.46	2.40	2.34	2.30	2.23	2.15	2.07	2.02	1.98	1.94	1.89	1.84	1.78
23	4.28	3.42	3.03	2.80	2.64	2.53	2.44	2.37	2.32	2.27	2.20	2.13	2.05	2.00	1.96	1.91	1.86	1.81	1.76
24	4.26	3.40	3.01	2.78	2.62	2.51	2.42	2.36	2.30	2.25	2.18	2.11	2.03	1.97	1.94	1.89	1.84	1.79	1.73
25	4.24	3.39	2.99	2.76	2.60	2.49	2.40	2.34	2.28	2.24	2.16	2.09	2.01	1.96	1.92	1.87	1.82	1.77	1.71
30	4.17	3.32	2.92	2.69	2.53	2.42	2.33	2.27	2.21	2.16	2.09	2.01	1.93	1.88	1.84	1.79	1.74	1.68	1.62
40	4.08	3.23	2.84	2.61	2.45	2.34	2.25	2.18	2.12	2.08	2.00	1.92	1.84	1.78	1.74	1.69	1.64	1.58	1.51
60	4.00	3.15	2.76	2.53	2.37	2.25	2.17	2.10	2.04	1.99	1.92	1.84	1.75	1.69	1.65	1.59	1.53	1.47	1.39
120	3.92	3.07	2.68	2.45	2.29	2.18	2.09	2.02	1.96	1.91	1.83	1.75	1.66	1.60	1.55	1.50	1.43	1.35	1.25
∞	3.84	3.00	2.60	2.37	2.21	2.10	2.01	1.94	1.88	1.83	1.75	1.67	1.57	1.51	1.46	1.39	1.32	1.22	1.00

TABLE 6(b) Values of $F_{0.01}$

$\nu_1 = $ Degrees of freedom for numerator

$\nu_2 =$ Degrees of freedom for denominator	1	2	3	4	5	6	7	8	9	10	12	15	20	25	30	40	60	120	∞
1	4,052	5,000	5,403	5,625	5,764	5,859	5,928	5,982	6,023	6,056	6,106	6,157	6,209	6,240	6,261	6,287	6,313	6,339	6,366
2	98.50	99.00	99.17	99.25	99.30	99.33	99.36	99.37	99.39	99.40	99.42	99.43	99.45	99.46	99.57	99.47	99.48	99.49	99.50
3	34.12	30.82	29.46	28.71	28.24	27.91	27.67	27.49	27.35	27.23	27.05	26.87	26.69	26.58	26.50	25.41	26.32	26.22	26.13
4	21.20	18.00	16.69	15.98	15.52	15.21	14.98	14.80	14.66	14.55	14.37	14.20	14.02	13.91	13.84	13.75	13.65	13.56	13.46
5	16.26	13.27	12.06	11.39	10.97	10.67	10.46	10.29	10.16	10.05	9.89	9.72	9.55	9.45	9.38	9.29	9.20	9.11	9.02
6	13.75	10.92	9.78	9.15	8.75	8.47	8.26	8.10	7.98	7.87	7.72	7.56	7.40	7.30	7.23	7.14	7.06	6.97	6.88
7	12.25	9.55	8.45	7.85	7.46	7.19	6.99	6.84	6.72	6.62	6.47	6.31	6.16	6.06	5.99	5.91	5.82	5.74	5.65
8	11.26	8.65	7.59	7.01	6.63	6.37	6.18	6.03	5.91	5.81	5.67	5.52	5.36	5.26	5.20	5.12	5.03	4.95	4.86
9	10.56	8.02	6.99	6.42	6.06	5.80	5.61	5.47	5.35	5.26	5.11	4.96	4.81	4.71	4.65	4.57	4.48	4.40	4.31
10	10.04	7.56	6.55	5.99	5.64	5.39	5.20	5.06	4.94	4.85	4.71	4.56	4.41	4.31	4.25	4.17	4.08	4.00	3.91
11	9.65	7.21	6.22	5.67	5.32	5.07	4.89	4.74	4.63	4.54	4.40	4.25	4.10	4.01	3.94	3.86	3.78	3.69	3.60
12	9.33	6.93	5.95	5.41	5.06	4.82	4.64	4.50	4.39	4.30	4.16	4.01	3.86	3.76	3.70	3.62	3.54	3.45	3.36
13	9.07	6.70	5.74	5.21	4.86	4.62	4.44	4.30	4.19	4.10	3.96	3.82	3.66	3.57	3.51	3.43	3.34	3.25	3.17
14	8.86	6.51	5.56	5.04	4.69	4.46	4.28	4.14	4.03	3.94	3.80	3.66	3.51	3.41	3.35	3.27	3.18	3.09	3.00
15	8.68	6.36	5.42	4.89	4.56	4.32	4.14	4.00	3.89	3.80	3.67	3.52	3.37	3.28	3.21	3.13	3.05	2.96	2.87
16	8.53	6.23	5.29	4.77	4.44	4.20	4.03	3.89	3.78	3.69	3.55	3.41	3.26	3.16	3.10	3.02	2.93	2.84	2.75
17	8.40	6.11	5.18	4.67	4.34	4.10	3.93	3.79	3.68	3.59	3.46	3.31	3.16	3.07	3.00	2.92	2.83	2.75	2.65
18	8.29	6.01	5.09	4.58	4.25	4.01	3.84	3.71	3.60	3.51	3.37	3.23	3.08	2.98	2.92	2.84	2.75	2.66	2.57
19	8.18	5.93	5.01	4.50	4.17	3.94	3.77	3.63	3.52	3.43	3.30	3.15	3.00	2.91	2.84	2.76	2.67	2.58	2.49
20	8.10	5.85	4.94	4.43	4.10	3.87	3.70	3.56	3.46	3.37	3.23	3.09	2.94	2.84	2.78	2.69	2.61	2.52	2.42
21	8.02	5.78	4.87	4.37	4.04	3.81	3.64	3.51	3.40	3.31	3.17	3.03	2.88	2.79	2.72	2.64	2.55	2.46	2.36
22	7.95	5.72	4.82	4.31	3.99	3.76	3.59	3.45	3.35	3.26	3.12	2.98	2.83	2.73	2.67	2.58	2.50	2.40	2.31
23	7.88	5.66	4.76	4.26	3.94	3.71	3.54	3.41	3.30	3.21	3.07	2.93	2.78	2.69	2.62	2.54	2.45	2.35	2.26
24	7.82	5.61	4.72	4.22	3.90	3.67	3.50	3.36	3.26	3.17	3.03	2.89	2.74	2.64	2.58	2.49	2.40	2.31	2.21
25	7.77	5.57	4.68	4.18	3.85	3.63	3.46	3.32	3.22	3.13	2.99	2.85	2.70	2.60	2.54	2.45	2.36	2.27	2.17
30	7.56	5.39	4.51	4.02	3.70	3.47	3.30	3.17	3.07	2.98	2.84	2.70	2.55	2.45	2.39	2.30	2.21	2.11	2.01
40	7.31	5.18	4.31	3.83	3.51	3.29	3.12	2.99	2.89	2.80	2.66	2.52	2.37	2.27	2.20	2.11	2.02	1.92	1.80
60	7.08	4.98	4.13	3.65	3.34	3.12	2.95	2.82	2.72	2.63	2.50	2.35	2.20	2.10	2.03	1.94	1.84	1.73	1.60
120	6.85	4.79	3.95	3.48	3.17	2.96	2.79	2.66	2.56	2.47	2.34	2.19	2.03	1.93	1.86	1.76	1.66	1.53	1.38
∞	6.63	4.61	3.78	3.32	3.02	2.80	2.64	2.51	2.41	2.32	2.18	2.04	1.88	1.77	1.70	1.59	1.47	1.32	1.00

TABLE 7 Random Digits*

Row 1	1306	1189	5731	3968	5606	5084	8947	3897	1636	7810
2	0422	2431	0649	8085	5053	4722	6598	5044	9040	5121
3	6597	2022	6168	5060	8656	6733	6364	7649	1871	4328
4	7965	6541	5645	6243	7658	6903	9911	5740	7824	8520
5	7695	6937	0406	8894	0441	8135	9797	7285	5905	9539
6	5160	7851	8464	6789	3938	4197	6511	0407	9239	2232
7	2961	0551	0539	8288	7478	7565	5581	5771	5442	8761
8	1428	4183	4312	5445	4854	9157	9158	5218	1464	3634
9	3666	5642	4539	1561	7849	7520	2547	0756	1206	2033
10	6543	6799	7454	9052	6689	1946	2574	9386	0304	7945
11	9975	6080	7423	3175	9377	6951	6519	8287	8994	5532
12	4866	0956	7545	7723	8085	4948	2228	9583	4415	7065
13	8239	7068	6694	5168	3117	1568	0237	6160	9585	1133
14	8722	9191	3386	3443	0434	4586	4150	1224	6204	0937
15	1330	9120	8785	8382	2929	7089	3109	6742	2468	7025
16	2296	2952	4764	9070	6356	9192	4012	0618	2219	1109
17	3582	7052	3132	4519	9250	2486	0830	8472	2160	7046
18	5872	9207	7222	6494	8973	3545	6967	8490	5264	9821
19	1134	6324	6201	3792	5651	0538	4676	2064	0584	7996
20	1403	4497	7390	8503	8239	4326	8022	2914	4368	4529
21	3393	7025	3381	3553	2128	1021	8353	6413	5161	8583
22	1137	7896	3602	0060	7850	7626	0854	6565	4260	6220
23	7437	5198	8772	6727	8527	6851	2709	5992	7383	1071
24	8414	8820	3917	7238	9821	6073	6658	1280	9643	7761
25	8398	5224	2749	7311	5740	9771	7826	9533	3800	4553
26	0995	8935	2939	3092	2496	0359	0318	4697	7181	4035
27	6657	0755	9685	4017	6581	7292	5643	5064	1142	1297
28	8875	8369	7868	0190	9278	1709	4253	9346	4335	3769
29	8399	6702	0586	6428	7985	2979	4513	1970	1989	3105
30	6703	1024	2064	0393	6815	8502	1375	4171	6970	1201
31	4730	1653	9032	9855	0957	7366	0325	5178	7959	5371
32	8400	6834	3187	8688	1079	1480	6776	9888	7585	9998
33	3647	8002	6726	0877	4552	3238	7542	7804	3933	9475
34	6789	5197	8037	2354	9262	5497	0005	3986	1767	7981
35	2630	2721	2810	2185	6323	5679	4931	8336	6662	3566
36	1374	8625	1644	3342	1587	0762	6057	8011	2666	3759
37	1519	7625	9110	4409	0239	7059	3415	5537	2250	7292
38	9678	2877	7579	4935	0449	8119	6969	5383	1717	6719
39	0882	6781	3538	4090	3092	2365	6001	3446	9985	6007
40	0006	4205	2389	4365	1981	8158	7784	6256	3842	5603

* From Donald B. Owen, *Handbook of Statistical Tables.* Reading, Mass: Addison Wesley, 1962.

TABLE 7 Random Digits (continued)

Row 1	4611	9861	7916	9305	2074	9462	0254	4827	9198	3974
2	1093	3784	4190	6332	1175	8599	9735	8584	6581	7194
3	3374	3545	6865	8819	3342	1676	2264	6014	5012	2458
4	3650	9676	1436	4374	4716	5548	8276	6235	6742	2154
5	7292	5749	7977	7602	9205	3599	3880	9537	4423	2330
6	2353	8319	2850	4026	3027	1708	3518	7034	7132	6903
7	1094	2009	8919	5676	7283	4982	9642	9235	8167	3366
8	0568	4002	0587	7165	1094	2006	7471	0940	4366	9554
9	5606	4070	5233	4339	6543	6695	5799	5821	3953	9458
10	8285	7537	1181	2300	5294	6892	1627	3372	1952	3028
11	2444	9039	4803	8568	1590	2420	2547	2470	8179	4617
12	5748	7767	2800	6289	2814	8281	1549	9519	3341	1192
13	7761	8583	0852	5619	6864	8506	9643	7763	9611	1289
14	6838	9280	2654	0812	3988	2146	5095	0150	8043	9079
15	6440	2631	3033	9167	4998	7036	0133	7428	9702	1376
16	8829	0094	2887	3802	5497	0318	5168	6377	9216	2802
17	9845	4796	2951	4449	1999	2691	5328	7674	7004	6212
18	5072	9000	3887	5739	7920	6074	4715	3681	2721	2701
19	9035	0553	1272	2600	3828	8197	8852	9092	8027	6144
20	5562	1080	2222	0336	1411	0303	7424	3713	9278	1918
21	2757	2650	8727	3953	9579	2442	8041	9869	2887	3933
22	6397	1848	1476	0787	4990	4666	1208	2769	3922	1158
23	9208	7641	3575	4279	1282	1840	5999	1806	7809	5885
24	2418	9289	6120	8141	3908	5577	3590	2317	8975	4593
25	7300	9006	5659	8258	3662	0332	5369	3640	0563	7939
26	6780	2535	8916	3245	2256	4350	6064	2438	2002	1272
27	2914	7309	4045	7513	3195	4166	0878	5184	6680	2655
28	0868	8657	8118	6340	9452	7460	3291	5778	1167	0312
29	7994	6579	6461	2292	9554	8309	5036	0974	9517	8293
30	8587	0764	6687	9150	1642	2050	4934	0027	1376	5040
31	8016	8345	2257	5084	8004	7949	3205	3972	7640	3478
32	5581	5775	7517	9076	4699	8313	8401	7147	9416	7184
33	2015	3364	6688	2631	2152	2220	1637	8333	4838	5699
34	7327	8987	5741	0102	1173	7350	7080	7420	1847	0741
35	3589	1991	1764	8355	9684	9423	7101	1063	4151	4875
36	2188	6454	7319	1215	0473	6589	2355	9579	7004	6209
37	2924	0472	9878	7966	2491	5662	5635	2789	2564	1249
38	1961	1669	2219	1113	9175	0260	4046	8142	4432	2664
39	2393	9637	0410	7536	0972	5153	0708	1935	1143	1704
40	7585	4424	2648	6728	2233	3518	7267	1732	1926	3833

TABLE 7 Random Digits (continued)

Row 1	0197	4021	9027	7327	9212	7017	8060	6216	1942	6817
2	9719	5336	5532	8537	2980	8252	4971	0110	6209	1556
3	8866	4785	6007	8006	9043	4109	5570	9249	9905	2152
4	5744	3957	8786	9023	1472	7275	1014	1104	0832	7680
5	7149	5721	1389	6581	7196	7072	6360	3084	7009	0239
6	7710	8479	9345	7773	9086	1202	8845	3163	7937	6163
7	5246	5651	0432	8644	6341	9661	2361	8377	8673	6098
8	3576	0013	7381	0124	8559	9813	9080	6984	0926	2169
9	3026	1464	2671	4691	0353	5289	8754	2442	7799	8983
10	6591	4365	8717	2365	5686	8377	8675	9798	7745	6360
11	0402	3257	0480	5038	1998	2935	1306	1190	2406	2596
12	7105	7654	4745	4482	8471	1424	2031	7803	4367	6816
13	7181	4140	1046	0885	1264	7755	1653	8924	5822	4401
14	3655	3282	2176	8134	3291	7262	8229	2866	7065	4806
15	5121	6717	3117	1901	5184	6467	8954	3884	0279	8635
16	3618	3098	9208	7429	1578	1917	7927	2696	3704	0833
17	0166	3638	4947	1414	4799	9189	2459	5056	5982	6154
18	6187	9653	3658	4730	1652	8096	8288	9368	5531	7788
19	1234	1448	0276	7290	1667	2823	3755	5642	4854	8844
20	8949	8731	4875	5724	2962	1182	2930	7539	4526	7252
21	4357	4146	8353	9952	8004	7945	1530	5207	4730	1967
22	5339	7325	6862	7584	8634	3485	2278	5832	0612	8118
23	6583	8433	0717	0606	9284	2719	1888	2889	0285	2765
24	6564	3526	2171	3809	3428	5523	9078	0648	7768	3326
25	4811	1933	3763	6265	8931	0649	8085	6177	4450	2139
26	6931	7236	1230	0441	4013	1352	6563	1499	7332	3068
27	8755	3390	6120	7825	9005	7012	1643	9934	4044	7022
28	6742	2260	3443	0190	9278	1816	7697	7933	0067	2906
29	6655	3930	9014	6032	7574	1685	5258	3100	5358	1929
30	8514	4806	4124	9286	0449	5051	4772	4651	0038	1580
31	8135	5004	7299	8981	4689	1950	2271	2201	8344	3852
32	4414	6855	0127	5489	5157	6386	7492	3736	7164	0498
33	3727	7959	5056	5983	8021	0204	7616	4325	7454	5039
34	5434	7342	0314	7525	0067	2800	6292	4706	3454	6881
35	7195	8828	9869	2785	3186	8375	7414	7232	0401	2483
36	2705	8245	6251	9611	1077	0641	0195	7024	6202	3899
37	1547	8981	4972	1280	4286	5678	0338	8096	8284	7010
38	3424	1435	1354	7631	7260	7361	0151	8903	9056	8684
39	8969	7551	3695	4915	7921	2913	3840	9031	9747	9735
40	5225	8720	8898	2478	3342	9200	8836	7269	2992	6284

TABLE 7 Random Digits (continued)

Row 1	6432	9861	1516	2849	2539	2208	4595	8616	6170	5865
2	3085	5903	8319	2744	0814	7318	8619	7614	3265	5999
3	0264	1246	3687	9759	6995	6565	3949	1012	0179	0059
4	8710	2419	6065	0036	9650	2027	6042	5467	1839	5577
5	5736	9001	3132	4521	9973	5070	8078	4150	2276	5059
6	7529	1339	4802	5751	3785	7125	4922	8877	9530	6499
7	5133	7995	8030	7408	2186	0725	5554	5664	6791	9677
8	3170	9915	6960	2621	6718	4059	9919	1007	6469	5410
9	3024	0680	1127	8088	0200	5868	0084	6362	6808	3727
10	4398	3121	7749	8191	2087	8270	5233	3980	6774	8522
11	0082	5419	7659	2061	2506	7573	1157	3979	2309	0811
12	4351	6516	6814	5898	3973	8103	3616	2049	7843	0568
13	3268	0086	7580	1337	3884	5679	4830	4509	9587	2184
14	4391	8487	4884	1488	2249	6661	5774	7205	2717	7030
15	7328	0705	0652	9424	7082	8579	5647	5571	9667	8555
16	3835	2938	2671	4691	0559	8382	2825	4928	5379	8635
17	8731	4980	8674	4506	7262	8127	2022	2178	7463	4842
18	2995	7868	0683	3768	0625	9887	7060	0514	0034	8600
19	5597	9028	5660	5006	8325	9677	2169	3196	0357	7811
20	3081	5876	8150	1360	1868	9265	3277	8465	7502	6458
21	7406	4439	5683	6877	2920	9588	3002	2869	3746	3690
22	5969	9442	7696	7510	1620	4973	1911	1288	6160	9797
23	4765	9647	4364	1037	4975	1998	1359	1346	6125	5078
24	3219	2532	7577	2815	8696	9248	9410	9282	6572	3940
25	6906	8859	5044	8826	6218	3206	9034	0843	9832	2703
26	7993	3141	0103	4528	7988	4635	8478	9094	9077	5306
27	2549	3737	7686	0723	4505	6841	1379	6460	1869	5700
28	3672	7033	4844	0149	7412	6370	1884	0717	5740	8477
29	2217	0293	3978	5933	1032	5192	1732	2137	9357	5941
30	3162	9968	6369	1258	0416	4326	7840	6525	2608	5255
31	1758	1489	2774	6033	9813	1052	1816	7484	1699	7350
32	6430	8803	0478	4157	5626	1603	1339	4666	1207	2135
33	4893	8857	1717	1533	6572	8408	2173	4754	0272	1305
34	1516	2733	7326	8674	9233	1799	5281	0797	0885	0947
35	4950	3171	5756	3036	9047	8719	8498	1312	7124	4787
36	0549	6775	9360	6639	0990	0037	7309	4702	0812	4195
37	1018	7027	7569	7549	2539	2315	8030	7663	3881	8264
38	2241	9965	9729	7092	4891	9239	0738	1804	3025	1030
39	1602	0708	2201	9848	6241	1084	8142	8555	7291	5016
40	5840	8381	1549	9902	6935	3681	6420	0214	8489	5911

TABLE 7 Random Digits (continued)

Row 1	1676	0367	7484	1595	5693	3008	9816	7311	6162	1024
2	6048	4175	8940	9029	8306	8892	4127	1709	4043	6591
3	5549	9621	2563	0515	0560	9021	0632	4309	4044	7010
4	5317	4584	9418	4600	0640	9668	6379	6515	6310	7916
5	2532	7784	6469	4793	5957	4123	6555	3237	6915	6960
6	2300	5412	3106	4877	6936	4109	8060	1896	6881	7028
7	1499	8699	4534	5367	7557	2701	2587	2521	2159	6991
8	6201	3791	2946	2863	5684	5517	7448	2227	8991	7505
9	6839	9736	8312	8068	7339	5395	9559	3416	6169	5484
10	0092	5537	1933	3186	8482	6680	2656	1864	4535	2193
11	1862	3253	6515	6299	2929	2219	9145	7511	2146	4962
12	9886	6744	3097	8894	0446	3494	8211	1723	6138	3181
13	5289	9071	1231	0651	9109	7448	2228	9700	0224	4595
14	2685	7104	7193	5506	2993	7028	4830	3866	8698	0277
15	6055	7092	4786	6847	4543	7448	2017	4114	8385	3625
16	4092	4995	0280	9371	3375	3503	4496	8642	5388	1831
17	5951	4937	3670	5797	5030	6524	2265	7748	7875	6976
18	7687	3849	4821	2373	1157	4208	3623	9399	7349	6663
19	9866	3463	2055	4872	2702	1807	9056	8576	4237	8757
20	3193	3011	8899	6721	0086	2623	7977	7578	4024	1997
21	9181	7365	9135	1669	2007	7784	6363	6913	6017	6588
22	9459	2175	5728	4933	0111	6703	1234	2410	1620	4859
23	9874	5278	2849	3163	6372	2600	9887	7060	3919	1111
24	7729	2099	7513	2774	6030	8260	9023	1368	9513	6122
25	4699	8102	3001	7947	1659	6571	1969	7152	7356	1062
26	1872	7244	3954	7422	2688	8649	0156	1965	5012	2461
27	9636	0123	2438	1757	4204	1650	2486	0002	4724	7412
28	6403	9054	7632	7469	8973	3332	0294	5062	0303	7315
29	4433	3293	2314	7431	2389	4094	5062	0118	0046	6070
30	2361	3933	8026	0431	8012	3214	8927	7355	0585	7638
31	4077	8463	6580	6983	0181	3327	6812	1755	3387	4569
32	6678	0006	3686	8478	9187	2291	9032	9852	1450	7940
33	6499	2582	5207	4627	0456	4245	3583	8996	1006	5839
34	6663	9021	0319	7908	1241	9977	7042	6923	2539	2103
35	9999	4503	6105	5525	1068	6272	7036	0200	6291	2841
36	9048	6982	3845	6865	9029	8700	0349	3416	8236	1129
37	5136	9653	3654	2863	5565	8923	5596	8389	9927	9092
38	9906	1070	5693	3012	1218	7309	4361	3041	4327	8423
39	4198	7035	8182	6270	6461	2079	2998	5507	9605	6734
40	2030	5878	8989	6789	4359	1820	5063	9199	7751	6337

TABLE 8 Operating Characteristic Curves for Tests About Means*

(a) One-tail tests based on normal distribution; $\alpha = 0.05$.

(b) One-tail tests based on normal distribution; $\alpha = 0.01$.

*Reproduced from the 2nd edition of *Engineering Statistics* by A. H. Bowker and G.J. Lieberman, Prentice-Hall, Inc., 1972, with the permission of the authors and publishers.

TABLE 8 Operating Characteristic Curves for Tests About Means (Continued)

(c) Two-tail tests based on normal distribution; $\alpha = 0.05$.

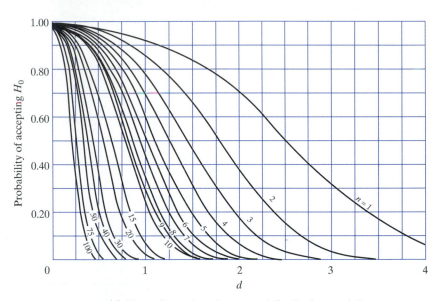

(d) Two-tail tests based on normal distribution; $\alpha = 0.01$.

TABLE 9(a) 95% Confidence Intervals for Proportions*

* This table is reproduced from Table 41 of the *Biometrika Tables for Statisticians*, Vol. I (New York: Cambridge University Press, 1954), by permission of the *Biometrika* trustees.

Table 9(b) 99% Confidence Intervals for Proportions*

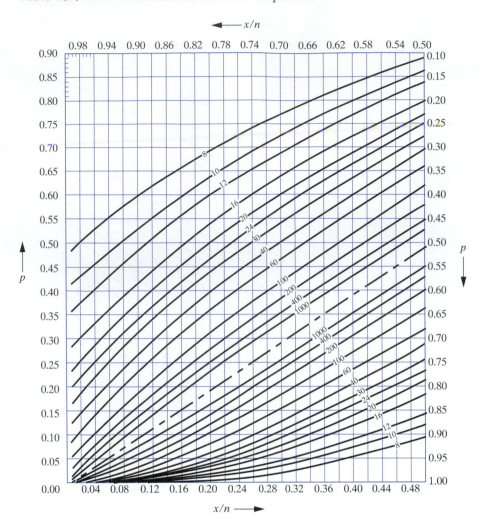

* This table is reproduced from Table 41 of the *Biometrika Tables for Statisticians*,
Vol. I (New York: Cambridge University Press, 1954), by permission of the
Biometrika trustees.

TABLE 10 Critical Values of D*

Sample size n	$D_{.10}$	$D_{.05}$	$D_{.01}$
1	0.950	0.975	0.995
2	0.776	0.842	0.929
3	0.642	0.708	0.828
4	0.564	0.624	0.733
5	0.510	0.565	0.669
6	0.470	0.521	0.618
7	0.438	0.486	0.577
8	0.411	0.457	0.543
9	0.388	0.432	0.514
10	0.368	0.410	0.490
11	0.352	0.391	0.468
12	0.338	0.375	0.450
13	0.325	0.361	0.433
14	0.314	0.349	0.418
15	0.304	0.338	0.404
16	0.295	0.328	0.392
17	0.286	0.318	0.381
18	0.278	0.309	0.371
19	0.272	0.301	0.363
20	0.264	0.294	0.356
25	0.24	0.27	0.32
30	0.22	0.24	0.29

* Adapted from F. J. Massey, Jr., "The Kolmogorov-Smirnov test for goodness of fit," *J. Amer. Statist. Ass.,* Vol. 46 (1951), p. 70, with the kind permission of the author and publisher.

TABLE 11* Values of $\mathcal{Z} = \dfrac{1}{2}\ln\dfrac{1+r}{1-r}$

r	0.00	0.01	0.02	0.03	0.04	0.05	0.06	0.07	0.08	0.09
0.0	0.000	0.010	0.020	0.030	0.040	0.050	0.060	0.070	0.080	0.090
0.1	0.100	0.110	0.121	0.131	0.141	0.151	0.161	0.172	0.182	0.192
0.2	0.203	0.213	0.224	0.234	0.245	0.255	0.266	0.277	0.288	0.299
0.3	0.310	0.321	0.332	0.343	0.354	0.365	0.377	0.388	0.400	0.412
0.4	0.424	0.436	0.448	0.460	0.472	0.485	0.497	0.510	0.523	0.536
0.5	0.549	0.563	0.576	0.590	0.604	0.618	0.633	0.648	0.662	0.678
0.6	0.693	0.709	0.725	0.741	0.758	0.775	0.793	0.811	0.829	0.848
0.7	0.867	0.887	0.908	0.929	0.950	0.973	0.996	1.020	1.045	1.071
0.8	1.099	1.127	0.157	1.188	1.221	1.256	1.293	1.333	1.376	1.422
0.9	1.472	1.528	1.589	1.658	1.738	1.832	1.946	2.092	2.298	2.647

* For negative values of r put a minus sign in front of the corresponding $\mathcal{Z}$'s, and vice versa.

TABLE 12(a) Values of r_p for $\alpha = 0.05$*

d.f. \ p	2	3	4	5	6	7	8	9	10
1	17.97								
2	6.09	6.09							
3	4.50	4.52	4.52						
4	3.93	4.01	4.03	4.03					
5	3.64	3.75	3.80	3.81	3.81				
6	3.46	3.59	3.65	3.68	3.69	3.70			
7	3.34	3.48	3.55	3.59	3.61	3.62	3.63		
8	3.26	3.40	3.48	3.52	3.55	3.57	3.57	3.58	
9	3.20	3.34	3.42	3.47	3.50	3.52	3.54	3.54	3.55
10	3.15	3.29	3.38	3.43	3.47	3.49	3.51	3.52	3.52
11	3.11	3.26	3.34	3.40	3.44	3.46	3.48	3.49	3.50
12	3.08	3.23	3.31	3.37	3.41	3.44	3.46	3.47	3.48
13	3.06	3.20	3.29	3.35	3.39	3.42	3.46	3.46	3.47
14	3.03	3.18	3.27	3.33	3.37	3.40	3.43	3.44	3.46
15	3.01	3.16	3.25	3.31	3.36	3.39	3.41	3.43	3.45
16	3.00	3.14	3.23	3.30	3.34	3.38	3.40	3.42	3.44
17	2.98	3.13	3.22	3.28	3.33	3.37	3.39	3.41	3.43
18	2.97	3.12	3.21	3.27	3.32	3.36	3.38	3.40	3.42
19	2.96	3.11	3.20	3.26	3.31	3.35	3.38	3.40	3.41
20	2.95	3.10	3.19	3.25	3.30	3.34	3.37	3.39	3.41
24	2.92	3.07	3.16	3.23	3.28	3.31	3.35	3.37	3.39
30	2.89	3.03	3.13	3.20	3.25	3.29	3.32	3.35	3.37
40	2.86	3.01	3.10	3.17	3.22	3.27	3.30	3.33	3.35
60	2.83	2.98	3.07	3.14	3.20	3.24	3.28	3.31	3.33
120	2.80	2.95	3.04	3.12	3.17	3.22	3.25	3.29	3.31
∞	2.77	2.92	3.02	3.09	3.15	3.19	3.23	3.27	3.29

* This table is reproduced from H. L. Harter, "Critical values for Duncan's new multiple range test." It contains some corrected values to replace those given by D. B. Duncan in "Multiple Range and Multiple F Tests," *Biometrics*, Vol. 11 (1955). The above table is reproduced with the permission of the author and the editor of *Biometrics*.

TABLE 12(b) Values of r_p for $\alpha = 0.01^*$

d.f. \ p	2	3	4	5	6	7	8	9	10
1	90.02								
2	14.04	14.04							
3	8.26	8.32	8.32						
4	6.51	6.68	6.74	6.76					
5	5.70	5.90	5.99	6.04	6.07				
6	5.24	5.44	5.55	5.62	5.66	5.68			
7	4.95	5.15	5.26	5.33	5.38	5.42	5.44		
8	4.74	4.94	5.06	5.13	5.19	5.23	5.26	5.28	
9	4.60	4.79	4.91	4.99	5.04	5.09	5.12	5.14	5.16
10	4.48	4.67	4.79	4.88	4.93	4.98	5.01	5.04	5.06
11	4.39	4.58	4.70	4.78	4.84	4.89	4.92	4.95	4.97
12	4.32	4.50	4.62	4.71	4.77	4.81	4.85	4.88	4.91
13	4.26	4.44	4.56	4.64	4.71	4.75	4.79	4.82	4.85
14	4.21	4.39	4.51	4.59	4.66	4.70	4.74	4.77	4.80
15	4.17	4.34	4.46	4.55	4.61	4.66	4.70	4.73	4.76
16	4.13	4.31	4.43	4.51	4.57	4.62	4.66	4.70	4.72
17	4.10	4.27	4.39	4.47	4.54	4.59	4.63	4.66	4.69
18	4.07	4.25	4.36	4.45	4.51	4.56	4.60	4.64	4.66
19	4.05	4.22	4.33	4.42	4.48	4.53	4.57	4.61	4.64
20	4.02	4.20	4.31	4.40	4.46	4.51	4.55	4.59	4.62
24	3.96	4.13	4.24	4.32	4.39	4.44	4.48	4.52	4.55
30	3.89	4.06	4.17	4.25	4.31	4.36	4.41	4.45	4.48
40	3.82	3.99	4.10	4.18	4.24	4.29	4.33	4.38	4.41
60	3.76	3.92	4.03	4.11	4.18	4.23	4.37	4.31	4.34
120	3.70	3.86	3.97	4.04	4.11	4.16	4.20	4.24	4.27
∞	3.64	3.80	3.90	3.98	4.04	4.09	4.13	4.17	4.21

* This table is reproduced from H. L. Harter, "Critical values for Duncan's new multiple range test." It contains some corrected values to replace those given by D. B. Duncan in "Multiple Range and Multiple F Tests," *Biometrics*, Vol. 11 (1955). The above table is reproduced with the permission of the author and the editor of *Biometrics*.

TABLE 13 Control Chart Constants*

Number of observations in sample, n	Chart for averages			Chart for standard deviations						Chart for ranges					
	Factors for control limits			Factor for central line	Factors for control limits				Factor for central line	Factors for control limits					
	A	A_1	A_2	c_2	B_1	B_2	B_3	B_4	d_2	D_1	D_2	D_3	D_4
2	2.121	3.760	1.880	0.5642	0	1.843	0	3.267	1.128	0	3.686	0	3.267
3	1.732	2.394	1.023	0.7236	0	1.858	0	2.568	1.693	0	4.358	0	2.575
4	1.500	1.880	0.729	0.7979	0	1.808	0	2.266	2.059	0	4.698	0	2.282
5	1.342	1.596	0.577	0.8407	0	1.756	0	2.089	2.326	0	4.918	0	2.115
6	1.225	1.410	0.483	0.8686	0.026	1.711	0.030	1.970	2.534	0	5.078	0	2.004
7	1.134	1.277	0.419	0.8882	0.105	1.672	0.118	1.882	2.704	0.205	5.203	0.076	1.924
8	1.061	1.175	0.373	0.9027	0.167	1.638	0.185	1.815	2.847	0.387	5.307	0.136	1.864
9	1.000	1.094	0.337	0.9139	0.219	1.609	0.239	1.761	2.970	0.546	5.394	0.184	1.816
10	0.949	1.028	0.308	0.9227	0.262	1.584	0.284	1.716	3.078	0.687	5.469	0.223	1.777
11	0.905	0.973	0.285	0.9300	0.299	1.561	0.321	1.679	3.173	0.812	5.534	0.256	1.744
12	0.866	0.925	0.266	0.9359	0.331	1.541	0.354	1.646	3.258	0.924	5.592	0.284	1.716
13	0.832	0.884	0.249	0.9410	0.359	1.523	0.382	1.618	3.336	1.026	5.646	0.308	1.692
14	0.802	0.848	0.235	0.9453	0.384	1.507	0.406	1.594	3.407	1.121	5.693	0.329	1.671
15	0.775	0.816	0.223	0.9490	0.406	1.492	0.428	1.572	3.472	1.207	5.737	0.348	1.652

* Reprinted with permission from the American Society for Testing and Materials, 1916 Race Street, Philadelphia, Pa., 19103.

TABLE 14(a) Factors for Two-Sided Tolerance Limits*

P n	$1 - \alpha = 0.95$			$1 - \alpha = 0.99$		
	0.90	0.95	0.99	0.90	0.95	0.99
2	32.019	37.674	48.430	160.193	188.491	242.300
3	8.380	9.916	12.861	18.930	22.401	29.055
4	5.369	6.370	8.299	9.398	11.150	14.527
5	4.275	5.079	6.634	6.612	7.855	10.260
6	3.712	4.414	5.775	5.337	6.345	8.301
7	3.369	4.007	5.248	4.613	5.488	7.187
8	3.136	3.732	4.891	4.147	4.936	6.468
9	2.967	3.532	4.631	3.822	4.550	5.996
10	2.839	3.379	4.433	3.582	4.265	5.594
11	2.737	3.259	4.277	3.397	4.045	5.308
12	2.655	3.162	4.150	3.250	3.870	5.079
13	2.587	3.081	4.044	3.130	3.727	4.893
14	2.529	3.012	3.955	3.029	3.608	4.737
15	2.480	2.954	3.878	2.945	3.507	4.605
16	2.437	2.903	3.812	2.872	3.421	4.492
17	2.400	2.858	3.754	2.808	3.345	4.393
18	2.366	2.819	3.702	2.753	3.279	4.307
19	2.337	2.784	3.656	2.703	3.221	4.230
20	2.310	2.752	3.615	2.659	3.168	4.161
25	2.208	2.631	3.457	2.494	2.972	3.904
30	2.140	2.549	3.350	2.385	2.841	3.733
35	2.090	2.490	3.272	2.306	2.748	3.611
40	2.052	2.445	3.213	2.247	2.677	3.518
45	2.021	2.408	3.165	2.200	2.621	3.444
50	1.996	2.379	3.126	2.162	2.576	3.385
55	1.976	2.354	3.094	2.130	2.538	3.335

(continued)

TABLE 14(a) Factors for Two-Sided Tolerance Limits* (Continued)

n \ P	1 − α = 0.95			1 − α = 0.99		
	0.90	0.95	0.99	0.90	0.95	0.99
60	1.958	2.333	3.066	2.103	2.506	3.293
65	1.943	2.315	3.042	2.080	2.478	3.257
70	1.929	2.299	3.021	2.060	2.454	3.225
75	1.917	2.285	3.002	2.042	2.433	3.197
80	1.907	2.272	2.986	2.026	2.414	3.173
85	1.897	2.261	2.971	2.012	2.397	3.150
90	1.889	2.251	2.958	1.999	2.382	3.130
95	1.881	2.241	2.945	1.987	2.368	3.112
100	1.874	2.233	2.934	1.977	2.355	3.096
150	1.825	2.175	2.859	1.905	2.270	2.983
200	1.798	2.143	2.816	1.865	2.222	2.921
250	1.780	2.121	2.788	1.839	2.191	2.880
300	1.767	2.106	2.767	1.820	2.169	2.850
400	1.749	2.084	2.739	1.794	2.138	2.809
500	1.737	2.070	2.721	1.777	2.117	2.783
600	1.729	2.060	2.707	1.764	2.102	2.763
700	1.722	2.052	2.697	1.755	2.091	2.748
800	1.717	2.046	2.688	1.747	2.082	2.736
900	1.712	2.040	2.682	1.741	2.075	2.726
1000	1.709	2.036	2.676	1.736	2.068	2.718
∞	1.645	1.960	2.576	1.645	1.960	2.576

* Adapted by permission from *Techniques of Statistical Analysis* by Columbia University Statistical Research Group, copyright 1947, McGraw-Hill Book Company, Inc., New York.

TABLE 14(b) Factors for One-Sided Tolerance Limits

n \ P	1 − α = 0.95			1 − α = 0.99		
	0.90	0.95	0.99	0.90	0.95	0.99
2	20.581	26.260	37.094	103.029	131.426	185.617
3	6.156	7.656	10.553	13.995	17.370	23.896
4	4.162	5.144	7.042	7.380	9.083	12.387
5	3.407	4.203	5.741	5.362	6.578	8.939
6	3.006	3.708	5.062	4.411	5.406	7.335
7	2.756	3.400	4.642	3.859	4.728	6.412
8	2.582	3.187	4.354	3.497	4.285	5.812
9	2.454	3.031	4.143	3.241	3.972	5.389
10	2.355	2.911	3.981	3.048	3.738	5.074
11	2.275	2.815	3.852	2.898	3.556	4.829
12	2.210	2.736	3.747	2.777	3.410	4.633
13	2.155	2.671	3.659	2.677	3.290	4.472
14	2.109	2.615	3.585	2.593	3.189	4.337
15	2.068	2.566	3.520	2.522	3.102	4.222
16	2.033	2.524	3.464	2.460	3.028	4.123
17	2.002	2.486	3.414	2.405	2.963	4.037
18	1.974	2.453	3.370	2.357	2.905	3.960
19	1.949	2.423	3.331	2.314	2.854	3.892
20	1.926	2.396	3.295	2.276	2.808	3.832
25	1.838	2.292	3.158	2.129	2.633	3.601
30	1.777	2.220	3.064	2.030	2.516	3.447
35	1.732	2.167	2.995	1.957	2.430	3.334
40	1.697	2.126	2.941	1.902	2.364	3.249
45	1.669	2.092	2.898	1.857	2.312	3.180
50	1.646	2.065	2.863	1.821	2.269	3.125
55	1.626	2.042	2.833	1.790	2.233	3.078
60	1.609	2.022	2.807	1.764	2.202	3.038
65	1.594	2.005	2.785	1.741	2.176	3.004
70	1.581	1.990	2.765	1.722	2.153	2.974
75	1.570	1.976	2.748	1.704	2.132	2.947
80	1.559	1.965	2.733	1.688	2.114	2.924
85	1.550	1.954	2.719	1.674	2.097	2.902
90	1.542	1.944	2.706	1.661	2.082	2.883
95	1.534	1.935	2.695	1.650	2.069	2.866
100	1.527	1.927	2.684	1.639	2.056	2.850
150	1.478	1.870	2.611	1.566	1.971	2.741
200	1.450	1.837	2.570	1.524	1.923	2.679
250	1.431	1.815	2.542	1.496	1.891	2.638
300	1.417	1.800	2.522	1.476	1.868	2.608
∞	1.282	1.645	2.326	1.282	1.645	2.326

TABLE 15 Sample Size Code Letters from MIL-STD-105D

Lot or batch size			General Inspection level		
			I	II	III
2	to	8	A	A	B
9	to	15	A	B	C
16	to	25	B	C	D
26	to	50	C	D	E
51	to	90	C	E	F
91	to	150	D	F	G
151	to	280	E	G	H
281	to	500	F	H	J
501	to	1,200	G	J	K
1,201	to	3,200	H	K	L
3,201	to	10,000	J	L	M
10,001	to	35,000	K	M	N
35,001	to	150,000	L	N	P
150,001	to	500,000	M	P	Q
500,001	and	over	N	Q	R

TABLE 16 Master Table for Single Sampling (Normal Inspection) from MIL-STD-105D

Acceptable quality levels (normal inspection)

Sample size code letter	Sample size	0.010		0.015		0.025		0.040		0.065		0.10		0.15		0.25		0.40		0.65		1.0		1.5		2.5		4.0		6.5		10		15		25		40		65		100		150		250		400		650		1000	
		Ac	Re	Ac	Re	Ac	Re	Ac	Re	Ac	Re	Ac	Re	Ac	Re	Ac	Re	Ac	Re	Ac	Re	Ac	Re	Ac	Re	Ac	Re	Ac	Re	Ac	Re	Ac	Re	Ac	Re	Ac	Re	Ac	Re	Ac	Re	Ac	Re	Ac	Re	Ac	Re	Ac	Re	Ac	Re	Ac	Re
A	2	↓	↓	↓	↓	↓	↓	↓	↓	↓	↓	↓	↓	↓	↓	↓	↓	↓	↓	↓	↓	↓	↓	↓	↓	↓	↓	↓	↓	↓	↓	↓	↓	0	1	1	2	2	3	3	4	5	6	7	8	10	11	14	15	21	22	30	31
B	3	↓	↓	↓	↓	↓	↓	↓	↓	↓	↓	↓	↓	↓	↓	↓	↓	↓	↓	↓	↓	↓	↓	↓	↓	↓	↓	↓	↓	↓	↓	0	1	1	2	2	3	3	4	5	6	7	8	10	11	14	15	21	22	30	31	44	45
C	5	↓	↓	↓	↓	↓	↓	↓	↓	↓	↓	↓	↓	↓	↓	↓	↓	↓	↓	↓	↓	↓	↓	↓	↓	↓	↓	↓	↓	0	1	1	2	2	3	3	4	5	6	7	8	10	11	14	15	21	22	30	31	44	45	↑	↑
D	8	↓	↓	↓	↓	↓	↓	↓	↓	↓	↓	↓	↓	↓	↓	↓	↓	↓	↓	↓	↓	↓	↓	↓	↓	↓	↓	0	1	1	2	2	3	3	4	5	6	7	8	10	11	14	15	21	22	30	31	44	45	↑	↑	↑	↑
E	13	↓	↓	↓	↓	↓	↓	↓	↓	↓	↓	↓	↓	↓	↓	↓	↓	↓	↓	↓	↓	↓	↓	↓	↓	0	1	1	2	2	3	3	4	5	6	7	8	10	11	14	15	21	22	30	31	44	45	↑	↑	↑	↑	↑	↑
F	20	↓	↓	↓	↓	↓	↓	↓	↓	↓	↓	↓	↓	↓	↓	↓	↓	↓	↓	↓	↓	↓	↓	0	1	1	2	2	3	3	4	5	6	7	8	10	11	14	15	21	22	30	31	44	45	↑	↑	↑	↑	↑	↑	↑	↑
G	32	↓	↓	↓	↓	↓	↓	↓	↓	↓	↓	↓	↓	↓	↓	↓	↓	↓	↓	↓	↓	0	1	1	2	2	3	3	4	5	6	7	8	10	11	14	15	21	22	30	31	44	45	↑	↑	↑	↑	↑	↑	↑	↑	↑	↑
H	50	↓	↓	↓	↓	↓	↓	↓	↓	↓	↓	↓	↓	↓	↓	↓	↓	↓	↓	0	1	1	2	2	3	3	4	5	6	7	8	10	11	14	15	21	22	30	31	44	45	↑	↑	↑	↑	↑	↑	↑	↑	↑	↑	↑	↑
J	80	↓	↓	↓	↓	↓	↓	↓	↓	↓	↓	↓	↓	↓	↓	↓	↓	0	1	1	2	2	3	3	4	5	6	7	8	10	11	14	15	21	22	30	31	44	45	↑	↑	↑	↑	↑	↑	↑	↑	↑	↑	↑	↑	↑	↑
K	125	↓	↓	↓	↓	↓	↓	↓	↓	↓	↓	↓	↓	↓	↓	0	1	1	2	2	3	3	4	5	6	7	8	10	11	14	15	21	22	30	31	44	45	↑	↑	↑	↑	↑	↑	↑	↑	↑	↑	↑	↑	↑	↑	↑	↑
L	200	↓	↓	↓	↓	↓	↓	↓	↓	↓	↓	↓	↓	0	1	1	2	2	3	3	4	5	6	7	8	10	11	14	15	21	22	30	31	44	45	↑	↑	↑	↑	↑	↑	↑	↑	↑	↑	↑	↑	↑	↑	↑	↑	↑	↑
M	315	↓	↓	↓	↓	↓	↓	↓	↓	↓	↓	0	1	1	2	2	3	3	4	5	6	7	8	10	11	14	15	21	22	30	31	44	45	↑	↑	↑	↑	↑	↑	↑	↑	↑	↑	↑	↑	↑	↑	↑	↑	↑	↑	↑	↑
N	500	↓	↓	↓	↓	↓	↓	↓	↓	0	1	1	2	2	3	3	4	5	6	7	8	10	11	14	15	21	22	30	31	44	45	↑	↑	↑	↑	↑	↑	↑	↑	↑	↑	↑	↑	↑	↑	↑	↑	↑	↑	↑	↑	↑	↑
P	800	↓	↓	↓	↓	↓	↓	0	1	1	2	2	3	3	4	5	6	7	8	10	11	14	15	21	22	30	31	44	45	↑	↑	↑	↑	↑	↑	↑	↑	↑	↑	↑	↑	↑	↑	↑	↑	↑	↑	↑	↑	↑	↑	↑	↑
Q	1250	↓	↓	↓	↓	0	1	1	2	2	3	3	4	5	6	7	8	10	11	14	15	21	22	30	31	44	45	↑	↑	↑	↑	↑	↑	↑	↑	↑	↑	↑	↑	↑	↑	↑	↑	↑	↑	↑	↑	↑	↑	↑	↑	↑	↑
R	2000	↓	↓	0	1	1	2	2	3	3	4	5	6	7	8	10	11	14	15	21	22	30	31	44	45	↑	↑	↑	↑	↑	↑	↑	↑	↑	↑	↑	↑	↑	↑	↑	↑	↑	↑	↑	↑	↑	↑	↑	↑	↑	↑	↑	↑

↓ = Use first sampling plan below arrow. If sample size equals, or exceeds, lot or batch size, do 100 percent inspection.

↑ = Use first sampling plan above arrow.

Ac = Acceptance number.

Re = Rejection number.

Answers to Odd-Numbered Exercises

Chapter 1

1.1 Statistical *population* could be air quality values for all U. S. based flights during period of study. The *sample* is the measurements from the 158 flights.

1.3. We used the first page of Table 7, row 11, and columns 17 and 18. We select 31, 4, 29, 21, and 24.

1.5 (a) $\bar{x} = 214.67$ (b) Below LCL.

Chapter 2

2.7 (a) 10.95, 11.95, 12.95, 13.95; (b) 10.45, 11.45, 12.45, 13.45, and 14.45; (c) 1.

2.9 The class frequencies are 3, 15, 24, 12, and 6.

2.11 (a) 11.5, 20.5, 29.5, 38.5, 47.5, 56.5, 65.5; (b) 12–20, 21–29, 30–38, 39–47, 48–56, 57–65.

2.13 The cumulative "less than" frequencies are 0, 10, 20, 29, 40, 52, 62, 68, 72, 76, 77, 79, 80.

2.15 The cumulative "less than" frequencies are 0, 4, 17, 35, 60, 80, 94, and 100.

2.17 The cumulative "or more" frequencies are 60, 45, 33, 22, 15, 7, 2, and 0.

2.19 No, because we tend to compare areas; the large sack should be modified so that its area is double that of the small sack.

2.23

```
2 | 67  88  95
3 | 55  70  91  83  17
4 | 05  19  34  62
5 | 40  08
6 | 12
```

2.25

```
2 | 2  1
2 | 8  6
3 | 2  4  3  4
3 | 6  6  7  9  5  5  5  5  8
4 | 3  3  0  0  4  2  1  1
4 | 9  6  8  5  8  5  5  5  7  7
5 | 0  1  2  3  1  4  1  3  2  2  0  3  4  0
5 | 6  5  6  7  7  9  6  5  5  9  8
6 | 2  0  2  3  4  0  1  1  0  2  1
6 | 5  7  8  5  8  7  9  8  5
7 | 2  3  4  0  4  3  4  0
7 | 9  8  6  5  6  7
8 | 4  2  0  2
8 | 8  5
```

2.27 (a) $\bar{x} = -3$ (b) $s = 2.94$ (c)   hole too small on average.

2.29 (a) $\bar{x} = 0.1673$ (b) $s = 0.0832$ (c)   No major difference.

2.31 No, the total earnings are only $375,000.

2.33 (a)   35;   (b)   34.5.

2.35 (a)   8;   (b)   9.

2.37 $\bar{x} = 30.91, Q_1 = 30.4, Q_2 = 30.85, Q_3 = 31.2$.

2.41 (a) $\bar{x} = 30.25$ and $s = 11.15$;   (b) $\bar{x} = 30.0$ and $s = 10.99$.

2.43 $\bar{x} = 5.18, s = 2.684$ and $V = 51.8\%$.

2.45 $V = 2.63\%$ for the price of copper and $V = 7.85\%$ for the price of coal; the price of coal is relatively more variable.

2.49 (a)   11.375;   (b)   27.45;   (c)   4.995.

2.51 (a) $Q_1 = 14.95, Q_3 = 22.83$, and the interquartile range is 7.88;
(b) $Q_1 = 7.33, Q_3 = 16.06$.

2.53 (a)   73.0;   (b)   43.64%.

2.55 (a) $Q_1 = 1712, Q_2 = 1863, Q_3 = 2061$;   (c) $Q_1 = 69.5, Q_2 = 70.55, Q_3 = 71.80$.

2.57 (a)   The class frequencies are $1, 8, 19, 17, 9, 3$, and 1.

2.59 (a) $\bar{x} = 5.4835$ and $s = 0.19042$;   (b)   median is $5.46, Q_1 = 5.34$ and $Q_3 = 5.63$;   (c)   there is no apparent trend.

2.61 (a)   median = 0.40, maximum = 0.57, minimum = 0.32 and the range = 0.25;   (b)   median = 0.51, maximum = 0.63, minimum = 0.47 and the range = 0.16.

2.63 (a) $Q_1 = 18.0, Q_2 = 27.0, Q_3 = 30.0$;   (b)   minimum = 12, maximum = 48, range = 36 and the interquartile range = 12.0.

2.65 (a) $Q_1 = 19, Q_2 = 28, Q_3 = 55$;   (b)   minimum = 12, maximum = 63, range = 51, and the interquartile range = 36.

2.69 The coefficient of variation is 5.22% for the first student and 6.73% for the second student, so the first student is more consistent.

2.71 (a) $Q_1 = 497.2, Q_2 = 602.0, Q_3 = 743.3$;   (b)   895.8

Chapter 3

3.1 (b) $R = \{(0, 0), (1, 1), (2, 2)\}, T = \{(0, 0), (1, 0), (2, 0), (3, 0)\}$,
$U = \{(0, 1), (0, 2), (1, 2)\}$.

3.3 (a) $R \cup U = \{(0, 0), (1, 1), (2, 2), (0, 1), (0, 2), (1, 2)\}$ is the event that at least as many carbon dioxide lasers are suitable as solid crystal lasers;
(b) $R \cap T = \{(0, 0)\}$ is the event that none of the lasers is suitable;
(c) $\bar{T} = \{(0, 1), (1, 1), (2, 1), (3, 1), (0, 2), (1, 2), (2, 2), (3, 2)\}$ is the event that at least one of the carbon dioxide lasers is suitable.

3.5 (a) $A \cup B = \{2, 3, 4\}$ is the event that work on the car is easy, average or difficult;   (b) $A \cap B = \{3\}$ is the event that work on the car is average;
(c) $A \cup \bar{B} = \{1, 3, 4, 5\}$ is the event that work on the car is not easy;
(d) $\bar{C} = \{1, 2, 3\}$ is the event that work on the car is very easy, easy or average.

3.7 (b) B is the event that 3 graduate assistants are present, C is the event that as many professors as graduate assistants are present, D is the event that altogether 3 professors or graduate assistants are present;
(c) $C \cup D = \{(1, 1), (1, 2), (2, 1), (2, 2)\}$, is the event that at most 2 graduate assistants are present;   (d) B and D are mutually exclusive.

3.9 Region 1 represents the event that the ore contains copper and uranium; region 2 represents the event that the ore contains copper but not uranium; region 3 represents the event that the ore contains uranium but not copper; region 4 represents the event that the ore contains neither uranium nor copper.

3.11 (a)   Region 5 represents the event that the windings are improper, but the shaft size is not too large and the electrical connections are satisfactory;   (b)   regions 4 and 6 together represent the event that the electrical connections are unsatisfactory, but the windings are proper;   (c)   regions 7 and 8 together represent the event that the windings are proper and the electrical connections are satisfactory;   (d)   regions 1, 2, 3, and 5 together represent the event that the windings are improper.

3.17 72.

3.19 (a)   1,680;   (b)   4,096.

3.21 720.

3.23 105.

3.25 (a)   55;   (b)   165.

3.27 280.

3.29 (a)   1/6;   (b)   1/18;   (c)   2/9;   (d)   1/18;   (e)   1/18;   (f)   1/9.

3.31 0.368.

3.33 45.

3.35 (a)   Yes;   (b)   no, sum exceeds 1;   (c)   no, $P(C)$ is negative;   (d)   no, sum is less than 1;   (e)   yes.

3.37 (b)   27/112, 45/112 and 5/14;   (c)   25/56, 5/16 and 27/112.

3.41 (a)   0.71;   (b)   0.72;   (c)   0.29;   (d)   0.28.

3.43 (a)   0.43;   (b)   0.67;   (c)   0.11;   (d)   0.59.

3.45 (a)   15/32;   (b)   13/32;   (c)   5/32;   (d)   23/32;   (e)   8/32;   (f)   9/32.

3.47 (a)   0.29;   (b)   0.18.

3.51 (a)   4 to 3;   (b)   19 to 1 against it;   (c)   4 to 1.

3.53 (a)   0.60;   (b) $0.75 \le p < 0.80$.

3.55 $P(I|D) = 2/3; P(I|\overline{D}) = 4/97$.

3.57 (a)   62/85;   (b)   74/84;   (c)   29/51.

3.59 (a)   0.4333;   (b)   0.5000;   (c)   0.4375.

3.65 (a)   33/59;   (b)   7/118;   (c)   45/118.

3.67 Yes.

3.69 (a)   1/256;   (b)   1/648;   (c)   1/243.

3.71 0.758.

3.73 0.068.

3.75 (a)   0.60;   (b)   0.20;   (c)   0.70.

3.77 (a)   0.686;   (b)   0.171;   (c)   0.0286.

3.79 0.28.

3.81 $0.20.

3.83 0.

3.85 93/16.

3.89 (a) $p > 1/6$;   (b) $p < 1/6$;   (c) $p = 1/6$.

3.91 3/4

3.93 Discontinue the operation.

3.95 (a) Expected useful life for FF, 28.5; for LWR 24; (b) for FF 6.25; for LWR 10.526.

3.97 (a) $\overline{A}$ = {(0, 0), (0, 1), (0, 2), (0, 3), (1, 0), (1, 1), (1, 2), (2, 0), (2, 1), (3, 0)} is the event that the salesman will not visit all 4 customers;
(b) $A \cup B$ = {(4, 0), (3, 1), (2, 2), (1, 3), (0, 4), (1, 0), (2, 0), (2, 1), (3, 0)} is the event that the salesman will visit all 4 customers or more on the first day than on the second day; (c) $A \cap C$ = {(1, 3), (0, 4)} is the event that he will visit all 4 customers but at most one on the first day;
(d) $\overline{A} \cap B$ = {(1, 0), (2, 0), (2, 1), (3, 0)} is the event that he will visit at most 3 of the customers and more on the first day than on the second day.

3.101 21.

3.103 (a) 0.56; (b) 0.26; (c) 0.06; (d) 0.76; (e) no.

3.105 There is a contradiction in his claim.

3.109 (a) 20/58; (b) 8/58; (c) 12/58; (d) 27/58.

3.111 Purposeful action is most likely.

3.113 (a) First job; (b) second job.

3.115 (a) 0.74; (b) 0.6923.

Chapter 4

4.1 1/12, 2/12, 3/12, 3/12, 2/12, and 1/12.

4.3 (a) No, sum exceeds 1; (b) yes; (c) no, $f(3)$ is negative.

4.5 $k = 16/31$.

4.9 .1176, .3025, .3241, .1852, .0595, .0102, .0007.

4.11 (a) 0.3169; (b) 0.1442; (c) 0.0861; (d) .0746; (e) .4862; (f) .7052.

4.13 27/128.

4.15 (a) 0.2969; (b) 0.0152; (c) 0.2061.

4.17 (a) 0.1501; (b) 0.7338; (c) 0.0982.

4.19 (a) 0.9571; (b) 0.7892; (c) 0.5614; (d) 0.3518.

4.21 0.3167.

4.23 (a) 0.4032; (b) 0.4536; (c) 0.1432.

4.25 (a) 0.15; (b) 0.0625.

4.27 (a) 0.1470; (b) 0.1468.

4.31 $\sigma^2 = 1.0$.

4.33 $\sigma^2 = 1.8$.

4.35 (a) $\mu = 2.8$ and $\sigma^2 = 0.84$.

4.37 (a) $\sigma^2 = 1.25$.

4.39 (a) $\mu = 338$ and $\sigma = 13$; (b) $\mu = 120$ and $\sigma = 10$; (c) $\mu = 24$ and $\sigma = 4.8$; (d) $\mu = 520$ and $\sigma = 13.49$.

4.43 (a) The probability of getting more than 95 or less than 49 left-hand breaks is less than or equal to 1/16.

4.49 0.0498, 0.1494, 0.2240, 0.2240, 0.1680, 0.1008, 0.0504, 0.0216, 0.0081, 0.0027.

4.51 (a) 0.242; (b) 0.087; (c) 0.937.

4.53 (a) 0.182; (b) 0.857; (c) 0.648.

4.55 0.007.

4.57 (a) 0.981; (b) 0.577; (c) 0.978.

4.59 (a) 0.0314; (b) 0.0121.

4.61 (a) 0.3010.

4.63 (a) 0.224; (b) 0.801; (c) .112.

4.65 (a) 0.216; (b) 0.108.

4.71 0.117.

4.73 (b) 0.195.

4.77 000–040, 041–170, 171–379, 380–602, 603–780, 781–894, 895–954, 955–982, 983–993, 994–997, 998–999.

4.79 (a) 0.04; (b) 0.

4.81 (a) 2.12; (b) 0.9856; (c) 0.9928.

4.83 (a) Yes; (b) Yes; (c) No, sum exceeds 1.

4.85 (a) 0.1468; (b) 0.1468.

4.87 (a) 0.5238; (b) 0.4190; (c) 0.0571.

4.89 (a) 0.72; (b) 0.72.

4.91 0.2707.

4.93 Probability at least 0.96.

4.95 0.5488.

4.97 (a) 0000–2465, 2466–5917, 5918–8334, 8335–9462, 9463–9857, 9858–9968, 9969–9994, 9995–9999.

Chapter 5

5.3 (a) 0.5904; (b) 0.024.

5.5 (a) 0.02; (b) 0.84.

5.7 (a) 0.556; (b) 0.09.

5.9 (a) 0.707; (b) 0.1339.

5.11 0.0916.

5.13 $\mu = 0.8$ and $\sigma^2 = 0.0267$.

5.15 $\mu = 4$ and σ^2 does not exist.

5.17 20,000 miles.

5.19 (a) 0.9332; (b) 0.1151; (c) 0.0154; (d) 0.9599.

5.21 (a) 2.37; (b) 1.23; (c) −0.37; (d) −2.02; (e) 1.81.

5.25 $\sigma = 19.88$.

5.27 (a) 0.7580; (b) 0.6578.

5.29 (a) 0.9568; (b) 0.7475; (c) 0.7201.

5.31 83.15%

5.33 $\mu = 2.984$.

5.35 (a) 0.049; (b) 0.008.

5.37 0.1841.

5.39 0.0808.

5.45 $F(x) = 0$ for $x \le \alpha$, $F(x) = \dfrac{x - \alpha}{\beta - \alpha}$ for $\alpha < x < \beta$, and $F(x) = 1$ for $x \ge \beta$.

5.47 50%

5.49 0.2646.

5.51 (a) 0.0807; (b) 0.0960.

5.53 0.5940.

5.55 (a) 0.049; (b) 0.799.

5.57 No relative maximum when $0 < \alpha < 1$; relative maximum at $x = 0$ when $\alpha = 1$.

5.59 (a) 25.9%; (b) 22.3%.

5.61 $e^{-\alpha t}$.

5.65 (a) $\mu = 0.2$; (b) 0.3164.

5.67 0.6321.

5.69 0.2057.

5.71 (a) $\dfrac{\binom{2}{x_1}\binom{1}{x_2}\binom{2}{2 - x_1 - x_2}}{\binom{5}{2}}$ for $x_1 = 0, 1, 2$, $x_2 = 0, 1$, and $0 \le x_1 + x_2 \le 2$;

(b) .7; (c) $f_1(0) = .3, f_1(1) = .6, f_1(2) = .1$;
(d) $f_1(0|0) = 1/6, f_1(1|0) = 4/6, f_1(2|0) = 1/6$.

5.73 (a) 1/4; (b) 1/24.

5.75 $F(x_1, x_2) = 0$ for $x_1 \le 0$ or $x_2 \le 0$,
$= \frac{1}{4}x_1^2 x_2^2$ for $0 < x_1 < 1$ and $0 < x_2 < 2$,
$= x_1^2$ for $0 < x_1 < 1$ and $x_2 \ge 2$,
$= \frac{1}{4}x_2^2$ for $x_1 \ge 1$ and $0 < x_2 < 2$, and $F(x_1, x_2) = 1$ for $x_1 \ge 1$ and $x_2 \ge 2$;
$F_1(x_1) = 0$ for $x_1 \le 0$, $F_1(x_1) = x_1^2$ for $0 < x_1 < 1$, and $F_1(x_1) = 1$ for $x_1 \ge 1$;
$F_2(x_2) = 0$ for $x_2 \le 0$, $F_2(x_2) = \frac{1}{4}x_2^2$ for $0 < x_2 < 1$, and $F_2(x_2) = 1$ for $x_2 \ge 2$;
they are independent.

5.77 $F(x, y) = 0$ for $x \le 0$ or $y \le 0$,
$= \frac{3}{5}x^2 y + \frac{2}{5}xy^3$ for $0 < x < 1$ and $0 < y < 1$,
$= \frac{3}{5}x^2 + \frac{2}{5}x$ for $0 < x < 1$ and $y \ge 1$,
$= \frac{3}{5}y + \frac{2}{5}y^3$ for $x \ge 1$ and $0 < y < 1$, and $F(x, y) = 1$ for $x \ge 1$ and $y \ge 1$.

5.79 (a) $f_1(x|y) = (x + y^2)/(5 + y^2)$ for $0 < x < 1$ and $f_1(x|y) = 0$ elsewhere;
(b) $f_1(x|\frac{1}{2}) = \frac{1}{3}(4x + 1)$ for $0 < x < 1$ and $f_1(x|y) = 0$ elsewhere;
(c) 11/18.

5.81 (a) 1/3; (b) $5/(6e) = 0.3066$.

5.83 (a) 0.3264; (b) 0.4712.

5.85 2.

5.87 $\mu = LW$ and $\sigma^2 = \frac{1}{12}(a^2 W^2 + b^2 L^2 + \frac{1}{12}a^2 b^2)$.

5.89 (a) 0; (b) 10.

5.91 (a) -6; (b) 25.

5.93 (a) 200; (b) 60.

5.109 (a) .4365; (b) .224.

5.111 $\mu = 3/8$ and $\sigma^2 = .0594$.

5.113 (a) .0062; (b) .1587; (c) .8664.

5.115 $Q_1 = 83.775, Q_2 = 102, Q_3 = 120.225$.

5.117 (a) .951; (b) .0025.

5.121 .1616.

5.123 (a) $f(x, y) = \binom{2}{x}\binom{2}{y}.7^{x+y}.3^{4-x-y}$, for $x = 0, 1, 2$ and $y = 0, 1, 2$.
(b) .2877.

5.125 (a) -150; (b) 60.

Chapter 6

6.5 (a) 15; (b) 300.

6.7 (a) $\mu = 0$ and $\sigma^2 = 26/3$.

6.9 The samples are 1 and 1, 1 and 2, 1 and 3, 1 and 4, 2 and 1, 2 and 2, 2 and 3, 2 and 4, 3 and 1, 3 and 2, 3 and 3, 3 and 4, 4 and 1, 4 and 2, 4 and 3, 4 and 4; the probabilities that $\bar{x}$ equals 1, 1.5, 2, 2.5, 3, 3.5, or 4 are 1/16, 1/8, 3/16, 1/4, 3/16, 1/8, and 1/16.

6.11 (a) It is divided by 2; (b) it is divided by 3/2; (c) it is multiplied by 3; (d) it is multiplied by 4.

6.15 approximately 0.628.

6.17 approximately 0.111.

6.21 $t = 1.15$: since $t_{0.10} = 1.476$ for 5 degrees of freedom, the data fail to reject the claim.

6.23 0.025.

6.25 0.02.

6.27 0.2873.

6.29 0.3125.

6.31 (a) 28; (b) 190.

6.33 (a) 6/7; (b) 18/19.

6.35 (a) less than .16; (b) .0124.

6.37 .0244.

6.39 .05.

6.41 Lack of independence. Longest lines are likely to occur together when the same cars must wait several light changes.

Chapter 7

7.3 (a) The medians are 4, 5, 4, 3, 5, 2, 3, 5, 3, 2, 3, and 4; the means are 4, 4.3, 4, 3.3, 4, 2, 2.7, 4, 3.3, 3, 3, and 4; (b) the frequencies are 2, 4, 3, and 3 for the medians, and 1, 5, 6, and 0 for the means.

7.5 $7899.4 < \mu < 15690.6$.

7.7 87.6%.

7.9 84.7%.

7.11 $n = 208$.

7.13 (a) $E = 22.14$; (b) $E = 4.46$.

7.15 99.82%.

7.17 $1.325 < \mu < 1.616$.

7.19 $4.83 < \mu < 6.72$.

7.21 $.5031 < \mu < .5089$.

7.23 $-0.34 < \mu < 8.34$.

7.25 (a) $\frac{1}{n}\sum_{i=1}^{n} x_i$; (b) $\frac{1}{n}\sum_{i=1}^{n} x_i$.

7.27 Type I; Type II.

7.29 (a) .1056; (b) .1056.

7.31 (a) .014; (b) .2327.

7.33 (a) 0.0087; (b) $\alpha \le 0.0087$.

7.35 $n = 47$.

7.37 (a) $\mu \neq 1250$; (b) $\mu < 1250$; (c) $\mu > 1250$.

7.39 $Z = 2.73$; reject H_0.

7.41 $Z = 2.08$; reject H_0.

7.43 $Z = 1.52$; cannot reject H_0.

7.45 $t = 4.79$; reject H_0.

7.47 $t = 3.087$; reject H_0.

7.49 $t = 2.11$; cannot reject H_0. The paradox is explained by the standard deviation, which has greatly increased.

7.51 (a) .80; (b) .09.

7.53 (a) .26; (b) .15; (c) .05.

7.55 (a) .92; (b) .79; (c) .56; (d) .30; (e) .12; (f) .05.

7.57 (a) .59; (b) .32; (c) .12; (d) .03; (e) .00.

7.59 n should be 40.

7.61 (a) Yes; (b) $17.843 < \mu < 19.949$; (c) $70.22 < \mu < 71.17$.

7.63 (a) $\mu = .006$ and $\sigma = .0036$; (b) .0475

7.65 $Z = 2.07$; the data fail to confirm the hypothesis that the men earn in excess of $20/week more than women.

7.67 $t = .96$; cannot reject H_0.

7.69 $t = 1.03$; cannot reject H_0.

7.71 $t = 2.205$; cannot reject H_0.

7.73 $0.0508 < \delta < 0.0552$.

7.75 (a) select 3 amplifiers by random drawing; (b) flip coin for each of the 6 amplifiers. If heads, channel 1 gets the modified power source.

7.77 Randomly select 25 cars, and install the modified air-pollution device. The other 25 cars use the current device.

7.79 $70.224 < \mu < 71.169$.

7.81 $24.92 < \mu < 27.88$.

7.83 $0.992 < \mu < 1.048$.

7.85 $n = 11$.

7.87 $-0.181 < \delta < -0.036$.

7.89 $0.007 < \delta < 0.150$.

7.91 (a) new dividing line $z = 2.210$; (b) .9999, .9984, .9864 , .9296, .7689, .50, .2311, .0704, .0136, .0016, .0001.

7.95 n should be 25.

7.97 (a) Randomly select 10 cars to use the modified spark plugs. The other 10 cars use the regular spark plugs; (b) select 7 specimens by random drawing, to try in the old oven.

7.99 $t = -1.99$ we would not reject $\mu_A = \mu_B$ at the level of significance $\alpha = .05$.

Chapter 8

8.1 (a) $s = 4.195$; (b) 4.341.

8.3 (a) 1.787; (b) 2.144.

8.5 $.082 < \sigma < .695$.

8.7 $\chi^2 = 5.832$; cannot reject H_0.

8.9 $\chi^2 = 115.886$; reject H_0.

8.11 $\chi^2 = 10.89$; cannot reject H_0.

8.13 $F = 1.496$; we cannot reject H_0.

8.15 $F = 2.42$; we cannot reject H_0.

8.17 (a) No, samples are not normal; (b) test equality of the standard deviations of the logarithms of the observations.

8.19 $1.52 < \sigma_1 < 2.20$ and $1.91 < \sigma_2 < 3.32$.

8.21 $\chi^2 = 19.21$; cannot reject H_0.

8.23 $\chi^2 = 72.22$; reject H_0.

8.25 $F = 2.797$; we cannot reject H_0.

Chapter 9

9.1 (a) $0.35 < p < 0.49$; (b) $0.352 < p < 0.488$.

9.3 (a) $0.52 < p < 0.64$; (b) $0.514 < p < 0.642$.

9.5 (a) $0.319 < p < 0.445$; (b) $E = 0.06$.

9.7 $E = 0.0885$.

9.9 $0.617 < p < 0.743$.

9.11 $n = 201$.

9.13 $n = 1,300$.

9.15 $0.513 < p < 0.639$.

9.17 $0.121 < p < 0.142$.

9.19 $z = 2.19$; reject H_0.

9.21 $z = -1.83$; cannot reject H_0.

9.23 $z = 1.489$; cannot reject H_0.

9.25 At most 3 or at least 12 heads; 0.0352.

9.27 $\chi^2 = 2.37$; cannot reject H_0.

9.29 $\chi^2 = 9.39$; reject H_0.

9.33 $-0.005 < p_1 - p_2 < 0.145$.

9.35 $0.170 < p_1 - p_2 < 0.374$.

9.39 $\chi^2 = 3.457$; cannot reject H_0.

9.41 $\chi^2 = 54.328$; reject H_0.

9.43 $\chi^2 = 0.657$; cannot reject H_0.

9.45 $\chi^2 = 9.185$; cannot reject H_0.

9.47 (a) 0.0375, 0.1071, 0.2223, 0.2811, 0.2163, 0.1013, and 0.0344; (b) 3, 8.6, 17.8, 22.5, 17.3, 8.1 and 2.8; (c) $\chi^2 = 1.264$; good fit.

9.51 (a) $0.115 < p < 0.275$; (b) $0.105 < p < 0.255$.

9.53 (a) $0.084 < p < 0.243$; (b) $0.077 < p < 0.223$.

9.55 (a) $0.075 < p < 0.217$; (b) $0.064 < p < 0.196$.

9.57 $p < 0.00424$.

9.59 $z = 0.807$; cannot reject H_0.

9.61 $z = -1.746$; reject H_0.

9.63 (a) $\chi^2 = 8.190$; reject H_0;

(b) $0.256 < p_1 < 0.611$; $0.108 < p_2 < 0.425$; $0.461 < p_3 < 0.806$.

9.65 $\chi^2 = 10.481$; cannot reject H_0.

9.67 $\chi^2 = 47.862$; reject H_0.

Chapter 10

10.1 $P(10 \, or \, more \,) = 0.2272$; cannot reject H_0.

10.3 $P(6 \, or \, fewer) = 0.3036$; cannot reject H_0.

10.5 $z = -3.91$; reject H_0.

10.7 $P(3 \, or \, fewer \,) = 0.1719$; cannot reject H_0.

10.9 $z = -0.10$; cannot reject H_0.

10.11 $z = 2.92$; difference is significant.

10.13 $z = 1.62$; cannot reject H_0.

10.15 $H = 26.0$; the populations are not identical.

10.17 $z = -0.244$; cannot reject H_0.

10.21 $z = -4.00$; reject H_0.

10.23 Maximum difference is about 0.22; cannot reject H_0.

10.25 $P(6 \, or \, more \,) = 0.0625$; reject H_0.

10.27 $z = -1.814$; reject H_0.

10.29 $H = 0.904$; cannot reject H_0.

10.31 $z = -1.797$; reject H_0.

10.33 $W_1 = 25$ so $U_1 = 19$; reject H_0.

10.35 $z = -2.248$; reject H_0.

Chapter 11

11.1 (b) $\hat{y} = 39.05 + 0.764x$; $\hat{y} = 65.8$.

11.3 (a) $11.87 < \beta < 17.11$;   (b) 39.97 to 63.71.

11.5 $t = -1.212$; cannot reject H_0.

11.7 (a) $\hat{y} = 0.0 + 2.0x$;   (b) $\hat{y} = 7.0$.

11.9 $t = 0.0$; cannot reject H_0.

11.11 7.23 to 12.39.

11.13 $22.37 < \beta < 27.49$.

11.15 (a) $\sum xy / \sum x^2$;   (b) 14.75.

11.17 $12.72 < \alpha < 33.08$.

11.19 (a) $\hat{y} = 3.39 + 0.679x$; $\hat{y} = 6.11$;   (b) $\hat{y} = 2.95 + 0.242x$; $\hat{y} = 5.61$.

11.23 (b) $\log_{10}\hat{y} = 4.842 + .0604x$ or $\hat{y} = 69{,}502.4(1.149)^x$ (c) 1,122,018.

11.25 44.86.

11.27 $\hat{y} = \exp[\exp(0.00041x + 1.21)]$

11.29 $\hat{\alpha} = 0.240$.

11.31 (a) $t = -2.28$; cannot reject $\beta_1 = 0$;   (b) $F = 38.59$; reject $\beta_2 = 0$.

11.35 $\hat{y} = 64.1$.

11.37 $\hat{y} = 2.266 + 0.225x_1 + 0.0623x_2$; $\hat{y} = 8.37$.

11.41 (a)   slight increase in variance;   (b)   U-shaped pattern.

11.43 A serious violation, time trend.

11.45 $z = 4.89$; reject $H_0 : \rho = 0$.

11.47 $z = 5.15$; reject $H_0 : \rho = 0$.

11.49 $.717 < \rho < .976$.

11.51 The first linear relationship is 1.9 times stronger.

11.53 (a) $0.395 < \rho < 0.885$;   (b) $-0.052 < \rho < 0.655$;   (c) $0.314 < \rho < .749$.

11.57 (a)   2812.4;   (b)   233.9;   (c)   0.958.

11.59 (a) $r_S = 0.697$;   (b) $r_S = 0.811$;   (c) $r_S = 0.915$.

11.61 $r_S = 0.39$; not significant.

11.65 $-57.2 < \alpha < 37.2$.

11.67 (a)   19.9 to 128.1 hours;   (b)   0.0 to 173.1 hours.

11.69 $.619 \pm .427$ or $.192 < \alpha < 1.046$

11.71 $\hat{\gamma} = 1.499$.

11.73 $\hat{\tau} = 0.9284$.

11.75 (a)   3.99 to 8.01 hours;   (b)   1.07 to 10.93 hours.

11.77 The first linear relationship is twice as strong.

11.79 (a) $0.446 < \rho < 0.923$;   (b) $-0.797 < \rho < -0.346$;   (c) $-0.173 < \rho < 0.476$.

11.81 (a) $\hat{y} = -0.0206 + 0.462x$;   (b) $0.43 < \beta < 0.50$;   (c) $t = -0.32$, cannot reject H_0.   (d)   The variance appears to increase somewhat with x.

Chapter 12

12.5 $F = 0.68$, not significant at the 0.01 level.

12.7 (a) $SS(Tr) = 204$, with 3 degrees of freedom; $SSE = 34$, with 11 degrees of freedom; $SST = 238$, with 14 degrees of freedom.   (b) $F = 22.0$, significant at the 0.05 level.

12.9 $F = 11.3$, significant at the 0.0 level.

12.11 $F = 15.7$, significant at the 0.05 level.

12.19 For technicians, $F = 0.64$, not significant at the 0.01 level; for days, $F = 0.77$, not significant at the 0.01 level.

12.21 (b) $SS(Tr) = 70$ with 3 degrees of freedom; $SS(Bl) = 136$, with 4 degrees of freedom; $SSE = 66$, with 12 degrees of freedom; $SST = 272$, with 19 degrees of freedom.   (c)   For treatments, $F = 4.24$, significant at the 0.05 level.

12.23 $F = 1.92$, not significant at the 0.05 level.

12.25 For machines, $F = 0.064$, not significant at the 0.05 level; for workers, $F = 1.346$, not significant at the 0.05 level; for replicates, $F = 6.217$, significant at the 0.05 level.

12.29

Tr 1	Tr 4	Tr 3	Tr 2
8	9	10	13

12.31

Method A	Method C	Method B
72	76	86

12.33 (a)

Thread 1	Thread 5	Thread 3	Thread 4	Thread 2
20.675	20.9	23.525	23.7	25.65

(b) $\alpha = 0.5, .05/(5 \cdot 4) = .0025, \mu_2 - \mu_1: 4.975 \pm 2.238$ with the same ± 2.238 applying for all pairs of means.

12.35   For Laboratories, $F = 6.55$, significant at the 0.05 level; for "along the rolling direction," $F = 1.29$, not significant at the 0.05 level; for "across the rolling direction," $F = 26.83$, significant at the 0.05 level.

12.37   For automobile size classes, $F = 414$, significant at the 0.01 level; for barrier impact speeds, $F = 99$, significant at the 0.01 level; for impact angles, $F = 17.5$, significant at the 0.01 level; for restraint systems, $F = 0.72$, not significant at the 0.05 level.

12.41   For track designs, $F = 6.44$, significant at the 0.01 level. The estimated effect of usage on breakage resistance is 0.39.

12.43 $F = 2.80$, not significant at the 0.05 level.

12.45   (b) $SS(Tr) = 56$, with 2 degrees of freedom; $SS(Bl) = 138$ with 3 degrees of freedom; $SSE = 32$, with 6 degrees of freedom; $SST = 226$, with 11 degrees of freedom.   (c)   For treatments, $F = 5.25$, significant at the 0.05 level; for blocks, $F = 8.63$, significant at the 0.05 level.

12.47   (a)   For fuels, $F = 0.35$, not significant at the 0.05 level.   (b)   For launchers, $F = 0.003$, not significant at the 0.05 level.

12.49   For flow, $F = 7.8$, significant at the 0.01 level; for precipitators, $F = 8.1$, significant at the 0.01 level.

12.51

Site E	Site B	Site C	Site A	Site D
3.70	6.77	14.20	21.30	26.73

12.53   For golf-ball designs, $F = 66.6$, significant at the 0.01 level; for golf pros, $F = 24.4$, significant at the 0.01 level; for drivers, $F = 2.7$, not significant at the 0.05 level; for fairways, $F = 73.3$, significant at the 0.01 level.

Chapter 13

13.1   Significant effects are temperature ($F = 11.5, \alpha = 0.01$), concentration ($F = 48.0, \alpha = 0.01$), and their interaction ($F = 3.8, \alpha = 0.05$). Optimal conditions for reflectivity are sulfone concentration at 10 grams per liter and bath temperature at 75°F. The 95% confidence interval for reflectivity is 37.32 to 46.02.

13.3   For detergents, $F = 0.05$, not significant at the 0.05 level; for engines, $F = 6.89$, significant at the 0.05 level; for interaction, $F = 0.81$, not significant at the 0.05 level.

13.5   For melt flow, $F = 8.65$, significant at the 0.01 level; for filter content, $F = 34.82$ significant at the 0.001 level; for interaction, $F = 3.99$, significant at the 0.05 level; for replicates, $F = 0.74$ not significant at the 0.05 level. A two-way table of means provides the summary.

13.7   Significant effects at the 0.01 level are specimen preparation (factor $C, F = 12.67$), and twisting temperature (factor $D, F = 86.51$). No other effects are significant at the 0.05 level. The F values for ingot locations (factor A) and slab positions (factor B) are 0.56 and 0.0008 respectively. For two-factor interactions AB, AC, AD, BC, BD, and CD, the corresponding F values are 0.09, 1.12, 1.20, 1.04, 0.09, and 0.98 respectively. The F values for three-factor interactions ABC, ABD, ACD, and BCD are 0.28, 0.53, 1.76, and 0.27 respectively. The F value for interaction $ABCD$ is 0.68.

13.11   (a) $SST = 110.4375, SS(Tr) = 103.9375, SS(Rep) = 1.5625, SSE = 4.9375$.
(b) $[A] = -1, [B] = -13, [C] = -25, [AB] = 3, [AC] = 3, [BC] = -29,$

$[ABC] = 3$;   (c) $SSA = 0.0625$, $SSB = 10.5625$, $SSC = 39.0625$, $SS(AB) = .5625$, $SS(AC) = .5625$, $SS(BC) = 52.5625$, $SS(ABC) = .5625$; (e) B, C, and BC are significant at the 0.01 level with corresponding F values of 14.9, 55.0 and 74.0.

13.13 The replication effect is significant at the 0.01 level with an F value of 9.1. The main effect B and the three-factor interaction ABC are significant at the 0.05 level with corresponding F values of 8.1 and 5.6 respectively. No other effects are significant at the 0.05 level.

13.21 (a) $SSE = SST - SS(Tr) = 138 - 118 = 20$, with 4 degrees of freedom. $MSE = 5$.

13.23 The 95% confidence intervals for effect A, B and interaction AB are 7 ± 9.8, 3 ± 9.8 and -1 ± 9.8 respectively. All the confidence intervals cover zero.

13.25 The 95% confidence intervals for oil viscosity, temperature, and oil viscosity $\times$ additive interaction are $1.2 \pm .39$, $-.9 \pm .39$ and $.4 \pm .39$, respectively. The 95% confidence intervals of all other effects cover zero. Conclusion: (1) changing temperature level from low to high decreases the engine wear; (2) need oil viscosity $\times$ additive table of means to summarize.

13.27 For rate, $F = 20.17$, significant at the 0.01 level; for additive, $F = 24.00$, significant at the 0.01 level; for nozzle, $F = 10.67$, significant at the 0.05 level; and for the rate $\times$ additive interaction, $F = 48.17$, significant at the 0.01 level.

13.29 (a)   Block 1: $a, b, c, abc, d, abd, acd, bcd$;

Block 2: $1, ab, ac, bc, ad, bd, cd, abcd$;

(b) Block 1: $1, bc, abd, acd$;

Block 2: a, abc, bd, cd;

Block 3: $b, c, ad, abcd$;

Block 4: ab, ac, d, bcd.

13.31 The B and C main effects are significant at the 0.01 level with F values of 11.9 and 27.8; the AD interaction is significant at the 0.05 level with an F value of 8.1; use combination of drugs A, B and C.

13.35 $1, ab, ac, ad, ae, af, bc, bd, be, bf, cd, ce, cf, de, df, ef, cdef, bdef, bcef, bcdf, bcde, adef, acef, acdf, acde, abef, abdf, abde, abcf, abce, abcd$ and $abcdef$. Each effect is aliased with its generalized interaction with $ABCDF$.

13.37 (a) $1, af, bf, ab, cf, ac, bc, abcf, df, ad, bd, abdf, cd, acdf, bcdf, abcd, ef, ae, be, abef, ce, acef, bcef, abce, de, adef, bdef, abde, cdef, acde, bcde, abcdef$.

13.41 The required half replicate includes treatment combinations $1, ab, ac, ad, bc, bd, cd$, and $abcd$. The MSE is 32.896 with 4 degrees of freedom. No effect is significant at the 0.05 level. The F values are 1.26 for $A = BCD$, 1.32 for $B = ACD$, 3.02 for $C = ABD$, 5.32 for $D = ABC$, 0.04 for $AB = CD$, 0.06 for $AC = BD$ and 0.46 for $BC = AD$.

13.43 (a)   For treatments, $F = 97.3$, significant at the 0.01 level;   (c)   significant effects at the 0.01 level are tenderizers ($F = 486.4$), cooking times ($F = 51.4$), cooking temperature ($F = 28.5$), and the tenderizer $\times$ time interaction ($F = 6.0$).

13.45 The AB interaction is significant at the 0.01 level with an F value of 19.0. No other effects are significant at the 0.05 level.

13.47 Changing temperature or pH or both from low to high increases the yield substantially. The 95% confidence intervals for factors A, B and interaction AB effects are 5.6 to 11.4, .6 to 6.4 and -4.4 to 1.4 respectively.

13.49 Significant effects at the 0.05 level are A and B with F values 45.63 and 7.74 respectively.

13.51 The largest number of blocks in which one can perform a 2^6 factorial experiment without confounding any main effect is 32. For example, we could confound on AB, BC, CD, DE, and EF.

13.53 (a) Block 1: 1, $bc, abd, acd, abe, ace, de, bcde$;

Block 2: $ab, ac, d, bcd, e, bce, abde, acde$;

Block 3: $b, c, ad, abcd, ae, abce, bde, cde$;

Block 4: $a, abc, bd, cd, be, ce, ade, abcde$.

(b) The intrablock SSE equals 401.875; A and E are significant at the 0.01 level with F values 12.7 and 17.3; B, C, AD, and ACD are significant at the .05 level with F-values 5.6, 6.0, 6.3, and 4.7.

13.55 We could use half the replicate that includes experimental condition 1. A and B are significant at the 0.01 level with F values of 73.0 and 23.3. C is significant at the 0.05 level with an F value of 10.0.

Chapter 14

14.1 (a) Central line $= 0.150, UCL = 0.153, LCL = 0.147$;

(b) central line $= 0.005, UCL = 0.010, LCL = 0$;

(c) $\bar{x}$: eighth, sixteenth, and seventeenth sample values outside limits; R: all sample values within limits.

14.3 (a) Central line $= 48.1, UCL = 50.3, LCL = 46.0$;

(b) central line $= 2.9, UCL = 6.7, LCL = 0$;

(c) process mean out of control, process variability in control;

(d) $z = -2.12$, there is a trend;

(e) no, process is not in control.

14.5 (a) $\bar{x}$: central line $= 21.7, UCL = 25.2, LCL = 18.2$; σ: central line $= 1.05, UCL = 3.74, LCL = 0$;   (b) yes, process is in control.

14.7 Central line $= 0.0017, UCL = 0.0042, LCL = 0$.

14.9 (a) Central line $= 0.037, UCL = 0.093, LCL = 0$.

14.11 Yes, central line for c chart is 4.9, $UCL = 11.6$, and $LCL = 0$.

14.13 We can assert with 95% confidence that 99% of the pieces will have yield strength between 36, 897 and 68,703 psi.

14.15 (a) 0.1063 ± 0.0008;   (b) 0.1063 ± 0.0001.

14.17 (a) $0.046, 0.139$;   (b) $0.059, 0.143$.

14.19 Producer's risk $= 0.143$, consumer's risk $= 0.082$.

14.23 $AOQL \approx 0.016$.

14.25 $\alpha = 0.15$.

14.27 Sample size is 32, acceptance number is 5, rejection number is 6.

14.29 $a_n = -1.67 + 0.19n, r_n = 2.14 + 0.19n$; reject on eighth trial.

14.31 (a) Central line $= 4.1, UCL = 4.17, LCL = 4.03$;

(b) central line $= 0.12, UCL = 0.25, LCL = 0$;

(c) $\bar{x}$: All sample values are outside limits: R: sixth sample value outside limits.

14.33 The standard is being met.

14.35 (a) $UCL = 3.48$, $LCL = 0$; (b) all the 10-foot sections are under control except the 19th section, which is out of the limits.

14.37 We can assert with 95% confidence that 90% of the interrequest times will be between 889 and 54,176 microseconds.

14.39 .992, .953, .879, .783, .677, .570, .469, .380, .303, .238, .185, .143, .109, .082, .062, .046, .034, .025, .019, .014; producer's risk = .217, consumer's risk = .082.

14.41 Sample size 20, acceptance number is 2, rejection number is 3.

14.43 (b) $L = 186.87$; (c) the cardboard strength data seems to be sampled from a normal distribution.

14.45 (a) 1.139; (b) 1.110.

14.47 (a) 1.60; (b) 1.548.

Chapter 15

15.1 $R = .9936$.

15.3 $R = .9983$.

15.5 (a)
$$f(t) = \begin{cases} \beta(1 - t/\alpha)\exp[-\beta(t - t^2/(2\alpha))] & \text{for } 0 < t < \alpha. \\ 0 & \text{elsewhere.} \end{cases}$$
$$F(t) = \begin{cases} 1 - \exp[-\beta(t - t^2/(2\alpha))] & \text{for } 0 < t < \alpha. \\ 1 - \exp[-\alpha\beta/2] & \text{for } t > \alpha. \end{cases}$$

15.7 (a) 0.6703; (b) 0.6703.

15.9 $n = 5$ and the failure rate is 3.94×10^{-4}.

15.11 (a) 0.6065; (b) 0.9502; (c) 0.3679.

15.13 (b) $F(x) = p\dfrac{1 - (1 - p)^x}{p} = 1 - (1 - p)^x$ for $x = 1, 2, 3, \ldots$; (c) .301.

15.15 (a) $3{,}253.1 < \mu < 38{,}005.6$; (b) $T_r = 40{,}970 < 45{,}767.5$; cannot reject H_0.

15.17 (a) $254.9 < \mu < 1{,}182.8$; (b) $T_r = 3{,}329$ and $1{,}642.7 < T_r < 5{,}921.3$, we cannot reject H_0.

15.21 2.003×10^5.

15.23 0.8758.

15.27 (a) 0.6753; (b) 0.4066.

15.29 83.3 hours.

15.31 2.003×10^5.

15.33 0.9520.

15.35 (a) 0.6667; (b) 0.50; (c) 0.9977.

Index